Lecture Notes in Computer Science 1061

Edited by G. Goos, J. Hartmanis and J. van Leeuwen

Advisory Board: W. Brauer   D. Gries   J. Stoer

Springer
Berlin
Heidelberg
New York
Barcelona
Budapest
Hong Kong
London
Milan
Paris
Santa Clara
Singapore
Tokyo

Paolo Ciancarini   Chris Hankin (Eds.)

Coordination Languages and Models

First International Conference
COORDINATION '96
Cesena, Italy, April 15-17, 1996
Proceedings

 Springer

Series Editors

Gerhard Goos, Karlsruhe University, Germany

Juris Hartmanis, Cornell University, NY, USA

Jan van Leeuwen, Utrecht University, The Netherlands

Volume Editors

Paolo Ciancarini
University of Bologna, Department of Computer Science
Pza. di Porta S. Donato, 5, I-40127 Bologna, Italy

Chris Hankin
Imperial College, Department of Computing
180, Queen's Gate, London SW7 2BZ, United Kongdom

Cataloging-in-Publication data applied for

Die Deutsche Bibliothek - CIP-Einheitsaufnahme

Coordination languages and models : first international
conference, coordination '96, Cesena, Italy, April 15 - 17, 1996 ;
proceedings / Paolo Ciancarini ; Chris Hankin (ed.). - Berlin ;
Heidelberg ; New York ; Barcelona ; Budapest ; Hong Kong ;
London ; Milan ; Paris ; Santa Clara ; Singapore ; Tokyo :
Springer, 1996
  (Lecture notes in computer science ; Vol. 1061)
  ISBN 3-540-61052-9
NE: Ciancarini, Paolo [Hrsg.]; GT

CR Subject Classification (1991): D.1.3, C.2.4, F1.2, D.2-4

ISBN 3-540-61052-9 Springer-Verlag Berlin Heidelberg New York

© Springer-Verlag Berlin Heidelberg 1996
Printed in Germany

Typesetting: Camera-ready by author
SPIN 10512685   06/3142 – 5 4 3 2 1 0   Printed on acid-free paper

Foreword

A new class of models, formalisms, and mechanisms for describing concurrent and distributed computations has emerged over the last few years. A characteristic feature of members of this class is that they are based on (generative) communication via a shared data space. They are called *coordination* languages and models.

This volume contains the proceedings of the First International Conference on Coordination Models and Languages (COORDINATION'96), held in Cesena (Italy) 15-17 April 1996.

In response to the call for papers, 78 papers were submitted to COORDINATION'96. All submitted papers were reviewed by at least 3 reviewers. The programme committee met at Imperial College (London) on 11 December 1995 and selected 21 regular papers. A further 10 papers were selected as short papers, to be presented at a poster session; these are included in this volume after the regular papers.

The programme committee invited Jean-Pierre Banâtre, Ugo Montanari, and Peter Wegner to give invited talks; these are included in this volume before the regular papers.

We thank all members of the programme committee and their sub-referees; they are listed on the following pages. We would also like to thank Roberto Gorrieri, the local arrangements chairperson, and Juarez Muylaert Filho and David Cohen for their assistance in processing the referees' reports. The following organisations provided sponsorship for the conference: Fondazione Cassa di Risparmio di Cesena, Italian National Research Council (C.N.R.), Comune di Cesena, Provincia di Forlì-Cesena, Olidata, Sun Microsystems, Silicon Graphics, Ascom TCS Safnat S.p.A., Link s.r.l., Libreria Minerva, and Cremonini Fabio s.r.l.. Finally, we would not have had the inspiration for arranging this conference had it not been for the EU-funded project COORDINATION; the project has provided partial financial support for a number of the European programme committee members.

April 1996   Paolo Ciancarini and Chris Hankin

Programme Committee

Gul Agha, University of Illinois, US
Jean-Marc Andreoli, Xerox Research Center, Meylan, FR
Marc Bourgois, ECRC, Munich, DE
Luca Cardelli, Digital SRC, Palo Alto, US
Paolo Ciancarini, University of Bologna, IT
Laurent Dami, University of Geneva, CH
David Stefan, Carnegie Mellon University, US
David Gelernter, Yale University, US
Chris Hankin, Imperial College, UK (Chair)
Jose Meseguer, SRI International, US
Daniel Le Métayer, INRIA/IRISA, Rennes, FR
Oscar Nierstrasz, Universität Bern (IAM), CH
António Porto, Uninova, Lisboa, PT
David Skadie, DIKU, Copenhagen, DK
Akinori Yonezawa, University of Tokyo, JP

Local Arrangements

Roberto Gorrieri, Bologna, IT

List of Referees

Birger Andersen	S. Bout	Sophie Pinchinat
Andrea Asperti	Valérie Issarny	Noel Plouzeau
Mark Astley	H.P. Barendregt	Shangping Ren
Uwe Borghoff	Nadeem Jamali	Philippe Rérolle
Paolo Bottoni	Jean-Marc Jezequel	M. Reynolds
Patricia Bournai	J.N. Kok	Olivier Radoux
Luis Caires	Tsung-Min Kuo	M. Rivell
Pierre-Yves Chevalier	Cosimo Laneve	Marco Roccetti
Juan Carlos Cruz	Niels Elgaard Larsen	Eva Bots
Luc Cherki	Patrick Lincoln	Davide Rogai
Joaquim-José Coutinho	Markus Lumpe	Jean-Guy Schneider
Steven Eker	William Mallon	Kees Schuerman
Babak Dehbaney	Nicole Müri-Ollet	Scott Smith
Laurence Fabiri	Cecilia Mascolo	Daniel Sannar
Daniela Fogli	T.E. Meijler	Jean-Pierre Talpin
Pascal Fradet	Antonio Messina	Günter Teege
Markus Frombers	Luis Monteiro	David N. Turner
Thom Frühwirth	Gilles Muller	Vasco Vasconcelos
D. Garlatta	Brian Nielsen	J.Y. Vion-Dury
Mauro Gaspari	Jacques Nové	Jan Vitek
Natalie Glance	D. Pagani	James Waldby
A. Gordon	Jens Palsberg	Gianluigi Zavattaro
Vineet Gupta	Irene Kersch	Vechie Yuck
A.A. Holzbacher	Atria Peterson	

Programme Committee

Gul Agha, University of Illinois, US
Jean-Marc Andreoli, Xerox Research Center Meylan, FR
Marc Bourgois, ECRC Munich, DE
Luca Cardelli, Digital SRC Palo Alto, US
Paolo Ciancarini, University of Bologna, IT
Laurent Dami, Université de Genève, CH
David Garlan, Carnegie Mellon University, US
David Gelernter, Yale University, US
Chris Hankin, Imperial College, UK (Chair)
Jose Meseguer, SRI International, US
Daniel Le Métayer, INRIA/IRISA Rennes, FR
Oscar Nierstarsz, Universitaet Bern (IAM), CH
António Porto, Uninova, Lisboa, PT
David Sands, DIKU, Copenhagen, DK
Akinori Yonezawa, University of Tokyo, JP

Local Arrangements

Roberto Gorrieri, Bologna, IT

List of Referrees

Birger Andersen	S. Hunt	Sophie Pinchinat
Andrea Asperti	Valerie Issarny	Noel Plouzeau
Mark Astley	R. Jagannathan	Shangping Ren
Uwe Borghoff	Nadeem Jamali	Philippe Rerole
Paolo Bottoni	Jean-Marc Jezequel	M Reynolds
Patricia Bournai	J.N. Kok	Olivier Ridoux
Luis Caires	Tsung-Min Kuo	M. Riveill
Pierre-Yves Chevalier	Cosimo Laneve	Marco Roccetti
Juan Carlos Cruz	Niels Elgaard Larsen	Eva Rose
Jose Cunha	Patrick Lincoln	Davide Rossi
Henrique Joao Domingos	Markus Lumpe	Jean-Guy Schneider
Steven Eker	Willem Mallon	Kees Schuerman
Nabiel Elshiewy	Narciso Marti-Oliet	Scott Smith
Alessandro Fabbri	Cecilia Mascolo	Daniel Sturman
Daniela Fogli	T.D. Meijler	Jean-Pierre Talpin
Pascal Fradet	Antonio Messina	Gunnar Teege
Markus Fromherz	Luis Monteiro	David N. Turner
Thom Fruehwirth	Gilles Muller	Vasco Vasconcelos
D. Galmiche	Brian Nielsen	J.Y Vion-Dury
Mauro Gaspari	Jacques Noye	Jan Vitek
Natalie Glance	D. Pagani	James Waldby
A. Gordon	Jens Palsberg	Gianluigi Zavattaro
Vineet Gupta	Remo Pareschi	Lenore Zuck
A.A. Holzbacher	Anna Patterson	

Contents

Invited Papers

Regular Papers

Short Papers

Parallel Multiset Processing:
From Explicit Coordination to Chemical Reaction

Jean-Pierre Banâtre

Irisa / Université de Rennes 1 / Inria
Campus de Beaulieu
35042 Rennes cedex - France

Abstract

The author has been involved for more than fifteen years in the design, study and implementation of coordination program structures. These structures were designed with a clear conviction that data structuring and program structuring were two closely related issues. Very early, it was recognized that data structuring was a key concept for the design of programs with a high potential for parallelism. This paper offers a personal perspective of this research activity, which culminated with the Gamma formalism.

1. Introduction

Parallelism is a powerful structuring concept that could facilitate program construction. As noted in [3], two kinds of parallelism have to be distinguished: physical parallelism and logical parallelism. Physical parallelism is related to the organisation of the computation on a set of processors. By logical parallelism, we mean the possibility of describing a program as a set of cooperating processes. In this paper, we are only concerned with logical parallelism.

The confusion between these two kinds of parallelism comes from the heritage of several decades of imperative culture and the impact of the Von Neumann model of computation. The sequencing operator, together with assignment, are the basic means of the machine, the role is of operation of the Von Neumann machine. They have been further developed with the introduction of the loop control structure and of the array data structure. Let us take the simple example of computing the maximum element of a set of values. In an imperative setting the set will be represented by an array $a [1 \ldots n]$ and a possible solution will be:

$$\text{max\_set} : m := a[1];$$
$$i := 1;$$
$$\text{while } i \neq n \text{ do } i := i + 1; \ m := \max(m, a[i])$$

while the condition $i \leq n$ holds, index i is incremented and a new local maximum is computed.

Two decisions have led to this highly sequential program : the choice of representing a set by an array, thus introducing an ordering between elements, and the use of a loop program structure for computing i and m.

Parallel Multiset Processing:
From Explicit Coordination to Chemical Reaction

Jean-Pierre Banâtre

Irisa / Universiti de Rennes 1 / Inria
Campus de Beaulieu
35042 Rennes cedex - France

Abstract:

The author has been involved for more than fifteen years in the design, study and implementation of coordination program structures. These structures were designed with a clear conviction that data structuring and program structuring were two closely related issues. Very early, it was recognized that set data structuring was a key concept for the design of programs with a high potential for parallelism. This paper offers a personal perspective of this research activity which culminated with the Gamma formalism.

1   Introduction

Parallelism is a powerful structuring concept that could facilitate program construction. As stated in [3], two kinds of parallelism have to be distinguished : physical parallelism and logical parallelism. Physical parallelism is related to the organisation of the computation on a set of processors. By logical parallelism, we mean the possibility of describing a program as a set of cooperating processes. In this paper, we are only concerned with "logical parallelism".

The confusion between these two kinds of parallelism comes from the heritage of several decades of imperative culture and the impact of the Von Neumann model of computation. The sequencing operator together with assignment are the basic means of abstracting the mode of operation of the Von Neumann machine. They have been further developed with the introduction of the loop control structure and of the array data structure. Let us take the simple example of computing the maximum element of a set of values. In an imperative setting, the set will be represented by an array a $[1 : n]$ and a possible solution will be :

$$\text{max\_set} : m := a[1];$$
$$i := 1;$$
$$*[i < n \rightarrow i := i + 1; m := max(m, a[i])]$$

while the condition $i < n$ holds, index i is incremented and a new local maximum is computed.

Two decisions have led to this highly sequential program : the choice of representing a set by an array, thus introducing an ordering between elements, and the use of a loop program structure for computing i and m.

The maximum element can in fact be computed by performing the comparisons of the elements in any order : every "confrontation" between two elements cancels the smaller one, and the unique remaining element will be the maximum. As will be seen later, this sentence describes an algorithm which can be readily written in Gamma [3].

The above example raises another crucial point. There is a very strong correlation between control structures and data structures. One knows that a variable, say v, represents a sequence whose successive elements verify a recurrence relationship of the form : $v_i = \varphi(v_{i-1})$, φ representing the body of the loop which computes v. It is also well-known that recursive data structures (like lists) are naturally exploited by using recursive control structures. In this paper, we will examine how appropriate control structures may be designed in order to carry out computations on general data structures such as multisets. Our aim will be the design of high-level programs which reflect the logical properties of the problem to solve, without any artificial sequentiality.

Section 2 describes coordinations structures which have been developed in order to process dynamic sets. Section 3 discusses the evolution from these structures to the Gamma formalism which is sketched in section 4.

2   Coordination structures for dynamic multiset processsing

This section gives an overview of work which was carried out fifteen years ago in a compiler design project [1,2]. In this context, it was recognized that proper control structures over proper data structures clearly enabled the user to better express the solutions of complex programming problems.

2.1   The notion of event

An event (called "future" in other contexts) can be seen as a single assignment variable [1]. The value of such variables may be requested in a computation before being actually produced. In this case, the computation demanding the value is simply suspended ; it is resumed when the value is known. Of course, the introduction of events comes with the possibility of dynamically creating processes. Here is a sample of program involving events and processes :

```
        begin
        (1)     event int x;
                ...
        (2)     activate (···x···);# process P₁#
                ...
        (3)     x ← 3
        (4)     activate (···x···);# process P₂#
                ...
        end
```

An event whose value is of type **integer** is declared in (1). In (2), the process P_1 is created. It will happen to be suspended, if x has not been assigned a value when it is accessed. The value 3 is assigned to x in (3) and finally a new process (say P_2) is created in (4). This process will not be interrupted because of x.

The concept of event has been largely used to simply solve the problem of forward referencing while constructing an Algol 68 compiler [1].

Another particular hard problem to deal with in the construction of compilers and operating systems is the management of dynamic identifier tables, i.e., tables whose cardinality cannot be known statically. Awkward sequential solutions are usually used (based on a priori fixed cardinality, which may reveal to be badly chosen or using dynamic data structures such as lists). Examining the very nature of these tables, it was clear that they would be better represented as sets rather than as arrays. Proceeding this way, they would also be naturally exploited in a parallel way.

Furthermore, the contents of these tables is built incrementally and their components can be seen as events whose values are determined as the computation progresses.

2.2 Dynamic sets of events

A set (say, s) of events of type **event m** is declared as **vse m** s ; vse stands for "varisized set of events". The generation of a new component belonging to s is expressed by $s \leftarrow v$, which means that one of the components of s gets its value, v. The cardinality of dynamic sets is itself an event. The value of this event is determined when some condition is realized during the computation. The primitive **close** s is used to signify that the vse s is completed.

Now we know how to declare and build vse's, but we haven't said yet how they can be exploited.

The control structure which was proposed in [2] acts as a process generator. As soon as a new element is introduced in a vse, s, new processes are generated which deal with s. Syntactically, this program structure can be described as :

for all elts of s **do** < process body > **od**

This peculiar loop acts as a process generator : when a new element s_j is added to s, an instance of < process body > dealing with s_j is spawn. In < process body >, s_j is referred to as **this** s ; this is simply a generic naming facility. Of course, several process generators may be associated to the same vse and elements s_j will, in general, be exploited by a "bunch" of processes.

In order to complete the above control structure, a coordination facility was added ; it allows the creation of an "epilogue" process, when **all** processes created by a given process generator have been completed. So the final format of our control structure is :

for all elts of s do < process body > **od**
at end < epilogue > **end**

More informations about *vse's* and associated control structures may be found in [2]. Next, we present an example illustrating the elegance of these data and program structures.

2.3 A general identifier binder

We consider the problem of associating an identifier to its declarations in a block structured language following the usual Algol/Pascal rules. For simplicity sake, we use the following grammar to describe the language :

```
< block >      ::= begin $ beg $ < body > end $ ed $
< body >       ::= < sentence > | < sentence >;< body >
< sentence > ::= var < identifier > $ var ident $ |
                    < identifier > $ occur ident $|
                    < block >
< identifier > ::= # usual notation for identifiers #
```

A block is a sequence of declarations and instructions. An instruction is either the occurrence of a variable or a nested block.

Symbols between $ are transmitted by the parser to the semantic analyser which performs identifier binding. Symbols produced by the parser are accessed sequentially by successive requests to the process *rsd* (for read syntactic data).

The solution we propose can be written as follows :

```
procpidentification = ((identifier → void) enclosing_block_search) void :
  begin
    vse identifier id_table ;
    procp search = (identifier x )void :
      begin
        activate
          (bool success := false ;
          for all elt of id_table
            do
              [x = this id_table → success := true
                □
              x ≠ this id_table → null
              ]
            od
          at end
            [ not success → enclosing_block_search (x)
              □
            success → print (x, "successfull binding")
            ]
          end
          )
      end search ;
    *[rsd ? symbol →
      [symbol = beg → identification (search)
        □
      symbol = (var, x) → id_table ← x
        □
      symbol = (occur, x) → search (x)
        □
      symbol = ed → close id_table
      ]
    ]
  end identification ;
```

Neither "identification" nor search are exactly procedures because they can create activities (processes) which may survive their own termination. For this reason, we prefix them with **procp** which recalls **procedure** and **process**. The notation (**identifier → void**) describes the functional type of the **procp** "enclosing_block_search". Otherwise, we have used a CSP-like notation [11] to describe process behaviour.

Several comments may be made about this program :

1. It does not introduce superfluous data structures (only *vse id_table* is used).
2. It makes an intensive use of coordination structures : recursion for dealing with block nesting, higher-order functions for transfering a computation from

recursion level $n+1$ to recursion level n. This is necessary for achieving proper binding.

3. The indentifier table is processed without introducing any artificial sequentiality.

4. In order to detect missing declarations, the compiler provides the procedure *mission_declaration*, defined as :

$$\text{proc missing\_declaration} = (\textbf{identifier } x) \textbf{ void :}$$
$$\textbf{begin}$$
$$\text{print } (x, \text{ "cannot be identified"})$$
$$\textbf{end missing\_declaration ;}$$

The initial call to identification is : *identification (missing_declaration)* ; If an identifier belonging to a block b cannot be bound to any declaration after invocation of search procedures associated with b and with all blocks enclosing b, the default procedure *missing_declaration* is invoked and produces the appropriate error message.

3   A smooth transition to Gamma

We believe that the above program is very elegant and clean ; it introduces as few data structures as possible and in particular, it avoids the use of intermediate data structures for emulating coordination structures.

However, dynamic sets of events are well adapted to the processing of very homogeneous sets because all the elements are associated with the same treatment. This may suggest that only a limited class of algorithms can be described with these structures. As far as software quality is concerned, one can realize that the provision of high-level data and coordination structures relieves the programmer from managing complex data structures. So, one can expect better quality programs.

Nevertheless, programs are seen as sets of processes which communicate and synchronize via events. It is recognized that reasoning and proving properties of such programs is very difficult, if not impossible, with the present tools. Then, our objective was to find more descriptive ways of computing over multisets. Further work was directed by the following observations :

1. The multiset is the less constraining data structure. There is no form of hierarchy in a multiset and there can be multiple occurrences of the same element.

2. A special ordering has been proposed on multisets [6]. Using such an ordering, it should be possible to prove termination properties.

3. In order to reason on multiset ordering, the computation should act as a multiset transformer.

Initial thinking let us to a proposal where a process was attached to every value of the multiset and a special value (weight) was associated to every such process [7]. Two processes could communicate if their respective weights were related by a certain condition. The computation was considered as stable as soon as all conditions were false. Those familiar with Gamma will identify the chaotic behaviour of Gamma computations. This approach was still operational in its spirit, but there was a first step towards property proving (termination).

During some years, there was not much progress till discussions with Daniel Le Métayer lead to the present day Gamma formalism. Daniel was quite influenced by functional programming and in particular by Backus's work on FP languages [8]. The locality principle that is often put forward to qualify Gamma behaviour comes directly from the functional world. Furthermore, the functional approach was very precious for our objectives in formal property proving. So, the synthesis between parallel multiset processing and functional programming gave birth to Gamma which is sketched in the next section.

4 A short trip in the Gamma world

The purpose of this section is not a new survey of the work achieved on Gamma [5]. We simply want to convey the spirit of the language through a short selection of examples. The interested reader can find in [5] a more comprehensive account of the work done on Gamma during the last ten years.

4.1 A short introduction to Gamma

The Gamma formalism was proposed ten years ago to capture the intuition of a computation as a global evolution of a collection of atomic values "interacting" freely. Gamma can be introduced intuitively through the chemical reaction metaphor. The unique data structure is the multiset which can be seen as chemical solution. A program is simply a pair (Reaction condition, Action). Execution proceeds by replacing in the multiset elements satisfying the reaction condition by the results of the action. The final result is obtained when a stable state is reached, that is to say when no more reactions can take place. The maximum element problem of the introduction can be solved by the following Gamma program :

$$\max : x, y \to y \Longleftarrow x \leq y$$

This program simply says that if two elements x, y are such that $x \leq y$, then these elements are replaced by y (the greater). Of course, nothing is specified about the order of evaluation of the comparisons. If several disjoint pairs of elements verify the condition, the corresponding reactions can be performed in parallel.

4.2 A selection of Gamma programs

We illustrate the Gamma style of programming through a set of selected examples, illustrating the elegance of the formalism.

Prime number generation

Goal : produce the prime numbers less than a given N.

Solution :
  primes $(N) = $ rem $\{2 \cdots N\}$
  rem $: x, y \rightarrow y \Longleftarrow$ multiple (x, y)

Number sorting

Goal : sort a set of numbers, each number being represented by a pair (index, value)

Solution :
  Sort $: (i, x), (j, y) \rightarrow (i, y), (j, x) \Longleftarrow (i > j) \wedge (x < y)$

Factorial

Goal : compute N !

Solution :
  factorial $(N) = $ fact $\{2 \cdots N\}$
  fact $: x, y \rightarrow x * y \Longleftarrow$ **true**

The majority element problem

Goal : compute the majority element of a multiset M. This element appears more than card $(M)/2$ times in the multiset. For simplicity sake, we assume that such an element exists. The operation **one of** extracts a random element from a multiset.

Solution :
  MAJ $= $ **one of** maj (M)
  maj $: x, y \rightarrow \{\} \Longleftarrow x \# y$

Convex hull

Goal : compute the smallest convext polygon containing a set of points in the plane

solution :
  convex $: P_1, P_2, P_3, P_4 \rightarrow P_1, P_2, P_3 \Longleftarrow P_4$ **inside** $< P_1, P_2, P_3 >$
  $Pi's$ are points and P_4 is "inside" $< P_1, P_2, P_3 >$ if P_4 is within the triangle they form.

The dining philosophers

Goal : solve the traditional dining philosopher problem.

Solution :
$$\text{phil} : \varphi_i, \varphi_j \rightarrow \phi_i \Longleftarrow j = i \oplus 1$$
$$\phi_i \rightarrow \varphi_i, \varphi_{i\oplus 1} \Longleftarrow \textbf{true}$$

This solution contains two rules describing the two possible transitions : a thinking philosopher is allowed to eat (he/she gets two forks $\varphi_i, \varphi_{i\oplus 1}$) or an eating philosopher i starts thinking (he/she releases two forks $\varphi_i, \varphi_{1\oplus 1}$). $\oplus$ represents addition modulo 5, if we consider five philosophers.

This small set of examples demonstrates the richness and power of the Gamma paradigm. Many more examples are presented in [3].

4.3 Systematic program construction in Gamma

The most attractive properties of Gamma (high-level data structuring, locality principle) have been exploited in the design of a derivation method which can be applied to develop totally correct Gamma programs [4].

The derivation method is inspired by the work of Dijkstra [9] and Gries [10]. The method is composed of four stages. The first one is the transformation of the specification and its split into and invariant and a termination condition. In the second stage, the reaction condition is derived from the termination condition. The third stage is the deduction of the action from the invariant and the termination condition. The last stage is the derivation of a well-founded ordering from the action and the invariant for proving termination.

We will not review in detail this method, we will simply sketch the derivation of a sorting algorithm.

Specification

A natural data structure to describe a sorted set of values is the sequence. This sequence must be encoded within a multiset ; we choose a multiset M of pairs (index, value), where $x.i$ of an element x gives the position of the value $x.v$ in the sequence. Let M_o be the initial multiset ; a possible specification of the result M is :

(1) $\forall x, y \in M, x \cdot i < y \cdot i \Longrightarrow x \cdot v \leq y \cdot v$
(2) $M \cdot i = \{1 \cdots \text{card } (M_0)\}$
(3) $M \cdot v = M_0$

1. Split of the specification

We may choose $I = (2) \wedge (3)$ because (2) and (3) can be established in a straightforward way from M_0. I means that values are evenly distributed on the range $1 \cdots$ card (M_0). The termination condition T is (1) which must hold at the end of the computation.

2. Reaction condition

The reaction condition can be derived in a straightforward way by negating T. So, we get :

$$R(x, y) = (x \cdot i < y \cdot i) \wedge (x \cdot v > y \cdot v)$$

3. Action

The action must transform the multiset while maintaining the invariant. A simple reasoning shows that the only possible choice is :

$$A(x, y) = \{(x \cdot i, y \cdot v), (y \cdot i, x \cdot v)\}$$

The elements $(x \cdot i, x \cdot v)$ and $(y \cdot i, y \cdot v)$ which are ill-ordered are replaced by $(x \cdot i, y \cdot v)$ and $(y \cdot i, x \cdot v)$ which are correctly ordered.

4. Well-founded ordering

In order to prove the termination of a Gamma program, we have to provide a well-founded ordering on multisets and to show that the application of the action decreases the multiset according to this ordering. We use a result of [6] allowing the derivation of a well-founded ordering on multisets from a well-founded ordering on elements of the multiset. Let $>$ be an ordering on S and $\gg$ be the ordering on multisets $\mathcal{M}(S)$ defined in the following way :

$$M \gg M' \Longleftrightarrow \exists X \in \mathcal{M}(S), \exists Y \in \mathcal{M}(S) \text{ such that }$$
$$(X \neq \{\} \wedge X \subseteq M \wedge M' = (M - X) + Y \wedge \forall y \in Y, \exists x \in X, x > y)$$

The ordering $\gg$ on $\mathcal{M}(S)$ is well-founded if and only if the ordering $>$ on S is well-founded.

In order to prove the termination of our *sort* program, we can use the following well-founded ordering [4] on the elements of the multiset :

$$(i, x) \sqsubseteq (i', x') \Longleftrightarrow i \geq i' \wedge x' \geq x$$

This completes the derivation of the program presented earlier in section 4.2.

The derivation strategy which has been quickly developed here, has been applied successfully to a lot of non-trivial examples as described in [4]. We believe that this formal derivation process was made possible by the fact that, in Gamma, a program is no longer a sequence of instructions modifying a state, but rather a multiset transformer operating on all the data at once.

5 Conclusion

This paper describes a personal view of the genesis of Gamma. It all happened because we were searching for paradigms that were relying on very few high-level data structuring facilities which do not introduce any non-logical dependencies between data. The multiset appears to be the ideal data structure. Then the question was : how to exploit multisets with language structures introducing no articial sequentiality and favoring formal reasoning. The outcome was this notion of dynamic set of events and its associate control structures which, after various influences, led to the Gamma formalism. We have stressed the simplicity and elegance of the Gamma formalism and of Gamma programs ; we have also shown how to develop Gamma programs from a specification in a systematic way. Much more could have been said (implementation, extensions $\cdots$), the interested reader find a review of past work and current perspectives on Gamma in [5].

Acknowledgments:

Many people have contributed to the work reported in this paper, most of them appear in the bibliography. I would like to mention two colleagues who had a major influence on this research : Laurent Trilling, now Professor at Grenoble University, who introduced me to the world of Programming and oriented some of my research directions ; Daniel Le Métayer, Research Director at Inria/Irisa for our common enthousiasm while discovering and developing the Gamma formalism.

References

[1] J.P. BANÂTRE, J.P. ROUTEAU AND L. TRILLING. AN EVENT-DRIVEN COMPILING TECHNIQUE, *Communications of the ACM*, VOL. 22-1, P. 34-42, JANUARY 1979.

[2] F. ANDRI, J.P. BANÂTRE AND J.P. ROUTEAU. A MULTIPROCESSING APPROACH TO COMPILE-TIME SYMBOL RESOLUTION, *ACM Transactions On Programming Languages And Systems*, VOL. 3-1, P. 11-23, JANUARY 1981.

[3] J.P. BANÂTRE AND D. LE MÉTAYER. PROGRAMMING BY MULTISET TRANSFORMATION. *Communications of the ACM*, VOL. 36-1, P. 98-111, JANUARY 1993.

[4] J.P. BANÂTRE AND D. LE MÉTAYER. THE GAMMA MODEL AND ITS DISCIPLINE OF PROGRAMMING. *Science of Computer Programming*, VOL. 15, P. 55-77, 1990.

[5] J.P. BANÂTRE AND D. LE MÉTAYER. GAMMA AND THE CHEMICAL REACTION MODEL : TEN YEARS AFTER. *Proceedings of the Coordination'95 workshop*, IC-PRESS, LONDON, 1996.

[6] N. DERSHOWITZ AND Z. MANNA. PROVING TERMINATION BY MULTISET ORDERING. *Communications of the ACM*, VOL. 22-8, P. 465-476, AUGUST 1979.

[7] J.P. BANÂTRE, M. BANÂTRE AND P. QUINTON. CONSTRUCTING PARALLEL PROGRAMS AND THEIR TERMINATION PROOFS. *Proc. Int. Conf. on Parallel Processing*. BELLAIRE, USA, AUGUST 1982.

[8] J.BACKUS. CAN PROGRAMMING BE LIBERATED FROM THE VON NEUMANN STYLE ? A FUNCTIONAL STYLE AND ITS ALGEBRA OF PROGRAMS. *Communications of the ACM*, VOL. 21-8, P. 613-641, AUGUST 1978.

[9] E.W. DIJKSTRA. *A discipline of programming*. PRENTICE HALL, ENGLEWOOD CLIFFS, NJ, 1976.

[10] D. GRIES. *The science of programming*. SPRINGER VERLAG, NEW-YORK, 1981.

[11] C.A.R. HOARE. COMMUNICATING SEQUENTIAL PROCESSES. *Communications of the ACM*, VOL. 21-8, P. 666-677, AUGUST 1978.

Graph Rewriting and Constraint Solving for Modelling Distributed Systems with Synchronization (Extended Abstract)

Ugo Montanari and Francesca Rossi

Università di Pisa, Dipartimento di Informatica
Corso Italia 40, 56125 Pisa, Italy
E-mail: {ugo,rossi}@di.unipi.it

Abstract. In this extended abstract we describe our approach to modelling the dynamics of distributed systems. For distributed systems we mean systems consisting of concurrent processes communicating via shared ports and posing certain synchronization requirements, via the ports, to the adjacent processes. We use graphs to represent states of such systems, and graph rewriting to represent their evolution. The kind of graph rewriting we use is based on simple context-free productions which are however combined by means of the synchronization mechanism. This allows for a good level of expressivity in the system without sacrificing full distribution. Moreover, to approach the problem of combining productions together, we suggest to exploit existing techniques for constraint solving. This is based on the observation that the combination problem can be modelled as a (finite domain) constraint problem. In this respect, we propose to use both local consistency techniques, to remove the possible redundancies in a system state, and a distributed backtracking search algorithm, as used in distributed constraint solving. Our method has two main advantages: first, it is completely formal and thus provides a precise description of the way a distributed system evolves; second, it also seems very promising from the performance point of view, since the techniques we propose to combine productions together have been proven very convenient in several cases.

1 Introduction

Among the many formalisms that can be chosen to represent distributed systems and their evolutions, we believe that graphs and graph grammars [Ehr78, Ehr87, SE94, SPvE92, CM95] are among the most convenient, both in terms of expressivity and of technical background. In fact, graphs describe in a natural way net topologies and data sharing, and moreover they possess a wide literature and technical results which make the whole field of graph rewriting very formal and its notions precisely definable. Therefore, consider a distributed system consisting of concurrent processes communicating via pieces of shared data (or channels, or ports). Then such a system can be represented as a graph where arcs (or in general hyperarcs) can represent processes (or subsystem abstractions) and nodes can represent the shared data.

Then, the evolution of such system can be modelled by graph rewriting: at each rewriting step a subpart of the current graph is chosen to evolve, and its evolution consists of being replaced by another graph. In the literature there are many graph rewriting formalisms, which range from the simplest context-free edge rewriting [Hab89] to the most general context-sensitive subgraph rewriting [Ehr78, Ehr87]. In order to choose one of them to model the evolution of a distributed system, we must make some assumptions on the system we want to model. For this paper, we assume that processes, in order to evolve, may require to synchronize with adjacent processes. That is, if two processes share a piece of data, then each of them may pose some conditions on this shared piece of information. If they agree on these conditions, then both of them (but not one of them alone) can evolve. Thus the evolution of a single process may happen only if the process is isolated, or if it does not require any synchronization to the adjacent processes.

A possible simple way to model process evolution in such kind of systems is to use a two-phase approach: first *context-free* process productions are specified (a set for each process), as well as synchronization requests for each of these possible moves. Then, *context-sensitive* subsystem rewriting rules are obtained by combining some context-free productions. These context-sensitive rules allow for the evolution of a subpart of the system consisting of several processes that agree on the synchronization on the shared data. Applying the rule means making all such processes (and not a proper subset of them) evolve, each with one of its context-free productions. Thus the resulting rewriting mechanism is not completely general, since it is obtained by combining context-free productions and not general ones. This may pose some restrictions on the way a system evolves, but it provides a natural formalism to model the behaviour of distributed systems with decentralized control. In fact, once the processes have agreed on how to behave on the shared data, they may move without any need of communicating with each other: each process needs only know its context-free productions.

This kind of synchronization and process evolution has been already considered in [DM87], and modelled via a special graph rewriting formalism, called *grammars for distributed systems* (GDS), where graphs represented not only the current state of the system but also its history, so to be able to derive concurrency and dependency information among the various computation steps. Also, a variation of GDSs which uses a more general rewriting mechanism allowing for system reconfiguration has been proposed in [CDM85]. In this paper we use instead a classical graph rewriting formalism, like that described in [Ehr87], since we are just interested in the present of the system, and not its history.

To make the above described model for distributed system rewriting realistic, one needs to give an effective, and possibly efficient, way to obtain the context-sensitive rewrite rules from the context-free productions (the so-called *rule-matching problem* [CDM85]). That is, one needs to say how a set of processes is chosen, their synchronization requirements checked, and the corresponding context-free productions combined to get the resulting context-sensitive rule. Of course, all these tasks are to be performed in a distributed way, since we assumed to be in a distributed environment.

In this respect, finite domain constraint problems [Mac88, Mon74], and the propagation and solution techniques associated to them [Mac88, Mon74, Mac77, Fre78, MF85, DP88], may be helpful. A finite domain constraint problem can be described as a set of variables taking values over corresponding finite domains, and a set of constraints. Each constraint involves a subset of the variables and specifies all the possible ways such variables can satify the constraint. That is, if a constraint involves k variables, then it will consists of a set of tuples, of length k, of values of the variable domains. Any other combination of values for the k variables which is not described by one of the tuples will violate the constraint. A solution for a constraint problem is an assignment to all the variables which satisfies all the constraints.

The idea here, already considered in [CDM85], is to represent the rule-matching problem in a distributed system as a constraint problem, where variables are associated to processes and constraints to ports (that is, sets of adjacent processes). The domain of a variable is then the set of all context-free productions for the corresponding process, and each constraint is satisfied by the tuples of context-free productions (one for each adjacent process) whose synchronization requirements agree on the considered port. In this kind of constraint problem, a solution is thus a choice of a context-free production for each process, such that all synchronization requirements are satisfied. Note that a solution does not necessarily make every process evolve. In fact, to model the case of a rewrite rule which synchronizes only a subset of the processes, we can assume that an *idle* production has been chosen for each inactive process.

Given this representation of the rule-matching problem as a finite domain constraint problem, it is natural to consider the techniques used to solve constraint problems of this kind. Usually, finite domain constraint problems are solved by a backtracking search over the tree of the possible alternatives for each variable: variables are assigned to elements of their domain, in some order, until a failure to satisfy (even a subset of) the constraints occurs; at that point, the assignment of the latest assigned variable is retracted and another assignment tried. Otherwise, a complete assignment is reached, which is a solution of the constraint problem, and the backtracking search assures that all solutions are tried.

To make the basic backtracking algorithm more efficient (although it always remains exponential in the worst case, since the problem is NP-complete), many *constraint propagation* (or *local consistency*) algorithms have been proposed in the literature [Mon74, Mac77, Fre78, MF85, DP88]. The basic idea behind such algorithms is the following: if, by looking at only some of the constraints of the constraint problem, one can see that there is no way to assign some variable to a value, then that assigment will never participate in any complete solution. Thus it can be eliminated. By iterating this removal until no more removals are possible in any variable domain, we get an algorithm which is polynomial, although exponential in the size (that is, number of variables) of the subsets of constraints considered at each step. This idea can be instantiated in several different ways depending on which and how many constraints one considers at each step. For example, by considering only one constraint at a time (and thus only the variables involved in such constraint), we have the so-called *arc-consistency* algorithm [Mac77]. More generally, by considering subsets of constraints involving k variables, we get the so-called *k-consistency* algorithm [Fre78]. It is clear how such algorithms may help the standard backtracking algorithm outlined above: if applied before starting the backtracking algorithm, then each variable has less alternatives; thus the branching factor of the search tree is smaller, causing failures to be discovered earlier. Therefore the process of finding a solution is faster.

In our formulation of the rule-matching problem as a finite domain constraint problem, eliminating values from a variable domain means eliminating, for a process, the choice of some of its context-free productions (because their synchronization requirements do not match with those of the productions of adjacent processes). This could lead to a great speed-up in the overall search for a solution, especially when the graph representing the current system state has special topologies [Fre88].

In classical constraint solving over finite domains, constraints are usually stored in one memory. Thus local consistency algorithms are usually centralized. However, it is easy to see that such algorithms have an intrinsic distributed nature, since one can consider agents corresponding to clusters of constraints, which represent the selected subproblems. Such agents know the tuples they allow and the domains of the variables they involve, and communicate among them via the shared variables. At each step of the algorithm (but several steps my occur simultaneously at different sites), an agent considers its constraints and the current domains of its shared variables, and possibly deletes some values from such domains. In particular, the arc-consistency algorithm can be implemented in a completely distributed environment, since each agent corresponds to just one constraint [ND95].

Once a local consistency algorithm has been applied over the current state of the system, so to possibly eliminate some redundant choices for the processes, one has however still the problem of solving the rule-matching problem, which, as said above, amounts to choosing a subset of the processes, and a context-free rule for each of them, so that all synchronization requirements of the chosen productions are satisfied. This can be done by a backtracking search algorithm (as described above), which however has to be distributed as well. Examples of ditributed version of such algorithm for finite domain constraint problems can be found in [YIDK92, Yok95]. Here we just give the basic ideas underlying all such algorithms.

Agents of the algorithm are processes, to be assigned one of their context-free productions, among the ones that are left after the application of some local consistency algorithm. We recall that each process has always the idle production, which for sure is still one of the possibilities after local consistency.

This allows to obtain partial solutions besides complete ones. Each agent knows the possible choices for its process and also the ports such a process shares with others. Assuming a fixed total ordering of the agents, each agent, concurrently to all the others, waits until new synchronization requirements are posted on the ports it shares with agents above it in the ordering. When this happens, it chooses one of its context-free productions which agrees with the requirements, and posts the corresponding new requirements on the ports the process shares with agents below it in the ordering. If it has no choice which satisfies such requirements, then it posts a failure on the ports the process shares with the agent which is the lowest one among those above it. When an agent sees one or more failures from below, it tries to make another choice, still compatible with the information coming from above. Attention has to be put to the fixed ordering of the agents, in order to avoid incorrect behaviours of such algorithm. In fact, if the order does not correspond to a line (that is, processes which are handled by agents which are one the successor of the other one in the ordering are not adjacent), then it is possible that failures are not communicated properly, and that thus a global failure is returned while instead there is a solution. Another way to solve this problem is to dinamically change the structure of the connections among agents, in particular by adding new connections whenever needed [YIDK92].

Once the rule-matching problem has been solved via the local consistency plus the distributed backtracking algorithm (and it is indeed possible to formally prove that such combination of techniques solves the rule-matching problem), each process has been assigned a context-free production and can now move according to the chosen production and independently of the others. This means that the processes can move all at the same time, or also at different times, but without regard of their relative speed, since the resulting state will always be the same (due to the context-free nature of the individual moves). We recall that processes whose chosen production is the idle one in practice do not move.

In the following of this extended abstract, the interested reader may find some details on (and/or pointers to) the formalisms and the techniques we informally described in the introduction, and on the way they can be used for our purposes. In particular, Section 2 gives the basic notions of graph and graph rewriting, and shows how to use graphs to model systems states and graph rewriting to model system evolution. Then, Section 3 defines constraint problems, local consistency algorithms, and distributed backtracking search, and shows how to model and efficiently solve the rule-matching problem using such notions and techniques. Finally, Section 5 concludes the paper summarizing the main points of our approach and pointing out its advantages.

2   Graphs and Graph Rewriting

In this paper we adopt the *algebraic* graph rewriting approach, as described in [Ehr87]. It is also called the *double-pushout* approach, since each graph rewrite rule is a pair of graph inclusions, and its application is described by a double pushout (where two of the arrows are the inclusions describing the rewrite rule to be applied) in the category of considered graphs. First we will give the basic notions of classical graph rewriting, according to this approach, and then we will show how to model distributed systems and their evolution via graph rewriting.

2.1 Basic Notions

By a *hypergraph*, or simply a *graph*, we mean a triple $G = (N, E, c)$, where

- N is a set of *nodes*,
- E is a set of *edges*,
- $c : E \to N^*$ is the *connection function* (thus each edge can be connected to a list of nodes).

If $G = (N, E, c)$ and $G' = (N', E', c')$ are two graphs, then a *graph (homo)morphism* $f : G \to G'$ is a pair of functions $(f_N : N \to N', f_E : E \to E')$ which preserve the connection functions (i.e., $c'(f_E(e)) = f_N^*(c(e))$, where f_N^* is the extension of f_N to lists). A *graph monomorphism* $f : G \hookrightarrow G'$ is a graph morphism such that both f_N and f_E are injective; moreover, f is a *graph isomorphism* if both f_N and f_E are isomorphisms.

Following the *algebraic approach* to graph grammars [Ehr78, Ehr87]), a graph production $p = (L \overset{l}{\hookleftarrow} K \overset{r}{\hookrightarrow} R)$ is a pair of graph monomorphisms having as common source a graph K, the *gluing graph*, indicating which arcs and nodes have to be preserved by the application of the production.

Given two graph morphisms $b : K \to B$ and $d : K \to D$, a pair $\langle h : B \to H, c : D \to H \rangle$ is called a *pushout* of $\langle b, d \rangle$ if:

- (commutativity property) $h \circ b = c \circ d$;
- (universal property)   for all graphs H' and graph morphisms $h' : B \to H'$ and $c' : D \to H'$, with $h' \circ b = c' \circ d$, there exists a unique morphism $f : H \to H'$ such that $f \circ h = h'$ and $f \circ c = c'$ (see Figure 1).

In this situation, H is called a *pushout object* of $\langle b, d \rangle$. Moreover, given arrows $b : K \to B$ and $h : B \to H$, a *pushout complement* of $\langle b, h \rangle$ is a pair $\langle d : K \to D, c : D \to H \rangle$ such that $\langle h, c \rangle$ is a pushout of b and d. In this case D is called a *pushout complement object* of $\langle b, h \rangle$.

Intuitively, graph H in Figure 1 is the pushout object of morphisms b and d if it is obtained from the disjoint union of D and B by identifying the images of K in D and in B.

A production p can be applied to a graph G yielding H (written $G \Rightarrow_p H$) if there is an *occurrence* of L in G, i.e., a graph morphism $g : L \to G$, and H is obtained as the result of the *double pushout* construction of Figure 2.

This construction may be interpreted as follows. In order to delete the occurrence of L in G, we construct the pushout complement of g and l, i.e., a pair $\langle k : K \to D, d : D \to G \rangle$ such that the resulting square is a pushout. Next, we have to embed the right-hand side R in D via a second pushout, which produces graph H. If $G \Rightarrow_p H$ we say that there is a *direct derivation* from G to H via p. From this informal explanation of a direct derivation, it should be clear that

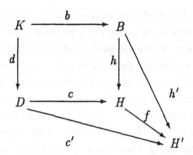

Fig. 1. Pushout diagram.

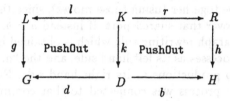

Fig. 2. Graph rewriting via double pushout construction.

the gluing graph K of the production is needed to specify how L and R are embedded in the larger graphs G and H, respectively.

A *graph rewriting system* is a set $\mathcal{R}$ of graph productions. A *derivation* from G to H over $\mathcal{R}$ (shortly $G \Rightarrow_{\mathcal{R}}^* H$), is a finite sequence of direct derivations of the form $G \Rightarrow_{p_1} G_1 \Rightarrow_{p_2} \ldots \Rightarrow_{p_n} G_n = H$, where $p_1, \ldots, p_n$ are in $\mathcal{R}$.

A graph production $p = (L \overset{l}{\hookleftarrow} K \overset{r}{\hookrightarrow} R)$ is *context-free* when graph L contains a single hyperarc, say of arity k, and k distinct nodes, and graph K contains only k nodes. This means that, when such production is applied, the hyperarc contained in L is deleted and replaced by graph R.

2.2   Graph Rewriting for Distributed Systems

It is easy to see how to model a distributed systems via a graph: processes are represented by arcs, and ports by nodes. The connection function specifies which ports are connected to which processes. Then, for each process there is a set of context-free productions, all of which have the hyperarc representing that process in their left member. Thus, all the productions associated to a process specify the possible moves for such process.

To model synchronization requirements, we need to slightly modify the way a production is defined, by adding some labels to the nodes in its left member. Assuming to have an alphabet of requirements, say A, then we need a partial function $f : nodes(L) \rightarrow A$, which associates a synchronization requirement to some of the nodes. In this way each move for a process poses some requests to the adjacent processes: that they move as well, and with matching synchronization requirements. Function f is partial since it is possible that, for a specific move, no requirement is posed on some of the ports adjacent to the process.

For the set of all context-free productions, we now have to get the set of all rewriting rules for the system. This is called the *rule-matching problem*. Each rule is obtained, as mentioned in the introduction, by merging some of the productions together while checking that such productions agree on the synchronization requirements. For example, consider two adjacent processes which share one port, such that no other process is connected to that port, and let us take one production for each of these two processes. Then each of such productions will pose a requirement over that port, say a and b. If $a \neq b$, then the two processes cannot move together (using those moves), since they do not agree on what should happen over that shared port. If instead $a = b$, then they can, via the context-sensitive graph rewriting rule which is obtained by taking the graph containing the two processes as its left hand side, and the "merging" of the right hand sides of the two productions as its right hand side. Note that we had to assume that no other process was connected to that common port. In fact, a move can be accomplished only if, for each port involved in the rewriting, all processes connected to it agree on the synchronization requirements.

Once all possible context-sensitive productions have been obtained, the distributed system can move using any one of them (via the double-pushout construction given above). Note however that, after the move, we have a different distributed system. Thus a new production-combination phase has to be performed in order to understand which are the subsequent possible moves.

Note also that, in order to specify the behaviour of a distributed system, one does not need to give the context-sensitive rewrite rules, but only the much simpler context-free productions. In fact, the problem of obtaining the rules (that is, the rule-matching problem) is left to the system. This makes the specification task much easier. However, the system may take a long time to solve such a complex problem (that, as noted earlier, has to be solved before being able to actually make a move). This is why in the following of this paper we will suggest some techniques to solve this problem in a distributed but efficient way.

3 Constraint Problems and Constraint Propagation

First we will give the basic notions for defining finite domain constraint problems and the related techniques for constraint propagation, and then we will show how to model the rule-matching problem as a constraint problem.

3.1 Constraint Problems

A (finite domain) constraint problem [Mac88, Mon74] consists of a set of variables ranging over a finite domain, and a set of constraints. A solution to such problem is an instantiation of all the variables such that all the constraints are satisfied. Formally, a (finite domain) constraint satisfaction problem (CSP) is a tuple

$$\langle V, D, C, con, def \rangle$$

where

- V is a finite set of *variables* (i.e., $V = \{v_1, \ldots, v_n\}$);
- D is a finite set of values, called the *domain*;
- C is a finite set of *constraints* (i.e., $C = \{c_1, \ldots, c_m\}$); C is ranked, i.e. $C = \bigcup_k C_k$, such that $c \in C_k$ if c involves k variables;
- *con* is called the *connection function* and it is such that $con : \bigcup_k (C_k \rightarrow V^k)$, where $con(c) = \langle v_1, \ldots, v_k \rangle$ is the tuple of variables involved in $c \in C_k$;
- *def* is called the *definition function* and it is such that $def : \bigcup_k (C_k \rightarrow \wp(D^k))$, where $\wp(D^k)$ is the powerset of D^k.

Function *con* describes which variables are involved in which constraint, while function *def* gives the meaning of a constraint in terms of a set of tuples of domain elements, which represent the allowed combinations of values for the involved variables. Then, the solution $Sol(P)$ of a CSP $P = \langle V, D, C, con, def \rangle$ is defined as the set of all instantiations of the variables in V (seen as tuples of values) which are consistent with all the constraints in C.

Local consistency algorithms [Mac88, Mon74, Mac77] remove from a CSP some domain elements or also some tuples from the constraint definitions if these objects are found to be inconsistent with some other object in the CSP. This is safe (that is, it does not change the set of solutions of the CSP), because local inconsistency implies global inconsistency, and thus such objects would never appear in any solution of the CSP. However, there may be objects (tuples and/or domain elements) which are inconsistent but are not recognized as such and therefore are not removed. Thus in general only local consistency is achieved (and not global consistency, which would mean that the problem is solved).

The first local consistency algorithms have been called arc-consistency [Mac77] and path-consistency [Mon74]. Later, both of them were generalized to the concept of k-consistency [Fre88]: a CSP is k-consistent if, for each k-1 variables, and values for them which are allowed by all the constraints involving subsets of them, and for each other variable, there is at least a value locally allowed for such k-th variable which is compatible with all the other k-1 variables. In this line, arc-consistency [Mac77] is just 2-consistency and path-consistency is 3-consistency.

A local consistency algorithm is an algorithm which achieves a certain degree of local consistency (2, 3, or k) in a constraint problem. This is usually done by an iterative scheme which stops only when no other domain value or tuple can be deleted. Here we will just consider local consistency algorithms which remove values from variable domains, and not tuples from constraints. This poses some limitations on the power of these algorithms, but it assures that no new constraint is added by them. In fact, it has been proved that in general achieving strong k-consistency may add constraints involving at most k-1 variables [Fre78]. The fact that no constraint is added makes the algorithm much more natural to be used in a distributed setting, where a change in the structure of the processes interconnection may be undesirable.

The simplest, but most of the times quite effective, local consistency algorithm is the one which achieves arc-consistency [Mac77]: only one constraint at a time is considered, and, for each variable connected to it, it is checked whether there is a value of its domain which is not compatible with any other value of the other variables (according to the constraint). If so, such value is deleted.

Local consistency algorithms are very useful because they are polynomial in the worst case (in the number of variables) [MF85] and at the same time they are able, in several cases, to remove many redundancies in the domains. This result can make the subsequent search algorithm, used to find solutions of the constraint problem, much faster.

Once the given constraint problem has been processed by a local consistency algorithm and some redundant values have been removed from each variable domain, we can now obtain all possible solutions of the current constraint problem. This can be done via a distributed backtracking search algorithm, where each of the concurrent agents corresponds to one variable (to be instatiated over its domain) and communicates with the other agents via the constraint topology. We will not go here into the detail of such an algorithm, pointing instead to an already developed algorithm presented in [YIDK92, Yok95].

3.2 Constraints for the Rule-Matching Problem

The rule-matching problem can be represented as a finite domain constraint problem as follows: variables represent processes and constraints represent ports (that is, sets of adjacent processes). The domain of a variable is the set of all context-free productions for the corresponding process, and the definition of a constraint is the set of tuples of context-free productions (one for each adjacent process) whose synchronization requirements match on that port.

A solution to this kind of constraint problem is, according to the above definition, a choice of a context-free production for each process, such that all synchronization requirements are satisfied. Thus such solution specifies a legal move of the distributed system, where each process proceeds according to the chosen production. This move is legal (that is, it corresponds to one of the rewriting rules that would be generated by merging some of the context-free production, as informally stated above) because it is obvious that no synchronization requirements is violated, otherwise some constraint would not be satisfied. It is possible to show that the number of solutions of the constraint problem is the same as the number of rewrite rules obtainable via the definition above. Thus this approach actually solves the rule-matching problem.

A distributed algorithm which takes the representation of the current state of the system and produces a finite domain constraint problem representing the current rule-matching problem can be easily outlined. In fact, variables are associated to processes, and constraints to ports. Since adjacent processes communicate via ports, also this information is directly and locally available.

It is now clear that local consistency algorithms can be applied to the constraint problem representing the current rule-matching problem in order to remove redundant values in the domain of the variables (that is, redundant choices for context-free productions which would never be used in any context-sensitive rewrite rule). The resulting problem (after the application of the chosen local consistency algorithm) therefore represents a new rule-matching problem (but equivalent to the given one, since it generates exactly the same possible moves), where some of the redundant context-free productions have been deleted.

In particular, the arc-consistency algorithm is the most natural in a distributed environment, since it has to deal with only one constraint at a time. Thus one may use a distributed version of this algorithm where a set of concurrent agents cooperate to remove redundant values from the variable domains, each agent corresponds to one of the constraints, and communication occurs via shared variables [ND95].

4 An Example

Let us know clarify the ideas described above via a simple but expressive example, adapted from [DM87]. Consider a distributed system representing a synchronous communication network connecting a number of stations. The system can increase its size dynamically but its topology is always tree-like. Each station may decide whether to request a communication or not. In a certain state of the system, a communication is established between two communication-ready stations.

There are three types of processes:

- process A represents a station which is ready to communicate,
- process B represents a station which does not want to communicate (thus it can only make the system increase its size or transform itself into a communication-ready station), and
- process C represents a communication switch with three ports, which has three possible ways to let the communication pass (by choosing any two of its three ports).

The context-free productions specifying how the single processes may evolve can be seen in Figure 3. The graphical way we represent these productions consists of specifying hypergraph L (the left hand side) and graph R (the right hand side). Multiple productions with the same left hand side are represented by giving the left hand side only once and separating the right hand sides by a bar. In a graph, nodes are circles and arcs are boxes, connected to as many nodes as their arity. The way nodes of L and R map to each other, for this example, should be clear from the picture. When a production has some synchronization requirements, they are written on the corresponding nodes of the right hand

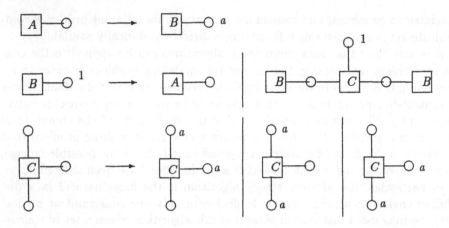

Fig. 3. A set of context-free productions.

side. For this example, there is only one kind of synchronization requirement, which we call a.

From Figure 3 we can see that:

- A can only transform itself into B, while synchronizing over the only node it is connected to.
- B can evolve in two different ways: it can either transform itself into A, or change the structure of the communication net by introducing a new switch. Two ports of such new switch are connected to B processes, while the other one is free. Note that these two moves do not need any synchronization. Thus B can move in isolation according to these two productions. After rewriting, all the nodes of the graph which are connected to the node marked 1 in the left hand side are attached to the node marked 1 in the right hand side. No marking has been used for the other production because the geometrical correpondence suffices.
- C can only move in a synchronized way: it can choose any pair of its three ports and decide to synchronize over such two ports.

The syncronization required by the only production for A means that the station represented by these A-process is chosen for the communication. In the same way, the choice of any of the productions for C means that communication passes through the two ports over which synchronization has occurred. Since rewriting can only occurr via these productions, any state of this system is a tree-like structure of C-processes with As or Bs at the leaves. Due to the synchronizations required by the productions, each context-sensitive rewriting rule for the system (whatever its current state is) involves either a single B-process (and it is specified by one of its context-free productions), or a subpart of the system consisting of two A-processes and a chain of C-processes. This subpart obviously specifies a path in the tree-like structure of the system which goes from one leaf to another one.

Thus the rule-matching problem, for this example, consists in the problem of choosing one of the possibly many paths going from one leaf labelled A to another leaf labelled A. Consider for example the states depicted in Figure 4 a) and b). In Figure 4 a), there are only two A-processes, and thus only one possible communication path (outlined by a bidirectional arrow). Instead, in Figure 4 b), there are three A-processes, and thus three possible communication paths.

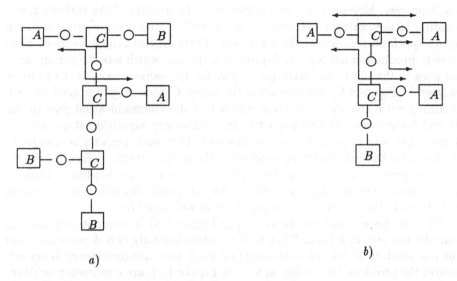

a)   b)

Fig. 4. Two states and the possible communication paths.

Consider now the state in Figure 4 b). The constraint problem corresponding to this state has as many variables as the processes (thus 6 variables), and as many constraints as the ports (thus 5 constraints). Each constraint connects only two variables, since every port of this example connects only two adjacent processes. The domain of each variable is the set of context-free productions available for the corresponding process. Thus, the domain corresponding to an A-process consists of just one production, that of a B-process consists of two productions, and that of a C-process consists of three productions (apart from the idle production which we did not explicitly specify in the example but which is always assumed to be a possible production for any process).

Consider now what an arc-consistency algorithm would do on this constraint problem. We recall that an arc-consistency algorithm looks at each variable, say x, and, for each other variable connected to it, say y, checks whether there are values in the domain of x which are not compatible with any other value for y. If so, that value for x is deleted. This continues until no more deletions are possible. In this case, consider the variable corresponding to the lower C-process. Since a port of such process is connected to a B-process, which does not have any production with synchronization, there is now way that C can use any one of its two productions which require synchronization over that port. Thus these two productions can be eliminated. Therefore the only production remaining for that C-process is the one which lets the communication pass through the upper and right ports of the process. No other pruning is done by the algorithm.

Consider now the state in Figure 4 a). In this case, the domain of the variable corresponding to the lower C-process becomes empty. In fact, since such process is connected to two B-processes, it cannot use any one of its three productions, since all of them require synchronization over one or two of the ports connected to a B-process. Moreover, because of this, also the domain of the variable corresponding to the central C-process is pruned. In fact, the two productions which require synchronization over the lower port of this process cannot be used. Thus the only production left for this C-process is the one which lets the communication pass in the upper and right port. Also, for the same reason as the pruning occurred in Figure 4 b), the domain of the upper C-process gets pruned as well, remaining with just the production which lets the communication pass in the left and lower ports. At this point the arc-consistency algorithm stops because no more pruning is possible. Notice, however, that such pruning is enough to directly solve the rule-matching problem without any search. In fact, all the C-processes present in the system have either one or zero possiblilities. Thus no choice has to be made: the C-processes with one possibility will move according to that, while the one with the empty domain will stay idle.

What we have noted for the system in Figure 4 a) is true not only for this example, but also in general. That is, if a system has only two A-processes (and thus one solution to the rule-matching problem), then arc-consistency is enough to solve the problem. Otherwise, as seen in Figure 4 b), arc-consistency achieves enough pruning to cut away from the search all the parts of the system which are not involved in any solution (that is, all those subtrees which do not contain any A-process). At this point, a distributed backtracking search algorithm can find all solutions, but searching only over the subparts of the system which for sure participate in some solution.

5   Conclusions

To summarize, we may list the main points of our proposal as the following ones:

- adopt *graphs* to describe system states and *graph rewriting* to describe system evolution;
- exploit *constraint problems* and the corresponding *local consistency* algorithms to remove redundancies in the description of a system state;
- use a *distributed backtracking search* algorithm, like those used for distributed constraint solving, to solve the rule-matching problem, and thus choose one possible move for the system. Such a move will in general involve several processes acting in synchrony.

The novelty of our approach is not in its individual ingredients, which have all being developed previously (apart from the need of small variations for making them fit for the desired distributed environment), but instead in the combination of all of them, which seems to us a convenient alternative way to model the dynamic of distributed systems, w.r.t. the methods usually used. In particular, the convenience of our proposal comes from various aspects:

- graphs are a very natural formalism for describing situations where there are agents or processes (that is, arcs) connected via ports (that is, nodes);
- graph rewriting allows for a faithful model of synchronized process evolution, since all the parts which belong to the left hand side of the same rewrite rule must be rewritten simultaneously, and thus synchronously;
- context-free graph rewriting is natural for distribution, since context-freeness assures that each process can evolve independently on the others (once the desired synchronization requirements have been checked and satisfied);
- constraint problems model very naturally the rule-matching problem, where there are processes with several choices (that is, variables with their domains) and synchronization requirements (that is, constraints);
- local consistency algorithms have been proved, by a long theoretical study and practical experimentation, to achieve a great amount of redundancy removal, and thus a great improvement in the solution process, in many cases, which are related for example to the structure of the constraint problem [Dec92], or to the semantics of the constraints [Mon74], or to the size of the domains [Dec92], or also to the tightness of the constraints [vBD94];
- distributed backtracking has been shown to be convenient when the structure of the process connection is not too dense [YIDK92]; thus in this cases the performance of this way of solving the rule-matching problem is feasible in practice.

References

[CDM85] A. Corradini, P. Degano, and U. Montanari. Specifying highly concurrent data structure manipulation. In G. Bucci and G. Valle, editors, *COMPUTING 85: A Broad Perspective of Current Developments*. Elsevier Science, 1985.

[CM95] A. Corradini and U. Montanari, editors. *Proc. SEGRAGRA95 (Joint COMPUGRAPH/SEMAGRAPH Workshop on Graph Rewriting and Computation)*. Elsevier, Electronic Notes on Theoretical Computer Science, 1995.

[Dec92] Rina Dechter. From local to global consistency. *Artificial Intelligence*, 55:87–107, 1992.

[DM87] P. Degano and U. Montanari. A model for distributed systems based on graph rewritings. *Journal of ACM*, 34(2), 1987.

[DP88] R. Dechter and J. Pearl. Network-Based Heuristics for Constraint-Satisfaction Problems. In Kanal and Kumar, editors, *Search in Artificial Intelligence*. Springer-Verlag, 1988.

[Ehr78] H. Ehrig. Introduction to the algebraic theory of graph grammars. In *Proc. International Workshop on Graph Grammars*. Springer Verlag, LNCS 73, 1978.

[Ehr87] H. Ehrig. Tutorial introduction to the algebraic theory of graph grammars. In *Proc. 3rd International Workshop on Graph Grammars*. Springer Verlag, LNCS 291, 1987.

[Fre78]   E. Freuder. Synthesizing constraint expressions. *Communication of the ACM*, 21(11), 1978.

[Fre88]   E. Freuder. Backtrack-free and backtrack-bounded search. In Kanal and Kumar, editors, *Search in Artificial Intelligence*. Springer-Verlag, 1988.

[Hab89]   A. Habel. *Hyperedge Replacement: Grammars and Languages*. PhD thesis, University of Bremen, 1989.

[Mac77]   A.K. Mackworth. Consistency in networks of relations. *Artificial Intelligence*, 8(1), 1977.

[Mac88]   A.K. Mackworth. *Encyclopedia of AI*, chapter Constraint Satisfaction, pages 205–211. Springer Verlag, 1988.

[MF85]   A.K. Mackworth and E.C. Freuder. The complexity of some polynomial network consistency algorithms for constraint satisfaction problems. *Artificial Intelligence*, 25, 1985.

[Mon74]   U. Montanari. Networks of constraints: Fundamental properties and application to picture processing. *Information Science*, 7, 1974.

[ND95]   T. Nguyen and Y. Deville. A distributed arc-consistency algorithm. In *Proc. of the CCP95 international workshop*, 1995.

[SE94]   H.J. Schneider and H. Ehrig, editors. *Graph Trasformations in Computer Science*. Springer Verlag, LNCS 776, 1994.

[SPvE92] M.R. Sleep, M.J. Plasmeijer, and M.C. van Eekelen, editors. *Term Graph Rewriting: Theory and Practice*. John Wiley & Sons, 1992.

[vBD94]   P. van Beek and R. Dechter. Constraint tightness versus global consistency. In *Proc. KR94*. Morgan Kaufmann, 1994.

[YIDK92] M. Yokoo, T. Ishida, E.H. Durfee, and K. Kuwabara. Distributed constraint satisfaction for formalizing distributed problem solving. In *Proc. IEEE International Conference on Distributed Computing Systems*, 1992.

[Yok95]   M. Yokoo. Asynchronous weak-committment search for solving distributed constraint satisfaction problems. In *Proc. CP95 (Principles and Practice of Constraint Programming)*. Springer-Verlag, LNCS 976, 1995.

Coordination as Constrained Interaction
(Extended Abstract)

Peter Wegner

1 Introduction

Protocols that coordinate interactive communication among software components have qualitatively different behavior from algorithms that progressively transform the state within a software component. Algorithm behavior is captured by Turing machines whose expressive power is that of computable functions. Coordination must handle temporal and other nonfunctional interactive properties that cannot be expressed algorithmically [We2]. For example, driving home from work can be viewed as a coordination problem that involves real-time coordination with other cars that cannot be expressed by noninteractive algorithms. Airline reservation systems and robots likewise must handle real-time coordination that cannot be expressed algorithmically. Coordination systems are open systems that must handle unpredictable external events that occur dynamically during the process of problem solving.

Coordination is constrained interaction: it constrains interaction protocols among communicating software components. Though explicitly specified coordination rules are limited by human ability to handle complexity, coordination patterns in nature and in practical software systems can be arbitrarily complex. Strongly constrained coordination models can be weaker than Turing machines, but models that express general-purpose interaction are more expressive than Turing machines [We1]. Practical coordination models must express not only simple static resource constraints specified by tokens of Petri nets or Prolog rewriting rules but also dynamic constraints of air traffic controllers and complex organizations. Coordination models can provide a unifying framework for World-Wide Web protocols like http, interface definition protocols for interoperability, and data exchange (DX) protocols for heterogeneous databases.

This extended abstract reviews some existing models of coordination from the viewpoint of an outsider looking in and considers the place of coordination in the broader context of models of interaction.

2 Coordination Models

Petri nets are a "pure" model of coordination. A Petri net has components (transitions) that fire by consuming resources at input places and delivering resources to output places. Resources are represented by multisets and coordination is realized by rewriting rules for multisets. Petri nets are flexible in expressing distributed coordination that depends on the availability of resources at distributed locations (places). They abstract away from specific data structures by permitting only a single data structure (tokens) and abstract away from algorithms by permitting only computation by execution.of coordination rules.

Petri net tokens are nonreusable resources better modeled by linear logic than by traditional logics. Linear logic provides a framework for coordination of nonreusable resources that admits both sequential and parallel coordination, illustrated by interaction abstract machines in [ACP].

Linda [CG] is a less abstract model of coordination that represents data by tuples (records) accessed by associative pattern matching. It realizes a blackboard model of coordination by processes that reside in and communicate through a shared tuple space. Its simple set of coordination commands for process input and output is compatible with a wide variety of algorithmic programming languages. It neatly separates coordination and computation, focusing on the complete and precise specification of coordination primitives that can be naturally embedded in algorithmic languages. The operational semantics of Linda's coordination primitives is examined in [CNY].

Object-oriented programming languages coordinate communication among objects by message-passing protocols. Coordination primitives in object-oriented languages are less flexible than in Petri nets in that protocols whose execution depends on inputs from several objects cannot be directly specified. Messages specify only pairwise coordination of components. Linda has even weaker coordination primitives, specifying only unary coordination of components with a shared tuple space. Both Linda and object-based systems can build up multiway coordination by composite coordination patterns. Object-oriented systems can simulate a shared tuple space by objects whose state consists of associatively addressed tuples.

Coordination of heterogeneous distributed components can be realized by megaprogramming languages [WWC] that specify coordination among megamodules by programs whose statements specify both the sequence of operations to be executed and the transformation of messages from the format of senders to a format acceptable to receivers. Megaprograms for simple coordination tasks can be very simple. However, coordination of distributed concurrently executing tasks with atomicity and real-time constraints can be arbitrarily complex.

Megaprograms are examples of "middleware" [Surv] interspersed between components to realize coordination. Models of coordination elevate middleware to a first-class status, corresponding to the role of management in large organizations. Middleware mediates among software components by transforming data and coordinating actions: the view of middleware as mediators is developed in [Wi]. Explicit coordination becomes more important as systems become large, just as explicit management structures are more important for large than for small companies. However, experience shows that simple typeless coordination systems like UNIX pipes or http are often more effective than more elaborate strongly-typed interface definition languages. Static type-compatilbility requirements that promote safety and efficiency appear to have an unacceptably high implementation cost in today's coodination technology.

Communication among heterogeneous components can be realized also by models of interoperability such as OMG's Common Object Request Broker Architecture [CORBA] and Microsoft's component object model [COM]. Interoperability solves the problem of reusability of resources specified in one environment by components in another environment. Most work on interoperability assumes a client-server, object-based model of communication [NT]. Coordination among heterogeneous distributed components may utilize protocols developed for client-server compatibility in more general contexts of coordination.

Coordination is concerned both with rules for scheduling and firing actions and with communicating and transforming data among components. Executing actions and communicating data, which require very different models (Petri nets and CORBA) need to be integrated:

coordination → firing rules + data exchange

Designers of coordination languages must address the following issues [Proc]:

1. What are the entities being coordinated? procedures, objects, processes, components of a specific type, subsystems;
2. What are the media (architectures) for coordination? blackboard model, client-server, Petri net, Pi calculus, CORBA, COM, UNIX pipes, middleware;
3. What are the protocols and rules of coordination? multiset rewriting rules, message send and receive, object request brokers, megaprogramming, HTML;

In [Proc] it was further suggested that coordination languages be classified according to the dimensions of scalability, encapsulation, decentralization, dynamicity, open-endedness, generativeness, and semantic richness. These dimensions were used to classify and justify design decisions of existing languages. Though these dimensions are useful, the design space for coordination is not well understood and more work is needed to characterize and explore it.

3 Models of Interaction

The design space for coordination can be embedded in the broader context of models of interaction. Interactive systems can be modeled by interaction machines definable by extending Turing machines with input and output actions (read and write statements). Interaction machines are open systems that model external events occurring during the process of computation, while Turing machines are closed, noninteractive systems that shut out the external world while computing an output from an input. Interaction machines have richer behavior than Turing machines because they can react to real-time interactive behavior not expressible by Turing machines.

Greater richness follows formally from the fact that input streams of interaction machines cannot be modeled by finite tapes, since they can always be dynamically extended. The computational distinction between Turing and interaction machines is expressed mathematically by that between enumerable finite sets of tapes and nonenumerable infinite sets of streams whose cardinality is that of the real numbers. It is entirely appropriate that the ability of interaction machines to express the "real" world is modeled mathematically by the "real" numbers. Infinite divisibility of continuous physical space and infinite extensibility of physical time give rise to dual nonenumerable abstractions of reality.

Real numbers are represented by infinite streams of digits that model infinite divisibility of continuous mathematical and physical space. Interaction machines turn this model inside-out, representing the external world by infinite streams of inputs. The infinite extensibility of outer temporal reality can be modeled by infinite divisibility of continuous space. Since the set of all infinite digit streams are in one-to-one correspondence with both the nonenumerable real numbers and the input streams of an interaction machine, interaction machines have a nonenumerable number of inputs.

Interaction machines cannot be specified by sound and complete logics: they are incomplete in the sense shown by Godel for the integers (the set of all true statements about them is not formally enumerable by theorems). Church's thesis that the intuitive notion of computing corresponds to formal computing by Turing machines is seen to be invalid or at least inapplicable, since interaction machines determine a very natural notion of computing more powerful than Turing machines. The Chomsky hierarchy of machines is extended beyond Turing machines to synchronous and asynchronous interaction machines, but mathematical characterization of machine behavior by sets or formal grammars cannot be similarly extended, showing that machines can specify more powerful forms of behavior than mathematical notations.

Nonenumerability captures the mathematical essence of interactive computing. Its operational essence is the control of actions by the external environment rather than by rules of inner computation. Interactive systems are operationally described by their observable behavior in terms of interaction histories.

Interaction histories of simple objects, like bank accounts with deposit and withdraw operations, are described by operation streams called traces. Operations whose effects depend on their time of occurrence, as in interest-bearing bank accounts, require time-stamped traces. Objects with inherently nonsequential interfaces, like joint bank accounts accessed from multiple automatic-teller machines, have inherently nonsequential interaction histories. Interaction histories of distributed systems, just like history in history books, consists of overlapping inherently nonsequential processes. Whereas interaction histories express the external unfolding of events in time, instruction-execution "histories" simply express an ordering of inner events of an algorithm without any relation to the actual passage of time.

Algorithms are time-independent transformations from inputs to outputs, while objects and interaction machines provide interactive services over time. Algorithmic time is measured by number of instructions executed rather than by the actual time of execution to provide a hardware-independent (abstract) measure of logical complexity. In contrast, the duration and the time that elapses between the execution of operations may be interactively significant. Operation sequences have temporal as well as functional properties, while instruction sequences have a purely functional semantics.

Interaction machines can model both the inner algoritmhic behavior and the inter-component coordination behavior of objects, software engineering applications, robots, intelligent agents, distributed systems, and networks like the internet and World-Wide Web. Coordination models of the World-Wide-Web that refine current HTML protocols represent a challenge with a great practical payoff. HTML has proved itself as a ubiquitous data interchange language with trivial coordination and data interchange protocols. Extending the coordination power of HTML, for example to hot Java, without impairing its universality is an important research problem.

Coordination languages express interactive properties of software systems. Petri nets and Linda are interactive formalisms. Interaction protocols expressed by multiset rewriting rules have control structures that cannot be entirely captured by algorithmic control structures. Inference rules of linear logic cannot be expressed by sound and complete models. There are many small indications that the tidy examples of simple coordination protocols are only the tip of the iceberg of a much larger and less tidy space of real-world coordination protocols that we have not even begun to explore. The extension of models of coordination from toy examples of multiset rewriting to real-world coordination of distributed system and software engineering is a challenging problem.

References

[ACP]   J. Andreoli, P. Ciancarini, and R. Pareschi, Interaction Abstract Machines. In Research Directions in Concurrent Object-Oriented Programming, Eds Agha, Wegner, Yonezawa, MIT Press, 1993.

[CG]   N. Carriero and D. Gelernter, Coordination Languages and Their Significance, CACM, Feb 1992.

[CNY]   Paolo Ciancarini, Oscar Nierstrasz, and Akinori Yonezawa, Proc. ECOOP '94 Workshop on Coordination Languages, LNCS 924, Springer Verlag, 1995, especially articles by Gelernter and Ciancarini.

[COM]   Kraig Brockschimidt, Inside OLE 2, 2nd edition, Microsoft Press, 1995.

[CORBA] Architecture and Specification, Revision 2.0, Object Management Group, July 1995.

[NT]   Oscar Nierstrasz and Dennis Tsichritzis Eds, Object-Oriented Software Composition, Prentice Hall, 1996. Especially Chapter 3 by Dimitri Konstantas.

[Proc]   Proceedings of First Annual Workshop on Coordination, Imperial College Dept of Computer Science, December 1994.

[Surv]   Research Directions in Software Engineering, Computing Surveys, June 1995.

[We1]   Peter Wegner. Interactive Foundations of Object-Based Programming. IEEE Computer, Oct. 1995.

[We2]   Peter Wegner. Foundations of Interactive Computing. Report CS-96-01, Jan 1996.

[Wi]   Gio Wiederhold. Mediation in Information Systems. Computing Surveys, June 1995.

[WWC]   Gio Wiederhold, Peter Wegner, and Stefano Ceri. Towards Megaprogramming. CACM Nov 1992.

The IWIM Model for Coordination of Concurrent Activities

Farhad Arbab

CWI
Department of Interactive Systems
Kruislaan 413, 1098 SJ Amsterdam, The Netherlands
Tel.: +31-20-592.4058
Fax.: +31-20-592.4199
Email: farhad@cwi.nl

Abstract. Exploiting the full potential of massively parallel systems requires programming models that explicitly deal with the concurrency of cooperation among very large numbers of active entities that comprise a single application. In practice, the concurrent applications of today essentially use a set of ad hoc templates to coordinate the cooperation of their active components. This shows the lack of proper coordination languages that can be used to explicitly describe complex cooperation protocols in terms of simple primitives and structuring constructs.

In this paper we present a generic model of communication and describe a specific control-oriented coordination language based on this model. The important characteristics of this model include compositionality, which it inherits from the data-flow model, anonymous communication, and separation of computation concerns from communication concerns. These characteristics lead to clear advantages in large concurrent applications.

1991 CR Categories: D3.3, D.1.3, D.3.2, F.1.2, I.1.3.
1991 AMS Subject Classification: 68N99, 68Q10.
Keywords and Phrases: concurrency, parallel computing, coordination languages, MIMD, models of communication.

1 Introduction

The primary concern in the design of a concurrent application must be its model of cooperation: how the various active entities comprising the application are to cooperate with each other. Eventually, a communication model must be used to realize whatever model of cooperation application designers opt for, and the concerns for performance may indirectly affect their design. Nevertheless, it is important to realize that the conceptual gap between the system supported communication primitives and a concurrent application must often be filled with a non-trivial model of cooperation.

The cooperation models of the real applications of today are essentially a set of ad hoc templates that have been found to be useful in practice. There is no paradigm wherein we can systematically talk about cooperation of active entities, and wherein we can compose cooperation scenarios such as (and as alternatives to) models like client-server, workers pool, etc., out of a set of primitives and structuring constructs. Consequently, programmers must directly deal with the lower-level communication primitives that comprise the realization of the cooperation model of a concurrent application. Because these primitives are generally scattered throughout the source code of the application and are typically intermixed with non-communication application code, the cooperation model of an application generally never manifests itself in a tangible form – i.e., it is not an identifiable piece of source code that can be designed, developed, debugged, maintained, and reused, in isolation from the rest of the application code.

The inability to deal with the cooperation model of a concurrent application in an explicit form contributes to the difficulty of developing working concurrent applications that contain large numbers of active entities with non-trivial cooperation protocols. In spite of the fact that the implementation of complex protocols are often the most difficult and error prone part of an application development effort, the end result is typically not recognized as a "commodity" in its own right, because the protocols are only implicit in the behavior of the rest of the concurrent software. This makes maintenance and modification of the cooperation protocols of concurrent applications much more difficult than necessary, and their reuse next to impossible.

The two most popular models of communication are shared memory and message passing. In the shared memory model, inter-process communication is only an implicit side-effect of the delay patterns imposed by the synchronization primitives on the processes that take turn to access and update certain common storage areas. Given the primary concern for communication among a set of cooperating processes, this implicit approach to information exchange is not conducive to explicit coordination. In contrast to the shared memory model, the message passing model uses primitives for explicit information exchange, which implicitly impose the required synchronization on the communicating parties.

Subordinating synchronization to information exchange makes the message passing model somewhat more flexible than the shared memory model and, therefore, it is the dominant model used in concurrent applications. However, both shared memory and message passing are too low-level to serve as a proper foundation for systematic construction of cooperation protocols as explicit, tangible pieces of software.

In §2, we show some of the shortcomings of a typical message passing model in this context. In §3, we present IWIM: a communication model that avoids these shortcomings and can be used in a paradigm to construct complex cooperation protocols. The impact of the IWIM model in separating communication and computation concerns is illustrated in §4. In §5 we describe MANIFOLD: a coordination language based on the IWIM model and illustrate some of its features. Although the IWIM model supports both synchronous and asynchronous forms of communication, the coordination language MANIFOLD uses asynchronous communication exclusively. This design decision was made to avoid the extra delays, reduced effective concurrency, and even unnecessary deadlocks that can result from synchronous communication in large concurrent systems[1]. A brief description of some related work appears in §6, and §7 is the conclusion of this paper.

2 The TSR Model of Communication

A common characteristic of most flavors of the message passing model of communication is the distinction between the roles they assign to the two active entities involved in a communication: the sender and the receiver. A sender s typically sends a message m to a receiver r. The identity of r is either statically known to s or it is dynamically evaluated at execution time. Sometimes, there is more than one receiver, i.e., the message m is multi-cast to a number of receivers, or it may even be broadcast to all active entities running in an application. One way or the other, the send operation is generally targeted to a specific (set of) receiver(s). A receiver r, on the other hand, typically waits to receive a message m from any sender, as it normally has no prior knowledge of the origin of the message(s) it may receive. We use the term *Targeted-Send/Receive*, or TSR, to refer to the communication models that share this characteristic. This encompasses theoretical models such as CSP[2], CCS[3], and the Actor model[4]; programming languages such as Occam[5], LOTOS[6], and various flavors of concurrent Object-Oriented and object-based languages; remote procedure call schemes; and programming tools such as PVM[7], MPI[8], P4[9], PARMACS[10], etc.

Consider the following simple example of a concurrent application where the two active entities (i.e., processes) p and q must cooperate with each other. The process p at some point produces two values which it must pass on to q. The process q, in turn, must perform some additional computation using the input it receives from p, and then pass on the result of this computation back to p. Note that it is perfectly meaningful to talk about the cooperation model of this application, independent of the actual processes involved, i.e., a specific p or q, or the computation they perform – as a matter of fact, this is exactly what we just did. The source code for this concurrent application looks something like the following:

```
process p:                          process q:

compute m1                          receive m1
send m1 to q                        let z be the sender of m1
compute m2                          receive m2
send m2 to q                        compute m using m1 and m2
do other things                     send m to z
receive m
do other computation using m
```

The first thing to notice in the above listing is that it is simultaneously both a description of what computation is performed by p and q, and a description of how they cooperate with each other. The communication concerns are mixed and interspersed with computation. Thus, in the final source code of the application, there will be no isolated piece of code that can be considered as the realization of its cooperation model, such that, e.g., we can use it as a module in another application where two other processes are to cooperate with each other in a similar fashion.

The second significant point to note in the above listing is the asymmetry between send and receive operations. Every send must specify a target for its message, whereas a receive can receive a message from any anonymous source. In our example, p must know q, otherwise, it cannot send a message to it. On the other hand, p does not (need to) know the source of the message it receives as m. And this ignorance is a blessing. If after receiving $m1$ and $m2$, q decides that the final result it must send back to p is to be produced by yet another process, x, p need not be bothered by this "delegation" of responsibility from q to x.

We can better appreciate the significance of the asymmetry between send and receive in a tangible form when we compare the processes p and q with each other. The assumptions hard-wired into q about its environment (i.e., availability and accessibility of other processes in the concurrent application) are weaker than those in p. The weaker dependence of q on its environment, as compared with p, makes it a more reusable process that can perform its service for other processes in the same or other applications.

Note, however, that q is not as flexible as we may want it to be: the fact that the result of its computation is sent back to the source of its input messages is something that is hard-wired in its source code, due to its final targeted send. If, perhaps in a different application environment, we decide that the result produced by q is needed by another process, y, instead of the same process, z, that provides it with $m1$ and $m2$, we have no choice but to modify the source code for q. This is a change only to the cooperation model in the application, not a change to the substance of what q does. The unfortunate necessity of modification to the source code of q, in this case, is only a consequence of its targeted send.

3   The IWIM Model of Communication

In §2 we made two observations about the direct use of the TSR model of communication in concurrent applications. To appreciate the combined effect of these two observations, it is illuminating to look at concurrent applications in general, using an anthropomorphic view. We may regard each process as an individual worker. When the TSR model is used directly, a worker must, naturally, know how to produce the (partial) results expected of him, *and* he also must either (1) know by name the workers he must deliver his results to, or (2) know how to find out the identities of those workers, e.g., know someone who knows them.

This dual concern by each worker leads to a tight coupling of the activities of a team of workers and intermixes production responsibilities of individual workers with the organizational/managerial responsibilities for the cooperation of the team as a whole. Furthermore, how such a team cooperates is only an implicit image induced by the rigid communication links, the knowledge of which is scattered among its members. This scenario works, and may even be very effective, for small teams of workers. However, the individual attention necessary to hand-craft the composite responsibilities of each worker makes it very difficult to use this approach in larger teams. Effective use of the resources of hundreds and thousands of workers requires a cleaner separation between organizational and production responsibilities, and a weaker dependence of individual workers on their environment.

In the following, we consider an alternative generic model of communication that, unlike the TSR model, supports the separation of responsibilities and encourages a weak dependence of workers on their environment. We refer to this generic model as the Idealized Worker Idealized Manager (IWIM) model[1]. Like the TSR model, the IWIM model is described only in terms of its most significant characteristics. As such, like the TSR model, it indeed defines not a specific model of communication, but a family of such models. Various members in this family can have different significant characteristics, e.g., with regards to synchronous vs. asynchronous communication.

3.1 Basic Concepts

The basic concepts in the IWIM model are *processes*, *events*, *ports*, and *channels*. A process is a *black box* with well defined ports of connection through which it exchanges *units* of information with the other processes in its environment. A port is a named opening in the bounding walls of a process through which units of information are exchanged using standard I/O type primitives analogous to read and write. Without loss of generality, we assume that each port is used for the exchange of information in only one direction: either into (input port) or out of (output port) a process. We use the notation $p.i$ to refer to the port i of the process instance p.

The interconnections between the ports of processes are made through channels. A channel connects a (port of a) producer (process) to a (port of a) consumer (process). We write $p.o \rightarrow q.i$ to denote a channel connecting the port o of the producer process p to the port i of the consumer process q.

Independent of the channels, there is an event mechanism for information exchange in IWIM. Events are broadcast by their sources in their environment, yielding an *event occurrence*. In principle, any process in an environment can pick up a broadcast event occurrence. In practice, usually only a few processes pick up occurrences of each event, because only they are *tuned in* to their sources.

The IWIM model supports *anonymous communication*: in general, a process does not, and need not, know the identity of the processes with which it exchanges information. This concept reduces the dependence of a process on its environment and makes processes more reusable.

A Process in IWIM can be regarded as a worker process or a manager (or coordinator) process. The responsibility of a worker process is to perform a (computational) task. A worker process is not responsible for the communication that is necessary for it to obtain the proper input it requires to perform its task, nor is it responsible for the communication that is necessary to deliver the results it produces to their proper recipients. In general, *no process in* IWIM *is responsible for its own communication with other processes.* It is always the responsibility of a manager process to arrange for and to coordinate the necessary communications among a set of worker processes.

There is always a bottom layer of worker processes, called *atomic workers,* in an application. In the IWIM model, an application is built as a (dynamic) hierarchy of (worker and manager) processes on top of this layer. Aside from the atomic workers, the categorization of a process as a worker or a manager process is subjective: a manager process m that coordinates the communication among a number of worker processes, may itself be considered as a worker process by another manager process responsible for coordinating the communication of m with other processes.

3.2 Communication Channel

A channel is a communication link that carries a sequence of bits, grouped into (variable length) *units.* A channel represents a reliable, directed, and perhaps buffered, flow of information in time. Reliable means that the bits placed into a channel are guaranteed to flow through without loss, error, or duplication, with their order preserved. Directed means that there are always two identifiable ends in a channel: a *source* and a *sink.* Once a channel is established between a producer process and a consumer process, it operates autonomously and transfers the units from its source to its sink.

If we make no assumptions about the internal operation of the producer and the consumer of a channel C, we must consider the possibility that C may contain some pending units. The *pending units* of a channel C are the units that have already been delivered to C by its producer, but not yet delivered by C to its consumer.

The possibility of the existence of pending units in a channel gives it an identity of its own, independent of its producer and consumer. It makes it meaningful for a channel to remain connected at one of its ends, after it is disconnected from the other.

In general, there are five different alternatives for a channel C in the IWIM model:

1. S channel: In this situation, we have the guarantee that there are never any pending units in C. This implies synchronous communication between the producer and the consumer of C through their respective ports. In this case it is meaningless to talk about a channel without a complete producer-consumer pair.
2. BB channel: In this situation, the channel is disconnected from either of its processes automatically, as soon as it is disconnected from the other.

3. BK channel: In this situation, the channel is disconnected from its producer automatically, as soon as it is disconnected from its consumer, but disconnection from its producer does not disconnect the channel from its consumer.

4. KB channel: In this situation, the channel is disconnected from its consumer automatically, as soon as it is disconnected from its producer, but disconnection from its consumer does not disconnect the channel from its producer.

5. KK channel: In this situation, the channel is not disconnected from either of its processes automatically, if it is disconnected from the other.

Furthermore, given that the last four types of channels may contain pending units, it is meaningful to reuse a channel of any one of these types for another communication after the breakup of the first.

The rationale behind these different channel types is to cover all possible basic channel behavior that cannot be "programmed" otherwise. The last four channel types support asynchronous communication. Given that a channel is an autonomous entity, it may be desirable to subject its behavior to certain boundary conditions. The basic boundary conditions that can reasonably affect the behavior of a channel are changes in its connections at its ends. We may or may not wish to have a channel immediately disconnect itself from its source or its sink as soon as its connection at its opposite end is broken; hence the above four channel types for the asynchronous case.

Note that not all concrete models in the IWIM family necessarily need to support all channel types described above, and some may include additional channel subtypes and/or impose further constraints on their behavior.

3.3 Primitives for a Worker

There are two means of communication available to a worker process: via its ports, and via events. The communication primitives that allow a process to exchange units through its ports are analogous to the traditional read and write I/O primitives. A process can attempt to read a unit from one of its input ports. It hangs if no unit is presently available through that port, and continues once the unit is made available. Similarly, a process can attempt to write a unit to one of its output ports. Again, it hangs if the port is presently not connected to any channel, and continues once a channel connection is made to accept the unit.

A process p can broadcast an event e to all other processes in its environment by *raising* that event. The identity of the event e together with the identity of the process p comprise the broadcast *event occurrence*. A process can also pick up event occurrences broadcast by other processes and react on them. Certain events are guaranteed to be broadcast in special circumstances; for example, termination of a process instance always raises a special event to indicate its death.

3.4 Primitives for a Manager

A manager process can create new instances of processes (including itself) and broadcast and react on event occurrences. It can also create and destroy channel (re)connections between various ports of the process instances it knows, including its own. Creation of new process instances, as well as installation and dismantling of communication channels are done dynamically. Specifically, these actions may be prompted by event occurrences it detects.

Each manager process typically controls the communications among a (dynamic) number of process instances in a data-flow like network. The processes themselves are generally unaware of their patterns of communication, which may change in time, by the decisions of a coordinator process.

4 Communication vs. Computation

Let us reconsider the example in §2, and see how it can be done in the IWIM model. Our example now consists of three processes: revised p, revised q, and a coordinator process c which is responsible to facilitate their communication. The source code for this version of the application looks something like the following:

```
process p:                      process q:                    process c:

compute m1                      read m1 from input port i1    ...
write m1 to output port o1      read m2 from input port i2    create the channel p.o1→q.i1
compute m2                      compute m using m1 and m2      create the channel p.o2→q.i2
write m2 to output port o2      write m to output port o1      create the channel q.o1→p.i1
do other things                                               ...
read m from input port i1
do other computation using m
```

In this example, the pattern of cooperation between the processes p and q is simple and static. Therefore, the responsibility of the coordinator process c is, indeed, very simple: perhaps, it first creates the processes p and q, establishes the communication channels defined above, and then may wait for the proper condition (e.g., termination of p and/or q) to dismantle these channels and terminate itself. Nevertheless, moving the communication concerns out of p and q and into c already shows some of the advantages of the IWIM model.

The processes p and q are now "ideal" workers. They do not know and do not care where their input comes from, nor where their output goes to. They know nothing about the pattern of cooperation in this application; they can just as easily be incorporated in any other application, and will do their job provided that they receive "the right" input at the right time. The cooperation model of this application is now explicit: it is embedded in the coordinator process c. If we wish to have the output of q delivered to another process, or to have yet another process deliver the input of p, neither p nor q, but only c is to be modified.

The process c is an "ideal" manager. It knows nothing about the details of the tasks performed by p and q. Its only concern is to ensure that they are created at the right time, receive the right input from the right sources, and deliver their results to the right sinks. It also knows when additional new process instances are supposed to be created, how the network of communication channels among processes must change in reaction to significant event occurrences, etc. (none of which is actually a concern in this simple example).

It is very likely that such ideal worker processes developed for one application can be used in other concurrent applications, with very different cooperation patterns. Removing the communication concerns out of worker processes enhances the modularity and the re-usability of the resulting software. Furthermore, the fact that such ideal manager processes know nothing about the tasks performed by the workers they coordinate, makes them generic and reusable too. The cooperation protocols for a concurrent application can be developed modularly as a set of coordinator processes. It is likely that some of such ideal managers, individually or collectively, may be used in other applications, coordinating very different worker processes, producing very different results; as long as their cooperation follows the same protocol, the same coordinator processes can be used. Modularity and re-usability of the coordinator processes also enhances the re-usability of the resulting software.

5 Manifold

MANIFOLD is a coordination language for writing program modules (coordinator processes) to manage complex, dynamically changing interconnections among sets of independent, concurrent, cooperating processes that comprise a single application[11, 12]. The conceptual model behind MANIFOLD is based on the IWIM model, described in §3. To our knowledge, presently, MANIFOLD is the only language or system based on the IWIM model. Specifically, the MANIFOLD model is a concrete version of the IWIM model where:

1. Each of the basic concepts of process, event, port, and channel in IWIM corresponds to an explicit language construct.
2. All communication is asynchronous. Thus, there is no synchronous communication channel (type S in §3.2), and raising and reacting to events do not synchronize the processes involved.
3. The separation of computation and communication concerns, i.e., the distinction between workers and managers, is more strongly enforced.

The MANIFOLD system consists of a compiler, a run-time system library, a number of utility programs, and libraries of builtin and predefined processes of general interest. A MANIFOLD application consists of a (potentially very large) number of processes running on a network of heterogeneous hosts, some of which may be parallel systems. Processes in the same application may be written in different programming languages and some of them may not know anything about MANIFOLD, nor the fact that they are cooperating with other processes through MANIFOLD in a concurrent application. Some of the processes will run as independent operating-system-level processes, and some will run together as light-weight processes (preemptively scheduled threads) inside an operating-system-level process. None of this detail is relevant at the level of the MANIFOLD source code, and the programmer need not know anything about the eventual configuration of his or her application in order to write a MANIFOLD program. The utility programs in the MANIFOLD system work on the object files produced by the (MANIFOLD and other language) compilers and take care of the proper composition of the executable files in an application; and of their mapping onto the proper actual hosts at run time (see §5.8).

MANIFOLD is a strongly-typed, block-structured, declarative, event driven language. The primary entities created and manipulated in a MANIFOLD program are processes, ports, events, and streams. The MANIFOLD system supports separate compilation. A MANIFOLD source file constitutes a program *module*, encapsulating all that is declared locally within its scope. A module can access entities defined in other modules by importing a definition that is exported by them, or share the ones declared as extern.

The MANIFOLD system runs on multiple platforms. Presently, it runs on IBM RS6000, IBM SP1/2, HP, SUNOS, Solaris, and SGI IRIX. Linux and Cray Unicos ports are under way. The system was developed with emphasis on portability and support for heterogeneity of the execution environment. It can be ported with little or no effort to any platform that supports a thread facility functionally equivalent to a small subset of the Posix threads, plus an inter-process communication facility roughly equivalent to a small subset of PVM.

5.1 Events

In MANIFOLD, once an event is raised by a source, it generally continues with its processing, while the event occurrence propagates through the environment independently. Any receiver process that is interested in such an event occurrence will automatically receive it in its *event memory*. The observed event occurrences in the event memory of a process can be examined and reacted on by that process at its own leisure and according to its own sense of priorities. The event memory of a process behaves as a set: there can be at most one copy of the occurrence of the same event raised by the same source in the event memory. If an event source repeatedly raises an event faster than an observer reacts on that event occurrence, the event memory of the observer induces an automatic sampling effect: the observer detects only one such event occurrence.

5.2 Streams

The asynchronous communication channels in MANIFOLD are called *streams*. A stream has an infinite capacity that is used as a FIFO queue, enabling asynchronous production and consumption of units by the processes connected to the stream as its source and sink.[1]. When the sink process of a stream requires

---

[1] The "infinite" capacity of a stream is not really as impractical as it seems. Once the volume of the units contained in a stream exceeds a threshold, its surplus is diverted into a file. An application that generates so much buffered information to fill up the capacity of the file system either needs a larger file system or a bit of restructuring to introduce some synchronization over the buffered information

a unit, it is suspended only if no units are available in the stream. The suspended sink process resumes as soon as the next unit becomes available for its consumption. The source process of a stream is never suspended because the infinite buffer capacity of a stream is never filled.

There are four primary types of streams in MANIFOLD, corresponding to the BB, BK, KB, and KK type channels in §3.2. Only KB and BK type streams can be reconnectable in MANIFOLD: once such a stream is disconnected from the process on its B-side, it can be reconnected to another source/sink on its dangling side.

Note that as in the IWIM model, the constructor of a stream between two processes is, in general, a third process. Stream definitions in MANIFOLD are generally additive. This means that a port can simultaneously be connected to many different ports through different streams. The flows of units of information in streams are automatically replicated and merged at outgoing and incoming port junctions, as necessary. Thus, a unit placed into a port that is connected to more than one outgoing streams is automatically duplicated, with a separate copy placed into each outgoing stream. Analogously, when a process attempts to fetch a unit from a port that is connected to several incoming streams, it obtains the first unit available in a non-empty incoming stream, selected non-deterministically.

5.3 Processes

The atomic workers of IWIM are called atomic processes in MANIFOLD. Any operating system-level process can be used as an atomic process in MANIFOLD. However, MANIFOLD also provides a library of functions that can be called from a regular C program running as an atomic process, to support a richer interface between the atomic process and the MANIFOLD world. An atomic process that takes advantage of this interface library is called a *compliant* atomic process.

Strong separation of computation concerns from communication concerns in MANIFOLD is achieved by not (directly) providing the usual computational capabilities of other programming languages in the MANIFOLD language. Furthermore, the interface library for the compliant atomic processes does not provide any means for an atomic process to perform coordination functions (i.e., the library does not contain functions that correspond to the primitives described in §3.4). Thus, atomic processes (compliant or not) can only produce and consume units through their ports, raise and receive events, and compute.

Manager/coordinator processes are written in the MANIFOLD language and are called manifolds. A manifold definition (i.e., the definition of a coordinator process in this language) consists of a header and a body. The header of a manifold (or atomic process definition) gives its name, the number and types of its parameters, and the names of its input and output ports. Parameters of a manifold can be manifold definitions, processes, events, and ports. The body of a manifold definition is a block.

A block consists of a finite number of states. Each state has a label and a body. The label of a state defines the condition under which a transition to that state is possible, in terms of a conjunction of patterns that can match with observed event occurrences in the event memory of the manifold. The body of a simple state defines the set of actions that are to be performed upon transition to that state. The body of a compound state is either a (nested) block, or a call to a parameterized subprogram known as a *manner* in MANIFOLD.

5.4 Manners

A *manner* is a parameterized subprogram that can be called by manifolds. Invocation of a manner never creates a new process: the processor executing the manner call enters the manner.

A manner consists of a header and a body. As for the subprograms in other languages, the header of a manner essentially defines its name and the types and the number of its parameters. A manner is either atomic or regular. The body of a regular manner is a block. The implementation of the body of an atomic manner is a C function that can interface with the MANIFOLD world through the same interface library as for the compliant atomic processes.

Parameters to a manner can be manifold definitions, processes, events, ports, and other manners. Manners embody coordination sub-protocols that can be used in various places within a MANIFOLD application. Thus, both general and application-specific higher-level abstract coordination protocols can be built out of the basic primitives in MANIFOLD as manners and stored in libraries.

5.5 State Transitions

The actions in a simple state body essentially correspond to the primitives described in §3.4: create and activate instances of (atomic and/or manifold) processes, raise (broadcast) events, post events (place an occurrence of the event in the event memory of the running manifold instance only), and construct and/or (re)connect streams between ports of various process instances. Upon transition to a state, the actions specified in its body are performed in a non-deterministic order. Conceptually, this is an atomic action and takes no time. Then, the state becomes *preemptable*: i.e., if the conditions for transition to another state are satisfied, the current state is preempted and a transition to a new state takes place. Preemption of a state preempts all streams constructed and/or (re)connected in that state.

Preemption of a stream breaks off the connection between the stream and its source and/or sink process at the B-end(s) of the stream. Thus, preempting a BB-type stream breaks the connections at both ends of the stream; preempting a BK-type stream breaks its connection with its source; preempting a KB-type stream breaks its connection with its sink; and a KK-type stream is not affected by preemption.

The event-driven state transition mechanism described above is the only control mechanism in the MANIFOLD language. More familiar control structures, such as the sequential flow of control represented by the connective ";" (as in Pascal and C), conditional (i.e., "if") constructs, and loop constructs can be built out of this event mechanism, and are also available in the MANIFOLD language as a convenience.

5.6 Coordination in Manifold

The crux of the coordination paradigm in MANIFOLD is to dynamically orchestrate the communications among sets of such processes *from the outside*, by *third party* specialized coordinator processes that are written in the MANIFOLD language. Furthermore, the coordinator processes must do their job with no knowledge of the internal details of the computations carried out by the processes whose cooperation they coordinate. The only information available to a coordinator process is the external behavior of the processes it coordinates, which contains the specification of their input and output sequences and the relative timing of the events they raise and/or expect. Coordinator processes not only can react to events of interest from other processes, they can also initiate actions on their own. Thus, in contrast to *reactive* coordination systems, (e.g., through the enforcement of constraints), coordination in MANIFOLD is *pro-active*.

We regard the clear separation (indeed, isolation) of computation and communication in MANIFOLD and its control-oriented approach to coordination of cooperation, essential and novel. The dynamic data-flow like network inherent in the IWIM model is an important component of MANIFOLD's control-oriented approach to concurrency. The compositional property of data-flow networks makes it possible to decompose the coordination of a complex, dynamic application into separate, simpler sub-coordination problems, and then combine them together. This is a significant issue in building massively concurrent applications.

5.7 Examples

It is beyond the scope of this paper to present the details of the syntax and semantics of the MANIFOLD language. However, because MANIFOLD is not very similar to any other well-known language, in order to appreciate the applicability of its underlying concepts to practical concurrent programming, it is essential to grasp the utility and the expressibility of some of its basic constructs. In this section we present two examples to illustrate the features and the capabilities of the MANIFOLD language and its underlying model.

Hello World! For our first example, consider a simple program to print a message such as "Hello World!" on the standard output. The MANIFOLD source file for this program contains the following:

```
manifold PrintUnits() import.
auto process print is PrintUnits.

manifold Main()
{
  begin: "Hello World!" -> print.
}
```

The first line of this code defines a manifold named PrintUnits that takes
no arguments, and states (through the keyword import) that the real definition
of its body is contained in another source file. This defines the "interface" to
a process type definition, whose actual "implementation" is given elsewhere.
Whether the actual implementation of this process is an atomic process (e.g., a
C function) or it is itself another manifold is indeed irrelevant in this source file.
We assume that PrintUnits waits to receive units through its standard input
port and prints them. When PrintUnits detects that there are no incoming
streams left connected to its input port and it is done printing the units it has
received, it terminates.

The second line of code defines a new instance of the manifold PrintUnits,
calls it print, and states (through the keyword auto) that this process instance
is to be automatically activated upon creation, and deactivated upon departure
from the scope wherein it is defined; in this case, this is the end of the application.
Because the declaration of the process instance print appears outside of any
blocks in this source file, it is a global process, known by every instance of every
manifold whose body is defined in this source file.

The last lines of this code define a manifold named Main that takes no parameters. Every manifold definition (and therefore every process instance) always has at least three default ports: input, output, and error. The definition
of these ports are not shown in this example, but the ports are defined for Main
by default.

The body of this manifold is a block (enclosed in a pair of braces) and contains only a single state. The name Main is indeed special in MANIFOLD: there
must be a manifold with that name in every MANIFOLD application and an
automatically created instance of this manifold, called main, is the first process
that is started up in an application. Activation of a manifold instance automatically posts an occurrence of the special event begin in the event memory of
that process instance; in this case, main. This makes the initial state transition
possible: main enters its only state – the begin state.

The begin state contains only a single primitive action, represented by the
stream construction symbol, "→". Entering this state, main creates a stream
instance (with the default BK-type) and connects the output port of the process
instance on the left-hand side of the → to the input port of the process instance
on its right-hand side. The process instance on the right-hand side of the → is, of
course, print. What appears to be a character string constant on the left-hand
side of the → is also a process instance: a constant in MANIFOLD is a special

process instance that produces its value as a unit on its output port and then dies[2].

Having made the stream connection between the two processes, main now waits for all stream connection made in this state to break up (on at least one of their ends). The stream breaks up, in this case, on its source end as soon as the string constant delivers its unit to the stream and dies. Since there are no other event occurrences in the event memory of main, the default transition for a state reaching its end (i.e., falling over its terminator period) now terminates the process main.

Meanwhile, print reads the unit and prints it. The stream type BK ensures that the connection between the stream and its sink is preserved even after a preemption, or its disconnection from its source. Once the stream is empty and it is disconnected from its source, it automatically disconnects from its sink. Now, print senses that it has no more incoming streams and dies. At this point, there are no other process instances left and the application terminates.

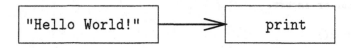

Fig. 1. The "Hello World" exmple in Manifold

Note that our simple example, here, consists of three process instances: two worker processes, a character string constant and print, and a coordinator process, main. Figure 1 shows the relationship between the constant and print, as established by main. Note also that the coordinator process main only establishes the connection between the two worker processes. It does *not* transfer the units through the stream(s) it creates, nor does it interfere with the activities of the worker processes in other ways.

Bucket Sort. Some of the dynamic capabilities of MANIFOLD can be seen in a program for sorting an unspecified number of input units. The particular algorithm used in this example is not necessarily the most effective one. However, it is simple to describe, and serves our purpose of demonstrating the dynamic aspects of the MANIFOLD language well. The sort algorithm is as follows.

There is a sufficiently large (theoretically, infinite) number of *atomic sorters* available, each of which is able to sort a bucket of $n > 0$ units very efficiently. (The number n may even vary from one atomic sorter to the next.) Each atomic sorter receives its input through its input port; raises a specific event it receives as a parameter to inform other processes that it has filled up its input bucket; sorts its units; produces the sorted sequence of the units through its output port; and terminates.

---

[2] Conceptually, constants are full-fledged process instances in MANIFOLD. However, in reality, they are implemented as only a block of memory.

49

The parallel bucket sort program is supposed to feed as much of its own input units to an atomic sorter as the latter can take; feed the rest of its own input as the input to another copy of itself; merge the two output sequences (of the atomic sorter and its new copy); and produce the resulting sequence through its own output port. Merging of the two sorted sequences can be done by a separate merger process, or by a subprogram (i.e., a manner) called by the sorter.

We assume our application consists of several source files. The first source file contains our Main manifold, as shown below. We assume that the merger is a separate process. The merger and the atomic sorter can be written in the MANIFOLD language, but they will be more efficient if they are written in a computation language, such as C. We do not concern ourselves here with the details of the merger and the atomic sorter, and assume that each is defined in a separate source file.

```
manifold PrintUnits() import.
manifold ReadFile(port in) import.
manifold Sorter import.

manifold Main()
{
    auto process read is ReadFile("UnsortedFile").
    auto process sort is Sorter.
    auto process print is PrintUnits.

    begin: read -> sort -> print.
}
```

The main manifold in this application creates read, sort, and print as instances of manifold definitions ReadFile, Sorter, and PrintUnits, respectively. It then connects the output port of read to the input port of sort, and the output port of sort to the input port of print. The process main terminates when both of these connections are broken.

The process read is expected to read the contents of the file UnsortedFile and produce a unit for every sort item in this file through its output port. When it is through with producing its units, read simply terminates. The process sort is an instance of the manifold definition Sorter, which is expected to sort the units it receives through its input port. This process terminates when its input is disconnected and all of its output units are delivered through its output port.

The manifold definition Sorter, shown below, is our main interest. In its begin state, an instance of Sorter connects its own input to an instance of the AtomicSorter, it calls atomsort. It also installs two *guards*, one on each of its input and output ports. The guard on the input port posts the event finished in an instance of Sorter after a first connection to the arrival side of its input is made, then all connections to the arrival side of its input are severed, and all units passed through this port are consumed. The guard on the output port posts the event `flushed` in an instance of `Sorter` after a connection is made to its arrival side, and all units arriving at this port have passed through.

```
manifold AtomicSorter(event) import.
manifold Merger() import.

manifold Sorter()
{
  event filled, flushed, finished.
  process atomsort is AtomicSorter(filled).
  stream reconnect KB input -> *.
  priority filled < finished.

  begin: (activate(atomsort),
          input -> atomsort,
          guard(input, a_everdisconnected!empty, finished),
          guard(output, a_everdisconnected, flushed)).

  finished: {
      ignore filled.  // possible event from atomsort

      begin: atomsort -> output.  // only output is that of atomsort
  }.

  filled: {
      process merge<a,b|output> is Merger.
      stream KK * -> (merge.a, merge.b).
      stream KK merge -> output.

      begin: (activate(merge),
              input -> Sorter -> merge.a,
              atomsort -> merge.b,
              merge -> output).

      finished:. // do nothing and leave this block
  }.

  end: {
      begin: terminated(void).  // wait for units to flush through output
      flushed: halt.
  }.
}
```

A full description of the `Sorter` manifold appears in [1] and takes about one and a half pages; due to space limitation, this description cannot be reproduced here. The following overview is meant to give an idea of the purpose of the other states of the `Sorter` manifold.

In the state labeled `filled`, the remainder of the input is diverted to a new instance of `Sorter`, and its output is sent to a merger process called `merge`, which also receives the output of `atomsort`. The state labeled `finished` deals with the terminal case of recursive instantiation in the `Sorter` manifold, when the last `atomsort` consumes the last input unit. The state labeled `end` ensures that an instance of `Sorter` waits until all output units are taken out of its output port, before it terminates.

An interesting aspect of the `Sorter` manifold is the dynamic way in which it switches connections among the process instances it creates. Perhaps more interesting, is the fact that, in spite of its name, `Sorter` knows nothing about sorting! If we change its name to X, and systematically change the names of the identifiers it uses to Y_1 through Y_k, we realize that all it knows is to divert its own input to an instance of some process it creates; when this instance raises a certain event, it is to divert the rest of its input to a new instance of itself; and to divert the output of these two processes to a third process, whose output is to be passed out as its own output.

What `Sorter` embodies is a protocol that describes how instances of two process definitions (e.g., `AtomicSorter` and `Merger` in our case) should communicate with each other. Our `Sorter` manifold can just as happily orchestrate the cooperation of any pair of processes that have the same input/output and event behavior as `AtomicSorter` and `Merger` do, regardless of what computation they perform. The cooperation protocol defined by `Sorter` simply doles out chunks of its input stream to instances of what it knows as `AtomicSorter` and diverts their output streams to instances of what it knows as `Merger`. `AtomicSorter` need not really sort its input units, `Merger` need not really merge them, and neither has to produce as many units through its output as it receives through its input port. They can do any computation they want.

As a concrete example of this notion of reusable coordinator modules, it is worth mentioning that one of our colleagues is using the exact same sort program described above as the coordination module for the parallel/distributed version of a dynamic domain decomposition algorithm. The original version of this algorithm is part of a package of numerical algorithms under development by another group at CWI[13]. No change to the coordination scheme described above is necessary to handle the single-grid version of the dynamic domain decomposition algorithm. Only a small change to the coordination modules is necessary to handle the multi-grid version of this algorithm.

5.8   Execution of Manifold Applications

A MANIFOLD application consists of one or more executable files, called *tasks*, each of which can run on a number of hosts, with the same or different hardware/software architectures. Conceptually, none of this information is relevant to the programmer at the level of the MANIFOLD language: all that a programmer sees are manifold definitions and process instances. However, the placement of the executable code for these manifold definitions in executable files (tasks) and the hosts on which these tasks can run, are details that must be specified at link and execution time, before a MANIFOLD application can run.

The MANIFOLD system includes a utility program called the MANIFOLD linker. The MANIFOLD linker expects an input file describing the composition of the executable files of an application and produces a set of C programs that contain the necessary link information for the tasks of the application, plus a set of specifications for how the final executable files should be linked. Each such executable file is created on a host with proper architecture by linking together the object files resulting from the output of the MANIFOLD compiler; the object files resulting from compiling the additional user C programs such as atomic processes and atomic manners; the object files produced by the MANIFOLD linker; and the proper libraries.

The execution of a MANIFOLD application starts by running any one of the executable files of the application on an appropriate host. This creates an instance of the task and passes it the command line parameters used in its invocation. Once running, the first invoked task instance in the application searches to locate a run-time configuration file for the application. (Normally, this configuration file is in the same directory where the executable file for the invoked task resides.) The contents of this configuration file tell the MANIFOLD run-time system what hosts are to be used for this run of the application, and which tasks can run on which of these hosts.

Next, the running task instance locates a task that contains the Main manifold of the application. An instance of this candidate task is started up on an appropriate host, and the first instance of the Main manifold of the application, known as the process main, is created in this task instance. Finally, the command line parameters used to invoke the application are passed on to main, and it is activated.

Other instances of manifolds and atomic processes are dynamically created as required during the life time of the application, and instances of tasks to contain them are also created as necessary on their appropriate hosts. A MANIFOLD application terminates when all processes created therein, except constants and a number of predefined special system processes have terminated.

6 Related Work

The survey by Malone and Crowston[14] characterizes coordination as an emerging research area with an interdisciplinary focus. They observe that coordination has been and is a key issue in many diverse disciplines other than computer science. Although tackling coordination problems in operating systems, parallel programming, and databases (to name but a few) has a long history in computer science, the notion of coordination as a research area and coordination languages as a serious topic are rather recent developments. Nevertheless, a number of models and systems have already appeared for coordination. Many of them deal with some limited aspect of coordination, or coordination in a specific and somewhat limited context.

HOP is a model for describing object composition patterns [15]. The main concepts in HOP are objects and ports. A HOP object is closer to the concept of an object in an object oriented language such as Smalltalk or C++, than to a process in IWIM or MANIFOLD. HOP objects are different than objects in typical object oriented languages primarily because they have ports. The underlying rationale for the concept of port in HOP is very similar to that of ports in IWIM and MANIFOLD: disallow access to foreign entities except through clearly designated boundary points (i.e., ports). However, the purpose of HOP is to directly model dependencies among objects and their composition, not to coordinate inter-object communication in the same sense as in IWIM and MANIFOLD.

Language support for the expression of certain kinds of multi-object coordination is presented in[16]. The main construct offered is a synchronizer, which is to be integrated into an object oriented concurrent language that adheres to the Actor model[4] of computation. Coordination patterns can be expressed as constraints that restrict invocation of a group of objects. Through invocation constraints, coordination patterns can be specified abstractly, independent of the protocols needed to implement them.

Enforcement of constraints is done by synchronizers, which are special objects that observe and limit the invocations accepted by a set of ordinary objects which are being constrained. This is somewhat similar to the idea of workers and managers in the IWIM model. As with managers in IWIM and manifolds in MANIFOLD, synchronizers can overlap: multiple separately specified synchronizers can constrain the same objects. Synchronizers themselves are not "real objects" in the sense that it is not possible to, recursively, constrain their behavior using other synchronizers, and ordinary objects cannot send messages to them as they do to other ordinary objects. In IWIM (and MANIFOLD) a manager (manifold instance) is externally indistinguishable from an ordinary worker (atomic process).

In an Actor-based language extended with synchronizers, as proposed in[16], the basic model of communication is a variant of the (asynchronous) TSR model, wherein the computation and communication concerns are mixed together in the same modules. In contrast, there is a clear separation of computation and communication concerns in IWIM (and MANIFOLD).

One of the best known coordination languages is Linda[17]. Linda uses a so called generative communication model, based on a shared tuple space[18]. In contrast to Linda, MANIFOLD is a "complete" language. The Linda model addresses only part of the underlying concerns of the IWIM model. There is a symmetry between the communication primitives in Linda, and the communication between processes is accomplished anonymously through the tuple space. However, there is nothing to prevent complete mixing of communication concerns with computation. There is no clear separation of workers and managers, as in IWIM. Unlike Linda, MANIFOLD encourages programmers to develop "pure coordination modules" separately and independently of the "pure computation modules" in their applications. This manifests the result of the substantial effort invested in the coordination component of an application in a tangible form as modular "pure coordinators" which can be reused in other applications. A significant difference between the underlying models of Linda and MANIFOLD can be characterized as a more data-oriented (Linda) versus a more control-oriented (MANIFOLD) approach to coordination of the cooperation among concurrent processes.

A number of parallel logic programming languages also exist that can, in principle, be used for coordination, in as much as logic clauses can represent the constraints and the protocols for concurrent execution of atomic goals (i.e., sequential computation fragments). This includes, e.g., Strand[19], PMS-Prolog[20], Shared Prolog[21], and Constraint Logic Programming languages[22]. Among them, Strand is different because of its emphasis on coordination constructs. Indeed, Strand is offered as a coordination language and, like Linda, has been used to augment imperative sequential languages such as C and Fortran, yielding Strand-C and Strand-Fortran.

The metaphor of Interaction Abstract Machines (IAMs)[23] and its underlying formal computational model, Linear Objects[24], present a paradigm for abstract modeling of concurrent agent-oriented computation. The operational semantics of the agents and their interactions is given in terms of the proof theory of Linear Logic. The notion of "property-driven communication" in IAMs is analogous to the concept of anonymous communication through ports and events in IWIM (and MANIFOLD). Furthermore, The fan-in and fan-out of the streams at ports in MANIFOLD can be seen as the equivalent of the notion of broadcasting on specific channels in IAMs, making the flow of units in the IWIM (and MANIFOLD) streams analogous to waves in IAMs.

Models such as IAMs, Linear Objects, the tuple space in Linda, Shared Prolog, and Blackboards[25] all propose a shared, open unrestricted data-structure (formally modeled as a multi-set) as an appropriate medium for communication in a concurrent or distributed data-driven system. The IWIM model, on the other hand, does not contain the notion of any central or shared entity, and is inherently a distributed model. Furthermore, IWIM supports a more control driven specification of coordination than these models.

7 Conclusion

In this paper, we illustrate the shortcomings of the direct use of communication models that are based on targeted-send and receive primitives in large concurrent applications. We propose that the gap between the requirements of concurrent applications and the communication primitives supported by the platform on which they are implemented must be filled with an explicit model of cooperation. More importantly, we argue that there is an urgent need for practical models and languages wherein various models of cooperation can be built out of simple primitives and structuring constructs.

We present the IWIM model as a more suitable basis for control-oriented coordination languages. The significant characteristics of the IWIM model include compositionality, which it inherits from data-flow, anonymous communication, and separation of computation concerns from communication concerns. These characteristics lead to clear advantages in large concurrent applications.

MANIFOLD is a specific coordination language based on the IWIM model. Some of the interesting properties of MANIFOLD are illustrated through simple examples in this paper. More experience is still necessary to thoroughly evaluate the practical usefulness of MANIFOLD. However, our experience so far indicates that MANIFOLD is well suited for describing complex systems of cooperating concurrent processes.

We believe it is possible and useful to go beyond MANIFOLD and develop languages and support environments that provide higher level abstractions, constructs, and tools for the development and debugging of the coordination components of massively concurrent applications. The ongoing work in our group on the visual programming language and environment based on MANIFOLD is one direction in which we pursue this goal. Our future work also includes using constraints to specify certain coordination concerns from which MANIFOLD code can be automatically generated.

References

1. F. Arbab, "Coordination of massively concurrent activities," Tech. Rep. CS–R9564, Centrum voor Wiskunde en Informatica, Kruislaan 413, 1098 SJ Amsterdam, The Netherlands, 1995.
2. C. Hoare, *Communicating Sequential Processes*. Prentice Hall International Series in Computer Science, New Jersey: Prentice-Hall, 1985.
3. R. Milner, *Communication and Concurrency*. Prentice Hall International Series in Computer Science, New Jersey: Prentice Hall, 1989.
4. G. Agha, *Actors: A Model of Concurrent Computation in Distributed Systems*. MIT Press, 1986.
5. INMOS Ltd., *OCCAM 2, Reference Manual*. Series in Computer Science, London — Sydney — Toronto — New Delhi — Tokyo: Prentice-Hall, 1988.
6. T. Bolognesi and E. Brinksma, "Introduction to the ISO specification language LOTOS," *Computer Networks and ISDN Systems*, vol. 14, pp. 25–59, 1986.
7. A. Geist, A. Beguelin, J. Dongarra, W. Jiang, R. Manchek, and V. Sunderam, "PVM 3 user's guide and reference manual," Tech. Rep. ORNL/TM-12187, Oak Ridge National Laboratory, September 1994.
8. J. J. Dongarra, S. W. Otto, M. Snir, and D. Walker, "An introduction to the MPI standard," Tech. Rep. CS-95-274, University of Tennessee, Jan. 1995.
9. R. Butler and E. Lusk, "User's guide to the p4 parallel programming system," Tech. Rep. ANL-92/17, Argonne National Laboratory, Oct. 1992. Version 1.4.
10. R. Hempel, H. Hoppe, U. Keller, and W. Krotz, "PARMACS v6.1 specification," tech. rep., PALLAS GmbH, Hermulheimer Strasse 10, D-50321, August 1995.
11. F. Arbab, I. Herman, and P. Spilling, "An overview of Manifold and its implementation," *Concurrency: Practice and Experience*, vol. 5, pp. 23–70, February 1993.
12. F. Arbab, "Manifold version 2: Language reference manual," Tech. Rep. preliminary version, Centrum voor Wiskunde en Informatica, Kruislaan 413, 1098 SJ Amsterdam, The Netherlands, 1995.

13. C. T. H. Everaars, P. W. Hemker, and W. Stortelder, "Manual of splds, a software package for parameter identification in dynamic systems," Tech. Rep. preliminary version, Centrum voor Wiskunde en Informatica, Kruislaan 413, 1098 SJ Amsterdam, The Netherlands, September 1995.

14. T. Malone and K. Crowston, "The interdisciplinary study of coordination," *ACM Computing Surveys*, vol. 26, pp. 87–119, March 1994.

15. L. Dami, "HOP: Hierarchical objects with ports," in *Object Frameworks* (D. Tsichritzis, ed.), Centre Universataire d'Informatique, University of Geneva, 1992.

16. S. Frolund and G. Agha, "A language framework for multi-object coordination," in *Proc. ECOOP '93*, vol. 707 of *Lecture Notes in Computer Science*, pp. 346–360, Springer-Verlag, 1993.

17. N. Carriero and D. Gelernter, "LINDA in context," *Communications of the ACM*, vol. 32, pp. 444–458, 1989.

18. D. Gelernter, "Generative communication in Linda," *ACM Transactions on Programming Languages and Systems*, vol. 7, no. 1, pp. 80–112, 1985.

19. I. Foster and S. Taylor, *Strand: New Concepts in Parallel Programming*. Prentice-Hall, 1990.

20. M. Wise, D. Jones, and T. Hintz, "PMS-Prolog: A distributed Prolog with processes, modules and streams," in *Implementations of Distributed Prolog*, Series in Parallel Computing, pp. 379–404, Wiley, 1992.

21. A. Borgi and P. Ciancarini, "The concurrent language Shared Prolog," *ACM Transactions on Programming Languages and Systems*, vol. 13, no. 1, pp. 99–123, 1991.

22. E. Shapiro, "The family of Concurrent Logic Languages," *ACM Computing Surveys*, vol. 21, pp. 412–510, September 1989.

23. J. Andreoli, P. Ciancarini, and R. Pareschi, "Interaction Abstract Machines," in *Trends in Object-Based Concurrent Computing*, pp. 257–280, MIT Press, 1993.

24. J. Andreoli and R. Pareschi, "Linear Objects: Logical processes with built-in inheritance," *New Generation Computing*, vol. 9, no. 3-4, pp. 445–473, 1991.

25. H. P. Nii, "Blackboard systems," in *The Handbook of Artificial Intelligence* (A. Barr, P. Cohen, and E. Feigenbaum, eds.), vol. 4, pp. 1–82, Addison-Wesley, 1989.

Sonia: an Adaptation of Linda for Coordination of Activities in Organizations

Mario Banville

Adaptive Information Systems
Centre for Information Technology Innovation (CITI)
Laval, PQ, Canada H7V 2X2
e-mail: banville@citi.doc.ca

Abstract: this paper presents Sonia, an adaptation of the Linda coordination language, to support organizational activities composed of people and software. This setting puts stress on the requirements for continuous operations in an open and heterogeneous environment where people play a major role. The goal is to take advantage of the expressiveness of Linda to support the inherent parallelism and need for coordination of workaday activities. A prototype has been built with which simple scenarios focusing on typical office work have been conducted and demonstrated to potential users from different backgrounds. The response was positive and encourages us to seek real scenarios to get more data to validate the usefulness of the mechanism.

1. Introduction

This paper presents the current state of our ongoing work on Sonia, an adaptation of the Linda coordination language, to support organizational activities composed of people and software. Although this possibility for coordination languages has been recognized long ago, most of its applications have been in the area of parallel processing where the goal is to get maximum performance from processors. The goal here is to take advantage of the expressiveness of Linda to support the inherent parallelism and need for coordination of workaday activities. So, issues of operating in such an environment will first be presented along with the interest in coordination languages like Linda as a potential solution. Next, a summary of Sonia and a discussion of the major decisions will follow. Lastly, the paper terminates with the presentation of a prototype, examples of application and current experiences with Sonia. The global goal of this work is to verify if such a coordination language would be applicable, understandable and easily used in such a setting.

2. Organizations, Information Systems and Coordination

The context for this work is the support of intra and interorganization activities typically referred to as groupware, workflow, electronic commerce, enterprise reengineering, information systems, etc. The focus on organizations is from the point of view of people working in team and using computer tools for their personal and interpersonal work. As information systems expand, almost every aspect of organizational activities are affected by computers. Programs, databases, electronic data interchange, word processors, form processing, fax, e-mail and so on are routinely used. Ironically, most software tools are used much in isolation from each other. At some point, to support organizational activities which are cooperative in nature, software tools of one must meet software tools of others. Coordination technology comes in as an enabler of relationships among people so that they can work together and control their processes.

Work of Strauss [ST93], a sociologist who contributed much to the interactionist approach of the Chicago school, is very interesting as a framework to understand the dynamic behavior of relationships in organizations. Foremost to his theory of action is the interplay of action and interaction, autonomy of actors, symbolic representation, work, history, planning and social worlds. This work is very general and not directly targeted at computers, but nevertheless it underlies the work presented in this paper. It shows that interactions play a central role, and Sonia is an attempt at providing an enabler for their articulation. This theory is used not so much as a metaphor for computer agent interactions, but more as a way to fit software as part of organizations.

Another useful and pragmatic approach at organizational activities comes from the domain of Computer Supported Cooperative Work (CSCW). CSCW is rich with such attempts and is very interesting for its balance between theory, practice and multidisciplinary fields. Figure 1 shows some of the characteristics typical of CSCW applications that have been extracted from the work of Blair and Rodden [BR92].

- most CSCW applications are distributed and open
- modes of cooperation: information exchange (messaging), information sharing (shared spaces)
- interactions: asynchronous, synchronous
- information: different types and media
- wide range of control techniques and inter-personal cooperation patterns:
  - various organizational contexts
  - different forms of cooperation must co-exist
  - structure of groups must be explicitly recognized
  - groups work in dynamic and unexpected ways
  - groups are themselves dynamic
  - control should be enabling rather than controlling

Fig. 1. Characteristics of CSCW applications

These characteristics are echoed by work of Hewitt on open systems in general [HE88]. What comes out is the distributed, heterogeneous and open nature of these systems. Communication is inherent, diversified and should be expressed explicitly.

The autonomy leads to a requirement for parallelism which makes it impossible to predict the exact behavior of other systems. As a consequence, asynchronous messaging must be supported, with proper tools to synchronize the activities and relationships in a flexible way. Centralized control, while practical in small scale settings, cannot answer all situations. So, decentralized control must be considered. This control should be enabling rather than constraining.

Through CSCW research, it became clear that current distributed systems present architectural limitations for cooperative work [BE95]. As a consequence, a fair amount of work in CSCW has been concentrated on architectural issues to answer such limitations, but too often as a secondary issue. In the end, we end up with underdeveloped distributed systems that can hardly communicate among themselves which is the opposite of the initial goal. It is interesting to see that other domains like Distributed Databases, Distributed Artificial Intelligence and Parallel Processing share many of these issues. Like in CSCW, solutions are developed in each of these fields. It is unrealistic to look for a single solution, but at some point, these applications have to find a common ground if they are to cooperate in organizational activities. So, work to tackle these common problems ought to be performed in its own right as advocated by Malone and Crowston [MC94] who proposed the field of Coordination for such a purpose.

The previous issues are rather wide in scope. In this paper, the goal is to concentrate on the basic issue of expressing parallelism, asynchronous messaging and flexible relationships that would favor the mixing of applications from which a diversified environment could be built dynamically. Such a solution must be simple so that it can be represented and understandable in an heterogeneous environment.

In this respect, a simple and expressive model from which to build is the one of coordination language of Gelernter and Carriero which led to Linda [CG89] [GC92]. This model comes and has mostly been applied to the field of parallel processing. The initial work considered the possibility of mixing people and software, but little work has been devoted to this aspect. The rest of this paper addresses this possibility by presenting an adaptation of Linda called Sonia. The name Sonia is used to avoid confusion with the current work on Linda. Effort has been put to minimize the changes to Linda so that its simplicity and its properties would be kept and if possible enhanced. Should this adaptation be considered minimal, it would be great. The important point is to see if it can express communication in a way that is meaningful and simple to people first, and then to apply it to the relationships among software tools. Wording and using proper metaphors for the context of users who do not consider their work as computer programming is very important. So, some features of Linda have been renamed, a liberty that one should consider in such a context. The ultimate goal is to let people manage their own processes and relationships.

3. Sonia, a Coordination Language

Figure 2 shows the elements of Sonia. As mentioned in the previous section, it has been influenced by the theory of action of Strauss [ST93]. Actors are autonomous and at the source of any action. These can be people or software tools. So, this setting is fundamentally heterogeneous. People from many backgrounds can intervene. Software tools can be designed in many languages and be running on many types of computer systems distributed over a network.

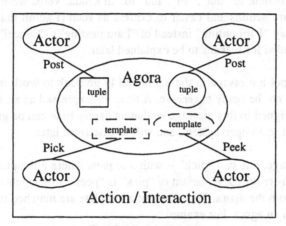

Fig. 2. Model of Sonia

When actors want to work together, interaction must proceed through communication and sharing of information. This is where an agora comes in. The agora draws on the idea of a public place where people meet to exchange ideas, information, goods and services. The agora behaves as a medium allowing sharing of information which makes possible relationships among actors. The place does not do the work itself, but is an enabler for cooperation. In Linda, this place is called a tuple space. The word agora was chosen to stress the social nature of coordination instead of a technical wording.

Actors communicate via the agora by posting and extracting messages in the agora. The messages are written as tuples of named values like:

Tuple(:shape "square" :color "red").

Note: many languages can interface to an agora, and each can have its own syntax. The exact syntax is not much of concern at this point; only the semantic is of concern here.

As opposed to Linda, in Sonia a tuple can be manipulated as a first-class object. This ability allows a tuple to be part of a tuple so that complex structures can be expressed. Types that can be used as values are: nil, any, number (integer and floating point), string (ISO Latin-1 and Unicode), time, delay, tuple, type, rule and array of these values. Their size and/or precision has no limit imposed by Sonia, but could be established dynamically by actors as a set of shared assumptions. For example, a string can be as large as you want and can accept any character. The same is true for a number so that no architectural restriction exists. The agora is also a first-class object which allows an actor to refer to as many agoras as need comes. This is quite important for many reasons to be discussed later, but the main one being that all actors of the world could certainly not communicate through a single agora.

Four operations are supported on an agora: "post", "pick", "peek" and "cancel". The first three are equivalent to "out", "in", and "rd" in Linda. Verbs were preferred since these operations are actions and easier to express as such (I admit that it is a bit cosmetic, but try to say "I am outing" instead of "I am posting"). "Cancel" is new. "Eval" has not been included for reasons to be explained later.

"Post" allows to put a message in the agora and to go back to work immediately. An actor may or may not be ready to receive. A time-out expressed as an absolute time or a delay can be assigned to this message so that an expiry time can be given. Time-outs are very important in an open system, and will be discussed later.

To extract a message, one can "pick" it with a request where a template describes the kind of tuple that is required. A variant of "pick" is "peek" which gets a message without removing it from the agora. The values of a template are matched to corresponding values of tuples in an agora. For example:

Template(:shape "square" :color any) would match

Tuple(:shape "square" :color "blue").

The rules governing the matching operation are:

(a) by value: compare for equality if the value of a template is not an Any, a Type or a Rule (the following rules),

(b) Type("aType"): accept a value of a specific type,

(c) Any: accept anything (polymorphism),

(d) Rule("aScript"): a comparison to evaluate on the value of a tuple so that complex expressions can be applied. Currently, this comparison is expressed in Smalltalk. For example,

Template(:shape any :color Rule("value = 'red' or: [value = 'blue']"))

would extract a tuple for any shape that is red or blue.

By default, tuples must have the same number of values as the template. A variation allows matching with tuples that have more values than a template. This opens the door for a generic template that matches tuples with optional values.

Rules (a) and (b) are the same than in Linda. Rules (c) and (d) are new. Such a template matching allows the relationship among actors to be very flexible. A client can put a message in an agora, and many actors can remove it so that they can team up on tasks. Changing the roles in the course of action is quite possible without any burden on the part of a client.

Like "post", "pick" can be assigned a time-out. If a time-out expires, the request ends up with nothing. Polling comes as a natural extension when a time-out of 0 is used.

"Cancel" allows the aborting of an outstanding "pick" or "peek", much as a "pick" allows the removal of a tuple. For example, a process may be waiting for a tuple, and, for some reason, another process may decide that this wait is no more required and would then use "cancel". A template is provided to "cancel" for matching to waiting requests. It can be used as a simple way to advise an actor waiting for a tuple to stop working (a variant of a Linda technique often called a poison pill).

4. Discussion and Issues of some of the Choices

4.1 Tuple as a List of Named Values

This may be a question of personal taste, but naming values of a tuple offers numerous advantages. It offers a natural and expressive meaning that maps very well with user interfaces (dialog, form, ...), programming languages (structure, record, ...), agent languages (KQML, ...) and external communication tools (e-mail, ...). Moreover, this idea is very close to semi-structured messages found in Information Lens [MG88] and Oval [ML92] which showed up as quite apt at representing both rigidly structured information suitable for software systems, and yet allow a very rich content structure suitable to people. This feature could be represented indirectly on top of Linda, but it is believed to be so useful that most operations on an agora would use it, so it is better to make it part of the coordination language itself.

Another benefit is that dependence on the order and the number of values is minimized. This makes possible the matching of a template to a tuple with more values than was requested so that extensions and optional values can be represented. In this proposition, two options are possible for matching a template to a tuple: the number of values of a tuple must be the same than the template, which avoids interference among simple signatures; or a tuple can have more values than a template in which case the signature of the template must be very discriminant.

When implementing Sonia, the use of names for tuple values is quite practical since it makes possible a fast discrimination of tuples (used to avoid a comparison with every tuples). The internal structure of an agora can make use of the list of names (a signature) for a fast access with hashing. Internally hashing tuples has already been recognized as a useful technique for implementing Linda efficiently (which is not so obvious after all). So, this adds one more trick for an efficient implementation.

4.2 Types of Values

When implementing a distributed and heterogeneous system, the choice of types to exchange is always a compromise; these types must be expressive which calls for various and complex types, and yet we must restrict ourselves to a minimal subset of concepts that can be easily represented and understood in many languages.

Currently, a small set of types that are very similar to basic types of many languages and distributed systems have been defined (nil, any, number, string, time, delay, tuple, type, rule, array). Any, type and rule are mainly used in a request template. Time and delay are not common in terms of basic types, but, as the section on time and time-out will show, time is fundamental in the coordination of activities and it seems reasonable to define it as a basic type. As in many computer languages, the ability to build composite types with the help of tuple and array is of great value to extend the basic types.

An important choice for heterogeneity of computer architectures and languages is to allow types of any size and precision; memory should be the only limit. While this feature is not so obvious to implement, it is believed to be feasible without too much compromise on performance. For numbers, this idea may look a bit surprising, but it allows the support of various and future computer architectures. If actors want to explicitly restrict their usage patterns to 32 bits integers, they are free to do so, independently from others with 64 bits architecture working on the same agora. It does not mean that every actors have to support types of any size, although it is quite feasible; their interface to Sonia may have specific restrictions which means that overflows may happen. Such overflows should be avoided through coordination among actors. An implementation of Sonia may also have restrictions, but the goal is to make the best effort to fully support this feature.

4.3 Time and Time-Out

The notion of time [WH72] is fundamental to the coordination of organizational activities (expressiveness) and vital for the operation in an open environment (errors). Currently, most distributed systems address the issue of location, but rarely the notion of timing. This notion in Sonia is central, and yet it is expressed in a simple way.

In terms of expressiveness, the uncoupling across time of Sonia, inherited from Linda, allows expression of relative ordering of processes leading to causal relationships. Understanding and giving meaning to the world depends on our interpretation of past events. The efficiency of our processes depends on a proper ordering of future events, which requires planning from past events. Much of these relationships are "logical", that is relative to the interaction with other processes. Moreover, the world is fundamentally real-time; any action takes time, and things, information and requests rarely last forever, even if the length of their life is unknown. Deadlines are part of almost every activity. So, Sonia extends Linda by supporting the expression of absolute time with Time and Delay types, and by providing time-outs on tuples and requests.

Another reason to include a time-out on operations is to react to errors and failures. For example, if a process fails, then how is it possible to behave in such a case? When running a single application, one simply stops, debugs and reruns it. But in an open environment, the rest of the world is not going to stop just because of a single faulty process. The only way to detect that a process is faulty is to detect a wrong behavior, or no behavior at all. So, time-out on operations is again a prerequisite. Time-out on requests avoids being blocked forever. Likewise, time-out on tuples avoids accumulation of debris. The "cancel" operation also allows premature termination of a request.

4.4 Matching Rules

The corner stone of Linda and Sonia is the associative memory model which comes from the matching mechanism. This is probably what distinguishes them most from other distributed systems. No specific addressing scheme is defined; instead, actors define their own addressing scheme by defining message content on which to match. This gives a huge flexibility in expressing relationships from one-to-one up to many-to-many.

This also implies that the choice of the matching rules is very important. Sonia keeps the two matching rules of Linda, namely matching on equality of values and their types. Polymorphism is possible by indicating that "any" type can be accepted as a value. There are good reasons for both strict type checking and polymorphism. Since the goal is to support heterogeneous computing, and that many languages have different stances in this respect, it is probably better to accept both and leave the choice to actors.

The last matching option, called Rule, where a script representing a comparison is executed on a value of a tuple comes from a need to match on something other than equality. Even equality is sometimes hard to define. For example, when strings are compared, is it case or non-case sensitive? Comparing floating points on an equality basis is not much use; ranges of values are often more appropriate. This facility also allows a set of specialized actors to clearly, simply and efficiently split messages among them. For example, an actor may process purchase orders for values equal to or above 5000 $, and another would process the others. An alternative would be to have a controller extract purchase orders, analyze their content and then split the work. This is a choice of distributed cooperative task sharing versus centralized control. The centralized control option implies more processes and more I/O. This facility is actually similar to an SQL query on a database. Sure it is possible to filter tuples (records) in actors, but this is more I/O intensive. Moreover, an agora (database engine) may be better tuned to that kind of filtering and run on a more powerful computer than actors. Another argument is that an agora is responsible to deliver messages as precisely as possible. Actors must have the ability to define exactly what they want without further filtering. In so doing, actors can concentrate on their work.

In Sonia, the script is currently expressed in Smalltalk because the first implementation uses this language, and is actually very appropriate in this respect. Of course, other languages could be chosen.

Executing such a script in an open environment raises integrity and security issues. First, such a script must absolutely not affect an agora nor the value of a tuple being compared. So, the execution of a script should be done in a private context shielded from external references. Should an exception happen when executing a script, it must be dealt with and be considered as a comparison that returns false. No script should enter in an infinite loop. A watchdog could detect such a behavior, but it is not easy to define an appropriate time limit. These questions are typical when using scripts in a distributed environment and shared with undertakings like Java, Telescript and even Postscript. These issues are probably better to be studied in their own respect independent of coordination languages.

A potential and efficient solution to the previous issues is to replace the script of a Rule by static functions defined by Sonia. For example, functions could be defined for <, <=, >, >=, string comparisons (case and non-case sensitive), etc. For more complex comparisons, a function could be defined to execute a script. In so doing, it could even be possible to support many languages.

4.5 No Eval

An important decision has been made of not including the "eval" operation found in Linda. This operation is used in Linda to create and execute processes and put their result in a tuple. Written with the previous examples syntax, it would give something like:

    eval Tuple(:shape doItShape() :color dotItColor()).

doItShape() and doItColor() are functions evaluated in parallel with other processes in a tuple space, and the result would be put in the tuple for posting.

It is clear that there must be a way to manage the creation of actors (processes), and the Linda approach is good for the purpose of parallel processing within an homogeneous application. But there are many reasons for keeping this external to Sonia. The first one is that distributing tasks among a set of processors is a coordination problem itself, and should be done on top of Sonia like other coordination applications. For example, one could have a set of actors representing each processor and providing a service of process creation. Many complementary ways to coordinate such work can be imagined.

For example, a sophisticated actor creation system based on a market driven algorithm like contract net [SM88] could be envisioned. An agora could even have a variety of such services at once.

The second reason is that a single mechanism for the creation of actors would probably not be sufficient and certainly not evolvable. For example, an actor could be a thread within a process, another process (program), a transaction in a database, a window receiving events within a thread, or a person... Again, a set of actors could provide all these options.

A third reason is that to be open, an agora must not restrict this creation from within. Instead, it must accept to be referenced by external actors. The extreme example would be someone accessing an agora directly (through an interface): is the person a child of an agora? Definitely not, and clearly actors and agoras can have different and independent life spans.

So the function of actor creation ought to be outside of Sonia. Any actor can create other actors based on an internal or an operating system service. But it is quite possible to have a package containing both Sonia and a library of actors for spawning other actors.

4.6 Agora as a First-Class Object

An agora can be viewed as a medium through which communication is possible. But, should all the actors of the world be required to go through a single agora, then things would become very bad. Such an agora would be a bottleneck, a restriction to scalability, a problem in coordinating the use of similar message signatures, an extreme exposure to faults and a security headache.

So, the use of many agoras, chosen on an affinity and functionality basis, sounds much more practical and natural. Making an agora as a first-class object allows an actor to refer to as many agoras as required. This also makes possible the use of specialized agoras optimized for particular uses and computer/network architectures (see [GE89] for a good source of ideas). All these implementations would share the same interface and concepts.

Next comes the question of the relationships among many agoras. In a sense, we could view the world as a federation of agoras. The current approach in Sonia is that it should remain outside the scope of the language. The relationships among agoras is a coordination problem. So it should be solved like other coordination problems; that is on top of Sonia with a dynamic mix of gateway actors. For example, an actor may be listening on an agora called "/France/TravelAgency" for a tuple like

```
Tuple(
   :to "/Canada/Tourism"
   :message Tuple(
      :requestForInfo "Skidoo trek"
      :replyTo "/France/TravelAgency"
   )
)
```

and relay the message to the "/Canada/Tourism" agora. Of course, a package containing both Sonia and a library of gateway actors could be offered as a whole.

This point contrasts with other propositions for multiple tuple spaces [AC93] [CA94] [GE89] [CI94] where creation and embedding of tuple spaces is treated internally to a tuple space. Interestingly, many of the ideas presented by these people would probably still be applicable or adaptable. Moreover, many schemes could be operational at the same time on the same agora and could be changed dynamically. Since these schemes are independent of Sonia, this discussion is left for further work.

4.7 Security

The current work on Sonia does not include security features, but in an open environment, security is very important. This choice was made because the first issue of this work on coordination languages is to develop cooperation mechanisms. So before developing a way to refrain relationships, this is better to find a way to express cooperative relationships. Security is also tricky so that it could easily deserve a whole paper on the subject. But, if we engage too far without taking care of security, we may end up with an unpractical solution. Instead, it has been chosen to present a spectrum of potential solutions. Their variety is considered as a good sign of a possible solution.

The first and obvious solution is to use private agoras for targeted groups. In other words, if you do not want others to know what you say, just do not tell them. Another option is to apply access rights at the interface. These rights could be applied for full access, or for a subset of operations. Existing security mechanisms of operating systems could probably be used. To restrict access to a subgroup only, the granularity of access rights could be finer by attaching them to tuples. Another avenue would be to have actors reserve the use of tuple and request signatures so that others would not use it. A last possibility would be to define a specific type for security that could be included in the content of a tuple. Such a tuple would be extracted only if a request could match this security attribute. Public key authentication and encryption systems could be used in such a way (albeit the load that it would incur).

5. Status of Current Work

5.1 Implementation

An implementation of Sonia has been developed in Smalltalk on top of Windows NT. Other languages and platforms could have been used. In addition, client interfaces have been created to other programming languages for UNIX environments. The main goal of this development is to prove the feasibility, to experiment with this mechanism to see its usefulness, and to demonstrate its working. So, this development focuses on simplicity and does not attempt to provide the most efficient, resilient, and feature rich system.

Figure 3 shows the major elements of the prototype and their operating relationships. Classes Tuple, TimeX and Delay are utility classes used when interfacing an Agora to represent a tuple, an absolute time and a delay, respectively. The centerpiece of the prototype is the Agora abstract class which describes the common interface to an agora. Three subclasses inheriting from Agora implement variations. LocalAgora is the corner stone since it manages and dispatches tuples and requests. Its reach does not extend beyond a Smalltalk workspace process. It allows experimenting with a rich set of types since any Smalltalk object with proper duplicate capability can be used in a tuple (most Smalltalk classes). The multi-processing and exception handling capability of Smalltalk are fully supported.

The class ServerAgora opens the gates of the workspace to offer an Agora on a network. It uses a Transport object to listen for incoming connections and can support many links. When a link is established, operations are relayed to a LocalAgora which was assigned at creation time. Many Transport protocols could be supported by subclassing Transport for different kinds of network. As of now, only TCP/IP is supported. The description of operations exchanged through the transport is encoded as a simple string which shields from any internal representation of objects and makes this exchange rather simple and readable (the specific encoding is out of scope of this paper).

Class RemoteAgora also uses Transport to connect to a ServerAgora. In so doing, any object can use a RemoteAgora like a local agora, albeit a little performance degradation. RemoteAgora does not depend on ServerAgora being implemented in Smalltalk; other implementations could be supported.

Any object can use any of the subclasses of Agora by creating new or referencing existing instances. Class AgoraBoard is a graphical application which references an Agora and provides a direct user interface. It is heavily used in demonstrations to present Sonia. Moreover, it can also execute Smalltalk code to show that manual operations can be processed automatically as well. Many such windows can be operating at the same time so that an agora can be populated with many cooperating actors. Class AgoraForm is another user interface that looks like a form processing application; it

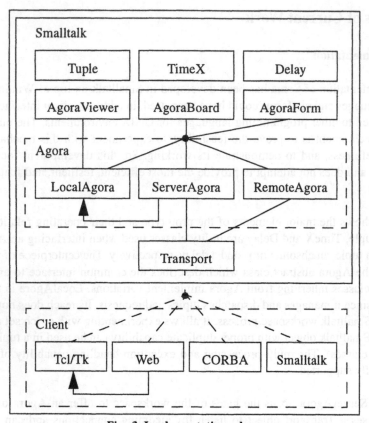

Fig. 3. Implementation schema

shows many fields which can be assigned names and values that can be operated on. Its purpose is to show that many interfaces are possible so that we can focus on functionality instead of ergonomic issues. By the same token, it suggests that work can be done to offer metaphors for user interaction.

Class AgoraViewer is a simple graphical viewer / debugger on a LocalAgora to which it is linked as a monitor. It receives events describing the operations occurring on an agora. These events can be kept in a trace for display / inspection and for saving in a file for later analysis. Stepping from event to event is possible since the agora operations continue only after the viewer returns from an event notification. As of now, this viewer supports only LocalAgora and cannot be used through a network.

Some client interfaces have been developed for other environments, platforms and programming languages. Figure 3 shows Tcl/Tk, Web, CORBA, and Smalltalk interfaces. The Smalltalk interface is the same than RemoteAgora plus Transport presented before, and has been repeated for the purpose of being complete. The Tcl/Tk interface works much the same than a RemoteAgora. It has been developed on a DEC Alpha with DEC UNIX operating system. The Web interface presents a form with fields where names and values of a tuple can be entered. Buttons allow posting, picking and peeking tuples / requests. This Web interface actually references an agora through the previous Tcl/Tk client interface. This interface is very practical since an agora can be used from almost any environment without programming. Moreover, many people are comfortable with the Web and get a glimpse of what can happen behind a Web interface. The last client interface is based on CORBA. This one opens the door to distributed objects written in many languages, C++ being the most often used in this class.

5.2 Lessons Learned Through Experimentation

Experimenting with Sonia has been limited to internal work in our lab with various simple scenarios focusing on typical office work. The intent was to convince ourselves first before advocating the idea to others. Then, before proceeding very far with Sonia, we wanted to know if the ideas could be grasped by a fair proportion of typical users with different backgrounds, both technical and organizational. This is a major issue since the goal is to propose a model that could be used by people in many different settings. Sonia has been demonstrated to many visitors (general public, current and potential partners) and people working at CITI. This paper actually follows this path in seeking feedback and comments. This process is not very scientific, but the end result allows us to adjust and to further the development of a prototype before engaging in field trials where more solid data could be gathered.

Figure 4 shows one of the scenarios that is used when demonstrating Sonia. It involves two persons, Frodo and Gandalf. Frodo sends an e-mail message to Gandalf with a purchase order for a car written in an EDIFACT format. Frodo knows nothing of Sonia and agoras, but his message is brought in an agora by an interface actor to an e-mail system. Gandalf could process this message manually, but being smart and efficient, he uses a filter on his mail that detects EDIFACT messages by looking at the subject field for the word EDIFACT. At this point, the mail is divided in two groups; tuples identifying a message to be read directly by Gandalf, and tuples destined to an EDIFACT actor. The EDIFACT actor then decodes the message (without even knowing that it comes from e-mail) and make it available in a tuple suitable for processing by other actors. In this case, order processing takes charge of it. The organization of order processing can be made of people and/or computer systems and be as complex as you want. The next steps go to delivery and invoicing which then communicate with Frodo via e-mail and a carrier. During such a presentation, the focus is on the interactions among actors, and what they actually do is not the point.

The reaction of people to such presentations is generally positive. The wording and the examples are very important. At the beginning, expressions like tuples and tuple spaces were used and caused some frowning... But when talking of agora, messages, social relationships and team work, things improved a lot. It seems to foster the best in ourselves. With examples related to their context, people seem to catch the idea well. In most cases, they see and propose ways of using it for their own work, and sometimes in creative and unforeseen ways. Almost surprisingly, this reaction is shared among com-

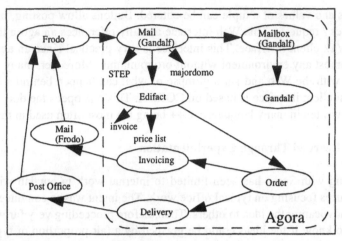

Fig. 4. Typical scenario

puter scientists, social scientists, managers, clerical workers, etc. As an example, a person saw a clear advantage of posting messages with time-outs. The idea was to post a limited number of airplane tickets made available to travel agents on a first come first served basis. With a time-out on tickets, a time limit on the offer could be expressed naturally. Such an example is not complete, but it shows that it can spark very nice ideas. The simple fact that tuples are now called tickets is meaningful. These ideas are very context dependent and shows the potential of letting people manage their processes.

One difficulty found when demonstrating Sonia is that people are not used to focus on the interactions. Sometimes, the attention diverged to the functionality of the actors at the expense of the interactions, for example the EDIFACT actor mentioned in the previous scenario, or the ability to filter e-mail messages. It may be positive if this means that confidence was reached and people were looking to do something useful. But I suspect that a culture of "ultimate integrated application" is in the way of a culture of "component building". Or people may simply not be used to such a freedom.

One more difficulty is to convey the relationships and the dynamic behavior among autonomous actors. Coding each actor in isolation does not say much of their roles in the global picture. During demonstrations, pictures showing the links between actors were used and definitely required. When programming these actors, such pictures were clearly beneficial. A tool to describe the relationships, visually or not, is required. Sonia does not have to provide such a tool, but instead such a facility could be built on top of Sonia. It could even be used to monitor the interactions among actors and behave like a debugger or a management layer. Moreover, formal methods of describing the interactions would certainly help to analyze the dynamic behavior of actors.

6. Conclusion

Coordination of activities in organizations puts stress on open distributed system architectures. In this respect, this paper presented a coordination language called Sonia which fosters simplicity, minimality and expressiveness of relationships, like her older sister Linda who provided much inspiration and guidance. Characteristics of this approach that answer concerns of organizational activities as presented in this paper are:

- action/interaction model: enables interactions, information exchange and sharing
- heterogeneity: people and different types of systems can talk to each other
- autonomy: each actor is free to act at her/his/its own will and pace (asynchrony) with support to synchronize their interactions
- flexibility: various degree of structure, dynamic set of actors and relations under the control of the actors
- time: supports the notion of relative and absolute time
- distribution and scaling: can be adapted to many network architectures, computer architectures and programming languages
- simplicity: few operations, simple and generic messages, open addressing scheme

Experience with Sonia is limited to internal work in our lab with various simple scenarios typical of office work. Much effort has been put at demonstrating a prototype to typical users with different backgrounds. The goal was to verify if it was simple enough for a majority of people and get feedback to further its development. The reaction was generally positive, and in most cases, people saw and proposed ways of using it for their own work, sometimes in creative and unforeseen ways.

This positive response gives confidence for further work. Development of the prototype will be extended to make it ready for real scenarios where more solid data could be gathered on its effectiveness. Work is also going on to build tools to represent the relationships among actors. To some extent, such tools could be used to manage the set of actors. Service advertizing and brokerage is also being pursued to ease the establishment of relationships.

7. Acknowledgments

Pierre Desjardins, the leader of the Adaptive Information Systems group within CITI, provided much freedom and support in making the existence of Sonia possible. He is also the person who developed the Tcl/Tk and Web interfaces presented in this paper. Work with Sylvie Bessette on activities in organizations was important in establishing the characteristics of such environments. Anne-Marie Tessier and François Lapointe provided guidance and feedback on the social nature of organizations.

8. References

[AC93] Gul Agha, Christian J. Callsen, "ActorSpaces: An Open Distributed Programming Paradigm", Proceedings of the 4th ACM Symposium on Principles and Practice of Parallel Programming, May 1993, pp. 23-32

[AG86] Gul A. Agha, "ACTORS: A Model of Concurrent Computation in Distributed Systems", The MIT Press, Cambridge, MA, USA, 1986

[BE95] Richard Bentley, "Flexible Architectures for CSCW System Support", Workshop on Software Architectures for Cooperative Systems, ACM SIGOIS Bulletin, April 1995, pp. 5-7

[BR92] Gordon S. Blair, Tom Rodden, "The Impact of CSCW on Open Distributed Processing", Report CSCW.8.92, Computing Department, Lancaster University, UK, 1992

[CA94] Christian J. Callsen, "Open Heterogeneous Distributed Computing", Ph.D. Thesis, R 94-2025, Institute for Electronic Systems, Aalborg University, Denmark, 1994

[CG89] Nicholas Carriero, David Gelernter, "Linda in Context", Communications of the ACM, April 1989, pp. 444-458

[CS93] Leigh D. Cagan, Andrew H. Sherman, "Linda unites network systems", IEEE Spectrum, December 1993, pp. 31-35

[CI93] Paolo Ciancarini, "Coordinating Rule-Based Software Processes with ESP", ACM Transactions on Software Engineering and Methodology, vol. 2, no. 3, 1993, pp. 203-227

[CI94] Paolo Ciancarini, "Distributed Programming with Logic Tuple Spaces", New Generation Computing, vol. 12, no. 3, May 1994, pp. 251-284

[GC92] David Gelernter, Nicholas Carriero, "Coordination languages and their significance (integration or separation)", Communications of the ACM, February 1992, p. 96 (12)

[GE89] David Gelernter, "Multiple tuple spaces in Linda", PARLE '89, Edited by E. Odjik, M. Rem and J.-C. Syre, Springer-Verlag, 1989, pp. 20-27

[HE88] Carl Hewitt, "Offices are open systems", Readings in distributed artificial intelligence, Morgan Kaufmann, 1988, pp. 321-329

[MC94] Thomas W. Malone, Kevin Crowston, "The interdisciplinary study of coordination", ACM Computing Surveys, vol. 26 no. 1, March 1994, pp. 87-119

[MG88] Thomas W. Malone, Kenneth R. Grant, Ramana Rao, David Rosenblitt, "Semistructured Messages are Surprisingly Useful for Computer-Supported Coordination", Computer-Supported Cooperative Work: A Book of Readings, Edited by Irene Greif, Morgan Kaufmann Publishers, 1988, pp. 311-334

[ML92] Thomas W. Malone, Kum-Yew Lai, Christopher Fry, "Experiments with Oval: A Radically Tailorable Tool for Cooperative Work", CSCW '92 Proceedings, 1992, pp. 289-297

[OM93] Object Management Group, "Object Request Broker Architecture", OMG TC Document 93.7.2, Framingham, MA, USA, 1993

[SM88] Reid G. Smith, "The contract net protocol: high-level communication and control in a distributed problem solver", in Readings in distributed artificial intelligence, Morgan Kaufmann, 1988, pp. 357-366

[ST93] Anselm Strauss, "Continual Permutations of Action", University of California Press, Berkeley, USA, 1993

[WH72] G. J. Whitrow, "The Nature of Time", Penguin Books, 1972

[WF87] Terry Winograd, Fernando Flores, "Understanding Computers and Cognition", Addison-Wesley, 1987

The TOOLBUS Coordination Architecture

J.A. Bergstra[1,2] and P. Klint[3,1]

[1] Programming Research Group, University of Amsterdam
P.O. Box 41882, 1009 DB Amsterdam, The Netherlands
[2] Department of Philosophy, Utrecht University
Heidelberglaan 8, 3584 CS Utrecht, The Netherlands
[3] Department of Software Technology
Centre for Mathematics and Computer Science
P.O. Box 4079, 1009 AB Amsterdam, The Netherlands

Abstract. Building large, heterogeneous, distributed software systems poses serious problems for the software engineer; achieving interoperability of software systems is still a major challenge. We describe an experiment in designing a generic software architecture for solving these problems. To get control over the possible interactions between software components ("tools") we forbid direct inter-tool communication. Instead, all interactions are controlled by a "script" that formalizes all the desired interactions among tools. This leads to a component interconnection architecture resembling a hardware communication bus, and therefore we will call it a "TOOLBUS".

We describe the coordination of tools in process-oriented "T scripts" featuring, amongst others, (1) sequential composition, choice and iteration of processes; (2) handshaking (synchronous) communication of messages; (3) asynchronous communication of notes to an arbitrary number of processes; (4) note subscription; (5) dynamic process creation. Most notably lacking are built-in datatypes: operations on data can only be performed by tools, giving opportunities for efficient implementation. In three large case studies, the TOOLBUS architecture has been used to build editor-interfaces with user-defined extensions, to study feature interaction in intelligent networks, and to build a simulator for traffic light control. We give an overview of these case studies and briefly sketch the evolution of the TOOLBUS design that incorporates the lessons we have learned from them.

1 Introduction

1.1 Motivation

Building large, heterogeneous, distributed software systems poses serious problems for the software engineer. Systems grow *larger* because the complexity of the tasks we want to automate increases. They become *heterogeneous* because large systems may be constructed by re-using existing software as components. It is more than likely that these components have been developed using different implementation languages and run on different hardware platforms. Systems become *distributed* because they have to operate in the context of local area networks.

It is fair to say that the *interoperability* of software components is essential to solve these problems. The question how to connect a number of independent, interactive, tools and integrate them into a well-defined, cooperating whole has already received substantial attention in the literature (see, for instance, [SvdB93]), and it is easy to understand why:

- by connecting existing tools we can reuse their implementation and build new systems with lower costs;

- by decomposing a single monolithic system into a number of cooperating components, the modularity and flexibility of the systems' implementation can be improved.

Tool integration is just one instance of the more general *component interconnection problem* in which the nature (e.g., hardware *versus* software) and granularity (e.g., natural number *versus* database) of components are left unspecified. As such, solutions to this problem may also increase our understanding of subjects like modularization, parameterization of datatypes, module interconnection languages, and structured system design.

In this paper we will pursue the more specific goal of integrating software components like user-interfaces, editors and compilers. It is generally recognized that the integration of such interactive tools requires three steps:

Data integration: how can tools exchange and share data structures representing application specific information? In its full generality, the data integration problem amounts to exchanging (complicated) data values among tools that have been implemented in different programming languages.

Control integration: how can tools communicate or cooperate with each other? The integration of the control of different tools can vary from loosely coupled to tightly coupled systems. A loose coupling is, for instance, achieved in systems based on broadcasting or object-orientation: tools can notify other tools of certain changes in their internal state, but they have no further means to interact. A tighter coupling can be achieved using remote procedure calls. The tightest coupling is possible in systems based on general message passing.

User-interface integration: how can the user-interfaces of the various tools be integrated in a uniform manner? [4] Two trends in the field of human-computer interaction are relevant here:

- User-interfaces and in particular human-computer dialogues are more and more defined using formal techniques. Techniques being used are transition networks, context-free grammars and events. There is a growing consensus that dialogues should be multi-threaded (i.e., the user may be simultaneously involved in more than one dialogue at a time).
- There is also some evidence that a complete separation between user-interface and application is too restrictive.

We will now first discuss related work (Section 2), and then we give an overview of the TOOLBUS co-ordination architecture (Section 3). A description and evaluation of three case studies (Section 4) and a discussion (Section 5) complete the paper.

2 Related work in coordination languages and tool integration

In this section we briefly sketch work in the field of coordination languages and tool integration and relate it to our approach. For a discussion of the design issues in coordination languages we refer to [GC92]. A survey of interdisciplinary aspects of coordination can be found in [MC94]

2.1 Data integration

In its full generality, the data integration problem amounts to exchanging (complicated) data values among tools that have been implemented in different programming languages. The common approach to this problem is to introduce an *intermediate data description language*, like ASN-1 [ASN87] or IDDL [Sno89], and define a bi-directional conversion between datastructures in the respective implementation languages and a common, language-independent, data format.

Instead of providing a general mechanism for representing the data in arbitrary applications, we will use a single, fixed, data representation based on term structures. We do not allow the exchange of arbitrary data structures, but insist that all data are represented in the same term format before they can be exchanged between tools. A consequence of this approach is that *existing* tools will have to be encapsulated by a small layer of software that acts as an "adapter" between the tool's internal dataformats and conventions and those of the TOOLBUS.

2.2 Control integration

The integration of the control of different tools can vary from loosely coupled to tightly coupled systems. A loose coupling is, for instance, achieved in systems based on broadcasting or object-orientation: tools can notify other tools of certain changes in their internal state, but they have no further means to interact. A tighter coupling can be achieved using remote procedure calls. The tightest coupling is possible in systems based on general message passing.

Broadcasting. The Field environment developed by Reiss [Rei90] has been the starting point of work on several software architectures for tool integration. In these broadcast-based environments tools are independent agents, that interact with each other by sending messages. The distinguishing feature of Field is a centralized message server, called *Msg*, which routes messages between tools. Each tool in the environment registers with *Msg* a set of message patterns that indicate the kinds of messages it should receive. Tools send messages to *Msg* to announce changes that other tools might be interested in. *Msg* selectively broadcasts those messages to tools whose patterns match those messages. Variations on this approach can be found in [Ger88, GI90]. In [Clé90] an approach based on signals and tool networks is described which has been further developed into the Sophtalk system [BJ93]. In [Boa93] the SPLICE system is described, a network-based approach in which each component is controlled by an "agent" and agents communicate with each other through global broadcasting. These and similar approaches lead to

---

[4] Some authors like, e.g., [Dal93], call this step *presentation integration*.

a new, modular, software structure and make it possible to add new tools dynamically without the need to adjust existing ones. A major disadvantage of most of these approaches is that the tools still contain control information and this makes it difficult to understand and debug such event-driven networks. In other words, there is *insufficient global control* over the flow of control in these networks. An approach closely related to broadcasting is *blackboarding*: tools communicate with each other via a common global database [EM88].

Object-orientation. Similar in spirit are object-oriented frameworks like the *Object Request Broker Architecture* proposed by the Object Management Group [ORB93] or IBM's *Common Blue Print* [IBM93]. They are based on a common, transparent, architecture for exchanging and sharing data objects among software components, and provide primitives for transaction processing and message passing. The current proposals are very ambitious but not yet very detailed. In particular, issues concerning process cooperation and concurrency control have not yet been addressed in detail. These efforts reflect, however, the commercial interest in reusability, portability and interoperability.

Remote procedure calls. In systems based on remote procedure calls, like [Gib87, BCL$^+$87], the general mode of operation is that a tool executes a remote procedure call and waits for the answer to be provided by a server process or another tool. This approach is well suited for implementing *client/server* architectures. The major advantage of this approach is that flow of control between tools stays simple and that deadlock can easily be avoided. The major disadvantage, however, is that the model is too simple to accommodate more sophisticated tool interactions requiring, for instance, nested remote procedure calls. See, for instance, [TvR85, BJ94] for an overview of these and related issues in the context of distributed operating systems.

General message passing. The most advanced tool integration can be achieved in systems based on general message passing. In SunMicrosystems' ToolTalk [TOO92], data integration as well as generic message passing are available. For each tool the names and types of the incoming and outgoing messages are declared. However, a description of the message interactions between between tools is not possible.

Another system in this category is Polygen, described in [WP92], where a separate description is used of the permitted interactions between tools. From this description, *stubs*[5] are generated to perform the actual communication. The major advantage of this approach is that the tool interactions can be described independently from the actual, underlying, communication mechanisms. The major disadvantage of this particular approach is that the interactions are defined in an ad hoc manner, that precludes further analysis of the interaction patterns like, for instance, the study of the dead lock behaviour of the cooperating tools.

The Manifold [AHS93] language uses events and datastreams through named ports as communication mechanisms. Coordination is described by means of transition-diagrams. The TOOLBUS has many objectives in common with Manifold, although the technical details are largely different: process descriptions based on prcess algebra versus transition diagrams, a different data model (terms versus bit strings), and different implementation techniques (direct interpretation of **T** scripts versus compilation and linkage-edit time configuration of modules).

The hardware metaphor. Although the analogy between methods for the interconnection of hardware components and those for connecting software components has been used by various authors, it turns out that more often than not approaches using the same analogy are radically different in their technical contents. For instance, in the Eureka Software Factory (ESF) a "software bus" is proposed that distinguishes the roles of tools connected to the bus, like, e.g., user-interface components and service components. As such, this approach puts more emphasis on the structural decomposition of a system then on the communication patterns between components. See [SvdB93] for a more extensive discussion of these aspects of ESF. A similar approach is Atherton's Software Backplane described in [Bla93], which takes a purely object-oriented approach towards integration.

In [Pur94], Purtillo proposes a software interconnection technology based on the "POLYLITH software bus". This research shares many goals with the work we present in this paper, but the perspectives are different. Purtillo takes the static description of a system's structure as starting point and extends it to also cover the system's runtime structure. This leads to a module interconnection language that describes the logical structure of a system and provides mappings to essentially different physical realizations of it. One application is the transparent transportation of software systems from one parallel computer architecture to another one with different characteristics. We take the communication patterns between components as starting point and therefore primarily focus on a system's run-time structure. Another difference is the prominent role of formal process specifications in our approach.

---

[5] Small pieces of interfacing software.

The notion of "Software IC's" is proposed by several authors. For instance, [Cox86] uses it in a purely object-oriented context, while [Clé90] describes a communication model based on broadcasting (see above).

Other paradigms. Various other solutions have been proposed. For instance, Linda [CG89] uses a shared tuple space as general mechanism for communication and synchronization. The language is based on two important principles: (a) computation and communication are orthogonal aspects of programming and should be treated independently; (b) flexibility through uncoupling of components. Various Linda implementations are available that extend existing programming languages with Linda's tuple operations. A related language is Gamma [BM90]; it is based on multiset transformations.

We see as a general disadvantage of these two particular approaches that the problem to be solved has to be moulded to fit the given datastructure (tuple/multiset) of the underlying coordination language. In our work we prefer to explore a process-oriented view on coordination.

Control integration in the TOOLBUS. The control integration between tools is achieved by using process-oriented "T scripts" that model the possible interactions between tools. The major difference with other approaches is that we use one, formal, description of *all* tool interactions. Coordination and computation are strictly separated: inside the TOOLBUS a varying number of parallel processes takes care of the coordination while all actual computation is performed in tools (and not in the TOOLBUS itself). We uncouple the coordination activities inside the TOOLBUS by using pattern matching to establish communication between processes rather than using explicitly named communication ports. We support heterogeneity, since tools implemented in different languages running on different machines can be coordinated by way of a single TOOLBUS.

2.3 User-interface integration

Two trends in the field of human-computer interaction are relevant here:

- User-interfaces and in particular human-computer dialogues are more and more defined using formal techniques. Techniques being used are transition networks, context-free grammars and events. There is a growing consensus that dialogues should be multi-threaded (i.e., the user may be simultaneously involved in more than one dialogue at a time) [Gre86].
- There is also some evidence that a complete separation between user-interface and application is too restrictive [Hil86].

We refer to [HH89] for an extensive survey of human-computer interface development and to [Mye92] for a more recent overview of the role of concurrency in languages for developing user-interfaces. Other approaches in this category that have some similarities with our approach are Abstract Interaction Tools [vdB88], Squeak [CP85], and the use of ESTEREL for control integration [Dis94]. Abstract Interaction Tools uses extended regular expressions to control a hierarchy of interactive tools. Squeak uses CSP to describe the behaviour of input devices like a mouse or keyboard when building user-interfaces. Experience with the Sophtalk approach we already mentioned earlier, has led to experiments to use (and extend) the synchronous parallel language ESTEREL for describing all control interactions between tools.

We will *not* address user-interface integration as a separate topic, but it turns out that the control integration mechanisms in the TOOLBUS can be exploited to achieve user-interface integration as well.

2.4 The relation with Module Interconnection Languages

Module Interconnection Languages [PDN86] and modules in programming languages are the classical solution to the problem of decomposing large software systems into smaller components. Modules can *provide* certain operations to be used by other modules and they can *require* operations from other modules. It is the task of the Module Interconnection Language (or the module mechanism) to establish a type-safe connection between provided and required operations. The dynamic behaviour of modules is usually not taken into account, e.g., the fact that the proper use of a "stack" module implies that first a "push" operation has to be executed before a "pop" operation is allowed.

The approach to component interconnection to be presented in this paper, *concentrates* on these dynamic, behavioural, aspects of modules. It shares many of the objectives of the work on "formal connectors" [AG94], where (untimed) CSP is used to describe software architectures. Their work is more ambitious than ours, since it aims at describing *arbitrary* software architectures, while we use a fixed (bus-oriented) architecture. The mechanisms we use to configure our bus architecture are, however, more powerful than the ones described in [AG94] (i.e., dynamic process creation, dynamic connection and disconnection of components, time).

2.5 Our approach

Requirements and points of departure. Before explaining our approach to component interconnection in more detail, it is useful to make a list of our requirements and state our points of departure.

To get control over the possible interactions between software components ("tools") we forbid direct inter-tool communication. Instead, all interactions are controlled by a "script" that formalizes all the desired interactions among tools. This leads to a communication architecture resembling a hardware communication bus, and therefore we will call it a "TOOLBUS". Ideally speaking, each individual tool can be replaced by another one, provided that it implements the same protocol as expected by other tools. The resulting software architecture should thus lead to a situation in which tools can be combined with each other in many fashions. We replace the classical procedure interface (a named procedure with typed arguments and a typed result) by a more general *behaviour description*.

A "T script" should satisfy a number of requirements:

- It has a formal basis and can be formally analyzed.
- It is simple, i.e., it only contains information directly related to the objective of tool integration.
- It exploits a number of predefined communication primitives, tailored towards our specific needs. These primitives are such, that the common cases of deadlock can be avoided by adhering to certain styles of writing specifications.
- The manipulation of *data* should be completely transparent, i.e., data can only be received from and send to tools, but inside the TOOLBUS there are no operations on them.
- There should be no bias towards any implementation language for the tools to be connected. We are at least interested in the use of C, Lisp, Tcl, and ASF+SDF for constructing tools.
- It can be mapped onto an efficient implementation.

The TOOLBUS. The TOOLBUS coordination architecture we are proposing in this paper can integrate and coordinate a fixed number of existing tools. We approach the problem of tool integration as follows:

Data integration: Instead of providing a general mechanism for representing the data in arbitrary applications, we will use a single, uniform, data representation based on term structures.

Control integration: the control integration between tools is achieved by using process-oriented "T scripts" that model the possible interactions between tools.

User-interface integration: we will *not* address user-interface integration as a separate topic, but we want to investigate whether our control integration mechanism can be exploited to achieve user-interface integration as well.

A consequence of this approach is that *existing* tools will have to be encapsulated by a small layer of software that acts as an "adapter" between the tool's internal dataformats and conventions and those of the TOOLBUS.

Compared with other approaches, the most distinguishing features of the TOOLBUS approach are:

- The prominent role of primitives for process control in the setting of tool integration. The major advantage being that complete control over tool communication can be achieved.
- The absence of built-in datatypes. Compare this with the abstract datatypes in, for instance, LO-TOS [Bri87], PSF [MV90, MV93], and μCRL [GP90]. We only depend on a free algebra of terms and use matching to manipulate data. Transformations on data can only be performed by tools, giving opportunities for efficient implementation.

In [BK94] we have applied a number of established techniques (i.e., process algebra [BK84, BW90], algebraic specification using ASF+SDF [BHK89, HHKR89], and C implementation) to approach the design of the TOOLBUS at various levels of abstraction. This has given rise to—even mutual—feedback between different levels.

3 Overview of the TOOLBUS coordination architecture

The global architecture of the TOOLBUS is shown in figure 1. The TOOLBUS serves the purpose of defining the cooperation of a fixed number of *tools* T_i ($i = 1, ..., m$) that are to be combined into a complete system.

The internal behaviour or implementation of each tool is irrelevant: they may be implemented in different programming languages, be generated from specifications, etc. Tools may, or may not, maintain their own internal state. Here we concentrate on the external behaviour of each tool. In general an *adapter* will be needed for each tool to adapt it to the common data representation and message protocols imposed by the TOOLBUS.

The TOOLBUS itself consists of a variable number of processes P_i $(i = 1, ..., n)$. The parallel composition of the processes P_i represents the intended behaviour of the whole system. Although a one-to-one correspondence between tools and processes seems simple and desirable, we do not enforce this and permit tools that are being controlled by more than one process as well as clusters of tools being controlled by a single process.

Inside the TOOLBUS, there are two communication mechanisms available. First, a process can send a *message* (using snd-msg) which should be received, synchronously, by one other process (using rec-msg). Messages are intended to request a service from another process. When the receiving process has completed the desired service it informs the sender, synchronously, by means of another message (using snd-msg). The original sender can receive the reply using rec-msg. By convention, the original message is contained in the reply.

Second, a process can send a *note* (using snd-note) which is broadcasted to other, interested, processes. The sending process does not expect an answer while the receiving processes read notes asynchronously (using rec-note) at a low priority. Notes are intended to notify others of state changes in the sending process. Sending notes amounts to *asynchronous selective broadcasting*. Processes will only receive notes to which they have *subscribed*.

The communication between TOOLBUS and tools is based on handshaking communication between a TOOLBUS process and a tool. A process may send messages in several formats to a tool (snd-eval, snd-do, and snd-ack-event) while a tool may send the messages event and value to a TOOLBUS process. There is no direct communication possible between tools.

3.1 Overview of T scripts

First, we address the data integration problem by introducing a notion of (untyped) *terms* as follows:

- An integer *Int* is a term.
- A string *String* is a term.
- A variable *Var* is a term.
- A single identifier *Id* is a term.
- $Id(Term_1, Term_2, ...)$ is a term, provided that $Term_1$, $Term_2$, ... are also terms.

Examples of terms are: 747, "flight simulator", and departure(flight(123), "12:35"). It is important to stress that terms provide a simple, but versatile, mechanism for representing arbitrary data.

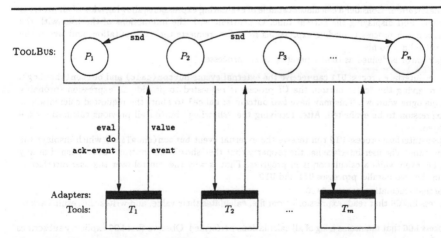

Fig. 1. Global organization of the TOOLBUS

A "T script" describes the complete behaviour of a system and consists of a number of definitions (for processes and tools) followed by one "TOOLBUS configuration".

A process definition is a named processes expression (see Figure 2 for an overview of the primitives used in process expressions). It has the form:

define *Pname Formals* = *P*

Primitive	Description
delta	inaction ("deadlock")
+	choice between two alternatives (P_1 or P_2)
.	sequential composition (P_1 followed by P_2)
*	iteration (zero or more times P_1 followed by P_2)
create	process creation
snd-msg	send a message (binary, synchronous)
rec-msg	receive a message (binary, synchronous)
snd-note	send a note (broadcast, asynchronous)
rec-note	receive a note (asynchronous)
no-note	no notes available for process
subscribe	subscribe to notes
unsubscribe	unsubscribe from notes
snd-eval	send evaluation request to tool
rec-value	receive a value from a tool
snd-do	send request to tool (no return value)
rec-event	receive event from tool
snd-ack-event	acknowledge a previous event from a tool

Fig. 2. Overview of TOOLBUS primitives.

Formals are optional and contain a list of formal parameter names. *P* is a process expression.

A TOOLBUS *configuration* is an parallel composition of processes and has the form:

toolbus(*Pname₁*, ..., *Pnameₙ*)

It describes the initial configuration of processes in the TOOLBUS. During execution, new processes can be created using the create primitive. Each process is identified by a unique, dynamically generated, process identifier.

3.2 Example: a calculator

Informal description. Consider a calculator capable of evaluating expressions, showing a log of all previous computations, and displaying the current time. Concurrent with the interactions of the user with the calculator, a batch process is reading expressions from file, requests their computation, and writes the resulting value back to file.

The calculator is defined as the cooperation of six processes:

- The user-interface process UI1 can receive the external events button(calc) and button(showLog). After receiving the "calc" button, the UI process is requested to provide an expression (probably via a dialogue window). This may have two outcomes: cancel to abort the requested calculation or the expression to be evaluated. After receiving the "showLog" button all previous calculations are displayed.
- The user-interface process UI2 can receive the external event button(showTime) which displays the current time. The user-interface has the property that the "showTime" button can be pushed at any time, i.e. even while a calculation is in progress. That is why the control over the user-interface is split in the two parallel processes UI1 and UI2.
- The actual calculation process CALC.
- A process BATCH that reads expressions from file, calculates their value, and writes the result back on file.
- A process LOG that maintains a log of all calculations performed. Observe that LOG explicitly subscribes to "calc" notes.
- A process CLOCK that can provide the current time on request.

TOOLBUS *script for the calculator.*

```
define CALC =
    ( rec-msg(calc, Exp) . snd-eval(calc,Exp) . rec-value(calc, Val) .
        snd-msg(calc, Exp, Val) . snd-note(calc, Exp, Val)
    ) * delta

define UI1 =
    ( rec-event(ui(U), button(calc)) . snd-eval(ui(U), dialogGetExpr).
      ( rec-value(ui(U), cancel)
      + rec-value(ui(U), expr(Exp)) . snd-msg(calc, Exp) .
          rec-msg(calc, Exp, Val) . snd-do(ui(U), displayValue(Val))
      ) . snd-ack-event(ui(U))
    + rec-event(ui(U), button(showLog)) . snd-msg(showLog) .
        rec-msg(showLog, Log) . snd-do(ui(U), displayLog(Log)) .
        snd-ack-event(ui(U))
    ) * delta

define UI2 =
    ( rec-event(ui(U), button(showTime)) . snd-msg(showTime) .
        rec-msg(showTime, Time). (snd-do(ui(U), displayTime(Time)) .
        snd-ack-event(ui(U)))
    ) * delta

define BATCH =
    ( snd-eval(batch, fromFile). rec-value(batch, expr(Exp)) .
        snd-msg(calc, Exp). rec-msg(calc, Exp, Val). snd-do(batch, toFile(Val))
    ) * delta

define LOG =
    subscribe(calc) .
    ( rec-note(calc, Exp, Val) . snd-do(log, writelog(Exp, Val))
    + rec-msg(showLog) . snd-eval(log, readLog) .
        rec-value(log, Log) . snd-msg(showLog, Log)
    ) * delta

define CLOCK =
    ( rec-msg(showTime) . snd-eval(clock, readTime) . rec-value(clock, Time) .
        snd-msg(showTime, Time)
    ) * delta
```

Different configurations of calculator. Observe that the above definitions allow us to generate the following five, meaningful, systems:

```
- toolbus(UI1, CALC, LOG)
- toolbus(UI1, CALC, LOG, BATCH)
- toolbus(UI2, CLOCK)
- toolbus(UI1, CALC, LOG, UI2, CLOCK)
- toolbus(UI1, CALC, LOG, BATCH, UI2, CLOCK)
```

3.3 An experimental TOOLBUS interpreter implemented in C

Implementation options. There are many methods for implementing the interpretation of **T** scripts, ranging from purely interpretative methods to fully compilational methods that first transform the **T** script into a transition table. The former are easier to implement, the latter are more efficient. For ease of experimentation we have opted for the former approach.

Another global implementation decision to be made is the way process communication is implemented. There are at least two options. First, one can use Unix "pipes" for this purpose, but this requires that all tools are child processes of the TOOLBUS interpreter and that interpreter and tools run on the same machine. Second, one can use general "socket" communication between processes. We have opted for this second approach to allow experiments with a client/server architecture where tools run on different machines and can be started at any moment *after* the TOOLBUS interpreter has been started. This requires that tools can take the initiative to make a connection with the TOOLBUS interpreter.

A final choice, is the way data are exchanged between TOOLBUS and tools. The data to be exchanged are *terms* and our approach will be to linearize a term (i.e., print it in prefix form) at the sending side and parsing it at the receiving side. In this way there is a completely standard way of sending and receiving terms which is independent of any implementation language.

The TOOLBUS *interpreter.* The TOOLBUS itself is implemented as a separate Unix process that interprets a given **T** script. The following steps are taken by the interpreter:

- Syntax analysis of the script.
- Typechecking of the script: this amounts to definition/use checking of names and detection of recursive use of named processes.
- Creation of tools: execute the tool as a separate Unix process. We also support the case the execution of a tool is started independently and that it will connect to the TOOLBUS later on. An input and an output channel are created between the TOOLBUS and each tool.
- Create the toolbus configuration as defined by the script. The TOOLBUS interpreter maintains a list of active processes.
- Execute:
  1. wait for an event coming from one of the tools;
  2. compute the effect of the event on the TOOLBUS state;
  3. perform any internal communication steps;
  4. perform any atomic actions.
  5. repeat.

4 Case studies

We have experimented with the TOOLBUS approach in several smaller case studies, like a multi-player game, graphics constraints, and a simple syntax-directed editing environment.

However, a better assessment can only be made by applying these concepts to larger, real-life, examples. Therefore we briefly summarize here the experiences gained in three recent case studies.

The first study concerns the translation of user-interface definitions to **T** scripts. The second one explores feature interactions in intelligent networks. In the third study, the TOOLBUS is used for simulating a real-time, distributed algorithm for traffic regulation.

4.1 An editor-interface with user-defined extensions

In [Koo92], the specification language SEAL is described for extending the user-interface of syntax-directed editors with user-defined menus and buttons. A major issue in this language (and its implementation) is how to connect parts of the user-interface with user-defined functionality and how to achieve appropriate enabling and disabling of user-interface elements.

In this first case-study [Oli94], SEAL descriptions of a user-interface are translated automatically into **T** scripts. The steps to achieve this are:

- Determine which tools are needed to support the notions provided by the SEAL run-time system.
- Determine a translation method from SEAL to **T** scripts. Two schemes have been experimented with: (a) a scheme in which each condition is evaluated by a (generated) process expression using the operators . and + to implement the Booleans operators in conditions; (b) a scheme in which the complete condition is sent to a condition tool for evaluation.
- Compile the "user-defined functions" (specified in ASF+SDF) to C using the techniques described in [KW93].

4.2 Feature interaction in intelligent networks

Intelligent Networks are telephone networks that provide a variety of services for extending the basic call process. An example of such a service is *call forwarding* that permits the redirection of incoming calls to another phone number. Another example is the rejection of calls coming from certain selected phone numbers. Such extra services can enhance or even modify the basic call process. A problem encountered in these networks is so-called *feature interaction*: the undesired interaction of services that have been activated during a call. The two examples just given illustrate this point: when combining them the result becomes unpredictable. With the increasing number of extra services being provided it becomes more and more difficult to predict interactions of a new service with existing ones.

To explore feature interactions in an experimental fashion, a telephone exchange based on the intelligent network model has been built using the TOOLBUS [Bul94]. Each telephone as well as each service are modeled as a tool.

4.3 A simulator for traffic light control

The starting point for this third case study [BKK] was a proprietary dynamic traffic regulation algorithm developed by the Dutch company *Nederland Haarlem* and a real-time process algebra specification of it. The problem at hand concerns the control of the traffic lights for a road crossing. Each road consists of three lanes for traffic, respectively, going straight on or turning to the left or to the right. Each lane is controlled by a separate traffic light. A simulation now consists of detecting incoming traffic, calculating a new state and duration for each traffic light based on given scheduling rules, and visualizing the global state of the road crossing, including the current traffic and the state of the traffic lights.

On closer inspection of the last issue, one can draw two conclusions:

– The execution speed of compiled ASF+SDF specifications is good, but the techniques used in this case study for interfacing them to the TOOLBUS were not yet sufficiently mature to give the desired performance. Interfacing involved several data conversions and Unix level process creations per invocation of the data tool. In the mean time we have solved this problem by considerably improving the efficiency of these interfacing techniques.

– From a more fundamental perspective, it is clear that one should not use *any* interprocess communication mechanism or data conversion to obtain, for instance, the addition of two integers as is done in the data tool in the third case study. Clearly, there is then a mismatch between the granularity of the desired operation and the overhead caused by the implementation techniques used.

A more interesting conclusion, therefore, is that we should make a distinction between the *logical design* of a system (as embodied by a **T** script and the tools it requires) and its *realization*. In the current TOOLBUS implementation these two coincide: the logical design is mapped onto an implementation with exactly the same structure. It is therefore interesting to explore the potentials of a TOOLBUS *compiler* that transforms a logical design into an implementation from which as much interprocess communication has been eliminated as possible. In the most extreme case, the generated implementation could be a single, monolithic, process without any interprocess communication left!

Primitive	Description
`if ... then ... fi`	guarded command
`if ... then ... else ... fi`	conditional
	expressions
`||`	communication-free merge (parallel composition)
`let ... in ... endlet`	local variables
`:=`	assignment
`delay`	relative time delay
`abs-delay`	absolute time delay
`timeout`	relative timeout
`abs-timeout`	absolute timeout
`rec-connect`	receive a connection request from a tool
`rec-disconnect`	receive a disconnection request from a tool
`execute`	execute a tool
`snd-terminate`	terminate the execution of a tool
`shutdown`	terminate TOOLBUS
`attach-monitor`	attach a monitoring tool to a process
`detach-monitor`	detach a monitoring tool from a process

Fig. 3. Overview of new TOOLBUS primitives.

4.5 Evolution of the TOOLBUS design

The above observations have encouraged us to extend the TOOLBUS design into a "Discrete Time TOOL-BUS" [BK95]. In Figure 3 we give a list of the new features. They can be categorized as follows:

The case study was motivated by the desire to reduce the long execution times needed when simulating the traffic regulation algorithm using standard process simulation tools and the need to visualize the large amounts of information produced by such simulations. The given real-time specification consists of a process part and a data part. Both require a different treatment in order to obtain a TOOLBUS based simulator. The process part is transformed as follows:

- The real-time specification is transformed into an untimed specification by introducing explicit time actions.
- The recursion used in the original specification is transformed into iteration.
- The specification resulting from the previous two steps is manually translated into a T script.

The data part consists of an algebraic specification of the data types needed in the process part. Since T scripts do not provide operations on data, it is mandatory to implement these data types as a separate tool. Two different approaches have been experimented with to obtain the data tool:

- Automatic compilation of the algebraic specification into C (also done in the first case study).
- Manual implementation of the data types in C.

As a last step, a user-interface has been built using Tcl/Tk.

4.4 Experiences

On the positive side, in all case studies except the second one concerning feature interaction, systems with the desired functionality and performance could be built at acceptable costs. This shows, at least, the potentials of the TOOLBUS for building complex systems and for integrating different implementation technologies. On the negative side, the following observations can be made (but see Section 4.5 for solutions to all of these problems):

- In the first case study, the lack of a conditional construct in combination with the absence of a built-in Boolean datatype resulted in a considerable increase of complexity of the generated T scripts. In the third study, the lack of a conditional construct complicated the translation somewhat.
- The way in which variables are treated in T scripts is overly restrictive: in *sending* actions all variables are replaced by their current value in the sending process; in *receiving actions* all variables get a value assigned as a result of the match with the sending action. Sometimes it is natural to combine these two mechanisms, e.g., the action rec-msg(V,W) in which we want to replace V by its current value *before* matching and assign a value to W *as a result of* matching. A solution is to mark all variables that should get a value as a result of matching, e.g., rec-msg(V,W?). In this manner, *two-way* data exchange can be realized during a single communication between two processes.
- In the second case study, the lack of a mechanism for dynamically executing (and naming) tools was a serious obstacle.[6] Without such a mechanism, all possible combinations of telephones and services have to be executed at the moment the TOOLBUS configuration is created, rather than executing them on a call-by-need basis.
- In the third case study, *time* is an essential aspect of the problem. Since it could not be modeled in the T script itself, a separate time tool had to be introduced.
- In the third case study, interfacing of a compiled algebraic specification with the TOOLBUS turned out to give unacceptable performance.
- *Expressions, assignment and, conditionals.* In response to the lack of built-in datatypes (and the resulting performance problems) we provide simple operations on terms (including operations on Booleans, integers and lists). Expressions can be used in assignments and as test in conditionals. In addition, a flexible type system has been introduced that smoothly integrates static and dynamic typing of variables.
- *Time.* Many of the applications we envisage need a notion of time so we provide features for defining (relative and absolute) delays and timeouts.
- *Dynamic execution, termination, connection and disconnection of tools.* Tools can not only be executed by the TOOLBUS, but they can also be executed externally (even on another computer) and be connected to the TOOLBUS later on. Similarly, tools can be terminated or disconnected.
- *Monitoring facilities*: the construction of heterogeneous, distributed, systems is not easy, therefore we provide primitives for the (distributed) debugging of such systems. Other applications of monitoring primitives are transaction monitoring, performance monitoring, and the logging and play back of complete interactive sessions.

---

[6] Recall that *processes* can be created dynamically, but all *tools* are executed at the moment of start up and cannot be executed dynamically.

The process CALC as shown earlier in Section 3.2, will now be written as follows:

```
process CALC is
  let Tid : calc, Exp : str, Val : int
  in
      execute(calc, Tid?) .
      ( rec-msg(compute, Exp?) . snd-eval(Tid, expr(Exp)) .
        rec-value(Tid, Val?) .
        snd-msg(compute, Expr, Val) . snd-note(compute(Expr, Val))
      ) * delta
  endlet

tool calc is {command = "./calc"}
```

Apart from a slight difference in concrete syntax, the following observations can be made about this fragment:

- Local variables are now explicitly declared (with their type) in a let construct. This is also the case for formal parameters of process and tool declarations.
- The notion of "result occurrence" of variables (denoted by ?) has been introduced in order to mark variable occurrences that lead to an assignment to that variable. This mechanism is fully integrated with term matching. See the discussion in Section 4.4.
- Tools are now explicitly executed by the script. Execution yields a tool identifier that identifies the tool instance just created.
- Tool declarations define an executable command, but may also define additional attributes of tools (e.g., their host machine). Each tool declaration introduces a new type as can be seen in the declaration of the variable Tid of type calc. Tool declarations can be parameterized.

The Discrete Time TOOLBUS has been implemented and it has been tested in a variety of new applications ranging from a C development environment for embedded systems, graphic constraints, multi-player games, and adapters for a variety of languages (e.g., ASF+SDF, Perl, Prolog, Python, Tcl).

A major test case our group is currently working on is the complete reengineering of the ASF+SDF Meta-Environment[Kli93]: given a formal description of some language (e.g., programming language, query language, mark up language, or other application language) the Meta-Environment generates an interactive programming environment for it. We use the TOOLBUS as the interconnection technology for connecting the various components involved (such as parser generators, syntax-directed editors, rewrite rule compilers, compiled specifications, and the like). By doing so, we will be able to assess the real benefits of this approach as stated in the introduction of this paper:

- By decomposing a single monolithic system into a number of cooperating components, the modularity and flexibility of the systems' implementation can be improved:
  - For each component we can select the optimal reengineering strategy (e.g., adapt the old component, re-implement it using the best tools available, buy it, etc.)
  - The components can be combined in new ways that were inconceivable in the old situation; rather than using a fixed skeleton for each programming environment generated, it becomes possible to tailor it towards specific needs.
- By connecting existing tools we can reuse their implementation and build new systems with lower costs. Typical examples we have encountered so far are the integration of existing tools for constructing user-interfaces and for constraint solving, as well as implementations of various programming languages.

5   Discussion

The TOOLBUS coordination architecture itself is a promising solution to the component interconnection problem, while the method used to arrive at its design has some merits of its own: the orchestrated use of process theory for design, algebraic specification for rapid prototyping, and C for experimental implementation, leads to a versatile framework for experimentation and implementation at affordable costs.

Case studies done so far, make clear that the expressive power of T scripts is acceptable: even sophisticated systems can be expressed concisely. We expect that the recently developed Discrete Time TOOLBUS is expressive enough to easily solve an even wider range of component interconnection problems. The simple approach we take compares favourably with other much more complex solutions like, e.g., the *Object Request Broker Architecture* as proposed by the Object Management Group [ORB93] or IBM's *Common Blue Print* [IBM93].

Regarding performance, the major lesson we have learned is that a distinction should be made between a *logical design* of a system and its subsequent implementation. Currently, the structure of the logical design is closely followed at the implementation level. More sophisticated implementation techniques involving the full compilation of T scripts can probably eliminate all overhead due to interprocess communication and data conversion.

Acknowledgements

We like to thank Doeco Bosscher, Thomas Bullens, Steven Klusener, Wilco Koorn, and Pieter Olivier for providing us with valuable feedback on our first TOOLBUS design.

References

[AG94]   R. Allen and D. Garlan. Formal connectors. Technical Report CMU-CS-94-115, School of Computer Science, Carnegie Mellon University, 1994.

[AHS93]   F. Arbab, I. Herman, and P. Spilling. An overview of Manifold and its implementation. *Concurrency: Practice and Experience*, 5:23–70, 1993.

[ASN87]   *Specification of Abstract Syntax Notation One (ASN-1)*. 1987. ISO 8824.

[BCL+87]   B. Bershad, D. Ching, E. Lazowsky, J. Sanislo, and M. Schwartz. A remote procedure call facility for interconnecting heterogeneous computer systems. *IEEE Transactions on Software Engineering*, SE-13:880–894, 1987.

[BHK89]   J.A. Bergstra, J. Heering, and P. Klint, editors. *Algebraic Specification*. ACM Press Frontier Series. The ACM Press in co-operation with Addison-Wesley, 1989.

[BJ93]   J. Bertot and I. Jacobs. Sophtalk tutorials. Technical Report 149, INRIA, 1993.

[BJ94]   F.M.T. Brazier and D. Johansen. *Distributed open systems*. IEEE Computer Society Press, 1994.

[BK84]   J.A. Bergstra and J.W. Klop. Process algebra for synchronous communication. *Information & Control*, 60:82–95, 1984.

[BK94]   J.A. Bergstra and P. Klint. The TOOLBUS—a component interconnection architecture. Technical Report P9408, Programming Research Group, University of Amsterdam, 1994.

[BK95]   J.A. Bergstra and P. Klint. The Discrete Time TOOLBUS. Technical Report P9502, Programming Research Group, University of Amsterdam, 1995.

[BKK]   D. Bosscher, A. S. Klusener, and J.W.C. Koorn. A simulator for process algebra specifications with the TOOLBUS. to appear.

[Bla93]   E. Black. The Atherton software backplane. In *[Dal93]*, pages 85–96, 1993.

[BM90]   J. Banatre and D.L. Metayer. Programming by multiset transformations. *Science of Computer Programming*, 15:55–77, 1990.

[Boa93]   M. Boasson. Control systems software. *IEEE Transactions on Automatic Control*, 38(7):1094–1106, 1993.

[Bri87]   E. Brinksma, editor. *Information processing systems–open systems interconnection–LOTOS–a formal description technique based on the temporal ordering of observational behaviour*. 1987. ISO/TC97/SC21.

[Bul94]   T. Bullens. private communication, 1994.

[BW90]   J.C.M. Baeten and W.P. Weijland. *Process Algebra*. Cambridge University Press, 1990.

[CG89]   N. Carriero and D. Gelernter. Linda in context. *Communications of the ACM*, 32(4):444–458, 1989.

[Clé90]   D. Clément. A distributed architecture for programming environments. In *Proceedings of the 4th ACM SIGSOFT Symposium on Software Development Environments*, pages 11–21, 1990. Sofware Engineering Notes, Volume 15.

[Cox86]   B. Cox. *Object-oriented programming: an evolutionary approach*. Addison-Wesley, 1986.

[CP85]   L. Cardelli and R. Pike. Squeak: a language for communication with mice. *Computer Graphics*, 19(3):199–204, 1985.

[Dal93]   R. Daley, editor. *Integration technology for CASE*. Avebury Technical, Ashgate Publishing Company, 1993.

[Dis94]   S. Dissoubray. Using Esterel for control integration. In *GIPE II: ESPRIT project 2177, Sixth review report*. january 1994.

[EM88]   R. Engelmore and T. Morgan, editors. *Blackboard systems*. Addison-Wesley, 1988.

[GC92]   D. Gelernter and N. Carriero. Coordination languages and their significance. *Communications of the ACM*, 35(2):97–107, 1992.

[Ger88]   C. Geretty. HP softbench: a new generation of software development tools. Technical Report SESD-89-25, Hewlett-Packard Software Engineering Systems Division, Fort Collins, Colorado, 1988.

[GI90]   D. Garlan and E. Ilias. Low-cost, adaptable tool integration policies for integrated environments. In *Proceedings of the 4th ACM SIGSOFT Symposium on Software Develpment Environments*, pages 1–10, 1990. Sofware Engineering Notes, Volume 15.

[Gib87]   P. Gibbons. A stub generator for multilanguage RPC in heterogeneous environments. *IEEE Transactions on Software Engineering*, SE-13:77–87, 1987.

[GP90]   J.F. Groote and A. Ponse. The syntax and semantics of μCRL. Technical Report CS-R9076, CWI, 1990.

[Gre86]   M. Green. A survey of three dialogue models. *ACM Transactions on Graphics*, 5(3):244–275, 1986.

[HH89]   H. R. Hartson and D. Hix. Human-computer interface development: concepts and systems for its management. *ACM Computing Surveys*, 21(1):5–92, 1989.

[HHKR89]   J. Heering, P.R.H. Hendriks, P. Klint, and J. Rekers. The syntax definition formalism SDF - reference manual. *SIGPLAN Notices*, 24(11):43–75, 1989.

[Hil86]   R. D. Hill.   Supporting concurrency, communication, and synchronization in human-computer interaction—the Sassafras UIMS. *ACM Transactions on Graphics*, 5(3):179–210, 1986.

[IBM93]   Open Blueprint Introduction. Technical report, IBM Corporation, December 1993.

[Kli93]   P. Klint.   A meta-environment for generating programming environments.   *ACM Transactions on Software Engineering and Methodology*, 2(2):176–201, 1993.

[Koo92]   J. W.C. Koorn.   Connecting semantic tools to a syntax-directed user-interface.   Technical Report P9222, Programming Research Group, University of Amsterdam, 1992.

[KW93]   J. F. Th. Kamperman and H.R. Walters. ARM, abstract rewriting machine. Technical Report CS-R93-30, CWI, 1993.

[MC94]   T.W. Malone and K. Crowston. The interdisciplinary study of coordination. *ACM Computing Surveys*, 26(1):87–119, 1994.

[MV90]   S. Mauw and G.J. Veltink. A process specification formalism. *Fundamenta Informaticae*, pages 85–139, 1990.

[MV93]   S. Mauw and G.J. Veltink, editors. *Algebraic specification of communication protocols*, volume 36 of *Cambridge Tracts in Theoretical Computer Science*. Cambridge University Press, 1993.

[Mye92]   B.A. Myers, editor. *Languages for developing user interfaces*. Jones and Bartlett Publishers, 1992.

[Oli94]   P. Olivier. SEAL versus the TOOLBUS. Master's thesis, Programming Research Group, University of Amsterdam, 1994.

[ORB93]   Object request broker architecture. Technical Report OMG TC Document 93.7.2, Object Management Group, 1993.

[PDN86]   R. Prieto-Diaz and J.M. Neighbors. Module interconnection languages. *The Journal of Systems and Software*, 6(4):307–334, 1986.

[Pur94]   J.M. Purtillo. The POLYLITH software bus. *ACM Transactions on Programming Languages and Systems*, 16(1):151–174, 1994.

[Rei90]   S. P. Reiss. Connecting tools using message passing in the Field programming environment. *IEEE Software*, 7(4), July 1990.

[Sno89]   R. Snodgrass. *The Interface Description Language*. Computer Science Press, 1989.

[SvdB93]   D. Schefström and G. van den Broek, editors. *Tool Integration*. Wiley, 1993.

[TOO92]   Designing and writing a ToolTalk procedural protocol. Technical report, SunSoft, june 1992.

[TvR85]   A.S. Tanenbaum and R. van Renesse.   Distributed operating systems.   *ACM Computing Surveys*, 17(4):419–470, 1985.

[vdB88]   J. van den Bos. Abstract interaction tools: a language for user interface management systems. *ACM Transactions on Programming Languages and Systems*, 14(2):215–247, 1988.

[WP92]   E. L. White and J. M. Purtilo. Integrating the heterogeneous control properties of software modules. In *Proceedings of the 5th ACM SIGSOFT Symposium on Software Development Environments*, pages 99–108, 1992. Software Engineering Notes, Volume 17.

Enhancing Coordination and Modularity Mechanisms for a Language with Objects-as-Multisets

Stefania Castellani * and Paolo Ciancarini

Dept. of Computer Science, Univ. of Bologna, Italy

Abstract. We introduce COOLL, a programming language combining the concepts of multiple tuple spaces and objects-as-multisets. COOLL extends Linear Objects (LO), an object oriented language based on the proof theory of Linear Logic (LL), with new mechanisms aiming at improving the ability of expressing coordination and modularity. Our goal is to explore the new mechanisms in the theoretical framework offered by Linear Logic.

1 Introduction

The technology of languages for programming distributed systems is still in its infancy. Most real distributed systems are being programmed using libraries of low-level communication constructs, often directly inherited from the operating system level. High-level distributed programming languages are needed. The designer of a new distributed language should take into account that a clear formal language definition is an important tool for avoiding design errors and supporting the construction of language tools and environments. Moreover the number of constructs to be inserted in a language should be small, to minimize the cost of complex implementation and improve usability of the language, but at the same time it should be complete enough to support a large number of programming techniques. One of the most interesting concepts for choosing a minimal set of parallel programming constructs is the concept of *coordination language* [9]. A coordination language consists of a small number of mechanisms for communication and process management that are orthogonal to mechanisms used to describe the internal computations of each (sequential) process. The most known coordination language is Linda; since its introduction a number of other coordination languages have been proposed, especially in the framework of logic programming. For instance, the combination of Linda with Prolog is being studied by several researchers [21, 8, 12].

Unfortunately, classic techniques for describing the semantics of sequential languages do not scale well for describing new distributed languages. Most languages in this class are formally defined by an operational semantics, but lack of declarative semantics. In this respect, one of the most interesting abstract

---

* This author is currently working at Rank Xerox Research Centre, Grenoble, France.

frameworks for describing distributed computations and their properties is Linear Logic (LL) [13]. Such a framework was exploited by Andreoli and Pareschi who introduced the first LL programming language, *Linear Object* (LO) [6]. They demonstrated how it is possible to use a fragment of LL to give a declarative semantics to an object-oriented language for distributed programming. More recently, alternative LL programming paradigms have been introduced [18, 14].

We start from the formal framework offered by LO to design a new coordination language, COOLL, which includes new coordination and modularity mechanisms but it is still based on (a fragment of) LL.

The paper has the following structure: in Sect.2 we describe shortly LO, and a programming example; in Sect.3 we discuss about the expressive power of LO; in Sect.4 we introduce COOLL; in Sect.5 we illustrate two examples that demonstrate the expressive power of COOLL for programming coordinated systems, showing in particular the use of the main new coordination mechanism in COOLL, called *virtual join*.

2 Linear Objects

Linear Objects (LO) is a language based on multiple tuple spaces and on an abstract notion of active communicating agents [5, 6, 4]. A computation in LO can be thought of as the evolution of a system of communicating agents; an agent state is represented by a multiset of atoms contained in a private context; agent's state transitions are expressed by multiset rewritings, and can be either state *transformations*, or *creations* of new agents, or *terminations*. Two forms of concurrency characterize LO computations: "inter" and "intra" agents concurrency [3]. Interagent concurrency is similar to independent AND parallelism in parallel logic languages [16]: each agent can compute independently from other agents. Intragent concurrency is similar to OR parallelism in parallel logic languages: each agent executes a program consisting of methods that are simultaneously active on a context. Each agent can test and modify its own context, but cannot access the context of other agents. Agents are dynamic entities, in fact they can terminate and can be dynamically created. Inter-object communication takes the form of *broadcasting*. Thus, LO effectively amalgamates the models of parallel computing by multiset rewriting as in Gamma [7] and in Maude [17], logic processes as "actor" objects [1], and explicit message passing as asynchronous broadcasting [19, 22]. At a theoretical level, this is accounted for by a rigorously defined semantics given in terms of the proof theory of LL.

2.1 Syntax of LO

LO syntax includes four connectives only taken from LL: @ ("par"), & ("with"), ⊤ ("top"), and ⊥ ("bottom"), plus the Linear Implication ("<> −").

The classes of Linear formulae *Goal* and *Method*, recursively built from the class *A* of atoms, can be described with the following BNF grammar:

$$Goal = A \mid Goal @ Goal \mid Goal \& Goal \mid \top \mid \bot$$
$$Method = Head \ [@ \ Tell] \ [@ \ \{P\_goal\}] \ <>- \ Goal.$$
$$Head = A \mid Head @ Head$$
$$Tell = \ ^\wedge A \mid \ ^\wedge A @ Tell$$

Some atoms in the left side of a method M can be marked by the *tell* marker "^", which denotes a form of broadcasting communication. *P_goal* is a conjunction of Prolog goals, that is system predicates to be evaluated in a single step.

An LO *program* is a set of methods and an LO *query* is a pair written $\langle P, G \rangle$ where P is a program and G is a ground goal. An LO *context* is a multiset of ground goals whereas a *flat context* is a multiset of ground atoms. An LO *sequent* is a pair written $P \vdash C$ where P is a program and C is a context.

2.2 Proof-Theoretic Semantics of LO

An LO computation is the execution of an LO query $\langle P, G \rangle$. This consists of searching a proof for the goal according to the program, called *target_proof*. Such a search generates a sequence of trees, graphically represented with the root at the bottom and growing upward. The nodes of a tree are labeled with LO sequents whereas the branches are obtained by instances of the inference figures of *Decomposition* and *Propagation* (see [5, 6]).

– Decomposition

$$[@] \ \frac{P \vdash G_1, G_2, C}{P \vdash G_1 @ G_2, C} \qquad [\bot] \ \frac{P \vdash C}{P \vdash \bot, C}$$

$$[\top] \ \frac{}{P \vdash \top, C} \qquad [\&] \ \frac{P \vdash G_1, C \quad P \vdash G_2, C}{P \vdash G_1 \& G_2, C}$$

– Propagation

$$[<> -] \ \frac{P \vdash G, C}{P \vdash \| Head @ Tell \|, C} \qquad \text{if } Head @ Tell <> - G. \in [P] \ .$$

A *target_proof* for a query $\langle P, G \rangle$ is a tree whose root is the sequent $P \vdash G$, $\overline{C}$, where $\overline{C}$ is a flat context, (an *answer context* to the query), and leaves are instances of $[\top]$.

Searching a Target_Proof for a Query. Let Π be a tree. The succession of the trees in the searching of a target_proof is built according to the mechanisms of Expansion and Instantiation [4]. This means that in the succession each tree Π_{i+1} is built from the tree Π_i according to these two mechanisms, defined as follows:

- Expansion:
  Let l be an open leaf of Π whose sequent matches the lower sequent of an inference figure. Let Π' be the tree obtained by expanding Π at node l with a branch (branches) to a new open leaf (leaves) labeled with the upper sequent (or sequents) of the selected inference figure. We have then:
  $\Pi \Longrightarrow_e \Pi'$.
- Instantiation:
  Let Π' be the tree obtained by adding an occurrence of a given ground atom to the context at each node of Π. We have then:
  $\Pi \Longrightarrow_i \Pi'$.

and the following rule:

The triggering of a method, whose left side contains only unmarked atoms, consists of applying the Expansion inference rule [<>−] according to the selected method. If the method left side contains marked atoms, the expansion step must be preceded by a step of the Instantiation mechanism for each marked atom.

This means that, in order to apply a method in an expansion step using the Propagation rule, unmarked atoms belonging to the left side of the method must be found in the context of the selected node. Unmarked atoms are added to such a context by first performing instantiation steps adding these atoms to all the nodes of the tree. A part from this situation, no other instantiation steps are allowed.

Target_proofs are searched in such a way that the bottom context in each occurrence of the propagation inference figure [<>−] contains only atoms ("focusing", see [2]).

A *Computation* for a query $\langle P, G \rangle$ is a sequence of trees $\Pi_0, \ldots, \Pi_n$ such that:

- Π_0 is reduced to a single node labeled with the sequent $P \vdash G$
- $\forall k = 0, \ldots, n-1 \quad \Pi_k \Longrightarrow_e \Pi_{k+1}$ or $\Pi_k \Longrightarrow_i \Pi_{k+1}$

A *Successful Computation* for a query $\langle P, G \rangle$ is a computation $\Pi_0, \ldots, \Pi_n$ where Π_n is a target_proof for the query.

The goal G in a query $\langle P, G \rangle$ is called an *initial_goal*.

2.3 LO Programming Example

To show a sample of LO programming style, we develop a program that coordinates a game of *Multiminds*, that is a multiplayer extension of Mastermind [20]. Playing a game of Multiminds consists of guessing a secret code, built by a game master using a given alphabet known to all players. The game master calls the players; when a player receives the call, it sends a new guess, computed using the past guesses. The game master checks the guess and, if the guess corresponds to the secret code, the player wins the game, otherwise the game master answers to the player giving the number of bulls (symbols corresponding in both the guess and the secret code) and cows (symbols that are in the code but in a different position). We have two types of agents: the `Coder` and the `Decoder`. The former describes the behaviour of the game master, the latter describes the behaviour of a player. From now on the logical symbol ⊤ is replaced by #t, and ⊥ by #b.

Program

```
coder(S) @ current(I) @ ^go(I) <>- coder(S).
```
   Coder calls the player ("go(I)").

```
coder(S) @ try(I,G) @ players(N) @ ^result(I,G,B,C) @
         {answer(S,G,B,C), C =\= 0, next_player(N,I,I1)} <>-
             coder(S) @ current(I1) @ players(N).
```
   Coder sends to the player I the answer (bulls B and cows C) to the guess G.

```
coder(S) @ try(I,G) @ ^victory(I,G) @
         {answer(S,G,B,C), C:=0} <>- #t.
```
   Player I has guessed the secret code with G. Coder, before ending, informs all the players.

```
decoder @ alp_l([A|List]) @ n_decod(N) @ {nextplayer(N,N1)} <>-
             decoder @ alp_l(List) @ n_decod(N1) &
             decoder(N) @ db([]) @ alph(A).
```
   Creation of the players

```
decoder(I) @ go(I) @ db(L) @ alph(A) @ ^try(I,G) @
             {compute(A,L,G)} <>-
             decoder(I) @ db(L) @ alph(A).
```
   After having received the message "go(I)" player I can start to play. It elaborates a guess G, sending it to the coder ("try(...)"), and waits for the answer.

```
decoder(I) @ result(I,G,B,C) @ db(L) <>-
             decoder(I) @ db([tried(G-[B,C])|L]).
```
   Player I stores the answer to the guess G ("result(...)").

```
victory(X,G) <>- #t.
```
   Player ends because the game is over.
   A possible implementation for the Prolog predicates **answer** and **compute** can be found in [20].
   An example of *Initial goal* with two players is the following goal:

```
coder([h,a,1,1,o]) @ players(2) @ current(0) &
decoder @ n_decod(0) @ alp_l([[1,o,1,h,a],[h,1,a,o,1]]).
```

3 Discussion

The programming example in the previous section shows the expressive power of LO for coordination problems, we need only a few methods in LO to describe the game, reusing a number of Prolog predicates conceived for the sequential solution in [20]. From the point of view of coordination, the dynamic cloning of an agent and broadcast are very powerful constructs, in particular broadcast introduces a sort of meta-level shared dataspace for object interaction [3]. Developing several coordination problems we found however some situations in which the LO solutions present expressivity problems.

As many parallel logic languages, LO methods can easily become verbose, especially when methods need to replicate atoms of the left side in their right side (see the fifth method in the example).

A LO program is a "flat" set of methods, which scope over every context. Actually, very often, a program is intended to define the behaviour of a group of agents, with different characteristics, that communicate among each other. That is, there is no notion of *identity*, that would allow a definition of an agent as an independent and addressable entity that cooperates with other agents, or of *modularity* that would simplify the design of a distributed implementation and also the task of writing a large program. Moreover, in LO there is a unique communication mechanism, namely broadcasting. Such a form of communication is admittedly very powerful; LO agents frequently use it to cooperate, however each agent must receive and store in its context also the messages for which it has no use, since le language lacks of any notion of identity, hence of addressable agent.

Although LO can be used as a coordination language in a very natural way, some coordination problems are not easily solvable. For instance, it is quite difficult to solve problems requiring the union of different contexts. This is a common situation in manipulating objects-as-multisets. In order to simulate the union of contexts, an LO programmer has to "take a snapshot" of the contexts to be merged, making accurate controls on their contents, then creating a new context, and finally deleting all the old contexts. Most of these operations imply time critic problems.

All these considerations encouraged us in extending the language, trying to give it a modular structure, and new coordination mechanisms aiming at improving the ability of expressing coordination, obtaining a new language, namely COOLL.

4 Design of COOLL

COOLL has been designed as an extension of LO, so it is based on multiple tuple spaces and on the vision of a computation as the evolution of a set of communicating agents. An important feature that characterizes COOLL with respect to LO is enhanced modularity. A COOLL program is composed of a set of theories, which are similar to *prototypes* i n object oriented languages [15]. A theory specifies the name of a type of agent and defines its behaviour with a set of methods. An agent, that is an instance of a theory, has a state represented by a multiset of atoms. An agent can change its state, terminate, create new agents that are instances of its own type (instances of the same theory), or synchronize the activities of two or more instances of its own type, replacing them with a new agent of the same type. Two forms of communication rule the cooperation between agents: broadcasting, like in LO, and the multicasting or *group* communication. The group communication allows an agent to send a message to a given type of agents, that are instances of the same theory.

COOLL agents can be thought then as objects, which have a name, can communicate between each other, create new objects or synchronize a set of objects of the same type. The synchrony has been achieved with the introduction of a new synchrony mechanism called "virtual join", a major novelty of COOLL with respect to LO.

4.1 Virtual Join

Virtual join in COOLL allows to synchronize the activities of a group of agents having some common features, simulating the union of contexts. A COOLL agent can cause the termination of other agents which are replaced by a new agent, that inherits their common features.

Syntactically, virtual joins are specified simply by allowing the use of the & not only on the right-hand side of methods, but also on their left-hand side, so that the syntax of *Head* becomes:

$$Head = A \mid Head @ Head \mid Head \& Head .$$

Operationally, the application of a rule of the form, say,

$$(p @ q) \& r <> - G \qquad (1)$$

is equivalent to the *simultaneous* application of the two rules

$$\begin{cases} p @ q <> - G \\ r <> - G \end{cases} \qquad (2)$$

on two different objects, followed by the *identification* of these two objects. This identification step is possible only if the two agents have exactly the same content after application of the rules (2). For example, rule (1) could apply to two agents of the form p, q, C and r, C, (sharing the *same* context C), producing a new object G, C.

Notice that from the point of view of Linear Logic, the formula (1) is equivalent to the conjunction (&) of the formulae (2). Using this, the behavior of the virtual join can easily be expressed in terms of proof construction mechanisms.

4.2 Theories, Group Communication, and the Read_Guard Mechanism

A COOLL program is a set of theories. A theory has a name and is a collection of methods which scope only on the contexts belonging to the agents representing the instances of that theory. COOLL methods in a theory describe the behaviour of a logic agent operating in a context containing the name of the theory. A theory has the following structure:

> **theory** *theory_name* <>−
>
>> *method*$_1$
>> #
>> ⋮
>> #
>> *method*$_n$.

With the introduction of the theory construct a program results in a set of modules addressable by name, so a COOLL computation can be naturally distributed among a set of elaboration nodes, one for each theory for example.

The theory structure allows to define an address space for the agents, and as a very natural consequence we introduced in COOLL a form of *group* communication (multicast) that allows an agent to send a message to a given type of agents, all the instances of a given theory. The broadcast communication will then be used only when the sender is not interested on the identities of the receivers. A COOLL method can contain then both broadcasting and group communications:

$$Communications = \; \hat{} A \mid !(dest, msg) \mid$$
$$Communications \; @ \; Communications$$

where **dest** is the name of the theory whose instances will receive **msg**.

Note that the group communication degenerates to a *point-to-point* communication if in the agent system the theory specified by **dest** will have only one instance.

The application of a method causes the deletion from a context of each atom in the left side of a method, then if the application of a method requires only the presence of these atoms, they will be specified both in the left and the right side of the method, to be reinserted in the context, after the application of the method. In a COOLL method there is the possibility of verifying the presence of a set of atoms in a context, without consuming them, with the *Read_guard* mechanism. The *Read_guard* is a multiset of atoms separated by @, enclosed between braces, in the Head of a method denoting the atoms that must be found in a context for the method triggering, and not removed from the context after the method application. Contrariwise, the atoms that must be found in the context for the method triggering, and removed from the context after the method application, form a multiset denoted as *In_guard*.

Moreover a COOLL method has been structured into three parts corresponding to the three phases of its application:

$$Conditions \; \langle c \rangle\text{-} \; Communications \; \langle c \rangle\text{-} \; Body$$

where *Conditions* specifies conditions for method triggering, *Communications* specifies intra-object coordination (broadcast and/or group communication), and *Body* defines a transition to a new configuration of the context. More precisely, a method can assume one of the following forms:

$$In\_guard \; [@ \; \{Read\_guard\}] \; [@ \; \{\{P\_goal\}\}]$$
$$\langle c \rangle\text{-} \; [Communications] \; \langle c \rangle\text{-} \; Outset$$

$$Contexts \; [@ \; \{Read\_guard\}] \; [@ \; \{\{P\_goal\}\}]$$
$$\langle c \rangle\text{-} \; [Communications] \; \langle c \rangle\text{-} \; Ground$$

where:

$$Outset = Ground \; | \; Contexts \; | \; \top \; | \; \bot$$
$$Contexts = \; Ground \; \& \; Ground \; | \; Ground \; \& \; Contexts \; .$$

Ground is a multiset of ground atoms separated by "@". *Contexts* is a conjunction of multiset of atoms.

The first type of method allows the agent, that triggers it, to replace in its context the atoms of the *In_guard* with another multiset of atoms (*Ground*), which can be empty ($\bot$), to create new instances of the theory (*Contexts*), or to terminate ($\top$).

The second type of method contains the application of the virtual join: agents indicated in *Contexts* terminate, and a new agent, inheriting their common context, replaces them. The agents to be synchronized must be all of the same type of the agent who triggers the method, and are identified by content with the multisets specified in *Contexts*.

An *initial_goal* specifies the set of the contexts associated to the initial agents as follows:

$$Goal = \star th\_name \; @ \; Ground \; \& \; Goal \; | \; \star th\_name \; @ \; Ground$$

where $\star$ denotes the name of a theory. An initial goal must specify one instance for each theory of the program.

All these conditions ensure that the group communication is associative and persistent: a message will be received when the receiver will be found in the agent system.

4.3 Proof-Theoretic Semantics

We describe now a proof-theoretic semantics that extends the similar semantics given for LO [6]: a COOLL program P can be mapped in a set of LL formulae and a COOLL computation consists of searching a proof tree for a given goal.

COOLL Programs as LL Formulae. Let P' be a COOLL program. P' is transformed into a set of LL formulae P as follows. Methods of each theory of P' are transformed inserting information belonging to the theory into the syntactic structure of methods according to the following rule:

Each method belonging to the theory th:

$$Head @ \{Read\_guard\} @ \{\{P\_goal\}\} \langle c \rangle\text{- } Communications \langle c \rangle\text{- } Outset$$

with $Outset = Ground \mid \top \mid \bot$, must be transformed in the method:

$$Head @ \{Read\_guard @th\} @ \{\{P\_goal\}\} \langle c \rangle\text{- } Communications \langle c \rangle\text{- } Outset.$$

Eliminating then the theory structure the program becomes a monolithic sequence of methods. Communications can be reduced to conditions over the context, like in LO, and the syntactic division between Conditions and Communications can be removed. The method M

$$M = Conditions \langle c \rangle\text{- } Communications \langle c \rangle\text{- } Body$$

can be rewritten as:

$$\underline{M} = Conditions @ Communications <>\text{- } Body .$$

Broadcasting communication is handled as in LO, whereas group communication is transformed into a particular broadcasting communication. In fact, we transform each group communication of the form `!(dest,msg)` into a communication of the form `^group(dest,msg)`, inserting then in the program a method:

`group(dest,msg) @ {dest} <>- msg.`

This method ensures that the message `msg` will be used only by the receiver `dest`.

Prolog goals, like in LO, can be seen as non consumable resources.

Read_guard can be eliminated according to the following rules:

1) A method of the form:

$$In\_guard @ \{Read\_guard\} @$$
$$\{\{P\_goal\}\} @ Communications <> - Ground.$$

must be transformed in the following method:

$$In\_guard @ Read\_guard @$$
$$\{\{P\_goal\}\} @ Communications <> - Ground @ Read\_guard.$$

2) A method of the form:

$$In\_guard @ \{Read\_guard\} @$$
$$\{\{P\_goal\}\} @ Communications <> - C_1 \& \ldots \& C_n.$$

must be transformed in the following method:

$$In\_guard @ Read\_guard @ \{\{P\_goal\}\} @ Communications <> -$$
$$C_1 @ Read\_guard \& \ldots \& C_n @ Read\_guard.$$

3) A method of the form:

$$C_1 \& \ldots \& C_n @ \{Read\_guard\} @$$
$$\{\{P\_goal\}\} @ Communications <> - C.$$

must be transformed in the following method:

C_1 @ *Read_guard* & ...& C_n @ *Read_guard* @ {{P_goal}} @
$$Communications <> - C @ Read\_guard.$$

Applying to a COOLL program P' the transformations above we obtain a set P of methods of the form:

$$Head @ Communications <>- Body.$$

where *Communications* contains only broadcasting communications.

COOLL Sequent System. A COOLL query is a pair $\langle P', G' \rangle$ where P' is a program and G' is a goal. Let P and G be respectively the set of LL formulae corresponding to P' and the goal transformed in a LL formula removing each occurrence of the special symbol $\star$. The abstract execution of $\langle P', G' \rangle$ consists of searching a proof tree for $\langle P, G \rangle$.

Such a search generates a sequence of trees whose nodes are labeled by sequents; each tree is built according to the inference rules given below. (In all figures C, C_1, and C_n denote contexts, whereas G, G_1, and G_2 denote goals.)

– Decomposition

$$[@] \frac{P \vdash G_1, G_2, C}{P \vdash G_1 @ G_2, C} \qquad [\bot] \frac{P \vdash C}{P \vdash \bot, C}$$

$$[\top] \frac{}{P \vdash \top, C} \qquad [\&] \frac{P \vdash G_1, C \quad P \vdash G_2, C}{P \vdash G_1 \& G_2, C}$$

– Propagation

$$[<> -_1] \frac{P \vdash G, C}{P \vdash \| In\_guard @ Communications \|, C}$$

if $In\_guard @ Communications <> - G. \in \lceil P \rceil$

$$[\&E] \frac{P \vdash A_1 \& ... \& A_n, C}{P \vdash A_i, C} \qquad \forall i = 1, ..., n$$

$$[<> -_2] \frac{P \vdash G, C}{P \vdash A_1 \& ... \& A_n, \| Communications \|, C}$$

if $A_1 \& ... \& A_n @ Communications <> - G. \in \lceil P \rceil$.

The Decomposition rules decompose complex formulae, like in LO, whereas the Propagation rules define how methods are triggered.

Definition 1 : *(Target_proof)*

A *target_proof* for a query $\langle P', G' \rangle$ is a tree such that its root is a sequent of the form $P \vdash G, \overline{C}$ where P and G are the COOLL program P' and the COOLL goal G' reduced to LL formulae, $\overline{C}$ is an *answer context* for the query and the leaf nodes are labeled with instances of the rule $[\top]$.

Searching a Target_Proof. A target_proof search can be described by the following mechanisms necessary to select the transition to be applied at each step of the sequence construction. Let Π be a tree.

– Expansion: let l be an open leaf of Π whose sequent isn't obtained applying the rule $[\&E]$. If a decomposition rule ($[@]$, $[\&]$, $[\top]$, $[\bot]$) or the first propagation rule $[<>-_1]$ can be applied at this node, then it is applied immediately. Let Π' be the tree obtained by expanding l with the upper sequents of the selected rule. We represent this evolution as: $\Pi \Longrightarrow_e \Pi'$.

– Synchronization: let $C_1 \& \ldots \& C_n @ \textit{Communications} <>- G.$ be an instance of a method of P. Let $l_1, \ldots, l_n$, be n nodes of Π having the sequents of the form $P \vdash C_i, \Delta$. We apply the composition rule $[\&E]$ to the nodes $l_1, \ldots, l_n$, obtaining the tree Π'. Then we apply the second propagation rule $[<>-_2]$ only to one of the nodes before transformed, leaving suspended the other ones, obtaining the tree Π''. We represent this evolution as: $\Pi \Longrightarrow_s \Pi''$.

– Instantiation: let Π' be the tree obtained by adding an occurrence of a given ground atom to the context at each node of Π. We represent this evolution as: $\Pi \Longrightarrow_i \Pi'$.

Instantiation must be applied when a method including communications triggers. In this case the instantiation steps must be followed by the Expansion or the Synchronization of the method.

We can define now COOLL computations.

Definition 2 : *(COOLL Computations)*

A COOLL *Computation* is a sequence of trees $\Pi_0, \ldots, \Pi_n, \Pi_f$ such that:

– Π_0 is the sequent $P \vdash G, \overline{C}$ where $\overline{C}$ is a still unspecified answer context
– $\forall k = 0, \ldots, n-1$ $\Pi_k \Longrightarrow_e \Pi_{k+1}$ or $\Pi_k \Longrightarrow_s \Pi_{k+1}$ or $\Pi_k \Longrightarrow_i \Pi_{k+1}$
– $\Pi_f = \Pi_n$ if building $\Pi_0, \ldots, \Pi_n$, the synchronization mechanism has never been applied. Otherwise Π_f is obtained completing Π_n, for each applied synchronization, as follows: if the synchronization has been applied to m nodes, the proof steps for the selected one among them must be replicated on the other $m - 1$ node.

Given a query $Q = \langle P, G \rangle$, a COOLL *Successful Computation* for Q is a computation $\Pi_0, \ldots, \Pi_n, \Pi_f$ such that Π_f is a *target_proof* for the query.

4.4 Synchrony

Synchronous mechanisms in a coordination language should be avoided, because the coordination concept is mostly based on asynchronous activities [9]; however, often it is very helpful to synchronize in a single step a number of independent activities. For instance, even in Linda there is a notion of synchrony, because an active tuple created with **eval** can contain several independent threads, and the tuple only appears in the tuple space when all activities are terminated, and also in the Swarm language [11] the synchrony relationship is used to group and simultaneously execute a set of transactions on a dataspace of logic tuples. The virtual join in COOLL and the synchrony relationship in Swarm present some differences. In COOLL the agents involved in a virtual join terminate and are substituted by a new agent. In Swarm if one of the transactions belonging to a given class of equivalence, defined by a synchrony relation, is selected for execution, all the transactions belonging to such a class are removed from the dataspace and then are executed all together. Each of them can have a different behaviour, and can be inserted again in the dataspace or can insert other transactions using a mechanism of continuations. The execution of a set of transactions bound by a synchrony relation can cause the creation of none, one or more transactions. In COOLL all synchronized agents terminate and they are replaced by one agent only, moreover they are all of the same type, that is they have the same behaviour. The agents that must be synchronized are statically declared in the program, while in Swarm synchrony relations among instances of transactions can be dynamically inserted and canceled from the relation space.

Apart from these differences, the virtual join in COOLL and the synchrony relation in Swarm both provide an explicit synchronous mechanism.

5 Programming in COOLL

To show how much the modularity allows to differentiate the behaviour of the various logic agents in a program, and how the virtual join, and the two forms of communication allow the coordination among them, we present now the COOLL version of a game of Multiminds, comparing it with the LO version. We will show then the solution of a simple synchronization problem.

5.1 Multiminds

The COOLL program consists of two theories: the former simulates the behaviour of the game master, the latter the behaviour of a player.

Program

```
theory coder <>-

  current(I) <c>- !(decoder,go(I)) <c>- #b
```

```
#
  try(I,G) @ {code(S) @ players(N)} @
                {{answer(S,G,B,C), C=\=0, next_player(N,I,I1)}}
                <c>- !(decoder, result(I,G,B,C)) <c>-
                current(I1)
  #
  try(I,G) @ {code(S)} @
                {{answer(S,G,B,C), C=:=0}}
                <c>- ^victory(I,G) <c>- #t.


theory decoder <>-

    alp_1([L|List]) @ n_decod(N) @ {next_player(N,N1)} <c>- <c>-
                        alp_1(List) @ n_decod(N1) &
                        id(N) @ db([]) @ alph(L)
  #
  go(I) @ {id(I) @ alph(A) @ db(L)} @
        {{compute(A,L,G)}} <c>- !(coder,try(I,G)) <c>- #b
  #
  result(G,B,C) @ db(L) <c>- <c>- db([tried(G-[B,C])|L])
  #
  victory(X,G) <c>- <c>- #t.
```

Such a COOLL program is more structured than the LO version. The theory concept allows to structure the code in two groups of methods describing the behaviour of the two kind of objects. Moreover the use of the group communications avoids that a decoder receives the guesses from the other decoders, while the victory is notified to all the players using broadcasting (note that in this case a group communication would had the same effect). The Read_guard avoids where it is possible the cancellation and the subsequent reinsertion of atoms that are not modified.

An example of *Initial goal* with two players is the following goal:

```
*coder @ code([h,a,1,1,o]) @ players(2) @ current(0) &
*decoder @ n_decod(0) @ alp_1([[1,o,1,h,a],[h,1,a,o,1]]).
```

5.2   Circles Changing Colour

The COOLL program of the circles changing colour describes the behaviour of coloured circles that change colour when they met. This program allows us to illustrate the use of the COOLL virtual join.

Program

```
    theory circle <>-
```

```
circle_list([C|L]) @ {radius(R)} <c>- <c>-
                circle_list(L) &
                centre(C) @ col(w) @ radius(R)
#
  centre(I,X) @ {radius(R)} @ {{X>0, X1 is X-R}}
                              <c>- <c>- centre(I,X1)
#
  centre(I,X) @ {radius(R)} @ {{X<0, X1 is X+R}}
                              <c>- <c>- centre(I,X1)
#
  centre(I,0) @ col(w) & centre(J,0) @ col(w)
                          <c>- <c>- centre(new,X) @ col(g)
#
  col(g) <c>- <c>- #t.
```

An *Initial goal* has the following form:

```
*circle @ circle_list([[1,5r],[2,-5r]]) @ radius(r).
```

We can represent the behaviour of the agents created by this goal in Fig.1, and Fig.2. At the beginning we have two objects having the same structure: they both are circles, with the same radius, and the same colour, white, but they are moving on opposite directions (see Fig.1); when they come in contact they are replaced by a new circle, which maintains the radius of its two predecessors, but has a new colour, namely grey (see Fig.2).

6   Conclusions

Which kind of applications can take advantage from COOLL features? The language can be applied to two classes of applications to build what we call "closed" and "open" coordination programs [10]. A *closed* coordination program uses parallelism aiming at gaining execution speed: in the general scheme, a number of agents, or workers, cooperate trying to explore a symbolic solution space without interaction with the external environment (parallel symbolic computing). We have implemented some closed coordination programs, as for instance a shortest path algorithm and some simulations. In fact, COOLL, being based on Prolog, is of course suitable for problems where massive symbolic computations dominate numeric computations. These applications take advantage of the features of both Prolog and Linda: the explorative style of programming supported by the former is enhanced by the power of controlling coordination supported by the latter [9].

The new features of COOLL fit well to problems in which several types of agents, with different behaviours, engage in intensive communication activities among each other. In fact, we found that COOLL is very useful as a tool for designing solutions to another class of problems, namely *open* coordination

a)

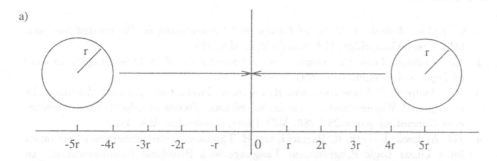

Fig. 1. two white circles are moving on opposite directions

b)

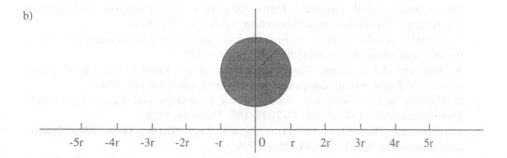

Fig. 2. white circles are replaced by a grey circle

programs. These are reactive programs which interact with an external environment including several users. More generally, we are exploring the suitability of COOLL for open system design, especially for "groupware" applications, i.e. for programs supporting the interaction of many users and tools, which are necessary in many distributed AI, office automation, and software engineering applications. For instance, this is the case of a program implementing a process-centered programming environment [10].

Acknowledgements This paper has been partially supported by the ESPRIT BRA 9102 "Coordination" project. We want to thank very much J.M. Andreoli and R. Pareschi for comments and discussions which were very helpful while we were writing this paper.

References

1. G. Agha. *Actors: A Model of Concurrent Computation in Distributed Systems.* MIT Press, Cambridge, MA, Cambridge, MA, 1986.

2. JM. Andreoli. Logic Programming with Focusing Proofs in Linear Logic. *Journal of Logic and Computation,* 2(3):297–348, 1992.

3. JM. Andreoli, P. Ciancarini, and R. Pareschi. Interaction Abstract Machines. In G. Agha, P. Wegner, and A. Yonezawa, editors, *Trends in Object-Based Concurrent Computing,* pages 257–280. MIT Press, Cambridge, MA, 1993.

4. JM. Andreoli, L. Leth, R. Pareschi, and B. Thomsen. True Concurrency Semantics for a Linear Logic Programming Language with Broadcast Communication. In *Proc. Conf. on Theory and Practice of Sw Development (TAPSOFT 93),* volume 668 of *Lecture Notes in Computer Science,* pages 182–198, France, 1993. Springer-Verlag, Berlin.

5. JM. Andreoli and R. Pareschi. Formulae as active representations of data. In *Actes du 9_{eme} Seminaire sur la Programmation en Logique,* Tregastel, France, 1990.

6. JM. Andreoli and R. Pareschi. Linear Objects: Logical Processes with Built-in Inheritance. *New Generation Computing,* 9(3-4):445–473, 1991.

7. JP. Banatre and D. LeMetayer. Programming by Multiset Transformation. *Communications of the ACM,* 36(1):98–111, January 1993.

8. A. Brogi and P. Ciancarini. The concurrent language Shared Prolog. *ACM Transactions on Programming Languages and Systems,* 13(1):99–123, 1991.

9. N. Carriero and D. Gelernter. Coordination Languages and Their Significance. *Communications of the ACM,* 35(2):97–107, February 1992.

10. P. Ciancarini. Distributed Programming with Logic Tuple Spaces. *New Generation Computing,* 12(3):251–284, May 1994.

11. H. Cunningham and GC. Roman. A Unity-Style Programming Logic for Shared Dataspace Programs. *IEEE Transactions on Parallel and Distributed Systems,* 1(3):365–376, July 1990.

12. K. DeBosschere and JM. Jacquet. Comparative Semantics of μLog. In D. Etiemble and J. Syre, editors, *Proc. Conf. on Parallel Architectures and Languages Europe (PARLE 92),* volume 605 of *Lecture Notes in Computer Science,* pages 911–926, Paris, France, 1992.

13. J. Girard. Linear logic. *Theoretical Computer Science,* 50:1–102, 1987.

14. N. Kobayashi and A. Yonezawa. A Concurrent Linear Logic Programming Paradigm. In *Proc. 10th Int. Symp. on Logic Programming,* pages 278–294. MIT Press, Cambridge, MA, 1993.

15. H. Lieberman. Using Prototypical Objects to Implement Shared Behavior in Object Oriented Systems. In N. Meyrowitz, editor, *Proc. ACM Conf. on Object-Oriented Programming Systems, Languages and Applications (OOPSLA),* volume 21:11 of *ACM Sigplan Notices,* pages 214–223, October 1986.

16. E. Lusk, DHD. Warren, et al. The Aurora OR-parallel Prolog System. In *Proc. Int. Conf. on Fifth Generation Computer Systems,* pages 819–830. ICOT, 1988.

17. J. Meseguer. A Logical Theory of Concurrent Objects and Its Realization in the Maude Language. In G. Agha, P. Wegner, and A. Yonezawa, editors, *Trends in Object-Based Concurrent Computing,* pages 314–390. MIT Press, Cambridge, MA, 1993.

18. D. Miller. A Multiple-Conclusions Meta-Logic. In *Proc. 9th IEEE Symp. on Logic In Computer Science (LICS)*, Paris, France, 1994. IEEE Computer Society Press.
19. K. Prasad. A Calculus of Broadcasting Systems. In S. Abramski and T. Maibaum, editors, *Proc. 16th Colloquium on Trees in Algebra and Programming*, volume 493 of *Lecture Notes in Computer Science*, pages 338–358, Brighton, UK, 1991. Springer-Verlag, Berlin.
20. L. Sterling and E. Shapiro. *The Art of Prolog*. MIT Press, Cambridge, MA, 1986.
21. G. Sutcliffe. Prolog-D-Linda v2: A New Embedding of Linda in SICStus Prolog. In F. DeBoesschere, J. Jacquet, and P. Tarau, editors, *Proc. Workshop on Blackboard-based Logic Programming*, pages 105–117, Budapest, Hungary, June 1993.
22. A. Tanenbaum, F. Kaashouek, and H. Bal. Parallel Programming Using Shared Objects and Broadcasting. *IEEE Computer*, 25(8):10–19, August 1992.

Towards a Compositional Method for Coordinating Gamma Programs

Michel Chaudron[1] and Edwin de Jong[2]

[1] Rijksuniversiteit Leiden, Department of Mathematics and Computing Science,
P.O. Box 9512, 2300 RA Leiden, Netherlands, chaudron@cs.leidenuniv.nl
[2] Hollandse Signaalapparaten B.V.,
P.O. Box 42, 7550 GD Hengelo, Netherlands, edejong@signaal.nl

Abstract. With the growing complexity of software, incurred by the widespread acceptance of parallel and distributed computer systems and networks, program design would benefit from clearly separating the correctness issues (the *computation*) from efficiency issues (the *coordination*). Gamma has shown to be a powerful and expressive programming model that allows the basic computations of a program to be expressed with a minimum of control. This enables the programmer to defer efficiency related decisions until a second stage in the design process. In support of this second activity we introduce in this paper a coordination language that exploits the highly nondeterministic behaviour of Gamma to impose additional control. Furthermore, we propose a compositional notion of refinement that can be used to reason about coordination of Gamma programs. This notion induces a number of refinement laws that can be used in an algebraic style of reasoning. Some examples are presented to illustrate application of these laws.

1 Introduction

The first and foremost requirement of a program is that it yields the correct answer. In many cases, the second requirement is that the answer is computed as fast as possible, or at least within reasonable time. With the growing complexity of software, incurred by the widespread acceptance of parallel and distributed computer systems and networks, program design would benefit from clearly separating the correctness issues (the *computation*) from efficiency issues (the *coordination*). The significance of treating the computational part of a program separately from coordination issues is discussed in [6]. An approach based on this separation of concerns consists of the following phases:

1. The construction of a program (or collection of programs) that performs the required computation, but does not impose premature constraints on the behaviour of the program,

2. Coordinate the computations of the program(s) into an efficient execution strategy. This is often achieved by exploiting some property of a particular order of execution.

In order to realize this approach, we need a programming model that supports the separation between computation and coordination. Existing programming models usually stress only one of these aspects. For instance, functional and logical programming languages emphasize their declarative nature and the advantages it has for proving correctness. In order to improve the efficiency, the programs have to be tailored to capitalize on the fixed execution strategies that are built in. With imperative languages, the programmer has complete control over the operational behaviour. Here, the control-flow is an integral part of the program, which makes it very difficult to focus on the correctness while abstracting from operational details.

Programming by multiset transformation, as exemplified by Gamma [5] has shown to be well suited to express the computations of a program without imposing premature constraints on the mode of execution. The minimal level of control yields some important advantages. First, Gamma programs are inherently parallel; in fact, it needs additional effort from the programmer to write sequential programs. Furthermore, the semantics of Gamma can be stated in a very clean and concise way, thus facilitating formal reasoning about programs. For this reason, Gamma is often put forward as an intermediate language in the program derivation process: first a Gamma program is specified which abstracts from operational details and which is therefore easier to prove correct. Subsequently, a specialized version of this program can be constructed by introducing additional control. A method for the derivation of Gamma programs was proposed in [4].

Though in [3] it has been demonstrated that the Gamma model can be implemented, the absence of control makes it very difficult to do this efficiently. Several efforts aimed at achieving more efficient executions of Gamma programs have been proposed.

In [12], Hankin et al. derive a number of refinement and equivalence laws by considering the input-output behaviour of Gamma programs induced by an operational semantics. The theory developed is used to design a method that imposes a "pipelining" execution order on programs. The main shortcoming of the calculus reported in [12] is that the laws described are not compositional; i.e. refining part of a program does not necessarily result in a refinement of the program as a whole. This limits the applicability of the laws. The following remedies have been put forward:

- In [17] a compositional semantics, based on transition traces, is given for some combining forms of Gamma programs. A more detailed study of the laws resulting from this semantics is given in [18].

- Another approach, presented in [11], uses a notion of equivalence based on bisimulation [15] to obtain compositional semantics.

- More general laws are obtained by focussing on a set of higher-level combining forms for Gamma, called *TROPES* [13]. The *TROPES* encapsulate typical forms of Gamma programs that have emerged from programming experience (e.g. [5]).

These approaches have in common that they try to improve the efficiency of a program by modifying the program itself. An alternative approach, that is adopted in this paper, is based on the idea of separating computation from coordination. The basic computation that is required to solve the problem at hand, is specified as a Gamma program which is proven correct. Then we exploit the highly nondeterministic behaviour of Gamma to improve the efficiency. This is done by using the coordination language presented in [10] that enables the programmer to control the otherwise chaotic execution of Gamma programs to the level of fully deterministic behaviour. The coordination component is specified separately from the Gamma program allowing more efficient versions of a program to be constructed while leaving the computational part unaffected.

Using this approach it is essential that the coordination component does not affect the established correctness of the original Gamma program. To meet this requirement, we present in this paper a method that opens up the opportunity for coordinating Gamma programs in a provably correct way. The method that we propose uses a transformational approach: Based on the semantics of schedules and a notion of refinement we derive laws that can be used to refine schedules while preserving correctness.

The paper is organized as follows. First we introduce the Gamma model (Section 2) and its coordination language (Section 3). In Section 4.1 we then propose a compositional notion of refinement that can be used in reasoning about the coordination component of a program. In Section 4.2 we derive a number of laws of refinement that support an algebraic style of reasoning. We illustrate these laws with some example applications in Section 5. We conclude the paper in Section 6 with some final remarks and directions for future research.

2 The Gamma Model

We start with a brief introduction to Gamma. For more details the reader is referred to [5] which includes a broad spectrum of example programs.

The uniform data structure in Gamma is the multiset. Multisets can be formed over arbitrary domains of values, including integers, reals, booleans and tuples. The simplest Gamma program is a conditional multiset rewrite-rule, written as $\bar{x} \to m \Leftarrow b$. Here $\bar{x}$ denotes a sequence of variables $x_1, \ldots, x_n$, m is a multiset expression, and b is a boolean expression. The free variables that occur in m and b are taken from $x_1, \ldots, x_n$.

Application of the rule $\overline{x} \rightarrow m \Leftarrow b$ to a multiset proceeds by replacing elements in the multiset satisfying the condition b by the elements that result from evaluating the multiset expression m. This step is repeated until no more elements are present that satisfy b.

For example, a Gamma program for sorting a sequence of numbers into ascending order is given by the following rule.

$$swap \,\widehat{=}\, (x,i),(y,j) \rightarrow (y,i),(x,j) \Leftarrow x > y \,\wedge\, i < j$$

The sequence is represented by a multiset consisting of value-index pairs. We assume the indices range from 0 to n. The program executes by exchanging ill-ordered values until there are no more pairs that satisfy this condition. At that point the resulting multiset represents a well-ordered sequence. It is important to note that the Gamma program does not specify in which order pairs of values are compared and exchanged. Disjoint pairs can be compared and exchanged in parallel, but this need not necessarily be the case. The Gamma program can be seen as the specification of a wide spectrum of more deterministic sorting strategies.

More complex Gamma programs can be built using two basic combinators. Individual rules can be composed into so-called *simple* programs [12] using the parallel combinator, denoted "+". The constituent rules in parallel composition are executed in any order (possibly in parallel) until none of the rules can be successfully applied. Simple programs can in turn be composed using the sequential combinator, denoted " $\circ$ ". If P_1 and P_2 are simple programs, then $P_1 \circ P_2$ first executes P_2 until its rules can no longer be applied, after which P_1 is executed on the resulting multiset.

The abstract syntax of Gamma programs can be specified as follows. We use r, R and P to range over the syntactic categories of multiset rewrite-rules, simple programs, and programs respectively.

$$\begin{aligned} r &::= \overline{x} \rightarrow m \Leftarrow b \\ R &::= r \mid R + R \\ P &::= R \mid P \circ P \end{aligned}$$

A configuration of a program P and a multiset M is written $\langle P, M \rangle$. To define the operational semantics of Gamma we use a labelled multi-step transition relation between configurations. A transition is written as $\langle P, M \rangle \overset{\sigma}{\rightsquigarrow} \langle P', M' \rangle$ where the label σ stands for the multiset substitution that transforms M into M'. A terminal configuration is written $\langle P, M \rangle \surd$.

The semantics of Gamma is collected in Figure 1. The multi-step transition relation is defined in terms of a single-step transition relation, that we distinguish by the subscript "1", i.e. $\langle P, M \rangle \overset{\sigma}{\rightsquigarrow}_1 \langle P, M' \rangle$. The various notations that we use in defining the semantics are best explained by considering the semantic rule for $r = \overline{x} \rightarrow m \Leftarrow b$:

if $\overline{v} \subseteq M \wedge b[\overline{x} := \overline{v}]$ then $\langle r, M \rangle \overset{\sigma}{\leadsto}_1 \langle r, M[\sigma] \rangle$ where $\sigma = m[\overline{x} := \overline{v}]/\overline{v}$

We write $b[\overline{x} := \overline{v}]$ to denote the boolean expression that results from replacing each free occurrence of x_i by v_i. By $M[\sigma]$ we denote the multiset that results from applying the substitution σ to M. More formally, let $M' = m[\overline{x} := \overline{v}]$, then $M[M'/\overline{v}] = (M \ominus \overline{v}) \oplus M'$, where $\oplus$ and $\ominus$ denote multiset addition and subtraction respectively. Note that for ease of notation we confuse the sequence $\overline{v}$ with the multiset consisting of the same elements as $\overline{v}$.

When multiple transitions transform disjoint parts of the multiset, then these transitions do not interfere with each other, hence they can also happen in parallel. This observation directly leads to the multi-step transition semantics of Gamma as defined in Figure 1. Formally the notion of non-interference can be defined in terms of the labels of the constituent transitions as follows. (In [8] a more liberal definition is given that reflects the possibility of concurrent reading of data.)

$$\langle \overline{x} \to m \Leftarrow b, M \rangle \overset{\sigma}{\leadsto}_1 \langle \overline{x} \to m \Leftarrow b, M[\sigma] \rangle \quad \text{if } \overline{v} \subseteq M \wedge b[\overline{x} := \overline{v}]$$
$$\text{where } \sigma = m[\overline{x} := \overline{v}]/\overline{v}$$

$$\langle \overline{x} \to m \Leftarrow b, M \rangle \sqrt{} \qquad \text{if } \neg(\exists \overline{v} \subseteq M : b[\overline{x} := \overline{v}])$$

$$\frac{\langle R_1, M \rangle \overset{\sigma}{\leadsto}_1 \langle R_1, M' \rangle}{\langle R_1 + R_2, M \rangle \overset{\sigma}{\leadsto}_1 \langle R_1 + R_2, M' \rangle} \qquad \frac{\langle R, M \rangle \overset{\sigma}{\leadsto}_1 \langle R, M' \rangle}{\langle R, M \rangle \overset{\sigma}{\leadsto} \langle R, M' \rangle}$$
$$\langle R_2 + R_1, M \rangle \overset{\sigma}{\leadsto}_1 \langle R_2 + R_1, M' \rangle$$

$$\frac{\langle R, M \rangle \overset{\sigma_1}{\leadsto} \langle R, M_1 \rangle}{\langle R, M \rangle \overset{\sigma_2}{\leadsto} \langle R, M_2 \rangle}{\langle R, M \rangle \overset{\sigma_1 \oplus \sigma_2}{\leadsto} \langle R, M[\sigma_1 \oplus \sigma_2] \rangle} \quad \text{if } M \models \sigma_1 \bowtie \sigma_2$$

$$\frac{\langle R_1, M \rangle \sqrt{}}{\langle R_1 + R_2, M \rangle \sqrt{}} \qquad \frac{\langle P_1, M \rangle \sqrt{}}{\langle P_1 \circ P_2, M \rangle \sqrt{}}$$

$$\frac{\langle P_1, M \rangle \sqrt{}}{\langle P_2, M \rangle \overset{\sigma}{\leadsto} \langle P_2', M' \rangle}{\langle P_2 \circ P_1, M \rangle \overset{\sigma}{\leadsto} \langle P_2', M' \rangle} \qquad \frac{\langle P_1, M \rangle \overset{\sigma}{\leadsto} \langle P_1', M' \rangle}{\langle P_2 \circ P_1, M \rangle \overset{\sigma}{\leadsto} \langle P_2 \circ P_1', M' \rangle}$$

Fig. 1. Structured Operational Semantics of Gamma

Definition 1. Given a multiset M and two multiset substitutions $\sigma_1 = M_1/N_1$ and $\sigma_2 = M_2/N_2$, we say that σ_1 and σ_2 are *independent* in M if $N_1 \oplus N_2 \subseteq M$. We write $M \models \sigma_1 \bowtie \sigma_2$ if σ_1 and σ_2 are *independent* in M.

The label assigned to a multi-step transition is a combination of the labels of the constituent transitions.

Definition 2. Given two multiset substitutions $\sigma_1 = M_1/N_1$ and $\sigma_2 = M_2/N_2$, the *composition* of σ_1 and σ_2 is defined as $\sigma_1 \oplus \sigma_2 = (M_1 \oplus M_2)/(N_1 \oplus N_2)$.

The semantics of Gamma as presented here, differs from the one in [12]. The latter uses a single step transition relation – suggesting an interleaved semantics. Improvements of the efficiency are often accomplished by introducing explicit sequentiality that reflects the causal relationships between consecutive computations. As mentioned before, our coordination language restricts the otherwise nondeterministic behaviour of Gamma programs, hence it cannot introduce new behaviour. Consequently, the semantics we choose for programs, limits the behaviours we can obtain using a coordination language. Because we want to distinguish between parallel and sequential execution at the coordination level, we need this distinction to be present in the semantics of Gamma.

3 Coordination of Gamma Programs

Gamma is an expressive and powerful programming model that allows the basic computations of a program to be expressed in a concise way and with a minimum of control. This enables the programmer to defer efficiency related decisions until a second stage in the design process. In support of this second activity we next introduce a coordination language that exploits the highly nondeterministic behaviour of Gamma to impose additional control with the objective to improve efficiency.

We refer to the programs that are written in the coordination language as *schedules* to emphasize the fact that they are not really programs but rather execution plans or harnesses for an existing program. A schedule is an expression representing an imperative statement over the rules from a Gamma program. The simplest schedule for a program P (next to skip which denotes the empty schedule) has the form $r \rightarrow s[t]$, where r is a rule from P and s and t denote arbitrary schedules. This schedule is executed by first attempting to execute the rule r; if this succeeds, then execution continues with the schedule s. If execution of r fails, then execution continues with t. As a notational convention, we write $r \rightarrow s[\text{skip}]$ as $r \rightarrow s$ and $r \rightarrow \text{skip}[\text{skip}]$ as r.

The coordination language provides a number of basic combinators that can be used to build more complex schedules. The complete set of combinators that is included in the kernel language is defined by the following abstract syntax for schedules.

$$s ::= \text{skip} \mid r \rightarrow s[s] \mid s; s \mid s\|s \mid c \triangleright s[s] \mid \,!s \mid S(\overline{v})$$

Schedules can be composed sequentially, using the combinator ";" and be put in parallel using "∥". The execution of a parallel composition $s\|t$ proceeds by a step performed by either s or t, or by a parallel step in which both s and t participate. For notational convenience, we write s^k, for $k \geq 0$, to denote k copies of schedule s composed in parallel. Furthermore, we use $\Pi_{i=1}^n s_i$ to denote $s_1\|s_2\| \ldots \|s_n$.

Execution of a Gamma program is such that the number of rules that may be executed varies dynamically with the number of available elements in the multiset. In order to describe this dynamic behaviour using schedules, the replication operator "!" is included. The schedule $!s$ denotes an arbitrary number of copies of s executing in parallel.

The occurrence of a schedule identifier $S(\overline{v})$ is accompanied by a corresponding schedule definition of the form $S(\overline{x}) \mathrel{\widehat{=}} s$. The free variables in s are taken from the sequence $\overline{x}$. Schedule definitions are included for structuring purposes, as well as a means to express recursive schedules. The use of recursion is typically accompanied by the use of a conditional schedule $c \triangleright s[t]$. Here, c represents a boolean expression that is independent from the multiset; if c evaluates to *true*, then schedule s is executed, otherwise execution continues with t. Analogously to the rule-conditional, $c \triangleright s[\text{skip}]$ is written as $c \triangleright s$.

Nondeterminism in Gamma arises at two levels:

1. at the selection of a rewrite-rule,
2. in selecting elements from the multiset.

The coordination language as introduced so far is only capable of resolving the first type of nondeterminism. The second type is resolved by *strengthening* the condition of a rewrite-rule. Consider a rule $r = \overline{x} \to m \Leftarrow b$. Rather than scheduling r directly, we can schedule a rule $r' = \overline{x} \to m \Leftarrow b'$, such that $b' \Rightarrow b$. Since b' is a strengthening of b, the rule r' exhibits restricted behaviour compared to r.

To illustrate, we return to the example sorting program consisting of the rule *swap*. A schedule that, for instance, exchanges neighbouring values only, will make use of a rule *swap'* which is obtained from the original rule by strengthening condition $i < j$ to $i = j - 1$ to get

$$swap' \mathrel{\widehat{=}} (x,i),(y,j) \to (y,i),(x,j) \Leftarrow x > y \wedge i = j - 1$$

To facilitate this process we shall adopt the notational convention that rule definitions are parameterized in the variables that are used to select elements from the multiset. For sorting this means that we define the rule

$$swap(i,j) \mathrel{\widehat{=}} (x,i),(y,j) \to (y,i),(x,j) \Leftarrow x > y \wedge i < j$$

A schedule that coordinates the sorting program such that it behaves like insertion sort, for instance, can now be specified as $InsertionSort(1)$ where

$$InsertionSort(i) \; \hat{=} \; (i \leq n) \rhd (Insert(i); InsertionSort(i+1))$$
$$Insert(i) \qquad \hat{=} \; (i > 0) \rhd (swap(i-1, i) \to Insert(i-1))$$

Here n denotes the length of the sequence. A well known parallel sorting algorithm (see e.g. [16]) is Odd-Even Transposition Sort. Coordination of the sorting program into a corresponding behaviour can be specified as $OddEvenSort(n)$ where

$$OddEvenSort(m) \; \hat{=} \; (m \geq 0) \rhd (Odd \; ; \; Even \; ; \; OddEvenSort(m-2))$$
$$Odd \qquad\qquad \hat{=} \; \Pi_{i=0}^{n \, \mathrm{div} \, 2 - 1} swap(2i+1, 2i+2)$$
$$Even \qquad\qquad \hat{=} \; \Pi_{i=0}^{(n+1)\mathrm{div}\, 2 - 1} swap(2i, 2i+1)$$

The operational semantics of the coordination language is defined in Figure 3 as a labelled multi-step transition relation between configurations which uses the structural congruence relation defined in Figure 2.

A configuration consists of a schedule-multiset pair $\langle s, M \rangle$. The label λ of a transition is either a multiset substitution or the special symbol ε which denotes an internal transition that does not affect the multiset. The semantics of schedules is defined in terms of the single-step semantics of Gamma from Figure 1. Note that the semantics of the conditional $c \rhd s[t]$ is defined by the structural congruence.

$skip; s \equiv s$	$skip \| s \equiv s$	$true \rhd s[t] \equiv s$ $!skip \equiv skip$
$s_1; (s_2; s_3) \equiv (s_1; s_2); s_3$	$s_1 \| (s_2 \| s_3) \equiv (s_1 \| s_2) \| s_3$	$false \rhd s[t] \equiv t$
	$s_1 \| s_2 \equiv s_2 \| s_1$	

Fig. 2. Structural Congruences for Schedules

$$\frac{\langle r, M\rangle\surd}{\langle r \to s[t], M\rangle \xrightarrow{\varepsilon} \langle t, M\rangle} \qquad\qquad \frac{\langle r, M\rangle \overset{\sigma}{\leadsto}_1 \langle r, M'\rangle}{\langle r \to s[t], M\rangle \xrightarrow{\sigma} \langle s, M'\rangle}$$

$$\frac{\langle s_1, M\rangle \xrightarrow{\lambda} \langle s_1', M'\rangle}{\langle s_1; s_2, M\rangle \xrightarrow{\lambda} \langle s_1'; s_2, M'\rangle} \qquad\qquad \frac{\langle s_1, M\rangle \xrightarrow{\lambda} \langle s_1', M'\rangle}{\langle s_1\|s_2, M\rangle \xrightarrow{\lambda} \langle s_1'\|s_2, M'\rangle}$$

$$\frac{\begin{array}{c}\langle s_1, M\rangle \xrightarrow{\lambda} \langle s_1', M'\rangle \\ \langle s_2, M\rangle \xrightarrow{\varepsilon} \langle s_2', M\rangle\end{array}}{\langle s_1\|s_2, M\rangle \xrightarrow{\lambda} \langle s_1'\|s_2', M'\rangle} \qquad \frac{\begin{array}{c}\langle s_1, M\rangle \xrightarrow{\sigma_1} \langle s_1', M_1\rangle \\ \langle s_2, M\rangle \xrightarrow{\sigma_2} \langle s_2', M_2\rangle\end{array}}{\langle s_1\|s_2, M\rangle \xrightarrow{\sigma_1\oplus\sigma_2} \langle s_1'\|s_2', M[\sigma_1\oplus\sigma_2]\rangle} \text{ if } M \models \sigma_1\bowtie\sigma_2$$

$$\frac{\langle s, M\rangle \xrightarrow{\lambda} \langle s', M'\rangle}{\langle !s, M\rangle \xrightarrow{\lambda} \langle s', M'\rangle} \qquad\qquad \frac{\langle s\|!s, M\rangle \xrightarrow{\lambda} \langle s', M'\rangle}{\langle !s, M\rangle \xrightarrow{\lambda} \langle s', M'\rangle}$$

$$\frac{\begin{array}{c}s \equiv t \\ \langle s, M\rangle \xrightarrow{\lambda} \langle s', M'\rangle \\ s' \equiv t'\end{array}}{\langle t, M\rangle \xrightarrow{\lambda} \langle t', M'\rangle} \qquad \frac{\langle s[\overline{x} := \overline{v}], M\rangle \xrightarrow{\lambda} \langle s', M'\rangle}{\langle S(\overline{v}), M\rangle \xrightarrow{\lambda} \langle s', M'\rangle} \text{ where } S(\overline{x}) \hat{=} s$$

Fig. 3. Structured Operational Semantics of Schedules

4 Refinement of Schedules

Our aim is to devise a design method for (parallel) programs where computation is clearly separated from coordination. An essential aspect of such a design method is the ability to reason about coordination. In our framework coordination is achieved by resolving nondeterministic choices in Gamma. As an instrument to eliminate nondeterminism, we propose in this section a notion of refinement for schedules. The problem of finding efficient execution strategies can be broken down in smaller steps by constructing successive refinements. With every subsequent step we gradually achieve more deterministic control.

First, we present a definition of refinement. We then derive a number of refinement laws that can be used in an algebraic style of reasoning about coordination. Applications of these laws will be illustrated in Section 5.

4.1 Refinement based on Simulation

We are interested in finding an ordering, denoted $\leqslant$, which relates schedules on the basis of their behaviour. The ordering should contain $s \leqslant t$ if s is a correct, more deterministic implementation of t.

To define this ordering, we adapt the definition of strong bisimulation, from [15], for our purposes. This requires the following modifications:

- Bisimulation induces an equivalence relation, while we require a (partial) ordering. Such an ordering can be obtained by breaking the symmetry of the definition of bisimulation. The definition thus obtained states that if $s \leqslant t$, then the actions of s can be matched by t. This is not sufficiently strong to preserve total correctness, because s may terminate prematurely (after displaying only a prefix of a behaviour of t). In order to handle termination behaviour properly we add the condition that s can only terminate, if t may terminate.

- Bisimulation is commonly used for models of concurrency where process and state are identified. In Gamma and also in its coordination language, communication is implicit through the use of the shared multiset. As a result, the behaviour of a program/schedule depends on the state of the multiset. Therefore we use configurations $\langle s, M \rangle$ rather than just schedules in our definition of simulation.

We now arrive at the following definition of simulation.

Definition 3. A binary relation $\mathcal{R}$ on schedules is a *simulation* if $(s, t) \in \mathcal{R}$ implies, for all λ and for all M,

$$i. \ \langle s, M \rangle \xrightarrow{\lambda} \langle s', M' \rangle \Rightarrow \exists t' : \langle t, M \rangle \xrightarrow{\lambda} \langle t', M' \rangle \ \wedge \ (s', t') \in \mathcal{R}$$
$$ii. \ s \equiv \mathsf{skip} \qquad\qquad\qquad \Rightarrow t \equiv \mathsf{skip}$$

We can now define our refinement relation $\leqslant$ as the maximal simulation:

Definition 4. $\leqslant = \bigcup \{ \mathcal{R} \mid \mathcal{R} \text{ is a simulation } \}$

We say that s is a refinement of t if $(s, t) \in \leqslant$. Analogously to Milner [15], $\leqslant$ can be shown to be the the greatest fixed point of the simulation relations.

For practical purposes it is desirable that our refinement relation is precongruent, allowing for a modular approach in reasoning about coordination. Precongruence of $\leqslant$ follows from Theorem 5 that states that $\leqslant$ is substitutive under all combinators of the coordination language.

Theorem 5. Let s_1, s_2, t_1 and t_2 be schedules such that $s_1 \leqslant t_1$ and $s_2 \leqslant t_2$, then $r \to s_1[s_2] \leqslant r \to t_1[t_2]$, $s_1; s_2 \leqslant t_1; t_2$, $s_1 \| s_2 \leqslant t_1 \| t_2$, $c \triangleright s_1[s_2] \leqslant c \triangleright t_1[t_2]$ and $!s_1 \leqslant !t_1$.

Proof. The proofs are in the style of [15] by determining appropriate simulations. Details can be found in [9]. To give a flavour of this proof, we sketch the proof of precongruence of $\|$.

Let $\mathcal{R} = \{(s_1\|t_1, s_2\|t_2) \mid s_1 \leqslant s_2, t_1 \leqslant t_2\}$. We use transition induction to show that $\mathcal{R}$ is a simulation.

i. According to the semantic rules in Figure 3, there are five possible transitions for $s_1\|t_1$. We consider only one case. The other cases are analogous.

   Assume that $\langle s_1, M\rangle \xrightarrow{\lambda} \langle s_1', M'\rangle$. Then by $s_1 \leqslant s_2$ follows $\langle s_2, M\rangle \xrightarrow{\lambda} \langle s_2', M'\rangle$ such that $s_1' \leqslant s_2'$. Hence $\langle s_2\|t_2, M\rangle \xrightarrow{\lambda} \langle s_2'\|t_2, M'\rangle$ and $(s_1'\|t_1, s_2'\|t_2) \in \mathcal{R}$.

ii. Assume that $s_1\|t_1 \equiv \text{skip}$. Then by the structural congruence $s_1 \equiv \text{skip}$ and $t_1 \equiv \text{skip}$. Then from $s_1 \leqslant s_2$ and $t_1 \leqslant t_2$ follows $s_2 \equiv \text{skip}$ and $t_2 \equiv \text{skip}$, hence $s_2\|t_2 \equiv \text{skip}$. $\square$

Using a standard technique, we define the equivalence $\cong$ on schedules associated with the refinement preorder.

Definition 6. $\cong \; = \; \leqslant \cap \leqslant^{-1}$

It follows that $\cong$ is a congruence relation on schedules. Also $\leqslant$, and hence $\cong$, can be proven to be substitutive under (recursive) schedule definitions [9].

4.2 Refinement Laws

We present a number of the basic refinement laws. These laws give additional insight into the algebraic properties of refinement. Furthermore, the laws give rise to an algebraic style of reasoning about schedules. Precongruence of $\leqslant$ guarantees the modular applicability of the laws.

We present the laws grouped per operator. The proofs of these laws can be found in [9]. Sequential composition forms a monoid with identity skip by laws (1), (2), and (3). Note that laws (1) and (3) immediately follow from structural congruence. Law (4) states that the rule-conditional distributes over the sequential operator. Parallel composition forms a commutative monoid with identity skip by laws (5),(6) and (7), which is immediate from structural congruence. Law (8) states that distributivity of the rule-conditional over parallel composition is a refinement.

(1) $\text{skip}; s \cong s$ (5) $\text{skip}\|s \cong s$
(2) $s; \text{skip} \cong s$ (6) $s_1\|s_2 \cong s_2\|s_1$
(3) $s_1; (s_2; s_3) \cong (s_1; s_2); s_3$ (7) $s_1\|(s_2\|s_3) \cong (s_1\|s_2)\|s_3$
(4) $r \to (s_1; t)[s_2; t] \cong (r \to s_1[s_2]); t$ (8) $r \to (s_1\|t)[s_2\|t] \leqslant (r \to s_1[s_2])\|t$

The main result concerning the combination of sequential and parallel composition, is law (9). It states that a synchronization point between parallel schedules can be introduced using the sequential operator to restrict behaviour. The special case (9') of law (9) states that sequential composition may be substituted for parallel composition.

$$(9) \quad (s_1 \| s_3); (s_2 \| s_4) \leqslant (s_1; s_2) \| (s_3; s_4)$$
$$(9') \quad s_1; s_2 \leqslant s_1 \| s_2$$

Replication is idempotent (11) and distributivity of "!" over "$\|$" (12) is a refinement. Laws (13) and (14) imply that $!s$ may be refined by s^k for an arbitrary $k \geq 1$.

$$(10) \quad !\text{skip} \cong \text{skip} \qquad\qquad (13) \quad s \leqslant !s$$
$$(11) \quad !(!s) \cong !s \qquad\qquad\quad (14) \quad s\|!s \leqslant !s$$
$$(12) \quad !(s_1\|s_2) \leqslant !s_1\|!s_2$$

Some basic laws involving the conditional operator follow easily from structural congruence.

$$(15) \quad false \triangleright s[t] \cong t$$
$$(16) \quad true \triangleright s[t] \cong s$$
$$(17) \quad \text{skip} \cong c \triangleright \text{skip}$$
$$(18) \quad (c \triangleright s_1)[t_1]; (c \triangleright s_2)[t_2] \cong c \triangleright (s_1; s_2)[t_1; t_2]$$
$$(19) \quad (c \triangleright s_1[t_1]) \| (c \triangleright s_2[t_2]) \cong c \triangleright (s_1\|s_2)[t_1\|t_2]$$
$$(20) \quad !(c \triangleright s[t]) \cong c \triangleright (!s)[!t]$$

Of the two types of nondeterminism in Gamma – (1) the selection of rules, and (2) the selection of elements from the multiset – the refinement laws only allow to resolve the former. The second type of nondeterminism involves strengthening of rules (as discussed in Section 3). Strengthening a rule is not always a refinement, i.e. it does not always preserve correctness because, even though strengthening preserves all safety properties, it may invalidate progress. Properties such as safety and progress cannot be used to prove refinement laws because with the definition of refinement we have, just as [11], discarded an essential feature of Gamma: the shared state. Hence, strengthening is not addressed by any of the laws. Work is in progress on a larger refinement relation that includes strengthening of rules. Yet the current notion of refinement has many interesting applications, as will be illustrated in the next section.

5 Application: Coordinating a Shortest Paths Program

We demonstrate application of the refinement laws by considering an example problem that is commonly known as the single source shortest paths problem. Pursuing separation between computation and coordination we shall first specify the basic computation that is required to solve the problem in Gamma. After that we shall relate several coordination strategies.

The problem description is as follows. Assume we are given a directed graph with vertices numbered 1 through n. A function L associates with every edge (u, v) a non-negative length $L(u, v)$. If there is no edge between vertices u and v, then we take $L(u, v) = \infty$. Also $L(u, u) = 0$ for all vertices u. Given a source vertex s, the problem is to determine for every vertex v, the length of a shortest path from s to v.

A Gamma program for solving this problem is given by the rule:

$$find(u,v) \stackrel{\frown}{=} (u,x),(v,y) \to (u,x),(v,x+L(u,v)) \Leftarrow x+L(u,v) < y$$

The multiset consists of pairs (v,x), where v is a vertex number and x is the length of a path from the source s to v. The initial multiset is given by: $M_0 = \{(s,0)\} \cup \{ (v,\infty) \mid 1 \le v \le n, v \ne s \}$.

Though the program performs the required computation, as can be proven formally using techniques from [4], it is hopelessly inefficient because of its unstructured search through the graph. We may coordinate the program's activities into a coherent (more deterministic) searching strategy by conducting a directed search on the graph starting from the source. From a given vertex u the search proceeds by an attempt to construct a shorter path to every adjacent vertex v (in no preferred order). If the attempt succeeds, the search is continued; otherwise the search at v is aborted. A schedule that expresses this strategy is given by $Search(s)$, where

$$Search(u) \stackrel{\frown}{=} Visit(1,u)$$
$$Visit(i,u) \stackrel{\frown}{=} (i \le n) \triangleright (find(u,i) \to Search(i)) \parallel Visit(i+1,u)$$

Note that the schedule still exhibits highly nondeterministic behaviour. The paths in the graph are traversed in any order (possibly in parallel). Using the refinement laws, however, we can transform the schedule into more deterministic versions. To illustrate, we shall derive a depth-first, a breadth-first, and a parallel breadth-first ordering from the schedule $Search$.

5.1 Depth-First Search

Using law (9') we may replace the parallel composition, which is at the basis of schedule $Search$, by a sequential composition. This results in a strategy where the vertices in the graph are visited in a depth-first order.

$$DepthFirst(u) \stackrel{\frown}{=} DFVisit(1,u)$$
$$DFVisit(i,u) \stackrel{\frown}{=} (i \le n) \triangleright (find(u,i) \to DepthFirst(i)); DFVisit(i+1,u)$$

The proof that the depth-first ordering is a correct refinement of the parallel strategy, i.e. $DepthFirst(s) \le Search(s)$, follows immediately using law (9').

5.2 Breadth-First Schedule

An alternative to law (9') to introduce sequential behaviour is presented by law (8). It appears that repetitive application of this law to the parallel composition of schedule $Search$ ultimately yields a breadth-first ordering.

As is standard, the schedule for a breadth-first search maintains a sequence of vertices that are yet to be visited. We write $v \cdot \overline{w}$ to denote the sequence $\overline{w}$ with the element v prepended, and $\overline{w} \cdot u$ for u appended to $\overline{w}$. We use $\langle\ \rangle$ to denote the empty sequence.

A breadth-first ordering can now be expressed as the following recursive schedule definitions:

$$BreadthFirst(\langle\ \rangle) \cong \mathsf{skip}$$
$$BreadthFirst(u \cdot \overline{w}) \cong BFVisit(1, u, \overline{w})$$

$$BFVisit(i, u, \overline{w}) \cong (i \leq n) \vartriangleright find(u, i) \rightarrow BFVisit(i + 1, u, \overline{w} \cdot i)$$
$$[BFVisit(i + 1, u, \overline{w})]$$
$$[BreadthFirst(\overline{w})]$$

The proof that breadth-first search is a correct refinement of the parallel strategy, i.e. $BreadthFirst(\langle s \rangle) \leqslant Search(s)$, is somewhat more involved than the case of a depth-first ordering, therefore we present it here as a more detailed example of application of the refinement laws.

The proof is largely based on the following intermediate result. We use $\overline{x} \# \overline{y}$ to denote the set of interleavings of sequences $\overline{x}$ and $\overline{y}$.

Lemma 7. *Let* $\overline{w}, \overline{w_1}$ *and* $\overline{w_2}$ *be sequence of vertices such that* $\overline{w} \in \overline{w_1} \# \overline{w_2}$, $i \geq 1$, *and* $1 \leq u \leq n$, *then* $BFVisit(i, u, \overline{w}) \leqslant BFVisit(i, u, \overline{w_1}) \| BreadthFirst(\overline{w_2})$

Proof. Let $\mathcal{R} = \{(BFVisit(i, u, \overline{w}), BFVisit(i, u, \overline{w_1}) \| BreadhtFirst(\overline{w_2})) \mid i \geq 1, 1 \leq u \leq n, w \in \overline{w_1} \# \overline{w_2}\}$. The result follows by showing that $\mathcal{R}$ is a simulation. The proof is by transition induction, as illustrated in the proof of Theorem 5. $\square$

Using Lemma 7 and law 8, we reason as follows:

$$BFVisit(i, u, \overline{w})$$
$$\cong \qquad\qquad\qquad\qquad\qquad\qquad\qquad\qquad\qquad\qquad\qquad def. BFVisit$$
$$(i \leq n) \vartriangleright find(u, i) \rightarrow BFVisit(i + 1, u, \overline{w} \cdot i)$$
$$[BFVisit(i + 1, u, \overline{w})]$$
$$[BreadthFirst(\overline{w})]$$
$$\leqslant \qquad\qquad\qquad\qquad\qquad\qquad\qquad\qquad\qquad\qquad\qquad Lemma\ 7$$
$$(i \leq n) \vartriangleright find(u, i) \rightarrow BFVisit(i + 1, u, \overline{w}) \| BreadthFirst(\langle i \rangle)$$
$$[BFVisit(i + 1, u, \overline{w})]$$
$$[BreadthFirst(\overline{w})]$$
$$\leqslant \qquad\qquad\qquad\qquad\qquad\qquad\qquad\qquad\qquad\qquad\qquad Laws\ 6,\ 8$$
$$(i \leq n) \vartriangleright (find(u, i) \rightarrow BreadthFirst(\langle i \rangle)) \| BFVisit(i + 1, u, \overline{w}) \qquad (*)$$
$$[BreadthFirst(\overline{w})]$$

Finally, we prove that $BreadthFirst(\langle s \rangle) \leqslant Search(s)$ as follows:

$$
\begin{array}{ll}
& BreadthFirst(\langle u \rangle) \\
\cong & \qquad\qquad\qquad\qquad\qquad\qquad\qquad\text{def. } BreadthFirst \\
& BFVisit(i, u, \langle \, \rangle) \\
\leqslant & \qquad\qquad\qquad\qquad\qquad\qquad\qquad\qquad\qquad (*) \\
& (i \leq n) \triangleright (find(u,i) \rightarrow BreadthFirst(\langle i \rangle)) \parallel BFVisit(i+1, u, \langle \, \rangle) \\
& \quad [BreadthFirst(\langle \, \rangle)] \\
\cong & \qquad\qquad\qquad\qquad\qquad\qquad\quad \text{def. } BreadthFirst, Law \ 5 \\
& (i \leq n) \triangleright (find(u,i) \rightarrow BreadthFirst(\langle i \rangle)) \parallel BFVisit(i+1, u, \langle \, \rangle)
\end{array}
$$

The latter schedule term can be seen to equal $Visit(i, u)$, by substituting $Search(i)$ for $BreadthFirst(\langle i \rangle)$ and $Visit(i, u)$ for $BFVisit(i, u, \langle \, \rangle)$. Hence the refinement $BreadthFirst(\langle s \rangle) \leqslant Search(s)$ follows from the schedule definitions of $Breadth$-$First$ and $Search$.

5.3 Parallel Breadth-first Search

We conclude the examples with a parallel version of breadth-first search that recursively divides the searching process into two if the amount of work exceeds some predefined threshold $k \geq 1$. A schedule that conducts this kind of search is a variation of the previous schedule and is defined as follows, where the schedule $BFVisit$ is the same as in Section 5.2

$$
\begin{array}{ll}
ParBF(\langle \, \rangle) & \cong \ \text{skip} \\
ParBF(\langle v_1, \ldots, v_m \rangle) & \cong \ (m > k) \triangleright ParBF(\langle v_1, \ldots, v_{m\,\mathrm{div}\,2} \rangle) \\
& \qquad\qquad\quad \parallel ParBF(\langle v_{m\,\mathrm{div}\,2\,+\,1}, \ldots, v_m \rangle) \\
& \qquad\quad [BFVisit(1, v_1, \langle v_2, \ldots, v_m \rangle)]
\end{array}
$$

We now arrive at the refinement ordering

$$
BreadthFirst(\langle s \rangle) \leqslant ParBF(\langle s \rangle) \leqslant Search(s)
$$

The proofs required are largely similar to the ones from Section 5.2, so we omit the details.

6 Related Work

The computational models of action systems [1] and UNITY [7] resemble that of Gamma in that a program, consisting of a set of actions, operates upon a shared storage by nondeterministically selecting actions for execution. This non-determinism in the selection of actions makes them in principle suitable for coordination by schedules.

The method for refinement of action systems [2] is based on the *weakest--precondition* calculus and proceeds by transforming an initial sequential program into a parallel one. Refinement of UNITY programs [14] also uses *wp*-based reasoning, but more prominently employs temporal logic. An initial (non-executable) specification is successively refined into a specification that is suitable for execution on a particular architecture.

In the approach we presented here, a Gamma program constitutes an executable specification of the input-output behaviour with high potential for parallelism. The freedom this offers for operational behaviour is subsequently handled by schedules. Hence, in contrast with action systems, we start with parallel behaviour and *decrease* the parallelism.

Furthermore, both action systems and UNITY change their initial program or specification to incorporate more operational detail. Using our approach, operational behaviour is specified using a coordination language, thereby achieving an explicit separation between computation and coordination.

7 Conclusion

Our aim is to develop a design method for (parallel) programs where computation is separated from coordination. The choice for Gamma as a language to specify the basic computations of a program is motivated by its highly nondeterministic and inherently parallel execution model. This enables the programmer to first concentrate on the computational aspects of a given problem. Efficiency issues are addressed in a second phase of the design process, where one or more optimized versions of the program are created using a coordination language. The coordination component is specified separately, leaving the computational part of the program unaffected.

Using such an approach, it is important that we are able to reason about coordination. In this paper we proposed a compositional notion of refinement that can be used to prove that one coordination strategy is a (totally) correct implementation of another. Our refinement relation is an adaptation of strong bisimulation to the shared state model. It induces a number of basic laws that, as we have illustrated, can be applied in an algebraic way of reasoning about coordination. The present notion of refinement is able to resolve only one type of nondeterminism in Gamma: the selection of rules. Research currently proceeds on a larger refinement relation that also supports the increase of determinacy in the selection of elements from the multiset.

Acknowledgements

We thank the referees and Henk Goeman for their helpful comments.

References

1. R.J.R. Back. *Correctness Preserving Program Refinements: Proof Theory and Applications*, volume Mathematical Centre Tracts 131. Mathematical Center, Amsterdam, 1980.
2. R.J.R. Back. Refinement calculus, part ii: Parallel and reactive programs. In *LNCS 430: Stepwise Refinement of Distributed Systems '89*, pages 67–93. Springer-Verlag, 1989.
3. J.-P. Banâtre, A. Coutant, and D. Le Métayer. A parallel machine for multiset transformation and its programming style. *Future Generation Computer Systems*, 4:133–144, 1988.
4. J.-P. Banâtre and D. Le Métayer. The GAMMA model and its discipline of programming. *Science of Computer Programming*, 15:55–77, November 1990.
5. J.-P. Banâtre and D. Le Métayer. Programming by multiset transformation. *Communications of the ACM*, 36(1):98–111, January 1993.
6. N. Carriero and D. Gelernter. Coordination languages and their significance. *Communications of the ACM*, 35(2):97–107, February 1992.
7. K.M. Chandy and J. Misra. *Parallel Program Design: A Foundation*. Addison-Wesley, 1988.
8. M. Chaudron. Schedules for multiset transformer programs. Technical Report 94-36, Rijksuniversiteit Leiden, Departement of Mathematics and Computing Science, P.O. Box 9512, 2300 RA Leiden, The Netherlands, December 1994.
9. M. Chaudron. Towards compositional design of schedules for multiset transformer programs. Technical Report 95-32, Rijksuniversiteit Leiden, Departement of Mathematics and Computing Science, P.O. Box 9512, 2300 RA Leiden, The Netherlands, November 1995.
10. M. Chaudron and E. De Jong. Schedules for multiset transformer programs. In *Coordination Programming: Mechanisms, Models and Semantics*. Imperial College Press, 1996. (to appear).
11. P. Ciancarini, R. Gorrieri, and G. Zavattaro. An alternative semantics for the calculus of GAMMA programs. In *Coordination Programming: Mechanisms, Models and Semantics*. Imperial College Press, 1996. (to appear).
12. C. Hankin, D. Le Métayer, and D. Sands. A calculus of GAMMA programs. In *5th International Workshop on Languages and Compilers for Parallel Computing*, *LNCS 757*, pages 342–355. Springer-Verlag, 1992.
13. C. Hankin, D. Le Métayer, and D. Sands. A parallel programming style and its algebra of programs. In *PARLE '93, LNCS 694*, pages 367–378. Springer-Verlag, 1993.
14. Singh A. K. Program refinement in fair transition systems. *Acta Informatica*, 30:503–535, 1993.
15. R. Milner. *Communication and Concurrency*. Prentice-Hall, 1989.
16. M. J. Quinn. *Parallel Computing: Theory and Practice (2nd ed)*. McGraw-Hill, 1994.
17. D. Sands. A compositional semantics of combining forms for gamma programs. In *LNCS 735, Formal Methods in Programming and Their Applications*, pages 43–56. Springer-Verlag, 1993.
18. D. Sands. Laws of synchronised termination. In *Proceedings of the First Imperial College Departement of Computing Workshop on Theory and Formal Methods*, pages 276–288. Springer-Verlag, 1993.

Introducing a Calculus for Higher-Order Multiset Programming

David Cohen and Juarez Muylaert-Filho

Department of Computing
Imperial College
London SW7 2BZ
England
email: {dyc, jamf}@doc.ic.ac.uk

Abstract. In this paper we introduce a higher-order calculus suitable for reasoning about programs written in many of the existing paradigms that adhere to the chemical reaction metaphor. The calculus draws its inspiration from Banâtre and Le Métayer's first-order language Gamma. However, the idea behind our calculus varies in that the so-called *reaction rules* are one-shot and are regarded as first-class citizens — in opposition to Gamma's n-shot rewrite rules. First a preliminary study of the basic properties of this new calculus is pursued, then we demonstrate that it is possible to translate the Lambda Calculus, first-order Gamma and higher-order Gamma terms into it.

1 Introduction

The intense interest surrounding parallelism in the Theoretical Computer Science community has given rise to several formalisms proposing alternative descriptions of parallel computation. The main objective of these investigations has been to offer tools for reasoning about parallel programs. In particular the focus of attention has recently shifted towards models of parallelism which incorporate nondeterminism such that execution of programs, in these models, is reminiscent of chemical reactions. This indeed is the basis for much of the work in so-called Coordination paradigms. Classic examples of such models and programming languages are: Swarm [9], Unity [4], Gamma [1], Cham [3] and Higher-Order Gamma [8].

In this paper we formulate a higher-order calculus suitable for reasoning about programs written in paradigms that adhere to this popular chemical reaction metaphor. An example of a (first-order) language is Gamma (abbreviated to FOG), introduced by Banâtre and Le Métayer in [1]. A Gamma program can be described as a multiset transformer. A set of *reaction rules* (consisting of an *action* function, and an associated predicate, the *reaction condition*) describe the program, while the data is collected in a multiset — a flexible data structure similar to a set but allows multiple occurrences of elements, sometimes referred to as a "bag". Execution of a FOG program amounts to replacing values in the data multiset according to a nondeterministically selected reaction rule, whenever those values satisfy its reaction condition, with the result described by its action.

For example, the FOG program below computes the maximum element of a multiset of integers:

$$max = (x, y) \rightarrow x \leftarrow x \geq y$$

The program is evaluated as follows: two arbitrary integers from the input multiset are selected and bound to x and y; if x$\geq$y then x is put back into the multiset and y is discarded. This process continues until all but one element have been consumed. The resulting singleton multiset is then the output of the program. Notice that the program max is executed as many times as there are two elements in the data multiset which satisfy its reaction condition. When the reaction condition fails, the program terminates. For this reason we call max an *n-shot* reaction rule. Typically a program would be composed of several reaction rules plus the data multiset, each rule potentially executing with others in parallel. Furthermore, complex programs might be constructed from the parallel and sequential combination of existing programs (see [7]).

In this paper we propose to promote reaction rules (in these paradigms of parallel nondeterministic "chemical" computing) to the status of first class citizens. This proposal leads us to the formulation of what we call **higher-order multiset machines** (*hmms*).

A *hmm* variable can be bound to an arbitrary reaction rule or a multiset of any description. The action part of a rule produces a multiset which might contain reaction rules and/or nested multisets, or it might be empty. It is important to point out that our reaction rules are one-shot, as opposed to the n-shot rules in FOG. Intuitively, a *hmm* "program" would be a multiset of reaction rules possibly with further nested multisets of reaction rules and so on. The execution of such a program would be performed by the reduction of this multiset of terms.

Viewing reaction rules as first-class citizens has a number of interesting consequences. First of all, similar in spirit to the λ- calculus, it is possible to encode numerals, truth-values, etc; that is to say, all "data values" can be encoded as reaction rules. Incidentally, we can translate λ-calculus terms into *hmm* in such a way that the reduction of these translated terms is faithful to their reduction in the λ-calculus. Secondly, we can devise combinators for recursion which allow us to have n-shot reaction rules as a *derived* feature of *hmm*, rather than a primitive one as in FOG. Thus it is possible to give a translation of FOG into *hmm*, including operators like sequential and parallel composition, without much difficulty.

The main motivation for this work was our dissatisfaction with the existing proposal for extending FOG to a higher-order language: Le Métayer's Higher-Order Gamma (HOG) [8]. Our main objection to it is that, although HOG is higher-order in a sense we will describe shortly, it retains a blatant distinction between a program and its data. We argue as follows. In HOG, the most important synthetic construct is the *configuration*: a pair of the form $[P, M]$ where P is a reaction rule and M its input data multiset. A program in HOG is a (possible nesting of) multiset(s) of configurations. Programs are evaluated in much the same way as FOG programs are, but M can contain configurations, and so on, to an arbitrary depth. Thus we have a notion of higher-orderness here in the sense that multisets may contain "active" elements (the configurations) which allow the writing of hierarchical programs. However, the distinction between program and data is still retained as P and M are separate entities in a configuration $[P, M]$, abusing the notion of higher-orderness as was originally introduced in traditional calculi such as the λ-calculus.

The work herein is intended to rectify this problem. As a by-product we show how to translate HOG programs into *hmm* terms. This ensures that we do not lose the computational power of HOG by moving to a more primitive calculus.

The rest of this paper is arranged as follows. In Section 2 we introduce the terminology and syntax we have adopted, describe reduction in our calculus and show that the λ-calculus can be translated into *hmm*. In Section 3 we introduce combinators for recursion and show how to make n-shot rules from 1-shot rules using those combinators. The fact that reaction rules are first-class citizens plays a major rôle in defining those recursion combinators. The translation of FOG is considered in Section 4 and in Section 5 we show how to translate HOG. Finally, in Section 6 we conclude our achievements and propose several avenues for further investigation.

2 The *hmm* Calculus

We begin by introducing the syntax and semantics of the calculus. The class of *hmm* terms and a nondeterministic reduction relation on these terms are defined and discussed. Then to show that the calculus is useful we investigate a translation of the λ-calculus into *hmm* and make some observations about matters arising from this investigation.

2.1 Syntax

The alphabet from which terms of the calculus are derived is:

$$x, y, z, \ldots \text{ variables from a countable set } Var$$
$$\{\!| \;\;|\!\} \text{ multiset braces}$$

$$,$$
$$\Leftarrow$$
$$\lambda$$

Terms of the calculus are defined formally as follows:

Definition 1. The class $\mathcal{G}$ of *hmm* terms is the least class satisfying:

1. $\{\!|\;|\!\} \in \mathcal{G}$;
2. if $x \in Var$ then $x \in \mathcal{G}$;
3. if $M_1, \ldots, M_n \in \mathcal{G}$ then $\{\!| M_1, \ldots, M_n |\!\} \in \mathcal{G}$;

4. if $M, N \in \mathcal{M}(\mathcal{G})$ then $\lambda \tilde{x}.M \Leftarrow N \in \mathcal{G}$ where $\tilde{x} = x_1, \ldots, x_n$, and $\mathcal{M}(\mathcal{G})$ denotes the set of multisets of terms from $\mathcal{G}$.

A term of the form $\lambda \tilde{x}.M \Leftarrow N$ is called a *reaction rule* and the multisets, M and N, in such a term are called the *action* and the *reaction condition*, respectively, in the style of Banâtre and Le Métayer's FOG [1]. Imitating the rôle of functions in the λ-calculus, reaction rules are promoted to the status of first-class citizens in *hmm*. There is no distinction between values and functions: they are all reaction rules.

As in the λ-calculus, the λ acts as a variable binder. We define the following two functions, one which yields the bound variables of a term, $BV : \mathcal{G} \to \wp(Var)$

$$
\begin{aligned}
BV(x) &= \emptyset \\
BV(\lambda \tilde{x}.M \Leftarrow N) &= \{\tilde{x}\} \cup BV(M) \cup BV(N) \\
BV(\{\!| M_1, \ldots, M_n |\!\}) &= \bigcup_{1 \leq i \leq n} BV(M_i)
\end{aligned}
$$

and one which yields its free variables, $FV : \mathcal{G} \to \wp(Var)$

$$
\begin{aligned}
FV(x) &= x \\
FV(\lambda \tilde{x}.M \Leftarrow N) &= FV(M) \cup FV(N) - \{\tilde{x}\} \\
FV(\{\!| M_1, \ldots, M_n |\!\}) &= \bigcup_{1 \leq i \leq n} FV(M_i)
\end{aligned}
$$

We insist that the variables in an abstraction are unique in their scope, e.g: an abstraction such as $\lambda x, x.x \Leftarrow P$ is not valid.

Definition 2. We use the symbol $\equiv$ to describe "syntactic equality" of terms. Furthermore we extend its power slightly by defining it to equate terms which are syntactically equal under a change of bound variables (in the same way as $\equiv_\alpha$ (α-congruence) does in the λ-calculus.)

We use the symbol $\uplus$ as a binary associative, commutative operator standing for the union of two (possibly nested) multisets of terms. The result of $M \uplus N$ is the multiset containing all the elements from both M and N.

Substitution of terms is defined as follows:

Definition 3. Substitution, $M[x := N]$, over terms in $\mathcal{M}(\mathcal{G})$ is defined by

1. $\{\!| |\!\}[x := N] \equiv \{\!| |\!\}$
2. $\{\!| x |\!\}[x := N] \equiv \{\!| N |\!\}$
3. $\{\!| y |\!\}[x := N] \equiv \{\!| y |\!\}$ if $x \not\equiv y$
4. $\{\!| (\lambda \tilde{y}.P \Leftarrow Q) |\!\}[x := N] \equiv \{\!| \lambda \tilde{y}.P[x := N] \Leftarrow Q[x := N] |\!\}$ if $\forall y_i \in \tilde{y} . x \not\equiv y_i$
5. $\{\!| \{\!| M_1, \ldots, M_n |\!\} |\!\}[x := N] \equiv \{\!| \{\!| M_1, \ldots M_n |\!\}[x := N] |\!\}$
6. $(\{\!| M |\!\} \uplus R)[x := N] \equiv \{\!| M |\!\}[x := N] \uplus (R[x := N])$

For convenience,

$$
\begin{aligned}
[\tilde{x} := \tilde{N}] \text{ can be written for } & [x_1 := N_1, x_2 := N_2, \ldots, x_n := N_n] \\
\text{or} \qquad & [x_1 := N_1][x_2 := N_2] \ldots [x_n := N_n]
\end{aligned}
$$

provided x_i are all distinct, and $\forall i < j \; x_i \notin N_j$.

We adopt Barendregt's variable convention, which states that all bound variables are different from free variables (see [2]), to avoid variable name clashes.

As in the λ-calculus, we can now formulate a substitution lemma which allows us to reorder substitutions:

Lemma 4 The Substitution Lemma.
If x and y are distinct variables, $x \notin FV(L)$ and M is a multiset of terms then

$$M[x := N][y := L] \equiv M[y := L][x := N[y := L]]$$

2.2 Reduction

In this section we describe the reduction relation on terms from the *hmm*-calculus. First we require an auxiliary definition:

Definition 5. The empty multiset $\{\![]\!\}$ is represented by the Greek letter ϕ. We will use $\{\!|\phi|\!\}$ to denote truth for the reaction condition of a reaction rule.

We think of the reaction condition of a term as a predicate which is waiting to be evaluated. The abstracted variables of the term must be bound, and all substitutions made, before its evaluation can take place. If the reaction condition reduces to $\{\!|\phi|\!\}$ then we say that it is true and the action term can be evaluated. We can now define the reduction relation over multisets.

Definition 6. The reduction relation $\rightarrowtail \subseteq \mathcal{M}(\mathcal{G}) \times \mathcal{M}(\mathcal{G})$ over multisets is described by the following theory:

$$\frac{M \rightarrowtail M'}{\{\![M]\!\} \rightarrowtail \{\![M']\!\}} \quad rec$$

$$\frac{M \rightarrowtail M'}{M \uplus R \rightarrowtail M' \uplus R} \quad par$$

$$\frac{P[\tilde{x} := \tilde{N}] \xrightarrow{*} \{\!|\phi|\!\}}{\{\!|\lambda\tilde{x}.M \Leftarrow P|\!\} \uplus \{\!|\tilde{N}|\!\} \rightarrowtail M[\tilde{x} := \tilde{N}]} \quad react$$

$$\frac{M \in \mathcal{M}(\mathcal{G}) \quad \nexists N . M \rightarrowtail N \quad FV(M) = \{\} \quad M \not\equiv \phi}{\{\![M]\!\} \rightarrowtail M} \quad hatch$$

$$\frac{M \rightarrowtail M'}{\{\!|\lambda\tilde{x}.M \Leftarrow N|\!\} \rightarrowtail \{\!|\lambda\tilde{x}.M' \Leftarrow N|\!\}} \quad decay$$

The rules of the reduction relation can be described as follows: *rec* allows the reduction of nested multisets. *par* states the fact that submultisets of the program multiset can reduce concurrently. *react* describes the way reduction of a term and its arguments is performed. *hatch* allows multiset braces (which behave in a similar way to Berry and Boudol's membrane[1] in [3]) to be removed under

---

[1] $\{\!|$ and $|\!\}$ act purely as a way of defining the required locality of some computation; such a multiset is then allowed to evolve locally until no further reactions are possible, whereupon the multiset is hatched.

certain conditions. This is the minimal collection of rules required to characterise reduction of multisets. A fifth rule, *decay*, is included to make the behaviour of the reduction relation "eager" in the sense that reductions are performed in the body (i.e. the action part) of abstraction terms.

The reduction process can be described informally as follows: a term reacts with a number of other terms, which are chosen nondeterministically from the multiset, by first testing its reaction condition; if this multiset reduces to $\{\!|\phi|\!\}$ (a multiset containing an empty multiset) then the action part of the term is added back into the original multiset, after the appropriate substitutions are performed, and all the reacting terms (the reaction rule and all its arguments) are removed from the original multiset (c.f. *react* rule). If the reaction condition fails then no change occurs. Notice that the dual of $\{\!|\phi|\!\}$ is any multiset of terms which does not reduce to $\{\!|\phi|\!\}$.

There are some important remarks to be made about the reduction relation at this stage:

- As can be seen in the definition of the syntax, an abstraction can be made over more than one variable. In this case all variables must be bound simultaneously for the subsequent reaction condition, and possible action, to occur (N.B: reaction rules with more than one argument **do not** accept one-argument at a time — unlike curried λ-terms);
- the reduction rules are *one-shot*, i.e. if a reaction is successful, the reacting term is not added back into the multiset after it has reduced (c.f. *react* rule). Later we will propose a way to encode recursion by devising a combinator similar to **Y** in the λ-calculus;
- we require that all variables in a multiset, representing a valid term, must be bound at some level. For this reason multisets containing unbound variables do not hatch.

A useful notion which crops up in our calculus is that of an inert multiset, i.e. a multiset that does not contain any terms which can react.

Definition 7. We say that a multiset M is *inert* iff there are no further reductions in that multiset:

$$M \text{ is inert} \iff \not\exists N . M \rightarrowtail N$$

Also, if there exists an N such that $M \overset{*}{\rightarrowtail} N$ and N *is inert*, then we say that "M has an *inert-form*" [2].

for example:

$$\{\!|\lambda x.\{\!|x|\!\} \Leftarrow \{\!|x|\!\}|\!\} \text{ is inert, and}$$

$$\{\!|\{\!|\lambda x.\{\!|x|\!\} \Leftarrow \{\!|x|\!\}|\!\}|\!\} \text{ has an inert form (the above example), but}$$

$$\{\!|\lambda x.\{\!|x,x|\!\} \Leftarrow \{\!|\phi|\!\}, \lambda x.\{\!|x,x|\!\} \Leftarrow \{\!|\phi|\!\}|\!\} \text{ does not have an inert form.}$$

---

[2] Note that a term may have more than one inert-form.

2.3 Translating the Untyped λ-Calculus

The *hmm*-calculus is obviously related to the λ-calculus both in syntax and semantics. In this section we explore that relationship and describe a translation of the λ-calculus into the *hmm*-calculus. The translation is important because it shows that the *hmm*-calculus can encode all λ-definable functions and thus it can be deduced that all Turing Computable functions are encodable in the *hmm*-calculus.

Familiarity with the λ-calculus will be assumed. We just recall the syntax of λ-terms as:

$$M ::= x \mid (\lambda x.M) \mid (MM)$$

The function Θ, which maps λ-calculus terms into *hmm*-calculus terms, can now be defined as follows:

$$\Theta(x) \quad = \{\!| x, \phi, \phi |\!\}$$
$$\Theta(\lambda x.M) = \{\!| \lambda x.\Theta(M) \Leftarrow \{\!| \phi |\!\} |\!\}$$
$$\Theta(MN) \quad = \{\!| \Theta(M), \lambda a_1, a_2.\Theta(N) \Leftarrow \{\!| \phi |\!\} |\!\}$$

Since there is no notion of application in *hmm*, the order of application between terms is, generally speaking, nondeterministic. This needs to be controlled in order to have a valid translation of the λ-calculus. Notice that we have defined the λ-calculus with single variable abstractions so the problem is overcome by encapsulating the argument term within an abstraction demanding two arguments concurrently. The correct sense of application between two *hmm* terms is then ensured and the encapsulating abstraction term is removed only after the application has been performed (this is due to the rule for Θ that translates variables). The application order is maintained by introducing braces around pairs of terms to indicate what this order is.

There is a close correspondence between reduction in the λ-calculus and the reduction of Θ-translated terms in *hmm*. The following example gives the translation of the term $\lambda x.xx$ and the reduction of the translated λ-expression $\Omega = (\lambda x.xx)(\lambda x.xx)$ to demonstrate that non-terminating reductions are possible in the *hmm*-calculus, despite the fact that rules are one-shot.

Example 1.

$$\Theta(\lambda x.xx) = \{\!| \lambda x.\Theta(xx) \Leftarrow \{\!| \phi |\!\} |\!\}$$
$$= \{\!| \lambda x.\{\!| \Theta(x), \lambda a_1, a_2.\Theta(x) \Leftarrow \phi |\!\} \Leftarrow \{\!| \phi |\!\} |\!\}$$
$$= \{\!| \lambda x.\{\!| \{\!| x, \phi, \phi |\!\}, \lambda a_1, a_2.\{\!| x, \phi, \phi |\!\} \Leftarrow \{\!| \phi |\!\} |\!\} \Leftarrow \{\!| \phi |\!\} |\!\}$$

Next, in order to perform the reduction of $\Theta(\Omega)$, we derive the following partial translation:

$$\Theta(\Omega) = \{\!| \Theta(\lambda x.xx), \lambda a_1, a_2.\Theta(\lambda x.xx) \Leftarrow \{\!| \phi |\!\} |\!\}$$
$$= \{\!| \{\!| \lambda x.\{\!| \{\!| x, \phi, \phi |\!\}, \lambda a_1, a_2.\{\!| x, \phi, \phi |\!\} \Leftarrow \{\!| \phi |\!\} |\!\} \Leftarrow \{\!| \phi |\!\} |\!\},$$
$$\lambda a_1, a_2.\Theta(\lambda x.xx) \Leftarrow \{\!| \phi |\!\} |\!\}$$

Now we can perform the necessary reduction steps

$$
\begin{aligned}
&\{\!|\{\!|\lambda x.\{\!|\{\!|x,\phi,\phi|\!\},\lambda a_1,a_2.\{\!|x,\phi,\phi|\!\} \Leftarrow \{\!|\phi|\!\}|\!\} \Leftarrow \{\!|\phi|\!\}|\!\}, \\
&\quad \lambda a_1,a_2.\Theta(\lambda x.xx) \Leftarrow \{\!|\phi|\!\}|\!\} \\
\rightarrowtail\ &\{\!|\lambda x.\{\!|\{\!|x,\phi,\phi|\!\},\lambda a_1,a_2.\{\!|x,\phi,\phi|\!\} \Leftarrow \{\!|\phi|\!\}|\!\} \Leftarrow \{\!|\phi|\!\}, \\
&\quad \lambda a_1,a_2.\Theta(\lambda x.xx) \Leftarrow \{\!|\phi|\!\}|\!\} & (hatch) \\
\rightarrowtail\ &\{\!|\{\!|\lambda a_1,a_2.\Theta(\lambda x.xx) \Leftarrow \{\!|\phi|\!\},\phi,\phi|\!\}, \\
&\quad \lambda a_1,a_2.\{\!|\lambda a_1,a_2.\Theta(\lambda x.xx) \Leftarrow \{\!|\phi|\!\},\phi,\phi|\!\} \Leftarrow \{\!|\phi|\!\}|\!\} & (react) \\
\rightarrowtail\ &\{\!|\{\!|\Theta(\lambda x.xx)|\!\},\lambda a_1,a_2.\{\!|\lambda a_1,a_2.\Theta(\lambda x.xx) \Leftarrow \{\!|\phi|\!\},\phi,\phi|\!\} \Leftarrow \{\!|\phi|\!\}|\!\} & (react) \\
\rightarrowtail\ &\{\!|\Theta(\lambda x.xx),\lambda a_1,a_2.\{\!|\lambda a_1,a_2.\Theta(\lambda x.xx) \Leftarrow \{\!|\phi|\!\},\phi,\phi|\!\} \Leftarrow \{\!|\phi|\!\}|\!\} & (hatch) \\
\rightarrowtail\ &\{\!|\Theta(\lambda x.xx),\lambda a_1,a_2.\{\!|\Theta(\lambda x.xx)|\!\}|\!\} \Leftarrow \{\!|\phi|\!\}|\!\} & (decay) \\
=\ &\Theta(\Omega)
\end{aligned}
$$

...

Which, like the β-reduction of Ω, loops indefinitely.

This correspondence between the two reduction relations can be precisely formulated by the following theorem:

Theorem 8. *If $M, N \in \Lambda$ then:*

$$
M \rightarrow\!\!\!\!\rightarrow_\beta N \iff \Theta(M) \overset{*}{\rightarrowtail} \Theta(N)
$$

where $\rightarrow\!\!\!\!\rightarrow_\beta$ is the usual reflexive, transitive closure of the one-step β-reduction relation, $\rightarrow\!\!\!\!\rightarrow_\beta$ (c.f. [2]), and $\overset{*}{\rightarrowtail}$ is the reflexive transitive closure of $\rightarrowtail$ (see Definition 6). The proof of this theorem is by induction on the definition of the reduction relation.

The following theorem further relates these two calculi by showing that all β-normal forms can be expressed as inert multisets in hmm :

Theorem 9. *if $M \in \Lambda$ then:*

$$
M \text{ is in } \beta\text{-normal form} \iff \Theta(M) \text{is inert}
$$

The proof is by induction on the structure of M.

This translation scheme is not the only valid framework within which interesting aspects of hmm can be described. We define the *Chemical Numerals* as an alternative way of representing numerals native to the hmm-calculus, as opposed to a translated numeral system from the λ-calculus. This system is presented as a variation on an interpretation of the Church Numerals (see [2]).

Definition 10 Chemical Numerals. Our numeral system, $\mathbf{ch} = ch_0, ch_1, \ldots$ is defined by the following terms:

$$
\begin{aligned}
ch_0 &\equiv \lambda x.\{\!|x|\!\} \Leftarrow \{\!|x|\!\} \\
ch_1 &\equiv \lambda f.\{\!|\{\!|f,\phi|\!\},\lambda x.\{\!|x|\!\} \Leftarrow \{\!|x|\!\}|\!\} \Leftarrow \{\!|f,\phi,\phi|\!\} \\
ch_2 &\equiv \lambda f.\{\!|\{\!|f,\phi|\!\},\lambda g.\{\!|\{\!|g,\phi|\!\},\lambda x.\{\!|x|\!\} \Leftarrow \{\!|x|\!\}|\!\} \Leftarrow \{\!|g,\phi,\phi|\!\}|\!\} \Leftarrow \{\!|f,\phi,\phi|\!\}
\end{aligned}
$$

...

and the usual successor, predecessor and test for zero functions:

$$Succ \quad \equiv \lambda n.\{\!|\lambda f.\{\!|\{\!|f,\phi|\!\}, n|\!\} \Leftarrow \{\!|f,\phi,\phi|\!\}|\!\} \Leftarrow \{\!|\phi|\!\}$$
$$Pred \quad \equiv \lambda n.\{\!|\lambda x.\{\!|x|\!\} \Leftarrow \{\!|\phi|\!\}|\!\} \Leftarrow \{\!|n|\!\}$$
$$IsZero \equiv \lambda n.\{\!|n,\phi|\!\} \Leftarrow \{\!|n,\phi|\!\}$$

During the construction of the Chemical Numerals, and the translation function Θ, we observed that a useful technique for guiding the reduction of terms can be formulated by way of two syntactic operations: $\mathtt{wrap}$ (e.g, in the definition of ch_0) and $\mathtt{unwrap}$(e.g, in the definition of $IsZero$). These operations generate terms which encapsulate the arguments within (respectively, release arguments from) an abstraction term. They are defined as follows:

Definition 11. $\mathtt{wrap}, \mathtt{unwrap} : \mathcal{M}(\mathcal{G}) \mapsto \mathcal{M}(\mathcal{G})$ are defined by:

$$\mathtt{wrap}(M) \quad \equiv \lambda x.\{\!|M|\!\} \Leftarrow \{\!|x|\!\}$$
$$\mathtt{unwrap}(M) \equiv \{\!|\phi, M|\!\}$$

Proposition 12. *Wrapping does not affect the reduction of a multiset. If M' is inert, then:*

$$M \overset{*}{\rightarrowtail} M' \;\Rightarrow\; \mathtt{unwrap} \circ \mathtt{wrap}(M) \overset{*}{\rightarrowtail} M'$$

The proof is straightforward.

3 Combinators for Recursion

A consequence of Theorem 8 is that the fixed point combinator **Y** of the λ-calculus can be translated into our calculus, with the same behaviour. This observation leads us to speculate on the possibility of defining an indigenous combinator for the hmm-calculus which can be used to describe other types of recursion.

In order to define one such combinator we use the syntactic functions $\mathtt{wrap}$ and $\mathtt{unwrap}$, from Definition 11, to make our combinators more readable. The wrapping precaution is necessary in the definition of the combinator because we want to ensure that reactions only occur between the function and its argument. We have no other way of guaranteeing that incorrect reductions will not occur[3]. We assume that any argument passed to $\mathtt{unwrap}$ has been previously wrapped. A first attempt at a combinator which we call $\mathcal{W}$, that takes a function and repeatedly applies it to an argument term, can then be defined by:

$$\mathcal{W} \equiv \{\!|U, U|\!\}$$

where

$$U \equiv \lambda a.\{\!|\lambda f.\{\!|\lambda x.\{\!|\{\!|\{\!|a, a|\!\}, f|\!\}, \mathtt{wrap}(\{\!|\mathtt{unwrap}(x), \mathtt{unwrap}(f)|\!\})|\!\}$$
$$\Leftarrow \{\!|\phi|\!\}|\!\} \Leftarrow \{\!|\phi|\!\}|\!\} \Leftarrow \{\!|\phi|\!\}$$

---

[3] On the other hand, if hmm were equipped with a type system, we could rely on types to ensure that reactions are well behaved.

Since both the function and the argument need to be wrapped before the combinator can begin its work, the combinator can only be used in a multiset that looks like this:

$$\{\!\{W, \mathtt{wrap}(f)\}\!\}, \mathtt{wrap}(a)\}\!\}$$

where f is the function to be applied and a is its argument. Notice that the fact that reaction rules are higher-order is crucial in the definition of W.

A combinator $\mathcal{Y}$, simpler than W, can be defined in such a way that the following behaviour can be obtained:

$$\{\!\{\mathcal{Y}, f\}\!\} \overset{*}{\rightharpoonup} \{\!\{f, \{\!\{\mathcal{Y}, f\}\!\}\}\!\}$$

It is defined as:

$$\mathcal{Y} \equiv \{\!\{T, T\}\!\}$$

where

$$T \equiv \lambda t.\{\!\{\lambda f.\{\!\{f, \{\!\{\{\!\{t, t\}\!\}, f\}\!\}\}\!\} \Leftarrow \{\!\{\phi\}\!\}\}\!\} \Leftarrow \{\!\{\phi\}\!\}$$

The drawback of both W and $\mathcal{Y}$ is that they do not stop reproducing, of their own accord, once f's reaction condition is false. To control this behaviour it is necessary that the details of the reaction rule (its action and reaction condition) are accessible to the combinator.

So, given a reaction rule of the form $\lambda \tilde{x}.\text{Act} \Leftarrow \text{React}$, we define a meta-function F to try to capture the behaviour we require. A first attempt at F is:

$$F \equiv \lambda \tilde{x}.\{\!\{\text{Act}, \{\!\{C, C\}\!\}\}\!\} \Leftarrow \text{React}$$

where

$$C \equiv \lambda a.\{\!\{\lambda \tilde{x}.\{\!\{\text{Act}, \{\!\{a, a\}\!\}\}\!\} \Leftarrow \text{React}\}\!\} \Leftarrow \{\!\{\phi\}\!\}$$

After close inspection it becomes clear that this is not a robust enough definition. The *decay* rule allows the multiset $\{\!\{C, C\}\!\}$ to reduce forever even though the term which encapsulates this multiset may reach a state where it is not able to react further.

We solve this problem by "wrapping" the C's in a similar way to the scheme described in Definition 11. Let $\tilde{y} \equiv \tilde{x}[x_i := y_i]$ (i.e. we rename all the variables in $\tilde{x}$). Then F and C become:

$$F \equiv \lambda \tilde{x}.\{\!\{\text{Act}, \{\!\{\tilde{x}, C, C\}\!\}\}\!\} \Leftarrow \text{React}$$

and

$$C \equiv \lambda \tilde{y}.\{\!\{\lambda a.\{\!\{\lambda \tilde{x}.\{\!\{\text{Act}, \{\!\{\tilde{x}, a, a\}\!\}\}\!\} \Leftarrow \text{React}\}\!\} \Leftarrow \{\!\{\phi\}\!\}\}\!\} \Leftarrow \text{React}$$

Unfortunately this translation also has a limitation. A rule can be constructed, such that the reaction condition is $\{\!\{\phi\}\!\}$ and the function demands a single argument, which makes this term for encoding recursion fail too. We solve this problem by introducing a tagging scheme using tuples which are discussed next.

3.1 Tuples and Tagging Data

In the λ-calculus it is possible to define an encoding of pairs, which can be generalised to n-tuples, in order to collect data together in a distinguishable way. We will now provide a scheme for encoding pairs in our calculus, together with first and second projection functions. n-tuples can be encoded by pairs in the standard way — by nesting pairs (i.e $(M_1, (M_2, \ldots (M_{n-1}, M_n) \ldots))$). But for our purpose pairs suffice anyway.

First we need to define two new variants of the functions wrap and unwrap given earlier:

$$\mathtt{wrap}'(M) \equiv \lambda x. \{|M|\} \Leftarrow \{|x, \phi|\}$$
$$\mathtt{unwrap}'(t) \equiv \{|t, \lambda y. \{|y|\} \Leftarrow \{|y|\}|\}$$

Then a pair can be defined by

$$(M, N) \equiv \lambda x, y. \{|\{|1, x, \mathtt{wrap}'(M)|\}, \{|2, x, \mathtt{wrap}'(N)|\}|\} \Leftarrow \{|y|\}$$

where (for $n = 1, 2$),

$$\pi_n \equiv \lambda x. \{|\pi_n', \phi, x|\} \Leftarrow \{|\phi|\}$$
$$\pi_n' \equiv \lambda y. \{|\lambda z. \{|\lambda a_1, a_2, a_3. \{|\mathtt{unwrap}'(z)|\} \Leftarrow \{|\phi|\}|\} \Leftarrow \{|\phi|\}|\} \Leftarrow \{|y = n|\}$$

are the projection functions.

We use tuples to imitate the distinction between programs and data. This will be of particular use later, when we translate FOG programs into the *hmm*-calculus. All data values in a multiset are now "tagged" by placing data in a pair: one element is the data value and the other is a tag identifying the data (you can think of tagging as a primitive form of typing). We assume an inexhaustible set of tags exists. So, for example, the number 2 is now represented by the pair $(2, t)$, where 't' is its associated tag.

In a similar way, again due to the translation of the λ-calculus, we can reliably extend our calculus with the syntax of First-Order logic ($\wedge, \vee$, etc...) and the basic arithmetic operations.

A reaction rule in *hmm* now needs to not only check the logical condition associated with the program clause, but also that the data is correctly tagged. So, for example, a reaction rule with action and reaction Act and React, respectively, that takes one argument whose data must be tagged with the tag t_n, say, would be written as the *hmm* term:

$$\lambda x. \{|\mathrm{Act}(\pi_1(x))|\} \Leftarrow \{|\mathrm{React}(\pi_1(x)) \wedge \pi_2(x) = t_n|\} \qquad (*)$$

We rewrite terms like this, with the help of pattern matching, so that they are clearer and more concise. The term would then be:

$$\lambda(d, t_n).\mathrm{Act}(d) \Leftarrow \mathrm{React}(d)$$

which would usually be further simplified to just:

$$\lambda(d, t_n).\mathrm{Act} \Leftarrow \mathrm{React}$$

It is important to note that this simplification can only be reliably used in multisets where all the data values are tagged and the rule $(*)$ is well behaved, as is the case in the FOG translation.

We modify the combinator F (from above) again, this time to take account of the fact that arguments must now be tuples:

$$F \equiv \lambda \overline{(x,t)}.\{|\text{Act}, \{|\overline{(x,t)}, C, C|\}|\} \Leftarrow \text{React}$$

$$C \equiv \lambda \overline{(y,t)}.\{|\lambda a.\{|\lambda \overline{(x,t)}.\{|\text{Act}, \{|\overline{(x,t)}, a, a|\}|\} \Leftarrow \text{React}|\} \Leftarrow \{|\phi|\}|\} \Leftarrow \text{React}$$

Notice that concurrent abstractions are still possible over tuples and $\overline{(x,t)} \equiv (x_1,t_1),\ldots,(x_n,t_k)$.

To make things clearer to read henceforth we shall abbreviate terms treated to this process of becoming n-shot by just annotating the ordinary abstraction term with a star $(*)$. So the reaction rule

$$\lambda^*(x,t).\{||\} \Leftarrow \{|\phi|\}$$

deletes all values from a multiset whose tag is t.

4 Translating First-Order Gamma

4.1 Translating Simple Programs

At the end of the previous section a combinator was proposed which became inert when the reaction condition could no longer be true. We will use this combinator in our translation of first-order Gamma. So, a simple FOG rule can be translated as the following multiset:

$$\{|\lambda^*(x,t),\ldots\{|\ldots|\} \Leftarrow \{|\ldots|\},\ldots < \text{data values} > \ldots|\}$$

In general the tupling scheme can be used to specify which elements of data a reaction rule is interested in.

We can now translate a *simple*[4] FOG program by collecting all these reaction rules and placing them in the multiset containing the tagged data values belonging to the FOG program (the tags are used to enumerate the type of a datum in the multiset).

A translated simple FOG program now looks like:

$$\{|F_1,\ldots,F_n,\ldots < \text{data values} > \ldots|\}|\}$$

where the F_i's are reaction rules that translate each re-write rule from the original Gamma program. We can now guarantee that reductions between rules are prohibited because of the tupling mechanism employed in writing the reaction rules and tagging the data values.

---

[4] By simple we mean a program that is built from a parallel composition of one or more basic reaction rules.

Example 2. The following is a translation of the Gamma program max (see Section 1 for the Gamma version).

$$\{\!|F_{\text{max}}, M|\!\}$$

where M is the multiset of data values,

$$F_{\text{max}} \equiv \lambda(x, \text{int}), (y, \text{int}).\{\!|(x, \text{int}), \{\!|(x, \text{int}), (y, \text{int}), C_{\text{max}}, C_{\text{max}}|\!\}|\!\} \Leftarrow \{\!|x \geq y|\!\}$$

and

$$C_{\text{max}} \equiv \lambda(x, \text{int}), (y, \text{int}).\{\!|\lambda a.\{\!|\lambda(u, \text{int}), (v, \text{int}).\{\!|(u, \text{int}), \{\!|u, v, a, a|\!\}|\!\}$$
$$\Leftarrow \{\!|u \geq v|\!\}|\!\} \Leftarrow \{\!|\phi|\!\}|\!\} \Leftarrow \{\!|x \geq y|\!\}$$

For a given multiset of numbers, say

$$\{\!|4, 6, 12, 3, 8, 9|\!\}$$

we assume the numbers are tagged — indicating they are integers. The maximum element can be found by placing F_{max} in the multiset and reducing it until it is inert.

$$\{\!|F_{\text{max}}, 4, 6, 12, 3, 8, 9|\!\}$$
$$\overset{*}{\rightarrowtail} \{\!|9, 4, 12, 3, 8, \{\!|6, 9, C_{\text{max}}, C_{\text{max}}|\!\}|\!\} \qquad \text{(react and par)}$$
$$\overset{*}{\rightarrowtail} \{\!|9, 4, 12, 3, 8, \{\!|\lambda a.\{\!|\lambda x, y.\{\!|x, \{\!|x, y, a, a|\!\}$$
$$\Leftarrow \{\!|x \geq y|\!\}|\!\} \Leftarrow \{\!|\phi|\!\}, C_{\text{max}}|\!\}|\!\} \qquad \text{(react and par)}$$
$$\overset{*}{\rightarrowtail} \{\!|9, 4, 12, 3, 8, \{\!|F_{\text{max}}|\!\}|\!\} \qquad \text{(react and par)}$$
$$\overset{*}{\rightarrowtail} \{\!|9, 4, 12, 3, 8, F_{\text{max}}|\!\} \qquad \text{(hatch and par)}$$
$$\cdots$$
$$\overset{*}{\rightarrowtail} \{\!|12, F_{\text{max}}|\!\}$$

At which point the computation halts because no further reductions are possible.

Henceforth we will use the alternative notation proposed in Section 3 for translations, so that F_{max} can be simply rewritten as:

$$\lambda^*(x, int), (y, int).\{\!|(x, int)|\!\} \Leftarrow \{\!|x \geq y|\!\}$$

4.2 Composition Operators

In [7] a calculus for Gamma programs was investigated in which properties of sequential ($\circ$) and parallel ($+$) composition were discussed. Informally speaking, for any two programs P_1, P_2 and some data multiset M, the sequential composition of P_1 and P_2 (written $P_1 \circ P_2$) applied to M is equivalent to the repeated application of P_2 to M until no further reactions with P_2 are possible. P_2 is then discarded and P_1 is repeatedly applied to the resultant multiset, M' say, until again no further reactions are possible — at which point the program terminates. Parallel composition of P_1 and P_2 (written $P_1 + P_2$) is equivalent to making a nondeterministic choice between these two programs, applying the chosen program to the multiset once, then repeating this choice and application process until neither programs can react with the data. An in-depth study of these operators for FOG can be found in [7].

In order to show that the *hmm*-calculus can describe these properties, we demonstrate how an encoding of these composition operators can be done. Below, assume that $P_i \equiv \lambda \tilde{p}_i . A_{\tilde{p}_i} \Leftarrow R_{p_i}$, for $i = 1, 2$ and also assume that they have been translated into *hmm* by the techniques described in the previous section.

Parallel composition is achieved by simply placing the two reaction rules in the same multiset as the data values (c.f the translation of FOG above). So, $(P_1 + P_2)(M)$, where $P_{1,2}$ are programs and M is the tagged data multiset, can be written quite simply as:

$$\{\!| P_1, P_2, M |\!\}$$

Sequential composition of programs, $(P_1 \circ P_2)(M)$, requires a little more detail. Borrowing the tagging technique used in the translation of first-order Gamma, we tag all terms representing data. We also introduce two flags associated with each rule: the *active* and *release* flags. The former indicates whether a rule should be executable at any particular time, by its presence in the multiset. The latter helps to activate a previously inactive part of the program.

The *terminator* term disables a reaction rule by consuming its active flag when the reaction condition of the rule with which it is associated is false for the entire multiset. It releases the "release" flag for that rule allowing the continuation of the program's execution. The *terminator* terms are defined as follows

$$terminator_i \equiv \lambda \delta, \mathbf{af}_i . \{\!| \delta, \mathbf{rf}_i |\!\}$$
$$\Leftarrow \{\!| \lambda x, y . \{\!| y |\!\} \Leftarrow \{\!| y |\!\}, \{\!| \lambda^*(x, d) . \{\!| |\!\} \Leftarrow \{\!| \phi |\!\}, \{\!| \neg \mathrm{React}_{P_n}(\delta) |\!\} |\!\} |\!\}$$

where the active flag for rule P_i is denoted by $\mathbf{af}_i$, and the release flag by $\mathbf{rf}_i$. The data multiset, M, is wrapped and represented by δ. The translation for $P_1 \circ P_2$ is thus

$$\{\!| \lambda \mathbf{rf}_2 . \{\!| \lambda^* \tilde{x}_{P_1}, \mathbf{af}_1 . \{\!| \mathbf{af}_1, \mathrm{Act}_{P_1} |\!\} \Leftarrow \{\!| \mathrm{React}_{P_1} |\!\}, \mathbf{af}_1, terminator_1 |\!\} \Leftarrow \{\!| \phi |\!\},$$
$$\lambda^* \tilde{x}_{P_2}, \mathbf{af}_2 . \{\!| \mathbf{af}_2, \mathrm{Act}_{P_2} |\!\} \Leftarrow \{\!| \mathrm{React}_{P_2} |\!\}, \mathbf{af}_2, terminator_2, \delta |\!\}$$

The above translations are fine as long as we do not nest composition operators. That is, the input program is *simple*. To generalise this translation to an arbitrary program, constructed from several levels of parallel and sequential composition operators, we exploit the tagging technique we used in the translation of the simple sequential composition above. The function that generalises this translation is defined recursively by $\mathcal{T}$ as follows, where the first argument is a list of release tags for which the residual[5] of the program in the second argument must wait.

$$T(\phi, (\tilde{x} \to A \Leftarrow R)_n)$$
$$= \{\!|\lambda\tilde{x}.A \Leftarrow R, \mathtt{af}_n, terminator_n|\!\}$$
$$T(\mathtt{rfs}, (\tilde{x} \to A \Leftarrow R)_n)$$
$$= \{\!|\lambda\mathtt{rfs}.\{\!|\lambda\tilde{x}.A \Leftarrow R, \mathtt{af}_n, terminator_n|\!\} \Leftarrow \{\!|\phi|\!\}|\!\} \quad \mathtt{rfs} \neq \phi$$
$$T(\mathtt{rfs}, P \circ Q)$$
$$= \{\!|T(\mathtt{r\_flags}(Q), P) \uplus T(\mathtt{rfs}, Q)$$
$$T(\phi, P_1 + \ldots + P_n)$$
$$= \uplus_{1 \leq i \leq n} T(\phi, P_i)$$
$$T(\mathtt{rfs}, P_1 + \ldots + P_n)$$
$$= \{\!|\lambda\mathtt{rfs}.\{\!| \uplus_{1 \leq i \leq n} T(\phi, P_i)|\!\} \Leftarrow \{\!|\phi|\!\}|\!\} \quad\quad\quad \mathtt{rfs} \neq \phi$$

The support function $\mathtt{r\_flags}$, which collects the flags of the residual part of the program is defined by

$$\mathtt{r\_flags}((\tilde{x} \to A \Leftarrow R)_n) = \{n\}$$
$$\mathtt{r\_flags}(P \circ Q) \quad\quad = \mathtt{r\_flags}(P)$$
$$\mathtt{r\_flags}(P_1 + \ldots + P_n) \quad = \bigcup_i \mathtt{r\_flags}(P_i)$$

In $P_1 + \ldots + P_n$, we assume, without loss of generality, that each P_i is either a sequential composition of some arbitrary programs, or a basic reaction rule.

As yet we have not formally proved that this translation is faithful. But an empirical study, by means of a Miranda™ program, has produced the expected results.

5 Translating Higher-Order Gamma

Before giving a translation of Le Métayer's higher-order Gamma we review its syntax and semantics. Configurations are used to unify a program and a multiset into one unit. A configuration consists of a record of named multisets and a (possibly empty) program. A simple program in higher order Gamma extracts elements from multisets and possibly produce new ones in their place.

The following BNF defines a syntax for the language:

---

[5] Formally, the residual of a program is defined as

$$residual(R, A) \quad = (R, A)$$
$$residual(P \circ Q) = residual(P)$$
$$residual(P + Q) = residual(P) + residual(Q)$$

as is given in [7].

$$
\begin{aligned}
\text{Conf} \quad &= \text{Passive} \mid \text{Active} \\
\text{Passive} \quad &= [\emptyset, \text{Env}] \\
\text{Active} \quad &= [\text{Prog}, \text{Env}] \\
\text{Env} \quad &= (V_1 = \text{Multexp}_1, \ldots, V_n = \text{Multexp}_n) \\
\text{Prog} \quad &= \text{Par} \mid \text{Prog} \circ \text{Par} \\
\text{Par} \quad &= \text{Sim} \mid \text{Par} + \text{Sim} \\
\text{Sim} \quad &= x_i : \text{Var}_{i_1}, \ldots, x_k : \text{Var}_{i_k} \\
&\quad \to \text{Seqexp}_1 : \text{Var}_{j_1}, \ldots, \text{Seqexp}_m : \text{Var}_{j_m} \\
&\quad \leftarrow C(x_1, \ldots, x_n) \\
\text{Seqexp} \quad &= \text{Exp}_1, \ldots, \text{Exp}_n \mid \emptyset \\
\text{Exp} \quad &= \text{Conf} \mid \text{Conf.Var}_i \mid x_i \mid \text{Arithexp} \mid \text{Boolexp} \mid \text{Multexp} \mid \ldots \\
\text{Multexp} &= \emptyset \mid \text{Multexp}_1 \uplus \text{Multexp}_2 \mid \text{Multexp}_1 - \text{Multexp}_2 \mid \{\text{Seqexp}\} \ldots
\end{aligned}
$$

Most of the above constructions are fairly straightforward. The semantics of HOG are similar to the semantics for FOG, apart from slight variations on the extensions proposed in [7]. The rules corresponding to the *hmm react* rule have very similar behaviour. The only difference is that once a program stops transforming the multisets (ie, all the multisets in the record are inert with respect to this program), the program is deleted from the configuration and replaced by an empty program.

The encoding of HOG follows naturally from the definitions of *hmm*. It is easy to see that *hmm* reaction rules encode Simple (*Sim*) HOG programs. Also, following the treatment in Section 4.2, parallel and sequential composition can be encoded in a straightforward manner. The semantics of $\rightarrowtail$ ensure that the same behaviour is observed in *hmm* as is in HOG.

In fact the only non-trivial part of the translation is in the encoding of the action of the fetch rule. In the operational semantics of HOG this rule is:

$$
[\emptyset, (V_1 = M_1, \ldots, V_k = M_k)].V_i \to M_i
$$

This named accessing of the labeled multisets can be mimicked in *hmm* by a neat trick using the tagging system we defined in Section 4. Given a configuration:

$$
[P, E]
$$

where

$$
E \equiv (V_1 = M_1, \ldots, V_k = M_k)
$$

we can translate E as follows: for each V_i we construct a unique tag corresponding to this variable name, call this tag t_i, then we place the translated multiset M_i and the tag in a pair so that we get a term that looks like:

$$
(M_i, t_i)
$$

The encoding of E in *hmm* is now just:

$$
E_h \equiv \biguplus_i \{\!| (M_i, t_i) |\!\}
$$

The fetch rule that performs the extraction of the i-th multiset from the environment can now be encoded by:

$$\{\!| \lambda x_1, \ldots, x_k.\{\!|\pi_1(x_i)|\!\} \Leftarrow \{\!|\pi_2(x_i) = t_i|\!\}, E_h|\!\}$$

where t_i is the tag associated with the multiset we wish to extract out of the possible k named multisets, as defined above. Alternatively a slightly more complicated version of the fetch rule can be devised using the flaging technique employed in the translation of sequential composition we gave earlier.

6 Conclusions

In this paper we formulated and investigated a primitive higher-order calculus aiming at being the "canonical" higher-order calculus for languages based on the chemical reaction metaphor. We showed that our calculus, called the hmm-calculus, could represent all computable functions by deriving a translation of the λ-calculus into it. We also showed that hmm contains all the ingredients that allow both FOG and HOG programs to be translated into it.

In summary, we have given what we believe are convincing arguments, in terms of their generality, for why hmm is a desirable calculus with which to explore further this area of Computing.

Of course, the work presented here is just the beginning. For example we haven't fully considered the relationship between hmm and Berry and Boudol's γ-calculus ([3]). In addition several avenues of further investigation exist which we feel are of interest and import. One such avenue would be to provide the hmm calculus with a compositional semantic model. A possible candidate would be the transition trace semantics, investigated for first-order Gamma programs in [10]. Also, we would like to extend the hmm calculus with a type discipline. Preliminary investigations into this matter have been presented in [5]. Finally, we would like to tackle the question of analysing programs written in hmm . This issue has been addressed by Hankin, Le Métayer and Sands in [7], for first-order Gamma. It would be very desirable to carry out a similar work for hmm programs. The basic calculus should be investigated more fully, like the λ-calculus has been, to give the calculus a more rigorous mathematical foundation.

Acknowledgements

Many thanks to Chris Hankin and Simon Gay for several discussions and for having read drafts of this paper. Our partners in the COORDINATION project also provided valuable input. The authors would like to acknowledge financial support through the COORDINATION ESPRIT project #9102.

References

1. J.-P. Banâtre and D. Le Métayer. The gamma model and its discipline of programming. In *Science of Computer Programming*, volume 15, pages 55–77. Elsvier Science Publishers, North Holland, 1990.
2. H. P. Barendregt. *The Lambda Calculus*. Elsevier Science Publishers, 1985.
3. G. Berry and G. Boudol. The chemical abstract machine. In *Theoretical Computer Science*, volume 96, pages 217–248. Elsvier, 1992.
4. K. Mani Chandy and Jayadev Misra. *Parallel Program Design*. Addison-Wesley, 1988.
5. D. Cohen. Higher order chemical machines. Master's thesis, Department of Computing, Imperial College of Science, Technology and Medicine, 1995.
6. C. Hankin, D. Le Métayer, and D. Sands. A calculus of gamma programs. In *Proc. of the 5th Workshop on Languages and Compilers for Parallel Computing*, number 757 in LNCS. Springer Verlag, 1992.
7. D. Le Métayer. Higher-order multiset programming. In *Proceedings of the First Annual Workshop*, COORDINATION, pages 103–123. ESPRIT, 1994.
8. G.-C. Roman and H. C. Cunnigham. A shared dataspace model of concurrency: Language and programming implications. In *Proceedings of the 9th International Conference on Distributed Computing Systems*, pages 270–279, 1989.
9. D. Sands. A compositional semantics of combining forms for gamma programs. In *Formal Methods in Programming and Their Applications*, number 735 in LNCS, pages 43–56. Springer Verlag, 1992.

μ^2Log: Towards Remote Coordination

Koen De Bosschere[1] and Jean-Marie Jacquet[2]

[1] Vakgroep Elektronica
Universiteit Gent, Belgium
email: kdb@elis.rug.ac.be
[2] Institut d'Informatique
University of Namur, Belgium
email: jmj@info.fundp.ac.be

Abstract. Modern computing is characterized, among others, by two major facts. On the one hand, methods are needed to master the ever growing complexity of information systems. On the other hand, distributed and open systems allow configurations to change dynamically and thus require tools to allow processes to cooperate, communicate and work in synergy.

A theoretical model μ^2Log, supported by an efficient implementation, is proposed to cope with these two problems. Following Linda, it offers tuple-based dataspaces as communication and coordination means and manipulates passive and active objects by the same kind of three basic primitives: *tell*, *read*, and *get* to respectively place, check the existence and remove an object. Our model supports multiple local dataspaces, multiple processes acting on these dataspaces as well as a distribution of these dataspaces and processes. Remote coordination is ensured by agents of some platforms granting access via aliases to other agents running on other platforms. As a result, a peculiar feature of our approach is that it neither requires a centralized server nor a centralized dataspace.

1 Introduction

As information systems ever grow more complex and are ever more integrated, mastering their complexity is one of the key issues in modern software engineering. One way to achieve this is to functionally decompose a system into tasks that only need a limited amount of interaction with their environment. The tasks are fully responsible for their part of the system and internally take care of all the aspects of it.

In sequential programming, this way of mastering the complexity has lead to the paradigm of object-oriented programming, where data structures are encapsulated in abstract entities called objects, together with the code that is allowed to use and to manipulate them. Object oriented programming has clear advantages when it comes to develop and maintain big applications because the possible interactions between the objects are clearly defined.

In the field of parallel and distributed programming, a similar way of mastering the complexity is advocated by the coordination languages. In their view, the basic building blocks are not objects anymore, but complete programs. These programs are responsible for a particular task, keep all the task-related data, and have a limited interaction with the other programs by means of a shared data space. In modern terminology, the self contained programs are called agents and the shared data space is called a Linda tuple space or a blackboard ([5]).

A coordination language only wants to offer a framework for multi-agent communication, and should ideally be completely independent from the underlying agent technology. It just forms an extra layer glueing together all the bits and pieces.

The coordination model based on a shared dataspace maps quite naturally on a hardware architecture with some form of shared memory. Indeed, the most powerful implementations of shared dataspace run on shared memory machines. The distributed implementations of the coordination model all rely on a kind of distribution of the tuple space over multiple machines, combined with a server process that keeps track of the operations on the shared dataspace. This server process is a bottleneck that harms the scalability of this approach. The server process is however needed in order to keep a global view on the shared dataspace.

Our approach for building distributed coordination is a truly distributed one. Each agent can have local dataspaces and multiple processes. Whenever an agent wants to use the dataspace of another agent, the owner agent must grant access, and from then on, the dataspace operations can directly be applied to the remote dataspace. There is neither a need for a centralized server process, nor for a centralized data space.

In this paper, for simplicity of the presentation, we shall concentrate on logic programs to code agents. However, the concepts we introduce can be naturally extended to other programming paradigms such as functional programming and object-oriented programming.

Our previous research in this area was mainly concerned with intra-agent communication. This is a form of communication where the processes of one agent must cooperate in order to solve a given problem. In this paper, we consider inter-agent communication where the agents are more loosely coupled. The intra-agent communication could typically be supported by a shared memory machine, whereas the inter-agent communication can be fully distributed on a network.

The remainder of this paper is structured as follows. Section 2 sketches a basic model, called μLog, embodying the very basic notions. Section 3 describes the real and distributed model $\mu^2 Log$. Section 4 defines formally the underlying language and section 5 gives the operational semantics. Section 6 proves its implementability by expliciting an efficient implementation. Finally, section 7 compares $\mu^2 Log$ with related work and section 8 draws our conclusion.

2 Basic Model

Our work is best explained by first introducing a primitive version which contains the very basic ideas. This version is called μLog. It has been presented in [1, 8] where operational, declarative and denotational semantics are also designed and compared.

2.1 Basic Concepts

There are three major ideas behind the design of μLog.

Pure communication via a shared data space. The first one, inspired from Linda ([6]), consists of regarding a computation as a set of processes floating around and acting on a shared space of data. The communication between these processes only occurs by means of this shared space using counterparts of the classical write and read operations: the primitive *tell* to put data, the primitive *get* to get data, and the primitive *read* to consult (in a non-destructive way) data. To keep the communication in its pure form via the dataspace and consequently to avoid implicit communication via shared variables, variables are renamed before being told or got.

Treating active and passive objects equally. The second basic idea, also inherited from Linda, considers active and passive objects equally. Hence, passive logic programming terms and active goals are manipulated by the above primitives regardless of their nature, telling, getting and reading goals being understood as creating corresponding processes, killing them, and checking their existence, respectively. We shall subsequently use the qualification *data* to refer either to a passive term or an active goal. Note that no confusion on the nature of a given data can arise since terms and goals are distinguished by their main functor which are respectively functions and predicates and thus of distinct classes. However, although this distinction is usual in theory, the practice of logic programming, exemplified by Prolog, has confused the two classes with clear advantages for meta-programming. In this context, in order to remove any ambiguity, we shall subsequently append the above primitives with a "t" or a "p" according as a passive term or an active process is actually under consideration.

Termination. The third feature, peculiar to μLog, consists of distinguishing two kinds of processes with respect to termination. A first class of processes, called *foreground*, are associated with goals that need to be successfully reduced in order to make the whole computation successful. They are to be considered as the initial goals on a blackboard. The other class of processes, called *background*, are considered as daemons with their interaction on the dataspace as unique point of interest. Hence their termination and failure is of no concern for the success of the computation. By convention, the initial query lists the foreground processes and all processes constructed during the computation are considered as background.

3 Distributed model

The recent advertisement on networks and, in particular, the internet and its associated tools and organization (e.g., netscape and www) have evidenced, if need still be, the interest and crucial importance of modular and distributed systems.

The classical approach to that end typically consists of distributing a single entity (say, in our context, a data space) and of using a manager to coordinate the individual pieces and let users think of the entity as a non-fractioned object.

We take a drastically opposite approach. Indeed, we propose a truly distributed approach avoiding the use of a master manager and rather making several μLog applications coordinate. This goal is subsequently reached in four steps:

i) the introduction of multiple blackboards,

ii) the distribution of blackboards on available computing resources,

iii) the introduction of aliases allowing access to non-local blackboards,

iv) the possibility of load balancing by moving blackboards between locations.

These points are discussed at the non-formal level in the remainder of this section. A formal description of the resulting language, called μ^2Log, is given in the next section.

3.1 Multiple blackboards

Concepts. To start with, it is important to make our terminology clear. As it results from section 2, any moment of an execution can be described by giving

- a dataspace;
- a collection of processes, accessing this dataspace and being manipulated by *tell*, *read* and *get* primitives;
- a substitution summarizing the bindings having been made.

We shall subsequently call such a four-component construct *a blackboard*. Accordingly, an execution in μLog is referred to as an execution of a blackboard.

The μ^2Log approach. With these definitions in mind, one could think of several blackboards being executed simultaneously. This is certainly a desirable feature because, in addition to modularity, it provides processes with private memories and allows communication to occur locally between processes.

Our approach relies on the following two design decisions:

- Blackboards are manipulated by the same kind of primitives as terms and processes, namely by tell, read and get primitives. Although the class of blackboards will be considered as disjoint from the class of terms and processes in theory, we shall follow the convention of section 2.1 and suffix tell and get primitives by "bb" to stress the operation on blackboards.
- Processes can access data and processes on any blackboard.

3.2 Distribution

Concepts. Distribution arises from the perception of the existence of different computing resources possibly located at different places. Naturally we are lead to spread the blackboards on these resources. Related to that is the possibility of launching several executions of our framework at several places and making them communicate. Both extensions are supported by the μ^2Log framework. To explain how this is done, let us adopt the following terminology.

- A *processor* consists of computing resources. Practically, it can be, in the context of a network of workstations, part of a machine identified by the machine name and a port name, or, in the context of a parallel machine, a set of processors.
- A *$\mu^2 Log$ application* or *application*, for short, consists of the executions of several blackboards launched by a common initial query.
- An *abstract machine* consists in a processor-application pair.

The μ^2Log approach. Our approach on this point is threefold:

- blackboards are created locally;
- an execution in μ^2Log is not composed of the execution of one blackboard as in μLog but of the concurrent executions of applications;
- the execution of a blackboard is made with respect to a program attached to the application to which the blackboard belongs;
- access to nonlocal blackboards takes place via special links.

3.3 Aliases

Concepts. The possible dynamic evolution of a distributed system may render it difficult to track the exact location of a particular blackboard. In order to conveniently adapt to this dynamic evolution, an extra indirection on the blackboard naming is desirable.

The μ^2Log approach. This is achieved in μ^2Log by introducing virtual blackboards as special blackboards containing no data and no processes but pointing to other (possibly virtual) blackboards.

3.4 Load balancing

Concepts. Finally, it often happens that the load of processors varies during the execution. It is then important for the efficiency of the whole execution to dynamically balance this load. To that end, parts of executions may need to migrate from one place to another. This task may be supported at the implementation level in a way hidden to the programmer. However, in interactive systems, it is also very useful to provide programming means to that end.

The μ^2Log approach. This point is also addressed in the μ^2Log model by means of a primitive to move a blackboard from one processor to another one. Coupled with virtual blackboards, this primitive offers a powerful programming means to physically move the real blackboard from one place onto another in a way completely transparent for the majority of processes.

4 The language

As usual in logic programming, the μ^2Log framework comprises denumerably infinite sets of *variables*, *functions* and *predicates*. They are referred to as *Svar*, *Sfunct* and *Spred*, respectively. The notions of term, atom, substitution, ... are defined therefrom as usual (see e.g. [9]). Their set is referred to as *Sterm*, *Satom*, *Ssubst*, ..., respectively.

The μ^2Log framework comprises two additional infinite sets, disjoint from the above ones, to cope with its distributed coordination goal: a set of *blackboard names*, referred to as *Sbbname*, and a set of *processor names*, referred to as *Spr*.

An application in μ^2Log is launched by a query or an initial goal being asked on a processor. As already suggested, an execution in μ^2Log generally consists of several queries being concurrently asked on various processors.

It will be useful to identify applications. To that end, a new infinite set of application names, distinct from the previous ones, is introduced. It is subsequently referred to as *Sappl*.

Abstract machines are then formally defined as follows.

Definition 1. An abstract machine is defined as a 3-tuple composed of

i) a processor,
ii) an application name,
iii) a program, composed of a set of Horn clauses whose bodies are general goals and therefore can contain blackboard primitives.

The program of the abstract machine identified by ma, is subsequently referred to as P_{ma}. The set of abstract machines is subsequently referred to as Sma.

Definition 2. Blackboard primitives and goals are defined as follows:

i) the blackboard primitives are constructs of the form

$$
\begin{array}{lll}
tellbb(bbn, bbt, bbg), & tellt(bbn, t), & tellp(bbn, p), \\
readbb(bbn), & readt(bbn, t), & readp(bbn, p), \\
getbb(bbn), & gett(bbn, t), & getp(bbn, p), \\
tellvb(bbn_1, bbn_2@ma_2) & relink(bbn_1, bbn_2@ma_2), & exch(bbn_1, bbn_2@ma_2)
\end{array}
$$

where bbn, bbn_1, bbn_2 are blackboard names, t is a term, p is a goal, bbt is a list of terms, bbg is a list of goals, and ma_2 is an abstract machine name;

ii) any atom and any blackboard primitive is a goal;
iii) Δ is a goal, representing the empty goal;
iv) if G_1 and G_2 are goals, then so are the sequential composition G_1 ; G_2 and the parallel composition $G_1 \parallel G_2$.

The queries also called *initial goals* or *igoal's*, for short, are non-empty lists of goals $[G_1, \ldots, G_m]$ sharing no variables. The sets of goals and initial goals are subsequently referred to as *Sgoal* and *Sigoal*, respectively.

As suggested, the construct *tellbb* is used to create a new (local) blackboard named bbn with the terms of bbt and the processes of bbg as initial terms and processes, respectively. Similarly, *tellt* and *tellp* add a term and a process to the specified blackboard. The *readbb*, *readt*, *readp* primitives are respectively employed to check the presence of a blackboard, of a term on a blackboard and of a process on a blackboard. The *get* primitives not only check a blackboard, term or process but also remove them. The primitive $tellvb(bbn_1, bbn_2@ma_2)$ is used to create a (local) virtual blackboard named bbn_1 pointing to blackboard bbn_2 on the abstract machine ma_2. The primitive $relink(bbn_1, bbn_2@ma_2)$ is used to relink the virtual blackboard bbn_1 to the (possibly virtual) blackboard bbn_2 on the abstract machine ma_2. Finally, the primitive $exch(bbn_1, bbn_2@ma_2)$ with bbn_2 intended to be a virtual blackboard is used to reverse the link between bbn_1 and bbn_2 and, if bbn_1 is not virtual, to physically move the active and passive data from bbn_1 to bbn_2, the latter becoming non-virtual in that case.

It is here worth noting that the communication between μ^2Log processes is designed to be strictly limited to blackboard communication. To that end, terms and processes are actually renamed before being placed on a blackboard. Similarly, initial goals are requested to share no variables. This design decision initially imposed by the purity of the model has turned out to be crucial for implementability purposes. Among others, problems caused by distributed backtracking (see e.g. Delta-Prolog problems in [11]) are avoided.

All blackboards created by the reduction of an application inherit the program of the application. This explains why the *tellbb* does not specify any program. Refinements could include the definition of the programs as sets of modules (as in [10]) from which *tellbb* could extract those which would be told on the blackboard and used by processes running on it. However, this is not essential for the purpose of this paper and is thus left for future work.

The μ^2Log framework distinguishes two kinds of processes. Processes that are created at blackboard start up time are called *foreground processes*. They correspond, one the one hand, to the parallel resolution of the goals of the considered initial goal, and, on the other hand, to the processes created together with a new blackboard. Note that the former case can actually be regarded as a specific case of the latter one. Indeed, foreground processes can be viewed as engendered by the creation of the first blackboard, subsequently called *init_app* following the name *app* of the considered application. These goals are requested to terminate to allow the whole computation to be considered as successful.

Processes that are created at run time on blackboards are called *background processes*. They act as daemons on the blackboards and have their effect on the blackboards as unique point of interest. Hence, their termination and failure is of no concern for the success of the computation. Non-terminating processes are important for providing internal services in parallel applications. They are automatically killed when the application terminates, i.e., when the foreground processes are all terminated.

Foreground and background processes are formalized as follows.

Definition 3. Foreground and background processes are constructs of the form $\leftarrow G \Diamond \theta$ and $\leftarrow\!\!\!\leftarrow G \Diamond \theta$, respectively, where G is a goal and θ is a substitution. A process is either a foreground process or a background process. It is denoted by an "$\Leftarrow$" arrow (as in $\Leftarrow G \Diamond \theta$) when there is no concern for its qualification of being foreground or background.

Convention 4. Given an igoal ig, we denote by $\overline{ig}$ the associated list of processes obtained by considering all the goals of ig as foreground processes and by associating each goal with the empty substitution ϵ.

5 Operational Semantics

We now formally describe the operational semantics of μ^2Log. The configurations to be considered are described in the next section. The transition rules are presented in section 5.2. A (formal) operational semantics together with the success set semantics are defined in section 5.3.

5.1 Configurations

Classically, configurations for languages are composed of the current statement to be solved accompanied by a state, summing up the results computed sofar. In our context, the contents of the blackboards sums up both the active components, corresponding to the statements, and the passive components, corresponding to the states. Configurations to be considered here thus report the current contents of the blackboards. According to sections 3 and 4, the description of each blackboard should include its name (bbn), its terms (bbt) and its processes (bbp), with each process being described by an expression of the form $\Leftarrow G \Diamond \theta$ where G is the goal to be solved and θ is the substitution summing up the values computed sofar for its variables. Note that, because processes do not share variables, it is possible to make local the bindings relative to the processes in a substitution associated with them. Moreover, this description should also include the name ma of the abstract machine on which it is running.

Virtual blackboards are special blackboards containing no terms and processes and pointing to other blackboards. Accordingly, the description for these blackboards does not contain bbt and bbp components. Furthermore, the bbn component is replaced by a construct of the form $bbn_1 \leadsto bbn_2$ to indicate that the blackboard under consideration, identified by bbn_1 is pointing to blackboard bbn_2.

Summing up, configurations are thus sets of elements of one of the following forms, corresponding respectively to real and virtual blackboards. For clarity, blackboard names, and abstract machines are grouped as in $bbn@ma$.

1. $\langle bbn@ma, bbt, bbp \rangle$.
2. $\langle bbn_1@ma_1 \leadsto bbn_2@ma_2 \rangle$.

The set of configurations is subsequently denoted by $Sconf$.

The transition rules allow to pick some processes and blackboards inside multi-sets and sets, respectively. For the ease of notation and to avoid any ambiguity, we will use the following two conventions.

On the one hand, the notation $m[\,]$ is introduced to denote a multiset where a place holder has been introduced at some place and the notation $m[e]$ is used to denote the multiset obtained from $m[\,]$ by substituting the place holder by the element e. Manipulations will possibly lead to derive from such a multiset m, similar multisets, noted m', where the place holder may be removed. In such a case, by abuse of notation, the expression $m'[e]$ is used to denote the multiset m', the element e thus being discarded. We will denote by $m_1 + m_2$ the multiset resulting from the union of the two multisets m_1 and m_2.

On the other hand, we will use the notations $\{\!|\ e\ |\!\}$, $\{\!|\ e_1\ e_2\ |\!\}$, and $\{\!|\ e_1\ e_2\ e_3\ |\!\}$ to respectively denote a set (not necessarily reduced to one, two or three elements) in which the element e, the elements e_1, e_2, and the elements e_1, e_2, e_3 have been selected. With respect to blackboards, by convention, e_1, e_2 and e_3 will be considered to denote the same element in case they have the same name. The notation $\{\!|\ |\!\}$ will be used to denote the above sets where the elements e, e_1, e_2, e_3 have been removed.

Finally, it turns out that the behavior of compound goals is determined by the behavior of elementary parts, namely of atoms and of blackboard primitives. The transition system can thus be defined by specifying the transition rules for the basic reductions of atoms and of blackboard primitives, and by giving the (classical) rules of composition for the compound goals. However, these last rules can be expressed directly in the former rules provided a suitable notion of context is introduced. Essentially, such a context determines, thanks to a place holder ∇, which atoms or blackboard primitives can be reduced in any goal. The resulting goal is then obtained from the goal under consideration by replacing the reduced atoms and blackboard primitives by their corresponding subgoals according to their reduction.

Definition 5. The contexts are the functions inductively defined on the goals by the following rules. They are typically represented by the letter c, possibly subscripted.

i) ∇ is a context that maps any goal to itself. For any goal G, this application is subsequently referred to as $\nabla[G]$.

ii) If c is a context and if G is a goal, then $(c \; ; \; G)$, $(c \parallel G)$, $(G \parallel c)$ are contexts. Their applications are defined as follows: for any goal G',

$$(c \; ; \; G)[G'] = c[G'] \; ; \; G$$
$$(c \parallel G)[G'] = c[G'] \parallel G$$
$$(G \parallel c)[G'] = G \parallel c[G']$$

In the above rules, we further state that the structure $(Sgoal, ; , \parallel , \triangle)$ is a bimonoid. Moreover, in the following, we will simplify the goals resulting from the application of contexts accordingly.

5.2 Transition rules

The operational behavior of $\mu^2 \text{Log}$ processes is formally defined as in [12] by means of a transition relation, itself specified by rules of the form

$$CC_1 \to CC_2 \quad \text{if} \quad Conditions,$$

that asserts the transition from the configuration CC_1 to the configuration CC_2 whenever the *Conditions* hold.

Definition 6. Define the transition relation $\to$ as the smallest relation of $Sconf \times Sconf$ satisfying the rules (A_g) to (Rel) of figures 1, 2, 3, 4, and 5. As usual, for the ease of reading, the more suggestive notation $CC_1 \to CC_2$ is subsequently employed instead of $\to (CC_1, CC_2)$.

Note that, thanks to the bimonoid structure imposed in definition 5, it is implicitly understood in the rules (A_g) to (Rel) that $(\triangle \; ; \; G)$, $(\triangle \parallel G)$, $(G \parallel \triangle)$ are to be interpreted as G. It is also assumed there that the foreground and background qualifications

(A_g) $\{ \langle n@ma, bt, m[\Leftarrow c[A]\Diamond\theta]\rangle \} \rightarrow \{ \langle n@ma, bt, m[\Leftarrow c[B]\gamma\Diamond\theta\gamma]\rangle \}$

$$if \left\{ \begin{array}{l} (H \leftarrow B) \text{ is a fresh renaming of a clause of } P_{ma} \\ H \text{ and } A \text{ unify with mgu } \gamma \end{array} \right\}$$

Fig. 1. Atom reduction

are respected by the "$\Leftarrow$" arrow that is that, in any rule, all the occurrences of the "$\Leftarrow$" arrow have to be replaced either by the "$\leftarrow$" arrow or by the "$\leftrightarrow$" arrow.

A word on the meaning of the above rules is in order. Rule (A_g) rephrases the usual reduction of an atom in our framework. Rule (T_b) describes the creation of a blackboard with the set of terms bbt and the foreground processes corresponding to the goals of bbp. Rule (T_v) describes the creation of a virtual blackboard. Rules (T_t) and (T_p) explain the writing of terms and processes on the blackboard, respectively. Writing to a virtual blackboard, and writing to a physical blackboard are modeled with one single transition by allowing chains of virtual blackboards of length 0 (obtained for $i = 0$). Rules (G_b), (G_v), (G_t), (G_p), (R_b), (R_v), (R_t) and (R_p) describe the reading of blackboards, virtual blackboards, terms and processes with or without consumption. Particularly notice the renamings in the rules (T_b) to (G_p). They ensure that processes communicate only via writing and reading of terms on the blackboard and not implicitly by means of shared variables.

Finally, for simplicity we have not given the rules for the cases when $n = bbn$ or $n = bbn_i$. In these cases, the blackboard operations are carried out on the blackboard that issued the operation in a completely analogous way.

5.3 Semantics

We are now in a position to define an operational semantics. In $\mu^2\text{Log}$, a successful computation is one for which all the foreground processes (of all the blackboards) have been reduced to empty goals, while some background processes are possibly still running on some blackboards. A first natural property to be reported by the operational semantics thus consists of the substitutions computed by those successful computations. However, it is also interesting to account for failed computations, which may actually result from three different reasons: infinite computations, the absence of suitable information on a blackboard, of links between blackboards or of blackboards (suspension) and the absence of suitable clauses (real failure). The proposed operational semantics will also tackle these features. To that end, it delivers for a set of concurrent applications not a set of substitutions but rather a set of so-called computational histories defined as words of substitutions, each one summing up the substitutions associated with the processes of the blackboards at the considered moment of the execution. Termination status marks are appended to indicate success, real failure or suspension.

Definition 7. A set of configurations is called *successfully terminated* iff all its foreground processes are of the form $\leftarrow \Delta\Diamond\theta$ for some substitution θ.

(T_b) $\{\!\!|$ $\langle n@ma, bt, m[\Leftarrow c[tellbb(bbn, bbt, bbg)]\Diamond\theta]\rangle \; |\!\!\} \rightarrow$
      $\{\!\!|$ $\langle n@ma, bt, m[\Leftarrow c[\Delta]\Diamond\theta]\rangle \; |\!\!\} \cup \{\langle bbn@ma, bbt', \overline{bbg'}\rangle\}$

$$if \left\{ \begin{array}{c} \text{no blackboard is identified by } bbn@ma \text{ in the initial configuration} \\ bbt' \text{ and } bbg' \text{ are respectively obtained from } bbt \text{ and } bbg \\ \text{by freshly renaming their elements individually} \end{array} \right\}$$

(T_v) $\{\!\!|$ $\langle n@ma, bt, m[\Leftarrow c[tellvb(bbn_1, bbn_2@ma_2)]\Diamond\theta]\rangle \; |\!\!\} \rightarrow$
      $\{\!\!|$ $\langle n@ma, bt, m[\Leftarrow c[\Delta]\Diamond\theta]\rangle \langle bbn_1@ma \rightsquigarrow bbn_2@ma_2\rangle \; |\!\!\}$

$$if \left\{ \text{ there exists a blackboard in the initial configuration identified by } bbn_2@ma_2 \right\}$$

(T_t) $\{\!\!|$ $\langle n@ma, bt, m[\Leftarrow c[tellt(bbn, t)]\Diamond\theta]\rangle \langle bbn_0@ma_0 \rightsquigarrow bbn_1@ma_1\rangle \cdots$
      $\langle bbn_{i-1}@ma_{i-1} \rightsquigarrow bbn_i@ma_i\rangle \langle bbn_i@ma_i, bt', bp'\rangle \; |\!\!\} \rightarrow$
      $\{\!\!|$ $\langle n@ma, bt, m[\Leftarrow c[\Delta]\Diamond\theta]\rangle \langle bbn_0@ma_0 \rightsquigarrow bbn_1@ma_1\rangle \cdots$
      $\langle bbn_{i-1}@ma_{i-1} \rightsquigarrow bbn_i@ma_i\rangle \langle bbn_i@ma_i, bt' + \{u\}, bp'\rangle \; |\!\!\}$

$$if \left\{ \begin{array}{l} u \text{ is a fresh renaming of } t \\ bbn_0 = bbn \\ 0 \leq i \end{array} \right\}$$

(T_p) $\{\!\!|$ $\langle n@ma, bt, m[\Leftarrow c[tellp(bbn, p)]\Diamond\theta]\rangle \langle bbn_0@ma_0 \rightsquigarrow bbn_1@ma_1\rangle \cdots$
      $\langle bbn_{i-1}@ma_{i-1} \rightsquigarrow bbn_i@ma_i\rangle \langle bbn_i@ma_i, bt', bp'\rangle \; |\!\!\} \rightarrow$
      $\{\!\!|$ $\langle n@ma, bt, m[\Leftarrow c[\Delta]\Diamond\theta]\rangle \langle bbn_0@ma_0 \rightsquigarrow bbn_1@ma_1\rangle \cdots$
      $\langle bbn_{i-1}@ma_{i-1} \rightsquigarrow bbn_i@ma_i\rangle \langle bbn_i@ma_i, bt', bp' + \{ \hookleftarrow q\Diamond\epsilon\}\rangle \; |\!\!\}$

$$if \left\{ \begin{array}{l} q \text{ is a fresh renaming of } p \\ bbn_0 = bbn \\ 0 \leq i \end{array} \right\}$$

Fig. 2. Tell reductions

Definition 8. The set of words formed from $Ssubst$ and whose finite elements are ended by one of the termination marks δ^+ (representing success), δ^s (representing suspension), and δ^- (representing failure) is referred to as $Sohist$. Its elements are called *operational histories*.

Definition 9. Given a set of configurations BB, we denote by $\Theta(BB)$ the union of the substitutions associated with the processes of BB. Note that because renaming is made before each operation on any blackboard and because processes are forced to share no variables, such a union consists of a well-defined substitution.

Definition 10. Let $\mathcal{P}_{nf}(Sapp)$ denote the set of finite sets of applications. Define the *operational semantics* as the following function $\mathcal{O} : \mathcal{P}_{nf}(Sapp) \rightarrow \mathcal{P}(Sohist)$: for any finite set of applications $S = \{<ig_1, pr_1, app_1, P_1>, \cdots, <ig_n, pr_n, app_n, P_n>\}$

$(\mathbf{R}_b)$ $\{\!\!\{\ \langle n@ma, bt, m[\Leftarrow c[readbb(bbn)]\lozenge\theta]\rangle\ \langle bbn@ma, bbt, bbp\rangle\ \}\!\!\} \rightarrow$
$\qquad \{\!\!\{\ \langle n@ma, bt, m[\Leftarrow c[\triangle]\lozenge\theta]\rangle\ \langle bbn@ma, bbt, bbp\rangle\ \}\!\!\}$

$(\mathbf{R}_v)$ $\{\!\!\{\ \langle n@ma, bt, m[\Leftarrow c[readbb(bbn)]\lozenge\theta]\rangle\ \langle bbn@ma \leadsto bbn'@ma'\rangle\ \}\!\!\} \rightarrow$
$\qquad \{\!\!\{\ \langle n@ma, bt, m[\Leftarrow c[\triangle]\lozenge\theta]\rangle\ \langle bbn@ma \leadsto bbn'@ma'\rangle\ \}\!\!\}$

$(\mathbf{R}_t)$ $\{\!\!\{\ \langle n@ma, bt, m[\Leftarrow c[readt(bbn,t)]\lozenge\theta]\rangle\ \langle bbn_0@ma_0 \leadsto bbn_1@ma_1\rangle \cdots$
$\qquad \langle bbn_{i-1}@ma_{i-1} \leadsto bbn_i@ma_i\rangle\ \langle bbn_i@ma_i, bt', bp'\rangle\ \}\!\!\} \rightarrow$
$\qquad \{\!\!\{\ \langle n@ma, bt, m[\Leftarrow c[\triangle]\lozenge\theta]\rangle\ \langle bbn_0@ma_0 \leadsto bbn_1@ma_1\rangle \cdots$
$\qquad \langle bbn_{i-1}@ma_{i-1} \leadsto bbn_i@ma_i\rangle\ \langle bbn_i@ma_i, bt', bp'\rangle\ \}\!\!\}$

$$if \begin{cases} \exists v \in bt' : \text{ any fresh renaming } v' \text{ of } v \text{ unifies with } t \\ \gamma \text{ is the mgu corresponding to the unification of } t \\ \qquad \text{and of some fresh renaming of such a term } v \\ bbn_0 = bbn \\ 0 \leq i \end{cases}$$

$(\mathbf{R}_p)$ $\{\!\!\{\ \langle n@ma, bt, m[\Leftarrow c[readp(bbn,p)]\lozenge\theta]\rangle\ \langle bbn@ma \leadsto bbn_1@ma_1\rangle \cdots$
$\qquad \langle bbn_{i-1}@ma_{i-1} \leadsto bbn_i@ma_i\rangle\ \langle bbn_i@ma_i, bt', bp'\rangle\ \}\!\!\} \rightarrow$
$\qquad \{\!\!\{\ \langle n@ma, bt, m[\Leftarrow c[\triangle]\lozenge\theta]\rangle\ \langle bbn_0@ma_0 \leadsto bbn_1@ma_1\rangle \cdots$
$\qquad \langle bbn_{i-1}@ma_{i-1} \leadsto bbn_i@ma_i\rangle\ \langle bbn_i@ma_i, bt', bp'\rangle\ \}\!\!\}$

$$if \begin{cases} \exists(\leftarrow G) \in bp' : \text{ any fresh renaming } G' \text{ of } G \text{ unifies with } p \\ \gamma \text{ is the mgu corresponding to the unification of } p \text{ and of some fresh} \\ \qquad \text{renaming of such a process } \leftarrow G \\ bbn_0 = bbn \\ 0 \leq i \end{cases}$$

Fig. 3. Read reductions

$$\begin{aligned} \mathcal{O}(S) = \ & \{\Theta(BB_0).\cdots.\Theta(BB_m).\delta^+ : (1,2,5,6)\} \\ & \cup \{\Theta(BB_0).\cdots.\Theta(BB_m).\delta^- : (1,3), not(5), not(7)\} \\ & \cup \{\Theta(BB_0).\cdots.\Theta(BB_m).\delta^s : (1,3,7), not(5)\} \\ & \cup \{\Theta(BB_0).\cdots.\Theta(BB_m).\cdots : (1,4,8)\} \end{aligned}$$

where $BB_0, \ldots, BB_m, \ldots \in \mathcal{P}(Sconf)$ and (1), ..., (8) stand for the following conditions:

(1) $BB_0 = \{\langle init\_app_1@ma_1, \emptyset, \overline{ig_1}\rangle, \cdots, \langle init\_app_n@ma_n, \emptyset, \overline{ig_n}\rangle\}$, where, $init\_app_i$ is the name of the initial blackboard corresponding to application app_i and ma_i is the triplet (pr_i, app_i, P_i),

(2) $BB_0 \rightarrow \cdots \rightarrow BB_m$,

(3) $BB_0 \rightarrow \cdots \rightarrow BB_m \not\rightarrow$,

(4) $BB_0 \rightarrow \cdots \rightarrow BB_m \rightarrow \cdots$,

(G_b) $\{\!|$ $\langle n@ma, bt, m[\Leftarrow c[getbb(bbn)]\Diamond\theta]\rangle$ $\langle bbn@ma, bbt, bbp\rangle$ $|\!\}$ $\rightarrow$
$\qquad \{\!|$ $\langle n@ma, bt, m[\Leftarrow c[\triangle]\Diamond\theta]\rangle$ $|\!\}$

(G_v) $\{\!|$ $\langle n@ma, bt, m[\Leftarrow c[getbb(bbn)]\Diamond\theta]\rangle$ $\langle bbn@ma \rightsquigarrow bbn'@ma'\rangle$ $|\!\}$ $\rightarrow$
$\qquad \{\!|$ $\langle n@ma, bt, m[\Leftarrow c[\triangle]\Diamond\theta]\rangle$ $|\!\}$

(G_t) $\{\!|$ $\langle n@ma, bt, m[\Leftarrow c[gett(bbn, t)]\Diamond\theta]\rangle$ $\langle bbn_0@ma_0 \rightsquigarrow bbn_1@ma_1\rangle$ $\cdots$
$\qquad \langle bbn_{i-1}@ma_{i-1} \rightsquigarrow bbn_i@ma_i\rangle$ $\langle bbn_i@ma_i, bt', bp'\}\rangle$ $|\!\}$ $\rightarrow$
$\qquad \{\!|$ $\langle n@ma, bt, m[\Leftarrow c[\triangle]\Diamond\theta]\rangle$ $\langle bbn_0@ma_0 \rightsquigarrow bbn_1@ma_1\rangle$ $\cdots$
$\qquad \langle bbn_{i-1}@ma_{i-1} \rightsquigarrow bbn_i@ma_i\rangle$ $\langle bbn_i@ma_i, bt'', bp'\rangle$ $|\!\}$

$$if \begin{cases} \exists v \in bt' : \text{ any fresh renaming } v' \text{ of } v \text{ unifies with } t \\ u \text{ is such a term } v \text{ in } bt' \\ \gamma \text{ is the mgu corresponding to the unification of } t \\ \qquad \text{and of some fresh renaming of } u \\ bt'' \text{ is } bbt \text{ where } u \text{ has been removed} \\ bbn_0 = bbn \\ 0 \leq i \end{cases}$$

(G_p) $\{\!|$ $\langle n@ma, bt, m[\Leftarrow c[getp(bbn, p)]\Diamond\theta]\rangle$ $\langle bbn_0@ma_0 \rightsquigarrow bbn_1@ma_1\rangle$ $\cdots$
$\qquad \langle bbn_{i-1}@ma_{i-1} \rightsquigarrow bbn_i@ma_i\rangle$ $\langle bbn_i@ma_i, bt', bp'\rangle$ $|\!\}$ $\rightarrow$
$\qquad \{\!|$ $\langle n@ma, bt, m[\Leftarrow c[\triangle]\Diamond\theta]\rangle$ $\langle bbn_0@ma_0 \rightsquigarrow bbn_1@ma_1\rangle$ $\cdots$
$\qquad \langle bbn_{i-1}@ma_{i-1} \rightsquigarrow bbn_i@ma_i\rangle$ $\langle bbn_i@ma_i, bt', bp''\rangle$ $|\!\}$

$$if \begin{cases} \exists(\hookleftarrow G) \in bp' : \text{ any fresh renaming } G' \text{ of } G \text{ unifies with } p \\ \hookleftarrow G'' \text{ is such a process } \hookleftarrow G \text{ in } bp' \\ \gamma \text{ is the mgu corresponding to the unification of } p \text{ and of some fresh} \\ \qquad \text{renaming of } G'' \\ bp'' \text{ is } bp' \text{ where the process corresponding to } \hookleftarrow G'' \text{ has been removed} \\ bbn_0 = bbn \\ 0 \leq i \end{cases}$$

Fig. 4. Get reductions

(5) BB_m is successfully terminated,

(6) BB_i is not successfully terminated for $1 \leq i < m$,

(7) there are $n' \in Sbbname$, $bt' \in \mathcal{M}(Sterm)$, $bg' \in Sbg$, $k, l \in \{1, \cdots, n\}$, $BB_{m+1} \in Sconf$, such that $BB_m \uplus \{< n'@ma_l, bt', bg' >\} -_{BB_m} \rightarrow BB_{m+1}$ where $-_{BB_m} \rightarrow$ indicates a transition due to a process of BB_m, and where Sbg denotes the set of (possibly empty) multisets of background processes,

(8) none of the $BB_i's$ is successfully terminated.

As usual, we assume that condition (6) is trivially verified in case $m = 0$.

The careful reader will have noticed that suspending read and get primitives have only been treated. However, it is easy to modify the above transition rules to account for non-suspending but failing versions of these primitives. Indeed, it is sufficient for that

(E$_1$) $\{\!| \ \langle n@ma, bt, m[\Leftarrow c[exch(bbn_1, bbn_2@ma_2)]\Diamond\theta]\rangle \ \langle bbn_1@ma, bbt, bbp\rangle$
$\quad\quad \langle bbn_2@ma_2 \rightsquigarrow bbn_1@ma\rangle \ |\!\} \ \rightarrow$
$\quad\quad \{\!| \ \langle n@ma, bt, m[\Leftarrow c[\triangle]\Diamond\theta]\rangle \ \langle bbn_1@ma \rightsquigarrow bbn_2@ma_2\rangle \ \langle bbn_2@ma_2, bbt, bbp\rangle \ |\!\}$

(E$_2$) $\{\!| \ \langle n@ma, bt, m[\Leftarrow c[exch(bbn_1, bbn_2@ma_2)]\Diamond\theta]\rangle \ \langle bbn_1@ma \rightsquigarrow bbn_3@ma_3\rangle$
$\quad\quad \langle bbn_2@ma_2 \rightsquigarrow bbn_1@ma\rangle \ |\!\} \ \rightarrow$
$\quad\quad \{\!| \ \langle n@ma, bt, m[\Leftarrow c[\triangle]\Diamond\theta]\rangle \ \langle bbn_1@ma \rightsquigarrow bbn_2@ma_2\rangle$
$\quad\quad \langle bbn_2@ma_2 \rightsquigarrow bbn_3@ma_3\rangle \ |\!\}$

(Rel) $\{\!| \ \langle n@ma, bt, m[\Leftarrow c[relink(bbn_1, bbn_3@ma_3)]\Diamond\theta]\rangle \ \langle bbn_1@ma \rightsquigarrow bbn_2@ma_2\rangle \ |\!\}$
$\quad\quad \rightarrow \{\!| \ \langle n@ma, bt, m[\Leftarrow c[\triangle]\Diamond\theta]\rangle \ \langle bbn_1@ma \rightsquigarrow bbn_3@ma_3\rangle \ |\!\}$

$\quad\quad\quad$ *if* $\big\{$ there exists a blackboard in the initial configuration identified by $bbn_3@ma_3$ $\big\}$

Fig. 5. Exchange and relink reductions

purpose to introduce an explicit fail configuration and to make transitions to that configuration for non-suspending primitives due to a lack of blackboards, terms or processes.

6 Implementation

In order to prove the feasibility of the concept, μ^2Log has been implemented in BinProlog. The resulting language is named MultiBinProlog accordingly; it is available by ftp at the address `ftp://clement.info.umoncton.ca/pub/MultiBinProlog`. MultiBinProlog runs under Solaris 2.5 and is a fast shared dataspace implementation in logic programming.

For the implementation of the blackboard, the threads library of Solaris 2.5 is used. The blackboard is just a chunk of memory that is managed by the blackboard access routines. Initially, a blackboard is 4 KB, but it can be dynamically extended to any size.

The blackboard routines update the blackboard data structure in a synchronized way. A blackboard consists basically of two lists: a list with waiting terms, and a list with waiting processes. Before accessing a blackboard, the blackboard primitives must first lock the blackboard to ensure exclusive access. The following algorithms are used to tell, get or read a term.

Algorithm: tell a term on the blackboard.

Input. A blackboard B and a term t.
Output. An updated blackboard B.
Method.

1. Lock blackboard B.
2. Take the oldest waiting process p on blackboard B.
3. If term t unifies with the term process p is waiting for, go to step 4, else go to step 6.

4. Communicate the term t with process p, resume process p and delete it from the list of waiting processes of blackboard B.
5. If process p was suspended by a destructive gett-operation, go to step 8.
6. Take the next oldest waiting process p on blackboard B and go to step 3 if such a process p exists.
7. Add term t to the blackboard B as the youngest waiting term.
8. Unlock blackboard B.

Algorithm: get or read a term from the blackboard.

Input. A blackboard B, a get or read operation o, and a timestamp ts.

Output. An updated blackboard B.

Method.

1. Lock blackboard B.
2. Take the oldest waiting term t that is not older than timestamp ts on blackboard B.
3. If term t unifies with the term the get or read operation o is associated with, go to step 4, else go to step 6.
4. If the operation o is a get operation, remove term t from the list of waiting terms of blackboard B.
5. Unlock blackboard B, and go to step 10.
6. Take the next oldest waiting term t on blackboard B and go to step 3 is such a term exists.
7. Add the operation o to the blackboard B as the youngest waiting process.
8. Unlock blackboard B.
9. Wait until this operation o is resumed due to the addition of a term to blackboard B by another process.
10. End of algorithm

The timestamp of the get or read operation keeps the age of the oldest term that can be read. Every term on the blackboard has a *timestamp*. The timestamp of the last term read is stored in the choice point associated with the blackboard manipulation routine. This value is used during backtracking to remember up to where the term list has been processed.

When tellt has found a waiting process to communicate a term with, it will directly write the result of the unification operation onto the heap of the suspended process. It can do so because (i) the blackboard is locked, and (ii) the owner of the heap is suspended. Hence, there is no need for synchronization, and all the relevant registers are accessible in memory.

The most distinguishing characteristic of this implementation is that the blackboard is completely passive, i.e., it is just a data structure. A passive approach offers considerable advantages over a process-based approach.

- It is more robust. Even after a crash, one can inspect the contents of the blackboard. This is more difficult if the blackboard contents are stored in a data structure that is passed around all the time.

- Communication with the blackboard does not need an intervention of a scheduler. Getting a term from the blackboard is nothing more than changing a number of fields of the blackboard data structure. In the process-based approach, the blackboard process must be activated before the communication can take place.
- In theory, a blackboard data structure can allow simultaneous updates of its substructures. A blackboard process can only handle one request at a time.

The distributed implementation uses the standard Unix RPC library to support the communication between virtual and remote blackboards (which can be either a physical or virtual blackboard). In order to grant access to external processes, an application must first create a *blackboard server*. This server is an RPC-server that accepts the blackboard requests from the remote virtual blackboards. Any incoming request is processed by a new lightweight thread. It is important to notice that this allows the local blackboard to remain passive. The threads created by the blackboard server are in no way different from the other background processes in the system. They both use the same blackboard access primitives. Since a new thread per incoming request is created, the access primitives are free to fail, suspend, etc. They do not disturb the normal operation of the blackboard.

On the client side, in order to create a virtual blackboard, a link must first be created with the blackboard server of the remote blackboard. Subsequent blackboard operations are forwarded to the blackboard server. The client will suspend until an answer is returned by the blackboard server. Hence, the client will not notice any behavioral difference between a (local) physical and a virtual blackboard (except for the performance). Almost all blackboard operations have the same semantics on physical and virtual blackboards, except a few. Killing a blackboard means physically removing it, except for a virtual blackboard where it means removing the virtual blackboard (but not the physical one so that the blackboard data are preserved).

7 Related Work

MultiBinProlog is certainly not the only Linda-like parallel logic programming language in existence today. Several Linda-like primitives have been incorporated in the languages Linda-D-Prolog [14], Sicstus Prolog [3] and FLiPSiDE [13]. None of these languages however feature such a tight integration between Prolog and the coordination component as $\mu^2 Log$ does.

Shared Prolog [2] and PoliS [5] also have such a tight integration and offer a similar functionality but they differ from $\mu^2 Log$ at the programming level. Programming in μLog is very close to programming in Prolog and requires only an adaptation for the blackboard related primitives, not for the Prolog part. In contrast, programming in Shared Prolog or PoliS requires to become familiar with pre-activation and post-activation parts, with guards and commitment, ..., and to think directly in parallel terms. Other differences are that the blackboard communication can only take place at specific places. Furthermore, processes in Polis are stateless meaning that sequential activations of the same process can only communicate by means of the shared dataspace, which is a serious performance drawback, especially in a distributed environment: the state of a process is a strictly local issue, and we believe that it is better not to keep this on a shared data space. Finally, the distinction between intra-agent and inter-agent communication has also been made in ESP [5]. There it is called closed and open communication. The open communication scheme is however not a natural extension of the closed communication scheme in that the access to a remote dataspace is limited to write access, and a special construct is needed (a shell) in order to have full access to a remote dataspace.

Linda [7] and Polis Prolog [4] support multiple tuple spaces in a similar way as μ^2Log does. However, our framework is more integrated as we use tell/read/get primitives not only to manipulate data, but also to manipulate processes and blackboards. PoliS is more restricted than μ^2Log in that a PoliS agent can only write to and not read from remote tuple spaces. This is a severe restriction that prohibits to use a tuple space to make information public on a network.

At the implementation level, a logic tuple space in PoliS is implemented as a Prolog process, and inter-tuple space communication takes place via a meta tuple space. Both the process and the meta tuple space form a bottleneck when it comes to large distributed applications. μ^2Log does not have this restriction because (i) a blackboard is a data structure, not a process, and several user processes can access different parts of the blackboard simultaneously, and (ii) remote blackboard communication is point to point between a user process and a blackboard, without the intervention of a meta-blackboard.

8 Conclusion

This paper describes μ^2Log at the language level, the semantic level and at the implementation level. μ^2Log is an extension of μLog with multiple blackboards that can be distributed, accessed, and even moved over a network. The concept of virtual blackboard is introduced to allow inter-application communication to take place in a convenient way and to allow blackboards to move to another location without disturbing the operation of processes operating on it. An operational semantics of the full set of blackboard primitives is presented, and an efficient implementation is discussed.

9 Acknowledgements

The authors are supported by the Belgian National Fund for Scientific Research as senior research assistants. They are grateful to B. Le Charlier and J. Van Campenhout for their support and advice. Part of this work has been carried out in the context of the INTAS project 93-1702 "Efficient Symbolic Computing".

References

1. K. De Bosschere and J.-M. Jacquet. Comparative Semantics of μLog. In D. Etiemble and J.-C. Syre, editors, *Proceedings of the PARLE'92 Conference*, volume 605 of *Lecture Notes in Computer Science*, pages 911–926, Paris, 1992. Springer-Verlag.
2. Antonio Brogi and Paolo Ciancarini. The Concurrent Language Shared Prolog. *ACM Transactions on Programming Languages and Systems*, 13(1):99–123, January 1991.

3. M. Carlsson, J. Widén, J. Andersson, S. Andersson, K. Boortz, H. Nilsson, and T. Sjöland. SICStus Prolog User's Manual. SICS technical report T91:11B, SICS, Kista, Sweden, 1991.
4. P. Ciancarini. Parallel Logic Programming using the Linda model of Computation. In Goos and Hartmanis, editors, *Proceedings of Research Directions in High-Level Parallel Programming Languages*. Springer Verlag, Mont Saint Michel, France, June 1991, pages 110–125.
5. P. Ciancarini. Distributed programming with logic tuple spaces. Technical report ublcs-93-7, University of Bologna, April 1993.
6. D. Gelernter. Generative Communication in Linda. *ACM Transactions on Programming Languages and Systems*, 7(1):80–112, January 1985.
7. David Gelernter. Multiple Tuple Spaces in Linda. In *Proceedings of the PARLE'89 Conference*, volume 365 of *Lecture notes on Computer Science*, pages 20–27, 1989.
8. J.-M. Jacquet and K. De Bosschere. On the Semantics of μLog. *Future Generation Computer Systems*, 10:93–135, 1994.
9. J.W. Lloyd. *Foundations of Logic Programming*. Springer-Verlag, second edition, 1987.
10. L. Monteiro and A. Porto. Contextual Logic Programming. In G. Levi and M. Martelli, editors, *Proc. 6th Int. Conf. on Logic Programming*, pages 284–302, Lisboa, 1989. The MIT Press.
11. L.M. Pereira, L. Monteiro, J. Cunha, and J.N. Aparício. Delta Prolog : A Distributed Backtracking Extension with Events. In G. Goos and J. Hartmanis, editors, *Proceedings of the Third International Conference on Logic Programming*, volume 225 of *Lecture Notes in Computer Science*, London, July 1986. Springer Verlag.
12. G. Plotkin. A Structured Approach to Operational Semantics. Technical Report DAIMI FN-19, Computer Science Department, Aarhus University, 1981.
13. D.G. Schwartz. *Cooperating Heterogeneous Systems: A Blackboard-based Meta Approach*. PhD thesis, Department of Computer Engineering and Science, Case Western Reserve University, 1993.
14. G. Sutcliffe and J. Pinakis. Prolog-D-Linda: An Embedding of Linda in SICStus Prolog. Technical Report 91/7, Department of Computer Science, University of Western Australia, 1991.

A Process Algebra Based on Linda*

Rocco De Nicola** and Rosario Pugliese

Dipartimento di Scienze dell'Informazione
Università di Roma "La Sapienza"
Via Salaria 113, 00198 Roma (ITALY)

Abstract. The problem of comparing and analyzing the relationships between distributed programs written in the same concurrent programming language is addressed. It arises each time one wants to establish program correctness with respect to a notion of "being an approximation of". We define a testing scenario for PAL, a process algebra which is obtained by embedding the Linda primitives for interprocess communication in a CSP like process description language. We present a proof system for PAL processes which is sound and complete with respect to the behavioural relation and illustrate how it works by giving a small example.

1 Introduction

The availability of sophisticated parallel hardware at a limited cost has led to a proliferation of languages aiming at taking advantage of the new computing capability. These programming languages are equipped with primitives for *interprogram communication* and permit designing concurrent and distributed programs.

A major problem to face is that concurrent and distributed programs are difficult to design and debug. The possible interactions which can occur when two or more concurrent programs are simultaneously executed may give rise to new unwanted behaviours and may lead to nondeterministic behaviour.

¿From the point of view of theoretical computer science, there had been several efforts to better understand concurrent systems and to develop methods for reasoning about concurrent programs in a rigorous and formal way. One of the theoretical approaches is the *algebraic* one; it rests on the notion of *Process Algebras* (CCS [23], ACP [2], CSP [18], etc.).

The idea underlying Process Algebras is that distributed systems may be modelled as sets of concurrent communicating processes. Their main aim is that of providing both description languages and techniques for verifying correctness.

---

* Work partially supported by EEC within the HCM Project EXPRESS, and by CNR within the project "Specifica ad Alto Livello e Verifica di Sistemi Digitali".
** Author's current address: Dipartimento di Sistemi ed Informatica, Università di Firenze, Via Lombroso 6/17, 50134 Firenze (ITALY).

The languages are based on sets of few basic constructs which have intuitive interpretations, such as nondeterministic or parallel composition and abstraction. They permit describing systems at various levels of abstraction.

Both the *specification* and the *implementation* of a system can be expressed in the same language. Here, by specification we mean a description of the expected behaviour of the system in terms of how it reacts to external stimuli, while by implementation we mean a more detailed description with informations about its logical or physical structure. The language does not differentiate between descriptions at different levels. There is no absolute distinction between the two concepts. Indeed, in a particular framework an expression of the language may be considered as a specification while in another one it may be perceived as an implementation.

Usually, the language is equipped with a behavioural relation over processes. This relation may be an equivalence saying that two processes have the "same" behaviour or a preorder saying that a process is an "approximation of" another one. Many "reasonable" relations had been considered, each of them deals with some observable features of the behaviour of processes and abstract away from others. Verification consists in analyzing the relationships between descriptions and implementations of systems. This task may be at least partially mechanized if it is possible to alternatively characterize the behavioural relations over processes by means of sets of laws.

The algebraic approach has so far mainly concentrated on languages with uninterpreted action symbols that use a synchronous paradigm for program interaction. Moreover, only a few well–established formal theories there exist for process algebras which handle some kind of data values.

In this paper we deal with programs which can manipulate values and can pass them to other programs asynchronously. Essentially, the language we consider, and that we shall call PAL (Process Algebra based on Linda), is obtained by substituting abstract action prefixes of a pure process algebra with the Linda primitives for process interaction. Linda [13, 7] is a member of a relatively recent generation of global environment parallel languages that differ from those of previous generations because they offer, and often require, explicit control of interactions. Indeed, a communication between different processes is obtained by accessing data in a common data space (tuple space), and data are content–addressable. Linda is a "coordination" language rather than a complete programming language; all of its primitives are devoted to coordinate interactions among programs. Linda primitives can be embedded in a (functional, imperative, logic, etc.) programming language to obtain a concurrent language. This renders Linda very general and leads to a family of concurrent languages based on Linda rather than to a single language.

The rest of the paper is organized as follows. In the next section we briefly introduce the main features of Linda. In section 3 we define the syntax of PAL, while in section 4 we introduce its operational semantics in SOS style [25]. A theory of testing [9] based on this operational semantics is described in section 5. In section 6 we present a proof system for PAL which is sound and complete with respect to the behavioural preorder. In section 7 by means of a small example we show how the proof system works. In the last section we discuss related work and future research.

2 A brief presentation of Linda

Linda [13, 7] is a coordination language that relies on an asynchronous and associative communication mechanism based on a shared global environment called Tuples Space (TS), a multiset of tuples. A *tuple* is a sequence of *actual fields* (value objects) and *formal fields* (variables) with the constraint that the first field be an actual field, called *logic* name (or *tag*). The basic interaction mechanism is *pattern–matching*. It is used to select a tuple in TS that matches a given tuple t. This operation permits selecting those tuples in TS with the same tag as t and with the same number of fields and such that corresponding fields have matching values or variables. Variables match any value of the same type and two values match only if identical. Over TS, we have four operations:

- **in**(t): the process executing this operation first evaluates t and then looks for a tuple t' matching t in TS . If and when t' is found, it is removed from TS; the corresponding values of t' are assigned to the variables of t and the process continues. If no matching tuple is found, the process is suspended until one is available.
- **read**(t) is similar to **in**(t), but it does not require removal of the matched tuple t' from TS.
- **out**(t): the process executing this operation evaluates t, adds it to TS and proceeds; this is a non–blocking operation.
- **eval**(t) is similar to **out**(t), but rather than forcing evaluation of t, the process executing **eval**(t) creates a new process that will evaluate t and then add the resulting tuple to TS. The tuple will not be available for matching until its evaluation is completed.

It is worth noting that nondeterminism is inherent in the definition of Linda primitives. It arises when more **in/read** operations are suspended waiting for a tuple; when such a tuple becomes available, only one of the suspended operations is nondeterministically selected to proceed. Similarly, when an **in/read** operation has more than one matching tuple one is arbitrarily chosen.

3 Syntax of PAL

Since we are mainly interested in analyzing the concurrent features of the language, we assume all values have the same data type and make simplifying assumptions on the set of expressions and boolean expressions used.

We assume a predefined syntactic category, *Exp*, of *value expressions*, ranged over by e, which contains a set of variable symbols, *Var*, ranged over by x, y, z, etc., and a non empty countable set of value symbols, *Val*, ranged over by v. We make use of the usual notion of closed expression, i.e. one without occurrences of variables, and a notion of *substitution*. In general, a substitution for variables is a function from Val to Exp which is almost everywhere the identity. We write $[e_1/x_1, \ldots, e_n/x_n]$ for the substitution σ whose non trivial domain is $\{x_1, \ldots, x_n\}$ and is defined by $\sigma(x_i) = e_i$. We write $\sigma[e/x]$ for denoting the substitution which is the same as σ except that x is mapped to e. We write $e[e_1/x_1, \ldots, e_n/x_n]$ for denoting the expression which is obtained by simultaneously substituting each occurrence of x_i in e with e_i.

Furthermore, we assume existence of a predefined syntactic category, $BExp$, of *boolean expressions*, ranged over by be, which contains at least the boolean values *false* (denoted by $f\!f$) and *true* (denoted by $t\!t$), the usual boolean operators $(\wedge, \vee, \ldots)$ and an operator, $=$, for testing equality of value expressions.

As usual, we assume a predefined countable set of process variables, which is denoted with $\mathcal{X}$ and ranged over by $X, Y, Z, \ldots$. Thus, the language has two kinds of variables, value and process variables and, correspondingly, two binding operators.

Free and bound process variables are defined as usual, $\text{rec} X.\_$ being the binding operator. Substitutions for process variables are mappings from process variables to terms and are ranged over by ξ.

Variables which occur in formal fields of t are bound by $\mathbf{in}(t).\_$ and $\mathbf{read}(t).\_$. Substitutions of value–expressions for variables are also extended to terms. We use $E\sigma$ to denote the term resulting from simultaneously substituting in E all free occurrences of x with $\sigma(x)$, with possible renamings for avoiding captures.

Definition 3.1 The set of (process) terms (ranged over by E, F) is generated from the following grammar:

$$
\begin{aligned}
E &::= \mathbf{nil} \mid \Omega \mid pre.E \mid \mathbf{if}\ be\ \mathbf{then}\ E_1\ \mathbf{else}\ E_2 \mid E_1\ op\ E_2 \mid X \mid \text{rec}\ X.E \\
pre &::= \mathbf{out}(ot) \mid \mathbf{in}(it) \mid \mathbf{read}(it) \mid \mathbf{eval}(E) \\
ot &::= e \mid !\, x \mid ot_1, ot_2 \\
it &::= e \mid !\, x \mid \star \mid it_1, it_2 \\
op &::= \oplus \mid \square \mid \,\|\, \mid \llcorner \mid \mid_c
\end{aligned}
$$

Let PAL (for *Process Algebra based on Linda*) denote the set of all terms which contain no free occurrences of value variables. We will call *processes* those PAL terms which contain no free process variables. These terms are also called *closed* terms. Let $\mathcal{P}$ (ranged over by P, Q, R etc.) denote the set of all processes.

In general, we will work with PAL terms, which will be also called value–closed terms. Therefore in the following $E, F, \ldots$ will range over PAL terms.

The language has a few operators for building up process terms from more basic ones.

– $\mathbf{nil}$ (*inaction*), denotes the term that cannot perform any action.
– Ω (*undefined*), denotes the term that may only compute internally.

- *pre.E* (*action prefix*), has a meaning that depends on *pre*. If this is not an output action, *pre.E* denotes a term that executes action *pre* and then behaves like *E*. If *pre* is an output action, *pre.E* denotes a term that can execute action *pre* in parallel with *E*.
- **if** *be* **then** E_1 **else** E_2 (*conditional*), denotes a term that acts like as E_1 if the boolean expression *be* evaluates to true and like as E_2 otherwise.
- $E[]F$ (*external choice*), denotes a term which behaves either like *E* or like *F* and the choice is controlled by the environment.
- $E \oplus F$ (*internal choice*), denotes a term which may autonomously decide to behave either like *E* or like *F*.
- $E|F$ (*parallel composition*), denotes the concurrent execution of *E* and *F*.
- $E \lfloor F$ (*left-merge*), denotes the concurrent execution of *E* and *F* but requires that the first action involve *E*.
- $E|_c F$ (*communication-merge*), denotes the concurrent execution of *E* and *F* but requires that the first action be a synchronization between *E* and *F*.
- rec*X.E* (*recursive definition*) has the same meaning as the term defined by the equation $X = E$ and it is used for describing recursive behaviours.

The communication primitives are those of Linda. This means that communications do not use channels but shared tuples. We have modified the Linda process creation primitive. The original definition of Linda permits process terms to compute values as fields of tuples but we have **eval**(*E*) where *E* is a process expression. However, in our formalism **eval(out(*t*).nil)** can be used to express the original **eval(*t*)**.

We distinguish between input and output tuples. We use "! *x*" for denoting a formal field whose variable is *x*, "*e*" for denoting an actual field which contains the value–expression *e* and, in the case of input tuples, "$\star$" for denoting a field which can match only with a formal field of output tuples. If *t* is a tuple then $|t|$ denotes the number of fields of *t* (i.e. the length of *t*), t_i denotes the field of *t* with index *i* ($1 \leq i \leq |t|$), *var(t)* the set of variables which occur in formal fields of *t*, *if(t)* the set of indexes of formal fields of *t* and *ia(t)* the set of indexes of actual fields of *t*.

4 Operational Semantics

The operational rules presuppose evaluation mechanisms for expressions and boolean expressions; let them be the functions $\mathcal{E}[\![\cdot]\!] : Exp \longrightarrow Val$ and $\mathcal{B}[\![\cdot]\!] : BExp \longrightarrow \{f\!f, t\!t\}$, respectively. We use $\mathcal{E}[\![e]\!]$ and $\mathcal{B}[\![be]\!]$ for denoting the values of the expression *e* and of the boolean expression *be* provided they are closed (i.e. have no free variables).

The evaluation mechanisms for output tuples and input tuples are given via the functions $\mathcal{O}[\![\cdot]\!] : OTpl \longrightarrow EOT$ and $\mathcal{I}[\![\cdot]\!] : ITpl \longrightarrow EIT$, respectively, defined in Figure 1. The tuples resulting after evaluation are, respectively, elements of the following two sets:

- *EOT, evaluated output tuples*, which is generated by the following rules:
  $ot ::= v \mid \star \mid ot_1, ot_2;$

$$\begin{array}{ll} \mathcal{O}[\![\,!\,x\,]\!] = \star & \mathcal{I}[\![\,!\,x\,]\!] = \,!\,x \\ \mathcal{O}[\![\,e\,]\!] = \mathcal{E}[\![\,e\,]\!] & \mathcal{I}[\![\,e\,]\!] = \mathcal{E}[\![\,e\,]\!] \\ \mathcal{O}[\![\,(t_1,t_2)\,]\!] = (\mathcal{O}[\![\,t_1\,]\!], \mathcal{O}[\![\,t_2\,]\!]) & \mathcal{I}[\![\,\star\,]\!] = \star \\ & \mathcal{I}[\![\,(t_1,t_2)\,]\!] = (\mathcal{I}[\![\,t_1\,]\!], \mathcal{I}[\![\,t_2\,]\!]) \end{array}$$

Fig. 1. Tuple Evaluation Functions

- *EIT, evaluated input tuples*, which is generated by the following rules:
  $it ::= v \mid !\,x \mid \star \mid it_1, it_2$.

Note that the evaluation mechanism for output tuples abstracts away from formals used in tuples; in that case it returns the symbol $\star$.

Furthermore, we will use the set *AEIT* of *patterns (abstract evaluated input tuples)* of input tuples which is generated from the following grammar:

$$t ::= v \mid ! \mid \star \mid t_1, t_2$$

and a function *patt* : $EIT \longrightarrow AEIT$ which returns the pattern of an evaluated input tuple and is defined by the following clauses:

$$patt(v) = v, \quad patt(!\,x) = !, \quad patt(\star) = \star, \quad patt(t_1, t_2) = (patt(t_1), patt(t_2)).$$

The function *patt* abstracts away from the formals used in input tuples; in that case, it returns the symbol !.

We modify the original pattern–matching mechanism of Linda (see section 2). We restrict matching by imposing that values in input tuples can match only with the same values in output tuples. This new mechanism permits to test which tuple has been selected by pattern–matching. So, for example, we are able to express **read**(t) in terms of **in**(t) and **out**(t). The original communication capability of Linda input primitives can be recovered by using the external choice operator []. For example, the Linda primitive **in**(! x, v) can access each tuple of the form (v', v) or $(v', !\,y)$, where $v' \in Val$ and $y \in Var$. In PAL we can obtain the same overall communication capability by composing the primitives **in**(! x, v) and **in**(! x, $\star$) by means of the operator []. Pattern–matching between input and output tuples is checked by means of predicate *match*. The rules defining predicate *match* over $EIT \times EOT$ are in Figure 2.

$$[t] \quad \begin{array}{ll} match(v, v) & v \in Val \\ match(!\,x, v) & v \in Val \\ match(\star, \star) & \\ \hline match(t_1', t_2'), & match(t_1'', t_2'') \\ \hline \multicolumn{2}{c}{match((t_1', t_1''), (t_2', t_2''))} \end{array}$$

Fig. 2. Matching Rules

In the following, if t, t' are evaluated tuples, indexes i and j are such that $1 \leq i \leq |t|$ and $1 \leq j \leq |t'|$, and $I \subseteq \{1, 2, \ldots, |t|\}$ then we will use the following notations for comparing tuples:

- $t =_i t' \Longleftrightarrow |t| = |t'| \wedge \forall j : j \neq i \Longrightarrow t_j = t'_j,$
- $t =_I t' \Longleftrightarrow |t| = |t'| \wedge \forall j \notin I : t_j = t'_j.$

We are, finally, ready to define the operational semantics of PAL.

Definition 4.1 The operational semantics of PAL is characterized by the extended labelled transition system $(\mathcal{P}, \mathcal{A}ct, \longrightarrow, \rightarrowtail)$ where:

- $\mathcal{P}$ (i.e. the set of PAL processes) is the set of *states*,
- $\mathcal{A}ct = \{t \mid t \in EOT\} \cup \{(t', t) \mid t' \in AEIT, t \in EOT\}$, ranged over by α, is the set of *actions* or *labels*,
- $\longrightarrow \subseteq \mathcal{P} \times \mathcal{A}ct \times \mathcal{P}$, the *action relation*, is the least relation defined by the rules in Figure 3,
- $\rightarrowtail \subseteq \mathcal{P} \times \mathcal{P}$, the *internal relation*, is the least relation defined by the rules in Figures 3 and 4.

Note that the names of formals of tuples do not affect the communication ability of processes. For this reason, in the labels of the transition system we abstract away from them (that is, they are not observable).

We use a complementation notation for actions. Actually, in PAL there can exist several complements of a given action. For example, both the input actions $((5, 7), (5, 7))$ and $((5, !), (5, 7))$ are complementary actions of the output action $(5, 7)$. More formally, we can say that a complementary action of α, denoted by $\overline{\alpha}$, is any element of the set $Comp(\alpha)$ defined by:

- $Comp(\alpha) = \{(t', t) \mid t' \in AEIT \wedge match(t', t)\}$, if $\alpha = t$;
- $Comp(\alpha) = \{t\}$, if $\alpha = (t', t)$.

Most of the operational rules are similar to those for TCCS in [15] and for ACP in [1]. However, we model the Linda Tuple Space not via a common passive component (for storing tuples that had been produced but not yet consumed), we use instead processes to model tuples. There are no sending operations. The asynchronous nature of the communication paradigm is rendered by permitting term P of **out**$(t).P$ to proceed before tuple t is actually accessed; that is, by transforming the term **out**$(t).P$ into $(\textbf{out}(t).\textbf{nil})|P$ (see rule **Red5** in Figure 4). Therefore, when tuples are used their producers are not obliged to take part in the communication.

Rule **AR1** in Figure 3 says that process **in**$(it).P$ consumes a tuple t' matching the tuple $\mathcal{I}[\![\, it \,]\!]$ resulting from the evaluation of it; this causes the substitution of the formals of the evaluated argument tuple $\mathcal{I}[\![\, it \,]\!]$ with the corresponding values of the matched tuple t' in P. The corresponding visible action carries information about the pattern used for reading and the tuple consumed. Rule **AR2** in Figure 3 says that process **read**$(it).P$ differs from **in**$(it).P$ because it makes available again the accessed tuple. The substitution resulting from a

$$\textbf{AR1} \quad \text{in}(it).P \xrightarrow{(patt(\mathcal{I}[\![it]\!]),t')} P[t'/\mathcal{I}[\![it]\!]] \qquad \text{if } match(\mathcal{I}[\![it]\!], t')$$

$$\textbf{AR2} \quad \text{read}(it).P \xrightarrow{(patt(\mathcal{I}[\![it]\!]),t')} \text{out}(t').P[t'/\mathcal{I}[\![it]\!]] \quad \text{if } match(\mathcal{I}[\![it]\!], t')$$

$$\textbf{AR3} \quad \text{out}(ot).\text{nil} \xrightarrow{\mathcal{O}[\![ot]\!]} \text{nil}$$

$$\textbf{AR4} \quad \frac{P \xrightarrow{\alpha} P'}{P[]Q \xrightarrow{\alpha} P'} \qquad\qquad \textbf{AR5} \quad \frac{P \xrightarrow{\alpha} P'}{Q[]P \xrightarrow{\alpha} P'}$$

$$\textbf{AR6} \quad \frac{P \xrightarrow{\alpha} P'}{P|Q \xrightarrow{\alpha} P'|Q} \qquad\qquad \textbf{AR7} \quad \frac{P \xrightarrow{\alpha} P'}{Q|P \xrightarrow{\alpha} Q|P'}$$

$$\textbf{AR8} \quad \frac{P \xrightarrow{\alpha} P'}{P\lfloor Q \xrightarrow{\alpha} P'\lfloor Q}$$

$$\textbf{AR9} \quad \frac{\mathcal{B}[\![be]\!] = tt, \quad P \xrightarrow{\alpha} P'}{\text{if } be \text{ then } P \text{ else } Q \xrightarrow{\alpha} P'} \qquad \textbf{AR10} \quad \frac{\mathcal{B}[\![be]\!] = ff, \quad Q \xrightarrow{\alpha} Q'}{\text{if } be \text{ then } P \text{ else } Q \xrightarrow{\alpha} Q'}$$

Fig. 3. SOS Rules for PAL: Action Relation

$$\textbf{Red1} \quad \Omega \rightarrowtail \Omega \qquad\qquad\qquad \textbf{Red2} \quad recX.P \rightarrowtail P[recX.P/X]$$

$$\textbf{Red3} \quad \frac{\mathcal{B}[\![be]\!] = tt, \quad P \rightarrowtail P'}{\text{if } be \text{ then } P \text{ else } Q \rightarrowtail P'} \qquad \textbf{Red4} \quad \frac{\mathcal{B}[\![be]\!] = ff, \quad Q \rightarrowtail Q'}{\text{if } be \text{ then } P \text{ else } Q \rightarrowtail Q'}$$

$$\textbf{Red5} \quad \frac{P \neq \text{nil}}{\text{out}(ot).P \rightarrowtail \text{out}(ot).\text{nil}|P} \qquad \textbf{Red6} \quad \text{eval}(P).Q \rightarrowtail P|Q$$

$$\textbf{Red7} \quad P \oplus Q \rightarrowtail P \qquad\qquad\qquad \textbf{Red8} \quad P \oplus Q \rightarrowtail Q$$

$$\textbf{Red9} \quad \frac{P \rightarrowtail P'}{P\lfloor Q \rightarrowtail P'\lfloor Q}$$

$$\textbf{Red10} \quad \frac{P \rightarrowtail P'}{P[]Q \rightarrowtail P'[]Q} \qquad\qquad \textbf{Red11} \quad \frac{P \rightarrowtail P'}{Q[]P \rightarrowtail Q[]P'}$$

$$\textbf{Red12} \quad \frac{P \rightarrowtail P'}{P|Q \rightarrowtail P'|Q} \qquad\qquad \textbf{Red13} \quad \frac{P \rightarrowtail P'}{Q|P \rightarrowtail Q|P'}$$

$$\textbf{Red14} \quad \frac{P \rightarrowtail P'}{P|_cQ \rightarrowtail P'|_cQ} \qquad\qquad \textbf{Red15} \quad \frac{P \rightarrowtail P'}{Q|_cP \rightarrowtail Q|_cP'}$$

$$\textbf{Red16} \quad \frac{P \xrightarrow{\alpha} P', \quad Q \xrightarrow{\bar{\alpha}} Q'}{P|Q \rightarrowtail P'|Q'} \qquad \textbf{Red17} \quad \frac{P \xrightarrow{\alpha} P', \quad Q \xrightarrow{\bar{\alpha}} Q'}{P|_cQ \rightarrowtail P'|_cQ'}$$

Fig. 4. SOS Rules for PAL: Internal Relation

$$[t] \quad \begin{aligned} &[v/v] = \lambda y.y \\ &[v/!x] = \lambda y.[y=x] \longrightarrow v,y \\ &[\star/\star] = \lambda y.y \\ &[(ot_1, ot_2)/(it_1, it_2)] = [ot_1/it_1] \circ [ot_2/it_2] \end{aligned}$$

Fig. 5. Substitution resulting after a successful matching

successful execution of a blocking (**in** or **read**) operation is defined by the rules in Figure 5.

Rule **Red6** in Figure 4 shows that **eval** really causes dynamic process creation. Rules **Red3** and **Red4** in Figure 4 and rules **AR9** and **AR10** in Figure 3 show that the conditional term **if** *be* **then** P **else** Q acts like P if the boolean expression *be* evaluates to true and Q otherwise. Rules **Red16** and **Red17** in Figure 4 deal with interprocess communication.

5   Testing Semantics

In this section we apply the standard theory of testing, as developed in [9, 15], to PAL.

We assume a special prefix, **success**, and a special label, ω, which are used to denote success. The operational rule which corresponds to this new action prefixing is: **success**.$P \xrightarrow{\omega} P$.

Observers (ranged over by o) are processes which can perform, in addition to the usual prefixes, the special action **success**.

Experiments are terms of the form $P|o$. To establish the result of an experiment $P|o$ we must consider all of its *computations*. A computation is a *maximal sequence* of internal transitions, i.e. a sequence

$$P|o = P_0|o_0 \rightarrowtail P_1|o_1 \rightarrowtail P_2|o_2 \ldots P_k|o_k \rightarrowtail \ldots$$

which is either infinite or such that its last configuration cannot perform any internal transition.

For every process P and observer o, we say P *must* o if for each computation

$$P|o = P_0|o_0 \rightarrowtail P_1|o_1 \rightarrowtail P_2|o_2 \ldots P_k|o_k \rightarrowtail \ldots$$

there exists some $n \geq 0$ such that $o_n \xrightarrow{\omega}$.

The *testing preorder* over PAL processes we are interested in is defined by:

$$P \sqsubseteq_M Q \text{ if for every observer } o, P \text{ must } o \text{ implies } Q \text{ must } o.$$

6   A Proof System for PAL

In this section we define a proof system for PAL processes which is sound and complete with respect to the behavioural preorder $\sqsubseteq_M$. In [27] we also define a denotational semantics for PAL based on a model which is a variant of Strong Acceptance Trees [15] and prove that the proof system is also sound and complete with respect to this model.

The proof system is based on equational laws plus two induction rules: one handling recursively defined processes and the other one dealing with input prefixes. The axioms and the inference rules of the proof system, which we call C, are shown in Figures 6, 7, 8, 9 and 10. Each equation $X = Y$ is an abbreviation for the pairs of inequations $X \sqsubseteq Y$ and $Y \sqsubseteq X$. We write $E_1 \sqsubseteq_C E_2$ ($E_1 =_C E_2$)

$$
\begin{aligned}
&\textbf{IC1}\ X \oplus (Y \oplus Z) = (X \oplus Y) \oplus Z \\
&\textbf{IC2}\ X \oplus Y = Y \oplus X \\
&\textbf{IC3}\ X \oplus X = X \\
&\textbf{IC4}\ \text{in}(t).X \oplus \text{in}(t).Y = \text{in}(t).(X \oplus Y) \\
&\textbf{IC5}\ \text{out}(t).\text{nil} \lfloor X \oplus \text{out}(t).\text{nil} \lfloor Y = \text{out}(t).\text{nil} \lfloor (X \oplus Y) \\
&\textbf{IC6}\ X \oplus Y \sqsubseteq X \\
\\
&\textbf{EC1}\ X \llbracket (Y \llbracket Z) = (X \llbracket Y) \llbracket Z \\
&\textbf{EC2}\ X \llbracket Y = Y \llbracket X \\
&\textbf{EC3}\ X \llbracket X = X \\
&\textbf{EC4}\ X \llbracket \text{nil} = X \\
\\
&\textbf{MIX1}\ \text{in}(t).X \llbracket \text{in}(t).Y = \text{in}(t).(X \oplus Y) \\
&\textbf{MIX2}\ \text{out}(t).\text{nil} \lfloor X \llbracket \text{out}(t).\text{nil} \lfloor Y = \text{out}(t).\text{nil} \lfloor (X \oplus Y) \\
&\textbf{MIX3}\ X \oplus (Y \llbracket Z) = (X \oplus Y) \llbracket (X \oplus Z) \\
&\textbf{MIX4}\ X \llbracket (Y \oplus Z) = (X \llbracket Y) \oplus (X \llbracket Z)
\end{aligned}
$$

Fig. 6. Inequations for sequential, nondeterministic processes

to indicate the fact that $E_1 \sqsubseteq E_2$ ($E_1 = E_2$) can be derived within the proof system C.

Figure 6 contains the standard equations for testing from [10, 15] and the additional laws **IC4**, **IC5**, **MIX1** and **MIX2** which, however, are modifications of similar laws in [10, 15].

$$
\begin{array}{ll}
\textbf{UND1}\ \Omega \sqsubseteq X & \textbf{UND4}\ \Omega | X \sqsubseteq \Omega \\
\textbf{UND2}\ X \llbracket \Omega \sqsubseteq \Omega & \textbf{UND5}\ \Omega \lfloor X \sqsubseteq \Omega \\
\textbf{UND3}\ X | \Omega \sqsubseteq \Omega & \textbf{UND6}\ X |_c \Omega \sqsubseteq \Omega
\end{array}
$$

Fig. 7. Inequations for Ω

Rule **UND1** in Figure 7 says that process Ω is less defined than every PAL process. The other laws deal with strictness of binary operators.

Laws in Figure 8 are essentially concerned with the various forms of parallel operators. They say that these operators are all derivable and thus that the only basic operators are **nil**, Ω, $\llbracket$, $\oplus$, $\text{in}(t)$. and $\text{out}(t).\text{nil} \lfloor$. Laws **PAR1** and **PAR2** are taken from [15]. Law **PAR3** is a modification of the interleaving law of [15] to take into account the communication paradigm used in PAL; we take advantage of the merge operators of the language. Like the corresponding interleaving law in [1], **PAR3** is a weaker version of the standard ACP axiom

$$
X | Y = X \lfloor Y + Y \lfloor X + X |_c Y
$$

which applies to *stable* processes only, i.e. processes with no initial internal transitions. Indeed, the general ACP law is not sound with respect to $\simeq_M$. For instance,

PAR1 $(X \oplus Y)|Z = (X|Z) \oplus (Y|Z)$
PAR2 $X|(Y \oplus Z) = (X|Y) \oplus (X|Z)$
PAR3 Let $X = \sum_{i \in I} \text{in}(t_i).X_i [] \sum_{k \in K} \text{out}(t_k).\text{nil} \lfloor X_k$
and $Y = \sum_{j \in J} \text{in}(t_j).Y_j [] \sum_{l \in L} \text{out}(t_l).\text{nil} \lfloor X_l$.
Then:
$X|Y = ((X \lfloor Y)[](Y \lfloor X)[](X|_cY)) \oplus (X|_cY)$ if $\text{COMM}(X,Y) \neq \emptyset$
$X|Y = (X \lfloor Y)[](Y \lfloor X)$ if $\text{COMM}(X,Y) = \emptyset$
where $\text{COMM}(X,Y) = \{(i,l) \mid \text{match}(t_i, t_l)\} \cup \{(j,k) \mid \text{match}(t_j, t_k)\}$
PAR4 $\text{out}(t).X = \text{out}(t).\text{nil}|X$

EVAL $\text{eval}(X).Y = X|Y$

LM1 $(X[]Y) \lfloor Z = X \lfloor Z [] Y \lfloor Z$
LM2 $(X \oplus Y) \lfloor Z = X \lfloor Z \oplus Y \lfloor Z$
LM3 $(\text{in}(t).X) \lfloor Y = \text{in}(t).(X|Y)$ if $var(t)$ are not free in Y
LM4 $(\text{out}(t).\text{nil} \lfloor X) \lfloor Y = \text{out}(t).\text{nil} \lfloor (X|Y)$
LM5 $\text{nil} \lfloor X = \text{nil}$
LM6 $X \lfloor \text{nil} = X$

CM1 $(X[]Y)|_cZ = (X|_cZ)[](Y|_cZ)$
     if $Z = \sum_{i \in I} \text{in}(t_i).Z_i [] \sum_{k \in K} \text{out}(t_k).\text{nil} \lfloor X_k$
CM2 $(X \oplus Y)|_cZ = (X|_cZ) \oplus (Y|_cZ)$
CM3 $X|_cY = Y|_cX$
CM4 $\text{nil}|_cX = \text{nil}$
CM5 $(\text{in}(t_1).X)|_c(\text{out}(t_2).\text{nil} \lfloor Y) = X[t_2/t_1]|Y$ if $match(t_1, t_2)$
CM6 $(\text{in}(t_1).X)|_c(\text{out}(t_2).\text{nil} \lfloor Y) = \text{nil}$ if $\neg match(t_1, t_2)$
CM7 $(\text{in}(t_1).X)|_c(\text{in}(t_2).Y) = \text{nil}$
CM8 $(\text{out}(t_1).\text{nil} \lfloor X)|_c(\text{out}(t_2).\text{nil} \lfloor Y) = \text{nil}$

Fig. 8. Axioms for PAL derived operators

if we take $P' = P|Q$ and $Q' = P \lfloor Q [] Q \lfloor P [] P|_cQ$ where $P = \text{in}(5).\text{out}(3).\text{nil}$ and $Q = \text{out}(5).\text{nil} \oplus \text{out}(7).\text{nil}$, by letting $o = (\text{in}(3).\text{success.nil})[](\text{in}(7).\text{success.nil})$ we get that P' *must o* and Q' *m/ust o*. Laws **PAR4** and **EVAL** are new and intuitively say that both the two unary operators $\text{out}(t)$ and $\text{eval}(E)$ are non blocking operators. In particular, law **PAR4** says that we do not need general output prefixing; nullary process operators of the forms $\text{out}(t).\text{nil}$ are sufficient. Like **PAR3**, **CM1** is a weaker version of a corresponding ACP axiom; it holds only if Z is stable. The condition on the syntactic structure of Z is necessary for the soundness of the law. For instance, if we take $P = \text{out}(5).\text{nil}$, $Q = \text{out}(7).\text{nil}$, and $R = \text{in}(5).\text{out}(3).\text{nil} \oplus \text{in}(7).\text{out}(3).\text{nil}$ then, by letting $o = \text{in}(3).\text{success.nil}$, we get that $(P[]Q)|_cR$ *must o* and $(P|_cR)[](Q|_cR)$ *m/ust o*. The remaining laws are obvious adaptations of similar laws of [2, 3, 1].

The laws in Figure 9 are new and characterize the communication paradigm of the language. The first one permits expressing the unary process operator $\text{read}(t)$ in terms of $\text{in}(t)$ and $\text{out}(t)$. Law **L2** is a generalization of law **MIX1** (actually **MIX1** can be derived from **L2** and **IC4**, but we have included it

$\boxed{\begin{array}{l}
\textbf{L1 } read(t).X = in(t).out(t').X \\[4pt]
\qquad \text{where } t' =_{if(t)} t,\; i \in if(t) \wedge t_i =!\, x \Longrightarrow t'_i = x \\[10pt]
\textbf{L2 } \dfrac{t' =_I t,\; var(t')\backslash var(t) \text{ are not free in } X}{in(t).X\,[\!]\,in(t').Y = in(t').\text{if } cond(t,t') \text{ then } X \oplus Y \text{ else } Y} \\[8pt]
\qquad \text{where } I = if(t') \cap ia(t),\; cond(t,t') = \wedge_{i \in I} var(t'_i) = t_i \\[10pt]
\textbf{L3 } \dfrac{t' =_I t,\; var(t')\backslash var(t) \text{ are not free in } X,\; var(t)\backslash var(t') \text{ are not free in } Y}{\begin{array}{l} in(t).X\,[\!]\,in(t').Y = in(t).\text{if } cond(t,t') \text{ then } X \oplus Y \text{ else } X \\ \qquad\qquad\qquad\qquad\;\; [\!]\; in(t').\text{if } cond(t,t') \text{ then } X \oplus Y \text{ else } Y \end{array}} \\[10pt]
\qquad \text{where } I_1 = if(t) \cap ia(t'),\, I_2 = if(t') \cap ia(t),\, I = I_1 \cup I_2 \neq \emptyset, \text{ and} \\
\qquad cond(t,t') = (\wedge_{i \in I_1} var(t_i) = t'_i) \wedge (\wedge_{i \in I_2} var(t'_i) = t_i) \\[10pt]
\textbf{L4 } \dfrac{t' =_I t,\; var(t')\backslash var(t) \text{ are not free in } X,\; var(t)\backslash var(t') \text{ are not free in } Y}{\begin{array}{l} in(t).X \oplus in(t').Y = in(t).\text{if } cond(t,t') \text{ then } X \oplus Y \text{ else } X \\ \qquad\qquad\qquad\qquad\;\; \oplus\; in(t').\text{if } cond(t,t') \text{ then } X \oplus Y \text{ else } Y \end{array}} \\[10pt]
\qquad \text{where } I_1 = if(t) \cap ia(t'),\, I_2 = if(t') \cap ia(t),\, I = I_1 \cup I_2 \neq \emptyset, \text{ and} \\
\qquad cond(t,t') = (\wedge_{i \in I_1} var(t_i) = t'_i) \wedge (\wedge_{i \in I_2} var(t'_i) = t_i)
\end{array}}$

Fig. 9. Linda Laws

for fluency of presentation). It allows us to delete a summand of an external choice by absorbing its behaviour in that of the other summand. The law can be applied only if the choice is an internal choice, i.e. a summand may access all the tuples the other summand may access. Law **L3** allows us to postpone an internal choice after a tuple has been accessed. Indeed, if both summands of an external choice can access common tuples then also an internal choice is needed. Thus, the law says that for both summands it is possible to access a common tuple without determining the next behaviour. Law **L4** rests on the same idea of **L3** and is a generalization of **IC4** (like **MIX1**, **IC4** is included for fluency of presentation). Laws **L3** and **L4** permit to transform a sum of input prefixed terms into an analogous sum of input prefixed terms. This new term is able to access every tuple the original term can access and each time the same tuple has been accessed it becomes the same term, whichever be the input operation performed.

The rules of the proof system are in Figure 10. Most of them are borrowed from [15] and should be self–explanatory. The main addition is the second part of rule **III** which is infinitary if Val, and then EOT, is infinite. Our proof system has two infinitary rules: rule **VI** is the usual infinitary rule for handling recursive terms and the second part of rule **III** for dealing with input prefixing. We have

$$\textbf{I} \quad \frac{}{E \sqsubseteq E} \qquad\qquad \frac{E_1 \sqsubseteq E_2, \quad E_2 \sqsubseteq E_3}{E_1 \sqsubseteq E_3}$$

$$\textbf{II} \quad \frac{E_1 \sqsubseteq E_1', \quad E_2 \sqsubseteq E_2'}{E_1 \ op \ E_2 \sqsubseteq E_1' \ op \ E_2'} \ \text{for every } op \in \{\oplus, [\!], |, \lfloor, |_c\}$$

$$\textbf{III} \quad \frac{E_1 \sqsubseteq E_2}{out(t).nil[\![E_1 \sqsubseteq out(t).nil[\![E_2}$$

$$\frac{E_1[t'/t] \sqsubseteq E_2[t'/t]}{in(t).E_1 \sqsubseteq in(t).E_2} \ \text{for every tuple } t' \in EOT : match(t, t')$$

$$\textbf{IV} \quad \frac{E_1 \sqsubseteq E_2}{recX.E_1 \sqsubseteq recX.E_2} \qquad\qquad \frac{}{recX.E = E[recX.E/X]}$$

$$\textbf{V} \quad \frac{E_1 \sqsubseteq E_2}{E_1\xi \sqsubseteq E_2\xi} \qquad\qquad \frac{}{E_1 \sqsubseteq E_2} \ \text{for every inequation } E_1 \sqsubseteq E_2$$

$$\textbf{VI} \quad \frac{\forall n > 0 : E_1^n \sqsubseteq E_2}{E_1 \sqsubseteq E_2}$$

$$\textbf{VII} \quad \frac{\mathcal{B}[\![be]\!] = tt}{\text{if } be \text{ then } E_1 \text{ else } E_2 = E_1} \qquad\qquad \frac{\mathcal{B}[\![be]\!] = ff}{\text{if } be \text{ then } E_1 \text{ else } E_2 = E_2}$$

$$\textbf{VIII} \quad \frac{\mathcal{O}[\![t]\!] = \mathcal{O}[\![t']\!]}{out(t).nil[\![E = out(t').nil[\![E} \qquad\qquad \frac{\mathcal{I}[\![t]\!] = \mathcal{I}[\![t']\!]}{in(t).E = in(t').E}$$

$$\textbf{IX} \quad \frac{x \in var(t), \quad y \text{ fresh}}{in(t).E = in(t[y/x]).E[y/x]}$$

Fig. 10. Proof System

added rule **VII** for dealing with conditional terms. Note that rules **VII** and **VIII** presuppose evaluation mechanisms for expressions, boolean expressions and tuples. Rule **IX** is an α–conversion rule for input prefixed term; substitutions are extended to tuples.

In [27] we prove that the proof system C is sound with respect to the preorder $\sqsubseteq_M$, i.e. for every processes P and Q, $P \sqsubseteq_C Q \implies P\sqsubseteq_M Q$. As usual, the soundness proof consists in checking that all the laws are satisfied by $\sqsubseteq_M$ and that the preorder $\sqsubseteq_M$ is preserved by the rules.

In [27] we also prove that the proof system C is complete with respect to the preorder $\sqsubseteq_M$, i.e. for every processes P and Q, $P\sqsubseteq_M Q \implies P \sqsubseteq_C Q$. The completeness proof, as usual, rests on the existence of certain standard forms for processes called Ω–sum forms (Ω–SF) and head normal forms ($hnfs$). Similar forms were already used in [9, 15, 16]. Intuitively, both these special forms aim to describe processes as an internal nondeterministic choice among a set of initial states. Each initial state is represented by the initial actions the process can perform and their corresponding derivates.

By using the proof system C every convergent process can be equated to a hnf. To avoid expressing the interaction ability of processes in terms of a possible infinite set (of those actions the process can do), we introduce the notion of *event*, which basically is either an output tuple or a pattern. Thus, the interaction ability of processes is expressed by the set of tuples the process is able to output and the set of patterns the process can use for accessing tuples. A hnf for PAL is either **nil** or a term P of the form $\sum_{A \in \mathcal{A}} \sum_{e \in A} P_e$ where $\mathcal{A}$ is a *saturated set* (see [15]), every $A \in \mathcal{A}$ is a *closed* set of events, i.e. for every input action (t_1, t_1') from state (which corresponds to) A it does not exists another input action (t_2, t_2') from state (which corresponds to) A such that $\forall t \in EOT : match(t_2, t) \Rightarrow match(t_1, t)$, and P is such that for every initial input actions (t_1, t) and (t_2, t) it can perform the terms obtained can be equated by means of the proof system C. Ω–SFs are used for equating every divergent finite process to Ω.

The following theorem summarizes our main results.

Theorem 6.1 For all process P, Q: $P \sqsubseteq_C Q$ if and only if $P \precsim_M Q$.

7 A small example

In this section we wish to show how the proof system can be used for a simple example. We consider some PAL processes that permit adding two arrays elementwise. We already assumed that the language is parameterized on a countable set of values, Val. Here, we require that Val be the *Natural Numbers*. Let A and B two arrays of n natural numbers. We shall consider PAL processes which add elementwise A and B leaving the result in an array C of the same length.

To better exploit the parallelism intrinsic in the problem, i.e. the fact that the computation of C_i depends only on A_i and B_i, the Linda style of programming suggests to represent every array as a *distributed data structure* [8]. Hence, we shall use a tuple for every single element of every array. To represent A we shall use n tuples with three fields: the first one contains the constant 0 which identifies the array, the second one the index i of the element and the last one the value A_i of the element. For arrays B and C we shall adopt a similar representation with the difference that we shall use 1 for identifying B and 2 for identifying C.

The processes we consider add elements of A and B with the same index, if they both exist, for any (finite) length arrays. Let us consider the PAL process

$$Q \equiv recX.\mathbf{in}(0, !\, x, !\, y).\mathbf{eval}(X).\mathbf{in}(1, x, !\, z).\mathbf{out}(2, x, y + z).\mathbf{nil}.$$

We want to show that process P_k obtained by putting in parallel k copies of Q is such that $P_k =_C Q$, that is $P_k = Q$ can be proven by means of syntactic transformations driven by the proof system C. We may think about Q as a process which executes on a single processor and is able to dynamically reproduce itself when a new element of array A is accessed. Each instance computes an element of array C. The number of instances which are concurrently active depends on the difference between the number of elements of A and that of elements of B which have been accessed. We may think about P_k as a really distributed process consisting of k copies of process Q which are simultaneously executed on k

different processors. In this sense P_k may be thought about as a more efficient and fault–tolerant solution of the problem than Q.

We formally define P_k as:

$P_2 \equiv Q|Q,$

$P_{j+1} \equiv Q|P_j$, for $j > 2$,

and by induction we prove that $P_k =_C Q$.

The completeness Theorem 6.1 says that the axioms together with the two induction rules presented in the previous section are sufficient to prove all the behavioural relationships between PAL processes. In practice it is often sufficient to use simpler induction rules. Here we use a powerful but simple form of induction for dealing with recursive terms, namely *Unique Fixpoint Induction* [15], which is expressed by the following rule:

$$\textbf{UFI} \qquad \frac{\text{E} = \text{F}[\text{E}/\text{X}]}{\text{E} = \text{rec} \text{X. F}} \qquad \text{where } X \text{ is guarded.}$$

In our setting a term is *guarded* whenever every process variable occurs within an input (i.e. blocking) prefixing. All terms we examine here are guarded thus **UFI** can be correctly used.

Firstly, we prove that $P_2 =_C Q$. The term Q is recursively defined and in order to show

$$P_2 = \text{rec} X.\textbf{in}(0,!\,x,!\,y).\textbf{eval}(X).\textbf{in}(1,x,!\,z).\textbf{out}(2,x,y+z).\textbf{nil}$$

we can use an instance of **UFI**. Hence, it is sufficient to deduce

$$P_2 = \textbf{in}(0,!\,x,!\,y).\textbf{eval}(P_2).\textbf{in}(1,x,!\,z).\textbf{out}(2,x,y+z).\textbf{nil}$$

that is, by applying **EVAL**,

$$P_2 = \textbf{in}(0,!\,x,!\,y).(P_2|\textbf{in}(1,x,!\,z).\textbf{out}(2,x,y+z).\textbf{nil}). \qquad (1)$$

This may be proven by using a standard strategy, consisting of expanding out the recursive definitions and applying the laws for parallel operators and the interleaving law **PAR3**.

By expanding out the recursive definitions and applying **EVAL** we get

$$\begin{aligned} P_2 &\equiv Q|Q \\ &= \textbf{in}(0,!\,x_1,!\,y_1).(Q|\textbf{in}(1,x_1,!\,z_1).\textbf{out}(2,x_1,y_1+z_1).\textbf{nil}) \\ &\quad |\textbf{in}(0,!\,x_2,!\,y_2).(Q|\textbf{in}(1,x_2,!\,z_2).\textbf{out}(2,x_2,y_2+z_2).\textbf{nil}). \end{aligned}$$

Since

$$Q = \textbf{in}(0,!\,x_1,!\,y_1).(Q|\textbf{in}(1,x_1,!\,z_1).\textbf{out}(2,x_1,y_1+z_1).\textbf{nil})$$

and

$$Q = \textbf{in}(0,!\,x_2,!\,y_2).(Q|\textbf{in}(1,x_2,!\,z_2).\textbf{out}(2,x_2,y_2+z_2).\textbf{nil}),$$

by applying the interleaving law **PAR3** we get

$$P_2 = \mathbf{in}(0, !\, x_1, !\, y_1).(Q|Q|\mathbf{in}(1, x_1, !\, z_1).\mathbf{out}(2, x_1, y_1 + z_1).\mathbf{nil})$$
$$[]\mathbf{in}(0, !\, x_2, !\, y_2).(Q|Q|\mathbf{in}(1, x_2, !\, z_2).\mathbf{out}(2, x_2, y_2 + z_2).\mathbf{nil}).$$

By applying rule **IX** for renaming the variables bound by input prefixes and equation **EC3** for coalescing the two summands of $[]$ we get the equation (1) and then we conclude that $P_2 =_C Q$.

Now, we prove the inductive step. We assume that $P_j =_C Q$. By applying rule **II** with hypothesis $Q \sqsubseteq Q$ and $P_j \sqsubseteq Q$ in the case of the operator $|$ we get

$$P_{j+1} \equiv Q|P_j \sqsubseteq Q|Q \equiv P_2 = Q.$$

In a similar way we can derive that $Q \sqsubseteq P_{j+1}$ and therefore we conclude that $P_k =_C Q$ for all $k \geq 2$.

8 Conclusions and Related Work

In this paper we have studied the impact of a theory of testing of [9] on a process algebra which permits programs to manipulate values and pass them to other programs asynchronously. The language is obtained by substituting uninterpreted actions of a CSP–like process algebra with the Linda primitives for process interaction.

Asynchronous variants of process algebras have been already considered for ACP [2], CSP [18], the π–calculus [24] and CCS [23]. Essentially these works have been followed two main lines that differ for the way non blocked output actions are modelled. They are rendered either as state transformers or as processes.

The variant of ACP [3, 4] and that of CSP [22] follow the first approach. They associate buffers (realized as state operators in ACP and as processes in CSP) to channels. These variants naturally describe environments in which outputs are modelled via unblocked sending primitives that make messages available for consumption.

The variants of the π–calculus [19, 20, 6, 14] and CCS [26] follow the second approach. They model outputs as concurrent processes. Also our work follows this approach. Output operations are modelled as internal moves which can always be performed (i.e. are non–blocking operations) and cannot change the structure of terms. For example, this means that

$$\mathbf{out}(t_1).(\mathbf{out}(t_2).\mathbf{nil}[]\mathbf{out}(t_3).\mathbf{nil}) \neq$$
$$(\mathbf{out}(t_1).\mathbf{out}(t_2).\mathbf{nil})[](\mathbf{out}(t_1).\mathbf{out}(t_3).\mathbf{nil}).$$

This seemingly differs from [5], where the law

$$\overline{a}.(\overline{b}.\mathbf{nil} + \overline{c}.\mathbf{nil}) = \overline{a}.\overline{b}.\mathbf{nil} + \overline{a}.\overline{c}.\mathbf{nil} \tag{2}$$

with a denoting input action on channel a and $\overline{a}$ denoting output action on the same channel, is considered a basic law in the case of asynchronous communications. Actually the difference is due only to the distinct choice operators of the languages. Indeed, the $+$ operator used in [5] can be used to describe both internal and external nondeterminism. For example, with the term $\overline{a}.b.\mathbf{nil} + c.\mathbf{nil}$

the sending of a would permit to reject c. In our setting, the corresponding term would be $(\overline{a}.b.\textbf{nil}[]c.\textbf{nil})\oplus\overline{a}.b.\textbf{nil}$. Output actions are dealt with just like the silent action of CCS in the translation from CCS to TCCS of [10]. Therefore, in our setting the sound version of law 2 is

$$\textbf{out}(t_1).((\textbf{out}(t_2).\textbf{nil}[]\textbf{out}(t_3).\textbf{nil})\oplus\textbf{out}(t_2).\textbf{nil}\oplus\textbf{out}(t_3).\textbf{nil})$$
$$= (\textbf{out}(t_1).\textbf{out}(t_2).\textbf{nil}[]\textbf{out}(t_1).\textbf{out}(t_3).\textbf{nil})$$
$$\oplus(\textbf{out}(t_1).\textbf{out}(t_2).\textbf{nil})\oplus(\textbf{out}(t_1).\textbf{out}(t_3).\textbf{nil}).$$

Only a few well–established theories for process calculi which explicitly manipulate values have been developed. The only addition to [3, 4], that we have already mentioned, are [16, 17, 21]. There a testing framework is developed for a variant of TCCS [10, 15] with value–passing. By and large, we have used methods similar to those of [16, 17, 21]. However, tuples based communication has rendered our work significantly different. Apart from the presence of non finitely branching transition system, that prompted introduction of the notion of event, we had to face additional complications, such as the inability of observers to perceive the differencies among patterns which access a given tuple.

As a future application of the study presented here we hope to be able to extend the approach to the case of an imperative Linda dialect. In [12] we have already studied an imperative language, L obtained by embedding the Linda primitives for interprocess communication in a simple sequential imperative language, SL. That work emphasizes the semantical formalization of the Linda communication paradigm on an imperative language. We succeeded in defining a testing scenario for L but we were unable to give alternative equational characterizations of the testing preorders. Obviously, this makes difficult and almost useless the practical usability of that framework for verifying programs, such as the example in [11] shows. In light of the study presented in [17], where the approach of [16] is also applied to an imperative language, the approach described in this paper seems to be more promising for defining a testing scenario for an imperative asynchronous language based on the Linda communication paradigm.

Acknowledgments We thank the anonymous referees for stimulating comments and Ernst-Rüdiger Olderog and Catuscia Palamidessi for helpful suggestions.

References

1. L.Aceto, A.Ingolfsdottir. A Theory of Testing for ACP. *Proceedings of CONCUR 91*, J.C.M. Baeten and J.F. Groote, editors, *LNCS* 527, pages 78-95, Springer-Verlag, Berlin, 1991.
2. J. Bergstra, J.W. Klop. Process Algebra for Synchronous Communication. *Information and Control*, 60:109-137, 1984.
3. J.A. Bergstra, J.W. Klop, J.V. Tucker. Process Algebra with Asynchronous Communication Mechanisms. *Proceedings of Seminar in Concurrency*, S.D. Brookes, A.W. Roscoe and G. Winskel, editors, *LNCS* 197, pages 76-95, Springer-Verlag, Berlin, 1985.

4. F.S. de Boer, J.W. Klop, C. Palamidessi. Asynchronous Communication in Process Algebra. *Proceedings of LICS*, 1992.
5. F.S. de Boer, C. Palamidessi. On the asynchronous nature of communication in concurrent logic languages: a fully abstract model based on sequences. *Proceedings of CONCUR'90, LNCS* 458, pages 99-114, Springer-Verlag, Berlin, 1990.
6. G. Boudol. Asynchrony in the π-calculus. *Unpublished manuscript*, INRIA Sophia–Antipolis, 1992.
7. N. Carriero, D. Gelernter. Linda in Context. *Communications of the ACM*, 32(4):444-458, 1989.
8. N. Carriero, D. Gelernter, J. Leichter. Distributed Data Structures in Linda. *Proceedings of the ACM Symposium on Principles of Programming Languages* (St. Petersburg, Fla., Jan.13–15), ACM, New York, pages 236-242, 1986.
9. R. De Nicola, M.C.B. Hennessy. Testing Equivalence for Processes. *Theoretical Computers Science*, 34:83-133, 1984.
10. R. De Nicola, M.C.B. Hennessy. CCS without τ's. *Proceedings of TAP-SOFT'87, LNCS* 249, pages 138-152, 1987.
11. R. De Nicola, R. Pugliese. Testing Linda: an Observational Semantics for an Asynchronous Language. Research Report: SI/RR - 94/06, Dipartimento di Scienze dell'Informazione, Università di Roma "La Sapienza", 1994.
12. R. De Nicola, R. Pugliese. An Observational Semantics for Linda. *Proceedings of STRICT'95*, pp.129-143, Jorg Desel (ed.), Series Workshops in Computing, Springer - Verlag, Berlin, 1995.
13. D. Gelernter. Generative Communication in Linda. *ACM Transactions on Programming Languages and Systems*, 7(1):80-112, 1985.
14. M. Hansen, H. Huttel, J. Kleist. Bisimulations for Asynchronous Mobile Processes. *Draft*, Department of Mathematics and Computer Science Aalborg University, 1994.
15. M.C.B. Hennessy. *Algebraic Theory of Processes*. The MIT Press, 1988.
16. M.C.B. Hennessy, A. Ingolfsdottir. A theory of communicating processes with value–passing. *Information and Computation*, 107(2)202-236, 1993.
17. M.C.B. Hennessy, A. Ingolfsdottir. Communicating processes with value–passing and assignment. *Journal of Formal Aspects of Computing Science*, pages 3:346-366, 1993.
18. C.A.R. Hoare. *Communicating Sequential Processes*. Prentice-Hall International, 1985.
19. K. Honda, M. Tokoro. An Object Calculus for Asynchronous Communication. *Proceedings of ECOOP'91, LNCS* 512, pages 133-147, Springer–Verlag, Berlin, 1991.
20. K. Honda, M. Tokoro. On Asynchronous Communication Semantics. *Proceedings of ECOOP'91, LNCS* 612, pages 21-51, Springer–Verlag, Berlin, 1991.
21. A. Ingolfsdottir. Semantic Models for Communicating Processes with Value–Passing. *Ph.D. Thesis*, University of Edinburgh, 1994.
22. H. Jifeng, M.B. Josephs, C.A.R. Hoare. A Theory of Synchrony and Asynchrony. *Proceedings of the IFIP Working Conference on Programming Concepts and Methods*, pages 446-465, 1990.
23. R. Milner. *Communication and Concurrency*. Prentice Hall International, 1989.
24. R. Milner, J. Parrow, D. Walker. A calculus of mobile processes, (Part I and II). *Information and Computation*, 100:1-77, 1992.

25. G.D. Plotkin. A Structural Approach to Operational Semantics. Technical Report DAIMI FN-19, Aarhus University, Dep. of Computer Science, Denmark, 1981.

26. R. Pugliese. A Process Calculus with Asynchronous Communications. In Proc. Italian Conference on Theoretical Computer Science '95, Ravello, 1995. (to appear)

27. R. Pugliese. Semantic Theories for Asynchronous Languages. *Ph.D. Thesis*, Draft, Università di Roma "La Sapienza", 1995.

Intra- and Inter-Object Coordination with MESSENGERS

Munehiro Fukuda
Lubomir F. Bic
Michael B. Dillencourt
Fehmina Merchant

Department of Information and Computer Science
University of California, Irvine

Abstract. MESSENGERS is a paradigm for the programming of distributed systems. It is based on the principles of autonomous messages, called Messengers, which carry their own behavior in the form of a program. This enables them to navigate freely in the underlying computational network, communicate with one another, and invoke pre-compiled node-resident functions. Coordination is facilitated at two distinct levels of abstraction: first, Messengers coordinate the invocation and the exchange of data among the various functions distributed throughout the network in both time and space (intra-object coordination); second, Messengers, each representing a high-level entity, can coordinate their behaviors among themselves (inter-object coordination). These principles, where an application is composed of autonomous, mobile entities whose behaviors may change dynamically and which can coordinate their actions among themselves, offer great flexibility in interacting with and manipulating the application at run time, as well as improved performance. This is illustrated using two concrete examples—a Toxicology simulation from medicine and a study of collective fish behavior from biology.

1   Introduction

In a recent article, Gelernter and Carriero [GC92] argued eloquently for an integration of *computing* with *communication* in programming languages. They observe that most existing programming languages focus primarily on computing, while leaving the aspects of communication (including I/O) and coordination to be handled outside the scope of the computing model, i.e., through ad hoc language extensions or library routines. Consequently, most distributed applications are collections of programs, where explicit communication primitives based on send/receive commands have been embedded for the purpose of coordination. They observe further that market forces of prepackaged software are already forcing a shift from creating new programs from scratch toward composing complex systems from existing program components. This will require the development of new coordination languages to facilitate the construction of such program ensembles.

In this paper we describe MESSENGERS, a coordination paradigm for distributed systems currently being developed by our research group. It is based on the concept of autonomous messages, which we refer to as *Messengers*[1] to differentiate them from ordinary passive messages. A Messenger, instead of carrying just data, contains a process, i.e., a program together with its current status information, including its program counter and local variables. Each node visited by the Messenger resumes the interpretation of the Messenger's program until a navigational command is encountered that causes it to leave the current node (or the Messenger terminates). The program, which may be arbitrarily complex, thus describes the behavior of the Messenger, allowing it to navigate through the network of nodes and to perform arbitrary functions at each of the nodes. Under the MESSENGERS paradigm, a distributed application is viewed as a collection of functions, whose coordination (i.e. invocation and exchange of data) is managed by groups of Messengers propagating autonomously through the computational network.

There is, however, a second aspect of coordination, which occurs at a higher level in certain classes of distributed applications. There, in addition to coordinating the invocation of individual functions that make up a complex behavior, it is sometimes necessary to coordinate the behaviors of the autonomous entities or objects themselves. This is typically the case when the application is described in terms of independent concurrent entities that coordinate their behavior in time and/or space. We refer to this level of coordination as *inter-object* coordination, while the coordination of functions that make up the behavior of an individual object will be called *intra-object* coordination. We will demonstrate that the MESSENGERS paradigm is effective at both levels of coordination.

2 The MESSENGERS Paradigm

MESSENGERS is a paradigm for distributed computing which, similar to other autonomous-message-based approaches [BFD96], departs from the conventional message-passing view by elevating messages to higher-level entities that embody some degree of autonomy or "intelligence" [Bic95, Fuk95b]. A message can be viewed as an object itself, which has its own identity and which can decide at run time where it wishes to propagate next and what tasks it is to perform there. The behavior of each Messenger is described by its program, which it carries along as it moves through the underlying computational network. MESSENGERS exhibits three novel characteristics that differentiate it from conventional message-based paradigms:

- *navigation autonomy* – the ability of each Messenger to navigate through the network, to replicate itself, and to decide what actions to take at each destination. This is achieved by providing navigational statements, which permit the Messenger to go to specific nodes in the network, follow specific

---

[1] We use capitalized lower-case when referring to the individual autonomous objects and upper-case for the entire system.

links emanating from the node in which it currently resides, or cloning itself to pursue independent paths.

- *intra-object coordination* – the ability of the MESSENGERS paradigm to serve as the coordination layer of software superimposed on other lower-level computations. This is achieved by having each Messenger invoke and control the execution of ordinary C functions residing on various nodes throughout the network; hence each Messenger orchestrates the execution of a group of precompiled components dynamically. This also offers great flexibility in choosing between interpreted code, which is slow but need not be distributed to all nodes a priori, and code compiled into native mode, which is much more efficient but must be made available on all nodes potentially visited by a Messenger

- *inter-object coordination* – the ability of Messengers, each representing a high-level entity in the application domain, to coordinate their respective actions to achieve complex collective behaviors. Spatial coordination is achieved by reading and writing of shared variables set up for this purpose in the nodes they visit. Temporal coordination is supported by special functions that access global virtual time, maintained by the system.

2.1 The MESSENGERS Language

During the course of executing an application, Messengers dynamically construct an application-specific logical network over a network of physical nodes (Sun Workstations in our present implementation). Multiple logical nodes can be mapped onto the same workstation. Each link of the logical network has a user-determined name and several (optional) weights. These are integer variables, which Messengers may use for navigation, for example in graph-based applications. Each node has a user-determined name and a system-wide address. It also contains a node variables area, which can be accessed by the visiting Messengers for the purpose of coordination among themselves.

The MESSENGERS paradigm supports three types of variables, referred to as *messenger, node,* and *network* variables [Fuk95b]. Messenger variables are local to and carried by the Messenger as it propagates through the logical network. Node variables are node-resident and are accessed via a node variable declaration carried by the Messenger. There is only one set of node variables in any given node and they are shared by all Messengers currently running in that node. Network variables describe the logical network, including node names, node addresses, link names, and link weights. All network variables are readable by any Messenger and all except for node addresses may also be modified. Link names and weights may be modified when traversing the corresponding link. Every Messenger program has the following form:

$$\downarrow$$

node variables declaration; messenger variables definition; $S_1; S_2; \dots S_n;$

Since node variables are stationary inside a node and thus shared by all Messengers, they are allocated only once by the first Messenger to arrive at that node. Subsequent Messengers then simply access these variables via their node variables declarations, which provide the mapping between the Messenger code and the corresponding node-resident values. The messenger variables definition, on the other hand, denotes private, messenger-carried variables and their data type. Network variables are predefined and referred to without explicit declaration. The declaration and definition formats are similar to those of the C Language and provide a variety of data types excluding pointer, union, and unsigned variables.

The remainder of a Messenger program consists of statements, denoted by S_i. The arrow is used to indicate the current statement, (i.e. the one to be interpreted next). This corresponds to a program counter in a conventional language and is saved in a status block, which is also carried by the Messenger as it migrates between different nodes. Each S_i is one of the following three types of statements:

Computation:

A Messenger may perform arbitrary computations using assignment and control statements from the C programming language. These statements are all interpreted by the current node.

1. *assignment*: The Messenger may read and update node and messenger variables, and read network variables. Arbitrary expressions are permissible in the assignment and include all of the common arithmetic and logic operators provided in C.
2. *control statement*: The Messenger may perform all the common control statements supported in C, such as if-then-else, while, do-while and break.

Navigation:

A Messenger may create new logical links and nodes, change or delete existing ones, and move arbitrarily though the network by following links or jumping to specific nodes.

1. *create(node, link, weight, physical)*: Create a *link* along which the Messenger moves, associate *weight* with this *link*, and create *node* on the *physical* node which the Messenger reaches. All parameters are optional. If omitted, the new node/link has no explicit name or weight and is created on a physical node chosen automatically by the system. Hence the last parameter allows the user to explicitly control the logical-to-physical node mapping.
2. *hop(node, link, weight, physical)*: Cause the Messenger to be forwarded to *node* on *physical* node along *link* if the link has the associated *weight*. As with *create*, all parameters are optional, which offers great flexibility in specifying the Messenger's next node destinations. If there are multiple destinations, a copy of the Messenger is propagated to each destination. For instance, *hop(node=a)* propagates the Messenger along all logical links emanating from the current node to all neighboring nodes named "a". If a node address is given as a node parameter, the Messenger jumps directly to the specified node. In addition, the parameters support "wild card" matching,

which results in a powerful multicast mechanism for each Messenger. For instance, *hop(node=*; physical='laguna')* sends a copy of the Messenger to all nodes on the physical node named 'laguna', regardless of any logical links.

3. *delete(node, link, weight, physical)*: Forward the Messenger as with *hop*, but also delete the links traversed by each copy of the Messenger. In addition, if this action erases all links from the departing node and there are no other Messengers currently residing in it, the node is also deleted.

Function Invocation:

This allows the Messenger to load and execute ordinary C functions, precompiled in native mode of and residing on the current physical node.

1. *exec(filename, arguments, [nowait])*: Invoke a precompiled function specified by *filename* as a separate concurrent process and pass *arguments* to it. If *nowait* is specified, the function may continue operating even after the Messenger has left the node (or has terminated).

2. *func(filename, function_name, in_arg, out_arg)*: Invoke a precompiled function specified by *filename* and *function_name* as part of the MESSENGERS interpreter, wait for its completion, and return the results back to the invoking Messenger program. The *in_arg* and *out_arg* are arguments passed to and returned from the function respectively. The invoked function also receives pointers to the node variable area and the memory space holding the messenger variables and thus can manipulate them directly. The loading of the function is triggered dynamically when it is invoked for the first time.

Each Messenger program written in the above high-level language is compiled into an internal machine-like language, which is understood by the MESSENGERS interpreter running in each node. The reason for this compilation is to simplify the task of the interpreter and to reduce the size of messages[Fuk95a].

2.2 The MESSENGERS Interpreter

The MESSENGERS system is implemented as a daemon running a language interpreter at each physical node. The interpreter exchanges Messengers with other interpreters, and multiplexes logical nodes mapped to its physical node.

For each new Messenger, the interpreter continues processing its statements until the interpreter encounters a statement that is navigational or functional, i.e., one that causes the Messenger to be removed from the current node or to be suspended when a precompiled function is invoked. Hence, exclusive operations are guaranteed between any two such statements. This non-preemptive scheduling strategy makes it easy to enforce critical sections but prohibits the use of infinite loops that do not periodically release the processor.

To support time-based coordination, required for example by simulation applications, the interpreters in the system are capable of maintaining global virtual time (GVT). Due to the associated overhead, this feature must explicitly be turned on and off by the user. Once activated, Messengers are able to utilize

GVT via a set of library functions (Section 2.3), which allow arbitrary application functions to be scheduled for future execution based on GVT and other constraints.

Within any given node, interpretation of Messengers continues (optimistically) until the interpreter exchanges Messengers with other interpreters. When a Messenger with an older time-stamp is received, the interpreter locally rolls the execution back to a state corresponding to the received time-stamp. Similar to database transaction processing, this is achieved by restoring an earlier consistent snapshot and reinterpreting all Messengers up to the point of the received time-stamp. In order to reduce the amount of computation required by the local rollback, once GVT is activated, the interpreter restricts the Messenger's migration to neighboring logical nodes only.

Nodes periodically send out messages to other neighbors that allow the system to collectively maintain the most recent stable GVT. This is used by each node to prune the data structures containing rollback information by discarding obsolete snapshots.

The general organization of the interpreter is then as follows. It alternates between two phases: Messenger interpretation and function execution. During the first phase, it makes a complete pass through the ready queue of Messengers and continues interpreting each until one of the following occurs: the Messenger terminates; the Messenger executes a navigational command causing it to move to another node; or the Messenger invokes a compiled function using *func()*. During the second phase, the interpreter calls all functions that have been scheduled as "future events" thus far. The above two phases are repeated until one of the following occurs: both the Messengers ready queue and the function scheduling queue are empty; an interval timer expires; or the local virtual time proceeds beyond a certain threshold. At that point, the interpreter enters an inter-daemon communication phase, which physically exchanges Messengers between workstations using Unix sockets. Thereafter, the interpreter continues with the Messengers interpretation phase as described above.

2.3 The MESSENGERS Library

The MESSENGERS environment provides a library of functions that extend the basic capabilities of the language and its interpreter as described so far. The coordination library is incorporated into the MESSENGERS interpreter as a set of node-resident functions, which may be called from Messenger's *func()* statement explained in Section 2.1 or called within any user-defined function invoked from *func()*. The coordination library's functions fall into two main categories: the first support the control of Messengers at run time; the second support inter-object coordination relative to GVT. This time-based coordination complements the space-based coordination achieved through shared node variables and is of great importance not only to simulation but also to other parallel processing problems, such as distributed termination and barrier synchronization. The following lists the most important library functions:

Functions for Messengers Control:

Since Messengers are created and destroyed at run time, several functions have been provided to support these tasks. The creation of new Messengers is accomplished using the functions *inject()* and *duplicate()*. The former creates a Messenger from a file containing the Messenger's behavior. It may also supply arbitrary initial parameters to the newly created Messenger. The function has two forms, depending on its intended use: one may be invoked from the Unix shell, thus allowing the user to create new Messengers on the fly; the other is used inside Messengers programs, thus allowing Messengers to create progenies at run time.

The function *duplicate()* allows a new Messenger to be created by cloning. It is provided mainly for performance reasons, since it replicates an existing behavior and hence does not involve the file system. The creation of Messengers using this function should not be confused with the replication of Messengers during navigation. The latter is implicit and is the result of the Messenger's following multiple logical links during a *hop()* statement. The function *duplicate()*, on the other hand, causes an explicit creation of a new Messengers inside a node.

A Messenger may terminate itself by executing the command *exit* or it may be killed by another Messenger using a function *kill(mid)*, where *mid* is the victim's internal identifier. This is known to its creator (in a way similar to a Unix fork) and may also be passed explicitly to other Messengers. A Messenger can find its own *mid* by calling *getmid()*.

Virtual Time Control:

Maintaining GVT imposes significant overhead on each processor due to the need for additional inter-processor communication and possible rollbacks. Hence the user has the option turn this feature on or off as needed by a given application. The virtual time control functions, *gvt_start()* and *gvt_stop()* are provided for this purpose.

Scheduled Function Invocation:

When GVT is active, any user-defined function may be scheduled to execute in the future relative to the GVT. The function invocation is scheduled as a future event. However, it remains an integral part of the invoking Messenger's behavior. In other words, the invoking Messenger is suspended until the function executes. At that time, the same function may be scheduled again as a future event or control returns to the interpreted Messenger's program.

The scheduling of a future invocation of a function may be based on a specific GVT value, on a predicate, or on a combination of both. The following is a list of the possible options:

1. *Schedule at a specific time:* The function will be invoked when GVT reaches the specified time value. That is, the Messenger schedules its wake-up call at a certain point in time.
2. *Schedule when node variable satisfies predicate:* The function will be invoked when a specified node variable satisfies a given condition, for example, when $N > 0$. That is, the Messenger schedules its wake-up call based on a predicate

over a node variable. This is implemented in the interpreter by checking the appropriate predicate each time it processes the future event queue. When not satisfied, the event remains in the queue. A maximum wait interval (using GVT) may also be specified, at which time the event is canceled. This form of scheduling corresponds to a signaling mechanism between Messengers since the condition can be made true only by some other Messenger.

3. *Schedule adaptively based on messenger variable:* Unlike node variables considered in the previous case, messenger variables are local to a Messenger and thus can only be changed by that Messenger. Hence a Messenger cannot suspend itself to wait for a messenger variable to satisfy a predicate. Instead, the rate of invocation of the function computing the variable is varied based on certain predicates involving that variable. In general, the interval at which the function is reinvoked is increased (e.g., doubled) at each invocation as long the predicate is satisfied, and it is decreased while the predicate is false. This permits the rate of function invocation to be continuously and automatically adjusted based on a predicate involving a given messenger variable. The predicate itself may take on three basic forms: (1) it involves only the currently computed value of the messenger variable; that is, as long as the variable M satisfies some predicate $P(M)$, the invocation interval (sampling rate) keeps increasing; (2) it involves the current and the last value of the variable, that is, it considers the estimated first derivative of the variable (its slope) based on its current and previous value; as long as the rate of change (M') of the variable M satisfies some predicate $P(M')$, the invocation interval keeps increasing; (3) it involves the current and the last two values of the variable, that is, it estimates the rate of change of the variable's slope (i.e., the second derivative, M'') over the last two intervals; that is, as long as M'' satisfies some predicate $P(M'')$, the interval keeps increasing.

The following sections illustrate the different types of coordination that are possible within the MESSENGERS paradigm. This includes (1) intra-object coordination achieved by dynamically invoking functions using *func()* or *exec()* as part of a Messenger's behavior; (2) spatial inter-object coordination achieved by reading and writing node-resident variables by different Messengers; and (3) temporal inter-object coordination achieved by utilizing the above GVT-based library functions.

3   Intra-Object Coordination

In this section we illustrate how a distributed application can be structured as a collection of functions, residing on different nodes of a network, where the invocation of these functions and the exchange of data among them is orchestrated by Messengers. We consider an application in Toxicology simulation, which we have been developing in collaboration with UCI's school of Medicine [RA84, FMB+96].

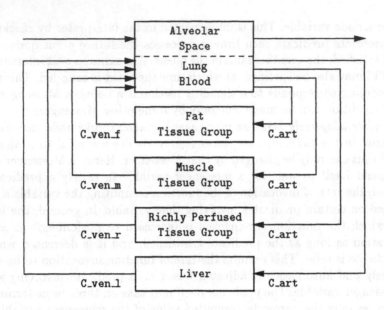

Fig. 1. A Toxicology Model

Simulating biological and physiological processes in living organisms is of great interest to many branches of medicine, biotechnology, and pharmacology. In particular, understanding how chemical substances that are inhaled, ingested, or infused intravenously are distributed through a human or animal body over time, their accumulation in different organs and their metabolism is essential in the development of new drugs and studying the health risks imposed by our changing environment. Research in Toxicology has produced a number of useful models that allow such processes to be simulated on computers. The most advanced models, referred to as pharmaco-kinetic models, attempt to faithfully reproduce the actual physiological processes that take place in a living organism. A model is typically represented as a collection of boxes, each representing a distinct organ or a group of organs having similar physiological characteristics. These are then interconnected by directed links, which represent the flow of fluids, in particular, blood.

Figure 1 shows an example of a simple model. The lung consists of two compartments – the alveolar space represents the area into which outside air is inhaled. Oxygen as well as other chemical compounds are then passed to the lung blood compartment and from there they are carried to all the other organ groups in the body. Each organ group retains some portion of the chemicals based on their size, the volume of incoming blood, and their tissue-specific physiological processes. These values are typically constants and are kept with each organ. The concentration of the chemical in the blood, on the other hand, which also plays an important role in determining how much of the chemical is retained in a given organ, is a variable and must be carried between the organs according to the blood flow. C_{art} in Figure 1 represents the arterial concentration of the chemical being modeled. Each organ changes this concentration based on its specific parameters and hence the outgoing (venal) concentrations C_{ven} are all distinct. They are again combined in the lung, thus completing the basic cycle.

Some organs, notably the liver, also carry out metabolic functions, which may change some portion of the original chemical compounds into others chemicals. For example, styrene, which is inhaled from the air is metabolized into styrene oxide and hence the model must be able to account for multiple chemicals circulating through the body and continuously changing from one to another.

All of the above processes, i.e. the metabolism and the retention of chemicals in organs, are described by sets of differential equations. The objective of the simulations is to solve these equations over a given simulated time interval to predict the levels of certain variables, such as the concentrations of toxins in the various organs, as functions of time. Originally, the models were implemented in conventional simulation languages as simple integration routines driven by a fixed time increment. Using such a continuous time-driven simulation, it is very difficult to improve its performance through parallelization. Furthermore, it is impossible to interact with the simulation process, for example, by altering some of the equations or constants, once execution has started.

Our implementation uses MESSENGERS as a control language to coordinate the operation and interaction of compiled node-resident functions, which carry out the actual computations of the model. The basic approach is to map each organ onto a separate node (running the MESSENGERS interpreter). This node contains the necessary sets of differential equations and constants, precompiled as C functions, describing the organ's behavior. The toxin-carrying fluids, such as blood, are implemented as waves of consecutive Messengers, which cycle through the organism along the predefined paths, thus mimicking the actual flow through the body over time. As they pass through the organs, they trigger the execution of the appropriate functions to compute the new concentrations and other values for the current simulated time increment.

Advantages

There are two primary advantages of the MESSENGERS-based implementation over other approaches. The first is the ability to manipulate the model dynamically at run time; the second is performance due to parallelism and the ability to perform discrete-event rather than time-driven simulation.

Dynamic Model Manipulation: Most existing simulation and modeling tools require the entire experiment to be set up *a priori*; only the final output may be used as feedback for the next experiment. Hence it is difficult to make incremental progress by backtracking to an earlier point and continuing the experiment in a different direction. MESSENGERS, on the other hand, permits not only parameters to be changed at run time but also the functional composition of the model itself. This is because a given simulation model is a collection of functions whose invocation is triggered by Messengers circulating through the model. Thus each simulation run is composed dynamically from the node-resident functions, depending on the programs carried by the Messengers. This gives the user great flexibility in interacting with the model—it allows both the definition and the state of a simulation experiment to be modified at run time by terminating existing Messengers and injecting new ones as necessary. Hence intermediate results observed from the current simulation run may be used as immediate feedback to steer the ongoing experiment.

Assume for example that the user wishes to modify a given organ's behavior, e.g., the liver in Figure 1, to compute its venous concentration using not only the kinetic flow equation but to also include metabolism. This would be achieved by terminating the Messenger passing through that organ and replacing it with one that included a call to the appropriate metabolic equations as part of its computation. With existing simulation control language approaches, the decision to add a metabolic step to an organ would require a major revision and recompilation of the entire model.

Performance: One of the main advantages of a MESSENGERS implementations is the inherent resulting parallelism. In the above model, each organ is logically a separate computational node and thus may be mapped onto a distinct computer, subject to communication overhead, which must be weighed against the gains from parallel execution.

Another major performance improvement can be achieved by a paradigm shift from a time-driven to an event-driven simulation, which is much easier to do with MESSENGERS than with conventional approaches. Most existing pharmaco-kinetic models are time-driven. That is, the differential equations are discretized and their solutions are derived by an integration process that cycles through all organs and recomputes the changes at each constant time step Δt, chosen as one of the simulation parameters. With MESSENGERS, it is easy to reproduce this time-driven behavior. In the above example, the lung node can serve as the time keeper. Initially, a wave of Messengers is sent along the arterial links. Each of these, having triggered and completed all the necessary computations in its respective node, returns along the venous links back to the lung node where it deposits its concentration value. The last Messenger to arrive triggers the next cycle of the simulation, which combines the individual concentrations, computes the next Δt, and causes the next wave of Messengers to leave the lung node. Hence this implementation mimics exactly the original time-driven simulation.

The main difficulty with a time-driven simulation is the choice of an appropriate Δt increment, which represents a trade-off between the model's fidelity and speed. Most time-driven simulations assume a constant Δt for the entire run. Better results may be obtained by varying Δt in response to the rate of change in the computed variables to automatically adjust the fidelity of the model. This improved version, however, is still very wasteful of computational resources. The reason is that the rate of change in the different parts of the model is not uniformly distributed yet a time-driven implementation requires that all nodes recompute their state at every step. As a result, even nodes where minimal or no changes occurred must still perform the same amount of computation as nodes where changes are significant.

The solution to this problem is to make the simulation event- rather than time-driven, which is accomplished by sending Messengers between nodes only when certain critical variables change by a given threshold increment. This not only distributes message traffic more evenly but actually reduces the total traffic volume, since changes are propagated among nodes only when they become significant. At the same time, the model's fidelity increases, since its precision does not depend on an arbitrary time increment (which must be chosen conservatively small to account for the most rapidly changing variables) but reflects the actual current changes. Using the MESSENGERS paradigm, it is simple to make a transition form a time-driven to an even-driven simulation, since the basic concept of Messengers circulating through the system is present in both cases. That is, each Messenger uses the scheduling function (time- or value-based) presented in Section 2.3 to determine its next step. In a conventional implementation, on the other hand, the fundamental structure must be changed to replace the global cycle inherent to time-driven simulation by a continuous event time line characteristic of event-driven simulations.

4 Inter-Object Coordination

In this section we consider a class of applications structured as collections of complex interacting entities. Typical examples of such applications are interactive battle simulations [Com94], particle-level simulations in physics [HE88], traffic modeling [Res94], and various individual-based simulation models in biology or ecology [HDP88, Vil92, HW92]. Related to the latter is also the study of collective behavior in AI, which investigates the mechanisms that result in complex and highly coordinated behaviors of groups of individuals, such as a school of fish or an ant colony, while each individual has only a very limited local knowledge of the "problem" and a set of simple rules to follow [Res94]. Finally, advanced graphics and animation applications, especially those involving large numbers of individuals, such as the animation of a flock of birds, have also taken advantage of individual-based modeling [Rey87].

To illustrate the type of problems we are concerned with in this section and to show how they are solved within the MESSENGERS paradigm, we consider the simulation of a school of fish. It has been observed that schools of fish are capable of performing complex maneuvers, for example, when avoiding a predator, without any particular individual taking on the role of a leader. The complex behavior of the entire school is the results of local interactions among neighboring fish.

In [HW92], a specific model has been formulated, where each fish periodically adjusts its position and velocity by coordinating its movement with up to four of its neighbors. Figure 2 illustrates the model components graphically. Each individual fish, shown as the black icon in the center of the illustration, has a certain radius (R3) of "visibility". Within this circle, excluding the dead angle area directly behind the fish, it first chooses a small number of neighbors, which

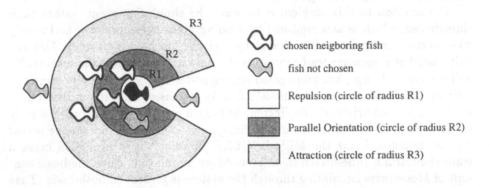

R3
R2
R1

$\bigcirc$ chosen neigboring fish

$\bigcirc$ fish not chosen

☐ Repulsion (circle of radius R1)

■ Parallel Orientation (circle of radius R2)

☐ Attraction (circle of radius R3)

Fig. 2. Ranges of the Basic Behavior of a Fish

it will use to recompute its own vector of motion, i.e., its speed and orientation. In the model at hand, the number of neighbors is four and they are chosen and prioritized according to certain rules. In particular, neighbors that are closest and those that are in front are preferred. In Figure 2, the four white fish icons indicate the chosen neighbors. Based on each of its neighbor's distance, speed, and orientation, the fish then determines a possible correction in its own speed and/or orientation. The following cases are distinguished:

1. *Repulsion* – if the neighbor fish is too close (within the circle of radius R1), the fish tries to avoid a collision by turing away.
2. *Parallel orientation* – if the neighbor fish is in the preferred range, i.e., between R1 and R2, the fish swims in the same direction and at the same speed as its neighbor.
3. *Attraction* – if the neighbor fish is too far away, i.e., between R2 and R3, the fish swims in the direction of its neighbor.

The individual speed and orientation corrections resulting from considering each of its neighbor are then combined, for example by computing their averages, to determine the new speed and orientation.

The above model, which is based on actual observations of fish behavior, is an example of collective intelligence: the graceful and highly complex movements of the entire school are the result of local interactions among individual neighboring fish. Similar models have been formulated to investigate other phenomena of collective behavior. For example, by defining rules for inter-species interaction, it is possible to study the various evasive maneuvers used by fish schools to avoid predators.

MESSENGERS is a natural paradigm for these types of applications. The simulated environment, which in the simplest case is a two-dimensional ocean, is partitioned and distributed over the network of processing elements. Figure 3 shows a partitioning using a homogeneous grid where each grid cell is mapped

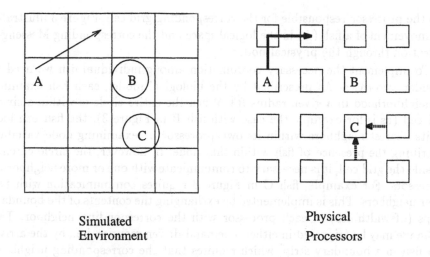

Simulated Environment	Physical Processors

Fig. 3. Logical and Physical Object Migration

onto one physical node. In our present implementation, the physical network is a LAN of workstations, implying a fully connected topology. Hence processors only need to keep track of their logical neighbors in the simulated space.

Each individual fish is then implemented as a Messenger, which carries its own behavior. In general, it could be programmed to "live" for a certain period of time, to interact with other members of the same species or with predators, to multiply, etc. In the application at hand, the objective is to study the collective school behavior. Hence the behavior of each individual fish is to swim indefinitely in the simulated space and to continuously adjust its speed and orientation by interacting with its nearest neighbors as dictated by the biological model. For this purpose, each Messenger representing a fish carries its current position (coordinates within the simulated environment) and motion vector at a given point t in the simulated time. Based on these and the relevant information about its nearest neighbors, it computes its new position and vector at time $t + \Delta$. It then schedules the reinvocation of its behavior function to occur at time $t + \Delta$ using a time-based scheduling function (Section 2.3), which suspends it until that time. When it is awakened the function computes its new position and vector, and again suspends itself until the next Δ interval has passed. The node interpreter services all events in the order of simulated time and hence all fish advance concurrently as the interpreter is multiplexed among the individual Messenger programs.

One important implication of the MESSENGERS paradigm is that the individual fish move not only within the simulated space but actually migrate among processors in the network. This occurs when a fish crosses the boundary of a grid cell. It not only computes the new coordinates but the corresponding Messenger performs a *hop* statement (Section 2.1), which causes it to transfer into the processor responsible for the corresponding grid cell. Figure 3 illustrates the movement of a fish (A) in the logical space and the corresponding Messenger migration through the physical nodes.

To implement the necessary coordination among individual fish we need to consider two cases. As prescribed by the biological model, each fish examines its neighborhood in a given radius R3. When the entire circle is within a single grid cell (as is for example the case with fish B in Figure 3), the fish can look for its nearest neighbors within its own processor by examining node variables describing the presence of fish within that node. If, however, the circle extends outside the grid cell, it is necessary to communicate with one or more neighboring processors. For example, fish C in Figure 3 requires communication with two other neighbors. This is implemented by exchanging the contents of the boundary strips (of width R3) of each processor with the corresponding neighbor. This exchange may be triggered in either a demand-driven manner, i.e., by the arrival of a fish in a boundary strip, which requires that the corresponding neighbor's boundary strip be examined, or in a data-driven manner, i.e., by automatically reporting any changes in the boundary strips to the corresponding neighbors.

Advantages

Analogous to the Toxicology application of Section 3, there are two primary advantages of the MESSENGERS-based implementation of the fish schooling simulation over other approaches. The first is the ability to describe new behaviors at run time; the second is performance due to parallelism, reduced communication and the ability to perform discrete-event rather than time-driven simulation.

Dynamic behaviors: With most existing simulations, the different types of entities that will be participating in a simulation must be set up *a priori*. To introduce a new entity, the simulation programs have to be modified, recompiled, and restarted. But to be most effective, the user should not only have the ability to introduce entities with known behaviors (developed at compile-time) but should also be able to create entities with new behaviors while the simulation is in progress. For instance, in a school of fish model, the user may wish to introduce new types of fish (e.g. a predator), or modify existing behaviors.

One of the advantages of the MESSENGERS' philosophy is that it is inherently open-ended in that its functionalities are not bounded by the number of predefined message types to which a node is able to respond. Instead, all functionalities are embodied in messenger programs and carried through the net. New entities can therefore be created and injected into the simulation space on the fly as the simulation is progressing. Similarly, existing behaviors may be changed by replacing Messengers on the fly.

Performance: To exploit parallelism, applications of the type described in this section need to deal with two important mapping issues: (1) how to divide the simulated environment (e.g. the ocean) over the processors, and (2) how to distribute the mobile objects (e.g. the fish). To reduce communication, it is imperative that the two be closely correlated. The reason is that only fish in close proximity in the logical space need to communicate with each other. If they are in close proximity in the physical space as well, only a very small number of processors, if any, need to exchange any information. This problem, which is a manifestation of the general proximity detection problem in simulation, can be seen in Figure 3. If all fish in a particular logical grid cell are always executing in the processor corresponding to that grid cell then a processor needs to communicate with only its local neighbors. For example, to examine the visibility range (radius R3) of fish C, it only need to communicate with two neighbors. In the case of fish B, no inter-processor communication is required. In general, the need to communicate depends on radius R3 relative to the grid cell size.

In a conventional message-based implementation of the problem, guaranteeing that the logical environment (including all mobile entities) is always perfectly correlated with the physical network is difficult to achieve due to the high cost of process migration. Hence objects are typically assigned to a given processor at the time of creation and remain stationary at that node for the duration of their execution. Due to their subsequent movement in the logical space, the logical neighbors of any given fish may reside on any processor. Hence each processor must either communicate with all other processors to detect the proximity of other fish, or some complex tracking mechanisms must be implemented. With MESSENGERS, on the other hand, the correlation requirement is satisfied automatically. Each Messenger representing a fish simply performs a *hop* statement when it detects that its new coordinates are outside the current grid cell. This causes it to migrate to the corresponding new processor. Since Messengers are inherently mobile in the physical space, this can be performed very efficiently.

In addition to the above dramatic reduction in inter-processor communication due to strict logical-to-physical space correlation, MESSENGERS also facilitate an easy transition from a time-driven to an event-driven simulation. The reason, which is analogous to that given for the Toxicology simulation in Section 3, is that each individual Messenger controls its own behavior. In a time-driven implementation it would recompute its position and schedule itself to wake up after a fixed time interval Δ using a time-based scheduling function. It is however just as simple to vary this interval by having each fish compute an appropriate Δ value at each step. For example, it could adjust Δ based on its current speed and/or the number of other fish in its neighborhood. This automatically adjusts the fidelity of the computation by invoking the relevant functions more frequently when necessary while not wasting unnecessary computational resources when changes are minimal. Making such a transition from a time-driven to an event-driven simulation in a conventional implementation is very difficult, since each is based on a fundamentally different organization.

5 Conclusions

We have presented a novel paradigm, called MESSENGERS, which is based on the concept of autonomous messages, each carrying a complete program to describe its behavior. These programs are interpreted by daemons running in each physical node of a network, which allows Messengers to navigate through the network, to communicate with one another, and to invoke precompiled node-resident functions. The MESSENGERS paradigm is related to other approaches that allow behaviors to be carried on messages. Among these are WAVE [Sap88], Java (Sun Microsystems), Telescript (General Magic), and various versions of "intelligent email". A survey and a classification of these systems based on their abilities to navigate autonomously and to coordinate the invocation of node-resident functions may be found in [BFD96].

In this paper we have focused on MESSENGERS' capabilities as a coordination paradigm, which can be exploited at two different levels of abstraction. First, each Messenger's behavior depends not only on the interpretive program it carries but also on the functions it may invoke and utilize when visiting a node. Hence the behavior of any given Messenger is determined by the composition of functions it invokes at run time. This capability, which we called intra-object coordination, allows us to view an application as a collection of distributed node-resident functions, whose invocation and data exchange is coordinated by the Messengers. Alternately, we can view an application as a collection of autonomous objects, each represented by a dynamically composed Messenger, which need to coordinate their actions among themselves in time and/or space. We refer to this level as inter-object coordination. We have shown, using concrete examples, that there are important classes of applications that can benefit greatly from the inherent flexibility and improved performance resulting from the MESSENGERS concept.

MESSENGERS is currently operational on a LAN of Sun-4 workstations interconnected by an Ethernet. Our current research efforts concentrate on the development of the two applications discussed in this paper and on further improvement of the MESSENGERS system itself, which includes the development of a graphics-based interface for the construction and control of simulation models, and on automatic load balancing to further improve performance. For additional information, the reader is referred to our WWW page: http://www.ics.uci.edu/~bic/messengers.html.

References

[BFD96] L. Bic, M. Fukuda, and M. Dillencourt. Distributed Computing using Autonomous Objects. *IEEE Computer*, (to appear) 1996.

[Bic95] L. Bic. Distributed Computing using Autonomous Objects. *5th IEEE CS Workshop on Future Trends of Distributed Computing Systems, Cheju Island, Korea*, August 1995.

[Com94] DIS Steering Committee. The DIS Vision: A Map to the Future of Distributed Simulation. *Institute for Simulation and Training*, 1994.

[FMB+96] M. Fukuda, K. L. Morse, L. Bic, M. Dillencourt, E. Lee, and D. Menzel. A Novel Approach to Toxicology Simulation based on Autonomous Objects. *SCS Western MultiConference, Simulation in the Medical Sciences, San Diego*, Jan 1996.

[Fuk95a]   M. Fukuda.   MESSENGERS: Intermediate Code Specification.   *Report MSGR-04, University of California, Irvine*, 1995.

[Fuk95b]   M. Fukuda. MESSENGERS: Language Specification and System Interface. *Report MSGR-01, University of California, Irvine*, 1995.

[GC92]   D. Gelernter and N. Carriero.   Coordination Languages and their Significance. *Communications of the ACM*, 35(2):97–107, February 1992.

[HDP88]   M. Huston, D. DeAngelis, and W. Post. New Computer Models Unify Ecological Theory. *BioScience*, 38(10):682–691, November 1988.

[HE88]   R.W. Hockney and J.W. Eastwood. *Computer Simulations using Particles.* IOP Publishing Ltd, Bristol, Great Britain, 1988.

[HW92]   A. Huth and C. Wissel. The Simulation of the Movement of Fish Schools. *Journal of Theoretical Biology*, 156:365–385, 1992.

[RA84]   J. C. Ramsey and M. E. Andeersen. A physiologically based description of the inhalation pharmacokinetics of styrene in rats and humans. *Toxicology and Applied Pharmacology*, 73:159–175, 1984.

[Res94]   M. Resnick. Changing the Centralized Mind. *Technology Review*, pages 33–40, July 1994.

[Rey87]   C.W. Reynolds. Flocks, Herds, and Schools: A Distributed Behavioral Model. *Computer Graphics*, 21(4):25–34, July 1987.

[Sap88]   P. Sapaty. WAVE-1: A New Ideology of Parallel and Distributed Processing on Graphs and Networks. *Future Generations Computer Systems*, 4(1), 1988.

[Vil92]   F. Villa. New Computer Architectures as Tools for Ecological Thought. *Trends in Ecology and Evolution (TREE)*, 7(6):179–183, June 1992.

Ariadne and HOPLa:
Flexible coordination of collaborative processes

Gert Florijn, Timo Besamusca, Danny Greefhorst

Utrecht University, Department of Computer Science
P.o. Box 80.089, 3508 TB Utrecht, the Netherlands
E-mail: *florijn@cs.ruu.nl*

Abstract. The Ariadne system and its modeling language HOPLa aim to provide generic support for hybrid collaborative processes, i.e. complex information processing tasks involving coordinated contributions from multiple people and tools. Ariadne should be usable for a wide variety of such processes and actively support people working in them and defining and managing them.

The basic concept in Ariadne is that of a process. It combines a shared workspace with mechanisms to control the growth and evolution of this workspace. The workspace holds tree-shaped data and is self-descriptive, in the sense that it holds the actual data but also the constraints (i.e. type definitions) that govern its structure. Nodes in the workspace can be marked as tasks to be performed and coordination operators and constraints, e.g. on the deadline or performer of a task, can be attached. Ariadne manages active processes and provides the interaction with the outside world. When tasks are enabled, actors are notified and results of their actions are stored in the workspace.

A key issue for Ariadne is flexibility. It should be easy for users to model and create new kinds of processes even if this happens during the work in the process itself. This is addressed in two ways. First, process workspaces can be adapted arbitrarily within the limits of type-definitions stored within them. Second, both process descriptions and running processes are HOPLa programs. This means that a running process can be stopped, arbitrarily modified (through editing of the program text) and continued whenever exceptions make this necessary and without the loss of any data that had already been produced.

1. Introduction

Coordination languages provide a new perspective on constructing computer programs. Instead of describing individual computations, a coordination language is used to glue together existing computations into new systems [Carriero92]. Given this scope, a coordination language does not have to be computationally complete, e.g. it does not have to provide things like arithmetic operations. Instead it should be "coordinationally complete", providing the means to create new computations and to organize and control their execution in dimensions like time and space.

Coordination and coordination languages have become popular in several fields. In this paper we focus on the application of coordination on supporting group work. In particular, we discuss computer support for hybrid collaborative processes. These are complex information processing activities that involve coordinated contributions by multiple users and computer agents. Typical examples of such processes are

- organizing and performing a poll among a group on a particular subject
- finding a suitable time-slot and location for a group meeting
- performing administrative procedures like travel expense reimbursement, granting loans, editing journals, or organizing the program committee for conferences
- keeping track of bug-reports in software and of their resolution
- carrying out a review of a draft report

All of these activities involve organized contributions by multiple users and tools. Instead of developing dedicated tools for specific activities, the main objective of our research is to create a generic environment that assists people in modeling, performing and managing a broad variety of such activities. This requires a more general coordination model by which

- the work can be decomposed into smaller steps
- the steps can be assigned to and performed by various people or tools
- the execution of steps can be coordinated (e.g. ordered in time)
- the results of steps are kept together for reference and use by future steps

The goal of our work is to define such a model and implement it in a system that provides active support for users working in and with such processes. For example, users who can perform a particular step in a process should be notified and possibly reminded later on. Since we would like (end-) users to define processes, the system should be as simple as possible, while remaining expressive enough to handle the variety of activities. Flexibility is also a key issue. The model (and system) should not only work for routine processes for which the steps to be performed and the data that is shared are well-known, but also for ad-hoc processes in which the steps and the associated data are defined on-the-fly.

In this paper we describe how the Ariadne system and its process modeling language HOPLa, address these issues. Section 2 provides some background and motivation. Sections 3, 4 and 5 discuss HOPLa and Ariadne in some detail. In section 3 we discuss the data model used to store the shared data in Ariadne processes. Section 4 discusses the mechanisms to define tasks and control their execution, while section 5 sketches the way in which processes are executed by Ariadne. In section 6 we discuss some examples and identify some shortcomings of the current system while section 7 provides some conclusions and discusses current research.

1.1. Acknowledgments

Doaitse Swierstra initiated the Ariadne project and provided helpful comments on earlier versions. Many thanks also to the anonymous referees for their comments.

2. Background and motivation

In this section we discuss the characteristics of hybrid collaborative processes and consider what is needed to support them. We also look at existing systems and evaluate them briefly.

2.1. Examples of collaborative processes

To set the scene for the rest of this paper, we first give some examples of the kind of collaborative processes we consider. First of all, there are many processes that are variations of the basic notion of an (electronic) conversation. Consider, for example, a negotiation-cycle in which two parties try to reach consensus on a certain topic, e.g. a supplier and a customer trying to reach agreement about the price of a product [e.g. Martial90]. Another example of such conversation-oriented processes is the Speech-Act model of conversations used in the Coordinator [Flores88]. Here users interact via typed messages and the system imposes structure on the conversation by limiting the types of messages that can be sent in reaction to an earlier message of a given type.

Many collaborative activities focus on the coordinated development of some electronic product, as in the Issue-Based Information System (IBIS) approach to structure group discussions [Conklin88]. In IBIS, a discussion is a hypertext web of nodes that either are Issues (discussion topics), Positions (opinions about the issues) and Arguments (that support or weaken positions). The IBIS-model also restricts the links that can occur in the web. Version management is another example of a product-centered process. It manages and records the evolution of a product, such as a computer program. Starting out with an initial version, changes made to the product result in new versions that are successors to the original.

A well-known class of office processes are routine administrative processes. As an example consider the handling of invoices in an office. When a service has been provided or a product delivered, an invoice is sent to the customer with the request to pay before a certain date. If the payment has been received within the given time-frame, the process is terminated successfully, otherwise a reminder has to be sent (typically by some information system) to the customer. Routine processes also occur in software development, e.g. a process that describes how modifications to an existing system must be developed and reviewed [Heimbigner91].

2.2. Common ingredients

While these processes appear to be very different, there are some fundamental similarities (see also [Ellis91]). First of all, they are collaborative: they are aimed at a particular goal and involve contributions by multiple actors. Secondly, they all involve data that is shared among the participants. For example, the two parties involved in a negotiation need to have an up-to-date picture of the latest offers and reactions, while in an IBIS discussion all people involved need access to the same discussion database. In the remainder of this paper we use the term *workspace* to refer to the shared data.

The final similarity is that all processes are organized in some way, by imposing constraints on the workspace and/or on the way of working. Constraining the workspace means that the shared data in the process has to meet some predefined structure (defined in a so-called *workspace model*), while constraining the way of working means that the work is broken down into tasks and that the execution of these tasks is coordinated. This includes defining when a task should be performed, e.g. by planning it for a particular moment in time or by defining dependencies on (specific results of) other steps. Similarly, constraints can be defined to control execution properties of tasks, such as who can/should perform it, which specific resources should/can be used, when the work should be finished (a deadline), or what the result should be. In the remainder we will use the term *process model* to refer to the decomposition in tasks and the constraints imposed on them for a particular process.

2.3. Variations

These common ingredients also allow us to identify some of the differences between actual collaborative processes (see also [Kaplan92]).

As far as the use of constraints is concerned, some processes just structure the data (e.g. IBIS) while stating little about the process. Others structure just the process (e.g. the negotiation-cycle) and still others structure both (e.g. administrative procedures). The detail of the models spans a wide spectrum, ranging from unstructured, via semi-structured to highly structured. If we consider the data in a process, for example, there can be no or hardly any constraints imposed (e.g. the versioning process does not state anything about the objects that are versioned), while on the other hand there can be very detailed constraints, as will typically be the case for the forms and databases used in an administrative process.

Finally, the moment at which the models are established can vary. For some cases, the models may be known and defined in advance, and not changed during the execution of a process (e.g. routinely executed administrative processes). In other situations, the models may be less obvious at the outset of process, because a lack of understanding of what is to be done or of a lack in experience with the particular situation (ad-hoc processes), but also because the way in which the work is done depends on the context where it is performed (so-called situation action [Suchman87]). In these situations, the workspace and/or process models may be created, refined and adapted during the work on a process itself. It can mean that constraints are added (e.g. more tasks are defined and scheduled, more structure is imposed on the workspace), but also that existing constraints are relaxed. A similar situation can occur in routine processes when some circumstances during execution differ from the expectations, e.g. when an important client demands a different payment period or a non-standard way of booking of an order. Handling such exceptions [Karbe90] can imply that a slightly modified or completely revised process model has to be adopted.

2.4. Computer support

There exists a large body of work on support of group work. In fact, the whole field of CSCW and groupware [e.g. Ellis91] is concerned with this. Both there and in the field of office systems, coordination of (human) activities has been studied from a theoretical perspective [e.g. Malone90] but also from a practical perspective. There are numerous models and systems aimed at supporting specific problems, like IBIS implementations [Conklin88], or tools for negotiations and conversations [Flores88].

Based on the similarities identified above, however, the notion of generic support for collaborative processes is an interesting, albeit challenging, possibility that has been proposed elsewhere too [Ellis94]. In fact, over the years several systems have been developed which can be parametrized to some extent. Since this paper does not provide room for a complete overview we consider only a few examples. OVAL [Malone92] and PAGES [Hämmäinen91] are messaging systems that allow the exchange of user-defined, semi-structured objects, while Lotus Notes provides a shared document database with the ability to define various types of semi-structured objects and related applications. Workflow management systems [Karbe90, Kreifelts91, Gulla94] can be parametrized by a process model. Similar systems have been put forward in the field of software engineering [e.g. Kaiser93]. Finally, systems like the Conversation Builder [e.g. Kaplan92] can structure both data and the way of working, and thereby support different kinds of collaborative processes.

2.5.   The Ariadne project

The problem with most existing systems is that they are focused on just one ingredient (i.e. data or process) and are frequently biased towards routine situations. Defining new workspace or process models is not a trivial matter and adaptation of these model within the context of a running process is almost always impossible. There are no adequate means to deal with exceptional situations and with situated or ad-hoc actions.

The aim of our research in the Ariadne project is to create an environment – called Ariadne – that provides generic support for hybrid collaborative processes. As follows from the discussion above, an important research goal is to provide support for a broad class of processes while offering the necessary flexibility to enable groups to handle exceptions and to organize ad-hoc work. In particular we want (end-) users to be able to define models for a particular activity and to adapt these models within the context of a running process.   Clearly this means that both the language used to describe models as well as the overall system should be simple to understand and use.

The core of our approach is a simple, flexible data model for workspaces augmented with mechanisms to define constraints that govern how this workspace grows and evolves. In the next two sections we discuss these aspects in some detail.

3.   Shared workspaces as flexible records

The shared workspace is the core of an Ariadne processes. It holds the data that is shared by the participants in the process. As we saw earlier, a fundamental requirement for the workspace is that it can hold both highly structured data (e.g. forms consisting of typed fields) but also unstructured or semi-structured objects (e.g. an E-mail message). HOPLa - the language used to define Ariadne processes [Besamusca95] - is based on the idea of flexible records, but extends it along several directions. In this section we give an overview both of the ideas behind flexible records and the way they are used in HOPLa.

3.1. Flexible records

Ψ–terms or *flexible records* [Ait-Kaci86] are a generalization of first-order terms as found in Prolog. They are record-like structures defined by the following rule:

$$d::= X: s(l_1 \Rightarrow d, K, l_n \Rightarrow d) \quad \text{with } n \geq 0$$

Here s is an element of a set S of sorts or typesymbols; it denotes the rootsymbol of this term. Each l_i denotes a feature, while X denotes an address that can be used to refer to this term. Terms can be represented textually. Consider the following "record" (parentheses for feature-less terms are omitted; upper-case names denote addresses):

```
P: person(name -> NM: id(first -> F: "Gert";
                         last  -> L: string);
           addr -> AD: address)
```

This defines a record with two features, one labeled `name` and one labeled `addr`. The name field refers to a term of type `id`, which again has two fields, `first` and `last`, while the `addr` feature denotes a value of type `address`. Typesymbols denote sets of values, such as `person`, `id` or `string`, or individual values, such as `"Gert"`. Individual values thus are represented as singleton-set types.

By using address references, sub-structures in a term can be shared. Consider a slightly different definition of a person record:

```
P: person(name-> NM: id;
           spouse -> S: person(spouse -> SS: P))
```

This defines a cyclic data structure (through the use of P) where the spouse of the spouse of a person refers to the original person.

3.2. The subtype relationship

Typesymbols are partially ordered to reflect subtyping or set inclusion, with a type T (or `any`) as top of the order and type ⊥ (or `none`) at the bottom. Typically the subtype relationship is (pre-) defined for individual values such as `"a"` and their natural type, i.e. `string`.

The subtype ordering on typesymbols also implies an ordering on terms, i.e. one term can be a subtype of another. A term x is a subtype of a term y (denoted as $x < y$) iff all of the following conditions hold

- the rootsymbol of x is a subtype of the rootsymbol of y
- for all features $l_y => d_y$ there is a $l_x => d_x$ with $d_x < d_y$, that is to say:
    - x has at least all the features defined in y and possibly more
    - terms in x denoted by features in y are subtypes of the corresponding terms in y

While maintaining the subtype relationship, a term can be modified in two ways. First, we can add new features, e.g. we can extend a person record with arbitrary features like "income", "age" or "employer" without breaking the subtype relationship with the person record defined above. Second, an existing typesymbol can be replaced by a subtype. This also holds for simple types and individual values so we can replace an occurrence of typesymbol `string` with a value such as `"a string"`.

3.3. HOPLa terms

Flexible records and the subtype rule provide the basis for defining and manipulating the workspace of an Ariadne process. Processes and their workspaces in Ariadne are defined using HOPLa (Hybrid Office Process Language). A HOPLa definition must provide all the information needed by the run-time system to initialize a workspace when a process is created and to maintain the workspace during the lifetime of a process. Obviously, this requires the definition of a term for the (initial) structure of the workspace, but also the typesymbols used in the term, and the subtype relationships among them.

To allow for this, a HOPLa definition consists of two ingredients: a definition of a term (the initial structure) and a set of type definitions or *termtypes*. A termtype defines a set of term values by listing a typesymbol plus the set of features that terms of this type at least should have. Termtypes are defined as subtypes of other termtypes. Consider the following definitions (note that term addresses are not required in HOPLa definitions):

```
Person(name -> string; age -> integer);
Emp<Person(manager -> Person);
```

Here we define two new termtypes (Person and Emp) where Emp is defined as a subtype of Person. Person has no explicit supertypes; it is an implicit subtype of the (predefined) termtype Any.

The HOPLa definition of a subtype can be seen as an explicit specification of the general subtype relation among terms. The < operator indicates that values (or instances) of the subtype must have at least all features defined in the supertype combined with all locally defined features. If there is overlap in the list of "inherited" features, the (terms denoted by) locally defined features must be subtypes of (terms denoted by) the inherited features. Instances of the subtype in that case will have the locally defined values. In the example, an Emp term will have three features, i.e. name, age and manager. For practical purposes, some types and subtype relations are predefined. In particular, HOPLa offers predefined types like integer and string, and accepts values of these types (e.g. constant numbers and constant strings) which are recognized as subtypes of the corresponding types.

The initial structure of the workspace is defined by a number of term definitions. These are just features that denote terms that are instances of termtypes defined earlier. When a workspace is created, the terms will be instantiated with all the features defined in the corresponding termtypes. Following that, the terms can be modified, where the subtyping constraints defined for flexible records apply. So, we can add features to a term or replace a term by a subtype. As an example, consider:

```
john -> Emp(name -> "John D.");
```

Here the instantiated term referred to by the name john will have the three features name, age and manager. In addition, its name feature is set to the string value "John Doe" which is a subtype of the predefined type string.

Note that HOPLa allows us to mix the definition of termtypes and of terms, as in:

```
peter -> Manager<Emp(car -> string)
```

This defines a new termtype `Manager` the values of which have an additional `car` feature, while at the same time defining a term of this type denoted by the name `peter`.

3.4. Collection terms

HOPLa extends the basic mechanisms of flexible records with constructors for collections. The idea is that we can define terms whose (unnamed) features refer to values of one particular termtype. In fact, we can distinguish various kinds of collections, like sets, bags or indexables. Some of these termtypes are predefined in HOPLa. The definition of a `Set` termtype for example looks like this:

```
Set(value -> set; type   -> Any)
```

where `set` is the built-in primitive type that holds the actual elements. A set value can be modified by adding (or removing) an element of the given type. A collection term is created by parametrizing one of the pre-defined termtypes with the type of the elements, i.e. by refining the `type` feature:

```
father -> Person(name->string; children->Set(type -> Person))
```

The actual collection is accessible via the `value` feature.

3.5. Constraints

Constraints explicitly define the set of values that are allowed for a particular feature. In defining constraints for an arbitrary type, it is possible to test for equality and inequality and standard comparison relations are possible for types that have an ordering on them. Membership check (in) and inclusion relations are provided too. In HOPLa we use a *set comprehension* to define a set of legal values, as in:

```
student -> Person(age -> { x | x <= 28 })
staff -> Team(employee -> Person(name -> FST: string);
              manager   -> Person(name -> {p | p != FST})))
```

In the first example the feature `age` is restricted to contain integer values less than or equal to 28. The second example states that the name of an employee should be different from the name of its manager.

4.   Coordinated actions

While flexible records provide us with the means to conveniently express the data involved in a collaborative process, we have not yet the ability to define a way of working, i.e. to define tasks to be performed within the context of a process. In Ariadne we have chosen to unify the definition of the workspace and of the process into one model. Conceptually, this model constrains the growth and evolution of the initial term. More pragmatically, tasks to be performed by people or tools are (directly associated with) terms in the workspace. The idea is that performing a particular task is governed by constraints and will result in an update of some piece of data that is stored in a particular place in the workspace. In the remainder of this section we will discuss this approach.

4.1.   Action terms

A task is viewed as the description of an action that is (to be) performed. In HOPLa we take the following information about an action into account:

- it is performed by one (or possibly multiple) actors.
- it involves performing a particular function or reaching a particular goal. In the case where a computer system performs an action, this can be described by a program or piece of code that should be performed.
- it is performed at a certain location (room, site, processor, etc.)
- it is started and terminated at a certain moment in time.
- it has an execution status, indicating whether it is disabled, enabled, busy or done.

We can summarize this in the following termtype

```
Action<Any(actor        -> Actor;   started    -> Time;
           terminated -> Time;   status     -> Status;
           location   -> Place;  function   -> Function)
```

Note that we assume in this paper that an action is performed by a single actor and performed at a single location. `Actor`, `Time`, `Status`, `Place` and `Function` refer to predefined termtypes representing actor values, time values, status values, location values and function values, respectively. Their definitions look like:

```
Actor(value -> string); Time(value -> integer); …
```

Instances of the `Action` termtype represent work that is to be done, is being done or has been done, depending on the progress in the process. To support this, action terms are recognized and handled by the Ariadne run-time system and the `status` feature determines what is to be done with them. When the run-time system determines that a particular action can be performed it sets its `status` from "disabled" to "enabled" and will try to find an actor that can perform it. If an actor decides to perform the activity, the system is informed, and it will mark the term as being "busy" and log the start time. Following that, the action term is open for user-activity that updates the features in the term (see chapter 5). When the system is informed that work on a particular action has been completed the status of the term is marked "done" and some additional features are set, e.g. the time the action was completed.

In updating these features, the normal subtyping rules apply. Thus it is fairly straightforward to impose constraints on the performance of actions. For example:

```
m     -> Action(actor -> Actor(value -> "florijn");
               terminated -> Time(value -> {x | x < 12345})))
```

indicates that this action can only be involve work by the given actor and should be terminated before a particular deadline. Of course, the Ariadne system can use constraints like these to actively inform people of work to be done and to remind them of deadlines.

4.2. Combining Actions and Data

In principle, we can use action terms to define a collection of tasks and to impose constraints on their execution. However, we do not yet have a way to capture or constrain the result of work on a task in the case it should produce some data.

To support this, HOPLa allows us to define a termtype that is a subtype of multiple other types. The same principles as with normal subtyping apply, with some additional constraints. First the set of feature labels in each of the supertypes should be disjunct. Second, features from shared ancestors are included only once in the instances of these types and constraints on them added by intermediate types should be mutually compatible.

Basically, the semantics of an action term is that it allows an actor to modify the values of all the features in the given action term. So if this term is also an instance of another type, the features of that type also become accessible and can be modified in accordance with the subtyping rules defined earlier. Now it is trivial to combine the workspace definition with the definition of tasks using the + operator. For example, in:

```
Aform<Any( name -> string;    age -> integer );
test-> AForm+Action(addr -> address)
```

test represents a term that will be open to user-activity that can set the features name, addr and age. Note that there is no fundamental requirement that either or all of these features are actually modified; there is just an opportunity to do so.

Turning "data" terms into actions does not work directly for built-in types like string or integer, since these have no features. However, this is corrected easily:

```
Integer<Data(value -> integer); String<Data(value -> string);
```

Here, Data refers to a predefined termtype (without features) that is used to identify data terms (as opposed to Action terms). Most of the termtypes seen earlier are defined as subtypes of Data. We can now define a form in which two fields can be modified by distinct user activities (note the explicit constraint on the actor that can perform the second action):

```
MForm(name -> String+Action;
        age -> Integer+Action(actor -> Actor(value -> "GHF")))
```

4.3. Coordination operators

The introduction of Action terms and the combination of them with data terms provides the basic mechanisms to define a process model for a process. What is lacking however is the means to define relationships between the actions. To handle this, we use a special kind of termtypes, called *coordination operators*. These operators are subtypes of termtype Action and are predefined. Basically, use of these types defines when the actions that are part of a term can be performed.

The three basic coordination operators and their meaning are:
- Serie: actions are performed sequentially, in the order of appearance in a term.
- Parl: actions can be performed concurrently.
- Unord: actions can be performed in random order, but only one can be "busy".

The operators are typically combined with normal terms. The reason for this is that the operators mainly manipulate the order in which data is produced, but do not influence the structure of that data. As an illustration, consider the following examples:

```
a -> Data+Parl(date -> Time+Action; age  -> Integer+Action)
b -> Data+Unord(date -> Time+Action; age  -> Integer+Action)
c -> Data+Serie(date -> Time+Action; age  -> Integer+Action)
```

The first expression (a) defines a form in which the date and the age can be acted upon (e.g. filled in) concurrently. In the second expression (b), either the date is filled in before the age or vice versa but work cannot take place on both actions at the same time, i.e. not both of these actions can be "busy". The last example (c) states that the age needs to be filled in after the date, i.e. the first action should be "done" before the second is "enabled".

Coordination operators can also be used in conjunction with sets. Consider:

```
x    -> Set+Serie(type -> ArbitraryForm+Action);
y    -> Set+Parl(type -> ArbitraryForm+Action);
```

In the first case (x) the elements to be added to the set must be added one at a time. As long as work continues on a particular element (i.e. as long as its status feature has not been set to "done") no other element can be added. In the second example (y) this is possible and work can be going on on multiple elements at the same time.

4.4. Composing coordination operators

The coordination operators are just "special" actions themselves. This means that we can combine these operators with other operators leading to larger structures:

```
f    -> Data+Serie(
    f1 -> Data+Parl(a -> Integer+Action;b -> String+Action)
    f2 -> Data+Serie(x -> Integer+Action;y -> String+Action))
```

The two "sub-forms" of f must be filled in sequentially, i.e. work on f1 must be completed before work on f2 can start. The actions on form f1 can occur in parallel, while for f2 two they must occur in sequence.

To combine coordination operators, we must define when such a term is considered "busy" or "done". These definitions are fairly intuitive. A term marked with Serie, Parl or Unord is "busy" when one of its component actions is "busy", and "done" when all its component actions are "done". However when we combine coordination operators with collections, it is not always obvious when terms should be marked as "done". Of course, if the elements of a collection are defined explicitly (e.g. through the use of set comprehensions), this is not a problem since the term is "done" if all its elements have been performed. However, in:

```
z -> Person+Serie(children -> Set+Parl(type->Person+Action);
                  age       -> Integer+Action)
```

it is not obvious when the setting of the children feature as a whole (i.e. this instance of the Parl operator) can be considered to be "done", so that the age field becomes enabled. In this case, the termination condition is typically outside the scope of the process definition itself. Therefore, users have indicate the "completion" of such a term by setting of the status feature of the term denoted by children.

4.5. Choices

In some situations, several actions - each with their own associated terms - could occur at a specific point along the process, but it is not known a priori which of these alternatives will occur. To model this, a coordination operator OneOf (again a subtype of Action) is defined which expresses that only one of its action components can actually occur during execution of a process. As soon as one of these alternatives is completed, the OneOf term is marked "done" too. As an example, consider the following form, where a choice can be made to provide a registration number or some personal info:

```
f -> Form+OneOf( registrationnr -> String+Action;
                 personalinfo   -> Person+Action)
```

To avoid superfluous work, it may be desirable to enforce early commitment, so that when one the alternatives is chosen (becomes "busy"), the rest of the alternatives become "disabled". Alternatively, we could let work on multiple alternatives proceed in parallel, which would allow the OneOf construct to be used to model an exception handler (e.g. work takes place on one alternative until it appears that something went wrong and another alternative is chosen). Currently, the first semantics is used.

5.   Processes and their execution

The previous two sections have defined all the ingredients that allow us to define Ariadne processes. It has become clear that we can view a process definition as a combination of termtypes and terms, including the definition of actions and their coordination. Technically, an Ariadne process can thus be seen as an Action term. However, to actually "run" a process some additional information is needed such as the actor which initiated the process and who is considered responsible for it. In addition, the run-time system must recognize processes and handle them accordingly. Therefore, a separate termtype Process is predefined as a subtype of Serie.

Given this definition, we can sketch the "interpretation" of processes as handled by the Ariadne system. First of all, the creation of a new process implies the instantiation of a Process term. Typically this is done by providing a HOPLa process definition consisting of termtype definitions and one initial term that is of type Process. Ariadne parses the program (after adding a prelude of standard, built-in type definitions), instantiates the initial term (by copying all the inherited attributes), logs some information in the term (such as the actor that initiated it) and then starts handling activities involved working in and managing this process.

This "process handling" involves two sides. On the one hand, we have to handle incoming events that represent, for example, the results of work on a particular action. On the other hand, we must signal certain situations in a process so that the system can actively support users, e.g. by informing actors that they can perform work on a certain action. Interaction between (the handler of) a process and users or computer programs is thus a fundamental requirement. It is done by exchanging messages across some communication medium like electronic mail or a direct network connection. The actual medium used is determined by the handler. The (incoming) messages ultimately take the form of a term, an instance of a HOPLa termtype Message, though the handler may create these messages from some other representation.

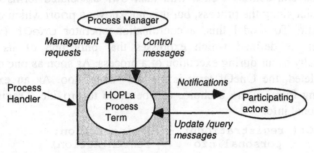

Figure 1: Ingredients of process handling

The handler parses incoming messages, checks whether they are acceptable and may send a response to the sender. We distinguish various kinds of messages. A *query-message* is a request to retrieve a part of the process (workspace) term. It contains a "path", identifying the sub-term wanted, and returns this term as HOPLa text. Such messages are always accepted. An *update-message* on the other hand corresponds to work within an action. Again, a path pointing to the action term in the process must be included, but in addition, features of that term can be set by giving their labels and the new values. Also, it should be indicated whether the action has been completed. In either case, the handler checks whether the update is acceptable, e.g. with respect to coordination operators and subtyping rules. If so, the term is updated.

When an action is completed, the process is reevaluated to determine whether new actions could be performed now. This being the case, we have to appoint the actor(s) that can/will perform the task and possibly allocate additional resources. While in some cases it may be precisely known (through constraints) which actor(s) and resources should be involved, this will typically not be the case. This means that the actor responsible for the process (the "process manager") will have to appoint the actor(s) and allocate the resources. Clearly, this can be done in many different ways. The process manager is sent a signal requesting the allocation, and must respond to this by means of a *control-message* that states the actual allocation. Now the appointed actor(s) can be notified that work has to be done. They can accept this by confirming that work has started (via an update message that sets the action status to "busy") or by immediately sending the results and completing the action.

Obviously, the Ariadne handler has to maintain state information about the interaction with the rest of the world. For example, it should be avoided that actors are notified repeatedly about the same action. This kind of information is again stored in the process term.

In addition to interaction with actors and checking constraints in the term, the system also provides some other functions, among which is the ability to save the complete process state (i.e. the complete term) in textual form on some file. This textual form is just plain HOPLa code, which combines the current state and all the information that was present in the original process definition (like the type definitions). This means that the process can be edited - and thus adapted - easily and then restarted.

6.   Examples

In the previous sections we have summarized the HOPLa mechanisms for describing collaborative processes and the way in which they are handled in Ariadne. In this section we illustrate the system by presenting some examples. At the same time we address some issues still to be resolved.

6.1.   Discussions

First we model an electronic discussion between a group of persons:

```
Discussion<Process(
        group -> Set+Action(type   -> Actor; value -> PS: set));
        discuss -> Thread<Data+Serie(
            message -> String+Action(actor -> { p | p in PS});
            replies -> Set+Parl(type -> Thread )))
```

When a process is performed with this definition, first the set of actors participating in this discussion has to be defined (by setting the feature group). After the group has been established, a string for the message feature has to be provided by one of the actors in the group. After that, replies can be added by members of the group, each of which is the beginning of a separate, parallel thread. Since there are no explicit termination conditions, this process will never "stop" automatically

Another variation on the basic conversation model is the negotiation-cycle. In a negotiation-cycle a supplier and customer try to reach consensus about some topic. The HOPLa representation of a simplified process looks like:

```
Negotiation<Process(
    prepare -> Data+Serie(
        supplier -> S: Actor+Action;
        customer -> C: Actor+Action);
    negotiate -> Proposal<Data+Serie(
        proposal -> String+Action(actor -> { s | s == S } );
            decision -> OneOf(
                accept -> Action(actor  -> {c | c == C});
                revise -> Data+Serie(
                    comment -> String+Action(actor -> {c| c == C});
                    revision -> Proposal))))
```

In the preparation phase the supplier and the customer actors must be identified. Following this the supplier has to create an offer. The customer can then indicate whether he is satisfied with the proposal. If so, the whole process is completed, otherwise the customer should give comments and there is going to be a revised proposal. Again, we assume that the data is represented as strings.

6.2.   Version Management

The purpose of a version management process is to organize the evolution of a particular data object by recording multiple versions and the derivation history of versions (i.e. the successor relation). We see that a version term holds some data (the data of the version) and a number of successors:

```
VersionTree<Process(
  root   -> Version<Data+Serie(
    data -> Data+Action;
    successors -> Set+Parl(type -> Version)))
```

Of course, further information could be recorded for versions like why it was created and what was changed. Also we could restrict the users who can perform these modifications by constraining the actor field.

The fact that we use the `Parl` operator for coordinating the creation of successors means that multiple "revisions" of one version can be active at any given moment in time. Once a user starts working on a new version a corresponding entry in the set is created which can be operated upon in parallel with others. An intuitive approach to model a more pessimistic "locking" behavior would be to replace the `Parl` operator with `Serie`, i.e. the successors feature is defined as

```
  successors -> Set+Serie(type -> Version)))
```

However, this does not work, because in this case the successors set is locked for further additions until the complete version history for the newly added version has been added. Since this process will never explicitly terminate, this will never occur. So, this definition implies that we have linearized development. A good solution for this problem is currently still being investigated.

6.3.   Electronic Voting

The purpose of the electronic voting example is to model the situation where a group of designated users are asked to vote on a particular topic. Users can make a choice from a set of options defined by the organizer of the vote.

```
ElectronicVote<Process(
  prepare -> Data+Parl(
      topic   -> String+Action;
      deadline-> D: Time+Action;
      choices -> Set+Action(type -> String;value -> CH: set);
      group   -> Set+Action(type -> Actor; value -> PS: set));
    votes   -> Set+Parl(
          type -> Vote<Data+Action(
                            choice -> {c | c in CH};
                            actor  -> {p | p in PS})))
```

The voting process consists of two parts; the preparation phase and the actual voting. In the preparation phase the topic, deadline, possible choices and the participants are set. In the voting phase, all participants as denoted by PS must cast a vote which is an element of the set CH of possible choices.

It should be noted that this definition is not precise enough, in that the constraints do not prevent actors from voting more than once. Furthermore the definition lacks the enforcement of a deadline. Basically what should happen is that the set of votes is marked "done" (i.e. no new entries can be made) once the deadline passes. The only way that is possible now is to let the status of the set be modifiable by an action and to let some computerized actor change the status when the deadline passes. Clearly, a more elegant solution to this problem would be desirable.

7.   Summary and current work

The Ariadne system - and its modeling language HOPLa - aims at providing generic support for hybrid collaborative processes. The examples discussed in this paper show that Ariadne and HOPLa can handle a broad variety of situations. The workspace and the process model can be specified in arbitrary detail while the resulting process definitions are still fairly simple and intuitive. The required flexibility is provided in two ways. First, process workspaces can be adapted arbitrarily within the limits of the type-definitions stored within them. Second, running processes are fundamentally the same as their definitions. Both are HOPLa programs and can be represented in textual form. Since a process is fully self-contained, this means that a running process can be arbitrarily modified (through editing) whenever exceptions give rise to this, and without the loss of information that has already been provided.

Work on Ariadne and HOPLa is continuing both on a conceptual and a practical level. Here we describe some of the topics that are currently being addressed.

As seen in section 6, there are some issues that are not handled properly by the current HOPLa definition. One problem area is the combination of coordination operators with collections, and in particular the control over the "locking" behavior for element actions and the termination condition for the collection itself. In fact, we are considering a more general mechanism by which the coordination of component actions and the completion conditions of coordination operators can be described explicitly. This would mean that users could to some extent define the behavior for the operators they want. This would also allow us to distinguish between the two different interpretations of OneOf (section 4).

Most HOPLa functionality described in this paper has been implemented in a preliminary prototype of an Ariadne process handler [Greefhorst96]. Work is currently underway to extend this prototype for use in a distributed environment. Another extension currently being studied is a tool that provides a graphical representation of HOPLa programs. This tool could visualize the actual state of an Ariadne process, but would also make the definition and adaptation of processes easier.

The self-descriptive, self-contained nature of Ariadne processes offers some potential advantages that have to be explored in more detail. For example, migration of processes is conceptually straightforward, in that a process could be sent to another Ariadne interpreter on another machine, and handled there. Users could even take a process along on a portable machine and bring it back later. Furthermore, the fact that processes can be viewed as (textual) data objects introduces the option of meta-processes, i.e. processes that operate upon other processes [Pemberton91].

The process handler (section 5) defines how an Ariadne process interacts with the outside world. It uses some communication mechanism, translates and handles incoming messages and turns state changes in the process into signals to the outside world. Obviously, we can envision multiple handlers that behave and present themselves in different ways. A trivial difference would be in the use of the communication mechanism, e.g. direct network connections vs. electronic mail, which might provide a basis to support both synchronous and asynchronous collaboration in the same process. But, also the information that is exchanged could be in different formats or be presented in different ways, and even the way in which process state changes are handled could be different. This leads to the notion of different *enactment styles* [e.g. Kaiser93]. For example, a more passive handler would let users decide which task they want to work on next and then try to meet the constraints needed to make that happen. In yet other cases the existence of a process model may be implicit- users only see a visual representation of some data in the workspace and modify it. In this case, the handler should track the activities performed by the users and check whether these correspond to (enabled) actions in the procedure. It is simple to implement different handlers explicitly and use them. But a more interesting opportunity however is to describe the enactment policy (including perhaps presentation aspects) in some high-level formalism and make them user-definable. This is an issue that is currently being studied.

Support for "process managers" is also being explored. As indicated before, process management involves the responsibility to allocate actors and other resources to particular tasks while meeting the constraints imposed in the process model. This requires some sort of database to store all the available resources and some approach to satisfy the constraints (see [Boerboom94] for some of the issues and potential solutions). An additional issue is how to appoint the best resource when multiple candidates are available. Clearly, making such choices requires a good overview of other running processes and the resources they (will) need. Also, the possibility of reflective processes [Bandinelli93], where Ariadne processes are used to perform these allocations, is being considered.

8.   References

[Ait-Kaci86]. H. Ait-Kaci, "Type Subsumption as a Model of Computation", in *Proc. of the 1st International Workshop on Expert Database Systems,* L. Kerschberg (Ed.), 1986.

[Bandinelli93] Sergio Bandinelli and Alfonso Fuggetta, "Computational Reflection in Software Process Modelling: the SLANG approach," in *Proceedings of the 15th International Conference on Software Engineering,* Baltimore, Maryland, 1993.

[Besamusca95] Timo Besamusca, "Defining a Coordination Language for Hybrid Office Processes," Master's thesis, University of Utrecht, Dept. of Computer Science, 1995.

[Boerboom94] Benno Boerboom, "Primitiva voor het modelleren van samenwerkings-processen," Master's thesis, University of Utrecht, Dept. of Computer Science, 1994.

[Carriero92] Nicholas Carriero and David Gelernter, "Coordination Languages and Their Significance," *Comm of the ACM,* vol. 32, no. 2, pp. 96–107, February 1992.

[Conklin88] Jeff Conklin and Michael L. Begeman, "gIBIS: A Hypertext Tool for Exploratory Policy Discussion," Technical Report STP-082-88, MCC, Software Technology Program, March 1988.

[Ellis91] C.A. Ellis, S.J. Gibbs, and G.L. Rein, "Groupware: Some Issues and Experiences," *Communications of the ACM*, vol. 34, no. 1, January 1991.

[Ellis94] C.A. Ellis and J. Wainier, "A Conceptual Model of Groupware," in *Proceedings CSCW'94.*

[Flores88] Fernando Flores, Michael Graves, Brad Hartfield, and Terry Winograd, "Computer Systems and the Design of Organizational Interaction," *ACM Transactions on Office Information Systems*, vol. 6, no. 2, pp. 153–172, April 1988.

[Gulla94] J. Gulla and O. Lindland, "Modelling Cooperative Work for Workflow Management," in *Proceedings CAiSE 94,* G. Wijers et. al. (Eds.), Utrecht, 1994.

[Greefhorst96] D. Greefhorst, "A Simulation Environment for Ariadne," Master's thesis, Utrecht University, Dept. of Computer Science, too appear, 1996.

[Hämmäinen91] Heikki Hämmäinen, et. al., "Distributed Form Management," *ACM Transactions on Information Systems*, vol. 8, no. 1, pp. 50–76, January 1990.

[Heimbigner91] Dennis Heimbigner and Marc Kellner, *Software Process Example for ISPW-7,* Anon. FTP from ftp.cs.colorado.edu, /pub/cs/techreports/ISPW7/ispw7.ex.ps, 1991.

[Kaplan92] Simon M. Kaplan, et.al., "Flexible, Active Support for Collaborative Work with ConversationBuilder," in *CSCW'92 - Proceedings of the ACM 1992 Conference on Computer-Supported Cooperative Work,* Toronto, Canada, 1992, pp. 378–385.

[Karbe90] B. Karbe and N. Ramsperger, "Influence of Exception Handling on the Support of Cooperative Office Work," in *Proceedings of the IFIP WG 8.4 Conference on Multi-User Interfaces and Applications,* Simon Gibbs and Alex A. Verrijn-Stuart (Eds.), Heraklion, Crete, Greece, 1990.

[Kaiser93] Gail E. Kaiser, Steven S. Popovich, and Israel Z. Ben-Shaul, "A Bi-Level Language for Software Process Modelling," in *Proceedings of the 15th International Conference on Software Engineering,* Baltimore, Maryland, 1993.

[Kreifelts91] Thomas Kreifelts, et.al., "Experiences with the DOMINO Office Procedure System," in *Proceedings of the Second European Conference on Computer-Supported Cooperative Work,* L. Bannon, M. Robinson, and K. Schmidt (Eds.), Amsterdam, the Netherlands, September 1991, pp. 117–130.

[Malone90] Thomas W. Malone and Kevin Crowston, "What is Coordination Theory and How Can It Help Design Cooperative Work Systems," in *CSCW'90 - Proceedings of the 1990 Conference on Computer-Supported Cooperative Work,* Los Angeles, California, October 1990, pp. 357–370.

[Malone92] Thomas W. Malone, Kum-Yew Lai, and Christopher Fry, "Experiments with Oval: A Radically Tailorable Tool for Cooperative Work," in *CSCW'92 - Proceedings of the ACM 1992 Conference on Computer-Supported Cooperative Work,* Toronto, Canada, November 1992, pp. 289–297.

[Martial90] Frank von Martial, "A Conversation Model for Resolving Conflicts among Distributed Office Activities," in *Proceedings of the 1990 Conference on Office Information Systems,* F. Lochovsky and R. Allen (Eds.), 1990.

[Pemberton91] Steven Pemberton and Lon Barfield, "The MUSA Design Methodology," Technical Report 91/12, Software Engineering Research Centre, December 1991.

[Suchman87] Lucy Suchman, *Plans and Situated Actions.* Cambridge University Press, 1987.

Coordination in the ImpUnity Framework

H.J.M. Goeman[1], J.N. Kok[1], K. Sere[2], R.T. Udink[3]

[1] Dept. of Computer Science, Leiden University,
P.O.Box 9512, 2300 RA Leiden, The Netherlands
{goeman,joost}@wi.leidenuniv.nl
[2] Dept. of Computer Science and Applied Mathematics,
University of Kuopio, P.O.Box 1627, FIN-70211 Kuopio, Finland
Kaisa.Sere@uku.fi
[3] Dept. of Computer Science, Utrecht University,
P.O.Box 80089, 3508 TB Leiden, The Netherlands

Abstract. The ImpUNITY framework is an extension of the UNITY framework. It contains several program structuring mechanisms and puts special emphasis on compositional refinement of both specifications and programs. It has an associated temporal logic, formal refinement notions, and program transformation rules. In this paper we show how coordination in the form of a shared tuple space between communicating ImpUNITY programs is modelled and used during formal program specification and refinement. We exemplify our formalism by a larger case study on a phone system where communication in the system is partly taken care of via a tuple space.

1 Introduction

Several examples of action based coordination languages have been presented in the literature. The shared dataspace language Swarm [4] is based on UNITY [3]. There are, however, some differences: a Swarm program is based on a dynamic set of nondeterministic transaction statements. The ensures relation and the fixed point property have been reformulated, but most of the UNITY theory can be directly applied to the Swarm-logic. The Gamma language [2, 5] is based on a multiset of actions that work on a shared tuple space. Gamma has an associated semantics, and refinement rules. These languages concentrate on the interaction with a shared tuple space.

Our main interest in this paper is to investigate how we can combine different systems and languages via a shared tuple space. The languages themselves can be for example standard imperative languages. Hence we study a framework, in which we can have both the possibility for communication via a shared tuple space, and more standard imperative programming constructs. Additionally we want to bring structure in the tuple space and the state spaces of the local programs, by allowing parts of them to be hidden and making it possible to restrict the access rights of different components to the tuple space.

We discuss how the ImpUNITY-framework can be used for this purpose. The ImpUNITY-framework was introduced in the paper [8] and in the thesis [6]. It is an extension of the UNITY-framework of [3] with the emphasis on formal refinement notions between programs and a collection of program structuring mechanisms. Moreover, the ImpUNITY framework supports compositional refinement of both specifications and programs. In this paper we extend this framework further and show how communication via shared tuple space is treated when specifying and deriving programs within this framework.

We show the practical applicability of our framework by deriving a specification for a phone system in a stepwise manner starting from a specification that gives properties for a shared tuple space and ending up with a network of programs describing the behaviour of the individual phones. The communication in this system is (partly) via a shared tuple space.

The overview of the rest of the paper is as follows. In section 2 we discuss the ImpUNITY Programming Language. Then in section 3 we introduce the ImpUNITY logic. Section 4 deals with coordination and in section 5 refinement notions are discussed. We also give some examples of program transformation rules. Then in section 6 we give the case study on the phone system. We end in section 7 with some concluding remarks.

2 The ImpUNITY Programming Language

In this section we discuss the ImpUNITY programming language. ImpUNITY can be seen as a mixture between UNITY and the language of the action system formalism. It has an associated temporal logic similar to the logic of UNITY [3] and it has formal refinement notions and the structuring mechanisms (procedures, local variables) of the the action system formalism [1].

As an example of an ImpUNITY program, consider the program *Buf* given in Figure 1. This program models a buffer that communicates with its environment by a procedure interface. Messages are put in the buffer by calling the procedure *flushin* and the buffer outputs messages by calling the procedure *flushout*. The *hide*-section of *Buf* specifies that variable b cannot be read by an environment and the modifier $[= \{b\}]$ in the *external*-section specifies that variable b cannot be written by an environment (formally $[= \{b\}]$ is a statement that assigns arbitrary values to variables not in $\{b\}$). The statement in the *assign*-section of *Buf* takes care of the output of the messages in b.

Formally, an ImpUNITY program consists of the following sections.

- The *external*-section, containing a statement (called a modifier) which specifies the way an environment is allowed to change the state. Typically, we will use modifiers of the form $[= Y]$, where Y is a set of variables. This modifier specifies that it is not allowed for an environment to change (other than via exported procedures) the values of variables in Y. The modifier is denoted by *external(F)*.
- The *hide*-section, containing a (possibly empty) set of program variables called a view. It specifies the variables that cannot be read by an environment. However, an environment can assign values to these variables. The view is denoted by *hide(F)*.

Program *Buf*
external [= {*b*}]
hide {*b*}
import proc *flushout*(*int*)
export proc *flushin*(*a* : *int*) = (*b* := *b* ++[*a*])
init *b* = [ ]
assign
    b ≠ [ ] → *flushout*(*hd*(*b*)); *b* := *tl*(*b*)
end{*Buf*}

Fig. 1. Buffer

- The *import*-section, containing declarations of procedures that are imported by the program. This set of imported procedures is denoted by *import*(*F*), and the definitions of these procedures must be provided by an environment.
- The *export*-section, defining procedures that are exported by the program. This set of procedure definitions is denoted by *export*(*F*).
- The *initially*-section, containing a predicate that specifies the possible initial states of the program. This predicate is denoted by *init*(*F*). There should exist at least one state that satisfies *init*(*F*).
- The *assign*-section, containing a set of statements that may contain calls to procedures in the *import*-section and the *export*-section. The set of statements is denoted by *assign*(*F*), statements are separated by the symbol ⫿.

The execution model is the UNITY execution model: statements are executed in a random order and there is a weak fairness assumption.

Parallel composition of programs is modelled by the union operator. Not all programs can be put together in a parallel composition. There are two main restrictions. In order to formulate them, we first need to introduce the standard refinement ordering. The idea is that statement S_1 is refined by statement S_2 (denoted by $S_1 \leq S_2$) if the amount of nondeterminism decreases. (In section 5 we introduce refinement notions for ImpUNITY programs. These are different from this refinement notion on statements.) Such a refinement ordering can be formally defined in terms of predicate transformers [6]. There are two main restrictions:

1. the modifier of each of the programs should be refined by every statement and by every procedure of the other programs (and the other way around), and
2. values of variables in the view of each of the programs should not be read by one of the statements or by one of the procedures of the other programs (and vice-versa).

If two ImpUNITY programs *F* and *G* satisfy these restrictions, then we can define their union *F*⫿*G*. The two assign sections are then put together such that

$assign(F\|G) \stackrel{\text{def}}{=} (assign(F)\cup assign(G))$. The other sections of the program follow directly (for example, the *hide*-section is the union of the two *hide*-sections).

3 The ImpUNITY Logic

The ImpUNITY logic is a UNITY-like logic. The logic is based on the UNITY-properties and takes the interference of environments into account. However, instead of using invariants of the program itself, we use invariants of programs in an environment.

There are two ways in which an environment can interfere with a program: an environment can execute its own statements (but these are restricted by the modifier in the external section of the program), and the environment can call procedures exported by the program. The first step in defining the ImpUNITY logic is the use of local invariants. A local invariant of a program is an invariant that cannot be falsified by an environment. For an ImpUNITY program F, we model the restriction on interference of an environment by $inter(F)$. Formally, (maximal) interference of a program F is defined by

$$inter(F) \stackrel{\text{def}}{=} (external(F)\Box approx(export(F)))^*,$$

where $approx(export(F))$ is an approximation of all possible calls to procedures in $export(F)$ obtained by the nondeterministic choice $\Box$ between all procedure bodies in which possible values for the formal parameters are substituted. The * denotes the nondeterministic choice between all finite iterations (sequential composition) of the statement. Hence, for our program in Figure 1 we have

$$inter(F) = skip\Box S\Box(S;S)\Box(S;S;S)\Box\cdots$$

where $S = ([= \{b\}]\Box\langle\Box a : a \in Int\rangle : (b := b +\!\!+[a])))$.

The fact that we can approximate a call to an imported procedure by $external(F)$ gives us a way to calculate standard UNITY properties of a program; we substitute $external(F)$ for each call to an imported procedure and treat the resulting program as a standard UNITY program. In this way it makes sense to write $(b = [\,])$ *unless false* for the program *Buf* of Figure 1.

Now we use the standard UNITY properties in the definition of properties in the ImpUNITY logic. In ImpUNITY we have one extra property $\rightarrow_{CM}$ called internal leadsto. The main motivation for the introduction of this property is that we want to have a property that satisfies

$$p \rightarrow_{CM} q \text{ in } F \wedge p \text{ unless } q \text{ in } G \Rightarrow p \rightarrow_{CM} q \text{ in } F\|G$$

In UNITY the *ensures* property satisfies this requirement, but $\mapsto$ does not satisfy it. Programs in ImpUNITY have more structure (in fact, parts of the program are not visible to an environment), and we can find a property between *ensures* and $\mapsto$ that satisfies this requirement. We discuss this property in detail in the appendix.

To distinguish properties in the ImpUNITY logic from the other properties, the new properties are subscripted by $*$, and properties in the standard UNITY logic of Chandy and Misra are subscripted by CM. We assume that the reader is familiar with the $invariant_{CM}$, $unless_{CM}$, $ensures_{CM}$ and $\mapsto_{CM}$ properties of UNITY.

Now we are able to introduce the ImpUNITY properties. The basic idea is simple: we use information contained in $inter(F)$ about the environment to derive more properties.

Definition 1. For ImpUNITY program F, properties of F are defined by

$$linvariant_* \ r \ in \ F \ \stackrel{\mathrm{def}}{=} \ r \Rightarrow inter(F)(r) \wedge invariant_{CM} \ r \ in \ F,$$
$$p \ unless_* \ q \ in \ F \ \stackrel{\mathrm{def}}{=} \ \langle \exists r : linvariant_* \ r \ in \ F : (p \wedge r) \ unless_{CM} \ q \ in \ F \rangle,$$
$$p \ ensures_* \ q \ in \ F \ \stackrel{\mathrm{def}}{=} \ \langle \exists r : linvariant_* \ r \ in \ F : (p \wedge r) \ ensures_{CM} \ q \ in \ F \rangle,$$
$$p \mapsto_* q \ in \ F \ \stackrel{\mathrm{def}}{=} \ \langle \exists r : linvariant_* \ r \ in \ F : (p \wedge r) \mapsto_{CM} q \ in \ F \rangle,$$
$$p \rightarrow\!\!\!\!\triangleright_* q \ in \ F \ \stackrel{\mathrm{def}}{=} \ \langle \exists r : linvariant_* \ r \ in \ F : (p \wedge r) \rightarrow\!\!\!\!\triangleright_{CM} q \ in \ F \rangle,$$

The properties defined above are UNITY-like properties in the sense that they can be used in a similar way as the standard UNITY properties. All theorems derived in [3] for properties of a single program also hold for the ImpUNITY properties. Furthermore, the theorems derived for the $ensures_{CM}$ property also hold for the $\rightarrow\!\!\!\triangleright_{CM}$ and $\rightarrow\!\!\!\triangleright_*$ properties. And then, the following substitution theorem holds.

Theorem 2. *Let F be an ImpUNITY program and let r be a predicate such that $linvariant_* \ r \ in \ F$. If for predicates p, p', q and q' both $r \Rightarrow (p = p')$ and $r \Rightarrow (q = q')$ hold, then*

$$p \ unless_* \ q \ in \ F \ = p' \ unless_* \ q' \ in \ F,$$
$$p \ ensures_* \ q \ in \ F = p' \ ensures_* \ q' \ in \ F,$$
$$p \mapsto_* q \ in \ F \ \ \ = p' \mapsto_* q' \ in \ F,$$
$$p \rightarrow\!\!\!\triangleright_* q \ in \ F \ \ \ = p' \rightarrow\!\!\!\triangleright_* q' \ in \ F.$$

The compositionality of the properties is expressed by the following theorem.

Lemma 3. *Let F and H be ImpUNITY programs. Then we have*

$$p \ unless_* \ q \ in \ F \| H \ \Leftarrow p \ unless_* \ q \ in \ F \ \bigwedge \ p \ unless_{CM} \ q \ in \ H,$$
$$p \ ensures_* \ q \ in \ F \| H \Leftarrow p \ ensures_* \ q \ in \ F \ \bigwedge \ p \ unless_{CM} \ q \ in \ H,$$
$$p \rightarrow\!\!\!\triangleright_* q \ in \ F \| H \ \ \ \ \Leftarrow p \rightarrow\!\!\!\triangleright_* q \ in \ F \ \bigwedge \ p \ unless_{CM} \ q \ in \ H.$$

$$p \ unless_* \ q \ in \ F \| H \ \Leftarrow p \ unless_* \ q \ in \ F \ \bigwedge \ p \ unless_* \ q \ in \ H,$$
$$p \ ensures_* \ q \ in \ F \| H \Leftarrow p \ ensures_* \ q \ in \ F \ \bigwedge \ p \ unless_* \ q \ in \ H,$$
$$p \rightarrow\!\!\!\triangleright_* q \ in \ F \| H \ \ \ \ \Leftarrow p \rightarrow\!\!\!\triangleright_* q \ in \ F \ \bigwedge \ p \ unless_* \ q \ in \ H.$$

4 ImpUNITY and Coordination

In this section we discuss how the ImpUNITY framework can deal with a form of coordination.

The first observation is that the ImpUNITY framework is rather abstract. The properties are based on predicates, and the form of statements is not specified. Also modifiers are just statements. Hence we can easily replace states based only on variables to for example states that describe besides the values of variables, also the contents of a shared tuple-space.

However, there is one section which mentions variables explicitly. This is the *hide*-section which gives a set of variables whose contents can not be read. It is useful to have hidden variables, but we like to generalize this idea so that it is also possible to hide part of the tuple-space.

We propose the following generalization: Let the *hide*-section contain a set of statements. The old set of variables Y is replaced by a set of statements, in which each statement assigns arbitrary values to all the variables in Y (one statement for each possible value). In addition we can add statements that put restrictions on the tuple-space. For example, one can specify in the *external* and *hide*-sections that only this program can write a certain type of tuples in the tuple space (by choosing a modifier that restricts the environment) and that the environment can only read this type of tuples.

Due to this generalization the definition of the union operator has to be modified. The second condition of the union operator is now as follows: For every statement S in the *hide*-section and for every statement T of the environment, we should have that when the execution of $S; T$ is started in an initial state, it either behaves like $T; S$ or like T. The same should hold for every procedure P of the environment: $S; P$ in an initial state either behaves like $P; S$ or like P. If S is an initialization of a local variable, this states that either it does not matter if we do this before or after statement T, or that it does not have influence at all.

For a typical coordination language we would assume that all the variables are local (that is, there are corresponding statements in the *hide*-section, and [= *Var*] is part of the modifier for the set of all variables *Var*).

We also have to add statements that manipulate the tuple space. In this paper we will only use statements that add and remove tuples, and that can check for the presence of tuples.

5 Program Refinement

The main idea behind the ImpUNITY approach is that we want to have a framework that supports the compositional refinement of both specifications and programs. The framework is shown in Figure 2.

First, a system is specified using the assumption that the program is a closed system (no interference from an environment). Then there are two ways to refine

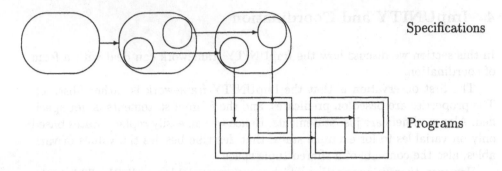

Specifications

Programs

Fig. 2. Program Design

the specification. A specification can be refined using the standard UNITY theorems. Moreover, a specification can be split into specifications of components using the compositional ImpUNITY properties. A specification of a component can again be refined using the standard UNITY theorems. As soon as a specification is specific enough, an ImpUNITY program is developed that satisfies the specification. This can be done independently for each component in the specification. Then, a program is transformed using refinement on the program level. The ImpUNITY framework has two notions of program refinement: observable refinement and a compositional notion of refinement. The observable notion of refinement is the natural notion of program refinement for programs that run in isolation. It expresses that all observable properties of a program are preserved, i.e. an ImpUNITY program F is refined by an ImpUNITY program G if G satisfies every specification that is also satisfied by F. This notion of program refinement is not compositional. The second notion of program refinement is compositional and says that an ImpUNITY program F is refined by an ImpUNITY program G if $G\|H$ satisfies every specification that is also satisfied by $F\|H$ for every environment H. For this notion of program refinement we give a number of program transformation rules.

Next we introduce the two notions of program refinement. Observational program refinement is based on observable properties, properties that do not refer to hidden variables. For coordination languages in which all variables are hidden this implies that the observational properties are only about the shared tuple-space.

Definition 4. For ImpUNITY program F and predicates p and q, observable properties of F are properties of F'

$$p \; unless_{obs} \; q \; in \; F \stackrel{\text{def}}{=} p \; unless_* \; q \; in \; F',$$
$$p \; ensures_{obs} \; q \; in \; F \stackrel{\text{def}}{=} p \; ensures_* \; q \; in \; F',$$
$$p \mapsto_{obs} q \; in \; F \stackrel{\text{def}}{=} p \mapsto_* q \; in \; F',$$

where F' is a program that is similar to F except that variables in $hide(F)$ are renamed such that they do not appear in p and q, and we also assume that $inter(F) = skip$.

Observable refinement is refinement of full programs. A full program is a program that can run in isolation, i.e. a program with an empty *import*-section. Observable refinement is defined as preservation of observable properties of a full program.

Definition 5. For full ImpUNITY programs F and G, G is an observable refinement of F, denoted by $F \sqsubseteq_O G$, if for all predicates p and q,

$$p \ unless_{obs} \ q \ in \ F \Rightarrow p \ unless_{obs} \ q \ in \ G,$$
$$p \mapsto_{obs} q \ in \ F \quad \Rightarrow p \mapsto_{obs} q \ in \ G.$$

The compositional notion of program refinement is observable refinement in any environment. We can use a more general form of program union that allows local variables of the components to be renamed before programs are composed. Note that this definition of program union is only unique up to local renaming. We say that a set of variables is local to an ImpUNITY program if the variables can neither be read nor written by the environment, and a set of variables is fresh if the variables are not read nor written by the program, and the program does not pose any restrictions on the use of the variables by the environment. We do not give the formal definitions. A local renaming is a renaming of a program where local variables are replaced by fresh variables.

Since observable program refinement concerns full programs, it is only interesting to examine environments for which the union results in a full program, that is a program in which there is no need for the import of procedures. Then, we define refinement $F \sqsubseteq G$ of ImpUNITY programs F and G as observable refinement in any environment for which the union leads to a full program.

For practical program refinement it is useful to have a collection of program transformation rules available. We give next some examples of such rules for ImpUNITY programs. For an overview, consult [6].

Statements that behave similarly, but differ only in their guards can be combined into one statement that is enabled if one of its components is enabled.

Transformation 6 (Combine statements)

Let F and G be ImpUNITY programs that only differ in their assign-sections. Let $U = \{p_i \rightarrow S \mid i \in I\}$ be a subset of $assign(F)$, and let statement $T \stackrel{def}{=} \langle \exists i : i \in I : p_i \rangle \rightarrow S$. If

$$assign(G) = assign(F) \setminus U \cup \{T\},$$

then $F \sqsubseteq G$.

Under certain conditions we are allowed to strengthen the guard of a statement. Here, we denote by $F \setminus S$ the program F from which statement S is removed from the *assign*-section.

Transformation 7 (Strengthening guard)
Let F be an ImpUNITY program and let $S = (p \to T)$ be a statement such that $S \in assign(F)$. Let G be the ImpUNITY program that only differs from F in the assign-section and

$$assign(G) = assign(F) \setminus \{S\} \cup \{S'\},$$

where $S' = (p \land q \to T)$. If

- $(q \land p) \Rightarrow inter(F)(q \lor \neg p)$,
- q $unless_{CM}$ $\neg p$ in $(F \setminus S)$, and
- $p \rightarrow_{CM} \neg p \lor q$ in G,

then $F \sqsubseteq G$.

The third transformation rule concerns the splitting of a statement.

Transformation 8 (Split statement)
Let F be an ImpUNITY program and let $S = (p \to T)$ be a statement such that $S \in assign(F)$. Let $\{q_i \mid i \in I\}$ be a set of predicates and let G be the ImpUNITY program that only differs from F in the assign-section and

$$assign(G) = assign(F) \setminus \{S\} \cup \{S_i \mid i \in I\},$$

where $S_i = (p \land q_i \to T)$ for $i \in I$. If

- $p \Rightarrow \langle \exists i : i \in I : q_i \rangle$,
- $p \land q_i \Rightarrow inter(F)(\neg p \lor q_i)$, for all $i \in I$, and
- q_i $unless_{CM}$ $\neg p$ in $(G \setminus S_i)$, for all $i \in I$,

then $F \sqsubseteq G$.

6 Phone System

In this section we derive a specification of a phone system via a number of refinement steps. We start from the following initial specification, consisting of a non-interference condition and two $unless_{CM}$ properties. The predicate $connection_{\{i,j\}}$ is true when $\langle connection, \{i,j\} \rangle$ is present in the tuple space, and $no\_connection_i$ is true when $\langle no\_connection, i \rangle$ is present in the tuple space.

Assume that there is no interference, i.e. that

$$inter(Phone) = skip$$

For all $i = 1, \ldots, n$

$no\_connection_i$ $unless_{CM}$ $\langle \exists j : j \neq i : connection_{\{i,j\}} \rangle$ in Phone

For all $i, j = 1, \ldots, n$, $i \neq j$,

$connection_{\{i,j\}}$ $unless_{CM}$ $no\_connection_i \land no\_connection_j$ in Phone

Let us now refine this specification to a program based on the finite state diagrams in Figure 3. These represent the distributed state space of the phone system with its possible transitions. There are n phones, called $phone_i$ for $i = 1, \ldots, n$. Every phone has $3+3n$ states, namely $1, 2, 3$ and $4_j, 5_j, 6_j$ $(j = 1, \ldots, n)$. The possible actions are as indicated in the diagram, with the following conventions. (In the diagram we have given names to most of the actions, but these names do not play a role in the rest of the paper.)

1. Transitions from a supernode represent transitions from each of its member nodes.
2. Solid transitions in the diagram for $phone_i$ result from the initiative of the user of $phone_i$.
3. Dotted transitions in the diagram for $phone_i$ result from the initiative of the user of $phone_j$, and are synchronized with solid transitions in the diagram for $phone_j$.

Here the intention is, that

1. $j.call_i : 1 \to 6_j$ in $phone_i$ is synchronized with $call_i : 2 \to 4_i$ in $phone_j$
2. $j.break : 4_j, 5_j, 6_j \to 3$ in $phone_i$ is synchronized with $break : 4_i, 5_i, 6_i \to 1$ in $phone_j$
3. $j.answer : 4_j \to 5_j$ in $phone_i$ is synchronized with $answer : 6_i \to 5_i$ in $phone_j$.

Let us first attach boolean variables to the states of $phone_i$ (for example $idle_i$ is true when $phone_i$ is in state 1).

1 $idle_i$
2 $ready\_to\_call_i$
3 $disconnected_i$
4_j $calling_{ij}$
5_j $speaking_{ij}$
6_j $called_{ij}$

Then we refine (using the standard UNITY theorems with the new ImpUNITY properties included) the first specification to a second specification, consisting of the following properties

$invariant_{CM}$ $connection_{\{i,j\}} = (calling_{ij} \lor speaking_{ij} \lor called_{ij})$ in Phone

$invariant_{CM}$ $no\_connection_i = (idle_i \lor ready\_to\_call_i \lor disconnected_i)$ in Phone

For $i, j = 1, \ldots, n, i \neq j$

$idle_i$ $unless_*$ $ready\_to\_call_i \lor \langle \exists j : j \neq i : called_{ij} \land calling_{ji} \rangle$ in Phone

$ready\_to\_call_i \rightarrow_* disconnected_i \lor idle_i \lor \langle \exists j :: called_{ji} \land calling_{ij} \rangle$ in Phone

$calling_{ij}$ $unless_*$ $\left(\begin{array}{l} (speaking_{ij} \land speaking_{ji}) \lor \\ (idle_i \land disconnected_j) \lor (idle_j \land disconnected_i) \end{array} \right)$ in Phone

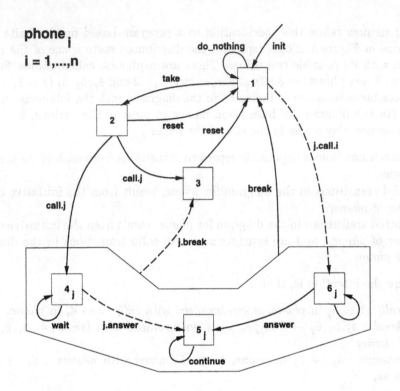

Fig. 3. The finite state diagrams of the phone system

$speaking_{ij}$ $unless_*$ $(idle_i \wedge disconnected_j) \vee (idle_j \wedge disconnected_i)$ in Phone

$called_{ij} \rightarrowtail_* \left(\begin{array}{l} (speaking_{ij} \wedge speaking_{ji}) \vee \\ (idle_i \wedge disconnected_j) \vee (idle_j \wedge disconnected_i) \end{array} \right)$ in Phone

$disconnected_i \rightarrowtail_* idle_i$ in Phone

Next, our goal is to derive n ImpUNITY programs, one per each phone in the system. Let us therefore distribute the previous properties over the phones. The phones will have properties as above, but we make each phone separately responsible for the progress properties $\rightarrowtail_*$. Let now $Phone = Phone_1 \square \cdots \square Phone_n$, where each $Phone_k$ has the following properties.

$ready\_to\_call_k \rightarrowtail_* disconnected_k \vee idle_k \vee \langle \exists j :: called_{jk} \wedge calling_{kj} \rangle$ in $Phone_k$

$disconnected_k \rightarrowtail_* idle_k$ in $Phone_k$

For $i, j = 1, \ldots, n$, $i \neq j$

$idle_i$ $unless_*$ $ready\_to\_call_i \vee \langle \exists j :: called_{ij} \wedge calling_{ji} \rangle$ in $Phone_k$

$calling_{ij}$ $unless_*$ $\left(\begin{array}{l} (speaking_{ij} \wedge speaking_{ji}) \vee \\ (idle_i \wedge disconnected_j) \vee (idle_j \wedge disconnected_i) \end{array} \right)$ in $Phone_k$

$speaking_{ij}$ $unless_*$ $(idle_i \wedge disconnected_j) \vee (idle_j \wedge disconnected_i)$ in $Phone_k$

For $i = 1, \ldots, n$, $i \neq k$

$ready\_to\_call_i$ $unless_*$ $disconnected_i \vee idle_i \vee \langle \exists j :: called_{ji} \wedge calling_{ij} \rangle$ in $Phone_k$

$disconnected_i$ $unless_*$ $idle_i$ in $Phone_k$

For $j = 1, \ldots, n$, $j \neq k$

$called_{kj} \rightarrow_* \begin{pmatrix} (speaking_{kj} \wedge speaking_{jk}) \vee \\ (idle_k \wedge disconnected_j) \vee (idle_j \wedge disconnected_k) \end{pmatrix}$ in $Phone_k$

For $i, j = 1, \ldots, n$, $i \neq j$ and $k \neq i$

$called_{ij}$ $unless_*$ $\begin{pmatrix} (speaking_{ij} \wedge speaking_{ji}) \vee \\ (idle_i \wedge disconnected_j) \vee (idle_j \wedge disconnected_i) \end{pmatrix}$ in $Phone_k$

Thus, we refine to a third specification, consisting of the properties of all the $Phone_i$ above together with the two $invariant_{CM}$ properties of the previous specification

$invariant_{CM}$ $connection_{\{i,j\}} = (calling_{ij} \vee speaking_{ij} \vee called_{ij})$ in $Phone$

$invariant_{CM}$ $no\_connection_i = (idle_i \vee ready\_to\_call_i \vee disconnected_i)$ in $Phone$

Finally, we make the step to an ImpUNITY program and find the following programs $Phone_i$ for each phone, where we define $Phone$ to be the union of the $Phone_i$'s.

We have two forms of communication between the programs $Phone_i$:

1. Communication via the tuple space (statements *add* and *remove* work on the tuple space, one of the guards, $connection_{\{i,j\}}$, checks whether the tuple $\langle connected, \{i,j\} \rangle$ is present in the tuple space).
2. Synchronous communication in the form of procedure calls ($Phone_i$ calls a procedure in $Phone_j$ which in turn calls a procedure in $Phone_i$.

All variables are local to $Phone_i$, so there is no communication between the phones via shared variables.

Program *Phone$_i$*
  external $[= \{idle_i, \ ready\_to\_call_i, \ disconnected_i\} \cup]$
            $\{calling_{ij}, speaking_{ij}, called_{ij} : j \neq i\}$
  hide $\{idle_i := \alpha, ready\_to\_call_i := \alpha, disconnected_i := \alpha : \alpha \in \{true, false\}\} \cup$
          $\{calling_{ij} := \alpha, speaking_{ij} := \alpha, called_{ij} := \alpha : j \neq i \wedge \alpha \in \{true, false\}\}$
  export
  proc $set\_speaking(j) = speaking_{ij}, calling_{ij} := true, false$
  ‖ **proc** $set\_calling(j) = calling_{ij} := true; remove(\langle no\_connection, i \rangle);$
                      $add(\langle connected, \{i, j\}\rangle)$
  ‖ **proc** $set\_no\_connection(j) = calling_{ij}, speaking_{ij}, called_{ij}, disconnected_i :=$
                              $false, false, false, true;$
                              $add(\langle no\_connection, i \rangle)$
  ‖ **proc** $check\_called\_for(j) = called_{ij} \rightarrow called_{ij}, speaking_{ij} := false, true;$
                                  $phone_j.set\_speaking(j)$
  ‖ **proc** $check\_idle\_for(j) = idle_i \rightarrow called_{ij}, idle_i := true, false;$
                              $remove(\langle no\_connection, i \rangle);$
                              $phone_j.set\_calling(i)$
  import $\langle \forall j : j \neq i : phone_j.set\_no\_connection, phone_j.check\_idle\_for \rangle$
        ‖ $\langle \forall j : j \neq i : phone_j.check\_called\_for, phone_j.set\_speaking \rangle$
        ‖ $\langle \forall j : j \neq i : phone_j.set\_calling \rangle$
  init $idle_i = true \wedge disconnected_i = false \wedge ready\_to\_call_i = false \wedge$
        $\langle \forall j : j \neq i : calling_{ij} = false \wedge speaking_{ij} = false \wedge called_{ij} = false \rangle$
  assign
  $idle_i \rightarrow skip \ \square \ ready\_to\_call_i, idle_i := true, false$
  ‖ $disconnected_i \rightarrow disconnected_i, idle_i := false, true$
  ‖ $\langle j : j \neq i : ready\_to\_call_i \rightarrow phone_j.check\_idle\_for(i)$
                          $\square$
            $ready\_to\_call_i, disconnected_i := false, true$
                          $\square$
            $ready\_to\_call_i, idle_i := false, true \rangle$
  ‖ $\langle ‖ j : j \neq i : connection_{\{i,j\}} \rightarrow skip$
                          $\square$
            $(calling_{ij}, speaking_{ij}, called_{ij} :=$
              $false, false, false;$
            $phone_j.set\_no\_connection(i);$
            $remove(\langle connected, \{i,j\}\rangle);$
            $add(\langle no\_connection, i \rangle);$
            $idle_i := true))$
  ‖ $calling_{ij} \rightarrow skip \ \square \ phone_j.check\_called\_for(i)$
  end$\{Phone_i\}$

Further refinements can be done using program refinement (for example using the transformation rules of the previous section). Following are examples of possible refinements. In the previous program the phones directly contact each other. In a first program refinement step we can introduce a switchboard, that serves as an intermediate between phones. Then in a second program refinement step we can distribute the switchboard, and introduce a protocol for the communication between the phones and the distributed switchboard. Hence, we then obtain an ImpUNITY program that models a mobile phone system.

7 Conclusions

We have shown that the ImpUNITY framework is suited to study coordination. Communication via a shared tuple space is a natural add to this formalism. In addition to this form of communication, the ImpUNITY framework has an associated logic and it gives (compositional) formal refinement notions for programs. Furthermore, the framework gives several possibilities to structure programs and state spaces (like procedures, and hiding of information).

We have shown the practical applicability of the ImpUNITY framework by deriving a specification for a phone system. Our initial specification gave properties only on the visible tuple space. The final program of this paper was a union of all the component programs, $Phone_i$. We included two forms of communication between ImpUNITY programs for this example, namely communication via the tuple space and communication via procedure calls. From a programming methodology viewpoint it might be better to use just one form of communication.

Acknowledgement Discussions with the representatives from the Nokia Mobile Phones Ltd gave the initial inspiration for the phone system case study.

References

1. R. J. R. Back and K. Sere. Action systems with synchronous communication. In E.-R. Olderog, editor, *Programming Concepts, Methods and Calculi*, volume A-56 of *IFIP Transactions*, pages 107–126. Elsevier, June 1994.
2. D. Le Métayer, C.L. Hankin, and D. Sands. Compositional semantics of a notation for composing parallel programs. Submitted for publication 1995.
3. K. Chandy and J. Misra. *Parallel Program Design: A Foundation*. Addison–Wesley, 1988.
4. H.C. Cunningham and G.C. Roman. A UNITY-style programming logic for a shared dataspace language. Technical Report WUCS-89-5, Dept. of Computer Science, Washington University, March 1989.
5. D. Le Métayer, C.L. Hankin, and D. Sands. A parallel programming style and its algebra of programs. In *PARLE'93*, volume 694 of *Lecture Notes in Computer Science*, Springer-Verlag, 1993.
6. R.T. Udink. *Program Refinement in UNITY-like Environments*. PhD Thesis, Utrecht University, September 1995.
7. R.T. Udink, T. Herman, and J.N. Kok. Progress for local variables in UNITY. In E.-R. Olderog, editor, *Programming Concepts, Methods and Calculi*, volume A-56 of *IFIP Transactions*, pages 127–146. Elsevier, June 1994.
8. R.T. Udink and J.N. Kok. ImpUNITY: UNITY with procedure and local variables. In B. Moller, editor, *Mathematics of Program Construction*, volume 947 of *Lecture Notes in Computer Science*, pages 452–472. Springer-Verlag, 1995.

Appendix: The Internal Leadsto property

In ImpUNITY we have one extra property $\rightarrowtail_{CM}$ called internal leadsto.

Definition 9. The property $\rightarrowtail_{CM}$ is the smallest relation *Prop* that satisfies the following conditions:

1. If p *ensures*$_{CM}$ q in F, then p *Prop* q in F.
2. If p *Prop* $(r \lor q)$ in F, r *Prop* q in F, and $(r \land \neg q) \Rightarrow inter(F)(\neg p \lor r \lor q)$, then $(p \lor r)$ *Prop* q in F.
3. If for any set W $\langle \forall w : w \in W : p_w \ Prop_{CM} \ q \ in \ F \rangle$, and

$$\langle \forall w : w \in W : (p_w \land \neg q) \Rightarrow inter(F)(\langle \forall i : i \in W : \neg p_i \rangle \lor p_w \lor q) \rangle,$$

then $\langle \exists w : w \in W : p_w \rangle$ *Prop* q in F.

There are two conditions in this definition. Both require something of $inter(F)$, and their intention is that we restrict the environment in such a way that we are able to prove p *unless* $(r \lor q)$ and r *unless* q of the environment for item 2, and for all i, p_i *unless* q of the environment for item 3.

The main motivation is that we want to have a property that satisfies

$$p \rightarrow q \ in \ F \land p \ unless_{CM} \ q \ in \ G \Rightarrow p \rightarrow q \ in \ F \| G$$

In UNITY the *ensures*$_{CM}$ property satisfies this requirement, but $\mapsto_{CM}$ does not satisfy it. Programs in ImpUNITY have more structure (in fact, parts of the program are not visible to an environment), and we can find a property between *ensures*$_{CM}$ and $\mapsto_{CM}$ that satisfies this requirement. Let us first sketch the problems with the $\mapsto_{CM}$ property. Assume $p \mapsto_{CM} q \ in F$ and $p \ unless_{CM} \ q \ in G$. We can have an intermediate predicate p' such that $p \mapsto_{CM} p' \ in F$ and $p' \mapsto_{CM} q \ in F$. Now $p \ unless_{CM} \ q \ in \ G$ guarantees nothing about what the environment is going to do in p'. It might for example go back to p, and we will not have $p \mapsto q \ in F \| G$. We can find a similar problem for the disjunctive closure of the $\mapsto_{CM}$ definition.

We want to have a definition scheme as for the $\mapsto_{CM}$ property, but by putting extra restrictions we hope to keep the compositionality. When we look in the UNITY book we find the following rule for unless

$$\frac{p \ unless_{CM} \ r \lor q, \ r \ unless_{CM} \ q}{p \lor r \ unless_{CM} \ q}$$

The idea is to use this rule for the transitive closure. We assume $p \lor r \ unless_{CM} \ q$ about the environment. What we need to know is that both $p \ unless_{CM} \ r \lor q$ and $r \ unless_{CM} \ q$ hold in the environment. That we know that $p \lor r \ unless_{CM} \ q$ holds for the environment is not sufficient. Therefore we need to find an extra condition on the environment. In fact, with a condition on the modifier and the exported procedures, we can restrict the environments, and hence we can achieve properties of the environment by putting the condition on $inter(F)$. Assume that (in Hoare triple notation) $\{r \land \neg q\} inter(F) \{\neg p \lor r \lor q\}$ or, equivalently, in weakest precondition notation, $\{r \land \neg q\} \Rightarrow inter(F)(\{\neg p \lor r \lor q\})$. Now we can prove the two unless properties ($p \ unless_{CM} \ r \lor q$ and $r \ unless_{CM} \ q$) of the environment.

1. The property $p \; unless_{CM} \; r \vee q$ is implied by $\{p \wedge \neg r \wedge \neg q\} inter(F)\{p \vee r \vee q\}$. This is implied by the property $p \vee r \; unless_{CM} \; q$ of the environment.

2. We prove $r \; unless_{CM} \; q$. We have the assumption about the environment $\{r \wedge \neg q\} inter(F)\{\neg p \vee r \vee q\}$ and the property $p \vee r \; unless_{CM} \; q$ (i.e. $\{r \wedge \neg q\} inter(F)\{p \vee r \vee q\}$ of the environment). Together (by taking the conjunction of the pre- and postconditions) they yield $\{r \wedge \neg q\} inter(F)\{r \vee q\}$, i.e. $r \; unless_{CM} \; q$.

Next we consider the third part of the definition. Assume about the environment $\langle \exists i :: p_i \rangle \; unless \; q$. We need for the environment for all i, $p_i \; unless \; q$, and hence it is sufficient to have $\{p_i \wedge \neg q\} inter(F)\{p_i \vee q\}$.

We know $\{\langle \exists i :: p_i \rangle \wedge \neg q\} inter(F)\{\langle \exists i :: p_i \rangle \vee q\}$. If we make the extra assumption $\{p_i \wedge \neg q\} inter(F)\{\langle \forall i :: \neg p_i \rangle \vee p_i \vee q\}$ then together (by taking conjunctions of pre- and postconditions) this yields for all i, $\{p_i \wedge \neg q\} inter(F)\{p_i \vee q\}$ i.e. $p_i \; unless_{CM} \; q$ for all i.

Compiler Correctness for Concurrent Languages

David S. Gladstein* ** and Mitchell Wand*

College of Computer Science, Northeastern University, 360 Huntington Avenue,
Boston, MA 02115, USA

Abstract. This paper extends previous work in compiler derivation and
verification to languages with true-concurrency semantics. We extend the
λ-calculus to model process-centered concurrent computation, and give
the semantics of a small language in terms of this calculus. We then define
a target abstract machine whose states have denotations in the same
calculus. We prove the correctness of a compiler for our language: the
denotation of the compiled code is shown to be strongly bisimilar to the
denotation of the source program, and the abstract machine running the
compiled code is shown to be branching-bisimilar to the source program's
denotation.

1 Introduction

Our original goal was to verify a compiler for Linda [8], using that language
as a representative of modern concurrent language design. Upon searching the
literature, we found a vast amount of work on models of concurrency, but little
that was obviously applicable to compiler derivation and verification. Accordingly
we decided to tackle first the more primitive "computation + communication"
model of systems like PVM [10] or Erlang [4]. Having done this, we expect
that our framework will be applicable to the more sophisticated, coordination
languages.

1.1 Compiler Derivation Methodology

A recipe [9, 31, 21] for compiling a source language into a target machine language
is as follows: The semantics of the source language is given as a compositional
translation $\mathcal{E}[\![\cdot]\!]$ from the source language to some metalanguage. The compiler
is defined by a compositional translation $C[\![\cdot]\!]$ from the source language to a
target language. This target language has a denotational semantics $\overline{(\cdot)}$ in the
same metalanguage as the source semantics. It also has a plausibly implementable operational semantics, typically given as an abstract machine for which the
target code is the machine language. The correctness of the compiler is expressed

---

* Work supported by the National Science Foundation under grant numbers CCR-
901463 and CCR-9304144.

** Author's current address: Invertebrates Department, American Museum of Natural
History, Central Park West at 79th Street, New York, NY 10024, USA.

as the equality of the denotational semantics of any source program p and the denotational semantics of its translation:

$$\mathcal{E}[\![p]\!] = \overline{\mathcal{C}[\![p]\!]} \tag{1}$$

The correctness of the abstract machine is expressed as an adequacy theorem relating the operational and denotational semantics of the target language:

$$\overline{Q} = N \text{ iff } Q \to^* F \text{ and } \overline{F} = N \tag{2}$$

for some final configuration F of the abstract machine. Combined, these theorems relate the denotational meaning of the source program to the answer obtained by executing the compiled code on the abstract machine:

$$\mathcal{E}[\![p]\!] = N \text{ iff } \overline{\mathcal{C}[\![p]\!]} = N \text{ iff } \mathcal{C}[\![p]\!] \to^* F \text{ and } \overline{F} = N \tag{3}$$

For the case of sequential languages, the metalanguage is usually some version of the λ-calculus, and the notion of equivalence is equality modulo α-renaming and β-reduction, which we write $\overset{\beta}{=}$.

In [30] this methodology is adapted to languages with parallelism. The metalanguage is chosen to be the λ-calculus extended with special operators that turn it into a process calculus. It is shown that β-equivalence $\overset{\beta}{=}$ extends to a strong bisimulation $\overset{\beta}{\simeq}$. This reduces the problem of ensuring bisimilarity to that of ensuring equality in the λ-calculus.

1.2 The Present Work

We want to derive and verify a compiler for a realistic concurrent language, so that running programs will be similar to those written, for example, using PVM [10] or Erlang [4]. Specifically, we shall include asynchronous buffered communication, and we shall allow for execution on multiple computers.

In [30], the calculus has an interleaving semantics, as does the abstract machine. Since we are interested in multicomputer implementations, the present work uses a true-concurrency model of computation. We show how to model concurrency in such a way as to retain the technical developments of [30], while also getting an abstract machine model which is plausibly implementable on a multicomputer.

The rest of the paper is organized as follows: Section 2 describes our conceptual model for true concurrency and gives the details of our metalanguage. Section 3 describes a small source language and gives its denotational semantics in the metalanguage. Section 4 specifies a target machine language and its denotational semantics, presents the compiler, and shows that the compiler preserves denotational semantics up to strong bisimulation (Theorem 3); this corresponds to condition (1). Section 5 presents an abstract machine that executes the target language, and proves its adequacy with respect to the denotational semantics (Theorem 9); this corresponds to condition (2). These theorems are combined in Theorem 10, which corresponds to condition (3). Section 6 briefly discusses a multicomputer Concert/C implementation of the abstract machine. Section 7 briefly considers related work. Section 8 outlines some possibilities for further research.

2 True Concurrency and Our Metalanguage

2.1 The Conceptual Model

Suppose we have a system with two states, and that the system evolves from one state to the other via some time consuming action. We might reasonably model this as a transition system with two states X and Y and a transition $X \xrightarrow{a} Y$.

Suppose now that we have two independent copies of that system, with transitions $X_1 \xrightarrow{a_1} Y_1$ and $X_2 \xrightarrow{a_2} Y_2$. To model their independent, concurrent operation, we might form their product as follows:

$$
\begin{array}{c|ccc}
 & X_1 & \xrightarrow{a_1} & Y_1 \\
\hline
X_2 & (X_1, X_2) & \xrightarrow{a_1} & (Y_1, X_2) \\
\downarrow a_2 & \downarrow a_2 & & \downarrow a_2 \\
Y_2 & (X_1, Y_2) & \xrightarrow{a_1} & (Y_1, Y_2)
\end{array}
$$

This is surely not what we want, since there is no concurrency. Even if we add a diagonal transition $(X_1, X_2) \xrightarrow{a_1 a_2} (Y_1, Y_2)$, there is a problem: the startings and endings of the activities represented by the transitions a_i are synchronized.

Rather than move to another mathematical representation of computation, we can recode our understanding by splitting the transitions. Whenever we have a durational action a represented by a transition $X \xrightarrow{a} Y$, we replace it with a new state $\langle a, X \rangle$ and two new new transitions $X \xrightarrow{a^+} \langle a, X \rangle$ and $\langle a, X \rangle \xrightarrow{a^-} Y$. Here the a^+ and a^- transitions are instantaneous, and the state $\langle a, X \rangle$ is a *durational state*, representing the time during which the system is doing the action a. If we apply this transformation to the previous example and take the interleaving product, we get the following:

$$
\begin{array}{c|ccccc}
 & X_1 & \xrightarrow{a_1^+} & \langle a_1, X_1 \rangle & \xrightarrow{a_1^-} & Y_1 \\
\hline
X_2 & (X_1, X_2) & \xrightarrow{a_1^+} & (\langle a_1, X_1 \rangle, X_2) & \xrightarrow{a_1^-} & (Y_1, X_2) \\
\downarrow a_2^+ & \downarrow a_2^+ & & \downarrow a_2^+ & & \downarrow a_2^+ \\
\langle a_2, X_2 \rangle & (X_1, \langle a_2, X_2 \rangle) & \xrightarrow{a_1^+} & (\langle a_1, X_1 \rangle, \langle a_2, X_2 \rangle) & \xrightarrow{a_1^-} & (Y_1, \langle a_2, X_2 \rangle) \\
\downarrow a_2^- & \downarrow a_2^- & & \downarrow a_2^- & & \downarrow a_2^- \\
Y_2 & (X_1, Y_2) & \xrightarrow{a_1^+} & (\langle a_1, X_1 \rangle, Y_2) & \xrightarrow{a_1^-} & (Y_1, Y_2)
\end{array}
$$

Here the two processes may start and stop their activities independently, and furthermore we have explicitly represented the possiblity that the two processes will be active at the same time. This matches our intuition about the behavior of independently executing computers.

The idea of modelling durational events by pairs of instantaneous transitions is certainly not new [16, 17]. Technical difficulties arise when applying this approach to autoconcurrent Petri nets [25, 14], but because the process-centered model of the next section by its very nature lacks autoconcurrency, we are able to use the split-transition representation.

2.2 The Calculus

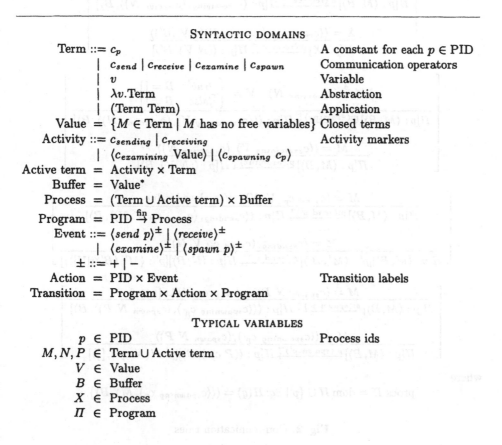

SYNTACTIC DOMAINS

Term ::= c_p	A constant for each $p \in$ PID
| c_{send} | $c_{receive}$ | $c_{examine}$ | c_{spawn}	Communication operators
| v	Variable
| $\lambda v.$Term	Abstraction
| (Term Term)	Application
Value $= \{M \in$ Term $\mid M$ has no free variables$\}$	Closed terms
Activity ::= $c_{sending}$ | $c_{receiving}$	Activity markers
| $\langle c_{examining}$ Value$\rangle$ | $\langle c_{spawning}\ c_p \rangle$	
Active term $=$ Activity $\times$ Term	
Buffer $=$ Value*	
Process $=$ (Term $\cup$ Active term) $\times$ Buffer	
Program $=$ PID $\overset{fin}{\to}$ Process	
Event ::= $\langle send\ p\rangle^{\pm}$ | $\langle receive\rangle^{\pm}$	
| $\langle examine\rangle^{\pm}$ | $\langle spawn\ p\rangle^{\pm}$	
$\pm$ ::= $+$ | $-$	
Action $=$ PID $\times$ Event	Transition labels
Transition $=$ Program $\times$ Action $\times$ Program	

TYPICAL VARIABLES

p	$\in$ PID	Process ids
M, N, P	$\in$ Term $\cup$ Active term	
V	$\in$ Value	
B	$\in$ Buffer	
X	$\in$ Process	
Π	$\in$ Program	

Fig. 1. Syntactic domains and typical variables for the calculus

Figure 1 shows the syntax of our calculus, which is based on an infinite set PID of process identifiers. The usual terms of the λ-calculus are extended with constants for each PID, as well as four communication operators. We also define four activity markers, to annotate processes engaged in durational activity. A process consists of a term (or a term together with an activity marker) and an input buffer. A program is a finite labelled collection of processes. The label of a program transition tells which process made a transition, as well as describing the transition.

Figure 2 gives the transition relation of our calculus; corresponding $^+$ and $^-$ transitions are grouped. The $^+$ transitions are "instantaneous computation" rules [7], in that the terms appearing in the transition may be related by an arbitrary number of β reductions. Within such a reduction sequence, the communication

$$\left[\begin{array}{c} M \stackrel{\beta}{=} (c_{receive}\ N) \\ \hline \Pi[p : \langle M, B\rangle] \xrightarrow{p:\langle receive\rangle^+} \Pi[p : \langle\langle c_{receiving}, (c_{receive}\ N)\rangle, B\rangle] \\[1em] X = \langle\langle c_{receiving}, (c_{receive}\ N)\rangle, (V::B')\rangle \\ \hline \Pi[p : X] \xrightarrow{p:\langle receive\rangle^-} \Pi[p : \langle(N\ V), B'\rangle] \end{array}\right]$$

$$\left[\begin{array}{c} M \stackrel{\beta}{=} (c_{examine}\ N) \quad V = \begin{cases} \ulcorner true\urcorner & B = [] \\ \ulcorner false\urcorner & B \neq [] \end{cases} \\ \hline \Pi[p : \langle M, B\rangle] \xrightarrow{p:\langle examine\rangle^+} \Pi[p : \langle\langle\langle c_{examining}\ V\rangle, (c_{examine}\ N)\rangle, B\rangle] \\[1em] M = \langle\langle c_{examining}\ V\rangle, (c_{examine}\ N)\rangle \\ \hline \Pi[p : \langle M, B\rangle] \xrightarrow{p:\langle examine\rangle^-} \Pi[p : \langle(N\ V), B\rangle] \end{array}\right]$$

$$\left[\begin{array}{c} M \stackrel{\beta}{=} (c_{send}\ c_{p'}\ V\ N) \quad V\ \text{a closed value} \\ \hline \Pi[p : \langle M, B\rangle] \xrightarrow{p:\langle send\ p'\rangle^+} \Pi[p : \langle\langle c_{sending}, (c_{send}\ c_{p'}\ V\ N)\rangle, B\rangle] \\[1em] M = \langle c_{sending}, (c_{send}\ c_{p'}\ V\ N)\rangle \\ \hline \Pi[p : \langle M, B\rangle][p' : \langle M', B'\rangle] \xrightarrow{p:\langle send\ p'\rangle^-} \Pi[p : \langle N, B\rangle][p' : \langle M', (B'@[V])\rangle] \end{array}\right]$$

$$\left[\begin{array}{c} M \stackrel{\beta}{=} (c_{spawn}\ N\ P) \quad p' \notin \text{procs}\ \Pi \cup \{p\} \\ \hline \Pi[p : \langle M, B\rangle] \xrightarrow{p:\langle spawn\ p'\rangle^+} \Pi[p : \langle\langle\langle c_{spawning}\ c_{p'}\rangle, (c_{spawn}\ N\ P)\rangle, B\rangle] \\[1em] M = \langle\langle c_{spawning}\ c_{p'}\rangle, (c_{spawn}\ N\ P)\rangle \\ \hline \Pi[p : \langle M, B\rangle] \xrightarrow{p:\langle spawn\ p'\rangle^-} \Pi[p : \langle(P\ c_{p'}), B\rangle][p' : \langle(N\ c_{p'}), []\rangle] \end{array}\right]$$

where

$$\text{procs}\ \Pi = \text{dom}\ \Pi \cup \{p \mid \exists q : \Pi(q) = \langle\langle\langle c_{spawning}\ c_p\rangle, M\rangle, B\rangle\}$$

Fig. 2. Communication rules

operators are uninterpreted; this trick of separating computational reductions from communication is due to [20]. We now describe each communication operation in turn.

The $c_{receive}$ operation fetches the head of the input queue, should it be nonempty. A process may try to read its input buffer at any time, but of course the operation cannot terminate until there is input. This is modelled by the $\langle receive\rangle^+$ transition always being enabled, and the $\langle receive\rangle^-$ transition requiring a nonempty input queue.

The $c_{examine}$ operation examines the input queue, returning $\ulcorner true\urcorner$ for empty and $\ulcorner false\urcorner$ otherwise. (The quasiquotation marks $\ulcorner\cdot\urcorner$ indicate a λ-calculus encoding of the datum, the details of which we leave unspecified.) The $\langle examine\rangle^+$ transition takes a snapshot of the state of the buffer, storing it in the activity marker. This snapshot is returned by the $\langle examine\rangle^-$ transition, rather than the actual state of the buffer. Thus this test is conservative: a result of $\ulcorner true\urcorner$ may or may not indicate an empty buffer, but a result of ⌜*false*⌝ always indicates a nonempty buffer.

The c_{send} operation sends a value to a process, or more accurately, puts it into the buffer of a process. Like the $\langle receive \rangle^+$ transition, the $\langle send \rangle^+$ transition is always enabled. The $\langle send \rangle^-$ transition is only enabled when the receiving process actually exists.

The c_{spawn} operation forks another process. The $\langle spawn \rangle^+$ transition is non-deterministic, because the process does not determine the PID of the new process in advance. The process makes a nondeterministic transition into the activity, recording the new, unused PID in the activity marker; a process id is considered to be in use once it is assigned to a fork activity.[1] The $\langle spawn \rangle^-$ activity actually establishes the new process.

A notion of equivalence for process-oriented calculi, called β-bisimilarity and written $\stackrel{\beta}{\simeq}$, was introduced in [30]. There the processes were λ-terms; two programs Π and Π' were related by $\stackrel{\beta}{\simeq}$ if dom Π = dom Π', and for each process p in the common domain, $\Pi(p) \stackrel{\beta}{=} \Pi'(p)$. This equivalence was proved to be a strong bisimulation.

The processes of our calculus are more complicated, being constructed of tuples and sequences of λ-terms. We therefore extend $\stackrel{\beta}{=}$ to cover tuples and sequences: $\langle M, N \rangle \stackrel{\beta}{=} \langle M', N' \rangle$ exactly when $M \stackrel{\beta}{=} M'$ and $N \stackrel{\beta}{=} N'$, and similarly $[M_1 \ldots M_n] \stackrel{\beta}{=} [M_1' \ldots M_{n'}']$ exactly when $n = n'$ and each $M_i \stackrel{\beta}{=} M_i'$. With this convention, we may write the definition of equivalence for our calculus:

Definition 1 (β-bisimilarity). Write $\Pi \stackrel{\beta}{\simeq} \Pi'$ if dom Π = dom Π', and at each p, $\Pi(p) \stackrel{\beta}{=} \Pi'(p)$.

We can then prove the following for $\stackrel{\beta}{\simeq}$:

Theorem 2. $\stackrel{\beta}{\simeq}$ is a strong bisimulation.

Proof. $\Pi \stackrel{\beta}{\simeq} \Pi'$ be given, and consider each rule for the transitions other than $\langle spawn \rangle^+$. The programs' corresponding processes are $\stackrel{\beta}{=}$, so by the transitivity of $\stackrel{\beta}{=}$, any rule which applies to Π applies to Π'.

For $\langle spawn \rangle^+$, the antecedent of the rule has the extra side condition $p' \notin$ procs $\Pi \cup \{p\}$. Clearly procs Π = procs Π', so any $\langle spawn \rangle^+$ transition open to one program is open to the other. □

3 Source Language Syntax and Semantics

The syntax of our source language is shown in Fig. 3, in which i ranges over identifiers and n over integers. We have the usual pieces of a functional language,

---

[1] Process ids which occur in a program Π but are not in procs Π are not considered to be in use. Hard-coded PIDs are not expressible in the source language of the next section, so this never happens in the translations of source language programs.

namely identifiers, constants, primitives, abstractions, and applications, as well as four new operators (**put, get, empty?,** and **spawn**) corresponding to the communication primitives.

$$p ::= a \qquad\qquad\qquad\qquad \text{Program}$$
$$a ::= (\textbf{rec } i(i)\ e) \qquad\qquad\quad \text{Abstraction}$$
$$e ::= n \mid i \mid a \mid (\textbf{if } e\ e\ e) \mid (e\ e) \mid (-\ e\ e) \qquad \text{Expressions}$$
$$\mid\ (\textbf{put } e\ e) \mid (\textbf{get}) \mid (\textbf{empty?}) \mid (\textbf{spawn } e)$$

Fig. 3. Source language syntax

The semantics of the language is given in Fig. 4. Expressions are translated compositionally into terms of our calculus, while programs are translated into entire programs. The environment is a map from identifiers to values; it represents the bindings of variables at the time the expression is evaluated. The continuation is a function mapping the value of the expression to the result of the program; it represents the remainder of the computation, which is waiting for the value of the expression. The translation is essentially a standard continuation-passing semantics; see [9, 22, 23] for detailed expositions. In what follows, when we have a term $(M_1 \ldots M_n)$, we will say that M_1 is in head position, or function position, and that M_n is in continuation position.

$$\mathcal{E}[i] = \lambda \rho \kappa. \kappa(\rho\, i)$$
$$\mathcal{E}[n] = \lambda \rho \kappa. \kappa(in_{int}\ulcorner n \urcorner)$$
$$\mathcal{E}[(\textbf{rec } i_1(i_2)\ e)] = \lambda \rho \kappa. \kappa(in_{clo}(\textit{fix } (\lambda p. \lambda v \kappa. \mathcal{E}[e](\rho[(in_{clo}\, p)/i_1][v/i_2])\kappa)))$$
$$\mathcal{E}[(\textbf{if } e_1\ e_2\ e_3)] = \lambda \rho \kappa. \mathcal{E}[e_1]\rho(\lambda b.(\textit{branch } b\ \mathcal{E}[e_2]\ \mathcal{E}[e_3])\,\rho\,\kappa)$$
$$\mathcal{E}[(e_1\ e_2)] = \lambda \rho \kappa. \mathcal{E}[e_1]\rho(\lambda f. \mathcal{E}[e_2]\rho(\lambda a.\textit{applicate } f\, a\, \kappa))$$
$$\mathcal{E}[(-\ e_1\ e_2)] = \lambda \rho \kappa. \mathcal{E}[e_1]\rho(\lambda v_1. \mathcal{E}[e_2]\rho(\lambda v_2.\textit{subtract } v_1\, v_2\, \kappa))$$
$$\mathcal{E}[(\textbf{put } e_1\ e_2)] = \lambda \rho \kappa. \mathcal{E}[e_1]\rho(\lambda v_1. \mathcal{E}[e_2]\rho(\lambda v_2.\textit{send } v_1\, v_2\, \kappa))$$
$$\mathcal{E}[(\textbf{get})] = \lambda \rho \kappa. c_{receive}\kappa$$
$$\mathcal{E}[(\textbf{empty?})] = \lambda \rho \kappa. c_{examine}\kappa$$
$$\mathcal{E}[(\textbf{spawn } e)] = \lambda \rho \kappa. \mathcal{E}[e]\rho(\lambda f. c_{spawn}(\lambda p'.\textit{boot } f\, p')\,(\lambda p'. \kappa\,(in_{pid}\, p')))$$
$$\mathcal{P}[a] = [p_0 : \mathcal{E}[a]\rho_0(\lambda f.\textit{boot } f\, c_{p_0})]$$

Fig. 4. Source language semantics

The clause for $(-\ e_1\ e_2)$ is typical. Each subexpression is evaluated, the value being bound to the argument variable of an explicit continuation. The values, together with the expression's continuation, are passed to the auxiliary term *subtract*. The auxiliary unboxes the values as necessary for the operation it implements, appeals to another term to do the actual arithmetic, and finally calls the continuation on the appropriately boxed result.

The **put** clause similarly evaluates its arguments and hands them to the term *send*, which proceeds as follows. The first argument should be a process id; it is unboxed, yielding a process term with c_{send} in function position. When the send operation has been completed, computation can continue as specified by the **put** expression's continuation. **put** expressions return *unit*.

The **get** clause is simply the process term with $c_{receive}$ in function position and the expression's continuation in continuation position. Thus upon completion of the receive operation, the expression will return the received value.

The **empty?** clause similarly returns the boolean value generated by the $c_{examine}$ primitive.

The c_{spawn} primitive operates on two arguments: a function to be spawned as a new process, and a continuation. Both arguments are functions, and both are to be called on the process id of the newly created process. The **spawn** clause evaluates its argument, which should yield a closure value representing the function to be spawned. The closure value itself is not of the right form for use by the c_{spawn} primitive, but the **spawn** clause wraps it in an abstraction which is; that abstraction handles the administrative task of boxing the new process id, and also providing the deadlocking continuation †. Likewise, the **spawn** expression's continuation is wrapped in an abstraction which boxes up the new process id before feeding it to the continuation.

The clause for an entire program expects that the program is in the form of a function to be spawned. It specifies that the function should be applied to an initial process id and installed as the one and only process, labelled with that process id.

We now turn to the auxiliaries, which are shown in Fig. 5. In the interest of brevity, we stop short of showing how to encode all of the auxiliary terms into λ-calculus. Rather we state the properties the encodings are expected to have; the details may be found in [13, 30]. The term **0** implements deadlock; it cannot communicate. The term † is then a deadlocking continuation.

The language uses four value domains (integers, PIDs, closures, and booleans), and a one-point domain *unit* for representing unspecified values. We omit definitions of the injection and projection terms; encodings as higher-order abstract syntax terms are given in [13]. Taken together, the injection (boxing) terms in_i and the projection (unboxing) terms out_j should have the property

$$out_j(in_i x)\kappa \stackrel{\beta}{=} \begin{cases} \kappa x & \text{if } i = j \\ \mathbf{0} & \text{otherwise} \end{cases}$$

Thus runtime type errors lead to immediate deadlock, while in the absence of type errors unboxing a value simply passes it to the current continuation. We also require that any attempt to unbox *unit* also leads to deadlock.

The term *subtract* makes use of a term *primitive_sub*, which we assume to have the property $(primitive\_sub \ulcorner m\urcorner \ulcorner n\urcorner) \stackrel{\beta}{=} \ulcorner m - n\urcorner$. The term *branch* makes use of a term *primitive_if* which should have the property that $(primitive\_if \ulcorner true \urcorner M N) \overset{\beta}{=} M$ and $(primitive\_if \ulcorner false \urcorner M N) \overset{\beta}{=} N$.

For later developments, we require an encoding of stacks: an infix constructor ::, an empty stack $\langle\rangle$, and a deconstructor *pop*. We also omit these encodings (which can be found in [13]), but they should have the property

$$pop \, v \, \kappa \overset{\beta}{=} \begin{cases} \kappa \, a \, x & \text{if } v \overset{\beta}{=} (a::x) \\ 0 & \text{if } v \overset{\beta}{=} \langle\rangle \end{cases}$$

$$
\begin{aligned}
\mathbf{0} &= \lambda v.v \\
\dagger &= \lambda v.\mathbf{0} \\
applicate &= \lambda va\kappa.out_{clo} \, v \, (\lambda f.f \, a \, \kappa) \\
branch &= \lambda b \, e_t e_f.out_{bool} \, b \, (\lambda v.(primitive\_if \, v \, e_t \, e_f)) \\
subtract &= \lambda v_1 v_2 \kappa.out_{int} \, v_1 (\lambda n_1.out_{int} \, v_2 \, (\lambda n_2.\kappa(in_{int} \, (primitive\_sub \, n_1 \, n_2)))) \\
send &= \lambda v_1 v_2 \kappa.out_{pid} \, v_1 \, (\lambda p.c_{send} \, p \, v_2 \, (\kappa \, unit)) \\
boot &= \lambda fp.applicate \, f \, (in_{pid} \, p) \, \dagger
\end{aligned}
$$

Fig. 5. Auxiliaries

4 Target Language Syntax and Semantics

To the extent that we could execute our calculus via an interpreter, the semantic map $\mathcal{E}$ gives an interpreter for our source language. To move towards a compiler, we separate the information which is known at compilation time from that which is not known until run time. In particular, we split the environment into a compile-time symbol table and a run-time display, and we split continuations into static instruction sequences and dynamic sequences of activation records. Furthermore, we introduce a run-time stack for storing intermediate results, instead of using continuations as, for instance, in the rule for $\mathcal{E}[\![(- e_1 \, e_2)]\!]$ where two explicit continuations were needed to bind the values of the subexpressions. This leads us to an abstract target machine whose state is a 4-tuple: a current instruction, a display of local variable bindings, a local stack of intermediate results, and a stack of suspended activation records.

The syntax of the target machine language and associated structures is given in Fig. 6. A system state is a finite map from process ids to process states. A process state is either a start state, a stopped state, or a computational state. A computational state consists of a control tuple and an input buffer. The control tuple may stand alone, or may be adjoined to an activity marker; its components were described in the previous paragraph.

The denotations of target machine language programs and states are given in Figs. 6 and 7, as a syntax-directed translation into the metalanguage. The translation follows the pattern established in [9].

The compiler of Fig. 8 translates source terms to target terms. To be correct, the denotation of the compiled code for an expression must match the denotation of the expression itself, after the difference between the compiled and "interpreted" codes' execution contexts are taken into account: the denotation of the compiled code $\mathcal{CE}[\![e]\!]$ for any expression e, symbol table Γ and instruction sequence π, when applied to a display u, local stack ζ, and continuation κ, must be equivalent to the semantic definition $\mathcal{E}[\![e]\!]$ when applied to the environment $u \circ \Gamma$ and a continuation that takes the value returned by e, pushes it on the local stack, and then executes the code sequence π on the resulting register values. This is expressed in the following induction hypothesis:

$$(\overline{\mathcal{CE}[\![e]\!]\Gamma\pi}) \overset{\beta}{=} \lambda u\zeta\kappa.\mathcal{E}[\![e]\!](u \circ \Gamma)(\lambda z.\overline{\pi}u(z::\zeta)\kappa) \tag{4}$$

This condition is easily verified by structural induction on e, after which the strong bisimilarity of the compiled code's denotation and the semantic definition follows directly:

Theorem 3 (Compiler Correctness). For any program p,

$$[p_0 : start\,\overline{\mathcal{CP}[\![p]\!]}] \overset{\beta}{\simeq} \mathcal{P}[\![p]\!]$$

.

5 The Target Machine and Its Correctness

We now present a small-step operational semantics for our abstract machine. We may separate the purely sequential rules from the communicating rules. The sequential rules, which only affect the "computational" part of a process state and not the buffer, may be conveniently expressed as rules for a 4-register machine, and then lifted to a rule expressing the transition of the entire process state. The computation rules and the lifting rule are given in Fig. 9. In addition, we assume that if the instruction is one of the ones in the figure, but the pattern for the rule does not match, we execute the default rule $\langle\langle\pi, u, z, k\rangle, b\rangle \rightarrow_1 \langle\texttt{stopped}\rangle$.

Figure 10 gives the small-step semantics for our abstract machine. Every durational action of each process of the machine is modelled by a pair of transitions, representing the start and end of the action. The pair of rules for τ transitions lifts the computation rules into the instantaneous transition model of computation, making explicit the possibility of the entire machine getting into states where many processes are computing (that is, in $\langle\texttt{computing}, X\rangle$ states) simultaneously. The other eight rules correspond in a straightforward way to the communication rules of Fig. 2.

In the previous section, we showed that the denotation of a compiled program matched the denotation of the program itself. This idea is captured in the following definition:

Syntax	Denotation	
$Q = [p : s]\ldots$	$[p : \bar{s}]\ldots$	System states
$s ::= \langle\mathtt{start}, \pi\rangle$	$start\ \bar{\pi}$	Process states
$\quad\mid\ \langle t, b\rangle$	$\langle \bar{t}, \bar{b}\rangle$	
$\quad\mid\ \langle\mathtt{stopped}\rangle$	0	
$t ::= c$	$\bar{c}$	Idle computation
$\quad\mid\ \langle\langle\mathtt{computing}\rangle, c\rangle$	$\bar{c}$	Active computation
$\quad\mid\ \langle m, c\rangle$	$\langle \bar{m}, \bar{c}\rangle$	Active communication
$c ::= \langle\pi, u, z, k\rangle$	$\bar{\pi}\,\bar{u}\,\bar{z}\,\bar{k}$	Computation state
$\pi ::= \langle\mathtt{fetch}, n, \pi\rangle$	$fetch\ \ulcorner n\urcorner\,\bar{\pi}$	Code sequences
$\quad\mid\ \langle\mathtt{pushint}, n, \pi\rangle$	$pushint\ \ulcorner n\urcorner\,\bar{\pi}$	
$\quad\mid\ \langle\mathtt{pushclosure}, \pi, \pi\rangle$	$pushclosure\ \bar{\pi}'\,\bar{\pi}$	
$\quad\mid\ \langle\mathtt{return}\rangle$	$return$	
$\quad\mid\ \langle\mathtt{call}, \pi\rangle$	$call\ \bar{\pi}$	
$\quad\mid\ \langle\mathtt{brtrue}, \pi, \pi\rangle$	$brtrue\ \bar{\pi}_t\,\bar{\pi}_f$	
$\quad\mid\ \langle\mathtt{sub}, \pi\rangle$	$sub\ \bar{\pi}$	
$\quad\mid\ \langle\mathtt{put}, \pi\rangle$	$put\ \bar{\pi}$	
$\quad\mid\ \langle\mathtt{get}, \pi\rangle$	$get\ \bar{\pi}$	
$\quad\mid\ \langle\mathtt{empty}, \pi\rangle$	$empty\ \bar{\pi}$	
$\quad\mid\ \langle\mathtt{spawn}, \pi\rangle$	$spawn\ \bar{\pi}$	
$\quad\mid\ \langle\mathtt{swap}, \pi\rangle$	$swap\ \bar{\pi}$	
$u ::= z$	$\bar{z}$	Displays
$z ::= \langle\rangle$	$\langle\rangle$	Stacks
$\quad\mid\ \langle v, z\rangle$	$(\bar{v}::\bar{z})$	
$k ::= \langle\mathtt{halt}\rangle$	$\dagger$	Continuations
$\quad\mid\ \langle\mathtt{frame}, \pi, u, z, k\rangle$	$\lambda v.\bar{\pi}\,\bar{u}(v::\bar{z})\bar{k}$	
$b ::= z$	$\bar{z}$	Buffers
$v ::= \langle\mathtt{int}, n\rangle$	$in_{int}\ulcorner n\urcorner$	Values
$\quad\mid\ \langle\mathtt{pid}, p\rangle$	$in_{pid}\,c_p$	
$\quad\mid\ \langle\mathtt{closure}, \pi, u\rangle$	$in_{clo}(\lambda v\kappa.\bar{\pi}(v::\bar{u})\langle\rangle\kappa)$	
$\quad\mid\ \langle\mathtt{bool}, 0\rangle$	$in_{bool}\ulcorner false\urcorner$	
$\quad\mid\ \langle\mathtt{bool}, 1\rangle$	$in_{bool}\ulcorner true\urcorner$	
$\quad\mid\ \langle\mathtt{unit}\rangle$	$unit$	
$m ::= \langle\mathtt{receiving}\rangle$	$\langle c_{receiving}\rangle$	Activity markers
$\quad\mid\ \langle\mathtt{emptying}, v\rangle$	$\langle c_{examining}\,\bar{v}\rangle$	
$\quad\mid\ \langle\mathtt{sending}\rangle$	$\langle c_{sending}\rangle$	
$\quad\mid\ \langle\mathtt{spawning}, v\rangle$	$\langle c_{spawning}\,\bar{v}\rangle$	
$\quad\mid\ \langle\mathtt{computing}\rangle$		

Fig. 6. System state syntax and denotations. Note that the rule for $\langle\langle\mathtt{computing}\rangle, c\rangle$ takes precedence over the rule for $\langle m, c\rangle$ which follows it.

Definition 4. We say that a program Π in our calculus and a system state Q correspond if $\Pi \stackrel{\beta}{=} \bar{Q}$. We write $\Pi \simeq Q$.

$$fetch\ n\ \pi = \lambda u\zeta\kappa.\pi u((dlookup\ u\ n)::\zeta)\kappa$$
$$pushint\ v\ \pi = \lambda u\zeta\kappa.\pi u((in_{int}\ v)::\zeta)\kappa$$
$$pushclosure\ \pi'\pi = \lambda u\zeta\kappa.\pi u(in_{clo}(fix\ (\lambda p.\lambda v\kappa.\pi'((in_{clo}\ p)::v::u)\langle\rangle\kappa)::\zeta)\kappa)$$
$$return = \lambda u\zeta\kappa.pop\ \zeta(\lambda v\zeta.\kappa v)$$
$$call\ \pi = \lambda u\zeta\kappa.pop\ \zeta(\lambda a\zeta.pop\ \zeta(\lambda f\zeta.applicate\ f\ a\ (\lambda v.\pi u(v::\zeta)\kappa)))$$
$$brtrue\ \pi_t\ \pi_f = \lambda u\zeta\kappa.pop\ \zeta(\lambda v\zeta.(out_{bool}\ v\ (\lambda b.(primitive\_if\ b\ (\pi_t u\zeta\kappa)\ (\pi_f u\zeta\kappa)))))$$
$$sub\ \pi = \lambda u\zeta\kappa.pop\ \zeta(\lambda v_1\zeta.pop\ \zeta(\lambda v_2\zeta.subtract\ v_1\ v_2(\lambda v.\pi u(v::\zeta)\kappa)))$$
$$put\ \pi = \lambda u\zeta\kappa.pop\ \zeta(\lambda v_1\zeta.out_{pid}\ v_1(\lambda p.c_{send}\ p\ v_2(\pi u(unit::\zeta)\kappa)))$$
$$get\ \pi = \lambda u\zeta\kappa.c_{receive}(\lambda v.\pi u(v::\zeta)\kappa)$$
$$empty\ \pi = \lambda u\zeta\kappa.c_{empty}(\lambda v.\pi u(v::\zeta)\kappa)$$
$$spawn\ \pi = \lambda u\zeta\kappa.pop\ \zeta(\lambda f\zeta.c_{spawn}(\lambda p'.boot\ f\ \dagger)(\lambda p'.\pi u((in_{pid}\ p')::\zeta)\kappa))$$
$$start = \lambda\pi.\pi\langle\rangle((in_{pid}\ c_{p_0})::\langle\rangle)\dagger$$
$$swap\ \pi = \lambda u\zeta\kappa.pop\ \zeta(\lambda v_1\zeta_1.pop\ \zeta_1(\lambda v_2\zeta_2.\pi u(v_2::(v_1::\zeta_2))\kappa))$$

Fig. 7. Denotational semantics of instructions

$$\mathcal{CE}[i]\Gamma\pi = \langle fetch, (slookup\ \Gamma i), \pi\rangle$$
$$\mathcal{CE}[n]\Gamma\pi = \langle pushint, n, \pi\rangle$$
$$\mathcal{CE}[(rec\ i_1(i_2)\ e)]\Gamma\pi = \langle pushclosure, (\mathcal{CE}[e](i_1::i_2::\Gamma)\langle return\rangle), \pi\rangle$$
$$\mathcal{CE}[(if\ e_1\ e_2\ e_3)]\Gamma\pi = \mathcal{CE}[e_1]\Gamma\langle brtrue, (\mathcal{CE}[e_2]\Gamma\pi), (\mathcal{CE}[e_3]\Gamma\pi)\rangle$$
$$\mathcal{CE}[(e_1\ e_2)]\Gamma\pi = \mathcal{CE}[e_1]\Gamma(\mathcal{CE}[e_2]\Gamma\langle call, \pi\rangle)$$
$$\mathcal{CE}[(-\ e_1\ e_2)]\Gamma\pi = \mathcal{CE}[e_1]\Gamma(\mathcal{CE}[e_2]\Gamma\langle sub, \pi\rangle)$$
$$\mathcal{CE}[(put\ e_1\ e_2)]\Gamma\pi = \mathcal{CE}[e_1]\Gamma(\mathcal{CE}[e_2]\Gamma\langle put, \pi\rangle)$$
$$\mathcal{CE}[(get)]\Gamma\pi = \langle get, \pi\rangle$$
$$\mathcal{CE}[(empty?)]\Gamma\pi = \langle empty, \pi\rangle$$
$$\mathcal{CE}[(spawn\ e)]\Gamma\pi = \mathcal{CE}[e]\Gamma\langle spawn, \pi\rangle$$
$$\mathcal{CP}[e] = (\mathcal{CE}[e]\langle\rangle\langle swap, \langle call, \langle return\rangle\rangle\rangle)$$

Fig. 8. The compiler

The goal now is to show that the successive states of a target machine running the compiled code for a program always correspond to the program's denotation. This amounts to showing that $\simeq$ is a branching bisimulation. We break the proof into several lemmas: we show first that silent transitions of the abstract machine correspond to β-reduction of terms in our calculus, and then that each observable transition of one system is justified by a corresponding transition in the other.

Lemma 5. If $s \to_1 s'$ then $\overline{s} \to_\beta^+ \overline{s'}$ via a reduction sequence containing at least one leftmost step.

$$\langle \text{start}, \pi \rangle \quad\rightarrow_0 \langle \pi, \langle\rangle, \langle\langle \text{pid}, p_0\rangle, \langle\rangle\rangle, \langle \text{halt}\rangle\rangle$$

$$\langle\langle \text{fetch}, n, \pi\rangle, u, z, k\rangle \quad\rightarrow_0 \langle \pi, u, \langle\langle clookup\; u\; n\rangle, z\rangle, k\rangle$$

$$\langle\langle \text{pushint}, n, \pi\rangle, u, z, k\rangle \quad\rightarrow_0 \langle \pi, u, \langle\langle \text{int}, n\rangle, z\rangle, k\rangle$$

$$\langle\langle \text{pushclosure}, \pi', \pi\rangle, u, z, k\rangle \quad\rightarrow_0 \langle \pi, u, \langle\langle \text{closure}, \pi', u\rangle, z\rangle, k\rangle$$

$$\langle\langle \text{return}\rangle, u, \langle v, z\rangle, \langle \text{frame}, \pi', u', z', k'\rangle\rangle \rightarrow_0 \langle \pi', u', \langle v, z'\rangle, k'\rangle$$

$$\langle\langle \text{call}, \pi\rangle, u, \langle v, \langle\langle \text{closure}, \pi', u'\rangle, z\rangle\rangle, k\rangle \rightarrow_0 \langle \pi', \langle\langle \text{closure}, \pi', u'\rangle, \langle v, u'\rangle\rangle, \langle\rangle,$$
$$\langle \text{frame}, \pi, u, z, k\rangle\rangle$$

$$\langle\langle \text{brtrue}, \pi_t, \pi_f\rangle, u, \langle\langle \text{bool}, true\rangle, z\rangle, k\rangle \quad\rightarrow_0 \langle \pi_t, u, z, k\rangle$$

$$\langle\langle \text{brtrue}, \pi_t, \pi_f\rangle, u, \langle\langle \text{bool}, false\rangle, z\rangle, k\rangle \quad\rightarrow_0 \langle \pi_f, u, z, k\rangle$$

$$\langle\langle \text{sub}, \pi\rangle, u, \langle\langle \text{int}, n\rangle, \langle\langle \text{int}, m\rangle, z\rangle\rangle, k\rangle \quad\rightarrow_0 \langle \pi, u, \langle\langle \text{int}, (m-n)\rangle, z\rangle, k\rangle$$

$$\langle\langle \text{swap}, \pi\rangle, u, \langle v, \langle w, z\rangle\rangle, k\rangle \quad\rightarrow_0 \langle \pi, u, \langle w, \langle v, z\rangle\rangle, k\rangle$$

$$\frac{\langle \pi, u, z, k\rangle \rightarrow_0 \langle \pi', u', z', k'\rangle}{\langle\langle \pi, u, z, k\rangle, b\rangle \rightarrow_1 \langle\langle \pi', u', z', k'\rangle, b\rangle}$$

Fig. 9. Computation rules

Lemma 6 (Sequential Simulation). If $Q \xrightarrow{\tau} Q'$ then $\overline{Q} \overset{\beta}{\simeq} \overline{Q'}$.

Lemma 7 (Communicating Simulation). If $a \neq \tau$, $Q \xrightarrow{a} Q'$ and $\Pi \simeq Q$, then there is a Π' with $\Pi \xrightarrow{a} \Pi'$ and $\Pi' \simeq Q'$.

Lemma 8 (Completeness). If $\Pi \xrightarrow{a} \Pi'$ and $\Pi \simeq Q$ then there is a Q_1 and a Q' with $Q \xrightarrow{\tau} \dots \xrightarrow{\tau} Q_1 \xrightarrow{a} Q'$, $\Pi \simeq Q_1$, and $\Pi' \simeq Q'$.

The proofs of Lemmas 5–7 are straightforward. The proof of Lemma 8 uses Lemma 5 and the completeness of quasi-leftmost reduction sequences for head normal forms; see [6, 30, 13] for details. Combining the lemmas gives the following:

Theorem 9 (Abstract Machine Correctness). $\simeq$ is a branching bisimulation.

Combining Theorems 3 and 9 we get:

Theorem 10 (Combined Correctness). For any program e, $\mathcal{P}[e]$ is branching bisimilar to $[p_0 : \langle \text{start}, \mathcal{CP}[e]\rangle]$.

This shows that the behavior given by the semantics is similar to the behavior of the target machine running the compiled program, as desired.

6 Implementation

To demonstrate that the small-step semantics is plausible, we coded an implementation in Concert/C [5], an extension of C which provides facilities for transmitting data structures between processes. Each process of the target machine

$$\left[\begin{array}{c} \dfrac{X \to_1 X'}{Q[p:X] \overset{\tau}{\to} Q[p:\langle \text{computing}, X\rangle]} \\[2em] \dfrac{X \to_1 X'}{Q[p:\langle \text{computing}, X\rangle] \overset{\tau}{\to} Q[p:X']} \end{array}\right]$$

$$\left[\begin{array}{c} \dfrac{X = \langle\langle\langle\text{get}, \pi\rangle, u, z, k\rangle, b\rangle}{Q[p:X] \xrightarrow{p:\langle receive\rangle^+} Q[p:\langle\langle\text{receiving}\rangle, X\rangle]} \\[2em] \dfrac{X = \langle\langle\text{receiving}\rangle, \langle\langle\langle\text{get}, \pi\rangle, u, z, k\rangle, \langle v, b\rangle\rangle\rangle}{Q[p:X] \xrightarrow{p:\langle receive\rangle^-} Q[p:\langle\langle\pi, u, \langle v, z\rangle, k\rangle, b\rangle]} \end{array}\right]$$

$$\left[\begin{array}{c} \dfrac{X = \langle\langle\langle\text{empty}, \pi\rangle, u, z, k\rangle, b\rangle \quad i = \begin{cases} 1 & b = \langle\rangle \\ 0 & b \neq \langle\rangle \end{cases}}{Q[p:X] \xrightarrow{p:\langle examine\rangle^+} Q[p:\langle\langle\text{emptying}, \langle\text{int}, i\rangle\rangle, X\rangle]} \\[2em] \dfrac{X = \langle\langle\text{emptying}, v\rangle, \langle\langle\langle\text{empty}, \pi\rangle, u, z, k\rangle, b\rangle\rangle}{Q[p:X] \xrightarrow{p:\langle examine\rangle^-} Q[p:\langle\langle\pi, u, \langle v, z\rangle, k\rangle, b\rangle]} \end{array}\right]$$

$$\left[\begin{array}{c} \dfrac{X = \langle\langle\langle\text{put}, \pi\rangle, u, \langle v, \langle\langle\text{pid}, p'\rangle, z\rangle\rangle, k\rangle, b\rangle}{Q[p:X] \xrightarrow{p:\langle send\, p'\rangle^+} Q[p:\langle\text{sending}, X\rangle]} \\[2em] \dfrac{X = \langle\text{sending}, \langle\langle\langle\text{put}, \pi\rangle, u, \langle v, \langle\langle\text{pid}, p'\rangle, z\rangle\rangle, k\rangle, b\rangle\rangle}{Q[p:X][p':\langle Y, b'\rangle] \xrightarrow{p:\langle send\ p'\rangle^-} \begin{array}{l} Q[p:\langle\langle\pi, u, \langle\langle\text{unit}\rangle, z\rangle, k\rangle, b\rangle] \\ {}[p':\langle Y, b'@\langle v, \langle\rangle\rangle\rangle] \end{array}} \end{array}\right]$$

$$\left[\begin{array}{c} \dfrac{X = \langle\langle\langle\text{spawn}, \pi\rangle, u, \langle\langle\text{closure}, \pi', u'\rangle, z\rangle, k\rangle, b\rangle \quad p' \notin \text{procs}\, Q \cup \{p\}}{Q[p:X] \xrightarrow{p:\langle spawn\, p'\rangle^+} Q[p:\langle\langle\text{spawning}, \langle\text{pid}, p'\rangle\rangle, X\rangle]} \\[2em] \dfrac{X = \langle\langle\text{spawning}, \langle\text{pid}, p'\rangle\rangle, \langle\langle\langle\text{spawn}, \pi\rangle, u, \langle\langle\text{closure}, \pi', u'\rangle, z\rangle, k\rangle, b\rangle\rangle}{Q[p:X] \xrightarrow{p:\langle spawn\, p'\rangle^-} \begin{array}{l} Q[p:\langle\langle\pi, u, \langle\langle\text{pid}, p'\rangle, z\rangle, k\rangle, b\rangle] \\ {}[p':\langle\langle\langle\text{call}, \text{return}\rangle, \langle\rangle, \langle\langle\text{pid}, p'\rangle, \langle\langle\text{closure}, \pi', u'\rangle, \langle\rangle\rangle\rangle\rangle, \\ \quad\langle\text{halt}\rangle\rangle, \\ {}[\langle\rangle]\rangle] \end{array}} \end{array}\right]$$

Fig. 10. Small step semantics

program was represented by a separate Concert/C process. The target machine states of Fig. 6 were transliterated into C structs. A straightforward interpreter implements those process transitions which do not involve interprocess communication, while message sending and spawning are implemented by the corresponding Concert/C facilities.

Taking the state of a Concert/C process to consist of its program counter together with the values of its program variables, we were able to argue that the collection of Concert/C processes is a simulation of the target machine: each state and transition of the collection of processes corresponds to a legal move of the target machine. Since we could not guarantee anything about the way our processes would be scheduled by the operating system, we were not able to argue that our implementation is complete for the target machine; however, we were able to show that the implementation is safe, in that it cannot deadlock unless the target machine can do so.

Had our machines' semantics been defined in the usual interleaving style, as in [30], the correctness proofs of the preceding sections would still have worked out; the difficulty comes in reasoning about the multicomputer implementation. As in the example of Sect. 2.1, the interleaving semantics specifies that the collection of processes must execute only one step at a time. The nature of a collection of computers, however, is to execute many steps simultaneously and without synchronization between the processors. In the absence of a locking mechanism preventing the computers from making independent progress, which would be silly, it is not clear how to draw a correspondence between the possible behaviors of the collection of computers and the semantic specification of the target machine. By contrast, the interleaved instantaneous transitions of the split-transition semantics captures precisely our understanding of the operation of the collection of computers.

The complete implementation is given in [13].

7 Related Work

The compiler derivation methodology sketched in Sect. 1.1 has been applied to yield correctness proofs for several compilers of modest size: a simple functional language [28, 27], a language with **while**-expressions [29], a language obeying stack-discipline and having nonlocal jumps [31], and core Scheme [9]. Two larger-scale systems have also been proven correct in great detail using these techniques: A complete implementation of Scheme is proven correct in [15], and a compiler for PreScheme, a Scheme-like language designed for systems programming, is proven correct in [21].

As discussed in [30], the literature contains a great deal of work on the mathematical and algebraic properties of models of concurrent computation, but very little about compiler correctness. We briefly discuss a few of the papers that are most closely related to our work; all of them use interleaving models of concurrency.

The Nielsons' formulation of process algebras for Concurrent ML [20] is the basis of the formulation of our calculus; most importantly, they originated the technique of separating computation and communication by having the computation treat the communication primitives as uninterpreted constants. They use a small-step semantics for both computation and communication, whereas we use a version of the instantaneous computation rule of [7]; this allows us to stay within the λ-calculus when considering computation alone.

Facile [11, 12] is a source language whose semantics is given by a compositional translation into the intermediate language "core Facile". Core Facile is based on the typed call-by-value λ-calculus, with channel-based communication and a call/cc operator. In [1], Amadio gives translations between several versions of this language, including a translation into an environment-based machine similar to ours. He proves the adequacy of his translations, in the sense that they do not confuse distinguishable programs. Both the computation and communication semantics of core Facile are given as a pure small-step semantics. This mixing of computation and communication makes the notion of observability more complicated, and requires considerable reasoning about administrative reductions, etc. Our formulation seems easier to reason about, because β-equivalence is automatically a bisimulation.

Milner shows in [18, 19] how λ-calculus can be translated into the π-calculus. Walker [26] translates two languages similar to POOL [2] into the π-calculus, but he gives no relation between his translations and any other semantics for the languages. CHOCS is used as an intermediate language in Thomsen's original article [24]; he translates the λ-calculus into CHOCS and shows that the translation preserves, but does not reflect, β-convertibility. He also gives a semantics for a toy language with procedures as a compositional translation into CHOCS.

Languages like ours which use the "computation + communication" paradigm naturally have substantial sequential components. Neither the π-calculus nor CHOCS is so well suited as the λ-calculus for generating reasonable code for the sequential portions of the language. By using the λ-calculus as an intermediate language, we are able to reuse large amounts of reasoning from sequential-language compiler proofs. Appel [3] gives further arguments for the use of λ-calculus as an intermediate language.

8 Future Work

In the course of this work, several avenues of further research became apparent.

Our account of asynchronous message passing is somewhat inaccurate, in that a process is blocked from the time it sends a message until the time the message is enqueued at the receiver's input buffer. We believe that this can be fixed by giving an account in which buffers and communication paths are reified, and all communication is synchronous; this approach would also apply to more sophisticated coordination mechanisms.

So far the communication and process control operations of our semantics have been equivalent to those provided by the underlying implementation system, in our case Concert/C. We need to give an account of high-level operations in terms of lower-level ones; refinement methods such as those of [21, 7] should be applicable.

References

1. R. M. Amadio. *Translating core Facile*. Technical Report ECRC-1994-3, ECRC, Feb. 1994.
2. P. America, J. de Bakker, J. N. Kok, and J. Rutten. Operational semantics of a parallel object-oriented language. In *Conf. Rec. 13th ACM Symposium on Principles of Programming Languages*, pages 194–208, 1986.
3. A. W. Appel. *Compiling with Continuations*. Cambridge University Press, Cambridge, 1992.
4. J. Armstrong, R. Virding, and M. Williams. *Concurrent Programming in Erlang*. Prentice Hall, 1993.
5. J. S. Auerbach et al. *Concurrent/C Tutorial and User's Guide: An Introduction to a Language for Distributed C Programming*. IBM T. J. Watson Research Center, June 1994.
6. H. P. Barendregt. *The Lambda Calculus: Its Syntax and Semantics*. North-Holland, 1984.
7. B. Bloom. Chocolate: Calculi of higher order communication and lambda terms. In *Conf. Rec. 21st ACM Symposium on Principles of Programming Languages*, pages 339–347, 1994.
8. N. Carriero and D. Gelernter. *How to Write Parallel Programs: A First Course*. MIT Press, 1990.
9. W. Clinger. The Scheme 311 compiler: An exercise in denotational semantics. In *Proc. 1984 ACM Symposium on Lisp and Functional Programming*, pages 356–364, Aug. 1984.
10. A. Geist et al. *PVM 3 User's Guide and Reference Manual*. Oak Ridge National Laboratory, May 1993.
11. A. Giacalone, P. Mishra, and S. Prasad. Facile: A symmetric integration of concurrent and functional programming. *International Journal of Parallel Programming*, 18(2):121–160, 1989.
12. A. Giacalone, P. Mishra, and S. Prasad. Operational and algebraic semantics for facile: A symmetric integration of concurrent and functional programming. In *Proc. ICALP '90*, volume 443 of *Lecture Notes in Computer Science*, pages 765–7780, Berlin, Heidelberg, and New York, 1990. Springer-Verlag.
13. D. Gladstein. *Compiler Correctness for Concurrent Languages*. PhD thesis, Northeastern University, Dec. 1994. Available via anonymous ftp from ftp.ccs.neu.edu as /pub/people/daveg/thesis.ps.Z.
14. R. Gorrieri and C. Laneve. Split and ST bisimulation semantics. *Information and Computation*, 118:272–288, 1995.
15. J. D. Guttman, V. Swarup, and J. Ramsdell. The VLISP verified scheme system. *Lisp and Symbolic Computation*, 8(1/2), 1995.
16. M. Hennessy. Axiomatising finite concurrent processes. *SIAM Journal of Computation*, 15(5):997–1017, 1995.
17. C. Hoare. *Communicating Sequential Processes*. Prentice Hall International, 1985.
18. R. Milner. Functions as processes. *Mathematical Structures in Computer Science*, 2:119–141, 1992.
19. R. Milner, J. Parrow, and D. Walker. A calculus of mobile processes (parts i and ii). *Information and Computation*, 100:1–77, 1992.
20. F. Nielson and H. R. Nielson. From CML to process algebras. In *Proceesings of CONCUR '93*, pages 493–508, Berlin, Heidelberg, and New York, 1993. Springer-Verlag.

21. D. P. Oliva, J. D. Ramsdell, and M. Wand. The VLISP verified PreScheme compiler. *Lisp and Symbolic Computation*, 8(1/2), 1995.

22. J. C. Reynolds. The discoveries of continuations. *Lisp and Symbolic Computation*, 6(3/4):233–248, 1993.

23. G. Springer and D. P. Friedman. *Scheme and the Art of Programming*. MIT Press, 1989.

24. B. Thomsen. A calculus of higher order communicating systems. In *Conf. Rec. 16th ACM Symposium on Principles of Programming Languages*, pages 143–154, 1989.

25. R. van Glabbeek and F. Vaandrager. The difference between splitting in n and $n + 1$ (abstract). In E. Best and G. Rozenberg, editors, *Proceedings 3rd Workshop on Concurrency and Compositionality*, Sankt Augustin, Germany, February 1991. GMD-Studien Nr. 191.

26. D. Walker. π-calculus semantics of object-oriented programming languages. In *Proc. Conference on Theoretical Aspects of Computer Software*, Lecture Notes in Computer Science, Berlin, Heidelberg, and New York, 1991. Springer-Verlag.

27. M. Wand. Deriving target code as a representation of continuation semantics. *ACM Transactions on Programming Languages and Systems*, 4(3):496–517, July 1982.

28. M. Wand. Semantics-directed machine architecture. In *Conf. Rec. 9th ACM Symposium on Principles of Programming Languages*, pages 234–241, 1982.

29. M. Wand. Loops in combinator-based compilers. *Information and Control*, 57(2–3):148–164, May/June 1983.

30. M. Wand. Compiler correctness for parallel languages. In *1995 Symposium on Functional Languages and Computer Architecture*, June 1995.

31. M. Wand and D. P. Oliva. Proving the correctness of storage representations. In *Proc. 1992 ACM Symposium on Lisp and Functional Programming*, pages 151–160, 1992.

A Software Environment for Concurrent Coordinated Programming

A.A. Holzbacher*

Laboratoire d'Informatique
Ecole Polytechnique
91128 Palaiseau
France
email: sandra@lix.polytechnique.fr

Abstract. In this paper, we present ConCoord: a software environment for Concurrent Coordinated programming. ConCoord contributes to concurrent programming in three ways. First, it separates programming into computation and coordination in order to reduce programming complexity. A ConCoord program is a dynamic collection of processes for either computation or coordination. Computation processes encapsulate conventional sequential computations. Coordination processes manage concurrency and only this. They handle dynamic evolution of the program structure depending on conditions on the program structure and execution state of processes. Second, ConCoord is targeted at networks of sequential and parallel machines. These networks support efficiently the exploitation of a diversity of concurrency grains on their different architectures. In order to take advantage of this feature, ConCoord provides linguistic support for heterogeneous concurrency exploitation. Third, reuse has being a primary concern in ConCoord's design. In our environment, sequential algorithms can be reused within computation processes. Concurrency management of concurrent algorithms can be reused within coordination processes. Both computation and coordination processes can be specified as parameterised reusable software components.

In this paper, we start by discussing the motivation and contributions of our work. Afterwards, we present ConCoord. This presentation details the contributions of ConCoord. It consists of two parts: one describes computation and the other coordination. We end the paper with comments on related work and conclusions.

1 Motivation

ConCoord's design derives from three main motivations: reducing concurrent programming complexity by separating programming into coordination and com-

---

* This work has been supported by the grant pf93 5416228 from the Spanish Ministry of Education and Sciences MEC.

putation, supporting heterogeneous concurrency exploitation, and promoting reuse.

Nowadays, concurrent programming remains a complex task. We believe that this complexity is partly due to a mixed treatment of sequential and concurrent aspects of programming within a unique programming language. Designers and programmers must deal with both aspects and hence be experienced in both sequential and concurrent programming. In this paper, we propose a software environment in which a program is decomposed into computation processes and coordination processes. In our environment, the design of a program requires experience in sequential and concurrent programming. However, the programming of single computation processes resembles sequential programming. The programming of coordination processes centers on concurrency management abstracting from computation details. In this way, the complexity of concurrency management is reduced.

We have chosen as target system for ConCoord networks of sequential and parallel machines. These networks appear as a good candidate to which distributed and parallel systems may converge in the future. They provide several advantages with regard to distributed and parallel systems. On these networks, distributed programming can exploit fine grain concurrency on the parallel machines widening in this way its application area. Parallel programming can gain computing power and memory at low price (see [Tur93]). Most existing programming languages or environments have been designed for an homogeneous concurrency exploitation which does not take full advantage of these networks. Parallel programming languages generally manage only fine grain concurrency; distributed programming languages center on coarse grain concurrency. Networks of sequential and parallel machines have the potential to support efficiently a variety of concurrency grains on their different architectures. ConCoord exploits this potential by supporting heterogeneous concurrency management.

Development of large applications requires reuse for reducing duplication of code and work. In the area of sequential programming, support for reuse ranges from packages for defining reusable components to generics for specifying parameterised reusable components (see [oD83]). In the area of concurrent programming, reuse has been treated in different ways. Some parallel programming languages give a set of reusable concurrent structures whose execution is guaranteed to be performant on particular architectures (see P^3L[DMO+92]). This solution hinders creation of new reusable components by the language users. Other programming languages provide linguistic support for defining reusable software components (see [Kra91, BWL89]). We have chosen this approach. In ConCoord, one can define reusable software components which can be parameterised or not. A sequential algorithm can be reused by means of a computation process. The concurrency management of a concurrent algorithm can be reused via a coordination process.

2 ConCoord

ConCoord is a software environment for Concurrent Coordinated programming. A ConCoord program describes a dynamic collection of sequential processes which communicate via message passing. Some of these processes are computation processes, other are coordination processes. A computation process executes conventional sequential computations and communication. It communicates with other processes without knowing the identity of its communication partners. Computation processes are unaware of the concurrency existing in the program. They are written in any sequential language with a few extensions for communication. The programming of computation components resembles sequential programming.

Coordination processes dynamically create and kill processes. They can also dynamically define, break and redefine bindings or channels between process ports. Coordination processes "coordinate" computation and other coordination processes, unaware of the implementation details of these processes. They cannot execute conventional sequential computations like numeric calculations. Coordination processes manage concurrency and only this. They are expressed in ConCoord's Coordination language: CCL.

The next sections present computation and coordination. They also describe ConCoord's support for heterogeneous concurrency exploitation and reuse.

2.1 Computation

In a program, a computation process is created or instantiated from a process type by a coordination process. Such a process type is named component and is defined in terms of a specification and an implementation. An abbreviated BNF for a component specification is shown below.

```
comp_spec  : component ['<'gen_param'>'] identifier ['('init_param')']
             ['{'interface'}']';'
interface  : ports_decl | states_decl | ports_decl interface
ports_decl : inport list_ports';' | outport list_ports';'
list_ports : '<'msg_type'>' identifier['['list_expr']'] [',' list_ports]
states_decl: states list_states [',' done'('param_types')']';'
list_states: identifier'('param_types')' [',' list_states]
```

A component may define: generic parameters, initialisation parameters and an interface. Generic parameters support the definition of parameterised reusable components and will be explained in section 2.1. Initialisation parameters are given values when the component is instantiated into a computation process. The interface specifies potential interactions of a computation process during its execution with other processes in the program.

```
component filter                        component func (int x, int y)
{                                       {
    inport <int> left;                      states done (int);
    outport <int> right, out;           };
    states new ();
};
```

Fig. 1. Two examples of components

An interface can define ports and states. In a concurrent program, process ports support collaboration between computation processes in the program computational goal. For this purpose, coordination defines bindings or channels between ports of computation processes. For example, coordination could create two processes f1 and f2 of type filter and bind the port right from f1 to the port left from f2. Arrays of ports are permitted but their use will not be commented here. We view communication via ports as computation and do not allow coordination processes to send or receive data via ports. When programming a component, ports are manipulated in a way similar to sequential in/out operations without awareness of concurrency. A computation process of type filter (see figure 1) receives values at its input port left and sends values at its ports right and out without knowing the identity or even existence of its communication partners.

States define possible states of execution of a component that may require some coordination action. In a single declaration, a component specifies its possible states and their parameter types. A component notifies of its state to coordination in an active way. For example, a process f1 of type filter explicitly sends its state new to coordination in order to inform that it has found a new value. Coordination may treat this notification by creating a new process filter and connecting it to some port of f1. There is a single pre-defined state done which represents the end of a component execution. A component may or may not define done. If it does so then it will always notify of the end of its execution. Otherwise, it won't notify of it at all and will have to be terminated by coordination.

Coordination specifies the execution of a computation process using only the information provided by the corresponding component specification.

Heterogeneous Concurrency Exploitation ConCoord components can represent different concurrency grains, ranging from functions to reactive processes. In figure 1, a component func expresses a function $f(x, y)$ which takes two integers x and y and returns an integer. The result of the function execution is passed as a parameter of the state notification done. Figure 1 also includes a reactive component filter.

In ConCoord, one can represent different concurrency grains by specifying ports and a state done. The processes derived from these concurrency grains must be mapped on the appropriate processors of the network of sequential and parallel machines. When a coordination process creates a process, it can specify its location on a processor of the network (see section 2.2). For example, a fine grain process like func could be mapped onto a processor of a parallel machine while a coarse grain one like filter onto a sequential machine. When mapping, other issues should also be taken into account like potential interactions between processes. Processes that may interact with each other heavily should be located close to each other if possible.

Computation Programming Languages A component implementation can be written in any sequential language with a few extensions for manipulation of ports and states whose abbreviated BNF appears below.

```
communication :    send_data | receive_data | guarded_receive
send_data      :    port_id '.' out '(' list_expr ')'
               |    port_id '.' send '(' list_expr ')'
receive_data   :    port_id '.' in '(' list_id ')'
port_id        :    identifier [ '[' list_expr ']' ]
state_notif    :    identifier '(' [ list_expr ] ')' | done '(' [ list_expr ] ')'
```

Ports manipulation is mainly supported by three operations for data transfer: in, out and send. A guarded receive is also provided but we won't detail it here. in blocks the computation process until some data is received. out blocks the computation process until its communication partner is ready to receive the data; send sends the data independently of the state of the communication partner. This semantics applies as long as a process port is bound to another process port. Ports binding or channel definition is the responsibility of coordination. If coordination has not bound a port of a computation process, any attempt of communication on that port by the process blocks the process until a binding is defined. Using this mechanism, coordination can prevent a computation process from interacting with other processes and guarantee consistency.

A process notifies of its state to coordination by naming one of its defined states and giving values to its parameters. For example, a process of type func (see Figure 1) can notify of its execution end and a result 10 with a statement: done(10). When a process sends a state, it remains blocked until coordination has treated it. This mechanism has two main advantages. It provides an up-to-date view of processes state to coordination. It also guarantees that a process that has notified of its state is in a safe state for being manipulated. This mechanism has the drawback that it can be time consuming. State notifications can be disabled within coordination. When states from a component are disabled, processes of the component type send states without blocking. From a design viewpoint, states must be chosen carefully and used only for coordination related states.

Operations for ports and states manipulations can be viewed as sequential in/out operations. They can be used with little knowledge of the concurrency existing in the program. Programming of components resembles sequential programming. When programming a component, one can either define new code or include existing sequential code. The latter supports integration and reuse of sequential programs into a concurrent program. As components have a well-defined specification which is separated from their implementation, different components can have implementations expressed in different programming languages. Nothing prevents a ConCoord program from being a multi-lingual application whose components are written in the language that better suits their functionality.

Reuse Reuse occurs at three different levels in the computation element of ConCoord. First, existing sequential code can be reused within a component. On the one hand, one can encapsulate a single sequential program into a functional component. On the other hand, one can assemble various sequential programs together with communication operations into a reactive component.

Second, components have various properties that make them reusable software items *per se*. Components have a well-defined specification and a separate definition of their implementation. Their implementation is self-contained code that does not use information about the execution context of the component. All these properties make components context-independent software items (see [Kra91]) which can be integrated or reused in different contexts or concurrent programs.

Third, components can be parameterised by data types. This feature resembles generics from Ada [oD83] and templates from C++ [Str91]. It supports parameterised reusable software items. We can for example define a generic version of filter, namely gen_filter which is parameterised by a type of data t_data for its input and output messages. Associated to this type of data, there could be an operation op to be applied to an incoming message in_msg from left in order to produce an out-coming message out_msg in right (i.e. out_msg = t_data::op (in_msg)).

```
component <t_data> gen_filter (t_data x, t_data y)
{  inport <t_data> left;
   outport <t_data> right, out;
   states done ();
};
```

2.2 Coordination

As already mentioned, a ConCoord program is a dynamic collection of computation and coordination processes. This collection has a hierarchical structure derived from creation. The root is a coordination process which is created at program start-up (see c1 in figure 2). The leaves are computation processes which cannot create any process (see p1, p2 and p3). The middle nodes are coordination processes (see c2). In the hierarchy, each coordination process supervises a domain or sub-collection of processes that it has created (e.g. c1 supervises c2 and p3). It defines dynamic evolution of its domain structure depending on conditions on its domain structure and on state of its domain processes. A coordination process manages its domain processes abstracting from their implementation details.

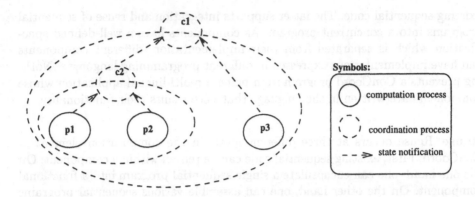

Fig. 2. Hierarchy of processes

It only uses the information provided by the specification of the process type. For example, c1 does not see c2's domain. When a process notifies of its state, this is only visible to its domain supervisor-coordinator.

Coordination processes are created or instantiated from a process type named coordinator. Coordinators are defined by means of a specification and an implementation. A coordinator specification is syntactically speaking equivalent to a component specification (see section 2.1) in which the keyword component has been replaced by coordinator. Semantically speaking there exist some differences which we explain below. In a coordinator, generic parameters serve for building parameterised coordinators and will be commented in section 2.2. Initialisation parameters are given values when a process of the coordinator type is created. The interface can define ports and states.

States have the same purpose in coordination as in computation. They permit a coordination process to notify of its execution state to its supervisor-coordinator. There can be user-defined or the pre-defined state done. In the case of a coordination process, the notification of done implies that the coordination process and all its domain processes have terminated.

In a coordinator, ports are only used to define bindings between computation processes belonging to different coordination domains. In figure 3, c2 has a port which supports a binding between ports of the computation processes p2 and p3. A coordination process cannot use its port for sending or receiving data. We remark that from an implementation viewpoint inter-domain communication (e.g. between p2 and p3) and intra-domain communication (e.g. between p1 and p2) will be supported in the same way[2]. The only difference between these two communications resides on the management of the bindings.

---

[2] In other words, inter-domain communication does not imply that messages have to go through the coordination process or processes that define the ports binding.

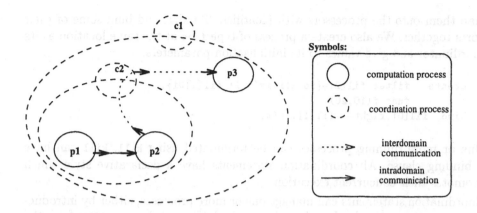

Fig. 3. Communication between computational processes

ConCoord's Coordination Language CCL A coordinator implementation is written in ConCoord's Coordination Language: CCL. CCL provides basic statements for manipulation of states notifications and coordination actions. It also gives structuring statements: conditional, alternative and repetition.

There are four statements for states manipulation. A coordination process sends its state to its supervisor-coordinator naming one of its defined states and giving values to its parameters. By means of **enable** and **disable**, a coordination process can enable or disable state notifications from processes of a certain process type in its domain. When states from a process type are disabled, processes of this type send states without blocking on the notification. With **empty**, a coordination process can consume all state notifications from a certain process type that are pending of treatment. **empty** unblocks all processes that originated the consumed states so they can continue their execution.

A coordinator specifies dynamic evolution of its domain structure in terms of coordination statements. Coordination statements support binding manipulation, process creation and process killing. Binding manipulation is provided by: **bind** for defining new bindings, **rebind** for modifying bindings and **unbind** for breaking bindings.

Process creation is supported by **create** which instantiates one or more processes from a component or a coordinator type. The instantiation can include definition of initialisation parameters. It can also specify a mapping expression (using @) to locate created processes on the processors of the network of sequential and parallel machines. ConCoord's users must define a configuration file with an integer identifier for each network processor. A mapping expression must evaluate to one of these identifiers. If no mapping expression is given, processes are located by default on the same processor as their supervisor-coordinator. **create** can have a binding clause which can be any binding manipulation. In the example below, we create two computational processes **fil[2]** of type **filter**, map them onto the processors with identifiers 0 and 1, and bind some of their ports together. We also create a process of type func at the same location as its coordinator and give values to its initialisation parameters.

```
create    filter fil[2]={forall i=(0,1) fil[i]@i},
          func f(10,20)
bind   fil[0].right--fil[1].left;
```

One or more running processes can be terminated using kill. kill can have a binding clause. All coordination statements have a declarative style which promotes their concurrent execution.

Coordination statements can manage one or more processes, either by introducing new processes in the domain or by manipulating running processes from the domain. CCL does not provide global variables to refer to running processes. Instead, CCL gives conditions on the domain structure which serve two purposes: checking domain state and selecting domain processes for later manipulation. An abbreviated BNF for conditions is shown below.

```
condition          :   one_condition [and condition]
one_condition      :   with_proc_sel | without_proc_sel
without_proc_sel   :   '('cardinality_cond')' | proc_type_id'.'any
                   |   proc_type_id'.'none
cardinality_cond   :   expr_using_cardinality_function_on_proc_type
card_function      :   card '('proc_type_id')' | card '('proc_var')'
with_proc_sel      :   sel '('list_proc_decl ['|' list_proc_cond]')'
                   |   '('list_id')'':'''('list_proc_decl ['|' list_proc_cond]')'
list_proc_decl     :   proc_type_id ['<'list_type_id'>'] identifier
                       [',' list_proc_decl]
list_proc_cond     :   one_proc_cond [and list_proc_cond]
one_proc_cond      :   struct_cond | not struct_cond
                   |   state_cond [and expr_on_state_parameters]
struct_cond        :   identifier'.'port_id '--' identifier'.'port_id
                   |   identifier'.'port_id '--'
                   |   identifier '!=' identifier | cardinality_cond
state_cond         :   identifier'.'state_id '('[list_expr]')'
                   |   identifier'.'done'('[list_expr]')'
                   |   identifier'.'any
```

Conditions can be combined using and. Conditions can select or not processes. Conditions with no process selection can query on the number of running processes using a pre-defined function card. They can also check the existence of state notifications from processes of a certain type using none or any.

Conditions with process selection declare process variables and are quantified. The keyword sel implies nondeterministic choosing of one process per process variable among all processes satisfying the condition. When this keyword is not used, all satisfying processes are selected in the process variables. In this case, the condition must be preceded by a tuple with the variables names. This tuple will be used later to refer to the relation stated by the condition. Conditions with process selections can query on domain structure and on state of domain processes. Domain structure is given by: binding state of process ports using the notation $--$, existence and number of running processes of a process type using card, and inequality of processes (e.g. p1 != p2). State of domain processes is provided by states which have been sent by the processes. The state can be a user-defined state, the pre-defined state done or any state (i.e. any). If a state has associated parameters, one can also include a condition on the parameters values.

Conditions can be used within two conditional statements: if and when, and an alternative statement choose. if executes one or more statements if its condition is satisfied. when blocks the coordination process until its condition is true and then executes one or more statements. choose resembles a guarded statement (see [Dij75]) and consists of various branches. Each branch defines a condition and its associated statements. Among the branches whose condition is satisfied, one is chosen nondeterministically and its associated statements are executed. choose blocks until at least one of its branch conditions is true. In all these statements, the conditions quantifiers only apply to the conditions. In the statements that will be executed if a condition is satisfied, one can access the processes selected via forall. forall allows different manipulations of the sets and relations of processes defined in the condition. We won't detail its use here for lack of space.

In the example below, $S1$ blocks the coordinator execution until there exist two different processes of type func that have notified of their execution end via done. When this is true, a new process of type func is created and initialised with the execution results of f1 and f2. $S2$ is executed if there are in the domain at least two processes of type filter, one of which has sent new and has its port right bound to the port left of the other. When $S2$ is executed, a new process of type filter is introduced between all pairs of processes satisfying the condition.

```
when sel(func f1, func f2 | f1.done(x) and f2.done(y) and f1!=f2)
   => create func new_f(x,y); // S1

if (fi1,fi2):(filter fi1, filter fi2 | fi1.new and fi1.right--fi2.left)
   forall (fi1,fi2)
      create filter new_fi
      rebind fi1.right--new_fi.left, new_fi.right--fi2.left; // S2
```

In the conditional and alternative statements, when a process is selected via a state condition, at the end of the statement execution the corresponding state is considered as treated. The process that originated the state can continue its execution. This is the case for processes selected in fi1 in $S2$. Furthermore, CCL provides a single repetition statement loop which can be combined with a statement exit. We emphasize that CCL first-class and unique programming paradigm is dynamic concurrency management. It does not support any conventional sequential computation like numerical calculations.

Heterogeneous Concurrency Exploitation Like components, coordinators can represent different concurrency grains by defining ports and the pre-defined state `done`. One can express both functional and reactive coordinators. We won't show any example of this because it is basically the same than for components. This section will center on CCL's support for a diversity of concurrency managements.

First, a coordination process can specify different kinds of scheduling for its domain processes, i.e. creation modes, execution orders and process termination. A creation mode can be either synchronous (e.g. `cobegin-coend`) or asynchronous (e.g. `fork`). In CCL, `create` is asynchronous. To simulate a synchronous creation, a coordinator can simply wait for the notifications of execution end of its domain processes as shown below.

```
create filter fi[10];
when (fi):(filter fi | fi.done and card(fi)==card(filter)) =>;
```

An execution order can be either sequential or concurrent. We remark that sequential execution is needed to exploit fine grain processes like functions. Concurrent execution of a collection of processes can be expressed by `create` which supports creation of various processes. Sequential execution can be expressed using the state `done`. The example below provides a sequential execution of three processes of type `func`. Each computation step is initialised with the results of the previous step.

```
create func f(1,2);
when sel(func f | f.done(x)) => create func f(x+1,x+2);
when sel(func f | f.done(x)) => create func f(x+1,x+2);
```

`kill` provides process termination. It can be used for concurrency exploitations like or-parallelism. An example would be a program that creates various processes to search some solution. Once a solution is found by one of the processes, all other processes are terminated.

Second, the alternative statement `choose` also provides means for concurrency exploitation. Domain conditions that require some coordination can be treated when they are satisfied independently of in which order this happens.

Finally, mapping expressions in `create` can be used to locate processes to the most appropriate processor in the network of sequential and parallel machines. The identification of "good" mappings is left to the program designer.

Reuse Coordinators are context-independent like components. They are defined by a separate specification and implementation. Their implementation is self-contained code that does not use any information about its execution context. Coordinators are *per se* reusable software items.

If generic parameters are not used, reusing a coordination implies reusing the coordinator itself and its domain processes. In other words, we will reuse the whole concurrent algorithm that is expressed by the coordinator, including its sequential computations. If one wants to reuse only the concurrency management of the concurrent algorithm, one can define generic parameters. A coordinator can have generic parameters that define data types and process types. The latter permits the specification of a coordinator parameterised by the type of processes it manipulates. We illustrate this feature with a generic dynamic pipeline whose specification is shown below.

```
coordinator<t_node,t_data> gen_dyn_pipeline
{  inport <t_data> in;
   outport <t_data> out;
   states error (), done ();
};
```

gen_dyn_pipeline has two generic parameters: type of processes which constitute the pipeline (t_node) and type of data exchanged by pipeline processes (t_data). It provides an input port in and an output port out. The first process in the pipeline gets messages from outside gen_dyn_pipeline's domain via in; all processes in the pipeline send messages to outside the domain via out. These two ports will be bound by the coordinator-supervisor of gen_dyn_pipeline as illustrated by the example in next the section.

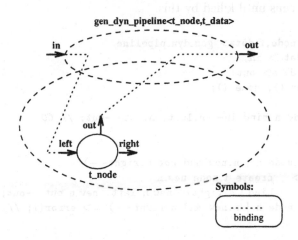

Fig. 4. Initial configuration of *gen_dyn_pipeline*

Below, we show the implementation of gen_dyn_pipeline. Initially, gen_dyn_pipe-line creates a process of type t_node and binds its ports left and out to its own ports in and out (see Figure 4 and statement *C0*). Each time that a process at the end of the pipeline sends a state new, a new process is added to the pipeline

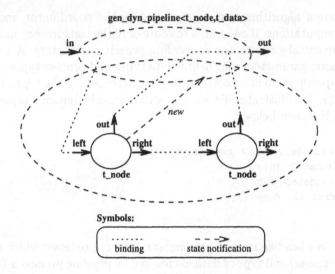

Fig. 5. Dynamic addition of a process to the pipeline in *gen_dyn_pipeline*

(see Figure 5 and statement *C1*). If a process notifies of this state without being the last one, the coordination process terminates originating a state **error** (see statement *C2*). **gen_dyn_pipeline** does not notify to its coordinator-supervisor of a state **done**; it runs until killed by this.

```
coordinator<t_node,t_data> gen_dyn_pipeline
{   inport <t_data> in;
    outport <t_data> out;
    states error (), done ();

    create t_node n bind in--n.left, n.out--out; // C0
    loop
    { choose
      { sel(t_node n | n.new and not n.right--)
            =>    create t_node new_n
                    bind  n.right--new_n.left, new_n.out--out; // C1
        sel(t_node n | n.new and n.right--) => error(); // C2
      };
    };
};
```

2.3   Example: The Primes Sieves of Eratosthenes

The primes sieve of Eratosthenes **sieves** computes the first n prime numbers and prints them (see [CG89, MDK92]). **sieves** is initialised by the value of n

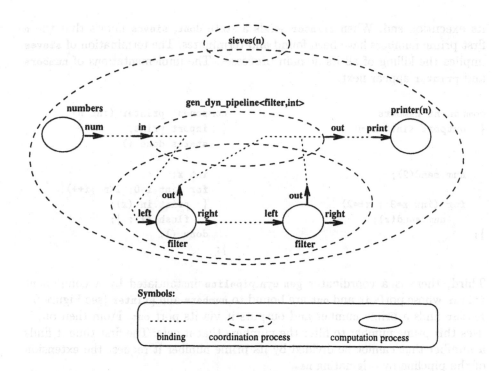

Fig. 6. Primes Sieve

and defines two states: error and done. The implementation of the coordinator sieves is shown below and illustrated in Figure 6.

```
use numbers, filter, printer;
coordinator sieves (int n)
{  states error (), done ();

    create   numbers nu, printer p(n), gen_dyn_pipeline<filter,int> gdp
    bind     nu.num--gdp.in, gdp.out--p.print;

    loop
    {  choose
       {  sel (gen_dyn_pipeline<filter,int> gdp | gdp.error) => error ();
          sel (printer p | p.done) => done ();
       };
    };
};
```

The primes numbers are computed by assembling three elements (see Figure 6). First, there is a component numbers which generates first a value 2 and from then on odd numbers. numbers runs it is killed by sieves or this ends its execution. Second, there is a component printer which prints n numbers and notifies of its execution end. When `printer` sends a state `done`, `sieves` knows that the n first prime numbers have been found and terminates. The termination of `sieves` implies the killing of all its domain processes. The implementations of `numbers` and `printer` appear next.

```
component numbers
{  outport <int> num;


  num.send(2);

  for (int x=3;; x+=2)
    num.send(x);
};
```

```
component printer (int n)
{  inport print;
   states done ();

   int x;
   for (int i=0; i<n ;i++)
   {  print.in (x);
      flush (x); };
   done ();
};
```

Third, there is a coordinator `gen_dyn_pipeline` instantiated by a component `filter` whose ports in and out are bound to `numbers` and `printer` (see Figure 6). `filter` finds a prime number and outputs it via its port `out`. From then on, it uses this prime number to filter the numbers that it gets. The first time it finds a number that cannot be divided by its prime number it request the extension of the pipeline by originating `new`.

```
component filter
{  inport <int> left;
   outport <int> right, <int> out;
   states new ();

   int prime, x = 0;
   left.in(prime);
   out.send (prime);
   while ((x%prime)=0) {left.in(x)};
   new ();
   right.send(x);
   for (;;)
   {  left.in(x);
      if (x%prime)!=0) then right.send (x); };
};
```

3   Related Work

The idea of decomposing concurrent programming into computation and coordination was first mentioned in [CG89] and has been used in various programming languages. Some of these languages do not enforce the decomposition by different programming languages for computation and coordination (see Caliban [CHK+93], Fortran-M [FC92], Linda [CG90], Occam [INM84] and PVM

[GBD$^+$94]). In these languages, sequential and concurrent aspects of programming are mixed within a unique programming context. Program design and maintenance are complicated.

Other programming environments enforce the decomposition by a linguistic separation but fail to support heterogeneous concurrency exploitation. First, there are environments which manipulate concurrency provided by functions. In these environments, a coordination language schedules functions written in a computation language which can be any conventional language. This approach leads to lack of support for reactive processes (e.g. Caliban[CHK$^+$93] and Delirium[LS90]), to simulation of reactive processes by means of recursion and streams within coordination (e.g. PCN[CT92] and Strand[FT90]) or to a limited number of pre-defined reusable constructs for coordination (e.g. P^3L[DMO$^+$92]). Second, some environments base their concurrency manipulation on reactive processes. In these environments, a coordination or configuration language manipulates processes written in a computation language which is a sequential language extended with communication (e.g. Darwin[MDK92], Durra[BDW$^+$92], Gerel[EW92]). In these environments, to express execution end of a functional process, one must send in a message the notification of execution end and the function results. Such a message does not actually guarantee that the process execution has terminated. ConCoord separates computation and coordination by means of different languages in a similar way than in environments with a configuration language. ConCoord extends the computation processes supported in these environments with a notification of execution end: the state done.

When providing linguistic separation, interactions between computation and coordination can be supported in various ways. First, coordination can read and modify state of computation processes (see Lomita[MCWB90]). This approach has an intruding style which hinders reuse. Second, coordination can view all communication between processes (see PRONET[LM82] and [Etz92]) and use this information for triggering changes. This approach can lead to inefficiency. Third, coordination can get events from processes (e.g. Durra[BDW$^+$92], Gerel[EW92], Manifold[AHS93]) and Regis[MDK94]). This approach retains the advantages of separating computation and coordination. In ConCoord, coordination and computation interact via states which differ from the events from these environments in two ways. First, events are raised asynchronously while states synchronously. Being synchronous, a state notification provides an up-to-date view of a process state. It also guarantees that the originator process is blocked and hence in a safe state to be coordinated. Second, in ConCoord, coordination can trigger changes by conditions on program structure and on states from various program processes. In the previous environments based on events, only one event is treated at a time.

One can view CCL's conditional statements as rules similar to the ones in coordination languages like LO[ACP92] and Gamma[BCM88]. A coordination domain resembles a structured multiset of processes in which the structure derives from bindings between process ports. Using the keyword sel, a CCL conditional statement can simulate a Gamma rule. In addition, when this keyword is not used, CCL can express changes on a whole set of multiset processes at the same time.

4 Conclusions

In this paper,we have presented ConCoord, a software environment for concurrent coordinated programming with three major contributions. First, ConCoord separates programming into computation and coordination in order to facilitate programming. Computation is expressed using a standard sequential programming language. Coordination is defined in a new language CCL whose unique programming paradigm is dynamic concurrency manipulation. A coordinator specifies dynamic evolution of a collection of processes abstracting from their implementation details. Second, ConCoord is targeted at networks of sequential and parallel machines. These networks have the potential to support a diversity of concurrency manipulations. In order to exploit this potential, ConCoord permits specification of different concurrency grains, process scheduling, and mapping expressions. Third, ConCoord supports a variety of reuses. Sequential algorithms can be reused using computation processes. Complete concurrent algorithms can be reused using a coordination process and its domain processes. Concurrency management of concurrent algorithms can be reused using a parameterised coordination process. Currently, we are implementing a prototype of ConCoord on top of Regis[MDK94]. Regis provides a configuration language Darwin which only supports a few dynamic changes on program structure.

References

[ACP92]   J.M. Andreoli, P. Ciancarini, and R. Pareschi. Interaction abstract machines. *Research Directions in Concurrent Object Oriented Computing*, 6:81–90, 1992.

[AHS93]   F. Arbab, I. Herman, and P. Spilling. An overview of Manifold and its implementation. *Concurrency: Practice and Experience*, 5(1):23–70, February 1993.

[BCM88]   J-P. Banâtre, A. Coutant, and D. Le Metayer. A parallel machine for multiset transformation and its programming style. *Future Generation Computer Systems*, 4:133–145, 1988.

[BDW+92] M.R. Barbacci, D.L. Doubleday, C.B. Weinstock, M.J. Gardner, and R.W. Lichota. Building Fault Tolerant Distributed Applications With Durra. In *Proc. of International Workshop on Configurable Distributed Systems*, pages 128–139. IEE London, 1992.

[BWL89]   J.P. Browne, J. Werth, and T. Lee. Intersection of parallel structuring and reuse of software components: A calculus of composition of components for parallel programs. In *Proc. International Conference on Parallel Processing*, pages 126–130. Penn. State Press 1989, 1989.

[CG89]   N. Carriero and D. Gelernter. Linda in context. *Communications of ACM*, 32(4):444–458, April 1989.

[CG90]   N. Carriero and D. Gelernter. *How to write parallel programs: A first course*. MIT Press, 1990.

[CHK+93] S. Cox, S-Y Huang, P. Kelly, J. Liu, and F. Taylor. Program transformations for static process networks. *SIGPLAN Notices*, January 1993.

[CT92]   K.M. Chandy and S. Taylor. *An Introduction to Parallel Programming*. Jones and Bartlett Publishers, 1992.

[Dij75]   E.W. Dijkstra.   Guarded Commands, Nondeterminancy and Formal Derivation of Programs. *Communications of ACM*, 18(8):453–457, 1975.

[DMO+92]   M. Danelutto, R. Di Meglio, S. Orlando, S. Pelagatti, and M. Vanneschi. A methodology for the development and the support of massively parallel programs. *Future Generation Computer Systems (North Holland)*, 8:205–220, 1992.

[Etz92]   G. Etzkorn.   Change programming in distributed systems. In *Proc. of International Workshop on Configurable Distributed Systems*, pages 140–151. IEE London, 1992.

[EW92]   M. Endler and J. Wei. Programming generic dynamic reconfigurations for distributed applications. In *Proc. of International Workshop on Configurable Distributed Systems*, pages 68–79. IEE London, 1992.

[FC92]   I. Foster and M. Chandy.   Modular Fortran: Introduction and language definition. Draft paper, June 1992.

[FT90]   I. Foster and S. Taylor. *Strand. New Concepts in Parallel Programming*. Prentice-Hall, 1990.

[GBD+94]   A. Geist,   A. Beguelin,   J. Dongarra,   W. Jiang,   R. Manchek,   and V. Sunderam. PVM 3 user's guide and reference manual. Technical report, Oak Ridge National Laboratory, 1994.

[INM84]   Ltd. INMOS. *occam Programming Manual*. Prentice-Hall International Series in Computer Science, 1984.

[Kra91]   J. Kramer. Configuration Programming: Exploiting Component Reuse in Distributed Systems. In P. Hall, editor, *Software Reuse and Reverse Engineering in Practice*. Chapman and Hall, 1991.

[LM82]   R.J. LeBlanc and A.B. Maccabe. The design of a programming language based on connectivity networks. In *Proc. of 3rd International Conference on Distributed Computing Systems*, pages 532–541. IEEE, 1982.

[LS90]   S. Lucco and O. Sharp. Delirium: An embedding coordination language. In *Proceedings of Supercomputing'90*, pages 515–524. IEEE, 1990.

[MCWB90]   K. Marzullo, R. Cooper, M. Wood, and K. Birman. Tools for Distributed Application Management. Technical report, Cornell University, 1990.

[MDK92]   J. Magee, N. Dulay, and J. Kramer. Structuring Parallel and Distributed programs. In *Proc. of International Workshop on Configurable Distributed Systems*, pages 102–117. IEE London, 1992.

[MDK94]   J. Magee, N. Dulay, and J. Kramer. Regis: A constructive development environment for distributed programs. *Distributed Systems Engineering Journal*, 1(5):304–312, September 1994.

[oD83]   United States Department of Defense. Reference manual for the Ada programming language. Technical report, 1983.

[Str91]   B. Stroustrup. *The C++ Programming Language*. Addison-Wesley, 1991.

[Tur93]   L.H. Turcotte. A Survey of Software Environments for Exploiting Networked Computing Resources. Technical report, Mississippi State University, 1993.

Designing a Coordination Model for Open Systems

Thilo Kielmann

Dept. of Electrical Engineering and Computer Science, University of Siegen
Hölderlinstr. 3, D-57068 Siegen, Germany
kielmann@informatik.uni-siegen.de

Abstract. Coordination models for closed concurrent systems like Linda and Gamma have been well established during the last few years. Closed systems typically are planned ahead and consist only of active components the behaviour of which is known in advance. In contrast, open systems are inherently heterogeneous and dynamically change their configuration over time. Models for coordinating software agents in open systems must therefore be able to cope with constantly changing configurations and new, unknown kinds of agents. In this paper, we identify the requirements of open systems with respect to coordination models and develop a coordination model suitable for these purposes.

1 Introduction

Open systems are systems in which new active entities (usually called "objects", "agents", or "actors") may dynamically join and later leave, i.e. evolving self-organizing systems of interacting intelligent agents [2, 10]. More precisely, open systems can be defined as being composed of software components which are *encapsulated* and *reactive* [31]. Components are called encapsulated if they have an interface that hides their implementation from clients; they are called to be reactive if their lifetime is longer than that of the atomic interactions (e.g. messages) which they execute. The fundamental property of open systems is their ability to cope with incremental adaptability, where encapsulation captures spatial incrementality by controlled propagation of local state changes and reactiveness enables temporal evolution by incrementally executing interactions.

A related important notion is the one of *open distributed systems*. It is defined in the upcoming ISO reference model of open distributed processing (RM–ODP) [15]. In the RM–ODP definition, *distributed systems* have to cope with *remoteness* of components, with *concurrency*, the *lack of a global state*, and *asynchrony* of state changes. In addition, *open distributed systems* are characterized by *heterogeneity* in all parts of the involved systems, *autonomy* of various management or control authorities and organizational entities, *evolution* of the system configuration, and *mobility* of programs and data.

Programming of open systems is primarily concerned with coordinating concurrently operating active entities. Concurrent programming languages based on the concept of *generative communication* [12] initiated the research area of *coordination* [14]. Today, the interaction between active entities in open systems is typically investigated based on this notion [4, 7].

Coordination as the key concept for modelling concurrent systems involves managing the communication which is necessary due to the distributed nature of a system, the expression of parallel and distributed algorithms, as well as all aspects of the composition of concurrent systems. We characterize coordination by the following notions: *agents* are active, self–contained entities performing *actions* on their own behalf. Actions are divided into two different classes: (1) *inter–agent actions* which perform the communication between different agents and hence are the subject of coordination models, and (2) *intra–agent actions* which are all actions belonging to a single agent like computations, low–level I/O operations or interactions with users. We call a collection (or a system of) interacting agents a *configuration*. Hence, *coordination* can be defined as managing the inter–agent activities of agents collected in a configuration.

The aim of this paper is to present a coordination model designed for the needs of open systems. For this purpose, we investigate the requirements imposed on coordination models by open (distributed) systems in Sect. 2 and emphasize the importance of generative communication in Sect. 3. Section 4 investigates related work before in Sect. 5 the design of our coordination model Objective Linda is presented some of the basic ideas of which have been introduced in another context in [19]. In Sect. 6 we finally illustrate Objective Linda's features by an example.

2 Coordination Models for Open Distributed Systems

As mentioned earlier, agents must be encapsulated and reactive in order to operate in open systems. Furthermore, coordination models which provide "the glue that binds separate activities into an ensemble" [14] have to reflect openness, too. Hence, coordination models for open systems have to satisfy the following requirements:

- At any time, agents must be allowed to enter or leave a configuration (**dynamics**). This implies that coordination laws must not rely on the existence of specific agents. The same holds for communication. Generative communication [12] by generating and consuming separate entities, usually contained in a specific computational space, is required in order to provide a suitable communication model (**generativeness**). On the other hand, it is also essential to protect a configuration from undesired interaction with agents outside (**encapsulation**).
  By the definition of open distributed systems, there is no overall compile time. Hence, it must be possible to program new agents during the runtime of an already existing system, i.e. specify a new agent's behaviour in a separate program (**decentralization**).
- Coordination models for use in heterogeneous environments must not rely on properties of specific hardware, programming languages or communication media like data types or their representations (**interoperability**).

Besides capturing the requirements of *what* to specify, the methods used *how* to model systems are essential in order to build large but still maintainable systems.

- A model suited for coordinating large systems must be as simple as possible. Hence, all agents should be modelled in a uniform way (**homogeneity**). For the purpose of large systems, it is vital to divide the overall configuration into smaller subconfigurations. Hence, it must be possible to treat entire configurations like single agents at a more abstract coordination level (**hierarchical abstraction**). Inter–agent actions have to be cleanly separated from intra–agent actions in order to distinguish between the concerns of coordination on one hand and of computations on the other (**separation of concerns**).

Encapsulation and reactiveness as central requirements of agents in open systems directly leads to object–based modelling. Objects are by their very nature open interactive systems. They can not (completely) be described algorithmically because they interact while computing [32]. Hence, specification of object–based systems is inherently incomplete and hence reflects openness.

The RM–ODP model which conceptually provides the basis for commercially available systems uses object–based modelling too; also because of the principal object properties of encapsulation and reactiveness. RM–ODP focuses on interaction between objects based on the client/server architecture: "They (objects) embody ideas of services offered by an object to its environments, that is, to other objects." [15] In RM–ODP, coordination between objects takes place via centralized instances, so called *traders* [16], which are repositories of service type definitions, used to identify offered and requested services.

Presumably the most prominent commercial system for open, object–based systems is the Common Object Request Broker Architecture (CORBA) [25]. Its central component, the Object Request Broker (ORB) acts as a trader in the sense of RM–ODP. Like other traders, the ORB provides references to server objects which in case of dynamically changing configurations may quickly turn into void ("dangling") references causing problems in open configurations. Today, client/server architectures are seen as the current intermediate step on the way from mainframe–oriented to collaborative (peer–to–peer) computing [22]. Nevertheless, service–oriented communication is an important paradigm for open distributed systems [1] and must hence be captured by coordination models. But because client/server communication is restricted to the exchange of request/reply pairs, other communication forms like e.g. for group communication can not be modelled adequately. Hence, coordination models for open systems need to be more general in their applicability.

3   The Role of Generative Communication

Generative communication as initially introduced in [12] is based on a shared data space, sometimes also called *blackboard*, in which data items can be stored ("generated") and later retrieved. This kind of communication inherently uncouples communicating agents: a potential reader of some data item does not have to take care about it (e.g. as with rendezvous mechanisms) until it really wants to read it. The reader even does not have to exist at the time of storing. The latter point directly leads to the other major advantage of generative communication: agents are able to communicate although they are anonymous to each other.

This uncoupled and anonymous communication style directly contributes to the design of coordination models for open systems: uncoupled communication enables to cope with dynamically changing configurations in which agents move or temporarily disappear. Anonymous communication allows to communicate with unknown agents. Hence it allows communication with incomplete knowledge about the system configuration which is a crucial demand of open systems. Due to this fact, coordination models based on generative communication are superior to message passing or trader–based schemes because these both rely on knowledge about a receiver's or server's identification.

Based on this observation, the LAURA model [30] has been developed in order to introduce generative communication into the RM–ODP model. In LAURA, agents using and offering services share a so–called *service space*. Here, *offer* and *request* forms are matched by LAURA's service type system which replaces RM–ODP's trading function. This model introduces uncoupled and anonymous communication into RM–ODP, but it does not help to overcome the rather restrictive communication scheme of request/reply pairs. Hence, a general–purpose coordination model for open systems needs further improvements.

4 Object–based Generative Models

As we have seen so far, coordination models for open systems must be based on generative communication and on object–based modelling. A model combining these two features covers the requirements of *dynamics, encapsulation, separation of concerns*, (and of course *generativeness*) as listed in Sect. 2. The need for *hierarchical abstractions* directly implies the presence of multiple object spaces. In the following, we will therefore investigate how far existing coordination models can cover the given requirements. We focus on two properties: (1) The object model of a system which determines how object matching can be performed, and (2) the introduction of multiple data spaces.

4.1 Shared Object Spaces

In the original Linda model [12] by which generative communication was introduced, the shared data space contains tuples of basic data types like numbers and character strings (and is hence called *tuple space*). The most important feature of Linda is the associative way of consuming tuples from the tuple space. This is done by providing a template which *matches* certain tuples. The template itself has a tuple structure and hence determines arity, types of the elements and optionally constant values for the elements of a matching tuple. Elements specified by type *and* value are called *actuals* whereas typed placeholders (without a value) are called *formals*.

The obvious similarity between tuples and the record structure of object implementations has led to early adaptations of the Linda model to object–oriented languages [17, 23]. In these systems, language–level objects are stored in shared data spaces and are retrieved using template objects which specify actuals and formals. This straightforward adaptation allows to use the Linda model from within object–oriented languages. But because object matching is based on the objects' implementation, the encapsulation property which is essential for the notion of objects is ignored in these systems.

The work in [28] attempts to overcome this deficiency by letting programmers specify so–called *important sets* denoting those parts of object implementations relevant to object matching. Although this approach abstracts from some irrelevant parts of implementations, matching is still based on it. Similarly, Bauhaus Linda [8] which is based on multisets as basic data structures, performs matching on multiset inclusion which also embodies the idea of matching based on relevant parts of the data items stored in the shared data space.

None of these models treats objects as completely encapsulated entities, hence they are not fully suited for open systems.

4.2 Multiple Data Spaces

The requirement of *hierarchical abstractions* (from Sect. 2) directly leads to the introduction of multiple data spaces arranged in nested hierarchies. Each data space can hence be treated as an agent as well as a configuration. Here, we discuss data spaces instead of object spaces because interesting approaches can also be found in models which are not based on objects.

Although there have been several proposals for introducing multiple data spaces to the Linda model, neither of them found broader acceptance. This might be due to the fact that generative communication with multiple data spaces implies a paradigmatical change. It can be seen to be in between the two extremes, denoted by message passing and the single–spaced Linda model [20]. In message–passing systems, senders have to know the name or address of the receiver. Hence, messages can only be sent to agents known by the sender. In Linda, producers of data entities only have to access the shared data space. It is up to the consumer to know which kinds of data entities are available. In systems with multiple data spaces, both variants must be combined: a producer of data items has to know the data spaces in order to put something inside whereas the consumer still has to know what kind of data is available. This setting degrades anonymity of communication and is most likely to be the main obstacle concerning general consensus about a suitable model with multiple data spaces.

One possible approach for introducing multiple data spaces is presented in [23]. Here, object spaces are simply first–class objects. They must hence be known by producers and consumers. This approach comes close to message passing and immediately leads to problems with dangling references if applied to open systems.

As an alternative to object–space references, the work in [13] uses a global naming scheme for tuple spaces (e.g. "*/root/sub1/sub2*") resembling Unix directory structures. This approach avoids dangling references but introduces problems with the global naming scheme in case of open systems in which name conflicts soon may arise. Additionally, problems may arise when some processes change the tuple space hierarchy (e.g. remove intermediate spaces like *sub1*) which may lead to invalid paths in use by other processes.

The work in [18] also introduces a global hierarchy of nested tuple spaces but refuses the global, static naming scheme. Instead, every active object knows tuple spaces by names which omit the hierarchy information (like *my_space* and *your_space*) and especially a relative name *context* denoting the next "outer" tuple space. This helps avoiding problems of [13] with the static global space hierarchy. Unfortunately, names for tuple spaces are still globally visible and hence may lead to naming conflicts, especially in open systems.

5 A Coordination Model for Open Systems

We will now introduce our coordination model Objective Linda which has been designed in order to be suited for open systems. We start with its language–independent object model, present its set of operations on object spaces which directly reflects openness, and complete by outlining how multiple object spaces can be handled cleanly in open systems.

5.1 Objective Linda's Object Model

Since the goal is to model open systems, a language–independent object model is necessary. In Objective Linda, objects to be stored in object spaces are self–contained entities; their interface operations only affect the encapsulated object state. The objects are instances of abstract data types which are described in a language–independent notation, called *Object Interchange Language* (OIL). Actual programs may hence be written in conventional object–oriented languages to which a binding of the OIL types (e.g. to language–level classes) can be declared. In OIL, all types have a common ancestor called *OIL_object* which defines the basic operations needed by all types. Types needed in application programs are then derived from *OIL_object* or its descendants. OIL allows subtyping such that an object of type S which is a subtype of T can be used whenever an object of T is expected. More precisely, OIL types are not related in a subtype relation but follow the *matching relation* [5] which slightly weakens the strong subtyping notion in order to allow operations which take parameters of *the–same* type (e.g. the famous *is_equal* function [9]). In order to avoid confusion with object matching in object spaces, we still call them "subtypes". OIL allows single as well as multiple subtyping and parameterized types. It is subject to the actual language binding to map these mechanisms to available language constructs. Because abstract data types can conceptually be used even in programming languages without objects at all (e.g. *C* or *Pascal*), it only depends on the programming language in use how simple and elegant OIL types and their relations are mapped onto the language.

In mixed–language environments of open distributed systems it is of course necessary to identify identical types across multiple language bindings. Naming schemes can in general not avoid name conflicts and consequently unintended name matches or mismatches [30]. Therefore, OIL types are identified by globally unique identifications making use of OSF DCE's [27] *Universally Unique ID's* (UUID's) which can easily be created from a host identification and a timestamp. Besides the identification of identical types it is of course also necessary to transport objects between agents operating in heterogeneous environments. For this purpose, techniques known as *object externalization* or *object imaging* [29] can be used. However, this issue belongs to the technical realization of the Objective Linda model and is hence beyond the scope of this paper.

Object Matching in Objective Linda. Objective Linda's object model treats objects as encapsulated entities which can only be accessed via their interface routines defined by the corresponding type. Hence, operations belonging to the coordination model must be based on the type interfaces, too. This fact is not only a restriction but also a major improvement with respect to other models: objects are treated based on their specification, rather than their implementation, which allows to completely abstract from implementation (data representation) details.

Consequently, object matching in Objective Linda is based on object types and the predicates defined by type interfaces. A potential reader has to specify the type of object it wishes to obtain from an object space and additionally a predicate (from the interface of the type) which selects the objects of a given type matching the specific request. Because OIL's subtype relations provide types which can be used as replacements for their supertypes, object matching will also consider objects of subtypes of the requested type.

As a toy example, consider two types: *linked_list* which has a subtype *double_linked_list* where type *linked_list* provides a predicate *nbr_items* giving the number of items in the list. A read request for an object of type *linked_list* for which the predicate *nbr_items = 3* holds will match any object of type *linked_list* containing three items which might in fact be a *double_linked_list*.

This kind of object matching ideally requires to have types and predicates as first–class entities in the programming language in use. Unfortunately, this is typically not the case with existing languages. Since the goal of this work is to model open systems which integrate existing tools and languages, it is not feasible to simply design yet another language and express the coordination model within it. Instead, the matching mechanism based on types and predicates must be expressed in existing languages in which only objects are available as first–class entities and hence as parameters to a matching operation.

Denoting the type of an object to be read from an object space is relatively simple because by passing an object as a parameter to a routine, its type can be taken as the desired one. Passing a predicate is a bit more difficult. One approach is to use so–called *function objects* [21] which realize specific predicates by implementing routines with predefined names (e.g. *eval*) operating on the types they have been tailored for.

Alternatively, the matching predicates can be directly integrated into the types on which they operate. Therefore, the type *OIL_object* provides a predicate *match* which takes an object of the same type as parameter and returns a boolean value deciding whether a given object matches certain requirements. This approach statically encodes object matching into the types themselves. Several variants of matching a type can be selected by presetting the encapsulated state of the object provided to a matching operation, which we call a *template object* in the following. In cases where a high degree of flexibility in matching predicates is needed, it is still possible to have specially tailored function objects as part of the template object's state. By this approach, matching flexibility is combined with a minimal amount of object types needed, because function objects are only introduced where necessary.

We illustrate this approach by a simple type taken from a real–world example. Figure 1 shows the code of a type *BARRIER_SYNC* which realizes objects being exchanged in a parallel computation between worker processes and a barrier for purposes of synchronization which is achieved by presence or absence of *BARRIER_SYNC* objects. In order to allow multiple barriers in an object space, it is necessary that *BARRIER_SYNC* objects contain an identification of the barrier object in charge. Barrier objects are active and consume *BARRIER_SYNC* objects using template objects containing their own identification. So, the *match* predicate checks for identical values of *barrier_id* in order to match the right objects. In the example, we use a binding to the Eiffel programming language.

```
class BARRIER_SYNC  inherit OIL_OBJECT redefine match end
creation create
feature barrier_id : STRING;
        create ( id : STRING ) is
            do  barrier_id := id;  end;
        match ( candidate : like current ) : BOOLEAN is
            do  Result := candidate.barrier_id = barrier_id;  end;
end -- class BARRIER_SYNC
```

Fig. 1. Complete code of an Eiffel class used for barrier synchronization

Evaluating Active Objects. According to Linda's *eval* operation, we will call the activity of an agent the *evaluation* of an active object. In favour of a homogeneous model, passive as well as active objects are characterized by their OIL type. The mechanism used to specify this activity is similar to object matching: the type *OIL_object* provides an operation called *evaluate* whose behaviour is refined by every type the objects of which will become active. As with *match*, behaviour can be individually parameterized by the object's state before it is evaluated.

Since the specification of abstract data types focusses on the objects of given types themselves rather than on protocols of interaction between them, its expressiveness is quite limited with respect to specifying behaviour of active objects. Methodologies for such specifications are subject to ongoing research. There already exist promising approaches for specifying behaviour based on message exchange in client/server like settings [24]. Unfortunately, behaviour specification of active objects based on generative communication is still unexplored. Hence, the expressiveness of Objective Linda's type specifications is limited in this respect.

5.2 Operations on Object Spaces

Besides the adaptation of the Linda model to object orientation, we also have to consider the operations on object spaces with respect to their suitability to open systems. The operations in the original Linda model have been designed without consideration of openness. As a consequence, the blocking operations for putting an object into an object space (*out*), for consuming an object (*in*), reading an object (*rd*), and activating a new active object (*eval*) assume unrestricted access to the data space and may hence block infinitely in case of object spaces in open systems (which are realized by several independent systems). Here, access to an object space may fail due to temporarily disconnected operation of a mobile host, transmission (line) errors, or missing access permissions.

Furthermore, the semantics of the non–blocking versions of *in* and *rd* (*inp* and *rdp*) imply access to a data space as a whole: these operations are defined to immediately return indicating a failure when there is no object matching a given request. This immediately introduces semantical problems in the presence of distributed or even open–implemented object spaces where parts of the object space simply may not be (temporarily) accessible. Hence, the semantics of such operations must be slightly modified for open systems: operation failure of *inp* and *rdp* should indicate "no such object could be found (in the moment)". This change reflects the fact that synchronization based on the absence of a certain object is impossible in open and hence possibly only partially available object spaces.

Infinitely blocking operations due to disconnected operation or missing access permissions is by no means a suitable behaviour. Instead, it is necessary to dynamically adapt the behaviour of an agent to the properties of its environment. This can preferably be done by introducing a *timeout* value which determines how long an operation should block before a failure will be reported. By adjusting this parameter, an agent can easily adapt its communication behaviour. A value indicating infinite delay leads to a blocking operation and can be used for object spaces which are known to behave like closed systems, e.g. object spaces which are local to the agent itself. A zero value yields a behaviour as *inp* and *rdp* with semantics as outlined above. All values in between can be used to adapt to different communication delays.

The *eval* operation for activating new agents also needs adaptation to open systems. In Linda, all elements of a tuple given as a parameter to *eval* are evaluated in parallel by new processes and each yields a single return value. After termination of all these processes, the tuple is converted into a passive one containing the processes' results. This operation views active processes as functions instead of encapsulated and reactive agents as they should be in a coordination model for open systems. As a consequence, the *eval* operation should get objects to be activated which are (like in Linda) invisible to *in* and *rd* operations and which simply disappear after termination. Hence, the behaviour of agents can only be observed by monitoring the passive objects produced and consumed by them.

Linda's ability to retrieve only one object at a time from an object space is simple and elegant, but unfortunately too restrictive. Just with these operations, it is, for example, impossible to implement the functionality of the trading function from RM–ODP which is able to provide a list of servers for a client's request. This is due to the fact that the semantics of the *rd* operation can not specify which object will be returned by several subsequent invocations; it might be e.g. the same object all the time. This impossibility is a consequence of uncoupled communication which is as such vital for open systems. Specifying any relation between the results of subsequent calls to *rd* would couple them. This would be similar to establishing a connection (or "session") between an object space and a requesting agent. Instead, an operation atomically retrieving several objects is necessary in order to cleanly introduce this functionality into the generative communication model.

Approaches to support reading of multiple objects have been reported in the literature. One approach, used in [13] and [18], treats tuple spaces as first–class entities and allows to produce snapshots of tuple spaces which can separately be investigated. Because these proposals can not selectively extract multiple objects, they are hardly applicable to larger systems in which snapshot sizes might soon become prohibitive apart from the fact that taking a snapshot of an open–implemented tuple space is close to impossible. Another approach is presented in [6] and introduces a *collect* operation which atomically returns all tuples matching a given template in a certain tuple space. This approach allows to select multiple objects to be consumed, but in the case of a RM–ODP trader, unrestrictedly returning the complete list of service providers might still be too much (e.g. with respect to memory size) or at least too inefficient.

There is also a demand for an *in* operation which atomically removes several objects from an object space. Applications for such an operation come from the field of synchronization problems. One example is atomic allocation of more than one resource at a time which can help avoiding deadlock situations. On the other hand, it is not necessary to put several objects atomically into an object space. After successful completion, a single *out* operation providing several objects can not be distinguished from a sequence of *out* operations providing one object each; the same holds for *eval*. Nevertheless, our *out* and *eval* operations take multiple objects to be stored and possibly activated. We introduce them in order to achieve a small and consistent set of powerful operations. Technically, Objective Linda's operations use objects of the type *Multiset* as a parameter for the objects to be stored (by *out* and *eval*) and as result type for the objects being matched (by *in* and *rd*). Here, a *Multiset* is a simple container type with the operations *put* and *get* and the predicate *nbr_items* denoting the number of items stored inside.

We can now introduce the set of operations on object spaces supported by Objective Linda. They are based on the following three design decisions. (1) Because objects in Objective Linda are self–contained entities and consequently contain no references to objects outside their encapsulated state, there is absolutely no sharing of data between them. Hence, the operations *out*, *eval* and *in* move objects between agents and objects spaces whereas *rd* returns clones of matching objects. (2) All operations dealing with multiple objects operate indivisibly: in case of failures the state of the object space in charge remains unchanged. (3) For reasons of "intellectual compatibility", we borrow the meanings of *in* and *out* from Linda which reflects the view of an agent operating on an object space; from the viewpoint of an abstract data type *object space*, the names of the *in* and *out* operations should have actually been exchanged. In the following, we will again use the syntax of an Eiffel language binding.

out (m : MULTISET ; timeout : REAL) : BOOLEAN

Tries to move the objects contained in *m* into the object space. Returns *true* if the operation could be completed successfully; returns *false* if the operation could not be completed within *timeout* seconds.

in (o : OIL_OBJECT ; min, max : INTEGER ; timeout : REAL) : MULTISET

Tries to remove multiple objects $o'_1 \ldots o'_n$ matching the template object *o* from the object space and returns a multiset containing them if at least *min* matching objects could be found within *timeout* seconds. In this case, the multiset contains at most *max* objects, even if the object space contained more. If *min* matching objects could not be found within *timeout* seconds, *Result.Void* is true.

rd (o : OIL_OBJECT ; min, max : INTEGER ; timeout : REAL) : MULTISET

Tries to return clones of multiple objects $o'_1 \ldots o'_n$ matching the template object *o* and returns a multiset containing them if at least *min* matching objects could be found within *timeout* seconds. In this case, the multiset contains at most *max* objects, even if the object space contained more. If *min* matching objects could not be found within *timeout* seconds, *Result.Void* is true.

eval (m : MULTISET ; timeout : REAL) : BOOLEAN

Tries to move the objects contained in *m* into the object space and starts their activities. Returns *true* if the operation could be completed successfully; returns *false* if the operation could not be completed within *timeout* seconds.

infinite_matches : INTEGER

Returns a constant value which will be interpreted as infinite number of matching objects when provided as *min* or *max* parameter to *in* and *rd*.

infinite_time : REAL

Returns a constant value which will be interpreted as infinite delay when provided as *timeout* parameter to *out*, *in*, *rd*, and *eval*.

This set of operations is the minimal one needed for operations in open systems. At the same time, it is powerful enough to express original Linda's operations as well as to reflect all requirements of open systems listed above. Objective Linda provides a minimal set of powerful operations in order to keep the model as simple as possible; but nevertheless it is still possible to add convenience operations (e.g. for frequently used special cases) to an OIL language binding or directly to application programs in order to simplify the programmer's task. Table 1 shows how the behaviour of Objective Linda's operations can be adapted by their parameters in order to match different requirements.

	min	*max*	*timeout*	behaviour
out			0	immediately fail on errors
			t	wait *t* sec. before failing on errors
			infinite_time	Linda's *out*
in	0	0	any	empty operation
	0	1	0	Linda's *inp*
	1	1	*infinite_time*	Linda's *in*
	1	*n*	any	consume up to *n* matching obj.
	1	*infinite_matches*	any	consume all matching objects
	infinite_matches	any	*t*	sleep *t* seconds
rd	0	0	any	empty operation
	0	1	0	Linda's *rdp*
	1	1	*infinite_time*	Linda's *rd*
	1	*n*	any	read up to *n* matching objects
	1	*infinite_matches*	any	read all matching objects
	infinite_matches	any	*t*	sleep *t* seconds
eval			0	immediately fail on errors
			t	wait *t* sec. before failing on errors
			infinite_time	Linda's *eval*

Table 1. Behaviour of Objective Linda's operations on object spaces

5.3 Multiple Object Spaces in Objective Linda

Configurations in Objective Linda consist of two kinds of objects, namely object spaces and OIL objects, the latter may be active as well as passive ones. Active objects have, from the moment of their activation on, access to two object spaces: (1) their *context* which is the object space on which the corresponding *eval* operation has been performed, and (2) a newly created object space called *self* which is directly associated to the object. With this basic mechanism, hierarchies of nested object spaces can be built providing hierarchical abstractions for sub–configurations. Before we explain how objects can get attached to more than these two object spaces, we illustrate this hierarchy and its basic applications in Fig. 2(a). Here, rounded boxes denote object spaces, boxes show passive objects, circles denote active ones. The *self* object spaces are shown close to the corresponding active objects. The *context* object spaces are the additional object spaces to which arrows are drawn.

In this abstracted example, object A has created object B by performing `self.eval`. This is the way how a computation may be decomposed into several subtasks. B has created a peer object C by invoking `context.eval`. This way, new computations can be started which are then performed without further control of the invoker. C has created a peer D by `context.out` which is hence simply a passive object. By consuming D, B may receive results from its peer C. E and F are located in object space C. The latter one must have created at least one of them; the other one might have also been created by its peer.

The restriction to exactly the *context* and *self* object spaces is not powerful enough in order to generally express coordination problems. There are four problems involved: (1) without implementing specialized routing agents, two agents with different *context* spaces could never communicate, (2) new agents would not be able to enter a given object space which contradicts openness, (3) mobile agents in open distributed systems could not move to other communication contexts, and (4) it should be possible to have more than one object space attached to an object in order to further structure computations.

The latter point can be handled by locally created object spaces which are then only known to their attached agents unless they make them available to others. But the problem of attaching to already existing object spaces needs further elaboration. This is due to the fact that object spaces are not part of agents but are accessed by references. This is necessary because object spaces must by their very nature be shared between agents. Consequently, object spaces must not be stored in object spaces; *Object_Space* cannot be a subtype of *OIL_object*.

Because object spaces must be accessed by reference, we have to minimize possible impacts of dangling references due to configuration changes in open systems. This is the reason for not introducing references to object spaces as subtypes of *OIL_objects*. Furthermore, it would hardly make sense to transfer language–level references between agents in separate address spaces, which is the typical case in open (distributed) systems.

This makes it necessary to introduce a construct which allows agents to attach to existing object spaces without using low–level references and which is based on the generative communication mechanism. Objective Linda therefore introduces a special subtype of *OIL_object* which is called *object space logical*. *Logicals* combine a reference to an object space with a logical identification such that an object space can be found by matching properties of *logical* objects. These properties can of course be specialized by subtyping to application needs, like numerical values, keywords, network addresses, geographical locations, or even "Uniform Resource Locators" (URLs) known from the World–Wide–Web.

Agents willing to let others attach to object spaces they are already attached to simply create a *logical* object including the reference to the object space to be made available which also contains a convenient logical identification for that object space. This *logical* is then *out*'ed to an object space. There, other agents may *rd* this *logical* like any other object; but the reference contained in it is useless for the agent in most of the cases (with different address spaces). Instead, an agent *a* willing to attach to object space *n* must call a special operation called *attach* on the object space *o* in which the corresponding *logical* object for *n* is stored. This operation has two effects: (1) *o* verifies that *n* can be attached to (is reachable, allows attachment, etc.), and (2) returns a reference to *n* which is locally useful to *a*. The *attach* operation can be introduced as follows:

attach (o : OS_LOGICAL ; timeout : REAL) : OBJECT_SPACE
　　Tries to get attached to an object space for which an *OS_LOGICAL* matching *o* can be found in the current object space. Returns a valid reference to the newly attached object space, if a matching object space logical could be found within *timeout* seconds; otherwise *Result.Void* is true.

As we have seen so far, configurations in Objective Linda consist of hierarchies of object spaces. Because attachment to further object spaces can only be accomplished using information available inside a configuration, all object spaces form a connected graph with a common root. Navigation in a configuration is based on information relative to other object spaces which is accessed via logical identifications. Subtyping applied to *logical* objects allows several identification mechanisms for object spaces to coexist and hence diminishes the need for global naming schemes.

The attachment of new agents to running configurations can also be performed using the mechanism introduced so far. Therefore, every agent has by default a *context* space by which it may attach to further object spaces. These default object spaces must of course be valid object spaces of a given configuration. The provision of such default object spaces is implementation dependent and may be based on object–space servers in the local network of a site. A typical example might be the entry point to an information system; roughly equivalent to a home page in the WWW.

Figure 2(b) illustrates this. Here, agent *O* has put a *logical* *O'* for its *self* space into *D* which locally serves as default context. Then, a new agent *N* performs an *attach* operation on *D* and gets access to *O*'s space, indicated by the dashed line.

With the addition of *logicals* and the *attach* operation, the coordination model for open systems is complete. To summarize, agents can get access in the following three ways: (1) attachment to *context* and *self* on creation, (2) creation of new locally associated object spaces, and (3) explicit execution of *attach* to already existing object spaces.

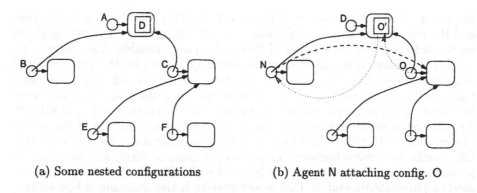

(a) Some nested configurations   (b) Agent N attaching config. O

Fig. 2. Hierarchical abstractions for configurations

6 Example: The Restaurant of Dining Philosophers

We will now illustrate Objective Linda's capabilities for expressing coordination problems in open systems. Therefore, we present a solution to the problem of *The Restaurant of Dining Philosophers* taken from [10]. This is an extension of Dijkstra's classical problem to open systems. In the restaurant, there is the table with n seats around. Between each two seats, there is exactly one chopstick on the table. Philosophers sitting down need two chopsticks (the ones left and right to their seat) in order to eat rice from the bowl on the table. So far, this is the classical synchronization problem. Additionally, philosophers can enter the restaurant, wait for a free seat, and leave the table after eating.

We extend the problem a bit and come to the following modelling: there are two kinds of agents in the system: a waiter who runs the restaurant with the name *The Philo and the Fork* and philosophers who come in and eat. Arriving philosophers try to enter the restaurant (*attach* to its object space), wait for a free seat and then try to atomically grab the two chopsticks next to their seat. After eating, they put the (now dirty) chopsticks back on the table, stand up, and leave the restaurant. The waiter has to do all the work in the restaurant; he starts his job by opening the door (putting a *logical* for his restaurant into his *context* space which is of a special subtype of $OS\_LOGICAL$ denoting restaurants). Then he sets up the table by putting chairs and chopsticks into his *self* object space. Until it is time to close the restaurant, the waiter looks for dirty chopsticks which he cleans and puts back on the table. In order not to forget closing time in case there are no philosophers producing dirty sticks, the *in* operation for the dirty sticks waits at most five minutes before the waiter can check again the wall clock. When closing time has arrived, the waiter closes the door (consuming the *logical* from the *context*), so that newly arriving philosophers can not get in any more. Then, the waiter waits until the last philosopher has gone (by waiting for n free seats) and can finally go home (terminate).

Below, we show our solution consisting of four Eiffel classes, namely *WAITER*, *PHILO*, *CHOPSTICK*, and *SEAT*. As it can be seen, Objective Linda provides a rather natural modelling to the problem. Philosophers simply have to know the name of the restaurant in order to get in. They then take any free seat and the two chopsticks next to the seat without having to know anything about seats, sticks, or even the number of them which are available. Also, there is no need to introduce artificial synchronization objects besides the seats and the chopsticks themselves. The waiter is the only one who knows how many seats (and sticks) are at the table; he can open and close the restaurant whenever he wants. The passive objects in our example are of types *SEAT* and *CHOP-STICK*. Seats simply contain a numerical identification and inherit the *match* routine from *OIL_OBJECT* which by default matches any object of the type. Chopsticks have more features. They may be clean or dirty, and they have a position between the seats on their left and right side. Furthermore, *myseat* is used to parameterize *match*. This *match* routine is also an example how matching can be parameterized by simple state changes of the template object before it is used for matching.

```
class PHILO   inherit OIL_OBJECT redefine evaluate end
creation make
feature evaluate is
    local r     : OBJECT_SPACE;
          l     : RESTAURANT_LOGICAL;
          s     : SEAT;
          m     : MULTISET;
          c1,c2 : CHOPSTICK;
          ok    : BOOLEAN;
    do !!l.create("the philo and the fork");
       r := context.attach(l,600);             -- wait at most 10 minutes for
                                                -- restaurant opening
       if not r.Void then                      -- entered the restaurant
           !!s.make;
           m := r.in(s,1,1,r.infinite_time);    -- wait for a free seat
           s := m.get;
           !!c1.make; c1.set_myseat(s.number);
           m := r.in(c1,2,2,r.infinite_time);   -- wait for 2 chopsticks
           c1 := m.get; c2 := m.get;
           eat;
           c1.mark_dirty; c2.mark_dirty;        -- sticks are dirty after eating
           m.put(c1); m.put(c2); m.put(s);      -- put dirty sticks back on table
           ok := r.out(m,0);                    -- and stand up
       end
    end                                         -- go home
end -- class PHILO

class CHOPSTICK   inherit OIL_OBJECT redefine match, make end
creation make
feature is_dirty, match_if_dirty      : BOOLEAN;
        leftseat, rightseat, myseat   : INTEGER;
        make is do is_dirty := false; match_if_dirty := false; end;
        mark_clean is do is_dirty := false; end;
        mark_dirty is do is_dirty := true; end;
        set_leftseat ( s : INTEGER ) is do leftseat := s; end;
        set_rightseat ( s : INTEGER ) is do rightseat := s; end;
        set_myseat ( s : INTEGER ) is do myseat := s; end;
        set_match_dirty is do match_if_dirty := true; end;
        match ( candidate : like current ) : BOOLEAN is
            do if match_if_dirty
               then Result := candidate.is_dirty;
               else Result := not candidate.is_dirty and
                              ( myseat = candidate.leftseat or
                                myseat = candidate.rightseat );
               end;
            end;
end -- class CHOPSTICK
```

```
class SEAT  inherit OIL_OBJECT
creation make, create
feature number : INTEGER;
        create ( n : INTEGER ) is do number := n; end;
end -- class SEAT

class WAITER  inherit OIL_OBJECT redefine evaluate end
creation make
feature evaluate is
    local l  : RESTAURANT_LOGICAL;
          i  : INTEGER;
          n  : INTEGER is 42;                    -- nbr of seats at the table
          s  : SEAT;
          c  : CHOPSTICK;
          m  : MULTISET;
          ok : BOOLEAN;
    do !!l.create("the philo and the fork");
       l.set_space(self); !!m.make; m.put(l);
       if context.out(m,0) then                  -- managed to open the door
          !!m.make;
          from i := 1; until i > n loop
             !!s.create(i);m.put(s);              -- get seats
             !!c.make; c.set_leftseat(i);         -- get sticks
             if i < n then c.set_rightseat(i+1);
                      else c.set_rightseat(1); end;
             m.put(c);
          end;
       ok := self.out(m,0);                       -- put seats and sticks to table
       from until closing_time                    -- serve philosophers:
          loop clean_sticks; end;
       !!l.create("the philo and the fork");
       m := context.in(1,1,1,                     -- close the door
                       context.infinite_time);
       clean_sticks;                              -- in case a philo dropped in
       !!s.create;                                -- wait until the last guest
       m := self.in(s,n,n,self.infinite_time);    -- has gone
       end
end                                               -- go home
clean_sticks is
local c   : CHOPSTICK;
      m,m2 : MULTISET;
do !!c.make;                                      -- replace dirty sticks by
   c.set_match_dirty;                             -- clean ones
   m := self.in(c,1,n,300);                       -- sleep at most 5 minutes
                                                  -- before rechecking wall clock
                                                  -- if it's closing time
   if not m.Void then
      from !!m2.create;                           -- clean sticks if we found some
      until m.nbr_items = 0 loop
         c := m.get;
         c.mark_clean;
         m2.put(c);
      end;                                        -- collect cleaned sticks in m2
      if m2.nbr_items > 0
         then ok := self.out(m2,0); end           -- put them back on the table
      end
   end
end
end -- class WAITER
```

7 Conclusion

The example of the restaurant of dining philosophers illustrated how well Objective Linda is suited to model coordination problems in open systems. This is primarily due to Objective Linda's three main contributions: (1) its object model which allows to build open systems from heterogeneous components which are modelled as encapsulated and reactive entities communicating in an uncoupled manner, (2) its set of object–space operations which directly reflect the requirements of openness, and (3) its model of multiple object spaces which on one hand provides hierarchical abstractions from configurations and on the other hand allows agents to simultaneously communicate via several object spaces.

We are currently experimenting with a prototypical class library implementing Objective Linda for clusters of workstations which is based on the PVM [11] package. First results are encouraging, so we are working on the evaluation of Objective Linda's concepts in a wider range of applications.

Acknowledgements

I am really grateful to Paolo Ciancarini, Bernd Freisleben, and Guido Wirtz for many encouragements and helpful discussions. Without them, my work would not be like it is.

References

1. Richard M. Adler. Distributed Coordination Models for Client/Server Computing. *IEEE Computer*, 28(4):14–22, 1995.
2. Gul Agha. *Actors: A Model of Concurrent Computation in Distributed Systems*. M. I. T. Press, Cambridge, Massachusetts, 1986.
3. Gul Agha, Peter Wegner, and Akinori Yonezawa, editors. *Research Directions in Concurrent Object–Oriented Programming*. MIT Press, Cambridge, Mass., 1993.
4. J. M. Andreoli, P. Ciancarini, and R. Pareschi. Interaction Abstract Machines. In Agha et al. [3], pages 257–280.
5. Kim B. Bruce, Angela Schuett, and Robert van Gent. PolyTOIL: A Type–Safe Polymorphic Object–Oriented Language. In Olthoff [26], pages 27–51.
6. Paul Butcher, Alan Wood, and Martin Atkins. Global Synchronisation in Linda. *Concurrency: Practice and Experience*, 6(6):505–516, 1994.
7. Christian J. Callsen and Gul Agha. Open Heterogeneous Computing in ActorSpace. *Journal of Parallel and Distributed Computing*, 21:289–300, 1994.
8. Nicholas Carriero, David Gelernter, and Lenore Zuck. Bauhaus Linda. In P. Ciancarini, O. Nierstrasz, and A. Yonezawa, editors, *Object-Based Models and Languages for Concurrent Systems*, number 924 in Lecture Notes in Computer Science. Springer, 1995.
9. Giuseppe Castagna. Covariance and Contravariance: Conflict without a Cause. *ACM Transactions on Programming Languages and Systems*, 17(3):431–447, 1995.
10. Paolo Ciancarini. Coordination Languages for Open System Design. In *Proc. of IEEE Intern. Conference on Computer Languages*, New Orleans, 1990.
11. G. A. Geist, A. L. Beguelin, J. J. Dongarra, W. Jiang, R. J. Manchek, and V. S. Sunderam. *PVM: Parallel Virtual Machine – A Users Guide and Tutorial for Network Parallel Computing*. MIT Press, 1994.
12. David Gelernter. Generative Communication in Linda. *ACM Transactions on Programming Languages and Systems*, 7(1):80–112, 1985.
13. David Gelernter. Multiple Tuple Spaces in Linda. In E. Odijk, M. Rem, and J.-C. Syre, editors, *PARLE'89, Parallel Architectures and Languages Europe*, number 366 in Lecture Notes in Computer Science, pages 20–27, Eindhoven, The Netherlands, 1989. Springer.

14. David Gelernter and Nicholas Carriero. Coordination Languages and their Significance. *Communications of the ACM*, 35(2):96–107, 1992.
15. ISO/IEC JTC1/SC21/WG7. Reference Model of Open Distributed Processing. Draft International Standard ISO/IEC 10746-1 to 10746-4, Draft ITU-T Recommendation X.901 to X.904, May 1995.
16. ISO/IEC JTC1/SC21/WG7. Information Technology – Open Distributed Processing – ODP Trading Function. Draft ISO/IEC Standard 13235, Draft ITU-T Recommendation X.9tr, July 1994.
17. Robert Jellinghaus. Eiffel Linda: an Object–Oriented Linda Dialect. *SIGPLAN Notices*, 25(12):70–84, 1990.
18. Keld K. Jensen. *Towards a Multiple Tuple Space Model*. PhD dissertation, Aalborg University, Dept. of Mathematics and Computer Science, Inst. for Electronic Systems, Fredrik Bajers Vej 7E, DK-9220 Aalborg Ø, Denmark, 1994.
19. Thilo Kielmann. Object–Oriented Distributed Programming with Objective Linda. In *Proc. First International Workshop on High Speed Networks and Open Distributed Platforms*, St. Petersburg, Russia, 1995.
20. Oliver Krone and Marc Aguilar. Bridging the Gap: A Generic Distributed Coordination Model for Massively Parallel Systems. In *Proc. of SIPAR Workshop on Parallel and Distributed Systems*, pages 109–112, Biel–Bienne, Switzerland, 1995.
21. Thomas Kühne. Parameterization versus Inheritance. In Christine Mingins and Bertrand Meyer, editors, *Technology of Object-Oriented Languages and Systems: TOOLS 15*, pages 235–245, Melbourne, Australia, 1994. Prentice Hall.
22. Ted G. Lewis. Where is Client/Server Software Headed? *IEEE Computer*, 28(4):49–55, 1995.
23. Satoshi Matsuoka and Satoru Kawai. Using Tuple Space Communication in Distributed Object-Oriented Languages. In *ACM Conference Proceedings, Object Oriented Programming Systems, Languages and Applications, San Diego California*, pages 276–284, 1988.
24. Oscar Nierstrasz. Regular Types for Active Objects. In O. Nierstrasz and D. Tsichritzis, editors, *Object-Oriented Software Composition*, chapter 4, pages 99–121. Prentice Hall, 1995.
25. Object Management Group. The Common Object Request Broker: Architecture and Specification. OMG Document Number 93.12.43, 1993.
26. Walter Olthoff, editor. *Proc. ECOOP'95*, number 952 in Lecture Notes in Computer Science, Århus, Denmark, 1995. Springer.
27. Open Software Foundation. Introduction to OSF DCE. Open Software Foundation, Cambridge, USA, 1992.
28. Andreas Polze. The Object Space Approach: Decoupled Communication in C++. In *Proc. of Technology of Object–Oriented Languages and Systems (TOOLS) USA '93*, Santa Barbara, 1993. Prentice Hall.
29. Satish R. Thatté. Object Imaging. In Olthoff [26], pages 52–76.
30. Robert Tolksdorf. *Coordination in Open Distributed Systems*. PhD dissertation, Technical University of Berlin, Berlin, Germany, 1994.
31. Peter Wegner. Tradeoffs between Reasoning and Modeling. In Agha et al. [3], pages 22–41.
32. Peter Wegner. Interactive Foundations of Object–Based Programming. *IEEE Computer*, 28(10), 1995.

CCE: A Process-Calculus Based Formalism for Specifying Multi-Object Coordination

Manibrata Mukherji[1] and Dennis Kafura[2]

[1] Department of Computer and Information Sciences, University of Delaware,
Newark, DE 19716, USA. Email : mukherji@cis.udel.edu
[2] Department of Computer Science, Virginia Tech, Blacksburg, VA 24061, USA.
Email : kafura@cs.vt.edu

Abstract. Coordination, the act of imposing a desired behavior on a group of autonomous, independently conceived agents, has been an important issue in the design and development of software systems, both *process-based* and *object-based*. In this paper, the Calculus of Coordinating Environments (CCE) is proposed to study coordination as the *behavioral* union of coordinated and coordinating agents. In CCE, the behavior of coordinated objects is expressed as agents in the Calculus of Communicating Systems (CCS) and the behavior of coordinating objects is expressed as agents (called CE agents) of an extension of CCS. Two composition rules are provided that capture the interaction among CE agents and CCS agents. The applicability of the new formalism is shown by specifying two simple coordination problems in CCE.

1 Introduction

In this paper, an abstract, formal approach, based on the Calculus of Communicating Systems (CCS) [1], for describing and reasoning about the coordination of a group of independently conceived, concurrent objects is developed. Such concurrent objects are the cornerstone of the concurrent object-oriented programming (COOP) paradigm. The formalism developed seeks to separate the coordination specification from the specifications of the objects being coordinated. The advantages of realizing such a separation are ease of specifying general-purpose objects, increasing the reuse potential of the specifications of both the objects and the coordinating agents, and gaining the ability to specify software systems by *composing* component specifications.

Studying coordination independent of the programming paradigms used to realize agents is relatively new. Several proposals ([2], [3], [4], [5], [6], [7], [8], [9]) have considered coordination and communication among software processes using high-level process-abstractions. Also, the issue of coordination among objects in object-oriented programming languages (OOPLs), both sequential and concurrent, has received significant attention recently ([10], [11], [12], [13], [14], [15], [16], [17], [18]). But, no endeavor has been made to propose formalisms that can capture the coordination among concurrent objects in a direct and simple way. Such a formalism would enable a semantic comparison of coordination constructs and a comparative study of related coordination schemes in concurrent object-oriented programming languages (COOPLs).

The different ways in which CCS (and its variants [19], [20]) may be used to specify coordination have two weaknesses. First, coordination is modeled at a very low level by making agents engage in explicit communications. Such low-level specifications are very poor candidates for specifying designs of software components that must satisfy software engineering criteria like *separation of concerns* and *reusability*. Also, when the coordinated behavior of the agents is determined using the Expansion Law of CCS, many terms are generated that represent incorrect coordination sequences among the agents. Second, the simplicity achieved by the CCS specification of an object group is not reflected by its corresponding object-based realization. That happens due to the lack of both a suitable formalism to capture multi-object coordination and a corresponding object-based implementation strategy.

Motivated by the above observations, the Calculus of Coordinating Environments (CCE) is proposed to study coordination as the *behavioral* union of coordinated and coordinating agents. CCE views a coordinating agent as a "container" agent that establishes a *transparent* boundary around the coordinated agents (through which the agents are visible to the environment) and elicits correct behavior from the group by *observing* actions of the coordinated agents and taking coordinating actions on them. The modeling of the *observe-coordinate* property of coordinating agents in CCE was inspired by the Theory of Contexts developed in [22]. Note that CCE is not claimed to be a general-purpose calculus. Instead, the goal is to augment the COOP paradigm by laying the foundation for a special-purpose calculus that enables the modeling of communication and coordination among concurrent objects.

The paper is organized as follows. Section 2 motivates the need for designing a high-level formal abstraction in CCS for specifying coordination. Section 3 introduces CCE. Sections 4 and 5 specify two coordination problems, a panel of two buttons and a vending machine, in CCE, respectively. Section 6 concludes the paper.

2 Modeling Object-Group Behavior in CCS

Autonomous agents can be coordinated in one of three ways. First, agents may bear the full responsibility of coordinating themselves and engage in explicit communication with each other for the purpose of coordination. Second, the responsibility of coordinating the agents may be delegated to a central group coordinator agent that hides the coordinated agents from the external environment. Third, the responsibility of coordination may be shared among the agents and a central group coordinator that does not hide the coordinated agents from the external environment. Each of these three ways of modeling coordination will be illustrated in this section using a simple coordination problem specified in CCS. The shortcomings of each of the CCS specifications will be discussed and the need for a better coordination abstraction will be shown.

The coordination problem considered is as follows: Two button agents are assumed to be working as a group to realize a panel of two buttons. Each button may be either in the depressed state or in the undepressed state. The environment in which the panel exists is assumed to provide the stimuli for changing the states of the buttons. The constraint that gives rise to the need for coordination is that at any point in time only one button may remain in the depressed state. Thus, when a button is depressed, the other button, if already depressed, must be undepressed.

2.1 Coordination Using Explicit Communication

One way of modeling the coordination among the two button agents is using explicit communication. In this scheme, a button, when depressed, queries the state of the other button and undepresses it, if it is already depressed. Although direct and straightforward, the explicit inclusion of the coordination functionality complicates the design of a button agent and prevents it from participating in groups where the implemented constraint is absent.

Coordination using explicit communication leads to the following specification of the panel of buttons in CCS:

$(B1 \mid B2)$, where
$B1 \stackrel{def}{=} depress1.(\overline{undepress2}.B1' + B1'); B1' \stackrel{def}{=} undepress1.B1$
$B2 \stackrel{def}{=} depress2.(\overline{undepress1}.B2' + B2'); B2' \stackrel{def}{=} undepress2.B2$

The CCS agents modeling the buttons, their ports, the environment in which they exist, and the relationship of their environment with the external environment is captured in Fig. 1. The agents exist in an environment that will be referred to as the **composition environment** that results due to the parallel composition of the two button agents. Unless explicitly hidden, the ports of the button agents are visible to the agents in the external environment. The agents are stimulated by actions originating in the external environment and the sequence of events resulting from such stimuli are controlled by the properties of the composition environment.

The rule of CCS that defines the properties of a composition environment is the *Expansion Law*. The latter rule defines how the behavior of agents, composed using the composition combinator, evolve. Using the Expansion Law, one may generate a *derivation tree* that depicts all possible sequences of actions that the agents in the composition environment may engage in. A partial derivation tree for the composition of the two button agents is shown in Fig. 2. The behavior of the composition as depicted by the leftmost path in the derivation tree in Fig. 2 is as follows:

$(B1 \mid B2) = depress1.depress2.((\overline{undepress2}.B1' + B1') \mid$
$\quad (\overline{undepress1}.B2' + undepress2.B2)) + \ldots$
$= depress1.depress2.\tau.(B1' \mid B2) + \ldots$

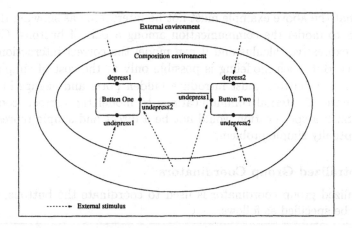

Fig. 1. The button agents, their ports, and the external environment.

The special action symbol τ captures the communication among complementary ports and is called an **internal action**. In the above case, the internal action is produced due to the handshake between the ports *undepress2* and *undepress2*.

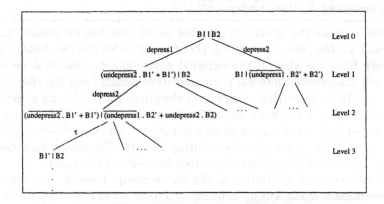

Fig. 2. A partial derivation tree for the composed button agents.

The above execution path represents an incorrect coordination sequence: on pressing button two after button one, instead of button one being undepressed, button two is undepressed. Note that the above inconsistent behavior of the group of buttons is not induced by the the external environment. Instead, it is the ability of composed agents to **engage in unrestricted internal communications** that leads to the inconsistent behavior. The inconsistent behavior would not have arisen if there was a way of specifying that after the input action at port *depress2*, there must be an internal communication between port *undepress1* of button agent *B2* and port *undepress1* of button agent *B1*.

Note that the above example must not be interpreted as showing the inability of CCS to model the communication among a pair of buttons. CCS is an extremely expressive calculus and it can model the correct interactions among the buttons. But, such modeling is possible only at the cost of simplicity and conciseness. The buttons must introduce hidden ports and engage in an elaborate sequence of internal communications to model the correct, coordinated behavior. Such a specification would not be a direct and simple representation of a conceptually simple problem.

2.2 Centralized Group Coordinators

If a centralized group coordinator is used to coordinate the buttons, then the group can be specified as follows:

$(B1 \mid B2 \mid GC) \backslash \{depress1, undepress1, depress2, undepress2\}$, where

$B1 \stackrel{def}{=} depress1.B1'$; $B1' \stackrel{def}{=} undepress1.B1$

$B2 \stackrel{def}{=} depress2.B2'$; $B2' \stackrel{def}{=} undepress2.B2$

$GC \stackrel{def}{=} depressButton1.\overline{depress1}.GC' + depressButton2.\overline{depress2}.GC''$

$GC' \stackrel{def}{=} depressButton2.\overline{undepress1}.\overline{depress2}.GC''$
    $+ undepressButton1.\overline{undepress1}.GC$

$GC'' \stackrel{def}{=} depressButton1.\overline{undepress2}.\overline{depress1}.GC'$
    $+ undepressButton2.\overline{undepress2}.GC$

Figure 3 shows the group coordinator agent, the button agents, and the hidden and visible ports. The group coordinator hides the two button agents completely from the view of the external environment. That is done neither to hide any complicated internal communication details from the clients of the group nor to hide the number of servers in the group (in which case a centralized group coordinator is the most desirable abstraction). Instead, the components are hidden so that a strict centralized control can be enforced over all communications inside the group thereby ensuring that the Expansion Law does not yield any terms that display uncoordinated behavior of the group.

In an object-based realization of the above group, however, the centralized group coordinator agent will be implemented as an object that has an interface consisting of the union of the interfaces of all the button objects. This replication of the interfaces could have been avoided if clients could communicate directly with the button objects and the group coordinator could observe the interactions instead of engaging in them. The replication of interfaces also has the side effects of altering the signatures of some operations of the components (for example, to disambiguate operations in different components that have the same name) and the inclusion of operations in the interface of the group coordinator that do not play any role in the coordination of the group (in order to ensure that a client does not have to send some messages to the group coordinator and some to the components). Thus, a different formalism is required to model group coordinators that do not hide communication complexity or the composition of a group.

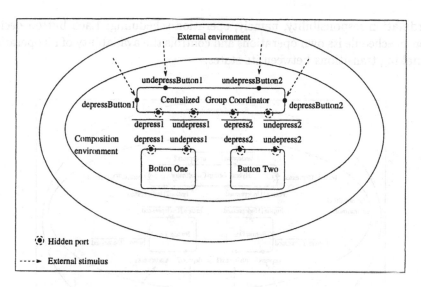

Fig. 3. The centralized group coordinator agent, the button agents, and the hidden and visible ports.

2.3 Hybrid Group Coordinators

Unlike a centralized group coordinator described above, a group coordinator that does not hide coordinated components and that allows components to share part of the coordination responsibility is called a *hybrid group coordinator*. Such group coordinators allow component agents to retain their autonomy by allowing them to interact with external agents and to make decisions about the availability of their own operations. In such a coordination scheme, the panel of buttons can be specified as follows:

$$(C \mid B1 \mid B2) \backslash \{button1Depressed, button1Undepressed,$$
$$button2Depressed, button2Undepressed\}, \text{ where}$$

$$B1 \stackrel{def}{=} depress1.\overline{button1Depressed}.B1'$$

$$B1' \stackrel{def}{=} undepress1.\overline{button1Undepressed}.B1$$

$$B2 \stackrel{def}{=} depress2.\overline{button2Depressed}.B2'$$

$$B2' \stackrel{def}{=} undepress2.\overline{button2Undepressed}.B2$$

$$C \stackrel{def}{=} button1Depressed.C' + button2Depressed.C''$$

$$C' \stackrel{def}{=} button2Depressed.\overline{undepress1}.C'' + button1Undepressed.C$$

$$C'' \stackrel{def}{=} button1Depressed.\overline{undepress2}.C' + button2Undepressed.C$$

Figure 4 shows the hybrid group coordinator agent, the button agents, and the hidden and visible ports. Since the ports of the button agents are not hidden, they communicate directly with external agents. For example, button one may be depressed by communicating with it at port *depress1*. By not hiding the ports of the button agents, the group coordinator allows buttons to share part of its coordination responsibility, namely, operation scheduling: Each button decides when to schedule its own operations and controls the availability of its operations by making transitions between its states.

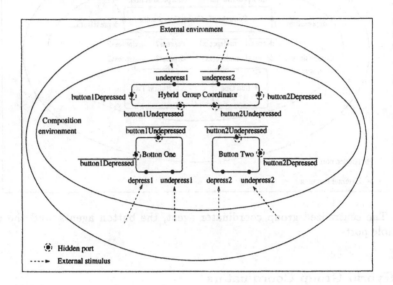

Fig. 4. The hybrid group coordinator agent, the button agents, and the hidden and visible ports.

Although the button agents do not communicate among themselves, they engage in internal communications with the group coordinator agent in order to inform it about every communication they participate in. Such interactions are necessary in order to determine whether a communication with an external agent is consistent with the constraints of the group. For example, after being depressed, button agent $B1$ explicitly engages in a communication with the group coordinator agent C at the output port $\overline{button1Depressed}$ before progressing with its computations. Since the latter port is restricted, the communication results in an internal action τ. This explicit communication with the central coordinator leads to complications when designing components since components must be designed with regard to their possible use in groups. If a component is not used in a group, then provisions must be made to capture its stand-alone behavior. An ideal approach would be to provide a formal abstraction that could *transparently observe* the operation scheduling decisions made by components thereby relieving them from engaging in such explicit internal communications.

The internal communications cause much more serious problems when the Expansion Law is used to expand the composition of the buttons and the coordinator by generating the following terms:

$$... = depress1.depress2.((button1Depressed.C' + button2Depressed.C'') \mid \overline{button1Depressed}.B1' \mid \overline{button2Depressed}.B2') + ...$$

$$= depress1.depress2.\tau.(C'' \mid \overline{button1Depressed}.B1' \mid B2') + \ldots$$
$$= depress1.depress2.\tau.\tau.(\overline{undepress2}.C' \mid B1' \mid$$
$$undepress2.\overline{button2Undepressed}.B2) + \ldots$$
$$= depress1.depress2.\tau.\tau.\tau.(C' \mid B1' \mid \overline{button2Undepressed}.B2) + \ldots$$

that represent the same incorrect coordination sequence that occurred in the case of explicit communication: when button two is depressed after button one, button two is undepressed instead of button one. The latter problem occurs because the depressing of button one is informed to the coordinator after the depressing of button two is informed. Terms corresponding to the correct sequence (informing the depressing of button one before informing the depressing of button two) are also generated along with the above incorrect sequence. Note that this must not be interpreted as a race condition in which button two succeeds in informing the group coordinator before button one can. Instead, the problem is due to the generation of every possible action of an agent in every possible order by the Expansion Law. Some of the alternatives must be prevented from occurring since they represent incorrect coordination of the components.

Even if only those terms are considered in which the occurrence of events at the button agents are informed to the group coordinator in the correct order, the continuous visibility of the *depress1*, *depress2*, *undepress1*, and *undepress2* ports to the external environment causes two problems. First, the following terms are generated:

$$\ldots = depress1.\tau.depress2.\tau.(\overline{undepress1}.C'' \mid$$
$$undepress1.\overline{button1Undepressed}.B1 \mid B2') + \ldots$$
$$= depress1.\tau.depress2.\tau.undepress1.(\overline{undepress1}.C'' \mid$$
$$\overline{button1Undepressed}.B1 \mid B2') + \ldots$$

that represent an incorrect coordination sequence. On depressing button two after button one, the coordinator's action of undepressing button one must be accepted by button one. Instead, in the above expression, button one decides not to interact with the coordinator and prepares to interact with the external environment thereby deadlocking the coordinator.

The second problem is that the following terms are generated:

$$\ldots = depress1.\tau.depress2.\tau.(\overline{undepress1}.C'' \mid$$
$$undepress1.\overline{button1Undepressed}.B1 \mid B2') + \ldots$$
$$= depress1.\tau.depress2.\tau.\overline{undepress1}.(C'' \mid$$
$$undepress1.\overline{button1Undepressed}.B1 \mid B2') + \ldots$$

that represent another incorrect coordination sequence in which the coordinator, instead of taking the coordinating action to undepress button one, decides to take it on the external environment thereby yielding an inconsistent state of the group. This happens due to the visibility of the *undepress1* port of the group coordinator to the external environment, as shown in Fig. 4.

2.4 Non-intrusive Hybrid Group Coordinators

The uncoordinated behavior associated with the hybrid group coordinator specified in the last section arose due to (i) the inability to control the order of occurrence of internal actions and (ii) the inability to control the visibility of those ports that are both participating in a dialogue with the environment and are being observed by the coordinator agent. What is required is a formalism that allows the specification of **non-intrusive**, hybrid group coordinator agents.

A hybrid group coordinator will be termed non-intrusive if it: (i) transparently observes events at specific ports of the coordinated agents, (ii) transparently initiates coordinating actions at specific ports of the coordinated agents, (iii) allows a **dynamic control** over the visibility of ports of the coordinated agents, and (iv) composes with coordinated agents to yield a pruned state-space. Event observation will be transparent if (i) a coordinator does not have to intercept requests for service from clients and (ii) a coordinated component does not have to engage in explicit communications to inform the occurrence of observed events to the group coordinator. Coordinating actions will be transparent if a coordinated component does not have to engage in interactions to explicitly trigger, accept, or respond to such actions. As a result, a non-intrusive hybrid group coordinator will be invisible to both the clients of the group and the components of the group. But note that such a coordinator is not expected to be any less complicated either in its specification or in its coordinating actions than a centralized group coordinator. The advantages of using non-intrusive, hybrid group coordinators over centralized ones are the ability to provide a distributed specification of the coordination among autonomous agents (an inherently distributed problem) and the simpler object-based implementations of such group coordinators.

The group of the button agents coordinated by a non-intrusive, hybrid group coordinator may be captured as shown in Fig. 5. Note that the button agents have no explicit ports to communicate with the group coordinator, the ports using which the group coordinator takes coordinating actions are hidden from the external environment, and the coordinator does not hide or replicate the interfaces of the buttons thereby allowing clients to communicate with components directly.

A new formalism is required to capture non-intrusive, hybrid group coordinators because the explicit-communication mode of interaction among agents in process-calculi like CCS is inadequate to capture the implicit, transparent mode of interaction required by these coordinators. Such a formalism is proposed in the following section.

3 A Calculus of Coordinating Environments

In this section, the Calculus of Coordinating Environments (CCE) is proposed. The prime contribution of the calculus is that it enables a simple and direct specification of non-intrusive, hybrid group coordinator agents, called **Coordinating Environment agents** (CE agents). CE agents coordinate compositions

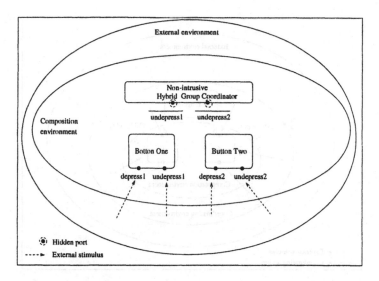

Fig. 5. The non-intrusive, hybrid group coordinator agent, the button agents, and the hidden and visible ports.

of CCS agents. The coordinated CCS agents have the two following properties: (i) they do not engage in any internal communications and (ii) they do not hide any of their ports explicitly.

The first property promotes the use of independently conceived agents that are unaware of the other participants in a group. The property also relieves a CE agent from the burden of dealing with τ actions that, as demonstrated in the last section, cause problems in coordinating groups. Instead, if two agents ever has to communicate, the CE agent implements that communication. The second property enables a CE agent to **control dynamically** the visibility of the ports of the CCS agents instead of permanently hiding them (as done by the restriction combinator of CCS).

Figure 6 captures the purpose of a coordinating environment and a CE agent at a very abstract level. The behavior of the coordinating environment is embodied in the CE agent that is **not visible to both the external environment and the coordinated agents.** A CE agent controls the composition environment so that the external environment may not take actions on the agents in the composition environment that may result in inconsistent states of the group. Instead, the CE agent, depending on the collective state of the agents in the composition environment, selectively exposes ports of the CCS agents to the external environment. Such selective exposure of ports is achieved through **observation: A port is exposed to the external environment only if the CE agent observes that port.** In Figure 6, only ports a and f are exposed to the external environment in the current state of the CE agent (that reflects the current state of the group). The set of exposed ports may change in a subsequent state of the group.

A CE agent may take a *coordinating action* by communicating with any of the

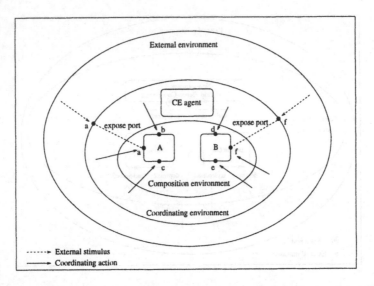

Fig. 6. The introduction of a coordinating environment between a composition environment and the external environment.

agents at any of their ports. These coordinating actions are internal communications that generate τ actions but the τ actions **do not escape the boundary of the coordinating environment**. The coordinating actions serve two important purposes: (i) they enable a CE agent to force component agents to change their states and (ii) they enable the replacement of direct communication among component agents by communications among the CE agent and the components.

3.1 The Operational Semantics of CCE

The operational semantics of CE agents is described by a labeled transition system (LTS). Let $\mathcal{A}$ be a set of names ($\alpha_0, \alpha_1 \dots$ range over $\mathcal{A}$) and $\bar{\mathcal{A}}$ be the corresponding set of *co-names* ($\bar{\alpha}_0, \bar{\alpha}_1, \dots$ range over $\bar{\mathcal{A}}$), as in CCS. Let $\mathcal{L} = \mathcal{A} \cup \bar{\mathcal{A}}$ be the set of labels and $Act_{CCS} = \mathcal{L} \cup \{\tau\}$ be the set of actions, as in CCS. Let $\mathcal{C}$ be the set containing all CE expressions ($C, D, \dots$ range over $\mathcal{C}$), $\mathcal{X}_{CE}$ be the set of CE variables (X, Y, ... range over $\mathcal{X}$), $\mathcal{K}_{C\mathcal{E}}$ be the set of CE constants ($C_0, C_1, \dots$ range over $\mathcal{K}_{C\mathcal{E}}$), let $ObsEv_{CE} = \mathcal{L}$, and let $CoordAct_{CE} = ObsEv_{CE} \cup \{\bigcirc\}$, where $\bigcirc \notin Act_{CCS}$ is a distinguished *no-action* symbol. Then, the operational semantics of CE agents is defined by $(\mathcal{C}, ObsEv_{CE} \times CoordAct^*_{CE}, \longmapsto)$ where the *transition relation* $\longmapsto \subseteq$ $(\mathcal{C}, ObsEv_{CE} \times CoordAct^*_{CE}, \mathcal{C})$. For $(C, (\alpha_0, \bigcirc), C') \in \longmapsto$, we write, $C \stackrel{(\alpha_0, \bigcirc)}{\longmapsto} C'$ and for $(C, (\alpha_0, \alpha_1 \dots \alpha_n), C') \in \longmapsto$, we write, $C \stackrel{(\alpha_0, \alpha_1 \dots \alpha_n)}{\longmapsto} C'$.

The operational semantics described above highlights several important properties of both CE agents and the coordinated CCS agents. First, the two-tuple $(\alpha_0, (\alpha_1 \dots \alpha_n))$ partitions an action of a CE agent into two distinct steps: *observation* followed by a *coordinating action sequence*. In $(\alpha_0, (\alpha_1 \dots \alpha_n))$, the

CE agent *observes* an action at port α_0 of a component CCS agent and takes actions at its ports α_1 through α_n, in that sequence, that are directed to one or more component agents. Note that these actions must be taken in a specific sequence because different sequences may result in different final states of the group. When n = 0, the coordinating action sequence is empty and is represented by the ◯ symbol. Thus, **a CE agent must observe an event** to progress with its computation but it **may not take a coordinating action** on making an observation.

The second important property that must be noted is that there is a **tight synchronization of the computation steps of a CE agent and those of the coordinated CCS agents.** The synchronization ensures that when a CE agent takes a sequence of coordinating actions, the component agents are ready to engage in such communications with the CE agent. In the absence of such a synchronization, the CE agent would not be able to progress thereby deadlocking the group.

The third important property that must be noted is that a CE agent **does not observe a τ action**. Since the communication among any pair of complementary ports is represented by a τ, a CE agent cannot distinguish between different τ actions. As a result, a CE agent **coordinates only those CCS agents that do not communicate among themselves.**

CE Agent Expressions CE agent expressions are formed using the following grammar:

$$C ::= 0 \mid X \mid (\alpha_0, p) \triangleright C \mid C + C \mid C\{\Phi_1, \Phi_2\} \mid fix(X = C)$$

where 0 is the no-action CE agent, $p \in CoordAct_{CE}^*$, $\triangleright$ is like the '.' (prefix) combinator of CCS, '+' is the non-deterministic choice combinator of CCS, $\Phi_1 : ObsEv_{CE} \rightarrow ObsEv_{CE}$ and $\Phi_2 : CoordAct_{CE} \rightarrow CoordAct_{CE}$ are two renaming functions, '{ }' is the renaming combinator like '[ ]' in CCS, and the recursion expression (denoted by *fix* which must be read as "the CE agent X such that $X \stackrel{def}{=} C$") allows recursive definition of CE agents. Thus, CE agent expressions are obtained using the familiar CCS combinators. The only difference is that a CE agent is not a CCS agent and hence cannot execute actions until it is composed, in a special way, with CCS agents.

The Transition Rules The transition rules for the CCE combinators are given below. The names *Act*, *Choice*, *Rel*, and *Rec* imply that the rules are associated with $\triangleright, +, \{ \}$, and *fix*, respectively. Also, $p \in CoordAct_{CE}^*$.

Act
$$\frac{}{(\alpha_0, p) \triangleright C \stackrel{(\alpha_0, p)}{\longmapsto} C}$$

Choice
$$\frac{C_j \stackrel{(\alpha_0, p)}{\longmapsto} C_j'}{\sum_{i \in I} C_i \stackrel{(\alpha_0, p)}{\longmapsto} C_j'} \quad j \in I$$

$$\textbf{Rel} \qquad \frac{C \overset{(\alpha_0, p)}{\longmapsto} C'}{C\{\Phi_1, \Phi_2\} \overset{(\Phi_1(\alpha_0), \Phi_2(p))}{\longmapsto} C'\{\Phi_1, \Phi_2\}} \qquad\qquad \Phi_2(\bigcirc) = \bigcirc$$

$$\textbf{Rec} \qquad \frac{C\{fix(X = C)/X\} \overset{(\alpha_0, p)}{\longmapsto} C'}{fix(X = C) \overset{(\alpha_0, p)}{\longmapsto} C'}$$

Note that $\Phi_2(\alpha_1 \ldots \alpha_n) = \Phi_2(\alpha_1) \ldots \Phi_2(\alpha_n)$. Also note that the relabeling operator enables the separate relabeling of both the ports at which observations are made and the ports at which coordinating actions are taken. This allows a CE agent to adjust its observations and actions to match any relabeling done to the ports of component agents.

The New Composition Combinator The interaction between CE agents and CCS agents is captured by introducing a new composition combinator in CCS that augments CCS agent expressions as follows:

$$P ::= \mathbf{0} \mid X \mid \alpha_0.P \mid \overline{\alpha_0}.P \mid \tau.P \mid P + P \mid P|P \mid P \backslash L \mid P\{f\} \mid$$
$$\qquad fix(X = E) \mid C[P_1]$$
$$P_1 ::= \mathbf{0} \mid X \mid \alpha_0.P_1 \mid \overline{\alpha_0}.P_1 \mid P_1 + P_1 \mid P_1|P_1 \mid P_1\{f\} \mid fix(X = E) \mid C[P_1]$$

where $f : Act_{CCS} \longrightarrow Act_{CCS}$ is a renaming function $(f(\tau) = \tau)$, C is a CE agent expression and [ ] is the new composition combinator (note that the usual renaming combinator, [ ], of CCS has been replaced by { }) that composes a CE-agent expression with a CCS-agent expression to yield a CCS-agent expression.

Note that the CCS agents coordinated by a CE agent may not have the form $\tau.P$ and may not use the restriction combinator. The hiding of ports from the external environment is achieved by not observing events at certain ports of the coordinated CCS agents. Unlike the permanent form of restriction achieved by the restriction combinator of CCS, CE agents allow a dynamic form of port restriction based on selective observation.

The two transition rules for [ ] that capture the interaction among CE agents and CCS agents are given below.

$$\textbf{Comp1} \qquad \frac{P \overset{\alpha_0}{\longrightarrow} P_1 \quad C \overset{(\alpha_0, \bigcirc)}{\longmapsto} D}{C[P] \overset{\alpha_0}{\longrightarrow} D[P_1]}$$

$$\textbf{Comp2} \qquad \frac{P \overset{\alpha_0}{\longrightarrow} P_1 \overset{\overline{\alpha_1}}{\longrightarrow} \ldots \overset{\overline{\alpha_n}}{\longrightarrow} P_{n+1} \quad C \overset{(\alpha_0, \alpha_1 \ldots \alpha_n)}{\longmapsto} D}{C[P] \overset{\alpha_0}{\longrightarrow} D[P_{n+1}]}$$

Rules *Comp1* and *Comp2* capture a step of computation by the composition of a CE agent and a CCS process-agent. In **Comp1**, the CE agent C does not take any coordinating action on the CCS agent P. Instead, the CE agent allows α_0 to escape its boundary and be available for interaction with the external environment. Note that in the latter process, P changes its state to P_1 and C changes its state to D.

Rule **Comp2** captures the **n-step coordinating action** property of CE agents. In an atomic step, a CE agent may observe an action at port α_0 and interact with the CCS agents P_1 through P_n at ports α_1 through α_n. The interactions with the CCS agents P_1 through P_n take place at complementary ports (for example, α_1 and $\bar{\alpha}_1$) but the resulting τ actions are consumed by the CE agent and are not allowed to escape its boundary. In the CCS agent resulting from the n-step coordinating action, $D[P_{n+1}]$, the CE agent has progressed by one step whereas the CCS agent P has progressed by (n+1) steps. The CE agent deliberately suppresses n states, P_1 through P_n, of the coordinated CCS agent. The latter suppression of states prunes the actions at the nodes P_1 through P_n in the derivation tree of P and selects only the path from P to P_{n+1} that is relevant for the correct coordination of the group.

4   The Panel of Buttons in CCE

Consider the two button agents defined below.

$B1 \overset{def}{=} depress1.B1'$; $B1' \overset{def}{=} undepress1.B1$
$B2 \overset{def}{=} depress2.B2'$; $B2' \overset{def}{=} undepress2.B2$

The button agents do not communicate either among themselves or with any group coordinator agent. Thus, they never engage in any internal communication in the composition environment. The same set of buttons were coordinated by a group coordinator in section 2.2. This section shows how a non-intrusive, hybrid group coordinator coordinates these two button agents.

Figure 7 shows a partial derivation tree for the composition of the two button agents defined above. In the tree, the leaf nodes are not expanded further because they already appear at other (expanded) internal nodes of the tree. Note that the state $B1' \mid B2'$ represents an incorrect state of the group in which both the buttons are depressed. Thus, the task of a group coordinator agent will be to suppress this state from being perceived by the external environment. Another important task of the group coordinator agent will be to block the transitions marked A and B. The path from the root of the tree to the leaf node marked Transition A represents a behavior of the group in which button two, being depressed after button one, is undepressed. Similarly, the path from the root of the tree to the leaf node marked Transition B represents a behavior of the group in which button one, being depressed after button two, is undepressed. According to the behavioral constraint imposed on the group, these two paths lead to inconsistent states of the group and hence, must be blocked.

Consider the CE agent defined below for coordinating the group of two button agents.

$noneDepressed \overset{def}{=} (depress1, \bigcirc) \triangleright button1Depressed+$
$\quad (depress2, \bigcirc) \triangleright button2Depressed$
$button1Depressed \overset{def}{=} (depress2, \overline{undepress1}) \triangleright button2Depressed$

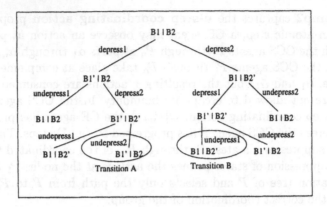

Fig. 7. A partial derivation tree for the composition of the button agents.

$$+(undepress1, \bigcirc) \rhd noneDepressed$$
$$button2Depressed \stackrel{def}{=} (depress1, \overline{undepress2}) \rhd button1Depressed$$
$$+(undepress2, \bigcirc) \rhd noneDepressed$$

The states of the CE agent model the different consistent states of the button agents it coordinates. The CE agent starts in the state *noneDepressed* in which none of the buttons are depressed. From that state, it has the option of observing an action either at the *depress1* port or at the *depress2* port. This observation amounts to the selective exposing of those two ports so that the external environment may communicate with them. No coordinating actions are associated with the latter observations. The state *button1Depressed* captures the relative configuration of the buttons in which button one is depressed and button two is undepressed. From this state, the CE agent either observes an action at the *undepress1* port or observes an action at the *depress2* port. In the former case, the CE agent makes a transition to the *noneDepressed* state without taking any any coordinating action and in the latter case, it makes a transition to the *button2Depressed* state after taking an output action at the port *undepress1*. The behavior from the state *button2Depressed* is analogous to the behavior of the CE agent from the state *button1Depressed*.

The behavior of the composition of the buttons with the CE agent is shown below.

$noneDepressed[B1 \mid B2]$
$= noneDepressed[depress1.B1' \mid depress2.B2']$
$= depress1.button1Depressed[B1' \mid depress2.B2']$
$\quad +depress2.button2Depressed[depress1.B1' \mid B2']$
$= depress1.button1Depressed[undepress1.B1 \mid depress2.B2']$
$\quad +depress2.button2Depressed[depress1.B1' \mid undepress2.B2]$
$= depress1.undepress1.noneDepressed[B1 \mid B2]$
$\quad +depress1.depress2.button2Depressed[B1 \mid B2']$
$\quad +depress2.undepress2.noneDepressed[B1 \mid B2]$
$\quad +depress2.depress1.button1Depressed[B1' \mid B2]$

Note that unlike the previous problem of incorrect coordination, in the above expansion, when button two is depressed after button one, button one is undepressed, button two remains depressed, and the CE agent is in a state in which it may either observe the undepressing of button two or the depressing of button one.

The composed behavior of the CE agent and the two button agents may be better understood by superposing their derivation trees, as shown in Fig. 8. The state $B1 \mid B2$ of the buttons corresponds to the state *noneDepressed* of the CE agent. From the latter state, the composition may evolve by either an input action at port *depress1* or an input action at port *depress2*. The state $B1' \mid B2$ of the buttons corresponds to the state *button1Depressed* of the CE agent. From the latter state, the composition may evolve by either an input action at port *undepress1* or an input action at port *depress2* followed by an internal action (that results due to a communication between the complementary ports *undepress1* and *undepress1*). The latter, one-step coordinating action takes the group directly to the state $B1 \mid B2'$ that corresponds to the state *button2Depressed* of the CE agent. Three important observations must be made: (i) the one-step coordinating action following the action at port *depress2* is not perceived by the external environment, (ii) the state $B1' \mid B2'$ of the buttons is rendered a transient, internal state that is not perceived by the external environment, and (iii) the inconsistent transition from the state $B1' \mid B2'$ through an input action at port *undepress2* is blocked by the CE agent. A similar explanation applies to the transitions in the right subtree of the root node in Fig. 8.

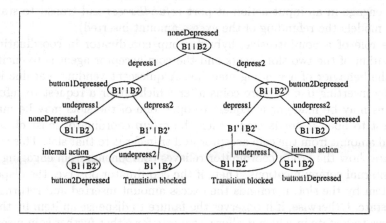

Fig. 8. The partial derivation tree for the composition of the CE agent and the two button agents.

5 Specifying a Vending Machine in CCE

Consider the two slot agents, *S1* and *S2*, and a coin acceptor agent, *CA*, defined below.

$$S1 \stackrel{def}{=} open1.amount1.(\overline{dispense1}.S1 + \overline{fail1}.S1)$$

$$S2 \stackrel{def}{=} open2.amount2.(\overline{dispense2}.S2 + \overline{fail2}.S2)$$

$$CA \stackrel{def}{=} insert.CA'$$

$$CA' \stackrel{def}{=} insert.CA' + refund.CA + \overline{insertedAmount}.CA' + refundExcess.CA$$

Slot *S1* starts with an input action at port *open1*. Next, it engages in another input action at port *amount1* (which models the transfer of an amount value to the slot). After the latter communication, the slot may perform an output action at port $\overline{dispense1}$ (which models the successful extraction of an item) or may perform an output action at port $\overline{fail1}$ (which models the failure of a slot to dispense an item). Slot *S2* behaves analogously. The coin acceptor agent *CA* starts with an input action at port *insert* and makes a transition to state *CA'*. In the latter state, it may engage in one of four actions. First, it may engage in an input action at port *insert* and remain in state *CA'* (which models the insertion of multiple coins). Second, it may engage in an input action at port *refund* and transit to state *CA* (which models the extraction of all inserted coins). Third, it may engage in an output action at port $\overline{insertedAmount}$ and remain in state *CA'* (which models reading the inserted amount from the coin acceptor). Fourth, it may engage in an input action at port *refundExcess* and transit to state *CA* (which models the refunding of the excess amount inserted).

The role of a non-intrusive, hybrid group coordinator in coordinating the composition of the two slot agents and the coin acceptor agent is to elicit from them the behavior of a vending machine. A quiescent vending machine is triggered by inserting one or more coins after which either a request to refund all the coins may be made or a request to open one of the slots may be made. If a request to open a slot is made, then the group coordinator must obtain the inserted amount from the coin acceptor and transfer it to that slot. This transfer illustrates how the group coordinator relieves components from engaging in explicit internal communications. Then, if the coordinator observes the dispensing of an item by the slot, it refunds the excess amount inserted and returns to its initial state. Otherwise, if it observes the failure to dispense an item by the slot, it returns to a state in which it allows requests for either further coin insertions, or refunding the inserted amount, or opening a slot.

The vending machine CE agent is defined below. Note, to increase readability, a semicolon separates two consecutive actions in a sequence of coordinating actions of the CE agent.

$$waitForCoins \stackrel{def}{=} (insert, \bigcirc) \triangleright processRequests$$

$$processRequests \stackrel{def}{=} (insert, \bigcirc) \triangleright processRequests$$

$$+(refund, \bigcirc) \triangleright waitForCoins$$
$$+(open1, insertedAmount; \overline{amount1}) \triangleright slot1Request$$
$$+(open2, insertedAmount; \overline{amount2}) \triangleright slot2Request$$
$$slot1Request \stackrel{def}{=} (\overline{dispense1, refundExcess}) \triangleright waitForCoins+$$
$$(\overline{fail1}, \bigcirc) \triangleright processRequests$$
$$slot2Request \stackrel{def}{=} (\overline{dispense2, refundExcess}) \triangleright waitForCoins+$$
$$(\overline{fail2}, \bigcirc) \triangleright processRequests$$

The behavior of the composition of the slot and coin acceptor agents with the CE agent is shown below.

$waitForCoins[S1 \mid S2 \mid CA]$
$= insert.processRequests[S1 \mid S2 \mid CA']$
$= insert.insert.processRequests[S1 \mid S2 \mid CA']$
    $+insert.refund.waitForCoins[S1 \mid S2 \mid CA]$
    $+insert.open1.slot1Request[(\overline{dispense1}.S1 + \overline{fail1}.S1) \mid S2 \mid CA']$
    $+insert.open2.slot2Request[S1 \mid (\overline{dispense2}.S2 + \overline{fail2}.S2) \mid CA']$
$= insert.insert.processRequests[S1 \mid S2 \mid CA']$
    $+insert.refund.waitForCoins[S1 \mid S2 \mid CA]$
    $+insert.open1.\overline{dispense1}.waitForCoins[S1 \mid S2 \mid CA]$
    $+insert.open1.\overline{fail1}.processRequests[S1 \mid S2 \mid CA']$
    $+insert.open2.\overline{dispense2}.waitForCoins[S1 \mid S2 \mid CA]$
    $+insert.open2.\overline{fail2}.processRequests[S1 \mid S2 \mid CA']$

The state $(S1 \mid S2 \mid CA)$ corresponds to the state *waitForCoins* of the CE agent. From the latter state, the composition may evolve by only an input action at port *insert*. The state $(S1 \mid S2 \mid CA')$ corresponds to the state *processRequests* of the CE agent. From the latter state, the composition may evolve by any one of four input actions at the ports *insert*, *open1*, *open2*, and *refund*. The actions at ports *insert* and *refund* takes the composition to the already expanded states $(S1 \mid S2 \mid CA')$ and $(S1 \mid S2 \mid CA)$, respectively. The actions at ports *open1* and *open2* result in a sequence of two atomic, unobservable, internal coordinating actions before resulting in the states $((\overline{dispense1}.S1 + \overline{fail1}.S1) \mid S2 \mid CA')$ and $(S1 \mid (\overline{dispense2}.S2 + \overline{fail2}.S2) \mid CA')$, respectively. The former state corresponds to the state *slot1Request* of the CE agent and the latter state corresponds to the state *slot2Request* of the CE agent. From $((\overline{dispense1}.S1 + \overline{fail1}.S1) \mid S2 \mid CA')$, the composition may evolve by either an output action at port $\overline{dispense1}$ or an output action at port $\overline{fail1}$. The former event causes an unobservable, internal coordinating action before resulting in the already expanded state $S1 \mid S2 \mid CA$ and the latter event results in the already expanded state $S1 \mid S2 \mid CA'$. The behavior from $(S1 \mid (\overline{dispense2}.S2 + \overline{fail2}.S2) \mid CA')$ is analogous to that from $((\overline{dispense1}.S1 + \overline{fail1}.S1) \mid S2 \mid CA')$.

6 Conclusions and Future Work

This paper addresses the issue of designing high-level formal abstractions for coordinating agents specified in CCS. The Calculus of Coordinating Environments (CCE) is proposed that extends CCS by providing a new composition combinator and a special agent called a Coordinating Environment (CE) agent. A CE agent coordinates the composition of multiple CCS agents by observing actions at specific ports of the coordinated agents and taking coordinating actions on them. A CE agent has a simpler object-based realization compared to a centralized group coordinator.

A working model for coordinating concurrent objects has been proposed that is based on the formal coordination abstraction proposed in CCE [23]. Among ongoing investigations are the formal properties of CCE and the applicability of formal specification schemes based on Communicating Sequential Processes [24] in modeling non-intrusive, hybrid group coordinators.

CCE is considered to be the first step towards a much more expressive calculus that will provide an integrated approach for specifying concurrency, communication, and coordination. An approach of future work would be to consider the *pi-calculus* [19] for modeling coordination among agents whose interconnection topology is dynamic. Another interesting avenue to pursue would be to utilize the Asynchronous CCS ([25]) to model coordination among agents that engage in asynchronous communication using messages. Such a calculus would capture more faithfully, the coordination among concurrently executing objects that are the cornerstone of the COOP paradigm.

References

1. R. Milner, *Communication and Concurrency*. Prentice Hall, 1989.
2. N. Carriero and D. Gelernter. Linda In Context. *Communications of the ACM*, April, 1989, Vol. 32, Number 4.
3. N. Francez, B. Hailpern, and G. Taubenfeld. Script: A Communication Abstraction Mechanism and its Verification. *Science of Computer Programming*, 6, 1986, pages 35 - 88, North-Holland.
4. A. W. Holt. Diplans: A New Language for the Study and Implementation of Coordination. *ACM Transactions on Office Information Systems*, Vol. 6, Number 2, pages 109-125, April 1988.
5. P. Ciancarini. Coordinating Rule-Based Software Processes with ESP. *ACM Transactions on Software Engineering and Methodology*, Vol. 2, Number 3, pages 203-227, July 1993.
6. D. C. Luckham et al. Partial Orderings of Event Sets and Their Application to Prototyping Concurrent, Timed Systems. *Journal of Systems Software*. Vol. 21, June 1993, pages 253-265.
7. M. H. Olsen, E. Oskiewicz, J. P. Warne. A Model for Interface Groups. In *Proceedings IEEE 10th Symposium on Reliable Distributed Systems*, pages 98-107, 1991.
8. ISA Project Core Team. ANSA: Assumptions, Principles, and Structure. In J. P. Warne, editor, *Conference Proceedings of Software Engineering Environments 1991*, University College of Wales, Aberystwyth, March, 1991.

9. F. Arbab, I. Herman, and P. Spilling. An Overview of Manifold and its Implementation. *Concurrency: Practice and Experience*, February 1993, Vol 1, Number 1.

10. A. Corradi and L. Leonardi. PO Constraints as Tools to Synchronize Active Objects. *Journal of Object-Oriented Programming*, pages 41-53, Oct. 1991.

11. C. Arapis. Specifying Object Interactions. In D. Tsichritzis, editor, *Object Composition*. University of Geneva, 1991.

12. I. M. Holland. Specifying Reusable Components Using Contracts. In O. Lehrmann Madsen, editor, *Proceedings ECOOP'92*, LNCS 615, pages 287-308, Utrecht, The Netherlands, July, 1992. Springer-Verlag.

13. R. Wirfs-Brock, B. Wilkerson, and L. Wiener. *Designing Object-Oriented Software.* Prentice Hall, 1990.

14. C. Atkinson, S. Goldsack, A. D. Maio, and R. Bayan. Object-Oriented Concurrency and Distribution in DRAGOON. *Journal of Object-Oriented Programming*, March/April 1991.

15. Mario Tokoro. Computational Field Model: Toward a New Computational Model/Methodology for Open Distributed Environment. In *Proceedings of the 2nd IEEE Workshop on Future Trends in Distributed Computing Systems*, Sept. 1990, Cairo, Egypt.

16. S. Frolund and G. Agha. A Language Framework for Multi-Object Coordination. In O. Nierstrasz, editor, *Proceedings ECOOP'93*, LNCS 707, pages 346-359, Germany, July, 1993. Springer-Verlag.

17. J. Van Den Bos and C. Laffra. PROCOL: A Concurrent Object-Oriented Language with Protocols, Delegation, and Constraints. *Acta Informatica*, Vol. 28, Number 6, 1991.

18. M. Aksit et al. Abstracting Object Interactions Using Composition Filters. *Proceedings of the ECOOP'93 Workshop on Object-Based Distributed Programming*, R. Guerraoui, O. Nierstrasz, and M. Rivelli editors, LNCS 791, pages 152-184, Kaiserslautern, Germany, July 1993. Springer-Verlag.

19. R. Milner, J. Parrow, and D. Walker. A Calculus of Mobile Processes, Parts I and II. Research Report. Laboratory for Foundations of Computer Science, University of Edinburgh, June 1989.

20. Oscar Nierstrasz. Towards an Object Calculus. *Proceedings of the ECOOP'91 Workshop on Object-Based Concurrent Computing*, M. Tokoro, O. Nierstrasz, P. Wegner, A. Yonezawa editors, LNCS 612, Springer-Verlag, Geneva, Switzerland, July 15-16, 1991.

21. D. Walker. Pi-Calculus Semantics of Object-Oriented Programming Languages. Research Report, University of Technology, Sydney. Sept. 1990.

22. K. G. Larsen. *Context-Dependent Bisimulation Between Processes*. Doctoral Dissertation. University of Edinburgh, 1986.

23. M. Mukherji. *Specification of Multi-Object Coordination Schemes using Coordinating Environments*. Doctoral Dissertation. Virginia Tech. July 1995.

24. C. A. R. Hoare, *Communicating Sequential Processes*. Prentice Hall, 1985.

25. K. Honda and M. Tokoro. An Object Calculus for Asynchronous Communication. In P. America, editor, *Proceedings ECOOP '91*, LNCS 512, pages 133-147, Geneva, Switzerland, July 1991. Springer-Verlag.

An Extensible Framework for the Development of Coordinated Applications

Enrico Denti, Antonio Natali, Andrea Omicini, Marco Venuti

LIA - DEIS - Università di Bologna
Viale Risorgimento, 2 – 40136, Bologna (Italy)
mailto:{edenti,anatali,aomicini,mvenuti}@deis.unibo.it
http://www-lia.deis.unibo.it/Staff/

Abstract. Distributed programming suffers from the lack of abstractions and tools required to handle and analyse the large amount of information characterising distributed systems. On the other hand, the separation of computation and coordination models definitely simplifies the design of a programming environment for distributed applications. Starting from this consideration, the $\mathcal{ACLT}$ coordination model extends the basic Linda kernel, by providing support for heterogeneous multi-agent systems, as well as for hybrid agent architectures integrating deduction and reaction. The design of the architectural support for the $\mathcal{ACLT}$ model led to the definition of a general-purpose scheme which is powerful enough to be used both for the system extension of the basic communication kernel and for building application-defined development tools. Such an approach is based on the idea of reactive communication abstractions, which can be programmed by agents according to a specification language which is rooted in the same model as the coordination language.

Keywords: Coordination models, Distributed programming environments, Extensible communication abstractions

1 Introduction

One of the main problems in developing distributed applications is the amount of information which has to be handled and analysed. Many aspects concerning concurrency, communication, synchronisation, sequential execution have to be taken into account altogether in order to get the whole picture of a distributed system. In particular, tools designed for the development of sequential applications do not suffice in a distributed environment: new tools, new abstractions are needed in order to cope with the complexity of distributed applications.

An effective approach to this problem consists in defining the *dimensions* of a distributed execution [9], where different *orthogonal* aspects are identified, each of which can be analysed independently and then combined so as to obtain the complete view of a system.

Coordination models like Linda [6] give then a relevant contribution to the definition of a framework for the development of distributed applications. With regard to this issue, two aspects are likely to have a strong impact:

i) the *separation* [8] between the computation and the coordination models;

ii) the concept of shared memory abstraction as a communication device, combined with the notion of *generative communication* [6].

According to (*i*), the aspects of communication can be considered separately from those of sequential execution. Thus, any computation model can in principle be integrated with coordination primitives, while retaining at the same time its basic operational semantics. Apart from the obvious conceptual economy of this approach, tools designed for the support of sequential programming are generally inadequate to capture distributed abstractions, but they can be re-used in order to describe the behaviour of the sequential components of a distributed system. As a further result, the definition of abstractions and tools for a distributed programming environment can now be concentrated on communication aspects only.

From the same viewpoint, the main consequence of (*ii*) is that communication channels can be re-interpreted as knowledge repositories, so that they can be used to get the whole picture of the communication state in a distributed application. With such an approach, one could build, for instance, a programming framework where a distributed application can be developed and executed keeping computation monitoring and communication monitoring separate.

$\mathcal{ACLT}$ (first presented in [12]) is a coordination model for multi-agent systems. Originating from research activities in the robotics field [15], $\mathcal{ACLT}$ is founded on a basic Linda-like kernel, extended with the notion of *logic tuple space* (see also [1, 4]) intended as the *theory of the communication*, along with the concept of *multiple tuple spaces* [7]. Tuples are first-order unitary clauses, and heterogeneous agents based on different technologies may exploit the logic theory represented by a tuple space according to their peculiar perception [5]. Non-logic agents (e.g. $\mathcal{ACLT}$-C agents) perceive the tuple space abstraction as a simple message repository, on which basic communication operations can be performed. Logic agents (e.g., $\mathcal{ACLT}$-Prolog agents), instead, can exploit logic tuple spaces as knowledge repositories which can be taken as bases for reasoning activities. For this purpose, the $\mathcal{ACLT}$ coordination language provides a small set of *demo* primitives allowing the design of hybrid agent architectures for logic agents, integrating deduction and reaction in a unique conceptual framework [12].

When facing the problem of providing a full-fledged programming environment for the $\mathcal{ACLT}$ model, two options are basically available:

- hardwiring the language and the supporting tools in an *ad-hoc* environment;
- defining a general-purpose extension scheme, such that the basic communication model can be enriched with new primitives (like the *demo* primitives), and the programming framework can be extended according to application needs.

The main aim of this work is to show how such a general-purpose scheme can be defined and exploited in a distributed programming environment like the $\mathcal{ACLT}$ supporting framework.

The proposed approach actually focuses on enhancing the communication abstraction. The basic idea is to shift the reactivity of the communication abstraction from the *communication state* to the *communication events*, lifting system observability from tuples to operations on tuples. Moreover, an event-(re)action scheme is defined allowing reactive activities to be associated to the basic communication operations. As a result, according to [11], *active* processes determine the behaviour of the distributed system, while *reactive* ones are in charge of the system monitoring.

Moreover, the supporting model provides a *specification language* meant to program the behaviour of the communication abstractions in terms of event reactions. Both supporting tools and language extensions can be built using this simple specification language, which is in turn based on the same communication model of the basic system: tuples and basic operations over tuple spaces. In particular, this work intentionally ignores the intricacies related to the definition of language extensions, by focusing instead on how such a specification language can be exploited to build supporting tools for distributed programming.

The paper is structured as follows. Section 2 discusses the role of the tuple space communication abstraction in a distributed programming environment like $\mathcal{ACLT}$. Section 3 introduces the general-purpose extension scheme upon which the $\mathcal{ACLT}$ multi-agent programming framework is built. This is then exploited in Section 4 to show how some simple support tools for the $\mathcal{ACLT}$ programming environment can be practically defined. Section 5 is devoted to final remarks and conclusions.

2 Enhancing the communication abstraction

From the viewpoint of the design of a distributed programming environment, the main consequence of the separation between the computation and the coordination models, discussed in [8], is that we can concentrate on the definition of abstractions and tools for communication only.

In the $\mathcal{ACLT}$ model, communication devices are represented by a multiplicity of named logic tuple spaces. A tuple space is a collection of first-order unitary clauses, uniquely identified by a ground term. So, the set of the logic tuple spaces can be read as the theory of the communication and taken as the view of the communication state in a distributed application.

However, such views are not enough for our purposes. In fact, they can provide static inter-process communication views [9] (i.e. views based on the content of the communication channel), showing the effects of interaction but not the interaction itself. Instead, it is widely acknowledged that distributed system monitoring calls for *dynamic* inter-process communication views, showing the *operations* performed on the communication channel. As a result, from the system viewpoint, the observability level should be moved from communication state observability to communication event observability. Since a logic tuple space can be seen as a communication channel view, the above requirement results in lifting the observability from tuples to operation over tuples.

Even though a tuple space may be perceived as a merely passive component, it *is* actually (implicitly) reactive, since it must be able, at least, to wake up suspended agents when a suitable new tuple is inserted. From this perspective, it seems natural to ground our general-purpose extension scheme on the *enhancement of the communication abstraction*, and in particular on the capability of specifying new tuple space behaviours.

Then, although a tuple space is intrinsically reactive to its state changes, as shown above, such a reactivity level is not enough, since it captures the effects of operations on tuple spaces, but not the operations themselves. So, primitives which do not result in a state modification, such as *read*, cause, by definition, no reaction at all.

Our approach is then to enhance the tuple space reaction level, making it sensitive to communication events rather than just to communication state changes. Although such an enhancement obviously concerns primarily the system level, the resulting ability should be made available also to the upper level of the application agents, thus providing the programmer with a flexible way to control the communication channel behaviour.

For this purpose, programmers should be provided with a *specification language* letting them specify tuple space reactions. For the sake of uniformity and conceptual economy, such a language should be based on the same model adopted for usual inter-agent communication, i.e. it should be expressed in terms of logic tuples and tuple spaces. The resulting architecture can be interpreted at two different abstraction levels: an *agent level*, and a *system level*, according to a model where all interactions, at both levels, can be modelled with the same basic coordination language.

3 An architecture for a multi-agent programming environment

As discussed above, in order to provide a general-purpose extension scheme for system programming, a notion of reaction to communication events has to replace the conventional, implicit notion of reaction to communication state changes. Moreover, a specification language is needed to capture the relevant events and to define the intended reactions of the communication devices.

3.1 The reaction model

The first idea of the proposed specification language is to provide the ability to define a set of logical events, each denoted by a unique name, and associated to physical events. Multiple physical events may correspond to the same logical event, and, conversely, multiple logical events may be associated to the same physical event.

Then, for each logical event, a set of distinct activities may be specified, which can be interpreted as independent, *reactive* agents. The activities of these agents, which are conceptually at a different level[1] from the application agents, are expressed in terms of a first-order logic coordination language, where only a subset of the coordination language available to logic agents can be used. For instance, a possible reaction might consist of a goal like in_noblock(p(a)), in_noblock(p(X)), out(pp(a,X)).

If multiple reactions are specified in response to a given logical event, they are all executed independently one from each other, in a non-deterministic way. In addition, any specified reaction is performed as an atomic action, thus providing a mechanism for expressing transactions. For instance, the example above produces either the deletion of two p/1 tuples and the addition of one pp/2 tuple, or it yields no effect at all.

Relevant events At the system level, the basic events to be intercepted are all those related to the communication primitives *in*, *out*, *read* and their variants.[2] However, *in* and *read* operations are conceptually different from *out* operations. In fact, while the latter simply adds a new tuple to a given tuple space, *in* and *read* can not conceptually be reduced to a single phase: rather, three distinct phases can be identified.

First, a tuple is sent by the agent to the tuple space. Then, the tuple space looks for a unifying tuple, and the agent possibly suspends its execution if no such tuple exists. Finally, when a unifying tuple is eventually found, the client agent is given such a tuple and subsequently resumes its execution.

While the second phase concerns only the internal tuple space behaviour, the first and the third phases represent two conceptually distinct events, which need to be intercepted separately. We will refer to the first phase, where only the tuple is considered, as the *pre* phase, and to the third phase, where only the unifying tuple is taken into consideration, as the *post* phase. Note, however, that since *out* operations imply no response from the tuple space, they can conceptually be thought of as performing the *pre* phase only.

Each communication event also features some natural properties, such as the name of the performing agent, the provided tuple, and the unifying tuple. Moreover, in a multiple tuple space environment such as $\mathcal{ACLT}$, the specification of the operation yielding a given reaction should involve the tuple space name, too.

---

[1] However, reactive agents do not constitute a meta-level, but rather a lower level with respect to the agent level. Actually, reactive agents can be conceived as a sort of kernel extension, allowing programmers to monitor typical kernel-level events, such as the occurrence of communication operations.

[2] The typical variants for *in* and *read* integrated in a logic language as Prolog are the *non-blocking in* and *read*, called also the *predicate versions* of the primitives [2]. These primitives (here, in_noblock and rd_noblock) replace the suspension semantics with the success/failure semantics, in that they fail (instead of causing the suspension of the performing agent) when no matching tuples exist.

The specification language Two kinds of special tuples (map/2 and react/2 tuples) constitute the proposed specification language, allowing the definition of

- the association between communication operations and logical events;
- the triggering of reactions in response to logical events.

This two-step specification allows multiple physical events to be associated to the same logical events and viceversa, multiple reactions can also be associated to the same logical event.

The first association is represented by a special tuple of the form

$$\text{map}(Operation, \; Event)$$

which captures the idea that each time the physical *Operation* is performed on the tuple space, a logical *Event* occurs.

If multiple *Operation*s are bound to the same *Event*, all the corresponding physical events will result in the same tuple space reaction. This could be useful, for instance, to build a simple tracer, in which case all operations should just be captured into the logical event **trace**, and handled somehow recording the performed operation.

If, on the other hand, one *Operation* is bound to multiple *Event*s, its occurrence will result in the triggering of a collection of logical events, which will be handled autonomously and asynchronously one from each other.

Reactive agents, or simply *reactions*, are specified through tuples of the form

$$\text{react}(Event, \; Goal)$$

where *Event* is the name of the logical event triggering the reactive agent, and *Goal* is the *body* of the reaction, that is the collection of primitive operations to be executed in order to perform the reaction.

Only a subset of the coordination primitives are allowed inside the body (*Goal*) of the reaction specification: in particular, suspensive operations (such as *in* and *read*) are obviously prohibited, due to the atomic action semantics of reactions. Instead, out, rd_noblock and in_noblock can be freely combined in a reaction body.

Moreover, it is not possible to nest goal demonstrations in *Goal*, by forcing the proof of an atomic formula with respect to a given logic theory. Instead, specific primitives can be used in a reaction body in order to test the intrinsic properties naturally featured by each relevant event, such as the tuple space involved, the name of the agent which caused the event, the provided tuple, the unifying tuple, and the phase of the current operation (*pre* or *post*, when applicable). As a result, also the following primitives can be used inside a reaction body:

- current_ts(?TS)
- current_tuple(?T)
- current_op(?Op)
- current_agent(?Ag)

```
- pre
- post
- success
- failure
```

Obviously, **pre** and **post** primitives succeed only in the *pre* and *post* phases, respectively. Correspondingly, **current_tuple** returns the provided tuple in the *pre* phase, and the unifying tuple in the *post* phase. Moreover, **success** fails only in the *post* phase of a failed non-blocking primitive, in which case **failure** succeeds.

If multiple reaction goals are associated to one given logical event, a new *reactive agent* is conceptually activated for each reaction goal. Since such reactions are conceptually independent, such agents might work sequentially, concurrently or in parallel to the one other, depending on the underlying system.

Example 1 (A simple tracer). In order to show the power of this specification language, we show here how a very simple tracer could be specified, which intercepts all possible actions over the tuple space (either modifying or not modifying its state) turning them into a common *trace* logical event, which is then handled by generating a visible tuple showing the occurred physical event.

For the sake of simplicity, we avoid here using multiple tuple spaces: instead, all communication primitives[3] are refered to the default $\mathcal{ACLT}$ tuple space.

```
map(rd, trace).
map(rd_noblock, trace).
map(nd_rd, trace).
map(in, trace).
map(in_noblock, trace).
map(nd_in, trace).
map(out, trace).

react(trace, (pre, current_op(Op), out(happened(Op)))).
```

Reactions as transactions Reactions are conceived as *atomic actions*. If all the primitives constituting a reaction specification succeed, then the reaction is brought to an end, and the side-effect operations possibly associated to it are triggered all at once. Instead, if even only one subgoal fails, the reaction is cancelled, having no effect at all. Thus, at the agent level, reactive agents are perceived as featuring a transaction semantics.

Instead, from a system level viewpoint, reactions can be seen as sequences of operations. In particular, the primitives constituting the body of a reaction are conceptually executed as a sequence. So, the relative order of the subgoal in a reaction body may influence the result of a reaction. However, this has no influence over the agent level of perception since reactions are atomic actions at that level. In particular, in case many side-effect operations occur in a successful

---

[3] Primitives nd_rd and nd_in allow non-deterministic suspension on more than one tuple, following the example of the SICStus Prolog Linda library [13]

reaction, then active agents would perceive such events as happening all at the same time, and producing a single transition of the tuple space state.

A further consequence of the atomicity of reactions is that they cannot be nested. Since the effects of a reaction R are actualised if and only if R is successfully ended, no further reaction to the relevant events which could occur in R can be fired until R is over, and the corresponding state transition is completed.

Example 2 (A simple reaction). For instance, the code below defines a reaction specifying that any **out** performed over the tuple space **world** should transform the tuple space **pqTS** by adding a new **a/1** tuple and transforming a tuple of the form **p(** t **)** possibly contained in **pqTS** into a tuple **q(** t **)**, where t is a generic term.

```
map(out, outEvent).
react(outEvent, (current_ts(world), current_agent(A),
                out(a(A))@pqTS,
                in_noblock(p(X))@pqTS, out(q(X))@pqTS)).
```

In case a tuple of the form **p(** t **)** exists, the reaction is successfully finished, and the transformation is completed as a transaction: the tuple space **pqTS** changes its state (two tuples inserted, one tuple removed) in a one-step transition. If no suitable **p/1** tuple exists, the reaction cannot be completed, consequently it produces no effect at all over **pqTS**, and no state change takes place in the system. In particular, even the **out(a(A))** operation, conceptually performed before the **in_noblock(p(X))**, gives no results in the case of **in_noblock** failure.

Moreover, in case this reactive agent succeeds, it results in three relevant events: two **out** and one **in_noblock**. In case some reactions are specified for these events too, they would be executed only after this reactive agent has successfully completed its task, with no nested reactions.

3.2   An abstract architectural reference model

In this Section we present an abstract architectural reference model, which captures all the concepts, components and functionalities needed to implement the proposed architecture for the support of the $\mathcal{ACLT}$ model. However, this model should not be intended as an immediate and direct transposition of the practically implemented architecture, but, rather, just as a (possibly inefficient and unoptimised) way to model the system behaviours.

In the previous Sections we showed that a multi-agent system organised around a tuple space abstraction for communication, synchronisation and coordination could be observed at (at least) two different perception levels, the (higher) agent level and the (lower) system level, where the reactive aspects of the tuple space behaviour are implemented.

Therefore, our architectural model should include a general-purpose scheme to support a flexible tuple space abstraction, where the same coordination model may conceptually be exploited both at the agent and at the system level. This means that the coordination abstraction should be designed, at some level, as an open kernel, with mechanisms allowing default behaviours and policies to be programmed so as to trigger new asynchronous (re)actions.

Unlike mechanisms typically used in the sequential programming language area, (such as traps, for low-level languages, and late binding, in higher-level languages like C++), which aim to support the design of open application agents, we require here that such a degree of openness is provided by the tuple space abstraction, thus transferring to the coordination device the responsibility of ensuring the necessary system flexibility.

Since the tuple space reactions are represented in the specification language described in the Subsection 3.1, which is based on the two special tuples map and react, the first issue is *where* such specifications should be stored. For this purpose, one of the tuple spaces is chosen as the *Specification Tuple Space* (*SpecTS* in the following), where specification tuples are deposited by agents by means of a series of out operations.

Since specification tuples are special only because of the way they are interpreted, we should determine which component of the system is in charge of such an interpretation. To this end, the concept of a special *system agent* is required. The system agent is notified of all events and - when needed - triggers the specified reactions. Then, each time a basic tuple space event occurs, the agent should check the specifications, translate it into the logical events bound to it, and activate as many reactive agents as the specified reacts. Notice that, because of the restricted language allowed in reaction goals, no synchronisation is possible between reactive agents, or between reactive agents and active (application) agents.

However, in order to trigger the specified behaviours, all tuple space events must somehow be made observable. With regard to this issue, everything goes as if the occurrence of any relevant event were matched by the insertion of an explicit *service tuple* in a special tuple space, called *Service Tuple Space* (*ServTS* in the following), visible only at the system level. A service tuple represents the operation to be performed along with all its properties, such as the operation phase (*pre* or *post*), the performing agent, the tuple space involved, and so on. This conceptually captures the new notion of observability of the communication processes, which is shifted from the communication state to the communication events, by using the same metaphors as the basic model.

Moreover, observability of the communication events is not achieved by intercepting and then reflecting such events to a meta-level which is in charge of their handling. Rather, it is obtained by coupling any occurrence of a relevant event with its representation in the form of a special tuple, which is directly perceived only at the level of the reactive agents (which is conceptually a lower level than the agent level). In this way, while the execution of a communication operation may trigger a multiplicity of further (asynchronous) computational threads in the form of atomic reactions, the behaviour of the communication operation itself remains unchanged. As a result, this model does not introduce any direct interference with the basic Linda coordination kernel.

For instance, the request for in(p(X,Y))@ts operation performed by an agent ag could be modelled by a service tuple of the form **service(in, pre, ag, ts, p(X,Y), ...)** put in the *ServTS*, representing to the *pre* phase of the **in** operation. Then, suppose the application agent **ag** suspends itself waiting for the answer: when it is finally awakened, it receives the resulting tuple (for instance, **p(a,6)**). This will be represented by the eventual appearance of a service tuple like **service(in, post, ag, ts, success(p(a,6)), ...)** in the *ServTS*, corresponding to the *post* phase of the **in**.

A major point here is that the *ServTS* should be thought as being conceptually different from the agent tuple spaces, since it is a conventional, state-reactive tuple space, with no event-reaction capabilities at all. If it were not so, the reaction handling mechanism would enter an endless loop, as the output of the service tuple would trigger a new event, which should be handled using the same protocol.

The system agent may then be considered as continuously waiting for service tuples in the *ServTS*, searching the *SpecTS* for specifications about the performed operation, and possibly forcing the execution of some reactive agents. This conceptual behaviour shows that reactive agents do not merit the full application agent status, since they are nothing more than mere asynchronous execution threads, like Shared Prolog [1] ephemeral agents. This is reflected, for instance, also by the fact that they don't even have a name: actually, a **current_agent** subgoal within the reaction goal would return the name of the application agent performing the tuple space operation.

Finally, it is worth noting that the conceptual architecture sketched here does in no way imply a centralised approach to the implementation of the *ACLT* distributed programming environment.

4 Building support tools

The general-purpose event-reaction mechanism proved to be effective in the design of programming support tools for the *ACLT* environment, which have been exploited also during the development of the *ACLT* system itself.

In order to monitor a distributed application effectively, one needs a method to watch the contents of a given tuple space (say, **world**) and to trace the operations performed by the application agents. These requirements have been met in the *ACLT* environment by providing two support tools: the *visualiser*, and the *tracer*.

4.1 The visualiser

Given that tuple spaces represent *views* of the inter-process communication state, the first issue is to provide a simple tool for the *visualisation* of the contents of a tuple space [9].

The *ACLT* visualiser is a tool designed to provide a dynamic mirroring of the contents of a given tuple space, and is built as an agent which monitors the contents of a tuple space and updates a visualisation (such as a terminal window) whenever the tuple space is modified. As could be expected, such behaviour can be achieved by suitably programming the tuple space reaction, so that a proper signal is raised whenever a tuple space modification event occurs. As a result, the visualiser can be designed as an endless loop waiting for such a signal, which is handled by correspondingly updating the visualisation.

Then, only two reactive behaviours (agents) are needed, one for each basic category of operations which can modify the tuple space content:

- a logical event to intercept *in* operations;
- another logical event to capture the single *out* operation.

Both events result in the emission of a tuple of the form

$$do(\mathit{Command}(\mathit{Tuple}))$$

telling the visualiser how to update the visualisation, into a separate tuple space visTS, used as a knowledge repository by the visualiser agent.

A possible event reaction specification needed for this purpose is the following:

```
map(out, outEvent).
map(in, inEvent).
map(nd_in, inEvent).
map(in_noblock, inEvent).

react(outEvent, (
    current_ts(world), current_tuple(T), out(do(add(T)))@visTS)).
react(inEvent, (post,
    current_ts(world), current_tuple(T), out(do(del(T)))@visTS)).
```

Although the specified reaction is similar in both cases, the one related to inEvent is constrained to be performed only in the *post* phase, when the matching tuple to be removed has been identified. Moreover, since the visualisation is not influenced by knowledge access operations (such as *read*), these primitives are not considered as relevant events.

Operationally, when activated over a given tuple space, the visualiser installs its event-reaction specification tuples in the *SpecTS* by means of a series of out operations. Then, it reads[4] and visualises the whole current tuple space content, and enter the endless loop waiting for do/1 tuples.

As a further result, once a distributed tuple space implementation is provided, the same mechanism used to design the visualiser can be taken as a basis to build an error recovery mechanism. By ensuring that the monitored and the visualiser tuple spaces are physically allocated on different machines, the "private copy" of the tuple space content maintained by the visualiser could be exploited to recover from a crash of the monitored tuple space, thus effectively enhancing the system robustness.

---

[4] Through the $\mathcal{ACLT}$ rd_all primitive.

Example 3 (Visualiser). To show the previously described visualiser working, let us consider a very simple multi-agent system, where three agents emy, ely, and evy communicate through a (initially empty) tuple space world. Suppose the system behaves as follows:

- agent emy suspends itself on tuple space world with a blocking in(a(X));
- subsequently, agent ely performs two operations on the tuple space world: first, an out(b(1)), then, a non-blocking in_noblock(a(1)).
- finally, agent evy performs two more operations on the tuple space world: first, an out(a(2)), then, a non-blocking rd_noblock(b(Y)).

The visualiser output is then determined by the following command tuples, recorded in tuple space visTS:

```
do(add(b(1))).
do(add(a(2))).
do(del(a(2))).
```

A careful implementation of this model, retaining the correspondence between the relative ordering of both agent level and system level events, would make tuple ordering in the visTS tuple space relevant, by implicitly providing some information about the temporal succession of operations.

4.2 The tracer

The simple visualisation of the tuple space content may be insufficient when analysing the correct behaviour of a set of agents and of their interactions. In fact, this would provide no information about knowledge access operations (i.e., *read*), nor would it allow non-blocking *in* operations, which may fail without removing any tuple, to be always detected.

Therefore, a different inspection tool is required, which monitors all tuple-space-related events. Again, such a tool should specify a set of proper event reactions, aimed to turn all operations into visible tracing tuples, such as the following:

```
map(out,        preEvent).
map(rd,         preEvent).
map(in,         preEvent).
map(nd_rd,      preEvent).
map(nd_in,      preEvent).
map(rd_noblock, preEvent).
map(in_noblock, preEvent).
map(rd,         awakeEvent).
map(in,         awakeEvent).
map(nd_rd,      awakeEvent).
map(nd_in,      awakeEvent).
map(rd_noblock, postEvent).
map(in_noblock, postEvent).
```

```
react(preEvent, (pre,
    current_op(Op), current_ts(Ts), current_tuple(T), current_agent(Ag),
    \+ T = trace(_,_,_,_),
    out(trace(agent(Ag), performs(Op),
        on_tuple(T), on_ts(Ts)))@trTS)).
react(awakeEvent, (post,
    current_op(Op), current_ts(Ts), current_tuple(T), current_agent(Ag),
    out(trace(agent(Ag), sleeping_on(Op),
        awaken_with(T), on_ts(Ts)))@trTS)).
react(postEvent, (post, success,
    current_op(Op), current_ts(Ts), current_tuple(T), current_agent(Ag),
    out(trace(agent(Ag), asking_for(Op),
        succeeds_with(T), on_ts(Ts)))@trTS)).
react(postEvent, (post, failure,
    current_op(Op), current_ts(Ts), current_tuple(T), current_agent(Ag),
    out(trace(agent(Ag), asking_for(Op),
        failed, on_ts(Ts)))@trTS)).
```

Here multiple logical events map the same physical event, in the same way as multiple physical events are mapped into the same logical event. For instance, an in operation is mapped both into a logical preEvent (which is actually executed only in the *pre* phase) and a logical awakeEvent (to be actually executed only in the *post* phase). In turn, the preEvent logical event maps practically all physical operations.

In order to provide a diagnostic tracing which is as expressive as possible, such mappings are closely tailored to the specific operation: so, for instance, two *post* events are provided, one for possibly suspensive operations and another one for non-suspensive operations with a success-or-failure semantics. An example could be an in_noblock operation, which is never suspensive, and triggers a more appropriate postEvent in its *post* phase rather than an awakeEvent. Notice the check in preEvent which is aimed to avoid tracing the trace tuples themselves, which would cause an endless loop.

Obviously, since tracing information is collected in the trTS tuple space, a visualiser like the one described in Subsection 4.1 might be used to make the tracing tuples visible.

Example 4 (Tracer). To show the previously-described tracer working, let us consider again the very simple multi-agent system introduced in the Example 3 on page 12. The tracer output results in the following sequence of tracing tuples in the tuple space trTS:

```
trace(agent(emy), performs(in),
                on_tuple(a(X)), on_ts(world)).
trace(agent(ely), performs(out),
                on_tuple(b(1)), on_ts(world)).
trace(agent(ely), performs(in_noblock),
                on_tuple(a(1)), on_ts(world)).
trace(agent(evy), performs(out),
                on_tuple(a(2)), on_ts(world)).
```

```
trace(agent(emy), sleeping_on(in),
                  awaken_with(a(2)), on_ts(world)).
trace(agent(evy), performs(rd_noblock),
                  on_tuple(b(Y)), on_ts(world)).
trace(agent(evy), asking_for(rd_noblock),
                  succeeds_with(b(1)), on_ts(world)).
```

As already noted in the Example 3, the tuple ordering in the trTS tuple space may be relevant, according to the peculiar implementation of the model, thus implicitly provide information about the temporal succession of traced operations.

4.3 Further remarks

The event-(re)action scheme defined in the previous Sections has also been exploited to extend the basic $\mathcal{ACLT}$ language. In particular, it has been used to provide a family of hybrid *demo* primitives [12] allowing reasoning activities over the evolving logic theory represented by a logic tuple space. The discussion of how such a complex system extension is achieved is outside the scope of this paper, and therefore will not be reported here.

5   Conclusions

In this work we have presented a framework for multi-agent system programming, based on the logic tuple space abstraction, which provides a notion of event reaction to tuple space operations which can be seen as the specification of low-level, asynchronous reactive agents.

One of the closest models known in the literature is represented by Shared Prolog, or ESP (Extended Shared Prolog) [1, 4, 3], whose main differences from $\mathcal{ACLT}$ are the following.

First, the neatness of the ESP model is by far superior to that of $\mathcal{ACLT}$, since ESP keeps sequential execution threads and communication operations clearly separate [3]. Instead, $\mathcal{ACLT}$ makes no syntactic restriction over the sequence of the operations performed by both active and reactive agents: even though this results in a less clean scheme, it seems more adequate to application environments (such as robotics [15]) where hybridness is a requirement [10] at any abstraction level.

Moreover, ESP agents are ephemeral, and express only reactive activities, while $\mathcal{ACLT}$ provides a framework where both active and reactive agents can be designed and combined.

Finally, ESP active tuples can be used only to model static inter-process communication views, since they react only to tuple space state modifications. Instead, the $\mathcal{ACLT}$ programming framework provides a specification language whose special tuples can also be used to model dynamic inter-process communication views, by allowing reactions to operations over tuple spaces to be captured, too.

This reaction mechanism has proved flexible enough to easily support the construction of effective support tools for system programming, which are needed to develop real distributed applications. Moreover, it has been used to extend the $\mathcal{ACLT}$ coordination language with hybrid primitives integrating deduction and reaction [12].

The $\mathcal{ACLT}$ multi-agent programming environment presented here has been mainly implemented on top of the SICStus Prolog system [14], and is currently working in a network of Sun, HP and Linux workstations. The actual implementation proved to be quite robust, and will probably be tested in advanced real application environments, in order to verify the effectiveness of the $\mathcal{ACLT}$ model.

References

1. A. Brogi and P. Ciancarini. The concurrent language, Shared Prolog. *ACM Transactions on Programming Languages and Systems*, 13(1), January 1991.
2. N. Carriero and D. Gelernter. How to write parallel programs: a guide to the perplexed. *ACM Computing Surveys*, 21(3):323–357, September 1989.
3. P. Ciancarini. Coordinating rule-based software processes with ESP. Technical Report UBLCS-93-8, Laboratory of Computer Science, University of Bologna, April 1993.
4. P. Ciancarini. Distributed programming with logic tuple spaces. *New Generation Computing*, 12, 1994.
5. E. Denti, A. Natali, A. Omicini, and M. Venuti. Logic tuple spaces for the coordination of heterogeneous agents. In *Proceedings of the First International Workshop "Frontiers of Combining Systems", FroCoS'96*, Munich, Germany, March 26–29 1996. Kluwer Academic Publisher.
6. D. Gelernter. Generative communication in Linda. *ACM Transactions on Programming Languages and Systems*, 7(1), January 1985.
7. D. Gelernter. Multiple tuple spaces in Linda. In *Proceedings of PARLE*, volume 365 of *LNCS*, 1989.
8. D. Gelernter and N. Carriero. Coordination languages and their significance. *Communications of the ACM*, 35(2):97–107, February 1992.
9. T.J. LeBlanc, J.M. Mellor-Crummey, and R.J. Fowler. Analyzing parallel program executions using multiple views. *Journal of Parallel and Distributed Computing*, 9:203–217, 1990.
10. D.M. Lyons and A.J. Hendriks. Planning for reactive robot behavior. In *Proc. of the IEEE Int. Conf. on Robotics and Automation*, Nice, France, May 1992.
11. D.C. Marinescu, J.E. Lumpp, T.L. Casavant, and H.J. Siegel. Models for monitoring and debugging tools for parallel and distributed software. *Journal of Parallel and Distributed Computing*, 9:171–184, 1990.
12. A. Omicini, E. Denti, and A. Natali. Agent coordination and control through logic theories. In *Topics in Artificial Intelligence - 4th Congress of the Italian Association for Artificial Intelligence, AI*IA'95*, volume 992 of *LNAI*, pages 439–450, Firenze, Italy, October 11–13 1995. Springer-Verlag.
13. Swedish Institute of Computer Science, Kista, Sweden. *SICStus Prolog Library*, 1994.

14. Swedish Institute of Computer Science, Kista, Sweden. *SICStus Prolog User's Manual*, 1994.
15. F. Zanichelli, S. Caselli, A. Natali, and A. Omicini. A multi-agent framework and programming environment for autonomous robotics. In *Proceedings of the International Conference on Robotics and Automation (ICRA '94)*, pages 3501–3506, S. Diego, CA, USA, May 1994.

Broadcasting in Time

K. V. S. Prasad*

Department of Computing Science
Chalmers University of Technology
S- 412 96 Gothenburg
Sweden
E-mail: prasad@cs.chalmers.se.

Abstract. In the calculus of broadcasting systems (CBS), speech is autonomous, but hearing takes place only when the environment speaks. This paper develops a timed CBS (TCBS) where no time may pass if there is speech pending. A process wishing to speak can be forced, by attaching a time-out to it, to first listen for a specified length of time. Those forced to wait for a long time can be seen as having low priority. This reading is consistent with PCBS, which is CBS with priorities. TCBS has an expansion theorem even if time is dense. A delay prefix operator can be derived up to weak bisimulation if time dependent behaviour is allowed.

TCBS casts, by contrast, light on handshake communication: on time abstracted bisimulation, and on the relations between time and priority, between expansion theorems and density of time, and between delays and time-outs.

1   Introduction

Broadcast vs. handshake. CBS [Pra95], a Calculus of Broadcasting Systems, is a simple and natural CCS-like calculus [Mil89] where processes speak one at a time and are heard instantaneously by all others. Speech is autonomous, contention between speakers being resolved non-deterministically, but hearing only happens when someone else speaks. CBS differs from almost all other process calculi, which use handshake (or rendezvous) communication. The change in communication primitive has far reaching consequences.

The first is that there is a natural way to run a CBS process: return a list of values it broadcasts. This allows CBS to be both a process calculus and a coordination language. It provides a small set of process constructors and functions to run these processes, both of which can be implemented on top of a host language, typically a functional language such as Haskell or SML. By contrast, there is no obviously correct way to stand back and let a CCS process run; in a straightforward interpretation, the user must interact with the process at each step. [Pra95] develops the basic theory of CBS and gives several programming examples.

---

* *Funding:* Swedish Government agency TFR and Esprit BRA CONCUR2.

[Pra95] also develops PCBS, which is CBS with priorities. Processes that wish to speak do so at some priority. This resolves contention between utterances of differing priorities. Hearing has no priority associated with it, since what a process hears is anyway decided by the environment. Things are much harder in CCS with priorities [CH90, CW91]. Here there is only one autonomous action, a completed handshake (written τ) which is silent. Priorities are associated with potential (i.e., non-autonomous or controlled) actions. This leads to obvious problems. A process p can do actions a or b and prefers a, say, but what use is this if the environment only allows b? Worse, what if the environment allows both actions, but prefers b?

Translated to a timed setting, the topic of the present paper, the difference in communication primitive can be illustrated as follows.

Consider the following classroom situation: the teacher gives the class two minutes to think about a question. The quickest student will answer, unless even this person takes more than two minutes, in which case the teacher will preempt the class. This can be described as a timed broadcast system with maximal progress, because people speak as soon as they are ready to. Handshake communication is illustrated by a marketplace, where buyer and seller must agree before a sale goes ahead. Each must wait for the other to appear; neither can expect in general to perform an action when it is ready.

Timed process calculi. There is now a plethora of these. A tutorial, [Hen92], notes that there is very little difference between untimed and timed languages. Current research finds little to say about the setting up of timed calculi, and focusses instead on more esoteric issues such as the abstract structure of time domains, the difficulties caused by dense time, and the like. But almost all timed calculi are based on handshake communication, even if occasional postulates such as "urgent actions" reveal the beginnings of dissatisfaction with it. As one might guess, setting up a timed calculus based on a different communication model turns out to be an instructive exercise.

Main results. This paper develops TCBS, a timed extension of CBS. TCBS shares several properties with existing timed calculi such as the Timed CCS of [Yi91] or TEPL, the simple timed calculus introduced in [Hen92].

As foreshadowed, it turns out that TCBS, a calculus with maximal progress and a time-out operator, is easier to set up than than timed handshake calculi with maximal progress [Yi91, HR90, Hen92]. Other main results are: a priority interpretation of TCBS is consistent with PCBS; TCBS has an expansion theorem even if time is dense. Delays and time-outs both fit into a more detailed calculus where each process keeps track of time. Yet the simpler TCBS without time dependence is expressive and powerful enough for many purposes. It is easier to read time as priority than the other way around, which suggests that time is more basic than priority, at least in this communication model. [Pra94] shows that strong bisimulation is the largest congruence contained in a bisimulation equivalence that ignores priority. The corresponding result for time is similarly simple for TCBS; it is a main result of [LY93].

Related work. There have been few comparisons of timed CCS with prioritised CCS. However, [Jef92b] gives a translation of timed algebra into a prioritised algebra where every action is time stamped.

Some confusion surrounds the expansion theorem for timed CCS [GL92, Hen92, Yi90, Yi91]. One influential view is that "in order to have expansion theorems in real-timed calculi, one should focus on calculi with time variables or similar notions" [GL92]. This is misleading. An expansion theorem for CCS is awkward with the delay operator (which is what [GL92] use) regardless of the density of time. To get an expansion theorem with the more powerful time-out operator (in CCS, the delay operator can be derived from the time-out), the density of time is indeed significant. Time variables, or some other means of keeping track of time, are needed if time is dense, but not if it is discrete.

Readership. Readers are assumed to be familiar with CCS [Mil89]. Familiarity with some timed process calculus and with one of [Pra93, Pra94, Pra95] would help.

2 The Syntax and Semantics of TCBS

TCBS is an extension of CBS [Pra95]. The treatment below is largely self contained, but concentrates only on the timed aspects.

The syntax and communication actions of TCBS processes are given in Table 1. TCBS is a framework or a coordination language, not a complete programming language. No syntax or computation rules are given for data expressions. The user chooses these for the application at hand. The evaluation of data is not represented, but is assumed to terminate, and closed data expressions merely stand for their values.

Types. Given the datatype α, the syntax defines inductively the set *Proc* α. Not every type α is permissible here: it must be possible to determine when two elements of α are equal. Further, α may not itself involve the type *Proc* β for any β, that is, this paper is restricted to first order TCBS.

A translator $\phi: Proc\ \beta \to Proc\ \alpha$ is specified by a pair of functions $\phi^\uparrow: \beta_\tau \to \alpha_\tau$ and $\phi_\downarrow: \alpha_\tau \to \beta_\tau$. That is, $\phi p \equiv \mathsf{Trans}\ \langle \phi^\uparrow, \phi_\downarrow \rangle\ p$, where Trans is the translation operator, always dropped in writing. Informally, $\_^\uparrow$ and $\__\downarrow$ are treated as projections yielding the components $\phi^\uparrow$ and $\phi_\downarrow$ of a translator ϕ.

The time domain. This is denoted $\mathbf{T}$. It can be taken to be either the natural numbers or the positive real numbers (including zero).

Defining equations and guardedness. This paper assumes that there is an unmentioned set of guarded constant definitions available for use in process terms.

Definition 1 Guardedness. Processes of the form 0, $!s$, $?f$ or $f\&s$ are guarded. If p and q are guarded, so are $p \mid q$ and if b then p else q. If p is guarded, so are $\delta : p$ and ϕp. If $A\ z \stackrel{\mathrm{def}}{=} p$ then $A\ d$ is guarded if $p[d/z]$ is. A definition $A\ z \stackrel{\mathrm{def}}{=} p$ is guarded if $p[d/z]$ is guarded for all d.

Let α be a datatype. Let τ be a distinguished value, $\tau \notin \alpha$, and α_τ be $\alpha \cup \{\tau\}$. Let $x : \alpha$ be a variable and $w : \alpha_\tau$ an expression.

Let β be another datatype. Let ϕ be specified by $\phi^\uparrow : \beta_\tau \to \alpha_\tau$ and $\phi_\downarrow : \alpha_\tau \to \beta_\tau$ satisfying $\phi^\uparrow \tau = \tau$ and $\phi_\downarrow \tau = \tau$.

Let δ, $\varepsilon \in \mathbf{T}$, the time domain (the natural numbers or the positive reals with zero).

Let b be a boolean expression. Then the elements of $Proc\ \alpha$ are given by

$$p ::= 0 \ \Big| \ !s \ \Big| \ ?f \ \Big| \ f\ \&\ s \ \Big| \ \delta : p \ \Big| \ p|p \ \Big| \ \phi p_\beta \ \Big| \ \text{if } b \text{ then } p \text{ else } p \ \Big| \ A\ d$$

where $f ::= [x]p$, $s ::= \langle w, p \rangle$, $p_\beta : Proc\ \beta$, and A ranges over constants, declared in (mutually) recursive guarded definitions $A\ z \stackrel{\text{def}}{=} p$, parameterised by a datatype ranged over by variable z and expression d.

The semantics below also uses p_i, p', p'', $p_i' : Proc\ \alpha$, $p_\beta' : Proc\ \beta$, and values $v : \alpha$, $w_\beta : \beta_\tau$, and $u : \alpha_\tau \cup \mathbf{T}$.

Tau	$p \xrightarrow{\tau?} p$
Guarded Sum	$!\langle w,p\rangle \xrightarrow{w!} p$ $\qquad\qquad$ $f\ \&\ \langle w,p\rangle \xrightarrow{w!} p$ $0 \xrightarrow{v?} 0 \quad !s \xrightarrow{v?} !s \quad ?[x]p \xrightarrow{v?} p[v/x] \quad [x]p\ \&\ s \xrightarrow{v?} p[v/x]$
Time	$0 \xrightarrow{\delta:} 0 \quad ?f \xrightarrow{\delta:} ?f \quad p \xrightarrow{0:} p \qquad \dfrac{p \xrightarrow{\delta:} p' \quad p' \xrightarrow{\varepsilon:} p''}{p \xrightarrow{(\delta+\varepsilon):} p''}$
Timeout	$\delta : p \xrightarrow{\delta:} p \qquad \dfrac{p \xrightarrow{v?} p'}{\delta : p \xrightarrow{v?} p'} \qquad \dfrac{p \xrightarrow{w!} p'}{0 : p \xrightarrow{w!} p'} \qquad (\delta+\varepsilon) : p \xrightarrow{\delta:} \varepsilon : p$
Compose[1]	$\dfrac{p_1 \xrightarrow{u\sharp_1} p_1' \quad p_2 \xrightarrow{u\sharp_2} p_2'}{p_1|p_2 \xrightarrow{u(\sharp_1 \bullet \sharp_2)} p_1'|p_2'} \ \sharp_1 \bullet \sharp_2 \neq \bot \qquad \begin{array}{c\|c c c} \bullet & ! & ? & : \\ \hline ! & \bot & ! & \bot \\ ? & ! & ? & \bot \\ : & \bot & \bot & : \end{array}$
Translate	$\dfrac{p_\beta \xrightarrow{w_\beta!} p_\beta'}{\phi p_\beta \xrightarrow{\phi^\uparrow w_\beta!} \phi p_\beta'} \qquad \dfrac{p_\beta \xrightarrow{\phi_\downarrow w?} p_\beta'}{\phi p_\beta \xrightarrow{w?} \phi p_\beta'} \qquad \dfrac{p_\beta \xrightarrow{\delta:} p_\beta'}{\phi p_\beta \xrightarrow{\delta:} \phi p_\beta'}$
Conditional[1]	$\dfrac{p_1 \xrightarrow{u\sharp} p_1'}{\text{if true then } p_1 \text{ else } p_2 \xrightarrow{u\sharp} p_1'} \qquad \dfrac{p_2 \xrightarrow{u\sharp} p_2'}{\text{if false then } p_1 \text{ else } p_2 \xrightarrow{u\sharp} p_2'}$
Define[1] $A\ z \stackrel{\text{def}}{=} p$	$\dfrac{p[d/z] \xrightarrow{u\sharp} p'}{A\ d \xrightarrow{u\sharp} p'}$

[1] $\sharp$, $\sharp_1$, $\sharp_2$ range over $\{!,?,:\}$. $\bot$ means "undefined" in the synchronisation algebra.

Table 1. The syntax of TCBS and the semantics of closed processes

Abbreviation	Meaning
$x?\,p$	$?[x]p$
$w!\,p$	$!\langle w, p\rangle$
$x?\,p \,\&\, s$	$[x]p \,\&\, s$
$f \,\&\, w!\,p$	$f \,\&\, \langle w, p\rangle$
$x?\,p \,\&\, w!\,p$	$[x]p \,\&\, \langle w, p\rangle$
$A \stackrel{\text{def}}{=} p$	$A\,() \stackrel{\text{def}}{=} p$ where $()$ is the only element of the type "Unit".

This paper often uses $f\,v$ for the function application $f(v)$.

NOTE the abuse of notation in the third, fourth and fifth lines. In the context of the operator $\&$ the subexpressions $x?\,p$ and $w!\,p$ stand for the abstraction $[x]p$ and the pair $\langle w, p\rangle$ respectively; outside of a $\&$ context, they stand for the processes $?[x]p$ and $!\langle w, p\rangle$ respectively.

Table 2. Syntactic abbreviations, freely used throughout.

Since every definition in this paper is guarded, so is every process. Examples of unguarded definitions are $p \stackrel{\text{def}}{=} p$, $p \stackrel{\text{def}}{=} \phi p$, $p \stackrel{\text{def}}{=} 2!\,q \mid p$ and $p \stackrel{\text{def}}{=} 2\!:\!p$. In the last example, it is not possible to determine p's response to hearing something from the environment—see Proposition 2 below. Thus prefixing by a timeout is not enough to ensure guardedness.

Induction on the structure of processes does not work for constant applications, because to prove the hypothesis for $A\,d$, the starting point is $p[d/z]$, which is not smaller than $A\,d$. But the proof of guardedness of $p[d/z]$ is smaller than that of $A\,d$. Induction can therefore be carried out on the depth of proof of guardedness of processes (abbreviated "induction on guardedness").

Open and closed processes. Let $x\!:\!\alpha$ be a (data) variable. Occurrences of x in p become *bound* in the *process abstraction* $[x]p$, and the scope of x in $[x]p$ is p. Bound variables are assumed to be renamed as necessary to avoid clashes under substitution. A process is *closed* if it has no free variables, and is *open* if it does. Thus $x?\,x!\,0$ is closed while $x!\,0$ is open. The set of all (open) processes is denoted $\mathbf{P}$, and the set of closed processes $\mathbf{P}_{cl}$.

Let $v\!:\!\alpha$ be a (data) value and let $p[v/x]$ denote the result of substituting v for x in p. The user has to supply the functions that substitute values for variables in data expressions. These functions extend from α to $\mathbf{P}$ in the evident way. For example, $(w!\,p)[v/x] = (w[v/x])!\,p[v/x]$ and $(\text{if }b\text{ then }p_1\text{ else }p_2)[v/x] = \text{if }b[v/x]\text{ then }p_1[v/x]\text{ else }p_2[v/x]$.

Only closed processes can communicate. Open ones cannot, by definition.

Communication actions. For each $w\!:\!\alpha_\tau$, there are relations $\xrightarrow{w!}$ and $\xrightarrow{w?}$ over *Proc* α. Also, for each $\delta \in \mathbf{T}$ there is a relation $\xrightarrow{\delta:}$ over *Proc* α. These are the least relations satisfying the axioms and inference rules in Table 1. Let $\sharp$, $\sharp_1$ and $\sharp_2$ range over $\{!, ?, :\}$ and u over $\alpha_\tau \cup \mathbf{T}$.

Expansion. Section 4 presents an extended guarded sum $f \mathbin{\&} \{s_i \mid i \in I\}$ with several *output branches*, needed (only) for an expansion theorem. This form is not needed for programming, which only needs at most one output branch as in the syntax presented here.

2.1 Examples and explanation

In (T)CBS, speech is autonomous, while hearing is a response to speech by the environment. TCBS incorporates *maximal progress*: time passes iff no process has anything to say, i.e., iff there are no autonomous actions available. Thus time actions in TCBS are like hearing in that they are not autonomous.

TCBS is built from CBS by augmenting the syntax by time-outs, and the semantics by the rules in the second box of Table 1, and by time instances of the other rules, notably

$$\frac{p_1 \xrightarrow{\delta:} p_1' \quad p_2 \xrightarrow{\delta:} p_2'}{p_1 \mid p_2 \xrightarrow{\delta:} p_1' \mid p_2'}$$

The processes 0 and $?f$ have nothing to say, and allow any amount of time to pass. If $?f$ hears v, it evolves to $f\,v$.

The process $f \mathbin{\&} (5+1)\,!\,p$ wishes to say 6 and become p. If it hears v immediately, it evolves to $f\,v$. It does not let time pass.

$$f \mathbin{\&} (5+1)\,!\,p \xrightarrow{6!} p \qquad\qquad f \mathbin{\&} (5+1)\,!\,p \xrightarrow{4?} f\,4$$

The process $\delta{:}(f \mathbin{\&} v!\,p)$ times out after δ units of time by saying v, and becomes p. Upto this time, it is prepared to hear v' and become $f\,v'$.

$$\delta{:}(f \mathbin{\&} (5+1)\,!\,p) \xrightarrow{\delta:} \xrightarrow{6!} p \quad \delta{:}(f \mathbin{\&} (5+1)\,!\,p) \xrightarrow{\varepsilon:} \xrightarrow{4?} f\,4 \text{ for } 0 \le \varepsilon \le \delta$$

Attaching a time-out to $?f$ achieves little; in fact, $\delta{:}(?f) \sim\ ?f$.

The next two examples show that care is needed when programming with time-outs. First, note the behaviour of $\delta{:}w!\,p$.

$$\delta{:}(5+1)\,!\,p \xrightarrow{\delta:} \xrightarrow{6!} p \quad \delta{:}(5+1)\,!\,p \xrightarrow{\varepsilon:} \xrightarrow{4?} (5+1)\,!\,p \text{ for } 0 \le \varepsilon \le \delta$$

Thus $\delta{:}(5+1)\,!\,p$ is *not* a good representation of a process that takes time δ to evaluate 5+1, for it does the evaluation immediately upon any interruption by the environment! The following attempt is not much better.

$$w!_\delta\,p \overset{\text{def}}{=} \delta{:}(x?\,w!_\delta\,p \mathbin{\&} w!\,p)$$

This yields the behaviour

$$(5+1)\,!_\delta\,p \xrightarrow{\delta:} \xrightarrow{6!} p \qquad (5+1)\,!_\delta\,p \xrightarrow{\varepsilon:} \xrightarrow{4?} (5+1)\,!_\delta\,p \text{ for } 0 \le \varepsilon \le \delta$$

where any interruption causes the evaluation to be restarted.

A process that takes δ to evaluate 5+1 is best represented by a *delay* operator (see Section 6).

Readers familiar with [Pra95] or [Pra94] can skip the rest of this section.

If both components of a parallel composition wish to speak, one is chosen arbitrarily. | is associative, and communication is synchronous. Whatever is said is heard instantaneously by all processes in parallel with the speaker.

$$?f \mid 5! \, p \mid y? \, y! \, 0 \xrightarrow{5!} \quad f \; 5 \mid \quad p \mid 5! \, 0$$
$$?f \mid 5! \, p \mid y? \, y! \, 0 \xrightarrow{4?} \quad f \; 4 \mid 5! \, p \mid 4! \, 0$$
$$?f \mid \delta \colon (5! \, p) \xrightarrow{\delta \colon} ?f \mid 5! \, p$$

All processes respond deterministically to what they hear; $w! \, p$ and $f \,\&\, w! \, p$ are deterministic also for speech. Contending speakers are the only source of non-determinism. This is captured by the extended guarded sum used for the expansion theorem (Section 4).

Finally, a translator ϕ is a pair $\langle \phi^\uparrow, \phi_\downarrow \rangle$. The process ϕp says $\phi^\uparrow 5$ if p says 5; its response to 4 depends on p's response to $\phi_\downarrow 4$. Translators do not affect the passage of time. Hiding and restriction are achieved by translation to τ, an aside appended to every data type. Asides are heard but always ignored. Translating functions must map τ to τ.

2.2 Properties of the calculus

Let $p \xrightarrow{u \natural}$ mean "$\exists \, p'$ such that $p \xrightarrow{u \natural} p'''$", and let $p \xrightarrow{u \natural}\!\!\!\!\!/ $ mean "$\not\exists \, p'$ such that $p \xrightarrow{u \natural} p'''$". The propositions below confirm that TCBS is well behaved.

First, some untimed properties. See [Pra95] for proofs and more detail.

Proposition 2 Input enabling and determinism. $\forall p, w, \exists! \, p'$ such that $p \xrightarrow{w?} p'$.

Definition 3. p/w, the image of p under w, is the unique p' such that $p \xrightarrow{w?} p'$.

For example,

$$(?f) \, / v = f \; v, \; p / \tau = p, \text{ and } (\delta p) \, / v = p / v$$

Proposition 4 Finite output branching. $\forall p$, the set $\{ w \mid p \xrightarrow{w!} \}$ is finite.

Proposition 5 Image finite. $\forall p, u, \natural$, the set $\{ p' \mid p \xrightarrow{u \natural} p' \}$ is finite.

To derive $5! \, 0 \mid x? \, 3! \, 0 \xrightarrow{5!} 0 \mid 3! \, 0$, the premise $x? \, 3! \, 0 \xrightarrow{5?} 3! \, 0$ is needed. But to derive any $\xrightarrow{5?}$ transition, no premises are needed that involve a $\xrightarrow{v!}$ for any v. The next proposition formulates this.

Proposition 6. For all w and w', $\xrightarrow{w?}$ transitions can be derived independently of $\xrightarrow{w'!}$ transitions.

Timing properties. All the propositions below can be proved by induction on guardedness.

Proposition 7 Time determinism. *If $p \xrightarrow{\delta:} p'$ and $p \xrightarrow{\delta:} p''$ then $p' \sim p''$.*

If the time domain is restricted to non-zero elements, the proposition can be strengthened to yield $p \equiv p'$. But $0 : p \xrightarrow{0:} p$ and $0 : p \xrightarrow{0:} 0 : p$, so processes are time deterministic only upto strong bisimulation equivalence $\sim$, defined in the next section.

Time determinism holds also for Timed CCS and TEPL.

Proposition 8 Time additivity. $p \xrightarrow{\delta:} \xrightarrow{\varepsilon:} r$ *iff* $p \xrightarrow{(\delta+\varepsilon):} r$.

So if $p \xrightarrow{\delta:}$ and $\varepsilon < \delta$ (i.e., $\exists \varepsilon' \neq 0$ such that $\varepsilon + \varepsilon' = \delta$) then also $p \xrightarrow{\varepsilon:}$.

Additivity is associated with density ("continuity" in [Yi91]). If time is discrete, then $\delta : p$ can be taken to be an abbreviation for $1^\delta : p$, $(\delta + \varepsilon) : p$ for $\delta : (\varepsilon : p)$, and $\xrightarrow{(\delta+\varepsilon):}$ for $\xrightarrow{\delta:} \xrightarrow{\varepsilon:}$. This makes the two "+" rules of Table 1 unnecessary, and the property of additivity a matter of definition. The property becomes interesting, and the rules necessary, only if a time interval can be divided infinitely finely. The non-zero naturals make a simple time domain for a calculus where further the rule $p \xrightarrow{0:} p$ is dropped. Such a calculus is enough to convey all the concepts of TCBS except the handling of dense time.

Additivity holds for Timed CCS; TEPL does not need it because it is a discrete timed calculus.

Proposition 9 Maximal progress. *If $p \xrightarrow{\delta:}$ for $\delta \neq 0$ then $\forall w$, $p \xrightarrow{w!} \!\!\!/$.*

Corollary 10. *If $p \xrightarrow{\delta:} \xrightarrow{w!}$ and $p \xrightarrow{\varepsilon:} \xrightarrow{w'!}$ then $\delta = \varepsilon$.*

Thus each process can be characterised by the maximum amount of time for which it can wait. This can be read as the "priority" of the process; the longer it can wait, the lower it's priority. This is explored in Section 5.

Proposition 11 Patience. *If $\forall w \; p \xrightarrow{w!} \!\!\!/$ then $\exists \delta \neq 0$, $p \xrightarrow{\delta:}$.*

Maximal progress and its inverse, patience, are much debated decisions with handshake communication. They seem natural here, as autonomous actions in (T)CBS are local, not composed of handshakes between possibly geographically separated components. A speaker has all the information it needs, and no reason to wait. Conversely, listening is a matter of waiting.

Maximal progress and patience hold for TEPL and Timed CCS. They need negative premises. In TEPL, $p \mid q \xrightarrow{\delta:}$ only if $p \mid q \xrightarrow{\tau} \!\!\!/$. Similarly for the time-out operator. [Yi91] codes negative premises into "timed sorts", used to say when the components of a parallel composition can communicate.

In TCBS, the basic dichotomy is between 0 and $?f$, which allow time to pass, and $!s$ and $f \& s$, which don't. The rest follows naturally from the way autonomy and communication are captured by parallel composition. Thus, as in

PCBS, the communication model yields a simple transition system with no need for negative premises.

In passing, note that some handshake calculi postulate "urgent actions" (usually with little physical interpretation). These have maximal progress but not patience.

Definition 12 Alert processes. A translator ϕ alerts if $\forall v\ \phi_\downarrow v \neq \tau$. A process p is alert if all translators occurring in p alert.

The following two properties hold only for alert processes.

Proposition 13 Persistence. *Let p be alert. If $p \xrightarrow{v?} q$ and $p \xrightarrow{\delta:} r$ then $r \xrightarrow{v?} q$.*

Proposition 14 Readiness. *Let p be alert. If $p \xrightarrow{\delta:} r$ and $r \xrightarrow{v?} q$ then $p \xrightarrow{v?} q$.*

These properties are illustrated by the process $p \stackrel{\text{def}}{=} 2\!:\!5!\,0$. Then $p \xrightarrow{2:} 5!\,0$, but also $p \xrightarrow{v?} 5!\,0$ for any value v.

To see why alertness is needed, let Deaf be a translator defined by Deaf $^\uparrow x = x$ and Deaf $_\downarrow x = \tau$. That is, Deaf lets through all outgoing values, but restricts all incoming ones. Then Deaf $p \xrightarrow{2:}\xrightarrow{v?}$ Deaf $(5!\,0)$, but Deaf $p \xrightarrow{v?}$ Deaf p.

Persistence applies only to non-autonomous actions. Most timed calculi do not have this property. In TEPL, which adds a time-out operator to CCS, the property holds only for the CCS subcalculus. In Timed CCS, which uses a delay prefix, the property holds for all processes, but in a weaker form, corresponding to "if $p \xrightarrow{v?}$ and $p \xrightarrow{\delta:} r$ then $r \xrightarrow{v?}$". This is uninteresting for TCBS because of input enabling.

Persistence says that time does not decrease input capability. Readiness says it does not increase it either. Readiness seems to be interesting only in TCBS.

Processes prefixed by delays, as in Section 7, are not persistent. Delay therefore cannot be expressed in TCBS using only alert processes. Alert processes are "time independent" in the sense that their responses to input are independent of when the input arives. With time dependence, TCBS can express delays.

3 Strong Bisimulation

Definition 15 Strong bisimulation for closed processes. $\mathcal{R} \subseteq \mathbf{P}_{cl} \times \mathbf{P}_{cl}$ is a strong bisimulation if whenever $p\mathcal{R}q$,
(i) if $p \xrightarrow{u\|} p'$ then $\exists q'$ such that $q \xrightarrow{u\|} q'$ and $p'\mathcal{R}q'$,
(ii) if $q \xrightarrow{u\|} q'$ then $\exists p'$ such that $p \xrightarrow{u\|} p'$ and $p'\mathcal{R}q'$

The largest strong bisimulation is an equivalence, denoted $\sim$. To show $p \sim q$, find a bisimulation $\mathcal{R}$ such that $p\mathcal{R}q$. All the laws below are shown this way.

Proposition 16 Some untimed laws.

1. *(a)* $x?\,0 \sim 0$
   (b) $(x?\,w!\,p)\ \&\ (w!\,p) \sim w!\,p$

2. *(a)* $0 \sim X$ *where* $X \stackrel{\text{def}}{=} x?X$

   (b) $w!p \sim X$ *where* $X \stackrel{\text{def}}{=} x?X \,\&\, w!p$

3. $(\mathbf{P}/\sim, |, 0)$ *is a commutative monoid.*

See [Pra95] for more laws.

CBS has no laws corresponding to the CCS + laws of associativity, commutativity, idempotence, and 0-identity, because the guarded sums have at most one output branch, and their input behaviour is deterministic.

$\sim$ is extended to process abstractions: $[x]p \sim [x]q$ iff $\forall v.\, p[v/x] \sim q[v/x]$. From $[x]p \sim [x]q$, it follows that $x?p \sim x?q$ and that $x?p \,\&\, s \sim x?q \,\&\, s$.

Proposition 17. $\sim$ *is a congruence for TCBS.*

Proposition 18 Timed laws.

1. $0{:}p \sim p$
2. $\delta{:}0 \sim 0$
3. $\delta{:}(?f) \sim ?f$
4. $\delta{:}(\varepsilon{:}p) \sim (\delta + \varepsilon){:}p$
5. $\delta{:}(p\,|\,q) \sim (\delta{:}p)\,|\,(\delta{:}q)$
6. *If* ϕ *alerts, then* $\delta{:}(\phi p) \sim \phi\,(\delta{:}p)$

The processes generated by 0, $!$, $?$, $\&$ and conditionals are called "finite guarded sums". [Pra95] shows that Laws 1(a) and 1(b) of Proposition 16 are the only axioms needed to axiomatise strong bisimulation for finite guarded sums. Adding timeout to this syntax yields "timed finite guarded sums". The axiomatisation has not yet been carried out for this version of TCBS; it is a conjecture that the above laws are enough. Suitable normal forms seem to be 0, $?f$, $\delta{:}(!s)$ and $\delta{:}(f\,\&\,s)$. The above laws are enough to put any timed finite guarded sum into normal form.

Time stamped actions. Let $\natural$ range over $\{!, ?\}$. The definition of $\sim$ matches $\xrightarrow{w\natural}$ and $\xrightarrow{\delta:}$ separately. In fact, only combinations of the form $\xrightarrow{\delta:}\xrightarrow{w\natural}$ need be considered. A reading is "$w\natural$ at time δ". Such a reading is useful when reading time as priority (Section 5). The action $\xrightarrow{w\natural}$ is represented as a combination where $\delta = 0$. The action $\xrightarrow{\delta:}$ is represented as a combination where $w\natural = \tau?$.

Definition 19 Time stamped bisimulation. $\mathcal{R} \subseteq \mathbf{P}_{cl} \times \mathbf{P}_{cl}$ is a time stamped bisimulation if whenever $p\mathcal{R}q$,

(i) if $p\xrightarrow{\delta:}\xrightarrow{w\natural}p'$ then $\exists q'$ such that $q\xrightarrow{\delta:}\xrightarrow{w\natural}q'$ and $p'\mathcal{R}q'$,

(ii) if $q\xrightarrow{\delta:}\xrightarrow{w\natural}q'$ then $\exists p'$ such that $p\xrightarrow{\delta:}\xrightarrow{w\natural}p'$ and $p'\mathcal{R}q'$.

Let the largest time stamped bisimulation be $\sim'$.

Proposition 20. $\sim = \sim'$

Proof. $\sim\subseteq\sim'$ is obvious. For the other direction, use time determinism.

A main result of [LY93] shows that *time abstracted bisimulation*, where the passage of time is ignored, yields an equivalence that is not a congruence. The largest congruence contained in this equivalence is strong bisimulation. For TCBS, this result is easy, as is the corresponding result for PCBS [Pra94]. Note that the only operator involved is $|$.

Definition 21 Time abstracted bisimulation. $\mathcal{R}\subseteq\mathbf{P}_{cl}\times\mathbf{P}_{cl}$ is a time abstracted bisimulation if whenever $P\mathcal{R}Q$,
(i) if $p\xrightarrow{\delta:}\xrightarrow{w\natural}p'$ then $\exists q',\varepsilon$ such that $q\xrightarrow{\varepsilon:}\xrightarrow{w\natural}q'$ and $p'\mathcal{R}q'$,
(ii) if $q\xrightarrow{\delta:}\xrightarrow{w\natural}q'$ then $\exists p',\varepsilon$ such that $p\xrightarrow{\varepsilon:}\xrightarrow{w\natural}p'$ and $p'\mathcal{R}q'$

The largest time abstracted bisimulation, denoted $\simeq$, is an equivalence, but not a congruence. For $3!_1\,p\simeq 3!_2\,p$, yet $3!_1\,p\,|\,5!_1\,q\xrightarrow{1:}\xrightarrow{3!}$, while for any δ, $3!_2\,p\,|\,5!_1\,q\xrightarrow{\delta:}\xrightarrow{3!}\not\rightarrow$. Let $\simeq^c$ be the largest congruence contained in $\simeq$.

Proposition 22. $\sim=\simeq^c$

Proof. It is easy to see that $\sim\subseteq\simeq$, and $\sim$ is a congruence. For the other direction, let $p\simeq^c q$, and let $p\xrightarrow{\delta:}\xrightarrow{w\natural}p'$. Then $q\xrightarrow{\varepsilon:}\xrightarrow{w\natural}q'$, and $p'\simeq^c q'$. But $\delta=\varepsilon$, otherwise a $|$ context can be found to distinguish p and q. Use Proposition 20.

4 Expansion

For this section, an extended calculus TCBS$_e$ is introduced where guarded sums have an *output tree*, a finite set of output branches instead of just one as in TCBS. The syntax of TCBS$_e$ is given by

$$p ::= \,!s \,\Big|\, f\,\&\,s \,\Big|\, \delta{:}p \,\Big|\, p\,|\,p \,\Big|\, \phi p_\beta \,\Big|\, \text{if } b \text{ then } p \text{ else } p \,\Big|\, A\,d$$

where $f ::= [x]p$ and $s ::= \{\langle w_i, p_i\rangle\,|\,i\in I\}$, where I is a finite set. The semantics below is extended from Table 1; the common parts are not repeated.

Guarded	$f\,\&\,s\xrightarrow{w_i!}p_i$	$\langle w_i,p_i\rangle\in s$	$[x]p\,\&\,s\xrightarrow{v?}p[v/x]$
Sum	$!s\xrightarrow{w_i!}p_i$	$\langle w_i,p_i\rangle\in s$	$!s\xrightarrow{v?}\,!s$

Now $!\emptyset$ says nothing and loops on all input. It corresponds to 0 in TCBS. Similarly, $f\&\emptyset$ corresponds to $?f$ in TCBS. Writing just $\langle w,p\rangle$ instead of $\{\langle w,p\rangle\}$, it is easily seen that TCBS is a subcalculus of TCBS$_e$.

TCBS$_e$ processes too have a unique response to each input. Again, p/w denotes the image of p under w (see Definition 3). Bisimulation extends naturally to TCBS$_e$, as do the notions of (timed) finite guarded sums.

First, the untimed expansion theorem. The finite number of output branches in a sum are enough for the expansion theorem below, since parallel compositions are finite. For legibility, $\{\langle w_i, p_i\rangle\,|\,i\in I\}$ is often written $\{w_i!\,p_i\,|\,i\in I\}$.

Proposition 23 Expansion theorem. *Let p, q be finite guarded sums. Then*

$$p_0 \mid p_1 \sim x? \, (p_0/x \mid p_1/x) \, \& \, \{w! \, (p'_r \mid p_{1-r}/w) \mid p_r \xrightarrow{w!} p'_r \text{ and } r = 0, 1\}$$

For example, the process $2! \, p \mid 7! \, q$ can be expanded into a guarded sum:

$$2! \, p \mid 7! \, q \sim x? \, (2! \, p \mid 7! \, q) \, \& \, \{2! \, (p \mid 7! \, q) \, , 7! \, (2! \, p \mid q)\}$$

Now, assuming the normal forms proposed earlier for timed finite guarded sums, the expansion theorem can be broken up into special cases.

Consider $\delta: p \mid \varepsilon: q$ where p, q are finite guarded sums. Assume that $\delta \leq \varepsilon$. Then $\delta: p \mid \varepsilon: q \sim \delta: (p \mid (\varepsilon - \delta): q)$. In the case $\varepsilon = \delta$, the composition is of the form $p \mid q$ where both components are just guarded sums. The case $\delta < \varepsilon$ results in a composition of the form $p \mid \delta: q$. Further, if p is of the form $?f$, it can be rewritten $p \sim \delta: p$, and the composition again reduces to one of just guarded sums. Thus there are only two cases to consider, the untimed theorem above, and

Proposition 24 Timed Expansion theorem. *Let $p \equiv f \, \& \, \{w_i! \, p_i \mid i \in I\}$, and $I \neq \emptyset$. Then*

$$p \mid \delta: q \sim x? \, (p/x \mid q/x) \, \& \, \{w_i! \, (p_i \mid (\delta: q) \, /w_i) \mid i \in I\}.$$

The existence of this theorem for TCBS calls for some comment, in the light of the discussion in the introduction.

[Hen92] points out that in TEPL, all agents without time-outs are persistent. Let the delay prefix "δ." be defined by the sole axiom $\delta. p \xrightarrow{\delta:} p$. Then $\delta. p$ is persistent as well. But the process $a. 0 \mid \delta. p$ is not persistent, for $a. 0 \mid \delta. p \xrightarrow{a} \delta. p$, but $a. 0 \mid \delta. p \xrightarrow{\delta:} a. 0 \mid p \xrightarrow{a} p$, i.e., after the time action, the agent no longer has an action to the same target state. Therefore CCS augmented by a delay prefix cannot yield an expansion theorem, even if time is discrete.

[Hen92] gets an expansion theorem using the time-out construct $p +_\delta q$ which behaves like p for δ and then becomes q. This is clearly not persistent.

[Yi91] gets around the problem by allowing time dependence: (in adapted notation) the action prefix is now written $a. f$ where f is a function from time to processes. The axioms are $a. f \xrightarrow{a} f \, 0$ and $a. f \xrightarrow{\delta} a. (\lambda t. f \, (t + \delta))$. The process $a. f$ is also not persistent. (It is weakly persistent).

Thus far it would appear that TCBS follows a path similar to that of [Hen92]. But [Hen92] only considers discrete time. What happens if time is dense? [GL92] motivate their study of dense time by showing that it is hard to get an expansion theorem using the delay prefix. This is misleading, since the impossibility here is independent of the density of time. However, their result holds. Roughly, the problem with dense time is this. For brevity here, CCS processes are written without trailing 0's, i.e., $a. 0$ is written just a. Consider the agent $(a +_{\delta + \delta'} q) \mid c$. The plausible expansion is

$$(a. c + c. (a +_{\delta + \delta'} q)) +_{\delta + \delta'} (q \mid c)$$

Consider the action
$$(a +_{\delta+\delta'} q) \mid c \xrightarrow{\delta} (a +_{\delta'} q) \mid c$$
The plausible expansion cannot match it

$$(a.c + c.(a +_{\delta+\delta'} q)) +_{\delta+\delta'} (q \mid c) \xrightarrow{\delta} (a.c + c.(a +_{\delta+\delta'} q)) +_{\delta'} (q \mid c)$$

The clock behind the action prefix does not tick.

It is difficult to demonstrate the "corresponding" situation in TCBS, but roughly speaking, the problem does not arise because input received by one component is also received by the other. Consider the expansion

$$\delta\colon(f \,\&\, v! \,p) \mid ?g \sim \delta\colon(x?\,(f\ x \mid g\ x)\,\&\, v!\,(p \mid g\ v))$$

When the second component receives input, the first one also loses its time-out. The fundamental differences in communication model mean that the result of [GL92] does not apply to TCBS.

5   Interpreting time as priority

. To avoid introducing the notation of PCBS, this section instead provides a priority reading of TCBS, and proves the necessary propositions to show that this reading is consistent.

An operational definition of the priority of a process has already been suggested: it is the longest time the process can wait. Corollary 10 shows that this is well defined. The highest priority processes, with priority 0, do not wait at all before saying what they want to. Processes with nothing to say have the lowest priority, "∞", and are willing to wait indefinitely.

Thus time actions can be interpreted as pauses to ensure that higher priority processes speak first. The priority of $3!_1\,p$ is 1 and that of $5!_2\,q$ is 2. In $3!_1\,p \mid 5!_2\,q$, the lower priority process is prevented from speaking first because the higher priority process times out before it is ready to do so. The latter needs a further wait of 1 unit, the former refuses, and therefore so does the composition.

Now every TCBS process can be assigned a syntactic priority. The proposition to follow checks that this agrees with the operational definition.

Definition 25. The priority $\pi(p)$ of a closed process p is given by the rules

$$
\begin{aligned}
\pi(0) &= \infty \\
\pi(?f) &= \infty \\
\pi(!s) &= 0 \\
\pi(f \,\&\, s) &= 0 \\
\pi(\delta\colon p) &= \delta + \pi(p) \\
\pi(p \mid q) &= \min(\pi(p), \pi(q)) \\
\pi(\phi p) &= \pi(p) \\
\pi(\text{if } b \text{ then } p_1 \text{ else } p_2) &= \text{if } b \text{ then } \pi(p_1) \text{ else } \pi(p_2) \\
\pi(A\ d) &= \pi(p[d/z]) \text{ where } A\ z \stackrel{\text{def}}{=} p
\end{aligned}
$$

Proposition 26. $p\xrightarrow{\delta:}$ iff $\delta \leq \pi(p)$.

Since $p\xrightarrow{\delta:}$ implies $\forall w$, $p\xrightarrow{\delta:}\xrightarrow{w?}$, the proposition above shows that a process is prepared to hear others of priority at least as high as its own.

Next, a syntax for a "PCBS" as a restriction of TCBS. Use timeouts only in the forms $\delta:!s$ and $\delta:(f\ \&\ s)$. The non-alert processes of TCBS cannot be put into this form, so "PCBS" is strictly a subcalculus of TCBS. The terms of "PCBS" annotate speech requests with priorities.

The priority of a process as defined above is merely that of its most urgent speech (a parallel composition may have more than one), as in the PCBS of [Pra95]: $\exists w$ such that $p\xrightarrow{\pi(p):}\xrightarrow{w!}$iff $\pi(p) \neq \infty$.

Finally, the semantics of TCBS can be cast into prioritised form by using time stamped actions as in Section 3. Read $\xrightarrow{\delta:}\xrightarrow{w\natural}$ as "do $w\natural$ at priority δ". This completes the interpretation of time as priority.

As with PCBS, this appears to suggest that hearing happens at a certain priority. Now $\xrightarrow{\delta:}\xrightarrow{w?}$ is interpreted as willingness to accept transmissions of that priority. Processes that cannot get an audience cannot speak! This explains how parallel composition respects priority.

Expansion theorem. The untimed theorem corresponds to the case where the two components have the same priority, so that priority can be ignored. The timed case has one component of higher priority. In PCBS, the component with lower priority cannot speak. All that matters is that it is of lower priority, it does not matter how much lower. This explains why the δ plays no role on the right hand side of the timed expansion theorem.

Comparison of "PCBS" with PCBS. The PCBS of [Pra95] takes priorities to be natural numbers. "PCBS" shows that they can be real numbers as well.

PCBS takes translators to be triples, with the first component specifying deprioritisation. "PCBS" suggests deprioritisation could usefully be separated out. PCBS then suggests that a static (or persistent) timeout is useful—an operator that attaches the timeout to every process the original one evolves to. It turns out that the notion of reversed translators is useful in CBS. The reverse of $\phi = \langle\phi^\uparrow, \phi_\downarrow\rangle$ is $\phi^R = \langle\phi_\downarrow, \phi^\uparrow\rangle$, and can be used to describe the environment as seen from inside the scope of ϕ. This suggests in turn a static timeout operator that also allows "inverse time". This is yet to be explored fully. Preliminary investigation suggests another, inverse, relation between time and priority.

6 Weak Bisimulation

Definition 27 Weak bisimulation for closed processes. $\mathcal{R} \subseteq \mathbf{P}_{cl} \times \mathbf{P}_{cl}$ is a weak bisimulation if whenever $p\mathcal{R}q$,

(i) if $p \xrightarrow{u\natural} p'$ then $\exists q'$ such that $q \xrightarrow{\tau!^* u\natural \tau!^*} q'$ and $p'\mathcal{R}q'$,

(ii) if $q \xrightarrow{u\natural} q'$ then $\exists p'$ such that $p \xrightarrow{\tau!^* u\natural \tau!^*} p'$ and $p'\mathcal{R}q'$

The largest weak bisimulation is an equivalence, denoted $\approx$. Because sums are guarded in (T)CBS, it is a congruence.

7 Delay prefixes and time-outs

Consider a *delay prefix*, $\delta.$, defined by the following rules.

$$(\delta + \varepsilon).p \xrightarrow{\delta:} \varepsilon.p \qquad\qquad \delta.p \xrightarrow{\delta:} p \qquad\qquad \delta.p \xrightarrow{v?} \delta.p$$

Now $\delta.p$ is neither persistent nor ready, and can therefore not be derived from alert processes in TCBS, since these are both persistent and ready. It is interesting to note that things are the other way around in TEPL.

Since non-alert processes show time dependence, it is an open question whether delay can be derived (at least upto $\approx$) from TCBS. It can if we explicitly allow time dependent behaviour.

7.1 Time dependence

Now suppose TCBS is extended to allow time dependence. This means firstly that the functions f for input are to be $\alpha \to \mathbf{T} \to Proc\ \alpha$. Define a function add_δ from processes to processes as below.

Definition 28.

$$
\begin{aligned}
\mathrm{add}_\delta\,(0) &= 0 \\
\mathrm{add}_\delta\,(!s) &= {!s} \\
\mathrm{add}_\delta\,(?f) &= {?}\,([v,t]f\ v\ (t+\delta)) \\
\mathrm{add}_\delta\,(f \,\&\, w!\,p) &= ([v,t]f\ v\ (t+\delta))\ \&\ w!\,p \\
\mathrm{add}_\delta\,(\varepsilon{:}\,p) &= \varepsilon{:}\,(\mathrm{add}_\delta p) \\
\mathrm{add}_\delta\,(p \mid q) &= \mathrm{add}_\delta p \mid \mathrm{add}_\delta q \\
\mathrm{add}_\delta\,(\phi p) &= \phi\,(\mathrm{add}_\delta p) \\
\mathrm{add}_\delta\,(\text{if } b \text{ then } p_1 \text{ else } p_2) &= \text{if } b \text{ then } \mathrm{add}_\delta p_1 \text{ else } \mathrm{add}_\delta p_2 \\
\mathrm{add}_\delta\,(A\ d) &= \mathrm{add}_\delta\,(p[d/z]) \text{ where } A\ z \overset{\text{def}}{=} p
\end{aligned}
$$

Next, the semantic rules are changed as below

$$(\delta + \varepsilon){:}\,p \xrightarrow{\delta:} \mathrm{add}_\delta\,(\varepsilon{:}\,p) \qquad \delta{:}\,p \xrightarrow{\delta:} \mathrm{add}_\delta p \qquad ?f \xrightarrow{\delta:} \mathrm{add}_\delta\,(?f)$$

$$?f \xrightarrow{v?} f\ v\ 0 \qquad\qquad f \,\&\, w!\,p \xrightarrow{v?} f\ v\ 0$$

Call the resulting calculus TCBS'. In TCBS', processes are neither persistent nor ready. The calculus is otherwise very like TCBS. Now consider the definition

$$X\ \delta \overset{\text{def}}{=} \delta{:}\,([v,t]\text{if } \delta = t \text{ then } p/v \text{ else } X\,(\delta - t)\ \&\ \tau!\,p)$$

It is easy to see that

$$X\ (\delta + \varepsilon) \xrightarrow{\delta:} X\ \varepsilon \qquad X\ \delta \xrightarrow{\delta:} v?\,(p/v)\ \&\ \tau!\,p \qquad X\ \delta \xrightarrow{v?} X\ \delta$$

Since $p \approx v?\,(p/v)\ \&\ \tau!\,p$, it follows that $X\ \delta \approx \delta.p$. Thus delay can be derived upto weak bisimulation using time dependence.

The translation from time to priority in [Jef92a] is similar in spirit to the derivation of $\delta . P$ here.

Finally, a curious continuation of the connection between time and priority. This paper would appear to have shown that time is more expressive than priority. But in fact the features of TCBS' can be mimicked by a version of PCBS where processes hear not just the highest priority transmission but also its priority, i.e., the priority annotation is no longer treated as only for deriving transitions, but is made available to receiving processes.

8 Examples

First, note that all the examples in [Pra95] of CBS are (degenerate) examples of TCBS. So are the prioritised examples, by reading priority as time. The main new techniqes is that time-outs can be used to detect termination.

Several simple protocols have been written and simulated in TCBS. Space does not permit their inclusion. The following brief description should give a taste of what is possible.

Example 1 Distributed search: Root of a monotonic function. Let **R** be the set of real numbers. Given a monotonically increasing function $f: \mathbf{R} \to \mathbf{R}$, and a $y: \mathbf{R}$, binary search is a sequential way to find the x within a given range such that $f\,x = y$ upto a desired accuracy. (If there is no such x, the program loops).

It is easy to parallelise the search by dividing the range into n sections. Let the process p_k compute $f\,x_k$, where x_k is the midpoint of the k'th. section. When p_k is done computing fx_k, it reports this value, and the range is adjusted. This may result in some processes finding that they are no longer in the range. For example, if p_k reports a positive value for $f\,x_k$, then the root is less than x_k, and all process p_l with $l > k$ abandon their current computation, and start a fresh one.

This description assumes computations can be interrupted. Otherwise, each round of computation has all processes ready to report, and all but the two nearest the root will find that they have completed a useless computation. So processes come up for communication several times during a computation, which is divided into grain sized bits. If a process has nothing to report for that round, it waits. If it does have something to say, it will to do so, unless it hears a better value.

The program is ommitted for lack of space. It has been run on a quasi-parallel implementation [RW93] of Haskell, which allows interesting experiments showing the effects of changing n and the grain.

9 Conclusions

This is a working paper, with many loose ends. However, it appears clear that the concepts proposed for TCBS are new and interesting. They are therefore reported here in preliminary form.

The main conclusions are as follows. Time is added easily to CBS, and significantly extends its power. The transition system for TCBS yields only those transitions that can actually take place.

TCBS is simple because only autonomous actions need be considered when deciding which process should act next. These actions are distinct and audible. By contrast, it is precisely the fact that there is only one autonomous action in CCS, and further that this action is the result of communication, that makes it difficult to add time to it. Negative premises are needed more or less explicitly.

Strong and weak bisimulations in TCBS are congruences, and yield observationally meaningful equivalences.

Time can be read consistently as priority. Delay can be derived from timeout upto weak bisimulation in a calculus with time dependence.

TCBS has an expansion theorem even if time is dense. This and other aspects of TCBS cast light, by contrast, on calculi with handshake communication.

Further work. Several gaps have been indicated in the paper. Various extensions of the calculus presented here have been tried; a stable version has yet to be reached incorporating all the avenues explored. Apart from this, work is in progress to move TCBS implementations to parallel implementations of Haskell. The simulator for untimed CBS has been proved correct w.r.t. the operational semantics of the language, as part of a project to develop proof methods for CBS programs. See [HPP95, AHP95] for some aspects. This work needs to be extended to TCBS.

References

[AHP95]   Jörgen Andersen, Ed Harcourt, and K.V.S. Prasad. A machine verified sorting algorithm. Preliminary version, 1995.

[CH90]   Rance Cleaveland and Matthew Hennessy. Priorities in process algebras. *Information and Computation*, 87, 1990.

[CW91]   Juanito Camilleri and Glynn Winskel. CCS with priority choice. In *Symposium on Logic in Computer Science*. IEEE, 1991.

[GL92]   Jens Chr. Godskesen and Kim G. Larsen. Real-time calculi and expansion theorems. In *FST&TCS'92*, 1992. Springer Verlag LNCS 652.

[Hen92]   Matthew Hennessy. Timed process algebras: a tutorial. In *Marktoberdorf Summer School on process design calculi*, 1992.

[HPP95]   Ed Harcourt, Pawel Paczkowski, and K.V.S. Prasad. A framework for representing value-passing parametric processes. Preliminary version, 1995.

[HR90]   Matthew Hennessy and Tim Regan. A temporal process algebra. Computer Science Internal Report 2/90, University of Sussex, 1990.

[Jef92a] Alan Jeffrey. *Observation Spaces and Timed Processes*. D.phil, Oxford University, 1992.

[Jef92b] Alan Jeffrey. Translating timed process algebra into prioritised process algebra. In *Nijmegen Symposium on Real-Time and Fault-Tolerant Systems*, 1992.

[LY93]   Kim Larsen and Wang Yi. Time abstracted bisimulation: Implicit specifications and decidability. In *Mathematical Foundations of Programming Semantics*, 1993.

[Mil89]   Robin Milner. *Communication and Concurrency*. Prentice Hall, 1989.

[Pra93]   K. V. S. Prasad. Programming with broadcasts. In *CONCUR*, August 1993. Springer Verlag LNCS 715.

[Pra94]   K. V. S. Prasad. Broadcasting with priority. In *ESOP*, April 1994. Springer Verlag LNCS 788.

[Pra95]   K. V. S. Prasad. A calculus of broadcasting systems. *Science of Computer Programming*, 25, 1995.

[RW93]   C. Runciman and D. Wakeling. Profiling parallelism. Internal report, Department of Computer Science, University of York, 1993.

[Yi90]   Wang Yi. Real time behaviour of asynchronous agents. In *CONCUR'90*, 1990. Springer Verlag LNCS 458.

[Yi91]   Wang Yi. *A Calculus of Real Time Systems*. PhD thesis, Chalmers University of Technology, June 1991.

Semantics of a Higher-Order Coordination Language

Matthias Radestock and Susan Eisenbach

Department of Computing
Imperial College of Science, Technology and Medicine
180 Queen's Gate, London SW7 2BZ
E-mail: {mr3,se}@doc.ic.ac.uk

Abstract. A distributed program can be viewed as a composition of three parts. Firstly, there is a coordination part which provides a hierarchical structure of components with dynamic binding. Secondly, there is the actual communication part which provides the interaction and synchronisation required by the system. Finally, there is the computation part providing the component programs.

Darwin is a language for describing distributed configurations in terms of component types, their instantiation to components with interfaces and the binding of those interfaces. A Darwin program thus defines a class of configurations. Although the language is very small it contains second-order constructs: component types can appear as parameters in the instantiation of other component types. Furthermore Darwin provides support for dynamic run-time instantiation of components. Component types therefore must have a run-time representation.

The coordination part of a distributed program has to be closely associated with the communication and computation part, as only the combination of the three will yield the complete program. On the semantic level we can achieve this by using the same formal description technique for all three. The π-calculus can serve as such a technique. The higher-orderedness of the coordination language can be captured by using the higher-order π-calculus. The semantics gives a precise meaning to Darwin programs. It turns out that by using the higher-order π-calculus this semantics can be expressed in a very concise and clear manner.

1   Introduction

The behaviour of an executing program should not come as a surprise to the writer of that program. Yet with programs that run on parallel and distributed systems, it is notoriously difficult to say with certainty what can be expected. Giving a formal specification of a programming language enables one to have that certainty; without a formal specification a language is defined by its compiler. Even with the best intentions several compilers for a language will lead to several variants. For any concurrent language designed to be implemented on very different architectures the importance of a formal language specification becomes paramount. But there is a problem with formality. Unless the world view that the formal system models is the same as that of the programming system it will be easier to execute a program than to prove useful properties about its behaviour. Therefore the underlying model that the specification language supports must be similar to that of the programming language.

The Darwin coordination language [3, 1, 2] is an interconnection language for defining configurations of programs in distributed systems. Darwin separates the description of the system structure from the algorithms used to describe individual processes. Thereby a process instantiation and reuse is permitted in different contexts. The separate structural description of the system is also of use during the design, construction, documentation and subsequent maintenance of a system. In essence, the structural description corresponds to the issue of *programming in the large* whereas the process description corresponds to *programming in the small*. The Darwin system grew out of Conic which has been used in large scale industrial projects[4]. An important characteristic of the Darwin system is that it enables systems to be configured dynamically.

Milner's π-calculus[6, 5] is designed to model concurrent computation consisting of processes which interact and whose configuration is changing. It does this by viewing a system as a collection of independent processes which may share communication links or bindings with other processes. Links have *names*. These names are the fundamental building blocks of the π-calculus.

In this paper we show that the π-calculus notions of processes and names have Darwin counterparts. Darwin is a higher-order language and derives much of its power from this higher-orderedness. It is therefore desirable for it to be captured in the semantics. However, attempts to define the semantics of such a language in terms of first-order definitions will either fail or produce complex definitions. The latter has a severe impact on the usefulness of the semantics for the analysis of programs. Fortunately the higher-orderedness in Darwin has a counterpart in the higher-orderedness of the higher-order π-calculus[9, 10]. This makes the higher-order π-calculus a good system for defining the semantics of Darwin. A further reason for choosing the π-calculus is the possibility of integrating the semantics of the coordination language with the semantics of the communication system and computational components of a distributed program. A π-calculus semantics of these has already been defined in our previous research[8]. The combination of the three will therefore enable us to define an integrated semantics for the whole distributed program.

2 Darwin

A distributed system consists of multiple concurrently executing and interacting computational components. The task of specifying the system as a collection of components with complex interconnection patterns quickly becomes unmanageable without the help of some structuring tools. The coordination language Darwin provides such a structuring tool. It has both a graphical and textual representation. Darwin allows distributed programs to be constructed from hierarchically structured specifications of components and their interconnections.

```
component Filter(int freq) {
    require in;
    provide out;
}
```

Fig. 1. Component type `Filter`

Composite components are constructed from the primitive computational components. Components interact by accessing services. This section gives a brief overview of Darwin.

2.1 Components and Services

Darwin views components in terms of both the services they provide to allow other components to interact with them and the services they require to interact with other components. For example, the component of Fig. 1 is a *filter* component which **requires** a single service *in* and **provides** a single service *out*. The diagrammatic convention used here is that filled in circles represent services provided by a component and empty circles represent services required by a component.

In general, a component may provide and require many services Provisions and requirements make up the *interface* of a component. It should be noted that the names of required and provided services are local to the component type specification. Components may be implemented and tested independently of the rest of the system of which they will form a part. This property is called *context independence* and permits the reuse of components during construction (through multiple instantiation) and simplifies replacement during maintenance. The example also illustrates the use of parameters of component types, e.g. *freq* in the example. These are passed to the underlying implementation of the component.

2.2 Composite Components

The primary purpose of the Darwin coordination language is to allow system architects to construct composite components from both basic computational components and other composite components. The resulting system is a hierarchically structured composite component which when elaborated at execution time results in a collection of concurrently (potentially distributed) executing computational component instances. Darwin is a declarative notation. Composite components are defined by declaring both the instances of other components they contain and the bindings between those components. Bindings, which associate the services required by one component with the services provided by others, can be visualised as filling in the empty circles of a component with the

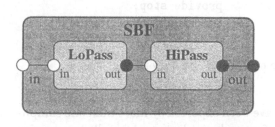

```
component SBF(int loFreq,
                int hiFreq) {
    require in;
    provide out;

    inst lo: LoPass(loFreq);
    inst hi: HiPass(hiFreq);

    bind lo.in -- in;
    bind hi.in -- lo.out;
    bind out    -- hi.out;
}
```

Fig. 2. Composite component type `SimpleBandFilter`

solid circles provided by other components. The example of Fig. 2 defines a band filter that is implemented in terms of a chain of a low pass filter and a high pass filter. The output of the low pass is bound to the input of the high pass. The **inst** statement is used for declaring sub-components.

Bindings between requirements and provisions are declared by the **bind** statement. Requirements which cannot be satisfied inside the component can be made visible at a higher level by binding them to an interface requirement as has been done in the example for the requirement *in* of the low pass which is bound to *in*. Similarly services provided internally which are required outside are bound to an interface service provision. In general, many requirements may be bound to a single provision. A particular requirement may be bound to a single provision only. It should be noted that a service may transmit or receive information or do both. The many requirements to a single provision binding pattern may thus describe either one-to-many or many-to-one communication depending on the interaction mechanism used to implement the service.

2.3 Name Server

Provisions and requirements can be **export**ed to and **import**ed from a *name server*. This feature of Darwin enables us to establish connections between program components and external components. The name-server can be viewed as a global name-space. Exported provisions are services that a component wants to make accessible to the outside world. To achieve this it *exports* the provision under a service description to the name server. The name server keeps track of all the exported provisions. Components in all programs connected to the name server can obtain access to these services by *importing* a handle from the name server. Imports are thus similar to requirements. To obtain the interface the requiring component queries the name server with a *service specification*. The name server will try to match this specification against the exported *service*

```
component Timer {                    component Stopwatch {
    export tick '1HzTick';               provide start;
}                                        provide stop;
                                         import seconds '1HzTick';
                                     }
```

Fig. 3. Example of exports and imports

descriptions. The same service can have been exported by more than one component and the name server must therefore make a selection. A handle to a service will be returned or the import will fail if there is no matching service known to the name server. The matching and selection policies can be arbitrarily complex, for instance by incorporating quality of service parameters. In the simplest case the matching function is *equality*, i.e. the required service specification has to be equal to the provided service description. The selection policy can just be random choice. A simple implementation may just queue requests for unavailable services until they become available.

In the example in Fig. 3 a `StopWatch` component is implemented by using a system `Timer` component that exports a 1Hz signal under the service description `1HzTick`. The two components could be part of different Darwin programs.

2.4 Generic Component Types

Darwin allows the specification of component type parameters that hold component types. Typically this is employed for achieving a higher degree of implementation flexibility – instead of having fixed component types for sub-components the types can be determined at the instantiation of the component, thus making the component type definition generic. The example in Fig. 4 illustrates this.

The `BandFilter` component type defines components that are capable of filtering out a frequency range of some input signal. If the lower bound of the frequency range is less or equal than the higher bound the filter will filter out all frequencies in that range. Otherwise it will filter out all frequencies outside that range. The filtering is accomplished by a combination of a low-pass and high-pass filter `LoPass` and `HiPass`. The types of these filters are determined by the context, thus enabling the configuration of `BandFilter` components with various implementations of filters. We could instantiate `BandFilter` with

```
    inst filter:BandFilter(LoPass1,HiPass1,10,20) .
```

The component type specified in the parameter declaration (in this case `Filter`) is required for static type checking – only component types with the same interface can be passed in.

Darwin is a higher-order language because it provides the ability to have component types as parameters to other component types. The example also shows how conditionals can be used in Darwin to create alternative configurations. Much of the expressive power of Darwin is derived from a combination of

```
component LoPass1(                component BandFilter(
   int freq) {                      component(Filter) LoPass,
                                     component(Filter) HiPass,
   require in;                       int loFreq, int hiFreq) {
   provide out;
}                                    require in;
                                     provide out;
component HiPass1(
   int freq) {                       inst lo: LoPass(loFreq);
                                     inst hi: HiPass(hiFreq);
   require in;
   provide out;                      when loFreq <= hiFreq {
}                                       inst mix: Mixer;
                                        bind lo.in    -- in;
component Mixer {                        bind hi.in    -- in;
   require in1;                          bind mix.in1 -- lo.out;
   require in2;                          bind mix.in2 -- hi.out;
   provide out;                          bind out      -- mix.out;
}                                    }
                                     when loFreq > hiFreq {
                                        bind lo.in -- in;
                                        bind hi.in -- lo.out;
                                        bind out   -- hi.out;
                                     }
                                  }
```

Fig. 4. Composite component type `BandFilter`

these two features. It enables the definition of component types with a very high degree of flexibility and reusability.

3 Darwin in Higher-Order π-calculus

When devising a semantics for a language, in a particular specification language, it is advantageous to have a simple mapping between the various concepts of the two languages. This significantly reduces the complexity of the semantics and simplifies reasoning. We believe that Darwin and the higher-order π-calculus are two such languages. Once the conceptual mapping has been established devising the semantics is in most cases straightforward.

3.1 Components, Instantiation and Decomposition

A *component type* definition in Darwin can be mapped to a process definition in the higher-order π-calculus. *Parameters* of the component type are treated as process parameters to the process definition. This higher-orderedness it not needed for basic type parameters but it significantly simplifies their modelling. The processes passed in represent constants as Darwin doesn't have any language constructs for manipulating variables. The higher-orderedness *is* required for the modelling of component type parameters though because component types are represented as processes. Components are created from their component types by instantiating the latter. In higher-order π-calculus this is expressed as an application of the actual parameters to the process definition of the component type.

```
component A(int x, component(B) y) ...
```

would be translated into a process equation

$$A(X, Y) \stackrel{\mathrm{def}}{=} \dots$$

and an instantiation

```
inst a:A(p, q)
```

would be expressed as

$$A(P, Q) \ .$$

Darwin components can be decomposed. The *decomposition* is specified in the component type definition. The instantiation of such a component type will cause all sub-components to be instantiated from their respective component types. The behaviour of the component is determined by the parallel interaction of the behaviour of the sub-components via the 'glue' – the bindings between interfaces of these components. This form of decomposition is expressed in the higher-order π-calculus as a parallel composition of all the instantiations, thus emphasising the parallelism inherent in the sub-components creation and the parallel existence and operation of these components.

```
inst a:A(p, q); b:B(r)
```

inside a component type definition can be translated into

$$A(P, Q) \mid B(R) \ .$$

3.2 Control Structures and Expressions

The Darwin language contains a **when** control structure which is used to make the creation of sub-components and the binding of interfaces conditional upon parameters. The interface specified by a component type is constant. All instances of a component type will thus have the same interface but possibly a different internal structure. The **when** statement evaluates a Boolean expression. All the variables, constants and operators of such an expression can be represented as processes in the higher-order π-calculus. The conditional itself is expressed as a process expression parameterised by the Boolean expression process and the processes representing the 'true' and 'false' branches. Only the higher-ordered version of the π-calculus allows us to express these constructs in such an elegant way.

```
when r<0 { inst a:A(p, q); }
```

has a higher-order π-calculus equivalent of

$$When(LessThan(R, Zero), A(P,Q), 0) \ .$$

[12, 11] provide a more detailed investigation into the definition of Booleans, Boolean functions and other standard data types.

3.3 Interfaces and Bindings

The *provisions* of a component represent services provided by that component. Other components can use these services once they have acquired a handle to them. *Requirements* represent the intention of a component to acquire such a handle. They turn into handles once a *binding* to a provision has been established through Darwin. In the higher-order π-calculus provisions and requirements can be expressed as *bound* and *unbound* names respectively. Names get bound (i.e. the requirements turn into handles) as a result of a communication. We can thus express a binding as a communication between the process representing the providing component with the process representing the requiring component.

The requirements and provisions of a Darwin component are the only interface between a component and the outside. A component encapsulates its sub-components, thus preventing direct outside access to them. During the instantiation of a component type, elements (i.e. provisions or requirements) of the sub-component interfaces can be bound to elements of interfaces of other sub-components or to elements of the interface of the containing component. This special case of *third party binding* (where the container component is the third party) is the only type of binding supported by Darwin. However, interfaces do have a run-time representation and the run-time system may thus support other types of binding. The third party binding requires the binding party to know the two other parties. This can be achieved by making the interface of components part of the left hand side of the defining process equation, i.e. making the provisions and requirements part of the parameter list. The responsibility for creating provisions and requirements then lies with the container component which is always the binding component. It must therefore be able to determine the interface of a sub-component from its component type. Hence the interface must be component type specific rather than instance specific, i.e. all instances of a component type must have the same interface. In Darwin this is enforced by disallowing the use of control structures in the interface declaration part of a component type definition.

```
component B(int z) { provide x; require y, w; }
```

is represented as

$$B(Z, x', y', w') \stackrel{\text{def}}{=} (\nu\, x)(!\overline{x'}(x).0 \mid y'(y).w'(w).B'(Z, x, y, w)) \ .$$

Provisions and requirements are both turned into communication links. The communication takes place with the binding component which is also the component that instantiated the process. The provisions of a component are made known to the binding component by communicating them along their respective communication links. The replication operator ensures that a provision can be bound to any number of requirements. Components wait to receive bindings for their requirements from the binding component through the respective communication links. Once all these bindings have been establish the process proceeds. Only primitive components (i.e. components with no sub-components) define new provisions. The provisions of composite components are obtained from the bindings. Similarly composite components do not wait for their requirements to be bound but only forward those bindings to the sub-components when they occur. The instantiation of sub-components in the container component

```
inst b:B(r); c:B(s);
```

is translated into

$$(\nu\ x_b, y_b, w_b, x_c, y_c, w_c)(B(R, x_b, y_b, w_b)\ |\ B(S, x_c, y_c, w_c))\ .$$

A binding

```
bind b.y--c.x, b.w--c.x;
```

translates to

$$x_c(a).\overline{y_b}(a).0\ |\ x_c(a).\overline{w_b}(a).0\ .$$

Bindings to the interface of the binding component, as in

```
bind p--b.x, c.y--q, r--q; ,
```

where p, q, r are elements of the interface of the binding component, are expressed as

$$x_b(a).!\overline{p'}(a).0\ |\ q'(a).\overline{y_c}(a).0\ |\ q'(a).\overline{r'}(a).0$$

where p', q', r' are obtained from the parameter list of the process definition (cf. above). The ! replication operator ensures that the outside can make multiple bindings to the provision.

3.4 Exports and Imports

The higher-order π-calculus is well-suited for defining the behaviour of name servers. However, it might be too low level for describing complex matching and selection policies. Also the name server functionality is not defined in Darwin but rather by the particular implementation. It therefore has to be treated as a 'black box' with a well-defined interface. The simplest name server interface that still allows arbitrarily complex matching and selection policies, just contains the two methods *export* and *import*. Both methods are expected to succeed, i.e. a name server must (eventually) accept all exported provisions and imported requirements will be queued until a matching service becomes available. This precise definition of the interface enables the definition of the higher-order π-calculus semantics for the **export** and **import** clauses in Darwin.

```
export x 'service1'; import y 'service2';
```

is translated into

$$\overline{export}(x, service1).0 \mid (\nu\, c)(\overline{import}(c, service2).c(y).P)$$

where P is the translation of the remaining part of the surrounding component type definition. The names *export* and *import* are globally scoped and form the interface to the name-server.

The operational semantics of the π-calculus defines that a communication event takes place whenever there is an input and output along the same channel. The execution of processes is suspended until such matches occur. If there are several input and output requests along the same channel, pairs are selected nondeterministically. Comparing this semantic definition to our specification for a simple name-server above we can observe that some of the name server functionality is part of the π-calculus semantics. This isn't surprising as the calculus is name based. For the simple case we can therefore eliminate the explicit name server altogether and translate the above program fragment into

$$!\overline{service1}(x).0 \mid service2(y).P\ .$$

We use the exported names as communication channels and utilise the replication operator to ensure that exported provisions can be imported multiple times.

4   The Higher-Order π-calculus Semantics of Darwin

The translation from Darwin into higher-order π-calculus is carried out by the semantic function $\mathcal{P}$ :: Darwin $\to$ HOπ. In order to translate the instantiation of component types we require information about the types. As the type definitions can appear in any order in the program the translation requires two passes. The fist pass determines the signatures of all component types and is of type $\mathcal{S}'$ :: Darwin $\to$ {CSig}. The signature contains all the formal parameters of a component type, and its interfaces and its type is thus CSig = (CName, [(TNAME, FName)], [PName], [RName]). The first field is the component type name, the second field is a list of formal parameter types and identifiers and the following fields are lists of names of provisions and requirements respectively. The second pass of the translation takes both the original Darwin program and the set of component type signatures and produces the higher-order π-calculus translation: $\mathcal{T}'$ :: Darwin $\to$ {CSig} $\to$ HOπ. The semantic function $\mathcal{P}$ is just

$$\mathcal{P}[\![p]\!] = \mathcal{T}'\, p\, (\mathcal{S}'\, p)\ .$$

Because there are two passes the processing of individual component type definitions can be carried out independently from each other. We can therefore rewrite $\mathcal{P}$ to

$$\mathcal{P}[\![p]\!] = \biguplus_{d \in D} d \text{ where } L = \mathcal{P}'[\![p]\!],\ \sigma = \mathsf{mapx}\ L\ (\lambda x.\mathcal{S}[\![x]\!]),$$
$$D = \mathsf{mapx}\ L\ (\lambda x.\mathcal{T}[\![x]\!]_\sigma)$$

$$S\left[\!\!\left[\begin{array}{l}\textbf{component}\\ c(t_1\ f_1, t_2\ f_2, \ldots, t_n\ f_n)\{B\}\end{array}\right]\!\!\right] = \begin{array}{l}(c, [(t_1, f_1), (t_2, f_2), \ldots, (t_n, f_n)], I_p, I_r)\\ \text{where } (\_, \_, I_p, I_r) = S[B]\end{array}$$

$$S[\textbf{provide } p; B] = \begin{array}{l}(\bot, \bot, [p] +\!\!+ I_p, I_r)\\ \text{where } (\_, \_, I_p, I_r) = S[B]\end{array}$$

$$S[\textbf{require } r; B] = \begin{array}{l}(\bot, \bot, I_p, [r] +\!\!+ I_r)\\ \text{where } (\_, \_, I_p, I_r) = S[B]\end{array}$$

$$S[x] = \begin{array}{l}(\bot, \bot, [], [])\\ \text{where } x \text{ is any Darwin construct}\end{array}$$

Fig. 5. Semantic function for the first pass

where $\uplus$ is a textual concatenation operator that combines individual higher-order π-calculus process definitions into one big higher-order π-calculus-'program'. The higher-order function mapx maps a function over the elements of a set or list. The function S has the type $S :: \mathsf{CTDef} \to \mathsf{CSig}$ and T has the type $T :: \mathsf{CTDef} \to \{\mathsf{CSig}\} \to \mathsf{HO}\pi$, i.e. they both translate a single component type definition. T produces a single defining equation in higher-order π-calculus for a component type definition. $P' :: \mathsf{Darwin} \to \{\mathsf{CTDef}\}$ is a simple parsing function that turns a Darwin program into a set of component type definitions. We can define it as

$$P'[\![ctdef]\!] = \{ctdef\}$$
$$P'[\![prog_1\ prog_2]\!] = P'[\![prog_1]\!] \cup P'[\![prog_2]\!]$$

since a Darwin program is a sequence of component type definitions and the smallest program contains just one such definition.

4.1 First Pass

The first pass of the translation of Darwin into higher-order π-calculus is accomplished by a semantic function (Fig. 5) that extracts the names of the formal parameters, provisions and requirements from a component type definition. The information is returned in a tuple of type CSig. The component type name and the names of the formal parameters can be obtained easily from the head of a component type declaration. For the names of provisions and requirements we have to scan the body of the declarations for **provide** and **require** clauses. As the interface declaration of a component type is the first part of the declaration body we terminate the function once we encounter a different Darwin construct. As a simplification we assume that the **provide** and **require** statements as well as **export**, **import**, **bind** and **inst** below only take one argument. The actual Darwin statements can normally take a list of arguments, e.g. **provide** p, q, r;. The expressiveness of Darwin doesn't suffer from this simplification as we can always transform such a statement into a list of statements, e.g. **provide** p; **provide** q; **provide** r;.

The ++ operator in the definition is the list concatenation operator. The names must be stored in lists rather than sets as during the second pass of the translation the elements will be identified by their position. Applying S to the BandFilter component from Fig. 4 we get the following result:

$$
S \begin{bmatrix} \begin{bmatrix} \texttt{component BandFilter(} \\ \texttt{component(Filter) LoPass,} \\ \texttt{component(Filter) HiPass,} \\ \texttt{int loFreq, int hiFreq)} \\ \texttt{\{...\}} \end{bmatrix} \end{bmatrix} = \begin{array}{l} (BandFilter, [\\ (\texttt{component(Filter)}, LoPass), \\ (\texttt{component(Filter)}, HiPass), \\ (\texttt{int}, loFreq), (\texttt{int}, hiFreq)], \\ [out], [in]) \end{array}
$$

4.2 Second Pass

The second pass of the translation is subdivided into two stages. The first stage splits the component type definition into a header and body part and extracts the header information containing all elements of the signature plus the exports and imports. Information provided by the first pass is only needed for the second stage which from the extracted header information, the definition body and the set of component type signatures generates a defining higher-order π-calculus equation for the component type.

$$
\mathcal{T}[\![c]\!]_\sigma = \mathcal{C}[\![b]\!]_\sigma(s) \text{ where } (s, b) = \mathcal{H}[\![c]\!]
$$

The first and second stage are represented by the semantic functions $\mathcal{H}$ :: CTDef $\rightarrow$ (CSig′, Darwin) and $\mathcal{C}$ :: Darwin $\rightarrow$ {CSig} $\rightarrow$ CSig′ $\rightarrow$ HOπ where CSig′ = (CSig, {(SName, PName)}, {(SName, RName)}). Unlike the names of the provisions and requirements in the signature, the exports and imports can be kept in a set rather than a list, because they're always referred to by name rather than by index. Each element of the set is a pair containing the service name and the name of the exported/imported provision/requirement.

First and Second Stage The definition of $\mathcal{H}$ (Fig. 6) resembles that of S (Fig. 5). As the component type definition of BandFilter (Fig. 4) doesn't include any exports or imports the application of $\mathcal{H}$ yields

$$
\mathcal{H} \begin{bmatrix} \begin{bmatrix} \texttt{component BandFilter(} \\ \texttt{component(Filter) LoPass,} \\ \texttt{component(Filter) HiPass,} \\ \texttt{int loFreq, int hiFreq)} \\ \texttt{\{...\}} \end{bmatrix} \end{bmatrix} = \begin{array}{l} ((BandFilter, [\\ (\texttt{component(Filter)}, LoPass), \\ (\texttt{component(Filter)}, HiPass), \\ (\texttt{int}, loFreq), (\texttt{int}, hiFreq)], \\ [out], [in]), \{\}, \{\}, \\ \texttt{inst lo: LoPass(loFreq);} ...) \end{array}
$$

The semantic function $\mathcal{C}$ (Fig. 7) translates the header information and embeds the translation of the remaining definition body. The latter is carried

$$\mathcal{H}\left[\!\!\left[\begin{matrix} \textbf{component} \\ c(t_1\ f_1, t_2\ f_2, \ldots, t_n\ f_n) \\ \{B\} \end{matrix}\right]\!\!\right] = \begin{matrix} ((c, [(t_1, f_1), (t_2, f_2), \ldots, (t_n, f_n)], \\ I_p, I_r), I_e, I_i, b) \\ \text{where } ((\_, \_, I_p, I_r), I_e, I_i, b) = \mathcal{H}[\![B]\!] \end{matrix}$$

$$\mathcal{H}[\![\textbf{provide } p; B]\!] = \begin{matrix} ((\bot, \bot, [p] \,+\!\!+ I_p, I_r), I_e, I_i, b) \\ \text{where } ((\_, \_, I_p, I_r), I_e, I_i, b) = \mathcal{H}[\![B]\!] \end{matrix}$$

$$\mathcal{H}[\![\textbf{require } r; B]\!] = \begin{matrix} ((\bot, \bot, I_p, [r] \,+\!\!+ I_r), I_e, I_i, b) \\ \text{where } ((\_, \_, I_p, I_r), I_e, I_i, b) = \mathcal{H}[\![B]\!] \end{matrix}$$

$$\mathcal{H}[\![\textbf{export } p\ s; B]\!] = \begin{matrix} ((\bot, \bot, I_p, I_r), \{(p, s)\} \cup I_e, I_i, b) \\ \text{where } ((\_, \_, I_p, I_r), I_e, I_i, b) = \mathcal{H}[\![B]\!] \end{matrix}$$

$$\mathcal{H}[\![\textbf{import } r\ s; B]\!] = \begin{matrix} ((\bot, \bot, I_p, I_r), I_i, \{(r, s)\} \cup I_i, b) \\ \text{where } ((\_, \_, I_p, I_r), I_e, I_i, b) = \mathcal{H}[\![B]\!] \end{matrix}$$

$$\mathcal{H}[\![x; B]\!] = \begin{matrix} ((\bot, \bot, [], []), \{\}, \{\}, x; b) \\ \text{where } (\_, \_, \_, b) = \mathcal{H}[\![B]\!] \\ \text{where } x \text{ is any Darwin construct} \end{matrix}$$

$$\mathcal{H}[\![x]\!] = \begin{matrix} ((\bot, \bot, [], []), \{\}, \{\}, x) \\ \text{where } x \text{ is any Darwin construct} \end{matrix}$$

Fig. 6. Semantic function for the first stage of the second pass

out by the semantic function $\mathcal{B}$ (Fig. 8). We use a Roman font for literal π-calculus names, e.g. C and F. The indices are variables that will be replaced with their real values, e.g. F_{f_1} will turn into F_{param1} if f_1 gets bound to **param1** in the equation. The equation in Fig. 7 may seem complicated, but the generated higher-order π-calculus definitions are actually rather small, as the **Filter** example illustrates:

$$C_{\text{Filter}}(F_{\text{freq}}, \text{out}', \text{in}') \overset{\text{def}}{=} (\nu\ \text{out})(!\overline{\text{out}'}(\text{out}).\mathbf{0}\ | \\ \text{in}'(\text{in}).C_{\text{Filter}}{}'(F_{\text{freq}}, \text{out}, \text{in}))$$

The definition of $\mathcal{C}$ captures the distinction between primitive and composite components in Darwin. A component is primitive if and only if the body of the component type definition contains only **provide, require, export** and **import** statements. As the first stage of the second pass parses exactly those constructs the second stage is invoked with an empty remaining component type definition body, denoted by $\bot$. The semantic function produces a reference to a process definition C'_c with the same signature as the process definition of the component type. C'_c identifies the π-calculus translation of the computational part of the primitive component. From the definition we can see that provisions, exports and imports are treated in parallel while requirements form a sequential composition. This is to ensure that the required names are bound in the remainder of the formula. The computational part of a primitive component is only invoked

$$C[\![b]\!]_\sigma(s) = C_c(F_{f_1}, F_{f_2}, \ldots, F_{f_{n_f}}, {p_1}', {p_2}', \ldots, {p_{n_p}}', {r_1}', {r_2}', \ldots, {r_{n_r}}') \stackrel{\text{def}}{=}$$

if $b = \perp$ then $(\nu\, p_1, p_2, \ldots, p_{n_p})(!\overline{{p_1}'}(p_1).0 \mid !\overline{{p_2}'}(p_2).0 \mid \ldots \mid !\overline{{p_{n_p}}'}(p_{n_p}).0 \mid$

$\qquad\qquad {e_1}'(x).!\overline{{e_1'}}(x).0 \mid {e_2}'(x).!\overline{{e_2'}}(x).0 \mid \ldots \mid {e_{n_e}}'(x).!\overline{{e_{n_e}'}}(x).0 \mid$

$\qquad\qquad {i_1}'(x).!\overline{{i_1'}}(x).0 \mid {i_2}'(x).!\overline{{i_2'}}(x).0 \mid \ldots \mid {i_{n_e}}'(x).!\overline{{i_{n_e}'}}(x).0 \mid$

$\qquad\qquad {r_1}'(r_1).{r_2}'(r_2).\ \ldots\ .{r_{n_r}}'(r_{n_r}).$

$\qquad\qquad C_c'(F_{f_1}, F_{f_2}, \ldots, F_{f_{n_f}}, p_1, p_2, \ldots, p_{n_p}, r_1, r_2, \ldots, r_{n_r}))$

$\quad$ else $\ {e_1}'(x).!\overline{{e_1'}}(x).0 \mid {e_1}'(x).!\overline{{e_2'}}(x).0 \mid \ldots \mid {e_{n_e}}'(x).!\overline{{e_{n_e}'}}(x).0 \mid$

$\qquad\qquad {i_1}'(x).!\overline{{i_1'}}(x).0 \mid {i_2}'(x).!\overline{{i_2'}}(x).0 \mid \ldots \mid {i_{n_e}}'(x).!\overline{{i_{n_e}'}}(x).0 \mid$

$\qquad\qquad B[\![b]\!]_\sigma(s)$

where $((c, [(t_1, f_1), (t_2, f_2), \ldots, (t_{n_f}, f_{n_f})], [p_1, p_2, \ldots, p_{n_p}], [r_1, r_2, \ldots, r_{n_r}]),$
$\qquad\quad \{(e_1', e_1), (e_2', e_2), \ldots, (e_{n_e}', e_{n_e})\}, \{(i_1', i_1), (i_2', i_2), \ldots, (i_{n_i}', i_{n_i})\}) = s$

Fig. 7. Semantic function for the second stage of the second pass

after all requirements have been bound, i.e. turned into handles. In case the component is composite the translation of the remaining definition body is processed in parallel with the exports and imports. Requirements are bound inside the translation of the definition body – and only if they are used in a binding. This ensures that the instantiation of component types doesn't get 'stuck' in cases where requirements are bound to provisions of the same component.

Translation of the Definition Body B :: Darwin $\to$ {CSig} $\to$ CSig$'$ $\to$ HOπ (Fig. 8) uses the ideas about the mapping of concepts from Darwin to higher-order π-calculus (cf. Sect. 3) in order to translate the remainder of the component type definition body. The most complicated of the defining equations is the one relating to the instantiation of component types. It is the place where the higher-orderedness of the higher-order π-calculus is needed in order to obtain a concise and intuitive definition.

It would be sufficient to pass in the component type name instead of the CSig$'$ structure s. We could then lookup the signature in σ. However, we would then not be able to verify whether an element in a **bind** statement has been correctly declared as a provision, requirement or import, as CSig doesn't contain information about exports and imports. Furthermore it would obscure what σ is *actually* needed for – to lookup the signatures of component types that are being instantiated.

There is the special case that the component type in the **inst** statement is not specified as a type identifier but is contained in a variable that has been passed in as a parameter to the current component. We identify this case by checking whether the component type part of the **inst** statement is contained in the parameter list of the current component type. The latter is obtained from

$$\mathcal{B}\left[\!\!\left[\begin{array}{l}\textbf{inst } c{:}t(e_1, e_2, \\ \ldots, e_n);\ B\end{array}\right]\!\!\right]_\sigma(s) = (\nu\, p_{1_c}, p_{2_c}, \ldots, p_{i_c}, r_{1_c}, r_{2_c}, \ldots, r_{j_c})$$
$$(C(a_1, a_2, \ldots, a_n, p_{1_c}, p_{2_c}, \ldots p_{i_c},$$
$$r_{1_c}, r_{2_c}, \ldots r_{j_c})|\mathcal{B}[\![B]\!]_\sigma(s))$$
$$\text{where } (t', \text{-}, [p_1, p_2, \ldots, p_i], [r_1, r_2, \ldots, r_j]) \in \sigma$$
$$t' = \text{if } t \in Q \text{ then } t'' \text{ else } t$$
$$(\mathbf{component}(t''), t) \in P$$
$$\{(t_1, f_1), (t_2, f_2), \ldots, (t_m, f_m)\} = P$$
$$Q = \{f_1, f_2, \ldots, f_m\}$$
$$C = \text{if } t \in Q \text{ then } \mathrm{F}_t \text{ else } \mathrm{C}_t$$
$$((\text{-}, P, \text{-}, \text{-}), \text{-}, \text{-}) = s$$
$$[a_1, a_2, \ldots, a_n] = \mathbf{mapx}\ [e_1, e_2, \ldots e_n]$$
$$(\lambda x.\mathcal{E}[\![x]\!]P)$$

$$\mathcal{B}[\![\textbf{bind } c_1.r{-}c_2.p;\ B]\!]_\sigma(s) = p_{c_2}(x).\overline{r_{c_1}}(x).0 \mid \mathcal{B}[\![B]\!]_\sigma(s)$$

$$\mathcal{B}[\![\textbf{bind } p_0{-}c.p;\ B]\!]_\sigma(s) = p_c(x).!\overline{p_0'}(x).0 \mid \mathcal{B}[\![B]\!]_\sigma(s)$$

$$\mathcal{B}[\![\textbf{bind } c.r{-}r_0;\ B]\!]_\sigma(s) = r_0'(x).\overline{r_c}(x).0 \mid \mathcal{B}[\![B]\!]_\sigma(s)$$

$$\mathcal{B}[\![\textbf{bind } r{-}p;\ B]\!]_\sigma(s) = p'(x).\overline{r'}(x).0 \mid \mathcal{B}[\![B]\!]_\sigma(s)$$

$$\mathcal{B}\left[\!\!\left[\begin{array}{l}\textbf{when}\,expr \\ \{block\};\ B\end{array}\right]\!\!\right]_\sigma(s) = \begin{array}{l}\mathrm{When}(\mathcal{E}[\![expr]\!]P, \mathcal{B}[\![block;B]\!]_\sigma(s), \mathcal{B}[\![B]\!]_\sigma(s)) \\ \text{where } ((\text{-}, P, \text{-}, \text{-}), \text{-}, \text{-}) = s\end{array}$$

Fig. 8. semantic function for the translation of the definition body

the CSig′ structure s. We use the signature of the component type specified in the type part of the parameter for determining the parameters of the instantiation. The higher-order π-calculus parameter identifier F_t is used for identifying the process to be instantiated. The higher-ordered constructs of the calculus are employed, because F_t is a *process variable* inside the process of the current component type which gets bound by the instantiation of that type. The instantiation parameters can be C expressions. $\mathcal{E}$ evaluates these expressions in order to obtain the values for the actual parameters.

The **bind** statement occurs in four variations and the semantic function accordingly has a defining equation for each of them. Finally there is the semantics of the **when** statement where *When* is the name of process that takes three processes as an argument. The first process is expected to represent a Boolean. If it is *true*, *When* evolves into the process specified in the second argument. Otherwise it evolves into the process specified by the third argument.

In applying C and $\mathcal{B}$ to the **BandFilter** component type we obtain its defining equation. For sake of clarity we have split the definition into four equations and

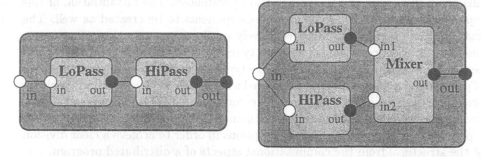

Fig. 9. Possible configurations of `BandFilter` components

carried out some optimisation on the processing of the **when** statements:

$$C_{\text{BandFilter}}(F_{\text{LoPass}}, F_{\text{HiPass}}, \overset{\text{def}}{=} (\nu\, \text{out}_{\text{lo}}, \text{in}_{\text{lo}})(F_{\text{LoPass}}(F_{\text{loFreq}}, \text{out}_{\text{lo}}, \text{in}_{\text{lo}}) \mid$$
$$F_{\text{loFreq}}, F_{\text{hiFreq}}, \qquad (\nu\, \text{out}_{\text{hi}}, \text{in}_{\text{hi}})(F_{\text{HiPass}}(F_{\text{hiFreq}}, \text{out}_{\text{hi}}, \text{in}_{\text{hi}}) \mid$$
$$\text{out}', \text{in}') \qquad \text{When}(\text{LessThanOrEqual}(F_{\text{loFreq}}, F_{\text{hiFreq}}),$$
$$C^1_{\text{BandFilter}}, C^2_{\text{BandFilter}})))$$

$$C^1_{\text{BandFilter}} \overset{\text{def}}{=} (\nu\, \text{out}_{\text{mix}}, \text{in1}_{\text{mix}}, \text{in2}_{\text{mix}})(C_{\text{Mixer}}(\text{out}_{\text{mix}}, \text{in1}_{\text{mix}}, \text{in2}_{\text{mix}}) \mid$$
$$\text{in}'(x).\overline{\text{in}_{\text{lo}}}(x).0 \mid \text{in}'(x).\overline{\text{in}_{\text{hi}}}(x).0 \mid$$
$$\text{out}_{\text{lo}}(x).\overline{\text{in1}_{\text{mix}}}(x).0 \mid \text{out}_{\text{hi}}(x).\overline{\text{in2}_{\text{mix}}}(x).0 \mid$$
$$\text{out}_{\text{mix}}(x).!\overline{\text{out}'}(x).0 \mid C^2_{\text{BandFilter}})$$

$$C^2_{\text{BandFilter}} \overset{\text{def}}{=} \text{When}(\text{GreaterThan}(F_{\text{loFreq}}, F_{\text{hiFreq}}), C^3_{\text{BandFilter}}, 0)$$

$$C^3_{\text{BandFilter}} \overset{\text{def}}{=} \text{in}'(x).\overline{\text{in}_{\text{lo}}}(x).0 \mid \text{out}_{\text{lo}}(x).\overline{\text{in}_{\text{hi}}}(x).0 \mid$$
$$\text{out}_{\text{hi}}(x).!\overline{\text{out}'}(x).0 \mid 0$$

5 Configurations

The Darwin compiler translates a Darwin specification (i.e. the coordination part of a program) into a language that can relate both to the process definitions of the primitive components (i.e. the computation part) and a run-time system specification (i.e. the communication part). Linked together they form an executable program. The Darwin specification and process definitions are parameterised. A Darwin program specifies a *class* of possible actual *configurations*. Initial parameters supplied at program startup determine which of these configurations will be established. For instance the instantiation of the `BandFilter` component type from Fig. 4 could result in two structurally different configurations (Fig. 9).

A configuration is created from a Darwin program by instantiating exactly one component type. The execution parameters supplied to the program identify this component type and its instantiation parameters. The instantiation of this top-level component will cause its sub-components to be created as well. The instantiation process continues recursively until component types of *primitive components* are encountered. These are types of non-composite components and hence they only specify interfaces. Unlike types for composite components, types of primitive components can be associated with *behaviour descriptions*, which are programs that during its execution can communicate with other programs along the bound interfaces of the primitive components. The behaviour descriptions are separated from the configuration descriptions in order to achieve a clear division of the structural from the computational aspects of a distributed program.

The execution of a Darwin program can thus be divided into two stages – instantiation and computation. *Instantiation* creates a configuration from a Darwin program and *computation* is the execution of programs associated with the primitive components in the thus established configuration. These programs communicate with each other using system and application domain specific Darwin communication libraries. Ultimately we are interested in the semantics of configurations because they, in combination with the communication and computation part, determine the behaviour of a program. The higher-order π-calculus semantics of Darwin is executable by applying the rewrite rules of the π-calculus. This elaboration covers the instantiation stage of a program and results in a configuration description, thus providing a smooth transition to the second stage of the execution.

6 Summary and Future Work

We have shown how the semantics of a coordination language can be defined in an elegant and concise way by using the higher-order π-calculus. The higher-orderedness of Darwin has been captured by using higher-order constructs of the calculus. A common problem when defining the semantics of a language is that concepts of the language are lost or at least not readily visible on the semantic level. However, we found a close correspondence between Darwin and higher-order π-calculus. The semantics can therefore retain many of the concepts of the language. Darwin is a language for describing configurations, i.e. *structural* aspects of a distributed application. Darwin programs make this structure explicit. The same can be said about the higher-order π-calculus semantics. This significantly simplifies reasoning on the semantic level. We are currently investigating this opportunity by employing automated tools such as PICT[7].

A further feature of the semantics is that it can be executed by applying the rewrite rules of the calculus. Execution means instantiation of a component type. The result is a configuration, described in terms of the higher-order π-calculus. This enables the integration of the semantics of the configuration, communication and computation part of a program, because the semantics of the latter two has been defined in terms of the π-calculus already (cf. [8]). Consequently the entire distributed application, with all it's aspects can be given a unified higher-order π-calculus semantics. We can reason about each part separately or in conjunction with the other parts. Because the calculus is executable we can even use it for simulation and experimental implementation of applications. This is particularly important for investigating the impact of changes in the coordination language or the communications system on the execution of a program. We are planning to use PICT and other higher-order π-calculus tools for that purpose.

7 Acknowledgements

We gratefully acknowledge the advice and help provided by the Distributed Software Engineering Research Section at the Imperial College Department of Computing, and the financial support provided by the EPSRC under grant ref: GR/K73282.

References

1. S. Eisenbach and R. Paterson. π-calculus semantics for the concurrent configuration language darwin. In *Proc. of the 26th Annual Hawaii Int. Conf. on System Sciences*, volume 2. IEEE Computer Society Press, 1993.
2. J. Kramer, J. Magee, M. Sloman, and N. Dulay. Configuring object-based distributed programs in REX. *IEE Software Engineering Journal*, 7(2):139–149, March 1992.
3. J. Magee, J. Kramer, and N. Dulay. Darwin/mp: An environment for parallel and distributed programming. In *Proc. of the 26th Annual Hawaii Int. Conf. on System Sciences*, volume 2. IEEE Computer Society Press, 1993.
4. J. Magee, J. Kramer, and M. Sloman. Constructing distributed programs in conic. *IEEE Transactions on Software Engineering*, 15(6), 1989.
5. R. Milner. The polyadic π-calculus: a tutorial. Technical Report ECS-LFCS 91-180, University of Edinburgh, October 1991.
6. Robin Milner, Joachim Parrow, and David Walker. A calculus of mobile processes, I and II. *Information and Computation*, 100:1–77, 1992. Also as Tech. Rep. ECS-LFCS 89-85/86, University of Edinburgh.
7. Benjamin Pierce, Didier Rémy, and David Turner. PICT: A typed, higher-order concurrent programming language based on the π-calculus, 1994. Available by anonymous FTP from pub/bcp on ftp.dcs.ed.ac.uk.
8. M. Radestock and S. Eisenbach. What do you get from a π-calculus semantics? In *Proc. of PARLE'94 Parallel Architectures and Languages Europe*, number 817 in Lecture Notes in Computer Science, pages 635–647. Springer-Verlag, 1994.
9. Davide Sangiorgi. From π-calculus to higher-order π-calculus – and back. Technical report, Computer Science Dept., University of Edinburgh, 1992.
10. Davide Sangiorgi. *Expressing Mobility in Process Algebras: First-Order and Higher-Order Paradigms*. PhD thesis, Computer Science Dept., University of Edinburgh, May 1993.
11. D. Walker. Some results on the π-calculus. In *Concurrency: Theory, Language, and Architecture*, Oxford, UK, September 1989.
12. D. Walker. π-calculus semantics of object-oriented programming languages. In *Conf. on Theoretical Aspects of Computer Software*, Tohoku University, Japan, September 1991.

Solving the Linda Multiple rd Problem

Antony Rowstron and Alan Wood*

Department of Computer Science, University of York,
York, YO1 5DD, UK.

Abstract. Linda is a co-ordination language that has been used for
many years. From our recent work on the model we have found a simple
operation that is widely used in many different algorithms which the
Linda model is unable to express in a viable fashion. We examine a
function which performs the composition of two binary relations. By examining how to implement this in parallel using Linda we demonstrate
that the current methods are unacceptable. A more detailed explanation
of the problem, which we call the *multiple* rd *problem* is then presented, together with some other algorithms which have the same problem. We then show how the addition of a primitive to the Linda model,
copy-collect, extends the expressibility of the model to overcome this
problem. This work builds on previous work on the addition of another
primitive called collect[1]. The parallel composition of two binary relations is then reconsidered using copy-collect and is shown to be more
efficient.

1 Introduction

Linda is an asynchronous model of concurrency, which allows parallel programs
to be developed which are highly decoupled; in other words each process knows
little or nothing about the other processes during computation.

Whilst working on the implementation of parallel image processing algorithms
in Linda[2] it became clear that the Linda model was unable to support a certain operation, which we will refer to as the *multiple* rd *problem*. The operation
however is one whose existence is often needed in parallel algorithms, where
information is stored in tuple spaces for many processes to non-destructively
access in parallel.

In order to demonstrate the problem we focus on the implementation of
several algorithms to perform the composition of two binary relations. However,
before considering the example, a brief overview of Linda is presented.

2 The Linda Model

The Linda model is described in detail in many papers[3]. The Linda Model
is intended to be an abstraction, and as such is independent of any specific
machine architecture. This has meant that alternatives and extensions to the

---

* {ant,wood}@minster.york.ac.uk

basic Linda model have been proposed and investigated. The extensions that are used currently in the York Linda kernel[4] are:

multiple tuple spaces The addition of multiple tuple spaces has been discussed for some time. Schemes based on hierarchies of tuple spaces have been suggested[5, 6], which involve the concept of active and frozen tuple spaces. The addition of multiple tuple spaces is achieved by incorporating a `tuple space` type and a primitive to create a new tuple space. For instance in ISETL-Linda[7], a type `bag` represents a tuple space, and the primitive `NewBag` creates values of type `bag`.

collect primitive A new tuple-space primitive, `collect`[1]. This primitive by its very nature requires multiple tuple spaces. Given two tuple space handles (`ts1` and `ts2`) and a tuple `template`, then `collect(ts1, ts2, template)` moves tuples that match `template` in `ts1` to `ts2`, returning a count of the number of tuples transferred.

3 Parallel Composition of Two Binary Relations

3.1 Introduction

In order to demonstrate the multiple `rd` problem, we will consider the implementation of an algorithm for the parallel composition of two binary relations. We will use a strategy that appears natural to the problem, and then consider how to implement it to overcome the multiple `rd` problem.

A binary relation is defined to be a set of ordered pairs. Given two binary relations, S and R, their composition, $R \circ S$, is defined to be:

$$\{(a, b) \mid (a, x) \in R \text{ and } (x, b) \in S\}$$

We assume that the elements of each set are held in separate tuple spaces, with each tuple representing an ordered pair. After performing the composition, a new tuple space will be created containing the resulting tuples. This is demonstrated in Figure 1.

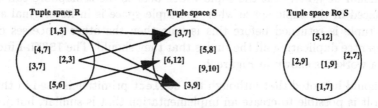

Fig. 1. Composition performed between two tuple spaces

3.2 Implementations

It is clear that an algorithm to do this can be implemented in parallel – every tuple in tuple space R is compared with every tuple in S in parallel. If the second item in a tuple from R matches the first item of a tuple in S, then a result tuple is placed in the result tuple space. At first sight it would appear that this problem is particularly well suited to Linda because of the matching element.

The most obvious solution is to have one worker for each element in the set R. Each of these workers will take a tuple from tuple space R. They will then attempt to find all tuples in tuple space S where the first element of the tuple is the same as the last element of the chosen tuple from tuple space R. It should be noted that any tuple in S may be needed by more than one worker process and any one process may need more than one tuple from S. Initially, the obvious idea is to use a rd. However, because more than one tuple from S may be required by a single process, repeated uses of the rd primitive might always return the same tuple. Therefore, how do the different workers access all the distinct tuples in tuple space S?

There are two basic approachs to the problem. We will outline each approach, and show the weaknesses that are inherent within them. In each case we present the ISETL-Linda[7] code for each worker.

Using tuples as semaphores The first solution to the problem is to use a tuple that acts as a semaphore (a lock tuple) on the tuple space S. Each worker takes a tuple from R, then attempts to grab the *lock* tuple in S. There is only one such tuple in the tuple space S, and therefore it acts like a binary semaphore. Once a worker has the tuple, it has unrestricted access to the tuple space S. The worker creates a template using the second element of the tuple read from R as the first element of the template. This template is then used by a `collect` to *move* all[2] the tuples that match the template in S to a local tuple space. Therefore, only tuples that are going to be used are moved from S. The worker then `in`s each tuple from the local tuple space and replaces the tuple back into S, and also outputs the composition result into a tuple space C. Finally, once all the tuples in the local tuple space have been processed and replaced into the tuple space S, the *lock* tuple is replaced in S. This means that S contains all the tuples it did when the worker started. It should be noted that the tuple which acts as the semaphore can only be replaced in the tuple space when the tuple space is in its original state. If the tuple is returned before this is true then the other processes can not guarantee duplicating all the tuples that they should. The ISETL-Linda code for a worker is shown in Figure 2.

It should be noted that although the `collect` primitive is used in this solution it is possible to create an implementation that is similar, but just uses the standard Linda primitives if the implementation supports a predicated

---

[2] In this case we can say all because the tuple space will be *inactive* if all processes adhere to using the semaphore tuple.

```
comp_worker := func(R,S,C);

    local my_val, my_ts, my_comb, dummy;

    my_ts := NewBag;
    my_val := lin(R,|[?int,?int]|);

    dummy := lin(S,|["lock"]|);

    todo := lcollect(S,my_ts,|[my_val(2),?int]|);
    while (todo > 0) do
      todo := todo - 1;
      my_comb := lin(my_ts,|[my_val(2),?int]|);
      lout(C,[my_val(1),my_comb(2)]);
      lout(S,my_comb);
    end while;

    lout(S,["lock"]);

    return ["TERMINATED"];
  end func;
```

Fig. 2. Worker using binary semaphore or lock tuple

version of in. If the implementation does not support the predicated in[3] then only the second approach (detailed below) can be used.

This solution is unacceptable because it creates a sequential bottleneck. If more than one process wishes to perform the operation at the same time then it produces a bottleneck, as first one process gets the semaphore and then the next. In the worst case, as is the situation here, the whole program degenerates into a sequential program. All the workers wish to access the tuple space at the same time but only one at a time can.

Streams The second approach is to use what is called a *stream*. This involves the addition of a new unique field to each tuple. This unique field then makes each tuple in the tuple space different. As long as the workers know how the unique field is generated (for example using a counter) each worker can access each tuple using a rd, and the accesses can occur concurrently. This is because all tuples are now distinct, and hence the rd primitive will never match multiple tuples as the unique field is specified in the template. The ISETL-Linda code for a worker is shown in Figure 3.

With this solution all the workers can perform the searching of the second tuple space in parallel. However, there are two problems with this approach that makes it unacceptable:

---

[3] Some implementations do not because of semantic problems with such a primitive.

```
comp_worker := func(R,S,C,NumTupS);

  local my_val, my_comb;

  my_val := lin(R,|[?int,?int]|);

  while (NumTupS > 0) do
    my_comb := lrd(S,|[NumTupS,?int,?int]|);
    NumTupS := NumTupS - 1;
    if (my_comb(2) = my_val(2)) then
      lout(C,[my_val(1),my_comb(3)]);
    end if;
  end while;

  return ["TERMINATED"];
end func;
```

Fig. 3. Worker using streams

- Every tuple in the tuple space requires a unique field to be added, and all the processes using the tuples must be aware of the unique field and how it is generated. This removes the natural use of a tuple space as the data structure, by adding another structure (a stream) to the tuples within it. In order to achieve this either the producer must be aware of the need to add this unique field, in which case the cost of adding the field is minimal, or the tuples have to be preprocessed before use, which incurs additional and unwanted time costs.

- It also largely negates the advantages of the tuple matching abilities of Linda. *Every* tuple in the stream structure *must* be read. If there are several thousands of tuples in a tuple space and only one percent actually match, then the cost of reading every tuple is enormous. If the implementation does not support a predicated version of rd then additional checking of the returned tuple will be required to see if the fields match. Even if the majority of tuples match, any tuple that does not match introduces unnecessary and unwanted time costs.

Table 1 presents the execution times on our system[4] of a sequential version of the problem (using tuple spaces), a version using a binary semaphore and a version using streams. In each case the cardinality of R was five, the cardinality of S was 50 and the number of elements that each element of R should have matched with in S was four, producing a set C with cardinality of 20. It should be noted that the time to alter the data structures and spawn the workers is not included in the execution times.

As can be seen none of the parallel versions represent a noticeable speed up of the sequential version. We call the problem observed here the *multiple* rd *problem*.

Version	Execution time in ticks (arbitrary units)
Stream version	11670
Sequential version	7885
Semaphore/Lock version	7143

Table 1. Experimental results

3.3 Generalisation of the problem

The multiple rd problem is not something that is exclusive to the parallel composition of two binary relations. We now present a fuller description of the multiple rd problem, and indicate some other areas where the problem can be observed.

This problem arises when multiple processes wish to *non-destructively read* a subset of the tuples in a tuple space. The repeated use of a rd in this situation is incorrect as it may result in the same tuple being read more than once. Within the "standard" Linda model the only solution to this problem is to use some sort of a binary semaphore or to use a stream, or some hybrid of the two methods. With the semaphore approach if a process wishes to read a subset of the tuples in the tuple space the process moves all the required tuples to a temporary tuple space, and then destructively reads them using an in and returns them to the original tuple space. If more than one process wishes to "read" a subset of the tuples in a tuple space then those *tuples* have to be "locked" whilst the copying is taking place because if any other processes were to try to copy the same tuples at the same time then both processes may fail to get a complete copy of all the possible tuples. The alternative, using a stream structure, requires the addition of a unique field to all the tuples and the reading of all tuples in a tuple space in order to detect all potential matches.

What makes this multiple rd problem more frustrating is that it would seem possible that several non-destructive reads of a tuple should be possible in parallel. Within the Linda model there is no notion of synchronisation between primitives, and hence two Linda primitives can be executed concurrently, and indeed the York Linda kernel[4] supports concurrent primitive operations.

We now consider other areas and algorithms where the multiple rd problem can be observed. Work on the parallel implementation of many different image processing algorithms in Linda has shown this to be a common problem. If, for example, a binary image is stored in a tuple space many image processing operations require to access only the pixels which have a value of one (or are "on"). Many low and intermediate level image processing operations use a repetitive process applied to every pixel, indicating that there will be many workers, sharing the image (for example the Hough transform). How can these multiple workers access the pixels with a value of one, without either checking every pixel[4] or locking the image? This is another example of the multiple rd problem.

Another example is in the use of persistent tuple spaces to store information. It has for a long time been suggested by some that persistent tuple spaces are a natural way to store information. Let us consider an example where a tuple space is being used to store information, perhaps tuples that contain names and addresses. What happens if several people concurrently wish to access the information? In the database world this would represent no problem: I wish to retrieve the addresses of all people whose name is "Smith". In a large database there are likely to be more than one tuple (record) which contains this name. The entire tuple space (database) would have to be locked or traversed in order to allow the retrieval of these tuples (records). This is clearly unacceptable.

4 The copy-collect primitive

In order to overcome the multiple rd problem we are investigating the use of an additional Linda primitive; copy-collect. It is similar to collect[1]:

copy-collect (ts1, ts2, template) This primitive *copies* tuples that match template from one specified tuple space (ts1) to another specified tuple space (ts2). It returns the number of tuples copied. This differs from a collect in that a collect *moves* the tuples, and therefore is a destructive operation on the source tuple space, where as copy-collect *copies* the tuples from the source tuple space, and is therefore non-destructive. If the source tuple space (ts1) is inactive (in other words no other processes are performing operations which modify its contents) then all the tuples which match the template will be copied from the source tuple space (t1). If a modifying operation is performed on the source tuple space at the same time then the outcome is nondeterministic, as it would be if an in and a rd, for example, where performed on the same tuple at the same time.

Linda is an asynchronous system, and therefore at the model level many operations can occur in parallel. Therefore, if two process happen to do a rd at the same time on the same tuple there is no reason why they could not be serviced concurrently. The copy-collect primitive is the same, many different processes can concurrently do a copy-collect and all these can be serviced concurrently. Therefore, many processes can *independently* and *asynchronously* produce a copy of a number of tuples in the same tuple space.

It might appear as though the primitive moves the bottleneck of using an explicit semaphore to lock a tuple space into the implementation - it appears to perform the same operations as indicated in the code fragment presented in Figure 2, except in the kernel. This of course can be the case. However, in our implementation the tuple space is distributed over many different processors

---

[4] In this case, if the image dimensions are known the image coordinates for each pixel acts as a unique field.

which can perform the operation in parallel. Therefore, the implementation is in effect locking several small sections of the tuple space and performing the operation in parallel. Hence, the effects of the bottleneck have been reduced. The cost of performing a `copy-collect` is similar to the cost of performing an in that blocks[4]. The primitive has been added to the York Linda kernel[4, 8].

5 Implementation - revisited

We can now reconsider the multiple `rd` problem, by examining how `copy-collect` would be used for the parallel composition of two binary relations. The new worker is shown in Figure 4. As with the first implementations each worker takes a tuple from tuple space R, and then uses the new primitive to copy all the tuples which it will require from tuple space S to a local tuple space. This is done by creating a template that will match all the tuples that are required and then performing a `copy-collect`. The copied tuples are then destructively read from the local tuple space, without affecting the source tuple space.

```
comp_worker := func(R,S,C);

    local my_val, my_ts, todo, my_comb;

    my_ts := NewBag;

    my_val := lin(R,|[?int,?int]|);
    todo := lcopycollect(S,my_ts,|[my_val(2),?int]|);
    while (todo > 0) do
        todo := todo - 1;
        my_comb := lin(my_ts,|[my_val(2),?int]|);
        lout(C,[my_val(1),my_comb(2)]);
    end while;

    return ["TERMINATED"];
end func;
```

Fig. 4. Code segment showing the worker using `copy_collect`.

Table 2 shows the execution times for the `copy-collect`, stream and semaphore version using the same data sets as for the first results presented in Table 1. As can be clearly seen the execution time for the `copy-collect` is significantly smaller than the other versions, and represents a speed up over the sequential version.

Table 2 also contains an additional result for a *coarser approach*. It had been suggested by an expert Linda programmer that the general approach that we were considering was a poor one, as it was too fine grained and consequently we should use a more coarse grained approach, where the contents of the set S are coded as a single tuple. All the workers start up, read a tuple from tuple space R as before but then read the single tuple in S, using some sort of local data structure to store the returned tuple and for the calculation of the matching elements. One of the underlying principles of our work is the abstraction away from large data structures with single processes and the use of a tuple space as a (distributed) data structure in its own right. Hence, although we could understand this view, we felt that it compromised this principle. However, we examined this approach and the execution time for the coarser version is shown in Table 2. As can be seen the execution time is comparable to the semaphore/lock version (and sequential) but the `copy-collect` version is still considerably faster.

Version	Execution time in ticks
Stream version	11670
Coarser approach	7244
Semaphore/Lock version	7143
`copy-collect`	4579

Table 2. Experimental results II

This has shown how the new primitive would be used, and it can be seen how it would work for all cases where a multiple `rd` is required, and therefore solves the *multiple* `rd` *problem*. In general, a worker creates a "local" copy of the tuples that it requires using a `copy_collect` and then destructively reads them from that local tuple space. For example, given a tuple space containing an image with each pixel a separate tuple (`[x_coord, y_coord, value]`) the command: `copy_collect(image_ts, local_ts, |[?int, ?int, 1])` would copy all the tuples with a value of one into the local tuple space.

6 Alternative proposals

As with any abstract model there have been many proposals to alter the model. One that is particularly of relevance here is the proposal for another primitive; `rd()all[9]`[5]. The informal semantics of `rd()all` are:

rd (template)all(function) This primitive will apply the *function* to all tuples in a tuple space that match the *template*.

Anderson[9] notes that there are specific problems with such a primitive. The suggestion is that the operation is not atomic, so essentially a cycle is created where a tuple is fetched, the function applied to it, and then the next

---

[5] The same primitive appears to have been suggested under a number of other names including
`rd*`.

tuple fetched. He states that this is due to the implementational difficulties of creating an atomic primitive. However, such a primitive raises much deeper questions whether it is perceived as atomic or non-atomic. What happens if the `function` removes tuples from the tuple space that the `rd()all` would match? What if the function adds tuples to the tuple space? Is there any reason why the function should not be executed in parallel? It would also imply that the primitive has the "interesting" ability to *livelock*, especially if it is not atomic. It is also unclear what information the primitive actually returns. However, it should also be noted that `rd()all` does not require multiple tuples spaces, and could be incorporated into systems with or without them.

There are however, a number of interesting things that this primitive does provide, such as the ability to unify across multiple templates. However, again the exact semantics are not specified, and this could be difficult to implement.

The `copy-collect` primitive is much simpler. It does not attempt to fold communication and computation into the same primitive. It also returns information which is very valuable to the programmer. The information allows the number of workers `evaled` to be controlled for example. If there are many tuples that match, more workers will be required than if fewer tuples match.

7 Conclusion

We have demonstrated the multiple `rd` problem, and have shown how the addition of a new primitive to the model can overcome the problem.

Since the focus of this paper is on the *need* for `copy-collect`, we have not given details of the implementation of the primitive. However, the primitive has been implemented in our distributed kernel. The cost in terms of messages between the different distributed sections of the tuple space is comparable to an `in`. It has been suggested that `copy-collect`, because of the duplication of the tuple spaces, may require large amounts of memory to cope with all the tuple duplication. Although currently physical duplication does occur in our implementation, a tuple storage method where tuples are not duplicated has been designed.

In order to ensure that the `copy-collect` performs as the informal semantics indicate, then the implementation *must* support the *ordering of* `out`s. That is if a single process creates a local tuple space and then performs two `out` operations, the tuple space must never contain the second tuple and not the first. We think that this is a logical thing to assume as an `out` is a non-blocking primitive and can therefore be considered atomic. However, some implementations[10] do not support the ordering of `out`s.

Recent work has shown that `copy-collect` has other uses as well as solving this problem[11]. One of the biggest problems for fine grained parallel programming using the Linda model is the need to add *extra* synchronisation. This extra synchronisation can often rapidly become a bottleneck, causing very poor scalability. We have successfully used the primitive to act as a means for polling the condition of processes, so each process maintains it own state tuple in a common tuple space. A `copy-collect` allows a broker process to interrogate the states tuples, without affecting the workers, and determine if termination has occurred.

Acknowledgements

During this work Antony Rowstron was supported by a CASE studentship from British Aerospace Ltd, and the EPSRC of the UK. The authors would like to thank Andrew Douglas for his comments, and Nicholas Carriero and David Gelernter for their advice on how they would implement the example algorithm.

References

1. P. Butcher, A. Wood, and M. Atkins. Global synchronisation in Linda. *Concurrency: Practice and Experience*, 6(6):505–516, 1994.

2. A. Rowstron and A. Wood. Implementing mathematical morphology in ISETL-Linda. In *IEE 5th International Conference on image processing and its applications*, pages 847–851, 1995.

3. N. Carriero and D. Gelernter. *How to write parallel programs: A first course*. MIT Press, 1990.

4. A. Douglas, A. Wood, and A. Rowstron. Linda implementation revisited. In P. Nixon, editor, *Transputer and occam developments*, Transputer and occam Engineering Series, pages 125–138. IOS Press, 1995.

5. D. Gelernter. Multiple tuple spaces in Linda. In E. Odijk, M. Rem, and J.-C. Syre, editors, *PARLE '89: Parallel Architectures and Languages Europe. Volume II: Parallel Languages*, pages 20–27. Springer-Verlang, Lecture Notes in Computer Science Volume 366, 1989.

6. S.C. Hupfer. Melinda: Linda with multiple tuple spaces. Technical Report YALEU /DCS/RR-766, Yale University, 1990.

7. A. Douglas, A. Rowstron, and A. Wood. ISETL-LINDA: Parallel programming with bags. Technical Report YCS 257, University of York, 1995.

8. A. Rowstron, A. Douglas, and A. Wood. A distributed Linda-like kernel for PVM. In J. Dongarra, M. Gengler, B. Tourancheau, and X. Vigouroux, editors, *EuroPVM'95*, pages 107–112. Hermes, 1995.

9. B. Anderson and D. Shasha. Persistent Linda: Linda + Transactions + Query Processing. In J.P. Banâtre and D. Le Métayer, editors, *Research Directions in High-Level Parallel Programming Languages*, volume 574 of *Lecture Notes in Computer Science*. Springer Verlag, 1991.

10. Scientific Computing Associates. *Linda: User's guide and reference manual*. Scientific Computing Associates, 1995.

11. A. Wood and A. Rowstron. Deadlock and algorithm design: Stable marriages in Linda. *Submitted to Parallel Processing Letters*, 1995.

Coordinating Distributed Objects with Declarative Interfaces

Narinder Singh[1] and Mark A. Gisi[2]

[1] Computer Science Department, Stanford University
Stanford, California 94305, USA
singh@cs.stanford.edu

[2] Software Technology Lab
Hewlett-Packard Laboratories
Palo Alto, California 94305
gisi@hplabs.hp.com

Abstract. This paper presents an architecture that supports coordination among loosely coupled distributed objects. The architecture has two components: objects that provide a declarative specification of their interface, and system programs that reason with these specifications to provide sophisticated interoperation services. Traditional object-oriented interoperation technologies rely on procedural interface specifications, which do not address the semantics of the operations supported by the object. In addition, traditional approaches provide limited support for automatic interoperation in a dynamic environment. For instance, a resource that is available at compile time may not be available at runtime, or a better resource may become available at runtime. Interoperation based on machine-processable specification of object interfaces reduces the coupling (interdependence) between a client and server, and also shifts the burden of coordination from the programmer to the system.

1 Introduction

A number of object-oriented technologies have been developed to support interoperation among applications distributed in an enterprise (e.g., CORBA [16, 17, 14, 15]). They enable objects residing in one application to be accessed by objects residing in another. They also enable an entire application to be represented as a single object.

These technologies provide a number of system services that support a model of programming that is similar to programming in a single process (address) space. Although objects may be distributed over a network, conceptually they are viewed as belonging to a single application. Programs are constructed by one or a small group of programmers who have complete knowledge about the kinds of interactions that take place among the objects. The relationship between objects can be described as being tightly coupled and static.

However, the single-process space abstraction is not always appropriate for modeling interactions that occur among distributed objects supporting different functions of an enterprise. Distributed systems that support one or more enterprises continually change and evolve over time, creating a dynamic environment. Furthermore, although objects that support different functions of an enterprise are required to interoperate from time to time, they often maintain high degrees of autonomy. That is, they do not relinquish total control to a central authority. Instead of viewing a collection of enterprise objects as belonging to a single application, it is more appropriate to view each object as maintaining a high degree of autonomy, that interoperates with other enterprise objects to support different threads of activity. For example, an activity might be a request to print a file, process a customer order, perform group scheduling, or obtain the latest temperature reading of a patient. The relationship between enterprise objects can be described as being loosely coupled and dynamic.

It is impossible for one or a small group of people to have complete knowledge about the different kinds of interactions that can take place during runtime. There is too much information and it changes too rapidly. A resource that is available at compile time may not be available during runtime, or a better resource may become available. Implementing objects that interact in dynamic runtime environments is a difficult task. We need to develop more sophisticated system services that assist object implementors in dealing with incomplete knowledge.

System services should be able to acquire, store, update and reason about existing resources and object capabilities. In order for them to reason about such information, we need a precise and semantically rich way of describing an object's capabilities and properties. Unfortunately, conventional procedural interfaces provide little semantic information in a machine-processable form.

We address this limitation by providing objects with a second declarative interface so that system services can utilize simple inferencing techniques to reason about them. A declarative interface can be used to provide a semantic description of a server object's capabilities and properties. It also enables client objects to describe their requests declaratively. A client can state "what" it would like as opposed to specifying "how" to achieve it. That is, the client describes what it would like, and it is the system's task to determine how to satisfy the request. This reduces the complexity of a client's implementation in two ways. First, the steps required to satisfy a request can change as the environment changes; therefore this logic does not need to be embedded in the client's implementation. Second, the client doesn't have to know about the precise details of the interfaces of the servers that are employed to satisfy the request, thereby reducing the coupling between client and server.

The ideas presented in this paper have been developed within a project focused on constructing distributed intelligent autonomous agents [8]. We believe a more restricted form of this work could be developed to extend existing distributed object models (e.g., CORBA and OLE). We describe the benefits of providing objects with a semantically rich declarative interface. We also describe services that utilize simple inferencing techniques to reason about existing resources that can assist object implementors in dealing with the complexities associated with large, evolving distributed environments.

2 Related Work

Conventional object models, e.g., CORBA [1, 16, 17] and the OLE/COM [14, 15], provide object communication infrastructures. Objects define their interfaces using a language referred to as IDL (Interface Definition Language). Figure 1 provides two simple interface definitions, one that translates a Microsoft WORD file to PostScript and the other that prints a PostScript file.

```
interface WordServices
{
    void TranslateWordToPostscript (in file wordFile, out file postscriptFile)
}

interface PrintServer
{
    void PrintPostscript(in file theFile)
}
```

Fig. 1. Interface Definition Language (IDL) Example.

IDL provides a syntax for object communication. In order to provide system services that support coordination, a mechanism is needed by which an object can provide semantic information that describes its behavior.

The ANSA project realized the limited expressive of IDL. They developed an architecture that supports interoperation among heterogeneous telecommunication services and distributed computer applications [10]. ANSA extended the expressiveness of IDL by enabling a server object to augment its specification with a collection of properties (name/value pairs). Properties provide semantic information that describe different instances of a service. For example, different instances of the print server in Fig. 1 could have properties describing its location within an enterprise (e.g., building and floor), the different paper formats it can handle (e.g., 8x11, 11x17, A4) and whether it can print in color or not. Figure 2 illustrates this extension to IDL.

In addition to supporting more expressive interface specification, ANSA also provides a system service called a trader [3], that utilizes this information to facilitate interoperation. A server registers an interface specification (along with a collection of properties) with the trader, and clients make requests to the trader to help find a particular instance of a server. With each request, the client provides values for those properties it cares about. The trader uses this information to search its repository for an instance of a server that matches the client's request. The trader then passes a reference to the server back to the client. The advantage is that the reference is located at runtime, when the lookup is delegated to the trader. This reduces the complexity of a client's implementation and adds flexibility because binding takes place at runtime.

```
interface PrintServer
{
    void PrintPostscript(in file theFile)
    Properties:
    {
      Building : {A, ..., F}
      Floor : {1, ..., 5}
      size8by11 : {true, false}
      size11by17 : {true, false}
      color : {true, false}
    }
}

interface WordServices
{
    void TranslateWordToPostscript (in file wordFile, out file postscriptFile)
}
```

Fig. 2. IDL Extended to Include Attributes.

3 Declarative Interfaces and Intelligent System Services

When an IDL specification is augmented with name/value pairs, an object's specification begins to resemble a declarative representation. Unfortunately, there are limits to how far IDL can be extended because it is inherently a syntactical representation. In this section we describe declarative interfaces and present a sophisticated system service called the facilitator, which utilizes simple inferencing techniques to reason about an object's capabilities. The facilitator is a system service that bridges the gap between objects that can provide services and objects that request those services.

In traditional systems, the object interface descriptions are in IDL, and the meaning of the IDL interface cannot be defined in IDL (e.g., the fact that a given interface returns the list price of a product). The meaning of the service provided by an object must be known by external means, and there is no support for standardizing or defining the semantics of the interfaces. This requires manual coordination between programmers in a standard CORBA-like environment to agree on the meaning of interfaces. In a large setting, no human can have such global knowledge, and the traditional coordination approaches break down. A declarative interface addresses these issues directly by providing a fixed semantics and by providing a mechanism for examining and defining the vocabulary used.

The system services provided by the facilitator are well suited to environments that are dynamic. In a dynamic environment, resources come and go, and it impossible to make decisions at compile time. The services provided by the facilitator are based on explicit runtime dynamic data about available services, including other applications, resources, and so forth. Facilitation services use these dynamic specifications at runtime to determine the best way to service a request. The thesis of the paper therefore is that by providing an object with a second semantically rich machine-processable specification, new high-level coordination services, that utilize simple inferencing techniques, can be constructed.

In this section we describe (1) the language for declarative specifications and (2) a new system service, the facilitator, that utilizes simple inference to manage the intelligent coordination among client and server objects.

3.1 A Declarative Specification Language

The language we use for describing a declarative interface, developed in the artificial intelligence (AI) community to support interoperation among distributed autonomous agents [7, 8], is called Agent Communication Language (ACL). The use of ACL in the facilitator architecture is described in Sect. 3.2.

An object provides the facilitator with a declarative description of its capabilities and properties at runtime by sending it a collection of ACL messages. ACL has three components: (1) a vocabulary (a domain-specific semantic part), (2) a content language called KIF (Knowledge Interchange Format), and (3) a communication (wrapper) language called KQML (Knowledge Query and Manipulation). An ACL message is a KQML message which consists of a communication directive and a semantic content expressed in terms of the vocabulary in KIF. The communication directive instructs the facilitator on how to process the content of the message. We describe the three components in the following subsections.

KIF and KQML were developed as part of the ARPA knowledge sharing effort, and both are being used by a number of different research groups. KIF has been standardized by ANSI and is currently under consideration for standardization by the ISO. KQML is being evaluated by the Object Management Group (OMG).

Vocabulary. The vocabulary of ACL is listed in a large and open-ended dictionary of words appropriate to common application areas (e.g., electronic commerce, medical industry, and so forth) [9]. Each word in the dictionary has an English description for use by humans in understanding the meaning of the word, and each word has formal annotations for use by programs. The dictionary is open ended to allow for the addition of new words within existing areas and in new application areas.

For example, consider an application where we wish to talk about files, and the translation of files from one format to another. We need to choose a vocabulary for file names, file types, file objects, and the translation of files. First, we need to select the names of individual files, e.g., we could choose "f1.tex" to be the name of a particular file, and similarly for other files. We need to choose symbols to refer to the types of files, e.g., latex, ps, dvi, rtf, word, etc. We also need to select a symbol for a function that maps the name of a file and its type to a file object, e.g., file. In addition we need to select a symbol for a relation that states that one file is the translation of another, e.g., translation.

Sharing information across a community demands agreement about the meaning of symbols, e.g., the meaning of the vocabulary for objects, functions, and relations in ACL. In a small setting (e.g., among a small group of programmers), it may be possible to mandate a single vocabulary for all objects to use in communication. However, in a large setting, this is impossible. More than likely, different communities in such an environment assign different meanings to the same symbols. Such an environment requires support for a collection of vocabularies. We have developed a framework for partitioning vocabularies (and defining mappings between them) based on a Name-Space Context Graph [19].

KIF. In the collaboration architecture we use KIF [6] as the representation language to record facts and properties. This is similar to ANSA, where it is possible to record the properties of objects, however, the KIF language is much more expressive. KIF is a prefix version of first-order predicate calculus with various extensions to enhance its expressiveness. The language has a well defined syntax and semantics.[3]

Sentences in KIF are composed from terms (similar to words in a natural language), which include words from a vocabulary, e.g., `"f1.tex"`, `translation`, `latex`, `dvi`, etc. Terms can be more complicated, as in the functional expression `(file "f1.tex" latex)`. The function `file` maps a file name and a file type to a file object.

First and foremost, KIF provides for the expression of simple data. For example, the sentences shown below encode facts in a printer database. The first states that `printer-1` is located in building 460. The second states that `printer-1` is on the fourth floor. The last two state that `printer-1` handles eight by eleven inch paper and eleven by seventeen inch paper.

```
(building printer-1 460)        (paper-size printer-1 8x11)
(floor printer-1 4)             (paper-size printer-1 11x17)
```

More complicated information can be expressed through the use of functional terms. For example, the first fact states that file `"f1.tex"` was modified on April 30, 1995. The second states that the size of `"f1.dvi"` is greater than one thousand bytes. The last fact states that the translation of a file `"f2.tex"` in `tex` format is the file `"f2.dvi"` in `dvi` format.

```
(modified (file "f1.text" latex) 4/30/95)
(> (size (file "f1.dvi" dvi)) 1000)
(translation (file "f2.tex" tex) (file "f1.dvi" dvi))
```

KIF includes a variety of logical operators to assist in the encoding of logical information (such as negations, disjunctions, rules, quantified formulas, and so forth). The expression shown below is an example of a complex sentence in KIF. Note that all symbols beginning with ? are universally quantified variables that can be instantiated to match any expression (subject to the rules of unification). It asserts that a printer is located in `hplabs` if it is building 460.

---

[3] The semantics of KIF is based on the standard Tarski semantics for first-order logic. There are special semantics for the quote operator to prevent paradoxes [6].

```
(<=  (location ?x hplabs) (building ?x 460))
```

One of the distinctive features of KIF is its ability to encode knowledge about knowledge, using the ˆ and , operators and related vocabulary. For example, the following sentence asserts that object scribe can handle printing any file that is in PostScript format. The use of commas signals that the variables should not be taken literally.

```
(handles scribe ˆ(print (file ,?x ps)))
```

KIF can also be used to describe procedures. Given the prefix syntax of KIF, such programs resemble Lisp or Scheme. The following is an example of a three-step procedure written in KIF. The first step ensures that there is a fresh line on the standard output stream; the second step is to print Hello! to the standard output stream; the final step is to add a carriage return to get to a new line.

```
(sequence (fresh-line t) (print ''Hello!'') (fresh-line t))
```

KIF defines a set of objects, functions, and relations whose meaning is fixed, e.g., numbers and arithmetic functions. However, it is important to note that KIF is open ended, i.e., users are free to define the meanings of any other symbols that are not predefined. The purpose of defining the predefined set of symbols is to ensure that all objects can start communicating in a simple base language, which they are free to extend.

KQML. We use KIF to write sentences which define what is true in our application domain. In a community of objects this alone is not sufficient. When an object communicates a KIF sentence to another it also needs to indicate its attitude towards it, e.g., "I am telling you that x is true," "I am telling you that x is no longer true," "is x true?," "find one instance for which x is true," "find all instances for which x is true," "print the file f," "perform action a," etc.

The purpose of KQML is to provide this extra linguistic layer to describe the attitude of the sending object towards the embedded KIF expression. Intuitively, each message in KQML is one piece of a dialog between the sender and the receiver, and KQML provides support for a wide variety of such dialog types.

As used in ACL, each KQML message is a list of components enclosed in matching parentheses [4]. The first word in the list indicates the type of communication (tell, ask-if, print, etc). The subsequent entries are KIF expressions appropriate to that communication, in effect the "arguments."[4]

The expression shown below is the simplest possible KQML dialog. In this case, there is just one message– a simple notification. The sender is conveying the enclosed sentence to the receiver. In general, there is no expectation on the sender's part about what use the receiver will make of this information.

```
A to B: (tell (= (size (file "f2.tex" tex)) 12678))
```

---

[4] The current KQML manual [4] provides a procedural semantics for the various communication types. Developing a more formal semantics for KQML is an area of ongoing research [13].

The following dialog is a little more interesting. In this case, the first message is a request for the receiver to execute the operation of printing a string to its standard i/o stream. The second message tells the sender that the request has been satisfied.

```
A to B: (perform (print ''Hello!'' t))
B to A: (reply done)
```

In the dialog shown below, the sender is asking the receiver a question in an ask-if message. The receiver then sends the answer to the original sender in a reply message.

```
A to B: (ask-if (> (size (file "f1.dvi" dvi)) (size (file "f1.ps" ps))))
B to A: (reply true)
```

In addition to the simple notifications, commands, and questions illustrated here, KQML also contains support for delayed and conditional operations, subscriptions, requests for bids, offers, promises, and so forth. Describing the complete list and their semantics is beyond the scope of this paper. Additional information can be found in [4].

KQML defines a set of performatives whose meaning is fixed, e.g., ask-if, tell, etc. However, it is important to note that, similar to KIF, KQML is open ended, i.e., users are free to define the meanings of any new performatives that are not predefined. The purpose of defining the predefined set of performatives is to ensure that all objects can start communicating in a simple base language, and they are free to extend this.

3.2 Intelligent Coordination Services

The CORBA Object Request Broker (ORB) provides the communication infrastructure but no support for coordination. The burden of coordination is placed entirely on the client programmer. Before a request can be satisfied, the client must identify the type of service, locate a reference to it and explicitly invoking the appropriate method passing it the require arguments. The ANSA trader reduces the burden by providing a yellow page service. It assists a client in locating an "instance" of a server that is most appropriate. The client still needs to know apriori what type of service it will need, which method to invoke and what the arguments the method are. The facilitator reduces the burden of coordination further. It can determine the type of service needed, identify an instance of that service and execute the appropriate methods. It can also create a new service by gluing together a number of existing services. The facilitator in effect reduces the interdependence of the client and server, since the client is not required to have explicit knowledge of the details of a server's interface.

A facilitator is a system service that can extend a distributed object model, similar to the ANSA trader (see Fig. 3). A facilitator is a lightweight service that is visible to those objects that wish to utilize it, and transparent to those that do not. Objects are free to register services and/or make requests to a facilitator or access objects directly using conventional method invocations (e.g., CORBA

ORB). In order to provide higher-level coordination services, objects will need semantically richer specifications than what ANSA's attribute extension of IDL can support. If an object chooses to utilize the facilitator it can communicate its ACL requests and/or specifications to the facilitator via the CORBA ORB.

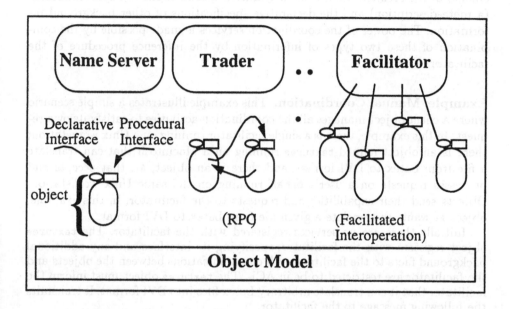

Fig. 3. Multiple system services extending an object model.

Scalability is an important concern with the facilitator architecture. In a small setting, a single facilitator can service a collection of objects (on the same or different machines). However, this is impractical in a large setting, where the single facilitator will be a bottleneck. In a large setting, there can be a collection of facilitators, typically one facilitator per machine. Each facilitator is connected to one or more neighboring facilitators, thus forming a graph of connected facilitators. Each facilitator also has a collection of objects directly connected to it. In order to support interoperation across the network, each facilitator informs each of its neighboring facilitators that it can directly handle all the capabilities of its directly connected objects and the capabilities of the other directly connected facilitators.

It should be noted that simple computations are performed by the facilitator if simple interface specifications are given to it. The operations of the facilitator are very efficient in these situations. The clients and servers can make the trade-off on how much work they wish the facilitator to perform by controlling the facts communicated to the facilitator and by controlling the power of the inference method used by the facilitator, which is one of: simple pattern matching, backward chaining without recursion, backward chaining, or model elimination.

In this section, we illustrate (with examples) several services provided by a facilitator, the interface specifications of objects, and the processing of object requests by a facilitator. In all the examples there is a single facilitator. Key elements of the architecture are the declarative specifications of object interfaces (a meta-description) and the declarative specifications of other background information. The power of the coordination services is made possible by the combination of these two types of information by the inference procedure of the facilitator.

Example: Manual Coordination. This example illustrates a simple scenario where a client object manages all the coordination activities to satisfy its own request. In this example, there is a single facilitator running on a Unix workstation; there is an object named textures running on a Macintosh that can translate a file from Latex to DVI format; and there is an object, A_1, that accepts and processes requests on a user's behalf running on the same Unix workstation. Objects send their capabilities and requests to the facilitator. In this example, object A_1 wants to translate a given file from Latex to DVI format.

Initially there are no services registered with the facilitator. The textures object registers with the facilitator, specifying its interface and any additional background facts to the facilitator. All communications between the objects and the facilitator are restricted to be in ACL. The textures object must inform the facilitator that it can translate arbitrary Latex files into DVI format. It transmits the following message to the facilitator:

```
(tell (handles textures ^(ask-one ,?y (translation (file ,?x latex)
                                                    (file ,?y dvi)))))
```

This is the declarative meta-description of the capability of textures. The performative handled is the standard ask-one KQML performative, which takes two arguments: a pattern argument and a sentence. In order to handle this performative, textures must return the first argument instantiated by a binding for the variables in a proof of the second sentence argument. The pattern in this example is ?y, and the sentence is (translation (file ,?x latex) (file ,?y dvi)). So the previous fact states that the textures object, when asked for one translation of a Latex file to a DVI file, will return the name of the DVI format file (?y).

The user interface object A_1 next registers with the facilitator. It has no capabilities, so it does not transmit any interface specifications to the facilitator. However, A_1 would like to find the translation of a file from Latex format to DVI format. In this example, A_1 will do all the work to perform the translation. It does this by first asking the facilitator if there is any object that can perform the translation (using the yellow-pages services of the facilitator), and it then sends the request to an object that can handle it.

Object A_1 first asks the facilitator if the following fact is true:

```
(handles ?a ^(ask-one ?result (translation (file ''f1.tex'' latex)
                                            (file ?result dvi))))
```

The facilitator uses its repository of information, which includes object interface specifications, to find a proof of this fact using backward inference. The proof is direct, since this fact matches the previous specification for object textures (repeated below) with the variable ?a bound to textures:

```
(handles textures ^(ask-one ,?y (translation (file ,?x latex)
                                             (file ,?y dvi))))
```

The facilitator informs object A₁ that textures can handle the request. A₁ next sends the following request to textures (using the communications support provided by the architecture):

```
(ask-one ?result (translation (file ''f1.tex'' latex) (file ?result dvi))))
```

textures translates the file ''f1.tex'' in Latex format to the file ''f1.dvi'' in DVI format, and returns this as the answer to A₁.

Example: Simple Content-Based Routing. This example is the same as the previous, except that the object representing the user (A₁) does not manage the coordination, but leaves this up to the facilitator. The example is the same as the previous example up to the point where A₁ makes the request. In the previous example, A₁ used the yellow-pages service of the facilitator to find an object that could handle a request. In this example, the facilitator gives A₁ the impression that it is directly achieving the request, and A₁ is unaware that textures will actually be used in the translation.

A₁ makes the following request to the facilitator:

```
(ask-one ?result (translation (file ''f1.tex'' latex) (file ?result dvi)))
```

The facilitator tries to find an object that can handle the quoted request:

```
(handles ?a ^(ask-one ?result (translation (file ''f1.tex'' latex)
                                            (file ?result dvi)))
```

The facilitator uses backward inference to try to prove this fact. The proof is direct, since this fact matches the previous specification for textures (repeated below) with the variable ?a bound to textures:

```
(handles textures ^(ask-one ,?y (translation (file ,?x latex)
                                             (file ,?y dvi))))
```

The facilitator passes the request from A₁ to textures. textures translates the file ''f1.tex'' in Latex format to the file ''f1.dvi'' in DVI format. The textures object returns the answer ''f1.dvi'', and this is the answer returned to A₁.

Note that in this example, A₁ makes the following request to the facilitator:

```
(ask-one ?result (translation (file ''f1.tex'' latex) (file ?result dvi)))
```

while in the previous example, A_1 made the following request to the facilitator:

```
(handles ?a ^(ask-one ?result (translation (file ''f1.tex'' latex)
                                            (file ?result dvi)))
```

and the second request to textures:

```
(ask-one ?result (translation (file ''f1.tex'' latex) (file ?result dvi))))
```

This example illustrates a small improvement with content-based routing; however, in general an arbitrary amount of intermediate effort can be saved by content-based routing, as illustrated by the next example.

Example: Simple Problem Decomposition. This example illustrates a case requiring problem decomposition. The scenario is the same as the previous example, except that there is a third object dvi2ps running on a different Unix workstation that can translate DVI format files to PostScript files. In this example, the user object A_1 requests the facilitator for the translation of a Latex file into a PostScript file. This requires first translating the file from Latex to DVI, and then translating the file from DVI to PostScript. A_1 is unaware of the sequence of operations taking place. It appears to A_1 that the facilitator is performing all the translations directly.

The example is the same as before up to the point when textures registers with the facilitator and sends its capabilities. Following this, dvi2ps registers with the facilitator and sends the following message:

```
(tell (handles dvi2ps ^(ask-one ,?y (translation (file ,?x dvi)
                                                  (file ,?y ps)))))
```

This is similar to the message sent earlier by textures to the facilitator. For this example, assume that the facilitator also knows the following background fact (some other object has informed the facilitator of this fact):

```
(tell (<= (translation (file ?x latex) (file ?y ps))
          (translation (file ?x latex) (file ?z dvi))
          (translation (file ?z dvi)   (file ?y ps))))
```

The general form for a conditional rule is (<= A B C), which means that A is true if B and C are true. The fact argument to the tell states that the translation of file ?x in Latex format is file ?y in PostScript format, if the translation from file ?x in Latex format is file ?z in DVI format, and the translation of file ?z in DVI format is file ?y in PostScript format. This rule in effect defines a simple transitivity relation.

The user interface object A_1 next registers with the facilitator. It has no capabilities, so it does not transmit any interface specifications to the facilitator. However, A_1 would like to find the translation of a file from Latex format to PostScript format. It sends the following message to the facilitator:

```
(ask-one ?result (translation (file ''f1.tex'' latex) (file ?result ps)))
```

The facilitator tries to find an object that can handle the quoted request:

```
(handles ?a ^(ask-one ?result (translation (file ''f1.tex'' latex)
                                            (file ?result ps))))
```

The facilitator uses backward inference to try to prove this fact. Unfortunately, no object can handle this request directly. However, the facilitator can use the transitive rule to decompose this request into the conjunction:

```
(and (translation (file ''f1.tex'' latex) (file ?z dvi))
     (translation (file ?z dvi)            (file ?result ps)))
```

The first conjunct is handled by the textures object, and it binds the variable ?z to the file ''f1.dvi''. This binding for ?z is plugged into the second conjunct, which is handled by the dvi2ps object, and it returns the variable ?result bound to ''f1.ps''.

The problem decomposition rule for this example is applicable only in the special case of translating Latex files to PostScript by first translating them to DVI format. The following, more powerful rule allows an arbitrary intermediate format (not just DVI):

```
(<= (translation (file ?x latex) (file ?y ps))
    (translation (file ?x latex) (file ?z ?f)
    (translation (file ?z ?f)    (file ?y ps))))
```

Note that this is a recursive rule, which can applied an arbitrary number of times. Content-based routing, in the presence of such rules, can tremendously reduce the complexity of problem solving compared with manual coordination.

Example: Defining New Primitive Performatives. In this example, we illustrate the definition of new performatives. The previous examples illustrated the use of the tell and ask-one primitive performatives of ACL. This example illustrates the definition of a conditional performative, though it possible to define simpler performatives without any conditions.

Performatives in ACL describe actions, as opposed to informational facts. It is important not to confuse informational facts with facts about actions. The purpose of informational facts is to define what is true, while the purpose of facts about actions is to define a procedure. For example, the fact (and P P) can be proved by proving P alone, while the action (sequence P P) cannot be satisfied by performing action P alone.

In this example, there is a single object called Scribe that can print files in PostScript format, as long as the size of the file is less than one megabyte. Scribe connects to the facilitator and sends it the following message:

```
(tell (<= (handles scribe ^(print (file ,?f ps)))
          (= (denotation ?f) ?fd) ; ?fd is the unquoted file name
          (< (file-size (file ?fd ps)) 1000000)))
```

The fact inside the tell in the above message states that Scribe can print any PostScript file as long as the size of the file is less than one million (bytes). The function file-size takes a file name as an argument and maps it to the size of the file in bytes. Scribe is defining a new performative `print`. It will handle all print requests of PostScript files (of a certain length), but how it does this is not specified or relevant.

The user object A₁ makes a request to the system to print a PostScript file by sending the facilitator the following message:

```
(print (file ''f1.ps'' ps))
```

The facilitator first searches for an object that can handle the quoted form of the above expression. It uses backward inference to find a proof for the fact:

```
(handles ?a ^(print (file ''f1.ps'' ps)))
```

The backward inference uses the interface description to conclude that the Scribe object can print the file ``f1.ps`` if the size of ``f1.ps`` is less than one megabyte. Assume that this is so, i.e., the following fact is true:[5]

```
(< (file-size "f1.ps" ps) 1000000)
```

The facilitator, therefore, concludes that Scribe can print the file ``f1.ps``. Next the facilitator sends a message to Scribe to print the file. Scribe prints the file, and when it is done, the successful indication of this is reported to the user object A₁.

Example: Defining Procedures from Existing Performatives. This example illustrates defining procedures in ACL, and it focuses on facts that specify a sequence of actions. The primitive actions are the KQML performatives, that include `ask`, `tell`, and other user-defined primitive performatives. From these primitives, it is possible to define more complex performatives as compositions of these (just as it is possible to define complex procedures from primitive statements in a programming language).

Every performative returns a value, e.g., the performative (`ask-one` <exp> <fact>) returns <exp> instantiated by a binding for the variables which make <fact> true. Performative definitions can be nested, where the evaluation is inside-out and a component performative is replaced by its value. This is similar to the inside-out evaluation of (+ (* 2 3) 4) in programming languages.

This example is identical to the previous, except that the user object A₁ wishes to print a Latex file. In this case A₁ sends the following message to the facilitator:

```
(print (file ''f1.tex'' latex))
```

Unfortunately the facilitator is unable to find an object that can handle this request, since the file is in Latex format, and the printer Scribe can only print files in PostScript format. One way of overcoming this is to define a procedure for printing that defines a sequence of actions: to print an arbitrary file, first translate it to PostScript format, and then print it. This is specified by the following fact describing a procedure:

---

[5] The size of a file is computed using procedural attachments, similar to the attachments for built arithmetic functions like addition and division.

```
(define ^(print (file ,?n ,?f) )
        ^(print (file (ask-one ?n2 (translation (file ,?n ,?f)
                                                 (file ?n2 ps))) ps)))
```

The general format for defining procedures is:

```
(define ^<performative-defined> ^<performative>)
```

A sequence of actions is defined by (sequence <a₁> ... <aₙ>), and conditional actions are defined by:

```
(cond <condition-1> <action-1> ... <condition-n> <action-n>)
```

In this example the definition of the new performative is nested. In this case, the name of the translated file is given by the inner performative:

```
(ask-one ?n2 (translation (file ,?n ,?f) (file ?n2 ps)))
```

The request from A_1 can now be handled. The facilitator cannot find an object that can handle the request directly; however, the facilitator uses the procedural definition above to find that the file can be printed if: 1) the file can be translated from Latex to PostScript (the inner performative in the definition), and 2) some object can print the resulting PostScript file. The process of handling these two steps was illustrated in previous examples. The transitive translation rule is used to translate the file from Latex to DVI, and then from DVI to PostScript. The PostScript file ''f1.ps'' can be printed directly by the printer Scribe since it is less than one megabyte long. The two steps are performed directly by the facilitator, and the indication of success is passed back to A_1.

Example: Vocabulary Translation. Hiding details about implementations reduces the coupling between a client and server. Unfortunately, with procedural interfaces, interaction between a client and server requires the client to have specific knowledge about the details of a server's interface. When a client makes a declarative request to the facilitator, the client is not required to know specific details about the interface of the server(s) that satisfies it. This further reduces the coupling between the client and server, which is particularly important when supporting interoperation among loosely coupled objects interacting in a dynamic environment.

This example illustrates the use of vocabulary translation to match a request with a server that can handle it.[6] A request is made with one vocabulary, while a service is provided with a different vocabulary. A translation rule is used automatically by the facilitator to map the request to the service. Such translation is not possible with a simple syntactic matching scheme.

Suppose that previously there was a different vocabulary for file translations, which is given below:

```
(file-translation <file1> <file2> <format1> <format2>)
```

---

[6] Vocabulary/interface translation should not be confused with file translation, which is what the vocabulary translation is being used to accomplish.

For example, previously we would have used:

```
(file-translation ''f1.tex'' ''f1.ps'' latex ps)
```

while the current use is:

```
(translation (file ''f1.tex'' latex) (file ''f1.ps'' ps))
```

The new vocabulary makes explicit the concept of a file by using the function file. When the vocabulary was updated, the interface for textures was also updated (as illustrated in the previous examples). Unfortunately, there is an object A0 (among others) that continues to use the old vocabulary. textures would like to continue supporting the old vocabulary. It does this by communicating the following message to the facilitator:

```
(tell (<= (file-translation ?file1 ?file2 ?format1 ?format2)
          (translation (file ?file1 ?format1) (file ?file2 ?format2))))
```

The fact embedded in the tell defines the mapping between the old and new vocabularies. Consequently, when A0 makes the request to the facilitator:

```
(ask-one ?result (file-translation ''f1.tex'' ?result latex ps))
```

The facilitator uses the previous translation rule in the process of its backward reasoning to translate the request. The request is translated to:

```
(translation (file ''f1.tex'' latex) (file ?result ps))
```

which is handled by textures. The processing from this point on is identical to that in the previous example.

This example illustrates that it is possible to modify the interface of an object, and still have the object support its old interface by using the translation capabilities of the facilitator.

These examples have illustrated the complex coordination behavior that is provided by the facilitator automatically in response to a request from a client. The client is not aware of the complicated sequence of events used to process the request. More generally, they also illustrate how semantically rich specifications significantly increase the ability of construct more sophisticated coordination services. That trying to add semantics to IDL by including name/value pairs is a good initial step but it is not sufficient.

4 Status

There is an API for the coordination architecture in C, C++, and Lisp. It hides all the details associated with network communication from the programmer. Each API uses TCP to communicate with the facilitator, but changing the communication protocol (e.g., to DCE) is a trivial task. The API has been used to support interoperation among applications running on UNIX, Macintosh System 7, and Windows NT. A prototype of the facilitator is implemented in Lisp and runs on Sun, Silicon Graphics, Hewlett-Packard Series 300/700 workstations and the Apple Macintosh.

The Logic Group in the Stanford University Computer Science Department, in conjunction with HP Labs in Palo Alto California, has been developing the facilitation architecture over the last five years. This system has been used in a collection of interoperation experiments, including an integrated design, manufacture, and diagnosis system for digital circuits[5], a multi-domain simulation of a robotic arm [2], and integrated CAD tools for civil engineering [12]. It is currently being used in the CommerceNet project [11], which provides smart search for product information using heterogeneous on-line catalogs, ordering, billing, etc.

5 Conclusion

In this paper we have presented an interoperation architecture based on declarative specification of object interfaces. Given machine-processable object specifications, it is possible to develop new system services that utilize simple inferencing techniques to facilitate interoperation among loosely coupled distributed objects. These services provide additional capabilities (content-based routing, problem decomposition, translation, etc.), and the automation of these services enables using the best information available at runtime.

The reduction in the coupling between a client and server is a consequence of describing requests declaratively. That is, a client describes a request in terms of what it would like, and not how to achieve it. This has the following advantages:

- The client is not required to know about which servers are needed to satisfy the request. This logic has been factored out of the client's implementation and placed in the facilitator, thereby reducing the complexity of the client's implementation.

- The client is no longer responsible for obtaining references to particular instances of the different servers.

- The client is not required to know the exact details about a server's interface.

There are a number of issues that must be addressed in order for declarative interfaces to gain acceptance. Standardizing on KIF and KQML is a good start, however, two problems arise: (1) traditional system programmers are not accustomed to providing declarative specifications, and (2) the syntax of KIF and KQML, which is based on nested parentheses, is not easy for humans to manipulate. The first is harder to solve, since it requires programmers to think about the objects, functions, and relations handled by an object. The second is easier to solve, since KQML and KIF are not meant to be processed by humans directly (this is similar to PostScript– humans use a drawing program to generate PostScript output). The problem can be addressed by developing APIs that map a traditional programming syntax into KQML and KIF.

Facilitated interoperation provides considerable flexibility, but at the expense of runtime efficiency. In small distributed environments, this approach may not be acceptable or needed. As the distributed systems become larger, more dynamic, and more decentralized, this approach may become not only reasonable but necessary.

References

1. Betz, M., "OMG's CORBA," *Dr. Dobb's Special Report,* Winter 1994/95.
2. Cutkosky, M. et al., "PACT: An Experiment in Integrating Engineering Systems," *Computer* 26, 1(1993), 28-37.
3. Deschrevel, J. P., "The ANSA Model of Trading and Federation," Architecture Projects Management, Cambridge, 1993.
4. Finin, T., and Wiederhold, G., et al., "Specification of the KQML Agent-Communication Language," available from the WWW with the URL http://www.cs.umbc.edu/kqml/kqmlspec/spec.ps, June, 1993.
5. Genesereth, M., "Designworld," in the *Proceedings of the 1991 IEEE International Conference on Robotics and Automation,* Sacramento, California, April 1991, pp. 2785-2788.
6. Genesereth, M. R., Fikes, R., et al., "Knowledge Interchange Format Version 3 Reference Manual" Logic92-1, Stanford University Logic Group, 1992.
7. Genesereth, M. R., and Ketchpel, S. P., "Software Agents," *Communication of the ACM,* Vol. 37, No. 7 July 1994.
8. Genesereth, M., Singh, N., and Syed, M., "A Distributed Anonymous Knowledge Sharing Approach to Software Interoperation," in the *Proceedings of the International Symposium on Fifth Generation Computing Systems,* 1994, pp. 125-139.
9. Gruber, T., "Ontolingua: A Mechanism to Support Portable Ontologies," KSL-91-66, Stanford Knowledge Systems Laboratory, 1991.
10. Herbert, A., "An ANSA Overview," *IEEE Network,* January/February 1994, pp. 18-23.
11. Keller, A., "Smart Catalogs and Virtual Catalogs," in *USENIX Workshop on Electronic Commerce,* August 1995.
12. Khedro, T., and Genesereth, M., "The Federation Architecture for Interoperable Agent-Based Concurrent Engineering Systems," *International Journal on Concurrent Engineering, Research and Applications,* pp. 125-131, 1994.
13. Labrou, Y., and Finin, T., "A Semantic Approach for KQML – a general purpose communication language for software agents," in *Third International Conference on Information and Knowledge Management,* 1994.
14. Microsoft Corporation, *OLE 2 Programmer's Reference: Creating Programmable Applications with OLE Automation,* Volume 2, Microsoft Press, Redmond, Wash., 1994.
15. Microsoft Technical Backgrounder OLE 2.0, 1994.
16. The Object Management Group, "The Common Object Request Broker: Architecture and specification," Revision 1.1, Document Number 91.12.1, December 1991.
17. Mowbray, T., *Essential CORBA: Systems Integration Using Distribute Objects,* Wiley, John & Sons, Inc., 1995.
18. Raj, R., Tempero, E., Levy, H., Black, A., Hutchinson, N. and Jul, E., "Emerald: A General-Purpose Programming Language", *Software-Practice and Experience,* vol 21, Number 1, January 1991.
19. Tawakol, O., and Singh, N., "A Name Space Context Graph for Multi-Context Systems," *Proceedings of the 1995 AAAI Fall Symposium Series,* Cambridge, Massachusetts, November, 1995.

Coordinating Services in
Open Distributed Systems with LAURA

Robert Tolksdorf

Technische Universität Berlin, Fachbereich 13, Informatik
Funktionales und Logisches Programmieren
Sekr. FR 6–10, Franklinstr. 28/29, D-10587 Berlin
Germany
e-mail: tolk@cs.tu-berlin.de
WWW: http://www.cs.tu-berlin.de/~tolk/

Abstract. Open distributed systems are computing systems that can be characterized by a heterogeneity of involved machine- and network architectures as well as of the data processed. They have to be able to integrate existing applications, to cope with the use of multiple programming-languages, and potentially high dynamics by joining and leaving components.

The coordination language LAURA is designed to facilitate the use and offer of services in such a system. It is based on a shared collection of forms describing offers, requests, and results of services, called the service-space. LAURA's operations permit the exchange of forms via the service-space, guided by a matching-rule based on a subtype-notion on service types. The uncoupled coordination paradigm inherited from LINDA allows it to meet the requirements of open systems.

An architecture for a distributed LAURA-system is described, that is scalable and can be adjusted to organizational borders. The architecture has been implemented on top of the ISIS toolkit.

1 Open Distributed Systems

Open distributed systems provide an infrastructure in which participants use and offer services from and to others. They do so at a very large scale – potentially world-wide – and with very few restrictions. The intention is to glue together resources that are already available for some participants but not accessible for all.

Whereas for a distributed system, a single application is distributed to several networked machines as in figure 1, an open distributed system is dynamically composed from non-dedicated hardware and software components, which may already be in use for other applications, as in figure 2. Components are able to join and leave the open system without restriction.

As these components work concurrently, communication and synchronization – in one word *coordination* – amongst them becomes necessary. A solution to the coordination problem in open systems has to provide the "glue" that holds together the components. It has to deal with several characteristics of the hardware and software components, such as:

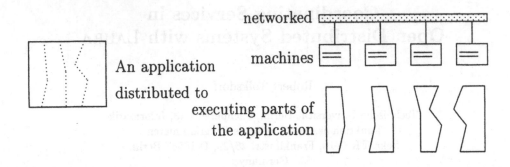

Fig. 1. Distributing an application

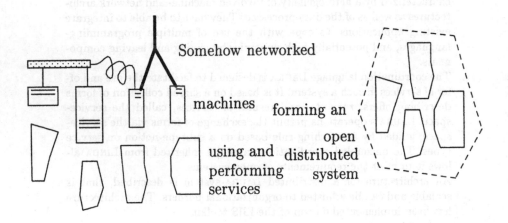

Fig. 2. Forming an open distributed system

- **Heterogeneity of machine-, network- and operating-system architectures** The machines on which the software components of an open system
  run, are heterogeneous, as they comprise different machine architectures and
  are from different vendors. They can include personal computers, workstations or mainframes. An open system has to deal with differences amongst
  them such as value representations.
  Coordinating open systems means to deal with these heterogeneities by making them transparent to the user and abstracting from their concrete out-
  forms when designing a coordination system.
- **Heterogeneity of programming languages used for software components** The software used in the open system can be programmed in different programming languages. One cannot assume that a language is available

across all hardware platforms involved or introduce a potentially world-wide restriction to use one language only.

Coordinating open systems means to abstract from the programming languages used for the software components and to introduce some linguistic means that focus on communication, synchronization, and services. It has to be abstract enough to cope with different models of computation materialized in languages.

- **Potential high dynamics by unrestricted joining and leaving components** An open distributed system has no time of beginning or end. It is formed by the components that joined it. In an open system there should be no restriction for components on when they join or leave. Examples can be the interactive start of some user interface component, or the replacement of a hard- or software component by another, newer one. No component should be forced to wait for some condition and no component should be hindered from leaving the system by some condition.

  Coordinating open systems means to avoid restrictions and to provide mechanisms that can deal with these dynamics. For example, no assumption on the availability of some component can be made. Even if it is in the system at some time, there is no guarantee that it will not leave quickly thereafter.

In this paper, we present a coordination language, called LAURA, which aims at coordinating services in open distributed systems. It is inspired from the conceptuation of the coordination language LINDA. In the next section, we review LINDA, which we will take as the starting point for our approach.

2 LINDA

LINDA is a language for coordination in parallel systems that has been studied from about the midst-eighties (Gelernter and Carriero, 92). The underlying view of a parallel system is that of an *asynchronous ensemble*, in which all work is performed by *agents*. Agents form an ensemble by coordinating their activity asynchronously via some media. The actual work they perform is carried out independently, asynchronously, and autonomously.

LINDA introduces an *uncoupled* communication paradigm which is based on the abstraction of a *tuple-space*. It acts as a shared store of data which is kept as *tuples* that are addressed associatively by a pattern used in a matching-mechanism to retrieve a tuple. It is unknown, which agent put the tuple into the tuple-space, thus communication partners remain anonymous to each other.

LINDA as a coordination language is embedded in some computational language, by which LINDA's coordination primitives are available available. The primitives out, inand rddeposit and retrieve tuples from the tuple-space. The selection of a tuple with respect to a given pattern provided for in- and rd-operations is governed by a *matching-rule*.

The following list identifies characteristic concepts of LINDA that we take as key-issues for solutions of the coordination problem in open systems:

- **Uncoupling of agents** The basic paradigm of communication is uncoupled in that the sending and receiving agents do not know about each other. This mechanism therefore needs no identification-scheme of agents, and is more abstract than a directed communication paradigm.
- **Associative addressing** An agent willing to receive data uses a pattern or template to address is associatively. It therefore does specify, *what data* it is interested in, not *what message* is wants to receive. The template makes a semantic statement, whereas "deliver message #1012 to me" is a syntactic statement.
- **Nondeterminism** Associative addressing by templates is non-deterministic, as it does not prescribe the choice of which data to select. During execution the choice finally has to be made, as concrete coordination has to be deterministic. However, the necessary choice is left to some mechanism "behind the stages". This late decision is appropriate to guide the choice by dynamic information.
- **Concurrency** Agents being coordinated in a system by LINDA perform their work implicitly concurrently. There are no assumptions on the order of execution or communication. The only requirement is induced by the potential blocking of in/rd: Data must be sent by some agent before it can be received.
- **Separation of concerns** LINDA was of the first languages to focus on co-ordination solely. It demonstrates that this separation of concerns leads to a solution of a coordination problem independent of how computation is performed. The benefits of this separation are concentration on a single problem and abstraction from the solution of other problems such as computation.

3 LAURA

In this paper we describe a design for the "glue" that enables us to coordinate an open system with the characteristics described. It is called LAURA and can be summarized for a first impression as follows.

We understand the software components in an open system as *agents* that use and offer *services* according to their functions. LAURA introduces the abstraction of a *service-space* shared by all agents which is a collection of *forms*. A form can contain a description of a service-offer, a service-request with arguments or a service-result with results.

The operations of the coordination language LAURA offer linguistic means to put and retrieve offer-, request- and result-forms to and from the service-space. When they are executed, a mechanism similar to LINDA's matching brings together offer-forms and request-forms and delivers the parameters to the service offerer. Result-forms are again matched with requests, so that results can be delivered to the requester. Figure 3 illustrates this abstraction for a set of components involved in a traveling ticket purchase system.

A main characteristic of our approach shows in the illustration: There are no visible connections amongst agents that offer and request services. An agent

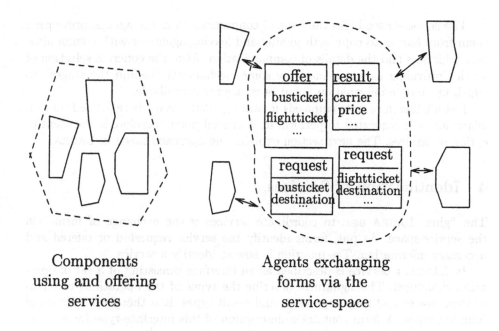

Components
using and offering
services

Agents exchanging
forms via the
service-space

Fig. 3. A service-space for a traveling ticket purchase system

knows only about the service-space where it exchanges forms. The service provider and the requester remain anonymous to each other. We claim that such an *uncoupled* coordination style is a well suited paradigm for open systems because of the following reasons.

In a conventional distributed system, one can assume that – due to its static nature – an agent that performs some service can repeat this at some time in the future. Therefore, it can be efficient to establish a connection between agents for the passing of multiple requests along that connection. If more than one agent offers the same service, it also may be convenient to choose a particular one and to memorize its identifier for further requests.

Both are impossible in open systems, since there is no guarantee that a known agent will be present at some later time. Establishing a connection hinders agents from leaving the system, which is an unwanted restriction. Memorizing a communication address for later use has the potential of leading to an error, because the agent could have left already.

Moreover, uncoupledness is part of the nature of open systems. There can be multiple offers of similar services by different agents. The decision on which particular service to use should be taken very late on the basis of information that is available at runtime only. With connections, the decision on what agent to communicate with is based on information about the past – the time of establishing the connection. This ignores new information such as the availability of a service-offerer which is cheap to communicate with.

The service-space hides the issue of connections from the agents, preventing them from having to cope with joining and leaving agents or with communication addresses and the details of communication. Also, the concrete selection of service providing agents is made by some mechanisms "behind the stages" to which up-to-date information about other agents is available.

LAURA therefore puts emphasis in stating *what service* is requested, not on *which agent* is requested to perform it. A crucial point therefore is the identification of services. The next section explains the approach taken in LAURA.

4 Identification of Services

The "glue" LAURA uses to coordinate services is the exchange of forms via the service-space. As put, forms identify the service requested or offered and necessary information. The question is how to identify a service.

In LAURA, a service is described as an interface consisting of a set of operation signatures. The signatures describe the types of the operations in terms of their names and their argument- and result-types. It is therefore a record of function-types. A form contains a description of this interface-type for service-identification. Putting a service-request form into the service-space triggers the search for a service-offer form so that the interface-type of the offer is in a matching relation to that of the request. We do not introduce names for service-types, which is different to what is done in other approaches, such as *direct naming* and *managed types*, as we call them.

ActorSpaces (Agha and Callsen, 93) use a direct naming system. Here, for some services named "mail", "mail-fast" and "simple-mail", the regular expression "*mail*" identifies any one out of those three. However, the name-portion "mail" still has to be known in advance. Such a scheme cannot be well-suited for open systems as they are dynamic in nature and as one cannot assume identical naming schemes at a world-wide scale.

A more dynamic scheme is defined for the ISO standard on open distributed processing ODP (ISO/IEC, 95). Here, a repository of type definitions is defined which is used to store interface types of services and relations amongst them. A subtype-relation amongst interface types can be explicitly declared or derived from subtyping rules. Offering or using a service is done via a trading function (ISO/IEC JTC1/SC21, 94) that stores offers and their types. It uses the type repository to determine relations amongst offered and requested types and provides a requester with the identifier of an object that offers an appropriate service. Our approach differs from the ODP scheme in that we do not introduce a repository of types and in that there is no connection between offerers and requesters visible to the agents.

In LAURA, no names are used at all for the identification of services or for the types of data involved in an operation. Instead, a service offered or requested is described by an interface signature consisting of a set of operations signatures. The operation signatures consist of a name and the types of arguments and parameters.

Similar to most approaches to interoperability we use an *interface description language* to notate the interface of a service. This is necessary to facilitate the usage of multiple programming languages. In LAURA interfaces are notated in the service type language STL. To illustrate an interface in STL, we express the type of a service offered or used by a traveling agency. It consists of three operations, getflightticket, getbusticket, and gettrainticket which take as arguments some identification of a credit-card, a travel date and a destination. All operations confirm the purchase and result in a price. getbusticket also results in the name of a bus-company. The interface of this service – to which we will refer as the "large-agency" – is expressed as:

```
(getflightticket:ccnumber*date*dest -> ack*price;
 getbusticket    :ccnumber*date*dest -> ack*price*line;
 gettrainticket :ccnumber*date*dest -> ack*price)
where
ccnumber          = string;
date              = <day,month,year>;
day               = number;
month             = number;
year              = number;
dest              = string;
ack               = boolean;
line              = string;
price             = <number,number>.
```

In Tolksdorf, 95a and Tolksdorf, 95b we formally defined a type-system which is used in the definition of the semantics of such interface definitions. This type system includes rules for subtyping and this subtyping is the key for LAURA's identification of services: Given the interface descriptions in forms, a service offer matches a service request, if the type of the interface offered is a subtype of the one requested.

Subtyping in LAURA is defined so that a type A is a subtype of B if all values of type A can be substituted when a value of type B is requested. The "values" we type are services. The subtyping enables us to use a service of type A if a service of type B is requested.

For the traveling example, the typing makes it possible to have an agency that offers bus-, train- and flight-tickets perform the purchase of a train-ticket when an agency is requested that offers bus- and train-tickets. It also rules out agencies offering bus- and flight-tickets to be selected for the purchase. When following interface description – to which we will refer as the "small-agency" – is contained in a service-form, the form matches a serve-form with the interface above, as their types are in a subtype-relation according to our type-system:

```
(getflightticket: ccnumber * date * dest -> ack * price;
 gettrainticket : ccnumber * date * dest -> price)
where
```

```
ccnumber      = string;
date          = <day,month,year>;
day           = number;
month         = number;
year          = number;
dest          = string;
ack           = boolean;
price         = <number,number>.
```

5 LAURA's Operations

We now review LAURA's operations in detail. In the examples, we assume that
the interfaces with which we illustrated STL above are abbreviated by the names
`large-agency` and `small-agency` which are locally known to agents and
which should not be misinterpreted as a service-name or global identifiers.

5.1 Operations for the Service Provider

A service is the result of an interaction between a service-provider and a service-
user. In LAURA, two operations coordinate this interaction for the service-provider, `serve` and `result`.

An agent that is willing to offer a service to other agents puts a serve-form
into the service-space. It does so by executing `serve`, which takes as parameters
the type of the service offered and a list of binding rules that define to which
program variables arguments for the service should be bound. For the example
large-agency, the operation would be formulated as

```
SERVE large-agency operation
(getflightticket: cc * <day,month,year> * dest ->
                  ack * <dollar,cent>;
 getbusticket    : cc * <thedate.day, thedate.month,
                  thedate.year> * dest ->
                  ack * <dollar,cent> * line;
 gettrainticket : cc * <day,month,year> * dest ->
                  ack * <dollar,cent>).
SERVE
```

This states that a service with the interface *large-agency* is offered and that
a code for the selected operation should be bound to the program variable
`operation`. In the case of the operation `gettrainticket`, the arguments
provided by the service-user should be bound to the program variables `cc`, `day`,
`month`, `year` and `dest`. Note that in contrast to the names used only for convenience in the definition of a service-interface, the names used in the binding
lists are those of variables that have to be declared properly in the program text
of the agent. The names used in the result-parts of the operations are ignored.

When a serve is executed, a serve-form is built from the arguments. Then, the service-space is scanned for a service-request form whose service-type matches the offered service by being a supertype. The code of the requested operation and the provided arguments are copied to the serve-form and finally bound to program variables according to the binding list. The serve-operation blocks as long as no matching request-form is found.

After performing the service requested, the service-provider uses result to deliver a result-form to the service-space. This operation looks similar to serve:

```
RESULT large-agency operation
(getflightticket: cc * <day,month,year> * dest ->
                  ack * <dollar,cent>;
 getbusticket    : cc * <thedate.day, thedate.month,
                  thedate.year> * dest ->
                  ack * <dollar,cent> * line;
 gettrainticket : cc * <day,month,year> * dest ->
                  ack * <dollar,cent>).
RESULT
```

Here, the names used in the argument parts of the binding lists are ignored. A result-form is built which consists of the service-interface and – depending on operation – a list of result values according to the binding list. For the case of a gettrainticket, they are taken from the program variables ack, dollar and cent. The agent is responsible to store the results of the service properly in those variables. The operation is performed immediately and the form is put into the service-space.

An agent that offers services usually operates in a loop consisting of the sequence serve–*perform the service*–result. However, LAURA makes no assumptions on this behavior nor enforces it. This is due to the fact that no assumptions on the programming language used for the agent and its execution model can be made. It can well be the case that multiple services are performed concurrently or that the order of service provision and result-delivery does not match the order of service-requests.

5.2 Using a Service

An agent that wants to use a service has to execute LAURA's third and last operation, service. Its arguments are the service-type requested, the operation requested, arguments for the operation and a binding-list. An example is

```
SERVICE small-agency
(getflightticket : cc * <thedate.day, thedate.month,
                  thedate.year> * dest ->
                  ack * <dollar,cent>;).
SERVICE
```

Here, a service with an interface *small-agency* is requested. The operation to be performed is getflightticket. The binding lists from both the argument- and result-part are used to access the arguments stored in the program variables cc, thedate.day, thedate.month, thedate.year and dest. The results of the service should be bound to ack, dollar and cent.

Up to now, we talked about a service-request form for the sake of simplicity. In fact, when executing service, two forms are involved: a service-put form and a service-get form. The first is constructed from the service-interface and the arguments and then inserted to the service-space. If another agent performs a serve-operation and the service-put- and serve-forms match, the arguments are copied as described above and the service-provider starts processing the requested operation.

The service-get form is constructed from the service interface and the binding list for the results. Then, a matching result-form is sought in the service-space and – when available – the results are copied and bound to the program variables.

When the request-form is entered to the service-space, it is matched with some serve-form, thus starting the execution of the requested service by some agent. When the result-form is retrieved, the results are bound to the local environment according to the binding list.

The interaction of agents coordinating services with LAURA consists either of putting a request for a service to the service-space, finding a matching offer form and copying of arguments or of trying to get the results of a service, by finding a matching result-form and copying of the results. This interaction is uncoupled, as service-provider and -user remain completely anonymous to each other. However, there remains the problem, that a result provides the results for a specific service.

5.3 Form-Transformations to Establish Logical Connections

Given that we have only two agents working on the service-space, the interaction as described will always succeed. When there are more service-users and -providers, the case can arise that two identical services are requested and result-forms for them are emitted by providers – or a single provider that processes services concurrently – to the service-space. In this case we want that the results of a service are given to the agent that requested it – which cannot be achieved if the interaction is implemented completely uncoupled and based on the matching of service-types only.

"Behind the stages" of LAURA there has to be some mechanism that turns the logical uncoupling into a concrete coupling for the period of time between the choice of some service-provider, the invocation of operations of this agent and the delivery of the service-effects – i.e. the results – to the service-user.

It does so by *form-transformations* that result in *unique forms* by the addition of some unique identifiers. When service is performed, LAURA generates this unique identifier and extends the form with it. serve stores this identifier within a LAURA-library – that has to be used by any agent – and extends the result-form with it. In this case there is only one result-form with that identifier and it can be retrieved by service. The resulting logical connection between provider and requester of a service is bound to the forms and does not require unique identifiers for agents. The logical connection does not imply a physical connection such as a communication channel but is manifested by the unique identifier in the form that then is used for the matching of unique forms.

Figure 4 shows a service interaction and the forms involved. The providing agent executes a serve with the offered interface I, a place holder for the operation code ?o and binding-rules for arguments ?a. The library transforms this serve-form into one with a place holder for a unique-identifier u prepended.

The service-user executes a service for a service with interface J, operation o with arguments a and binding-rules for the results ?r. The library generates unique put- and get-forms from these which include the unique identifier u. Then a match occurs when I is a subtype of J in which case the arguments and o are copied. The put-form is removed from the service-space and the serve-form delivered to the provider with arguments filled in with a. The library strips off u, stores it and binds the values from o and a according to the binding rules ?o and ?a.

The provider processes the service and performs a result with results r. The library prepends the stored u and inserts the unique result-form to the service-space. Here a second match occurs with the unique get-form and the results r are copied. The result-form is destroyed and the put-form delivered to the service-user. Here the library strips off the unique identifier and binds r according to the binding-rules ?r.

The following list highlights the characteristics of LAURA and how they meet the requirements of service-coordination in open distributed systems:

- **Separated focus on coordination** LAURA does focus on the coordination of services and introduces a complete language with respect to this task. Thereby, no assumptions are made on programming languages the implement the processing of services or their execution models. This is necessary to allow the use of multiple languages in an open system.
- **Uncoupled coordination** LAURA requires no form of coupling amongst service-user and -provider. The logical connection with unique identifiers is hidden and induces no physical connections. This is necessary to cope with the dynamics of joining and leaving agents in open systems.
- **Service identification by typed interfaces and subtyping** In LAURA services are identified by the type of their interfaces solely and selected based on a subtyping relation. This is necessary to avoid a global naming mechanisms and to make use of multiple offers for similar services.

6   An Architecture for LAURA

We have implemented LAURA to perform experiments with our approach in a UNIX-environment. We used the communication infrastructure provided by the ISIS-toolkit (Birman and Schiper et al, 91, Birman and Cooper et al, 90). Two

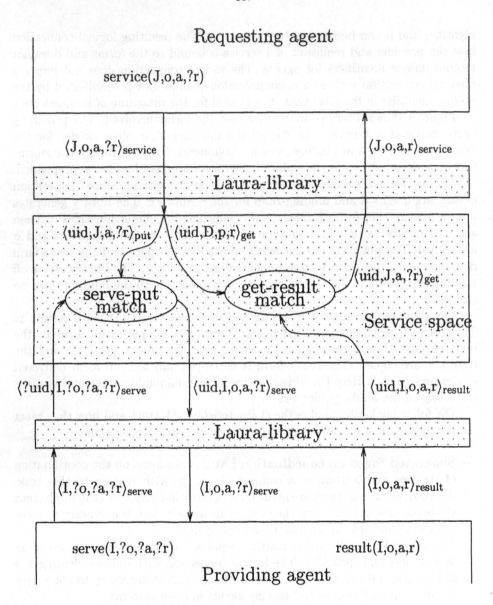

Fig. 4. Forms involved when coordinating a service

embeddings of LAURA 's primitives are provided, one for the programming language C and one for the script language of csh. A precompiler exists for these embeddings. External type-systems are provided by ISIS and by the external data representation XDR by Sun (Sun, 87).

Components programmed in a language with a LAURA-embedding connect to a LAURA kernel on the same machine using UNIX sockets. Calls for LAURA operations are transferred via this socket connection, using XDR for data representation in forms. Thereby, components programmed in different languages can coordinate their work.

The LAURA kernel keeps a local store of forms and performs matching on them. Besides serving the local components, it is connected to other kernels, running on distant machines. The distribution scheme allows coordination amongst distributed components by a partial replication scheme of forms.

6.1 A Distributed LAURA

The LAURA kernel implements operations that work on a shared collection of forms. For the case of a centralized implementation on one machine, two pools of elements are held and operations on them suffice for the implementation.

For a distributed implementation, the communication costs for replication and distributed search have to be balanced for efficiency. We chose a replication scheme similar to the one originally proposed for the S/NET Linda-implementation. The idea is to replicate elements only partially on subsets of all nodes. Within this subset, the search for an element can be performed locally. In contrast to a full replication, the costs for removing a replica decrease. In order to find an element from all subsets, only one node per subset has to be asked for a matching element. This decreases the communication costs.

The distribution scheme is as follows. Let N be the set of nodes that participate in the system. Subsets of nodes can form logical busses meaning that they have the availability to send and receive broadcasted messages to and from the nodes of this subset. There is a set of logical busses $A = (A_0, \ldots, A_n)$, called *add-busses* and a set of logical busses $R = (R_0, \ldots, R_n)$, called *remove-busses*. A node from N is a member of exactly one add- and one remove-bus, so that $\bigcap_{i=0}^{k} A_i = \emptyset$, $\bigcap_{i=0}^{k} R_i = \emptyset$, $\bigcup_{i=0}^{k} A_i = N$ and $\bigcup_{i=0}^{k} R_i = N$. Add- and removebusses are organized so that they form a grid in which an add-bus intersects all remove-busses and vice versa.

Given such an organization, the compromised replication scheme can be implemented by replicating an element that is added at some node over the add-bus which the node is part of and by trying to remove an element from the nodes of the remove-bus. As the remove-bus intersects all add-busses, the union of the replicas held by the nodes therein equals to the union of all elements that have been added in the system.

Moreover the organization has the advantage to localize the effect of an add – all add operations on distinct add-busses are completely independent. Also, searches on distinct remove-busses require no synchronization prior to the removal of a replica. Doing so takes advantage of the independencies formally defined in the previous chapter.

A request for a remove on a remove-bus does access all elements that are currently in the system. If the request fails, the remove-operation has to be stored in some remove-pool from which it is periodically re-issued on the remove-bus.

The delay between an **add** of an element and its removal in the next re-issuing-cycle can be accepted under the relaxed efficiency requirements given in open systems.

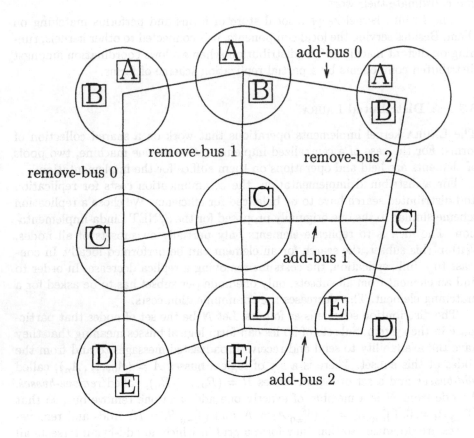

Fig. 5. A partial replication scheme

The organization is depicted in figure 5 for an example system. The nodes are represented by large circles with an element-storage contained in them. The lines represent logical busses as just described. The different layout of the element-stores reflects the fact that no distributed shared memory is established, as elements are not referenced by addresses. The local organization of this storage can be different from node to node.

The organization also allows for a parallel removal of as many distinct elements as there are remove-busses, even with LAURA kernels that operate purely sequentially.

However this organization always requires $n \cdot m$ nodes for n add- and m remove-busses, thus degenerating the system to one add- or remove-bus for –

say – 7 nodes which, in turn, corresponds to the organizations with full or no replication. Also, in an open system the number of nodes involved cannot be chosen in advance to the execution

We therefore introduce the notion of *pseudo-nodes* and design a protocol that handles joining and leaving nodes in order to maintain the described organization while meeting the requirements of open distributed systems.

As described, a node is member of exactly one add- and one remove-bus. This requirement can be upheld for any number of nodes, if we allow a node to have multiple identities in the system. We speak of a pseudo-node for a member of a bus that is simulated by another member on the same add-bus. This simulation is easy to achieve, as the element-replication on the add-bus requires no overhead and the simulating node only has to join a second remove-bus and handle remove-operations from there, too.

Figure 6 shows the evolving structure of the grid as two nodes join. Here, solid bullets represent real nodes, while hollow bullets stand for simulated nodes.

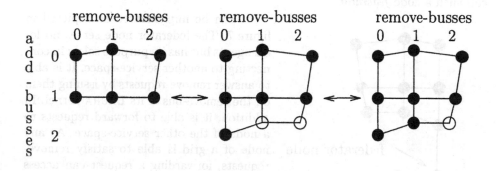

Fig. 6. The organization evolving by added nodes

The removal of nodes leads to the start of new simulated nodes, and finally to the removal of busses on which only simulated nodes exist.

Above we stated that we use the ISIS-toolkit as the communication-infra-structure for our experimental prototype. ISIS is a toolkit that uses *process groups* and *broadcasts* as the basic mechanisms to implement communication and synchronization in a distributed environment. A process group is a collection of processes that can be located on any node in the ISIS-system. A process can join and leave symbolic named groups. Communication is performed by broadcasts of messages to groups. These messages then are delivered to all members of the group.

The distributed organization we outlined in this section, fits well on ISIS mechanisms. We can map the logical busses directly on process-groups. Broadcasts then are messages sent to a process-group. The fault-tolerance of ISIS ensures that no broadcasts will be lost, which would be disastrous for our organization. The synchronization mechanisms ease greatly the implementation of the protocols described in the next sections.

6.2 Scaling and Federation

The distribution scheme outlined relies on a very uniform structure that is only relaxed by pseudo-nodes. Such a uniform structure cannot be guaranteed to be realizable in the light of the heterogeneity and scale of open distributed systems. Two requirements have to be met: First, an architecture for an open distributed system has to be scalable. Second, organizational borders – for example between enterprises that participate in the same system – have to be reflected. But it shows, however, that the structure we have chosen is not as uniform as it may look.

As any node in the service-space has access to the complete storage of forms, it may well communicate with another node from some other grid of nodes. We call such a node *federator*.

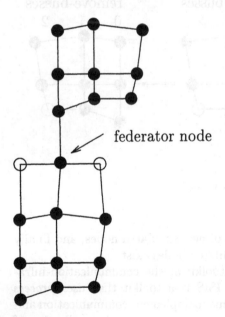

It can be implemented as depicted in figure 7. The federator node serves no local agents but has its purpose solely in connecting to another service-space. It is able to answer remove-requests by issuing them on the remove-bus of its LAURA kernel. In addition, it is able to forward requests to a node of the other service-space. As any node of a grid is able to satisfy remove-requests, forwarding a request can access all elements stored in another service-space.

Such an organization satisfies the requirements we described. First, it becomes possible to scale the service-space by connecting several smaller service-spaces with a grid of federators. The protocols for joining and leaving nodes remain untouched. Also, it is possible to take advantage of dedicated communication lines and protocols amongst the federators.

Second, these federators can be used as "entry-nodes" for LAURA kernels that exist in an organizational context. Having defined federators at each service-space allows it to introduce some form of access-control. It could be defined that the service-space of some enterprise provides services to a specific other one and neglects accesses by others. Our distribution scheme does not require additional protocols for the denial of operations, ignoring them suffices.

Fig. 7. A federator

The additional federator nodes do not necessarily have to run on a dedicated machine. Still, these schemes are only a logical structure that can be implemented on nodes that run another LAURA kernel.

7 Perspectives

LAURA will find its application in the ESPRIT Open LTR project PageSpace (Tolksdorf and Ciancarini, 95), where agents use and offer services concerning hypertext information entities on top of the World Wide Web. LAURA is one of the coordination languages under evaluation to provide the necessary coordination amongst these agents.

References

G. Agha and C. Callsen. ActorSpaces: An Open Distributed Programming Paradigm. In *Proceeding of the Fourth ACM SIGPLAN Symposium on Principles and Practice of Parallel Programming*, 1993.

K. Birman, R. Cooper, T. Joseph, K. Marzullo, M. Makgangou, K. Kane, F. Schmuck, and M. Wood. *The ISIS System Manual, Version 2.1*. The ISIS Project, 1990.

Kenneth Birman, André Schiper, and Pat Stephenson. Lightweight Causal and Atomic Group Multicast. *ACM Transactions on Computer Systems*, 9(3):272–314, 1991.

David Gelernter and Nicholas Carriero. Coordination Languages and their Significance. *Communications of the ACM*, 35(2):97–107, 1992.

ISO/IEC. Basic Reference Model of Open Distributed Processing – Part 1-4, 1995.

ISO/IEC JTC1/SC21. Information Technology – Open Distributed Processing – ODP Trading Function, WG7 Committee Draft, 1994.

Sun. XDR: External Data Representation standard. Request for Comments RFC 1014, Internet Engineering Task Force, June 1987.

Robert Tolksdorf. *Coordination in Open Distributed Systems*. Number 362 in VDI Fortschrittsberichte. VDI Verlag, 1995. PhD Thesis.

Robert Tolksdorf. Naming and typing in languages for coordination in open distributed systems. In Günter Hommel, editor, *Quality of communication based systems*, pages 147–162. Kluwer Academic Publishers, 1995.

Robert Tolksdorf and Paolo Ciancarini. Integrating Internet Services with a PageSpace. In *Proceedings of the ACM SIGCOMM '95 Workshop on Middleware*, 1995.

Visifold*: A Visual Environment for a Coordination Language

Pascal Bouvry and Farhad Arbab

CWI, Kruislaan 413, 1098 SJ Amsterdam, The Netherlands

1 Introduction

Parallel architectures are presently widely available. However developing correct and effective software on these machines is hampered by the lack of proper programming tools. Software engineering tools to assist programmers in writing correct and efficient code are needed. Managing concurrency among different processes adds much difficulty to classical sequential programming. This makes software engineering for parallel processing a crucial issue.

Visifold is a coordination language for orchestration of concurrent activities in massively parallel and distributed computing environments based on Manifold[Arb96]. Visifold is a graphical environment designed to produce Manifold programs. Manifold is a programming language based on the *Idealized Worker Idealized Manager* (IWIM) model[Arb96]. The basic components of Manifold are processes, events, ports and streams. A process is a black box with well defined ports of connection through which it exchanges units of information with the other processes in its environment.

Visifold is currently under development at CWI. Visifold includes a set of tools aimed to design, debug and tune concurrent programs: a program generator, automatic verification tool and monitoring/debugging tools. The program generator is already implemented and is running. In this paper, we first describe the Visifold project and an example of its use. In conclusion, we compare Visifold to some other existing tools.

2 Goals of the Visifold project

Visifold is a graphical programming environment for Manifold and it includes several parts:

- *Visual programming:* Automatic Manifold code production from an interactive graphic description;
- *Monitoring:*Visualization of a program execution ;
- *Debugging:* Different tools for debugging/tuning programs.

These components are described in more detail in the rest of this section.

---

* In memory of our lost friend and colleague Kim Korner who contributed the name Visifold and many of its concepts.

2.1 Visual Programming

In concurrent programming, program designers usually draw task graphs in order to clarify their ideas of different interacting tasks. Then they transform this graphic description into a textual one.

The transformation of graphic to textual representation can be done automatically. Visifold supports such graphical description and automatic code generation. Contrary to many other models, where the textual representation of process communication is coupled with the computational model, in Visifold, the description of process communication remains separate from computation and constitutes a communication protocol between processes. Communication protocols manifest themselves in special processes called coordinators.

Visifold, by its graphical nature, is at a higher level of abstraction than the Manifold language. Through direct manipulation of abstractions, program design becomes easier.

2.2 Monitoring

Tuning parallel programs to improve their performance is not easy. There are many non-trivial issues such as the mapping problem, which can be roughly described as how to distribute processes among processors. Monitoring can help to provide the insight through which proper decisions can be made. The underlying model of Visifold makes it easy to show the critical information obtained through monitoring a running application, in the same visual programming paradigm used for program generation.

2.3 Debugging

Many programming errors are avoided when Visifold is used because:

– Automatic code generation produces syntactically correct programs.
– Actions are restricted to coherent ones.
– Certain inconsistencies can be checked automatically.

Visifold offers off-line debugging facilities by allowing symbolic program execution and on-line debugging facilities by monitoring the real program execution on the target machine.

Presentation of the results of monitoring in the same visual programming paradigm automatically provides an animation of a running application. Many bugs, especially timing and synchronization errors in coordination protocols, can be detected by observing such animations. Special debug mode facilities such as stepping, traps, and replays, directly manipulated through the visual programming interface, provide high-level support for programmer interaction and inspection.

3 An example: The bucket sort

In this section, we illustrate some of the capabilities of Visifold through a program to sort a stream of units. A brief explanation and the Manifold version of this program appear in [Arb96]. Due to space limitations and the highly interactive character of Visifold, it is impossible to give a snapshot of all windows here.

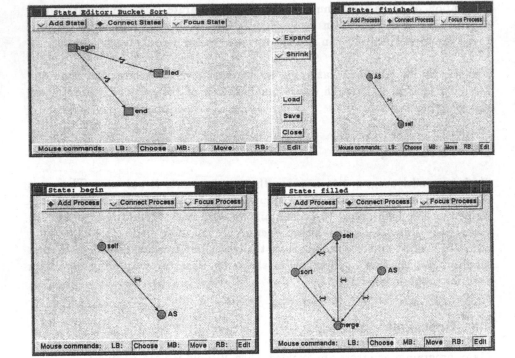

Fig. 1. State and dataflow editors of the bucket-sort coordinator

We show only the snapshots of the coordinator called "Sort" which is composed of four different states:

1. the "begin" state (cf fig 1, bottom left). This state connects the incoming stream to a first atomic sorter.
2. the "finished" state (cf fig 1, top right)., which is in charge of managing a normal termination of the atomic sorter. As all remaining data have been successfully sorted, the output of the atomic sorter will be directly connected to the coordinator output.
3. the "filled" state (cf fig 1, bottom right), which is in charge of managing the filled event raised by the atomic sorter. In this case a new instance of sorted is launched to manage the rest of the unsorted stream. The output of this

new Sort process and the output of the atomic sorter are both connected to a merger. The output of this merger will be connected to the coordinator is output.

4. the "end" state, which is in charge of managing a normal termination of the Sort coordinator until all units it has to deliver have passed through its output port.

4 Conclusion and Perspectives

Visifold is a visual programming environment for a coordination language. Visifold includes a visual programming tool plus monitoring and debugging tools. The visual programming tool, a graphical implementation of the IWIM model, has been implemented.

Visifold runs under X-Window and produces Manifold source code which runs on multiple-platforms: IBM SP, HP, IBM RS6000, SUN OS, SOLARIS, SGI IRIX, Linux and is being ported to Cray. The current implementation uses several thread packages (Posix threads, LWP, IRIX sprocs, etc.) and PVM 3.3.10.

There are similarities between Visifold and some other diagram-oriented tools. HeNCE2 [Ba94] is easy to use but is restricted to static graphs. Phred [BN94] and CODE [NB92] use state diagrams annotated with information on data and their accessibility. They merge dataflows and state diagrams resulting in a style of programming that is powerful but not easy. Visifold tries to find a balance between complexity/expressibility and simplicity. It combines the capabilities of Phred/CODE with the simplicity of HeNCE2. Visifold separates dataflows from state diagrams in a hierarchical fashion, such that each dataflow corresponds to a state. Furthermore, unlike in these other tools, in Visifold, a coordinator is a genuine process and can also be used as a worker by other coordinators.

Visifold is still under development at CWI. Our next goal is to program industrial code using Visifold and to develop the monitoring, debugging, and performance analysis tools based on the running Visifold graphical kernel.

References

[Arb96] Farhad Arbab. The IWIM model for coordination of concurrent activities. In Springer-Verlag, editor, *COORDINATION96*, LNCS, April 1996. Cesena (Italy).

[Ba94] Adam Beguelin and al. HeNCE: A user's guide version 2.0. 1994. Available by anonymous ftp on ftp.netlib.org.

[BN94] Adam Beguelin and Gary Nutt. Visual programming and determinacy: A language specification, an analysis technique, and a programming tool. *Journal of Parallel and Distributed Computing*, 1994.

[NB92] Peter Newton and James C. Browne. The CODE 2.0 graphical parallel programming language. In *Proc. ACM Int. Conf. on Supercomputing*, July 1992.

ALWAN: A Skeleton Programming Language*

Helmar Burkhart and Robert Frank and Guido Hächler

Informatics Department
University of Basel, Switzerland

Abstract. ALWAN is a parallel language and programming environment developed at the Parallel lab of the University of Basle (PUB). The
design goals of ALWAN are to increase the programmability of parallel
applications, enable performance portability, support the reuse of software components, and mixed-language programming. Parallel programs
consist of (sequential) calculation and (parallel) coordination parts. To
address the major difficulties in parallel programming, the ALWAN language provides high level constructs for the description of parallel coordination aspects such as data partitioning and distribution, process topology management and communication aspects. As ALWAN is intended
to specify only the coordination of an algorithm, it provides an interface
to other, widely used, sequential languages, such as C and FORTRAN.
Coordination skeletons and sequential building blocks are processed by
the programming environment (ALWAN compiler and support libraries)
which can automatically generate programs for various parallel architectures.

Language overview

To give a very brief introduction to some aspects of ALWAN we use a systolic
matrix multiplication program (figure 1), to which the line numbers in braces
refer. The algorithm operates on blockwise partitioned matrices placed on a
torus. After first prerotating the input matrices (which includes interactions),
local calculations and rotations (including interactions) alternate in a loop.

ALWAN is a subset of MODULA-2 with a small number of new concepts reflecting the necessities of parallel programming. The TOPOLOGY construct {32-62}
allows the programmer to specify parallel processes. Within a TOPOLOGY, which
is syntactically very much like a procedure. The INHERIT mechanism {33} allows
reusing typical topology properties predeclared in libraries which are written in
ALWAN . Interactions are expressed using the assignment operator, where either the source or the destination, specified by the @<location> constructor, is
on a neighbouring process {48,51,58,59}. A single neighbour (*direction*) is specified when the communication is direct, a set of processes (*group*) is specified
for collective communications. The ACTIVE ...DO statement determines which
processes initiate an interaction {47-52}.

---

* This research project is sponsored by the Swiss Priority Programme in Informatics
Research, Grant 5003-034357.

```
 1: MODULE Systolic;   (* GH 1.2.96 *)
 2: FROM TopoLib IMPORT Torus;
 3: FROM InOut IMPORT WriteString, WriteLn;
 4:
 5: TYPE
 6:   ElemType! = LONGREAL;
 7:   ParamType! = RECORD
 8:                     xDim_A, yDim_A,
 9:                     xDim_B, yDim_B: LONGINT;
10:                END;
11:   (* cf figure a *)
12:   PMatrix(x,y,p:INTEGER)! = ARRAY [0..y-1],[0..x-1] OF ElemType
13:                       PARTITIONED AS BLOCK(y CDIV p), BLOCK(x CDIV p);
14: (*** global variables ***)
15: VAR
16:   A_Matrix, B_Matrix, C_Matrix: PMatrix;
17:   M_Par                       : ParamType;
18:
19: (*** external functions ***)
20: PROCEDURE torusDim:LONGINT; EXTERNAL;
21: PROCEDURE setZero(VAR mat: PART OF PMatrix;
22:                     x,y,w,h: LONGINT); EXTERNAL;
23: PROCEDURE multiply(VAR a,b,c: PART OF PMatrix;
24:                     x_A, y_A, x_B: LONGINT); EXTERNAL;
25: PROCEDURE readParameter(VAR p:ParamType):LONGINT; EXTERNAL;
26: PROCEDURE writeElements(VAR elems: ARRAY OF ElemType;):LONGINT;
27:   EXTERNAL;
28: PROCEDURE readElements(VAR elems: ARRAY OF ElemType;
29:                     fileNo: LONGINT):LONGINT; EXTERNAL;
30:
31: (*** the parallel procedure ***)
32: TOPOLOGY SystolicMult(A,B: PMatrix; VAR C: PMatrix);
33:   INHERIT Torus(torusDim,torusDim); (* cf figure b *)
34:   VAR
35:     i : INTEGER;
36:
37:   BEGIN
38:     (* initialize the result matrix *)
39:     setZero($C, 0, 0, LENGTH($C,0), LENGTH($C,1));
40:     (* set elements not input to zero *)
41:     setZero($A,LAST_INDEX($A,2)+1,LAST_INDEX($A,1)+1,
42:             LENGTH($A,2),LENGTH($A,1));
43:     setZero($B,LAST_INDEX($B,2)+1,LAST_INDEX($B,1)+1,
44:             LENGTH($B,2),LENGTH($B,1));
45:     (* pre-rotation of A and B *)
46:     FOR i := 0 TO torusDim-2 DO
47:       ACTIVE row_id <= i DO (* cf figure e *)
48:         $A: $A@west;
49:       END;
50:       ACTIVE col_id <= i DO
51:         $B := $B@north
52:       END
53:     END;
54:     (* multiply and rotate *)
55:     FOR i := 0 TO torusDim-1 DO
56:       multiply($A,$B,$C,HIGH($A,2),HIGH($A,1),HIGH($B,2));
57:       IF i < torusDim-1 THEN
58:         $A := $A@west; (* cf figure f *)
59:         $B := $B@north
60:       END
61:     END
62:   END SystolicMult;
63:
64: (* controller code *)
65: BEGIN
66:   INPUT M_Par USING readParameter(..);
67:   IF M_Par.xDim_A = M_Par.yDim_B THEN
68:     DIM(A_Matrix,M_Par.xDim_A ,M_Par.yDim_A,torusDim);
69:     DIM(B_Matrix,M_Par.xDim_B, M_Par.yDim_B,torusDim);
70:     DIM(C_Matrix,M_Par.xDim_B, M_Par.yDim_A,torusDim);
71:     INPUT A_Matrix USING readElements(..,1); (* cf figure d *)
72:     INPUT B_Matrix USING readElements(..,2);
73:     SystolicMult(A_Matrix, B_Matrix, C_Matrix);
74:     OUTPUT C_Matrix USING writeElements(..)
75:   ELSE
76:     WriteString("Wrong dimensions.");
77:     WriteLn
78:   END
79: END Systolic.
```

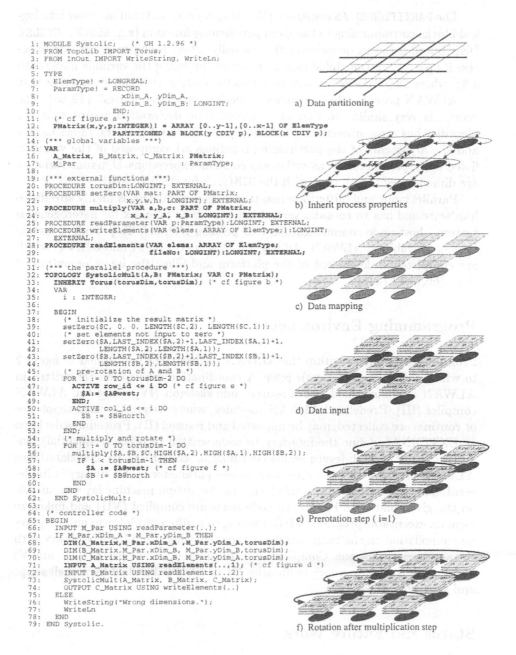

a) Data partitioning

b) Inherit process properties

c) Data mapping

d) Data input

e) Prerotation step (i=1)

f) Rotation after multiplication step

Fig. 1. Systolic Matrix Multiplication

The PARTITIONED AS construct {12,13} splits each index of an array into logical blocks corresponding to the given *partitioning* function (e.g. BLOCK, CYCLE). Distributed data can be viewed either globally, where each process is able to access its part using the global index, or locally (prefixing the variable name with a $), where all processes are able to access their parts with indices starting at 0.

ALWAN provides the possibility to declare "data templates" {12,13}. The syntax is very similar to that of a normal type declaration except that the identifier has a parameter list just like a procedure and that the range indices and the arguments of the partitioning functions are composed of the variables listed in the parameter list as well as any constant expressions. Dynamic variables are dimensioned at run time with the DIM(...) function {68-70}.

Parallel input and output are non-trivial. In general, this is highly specific to hardware and has to consider several issues such as byte sex for heterogeneous systems, host-node communication, true parallel I/O, etc. To provide a certain level of portability, ALWAN defines two constructs (INPUT and OUTPUT) which are completely independent of the platform and allow the input or output of data {66,71,72,74}.

Programming Environment

Program development within the ALWAN environment is outlined in figure 2 to which the Roman numerals refer. A coordination description (I) written in ALWAN is transformed into a source code skeleton (IV) using the ALWAN compiler (III). Predefined ALWAN modules, where frequently used topologies or routines are collected, may be imported and re-used (II). Procedures declared as EXTERNAL define the interface to code written in other (sequential) languages (V). The high-level parallel coordination constructs are translated into ALWAN library (VI) calls with appropriate parameters. This library is implemented for various machines, interfacing to the virtual machine layers available on the given platform. Finally, all code parts are compiled (VII) and linked to form an executable program (VIII). Porting to a different platform only requires a recompilation on the target machine, thus replacing the ALWAN library with the appropriate new one. Compilation of the different source parts (I, IV, and V) and linking to the appropriate libraries (II and VI) is handled by a shell script and generated make files.

Status and Future Work

The ALWAN compiler is implemented on various UNIX platforms. The full set of library routines has been implemented for PVM. To prove the feasibility of our approach, an intermediate version (no support of collective communication, inhomogeneous data, asynchronous communication, and run time checks) was implemented for PVM, MPI, CMMD, and NX and tested on CM5, SP1, Paragon and a workstation cluster containing NeXT and Sun workstations. The compiler

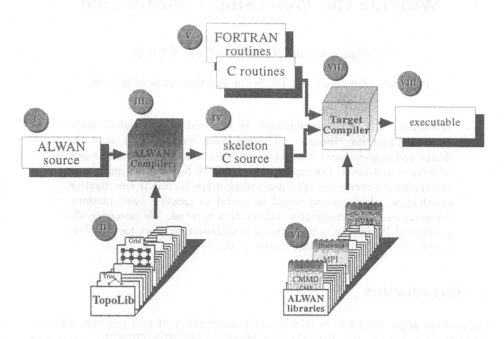

Fig. 2. System Overview

supports mixed-language programming in that the external routines may be written in either C or FORTRAN 77.

A full ALWAN implementation for PVM and MPI will be available in the first quarter of 1996. Further implementations will follow and include support for virtual shared memory systems.

The ALWAN tool suite is currently used within different projects: ALWAN is used within the ALPSTONE performance prediction environment. A library of sample parallel algorithms was built to be used as teachware. This library contains matrix multiplication variants and stencil algorithms (both using a torus topology), bitonic sort using a hypercube topology, divide and conquer sort on a tree, gaussian elimination and transitive closure of graph (Warshall algorithm) both on a farm. Other members of the laboratory use ALWAN to solve application problems (CFD code; image processing for computer-aided surgery). Another project extends ALWAN to support the creation of parallel services for industry standard client server environments.

Contact Person : Robert Frank and Guido Hächler,
  {frank|haechler}@ifi.unibas.ch
Home Page   : http://www.ifi.unibas.ch/~alwan
Reference   : Burkhart, H., Frank, R. and Hächler, G. (1996) Structured
          Parallel Programming: How Informatics Can Help Overcome
          the Software Dilemma, *Scientific Programming, Spring 1996.*

Weaving the Web Using Coordination

P. Ciancarini and R. Tolksdorf and F.Vitali

University of Bologna and TU Berlin and University of Bologna

Abstract. The rapid developments in the field of distributed, inter-networked systems, especially the World Wide Web (WWW), allow the design and implementation of rich environments including a wide variety of services and users. The capabilities of WWW however are quite weak to support the necessities of its demanding users, lacking in coordination capabilities, which instead would be useful to create a basic platform for groupware and cooperative information systems. We introduce the concept of PageSpace, a new kind of middleware support for the Web, which offers coordination capabilities to the WWW.

1 Introduction

Groupware applications have to support coordination of real persons, who are typically networked. The Internet and World Wide Web (WWW) are clearly becoming the major platform for geographically distributed groupware applications. However, the Web technology in its current state does not provide enough of the necessary support services and offers no conceptual framework for them.

Currently there are plenty of opportunities for new services to be provided on the network [1]. In fact the whole world of *middleware* is rapidly evolving [9]. By *Middleware* we designate those areas of software services which "sit" above the traditional network protocols, and provide means for extending the commonly available services to compose and coordinate new and old programs in complex software ensembles which offer innovative services. Coordination technology can be used to integrate services for the support of applications based on federated databases, geographically distributed information spaces (such as the WWW itself), and personal communication tools (eg. e-mail, news and even telephone and video devices).

The *PageSpace* is an abstraction which enhances the capabilities of current WWW middleware using the technology of coordination languages. The Page-Space is intended to support the design and implementation on the Web of open multiuser (groupware) software systems.

2 The WWW: current architecture and problems

The World Wide Web environment is the resulting illusion of several cooperating applications working together thanks to three simple mechanisms. A minimal client-server protocol, HTTP, allows clients to fetch data from servers, directly or through the activation of remote processes; a simple markup language, HTML, allows data to be collected in pages (or documents) and contains several types of formatting instructions, hypertext links, and form-like interactive objects; a world-wide naming scheme, URI, and its more known subset, URL, provide unique global identification of data collections and other network resources. The protocol ruling client-server interactions is so simple, unsafe, and inefficient that often it is necessary to introduce a *proxy*, an intermediate filter between WWW clients and servers, collecting all HTTP requests from the clients, and then delivering the results back to the clients. Proxies are used for caching frequent responses or for security reasons.

Essentially, two problems underline the limits of the current WWW implementation:

1. the volatile nature of resources locators, that makes existing addresses unstable and unreliable.
2. the intrinsic staticity of Web resources, that makes the WWW essentially a browsing mechanism rather than an interaction environment.

Ad-hoc extensions are being studied to account for these problems. However, in our opinion a more general software architecture could open the way for the WWW to offer scalable support to innovative applications.

3 The PageSpace as an integration platform

A number of distinct technologies contribute to the dynamic aspects of the Web: Common Gateway Interface (CGI) scripts are programs that are executed by the server upon request of the browser; server-side includes are extensions tags to HTML detected by the server before transferring a page and substituted with some dynamically generated information (e.g. the current date); application specific MIME-types are data types that cannot be displayed by the browser and that are usually fed to an external application; browser scripting languages are passed along with an HTML page and are executed by enhanced browsers (e.g. Java).

These mechanisms involve a number of protocols and different approaches (CGI protocol, server configurations, MIME setup etc.). In order to overcome such complexities and to add value to the Web as a platform for distributed, open applications, the PageSpace introduces two general issues:

- The Web is enhanced with support for active agents (brokers) which use and offer services. Also, the specialized viewer application is an integral part of an active page that is executed by the browser.
- The PageSpace provides means to coordinate all these activities. We apply coordination technology based on the tuple space paradigm.

The integration of an active Web by a uniform notion of activity and coordination serves another purpose: as the various distinct technologies listed above are replaced by a single framework, the development of distributed application running on top of the Web becomes easier. It becomes possible to model the WWW itself with all its clients, servers, proxies, and a number of additional tools as an uniform service-based framework.

4 Engineering the PageSpace

The Java language is rapidly becoming a *de facto* standard for scripting client-side applications on the WWW. Java is a sort of simplified object oriented language easily portable across several architectures. Many commercial and research browsers have announced Java support.

Java, although powerful, lacks of a general coordination model. Thus, the coordination of active agents within the PageSpace shall be expressed and implemented using a certain type of parallel programming languages, called *coordination languages*. Our basic idea is to augment Java with the coordination model offered by some coordination language. We are exploring two possible candidates for this task:

- SHADE, an object-based coordination language developed in Bologna [5], which includes the concepts of a shared object dataspace and objects-as-multisets. It has been designed to offer the abstraction of a shared object space that is both a repository for objects and a coordination media of services and of their clients. Inheritance is implemented by delegation. Coordination is driven by rules and is based on associative communication between an object and the object space.
- LAURA, a coordination language developed in Berlin [11] which extends the Linda's Tuple Space with the concept of services that can be associatively requested. LAURA has been designed to meet the requirements of open distributed systems, such as heterogeneity of hardware, networks, and software as well as to potential high dynamics of the system caused by joining and leaving components. It provides three coordination primitives that manipulate forms in a shared data space, called the service-space. These forms contain service-offers, -requests and -results. Services are identified by the types of their interfaces, matched according to a subtype relation. LAURA is implemented on top of the ISIS toolkit [3] and has been embedded into C and csh.

The PageSpace concept should be a conservative extension of the mechanisms used in WWW and retain their elegant and efficient simplicity; only minor extensions to the coordination languages chosen for the experiment are foreseen, and implementation will be based on existing standard components, such as communication toolkits, information brokers, public-domain WWW tools, etc.

5 Related approaches

Interestingly, there are already several examples of projects based on specific middleware for WWW geared towards integrating coordination. Some of these projects are aimed at improving the World Wide Web itself, some make use of it for specific purposes.

There are three different approaches at extending WWW for middleware applications:

- *at the server*, having HTTP requests activate CGI applications and return the output as an HTML page. For instance the WWW Linda Toolkit [10] is a simple interface between WWW and a Linda tuple space implementation providing access to a shared tuple space through an HTML form; in [2] a general architecture for integrating DCE middleware components into the WWW through CGI is proposed; in Web* HTML data and TCL script are mixed. Each script invocation is then substituted by its output on the server before sending the document to the client. External services are accessible through the CORBA-compliant Orbix system, which is completely interfaced with the Web* application.
- *at the client/browser*, having pages returned by the server "executed" by local applications (client's clients). For instance, in SHAREd Web [8], several concurrent applications are activated to create a complete collaborative environment for a team of designers working on a project; the WWWinda project [7] is building a flexible, modular WWW browser architecture based on the Linda programming language creating several independent tools, each implementing a different part of the whole WWW browser; some browsers add support for complete general purpose scripting language: HotJava and recent generation Netscape Navigators support Java, the Grail browser (`http://monty.cnri.reston.va.us/grail`) is built and extendible with Python, and the SurfIt! browser (`http://pastime.anu.edu.au/SurfIt/`) supports extensions and applets written in Safe-Tcl.
- *at the proxy*, having HTTP requests and responses collected and acted upon. For instance, OreO [4] is a proxy toolkit for creating generic filters between unmodified browsers and unmodified servers.

6 Conclusions

The PageSpace is an Open LTR project (the first one in software) involving Technische Universität Berlin (TUB) and the University of Bologna (UniBo). In this first phase, we are surveying advanced coordination applications of the WWW, studying the middleware necessary to support these applications, formulating it in terms of coordination primitives written in SHADE or LAURA, and developing a preliminary design and prototype of such a middleware.

With the prototype we intend to demonstrate how the PageSpace concept is suited for designing coordination systems at a world-wide scale by setting up a common framework and implementing typical agents that offer useful services.

We can envision several applications of PageSpace. We are currently concentrating on studying some in office automation, process centered environments, and concurrent engineering, which are directly grounded on rule-based, coordinated workflow frameworks and groupware applications.

- monitoring process-centered environments: documents are stored and retrieved representing the state of a software process [6].
- distributed auction bidding: the Web is used to sell and buy goods using stock exchange mechanisms [5].
- infotainment servers integrated in the WWW, implementing services such as the Internet Chess Server, a virtual chess club where games can be played, observed and commented.

Acknowledgements. We thank for support the EU Open LTR project Page-Space n. 20179. P. Ciancarini was also partially supported by Italian CNR.

References

1. R. Adler. Distributed Coordination Models for Client/Server Computing. *IEEE Computer*, 28(4):14–22, April 1995.
2. A. Beitz, R. Iannella, A. Vogel, Z. Yang, and T. Woo. Integrating WWW and Middleware. In R. Debreceny and A. Ellis, editors, *Proc. 1st Australian World Wide Web Conference*, Lismore, NSW, 1995. Norsearch Publishing.
3. K. Birman, A. Schiper, and P. Stephenson. Lightweight Causal and Atomic Group Multicast. *ACM Transactions on Computer Systems*, 9(3):272–314, 1991.
4. C. Brooks, M. S. Mazer, S. Meeks, and J. Miller. Application-Specific Proxy Servers as HTTP Stream Transducers. In *Electronic Proc. 4th Int. World Wide Web Conference "The Web Revolution"*, Boston, MA, December 1995.
5. S. Castellani, P. Ciancarini, and D. Rossi. The ShaPE of ShaDE: a coordination system. Technical Report UBLCS, Dipartimento di Scienze dell'Informazione, Università di Bologna, Italy, 1995.
6. P. Ciancarini. Modeling The Software Process Using Coordination Rules. In *Proc. 4th IEEE Workshop on Enabling Technology: Infrastructure for Collaborative Enterprises*, pages 46–53, Berkley Springs, WV, April 1995. IEEE Computer Society Press.
7. Y. Gutfreund, J. Nicol, R. Sasnett, and V. Phuah. WWWinda: An Orchestration Service for WWW Browsers and Accessories. In *Electronic Proc. of the 2nd Conf. on the WWW: Mosaic and the Web*, Chicago, IL, December 1994.
8. V. Kumar, J. Glicksman, and G. A. Kramer. A SHAREd Web To Support Design Teams. In *IEEE Third Workshop on Enabling Technologies: Infrastructure for Collaborative Enterprises*, Morgantown, WV, April 1994.
9. T. Lewis. Where is Client/Server Software Headed? *IEEE Computer*, 28(4):49–55, April 1995.
10. W. Schoenfeldinger. WWW Meets Linda. In *Electronic Proc. 4th Int. World Wide Web Conference "The Web Revolution"*, Boston, MA, December 1995.
11. R. Tolksdorf. *Coordination in Open Distributed Systems*. PhD thesis, Techniche Universitet, Berlin, Germany, December 1994.

Investigating Strategies for Cooperative Planning of Independent Agents Through Prototype Evaluation

E.-E. Doberkat and W. Hasselbring and C. Pahl

University of Dortmund, Informatik 10 (Software Technology)
D-44221 Dortmund, Germany
{doberkat|willi|pahl}@ls10.informatik.uni-dortmund.de

Abstract. This paper discusses the application of the prototyping approach to investigating the requirements on strategies for cooperative planning and conflict resolution of independent agents by means of an example application: the strategic game "Scotland Yard". The strategies for coordinating the agents, which are parallel algorithms, are developed with a prototyping approach using PROSET-Linda. PROSET-Linda is designed for prototyping parallel algorithms.

We concentrate on the techniques employed to elicit the requirements on the algorithms for agent interaction. The example application serves to illustrate the prototyping approach to requirements elicitation by means of a non-trivial instance for investigating algorithms for cooperative planning and conflict resolution.

1 Introduction

Cooperative planning of independent agents is a realistic problem which requires careful study. For concentrating on the essential aspects (plan generation, conflict resolution) we propose in this paper a prototypical approach which is realized for a strategic game called "Scotland Yard". This game has a number of cooperating detectives who chase a villain through London using different means of public transportation. The villain's moves are only partially visible. Each detective develops for each move a plan which may or may not conflict with the plans of fellow agents; if it does, the conflict has to be resolved before all the agents make their moves. There is no master detective who supervises plan generation in general (and conflict resolution in particular), so the detectives have to come to terms on their own.

Finding a clear and intelligible solution to plan generation and conflict resolution is certainly more important than obtaining directly a very efficient program — once a solution is found through exploration, it may be used as an executable specification for an efficient implementation. Consequently, we concentrate on conceptual aspects and implement our solution in a prototyping language.

Prototyping means modelling essential features, and strategies, which are certainly essential here, may very well be isolated textually from the rest of the code. Then it is easy to experiment with strategies and, equally important, easy to argue even informally about strategies: this is so since the very high level character of our prototyping language makes the details of a strategy rather transparent (which would not always be the case in programs written in one of the common production languages).

2 Prototyping Parallel Algorithms with PROSET-Linda

Cooperation is a central aspect in distributed artificial intelligence applications. Implementing cooperative planning algorithms is parallel programming, what is conceptually harder to undertake and to understand than sequential programming, because a programmer often has to focus on more than one process/agent at a time. Consequently, developing parallel algorithms is in general considered an awkward undertaking. The goal of the PROSET-Linda approach is to partially overcome this problem by providing a tool for prototyping parallel algorithms [5]. To support prototyping parallel algorithms, a prototyping language should provide simple and powerful facilities for dynamic creation and coordination of parallel processes.

In PROSET, the concept for process creation via Multilisp's futures [4] is adapted to set-oriented programming and combined with the coordination language Linda [3] to obtain the parallel programming language PROSET-Linda. Linda is a coordination language which provides means for synchronization and communication through so-called tuple spaces. The access unit in tuple spaces is the tuple, similar to tuples in PROSET. Several library functions are provided for handling multiple tuple spaces dynamically.

3 Design and Implementation of the Application

An important element to be realized in our implementation of the Scotland Yard game is a program structure being supportive of coordinating the program components. These components are a *graphical user interface*, a *rule component*, and finally a *planning component*. The graphical user interface, which has been realized with `Tcl/Tk` [6], displays the board together with other information, and handles the communication with the player. The rule component manages the board, supervises the correctness of the moves, and executes the moves. The planning component is realized by autonomous detectives. Two separate tuple spaces are used for communication (see Fig. 1). Planning among the detectives is done with a tuple space called `planboard`. The interaction with the rule component is realized through a tuple space called `ruleboard`.

It is possible to dynamically select the strategy to be used for each detective. All strategies can be used together in one game. Detectives using different strategies are able to cooperate.

The moves of the detectives have to be coordinated when conflicts arise or when the total effort should be optimized. Conflicts arise when two or more detectives want to move to the same location. Therefore, each detective computes

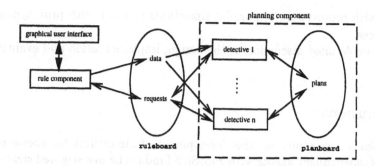

Fig. 1. Tuple spaces used for coordination.

a set of moves, each move is scored. If two detectives want to move to the same location with their best moves, i.e. their highest scored moves, the scores will determine, which detectives can execute his move and which detective has to select another move. The latter detective is the detective whose loss is smaller when he cannot execute his highest scored move. This loss is the difference between his best and his second best scored move.

4 Strategies and their Evaluation

Our goal is to implement and evaluate executable prototypes of cooperative planning algorithms to exploratively analyze the requirements on such algorithms. Several strategies have been implemented and evaluated. Examples are a simple randomized version for initial testing, the *minimal-distance* strategy tries to minimize the shortest paths from each detective to the possible positions of Mister-X, the *distance-sum* strategy tries to minimize the sum over all such paths, and a variation of the strategy presented in [1]. In another strategy, which we call *mixture*, each detective selects for every move randomly among the latter three strategies (excluding the random strategy). The high level of PROSET-Linda allowed us to easily experiment with different algorithmic variations.

Additional strategies varying the planning depth or the procedure of scoring the moves have been implemented. Others integrate elements of static valuations of positions into their planning algorithms. One strategy which considers not only the position of Mister-X but also the positions of the neighboring detectives to obtain a good distribution for avoiding conflicts has been proven to be most successful in the experimental evaluation at our department. A detailed discussion of the implemented and evaluated strategies is beyond the scope of this paper.

As an aside, we mention that some players studied the individual strategies of the detectives to base their movements on this knowledge to obtain better positions. Against such players, the *mixture* strategy is the most successful, because the player cannot rely on deterministic movements by the detectives.

Also, the graphical user interface changed during the evaluation according to the user's requests. We do not discuss this in detail here, because this paper is concerned with prototyping of parallel algorithms and not with prototyping of user interfaces.

For a more detailed discussion of the design, implementation and evaluation refer to [2].

5 Conclusions

We presented a case study for the development of algorithms for cooperation strategies of independent agents with PROSET-Linda. The investigated strategies for planning are only sketched in this short paper. The emphasis is on the prototypical development and evaluation of planning algorithms for independent agents.

The evaluation showed that not all algorithmic variations for the planning strategies are good candidates for further (more efficient) implementations with some lower-level language. If we had implemented *all* the algorithms directly with a production language, for example C with extensions for message passing, the implementation effort would have been higher. This is what prototyping is about: experimenting with ideas for algorithms and evaluating them to make the right decisions for the next steps in the development. Purely theoretic evaluations are often not possible in practice. However, the exact savings in time cannot be presented: This would require a similar project without prototyping for comparison.

The main technical contribution of this paper is demonstrating the flexibility of incorporating different approaches for planning and conflict resolution strategies for independent agents. This is made possible through the use of a very high-level language and the corresponding techniques for exploratively prototyping algorithms.

References

1. W. Becker and A. Zell. Cooperative planing of independent agents. Technical Report 5/91, University of Stuttgart, IPVR, Stuttgart, Germany, 1991.
2. E.-E. Doberkat, W. Hasselbring, and C. Pahl. Investigating strategies for cooperative planning of independent agents through prototype evaluation. Software-Technologie Memo Nr. 86, University of Dortmund, Dept. of Computer Science, Dortmund, Germany, December 1995.
3. D. Gelernter. Generative communication in Linda. *ACM Transactions on Programming Languages and Systems*, 7(1):80–112, January 1985.
4. R.H. Halstead. Multilisp: A language for concurrent symbolic computation. *ACM Transactions on Programming Languages and Systems*, 7(4):501–538, October 1985.
5. W. Hasselbring. *Prototyping Parallel Algorithms in a Set-Oriented Language*. Dissertation (University of Dortmund, Dept. Computer Science). Verlag Dr. Kovač, Hamburg, 1994.
6. J.K. Ousterhout. *Tcl and the Tk Toolkit*. Addison-Wesley Publishing, 1994.

A Case Study of Integration of a Software Process Management System with Software Engineering Environments for Process Monitoring and Management

Atsuo Hazeyama[1] and Seiichi Komiya[2]

[1] NEC Corporation
2-11-5 Shibaura Minato-ku Tokyo 108 Japan

[2] Information-technology Promotion Agency (IPA)
3-1-38 Shibakoen Minato-ku Tokyo 105 Japan

Abstract. The authors aim at constructing an integrated software project management system. They have thus far considered a framework to support schedule management of the whole project based on coarse-grained processes. However, a coarse-grained process is often composed of more fine-grained processes. Progress of a coarse-grained process can be often grasped as an accumulation of progress of more fine-grained processes. This paper clarifies a framework to support different granularity of processes integratedly and to manage processes of the whole project.

1 Introduction

With the advance of the informatization of society, the need for software development has been increasing. Furthermore, along with the trends toward increasing the scale and complexity in the software developed, it has become difficult to complete the development of such software in accordance with the quality as required, the deadline, and within budgetary limits. Large-scale software is usually developed by organizing a project to gather manpower and they are best carried out by adopting management-oriented approach. In such projects, coordination plays very important roles and therefore supporting coordination is important.

Coordination has been defined as the direction of individuals' efforts toward achieving common and authorized goals and the integration or linking together with different parts of an organization to accomplish a collective set of tasks[2].

There are two types in support of coordination by computers:

(1) generates solutions for coordination automatically.
(2) supports decision making for coordination, namely, collects data and processes them for decision making.

Coordination in software development is also categorized into the following four types:

(a) scheduling

(b) support of mutual consent

(c) version/configuration management

(d) workflow management

We have been aiming at constructing a model and system to support coordination work in software project management. We have proposed a model and system for schedule management of coarse-grained processes which took into account the characteristics of software projects, that is, the agents of software processes (humans) are usually engaged in plural activities concurrently [1]. Therefore the model represented not only the constraints on activities but also those between activities and workers (i.e., supported (2) for (a)).

Here coarse-grained processes mean activities to take several days or weeks to complete them, such as design, coding, test etc. Therefore schedule management of each worker was also done based on this type of processes. However coarse-grained processes might involve more fine-grained processes which do not appear in the schedule tables and progress of the coarse-grained process can be obtained by accumulating progress of the more fine-grained processes. For example, the divergence trend of bugs is one progress data for a system test of a software. It is calculated by accumulating the number of problem reports. If we can support bug resolution process, we will be able to get the data from the process. As project managers do not grasp the details of all the processes and each worker's schedule, collection of the process data is necessary for appropriate management and coordination. At this time, as the project size becomes large and/or process management cycle becomes short-term, data collection becomes hard work. Therefore automatic data collection becomes important (it is not essential but it becomes a powerful tool). For automatic data collection, the integration of a process management system and software development environments which development activities are performed is necessary.

In this paper, we will propose a model for integrating both coarse-grained processes of the whole project and fine-grained processes performed in a coarse-grained process for process monitoring and management of the whole project (i.e., supported (2) for (a) & (d)).

2 Support Model

This section proposes a model for integrating both coarse-grained process of the whole project and fine-grained process performed in a coarse-grained process for process monitoring and management of the whole project.

As we described in the previous section, we have thus far proposed a process model for software process management to manage processes we call coarse-grained in this paper. This model is composed of 5 major objects (activity, product, resource, role, project) and their relationships.

In order to manage both the coarse-grained processes and more fine-grained processes integratedly, workflow of each product object needs to be gone into details.

In the fine-grained processes, product object is transferred into workers. To represent the progress, finite state machine model is effective. Therefore we introduce an attribute "status" into product objects and represent state transitions on this attribute. We also introduced the relationship 'current_owner' between product objects and resource objects so that we can grasp who owns the product object at each state. Furthremore we introduce attributes "efforts estimation" and "work assignment period" to grasp the workload of each activity and each worker.

Fig. 1 shows the model for the integrated process management. Fig. 2 also shows an example finite state machine model for a product "problem report"(i.e., problem resolution process for debugging and test).

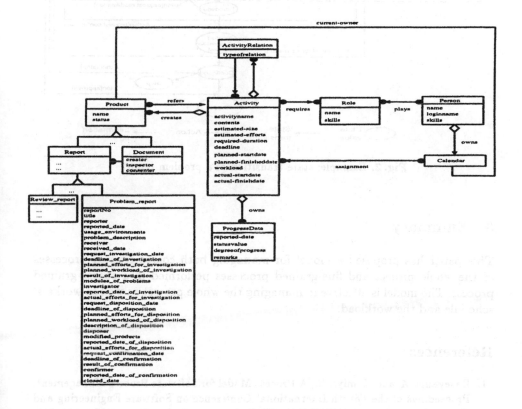

Fig. 1. Object model for integrated process management

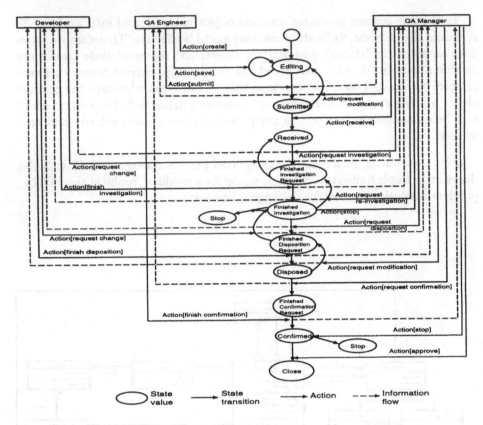

Fig. 2. Example: state transition of a problem report

3 Summary

This paper has proposed a model for managing both coarse-grained processes of the whole project and fine-grained processes performed in a coarse-grained process. The model is effective in managing the whole project as well as workers' schedule and the workload.

References

1. Hazeyama, A. and Komiya, S., A Process Model for Software Process Management, Proceedings of the Fourth International Conference on Software Engineering and Knowledge Engineering (SEKE'92), IEEE Computer Sosiety Press (1992) 582–589.
2. Kraut, R. E., and Streeter, L. A., Coordination in Software Development, Communications of ACM, Vol.38, No.3 (1995) 69–81.

Nepi: A Network Programming Language Based on the π-Calculus*

Eiichi Horita and Ken Mano

NTT Communication Science Laboratories, horita/mano@progn.kecl.ntt.jp

1 Introduction

We propose a network/distributed programming language called *Nepi*. Nepi is based on the π-calculus [5, 4], a process algebra having a facility for passing communication channels between processes. After giving the syntax of Nepi in Sect. 2, we give, in Sect. 3, the operational semantics of Nepi via a Plotkin-style transition system [7]. Then we describe a distributed implementation of Nepi in Sect. 4. First we introduce another calculus called the νπ-calculus, which is shown to be equivalent to the π-calculus at an appropriate level of abstraction; the νπ-calculus is more suited toward distributed implementation. Next, the implementation of Nepi is provided by implementing the νπ-calculus in Unix using standard facilities such as sockets.

Pierce and Turner developed *Pict*, a language based on the π-calculus, and provided a uniprocessor implementation of it [6]. As pointed out in [6], multiprocessor implementations of any language based on the π-calculus remain for future research. Our development of Nepi is an effort in this direction. With Nepi, two programs invoked as different OS processes residing in different machines in a network can communicate with each other. This is why we call Nepi a network programming language.

Berry and Boudol proposed a new kind of abstract machines, called the *chemical abstract machines* [1]. There, two abstract machines were introduced to describe the behavior of mobile processes specified in the π-calculus [1, Sect. 5.2]. One of these machines uses the concept of *name server*, which the νπ-calculus also uses. However, no formal comparison between the π-calculus and the abstract machines is given in [1], and actual implementations based on the abstract machines remain to be developed. The main contributions of our paper are the formal proof of the equivalence between the π-calculus and the νπ-calculus and an actual implementation of the latter in a network.

2 Syntax

The underlying framework of Nepi is the π-calculus, which is an algebraic calculus rather than a programming language. To develop a compiler, we need to specify a concrete syntax, which we give along the lines of the S-expression syntax of Lisp.

---

* This paper is an extended abstract of [2].

The phrase "let $(x \in) X$ be ..." introduces a set X with a variable x ranging over X. The set of natural numbers is denoted by ω. The power set of a set X is denoted by $\wp(X)$. For a set A, we write A^* to denote the set of finite sequences of elements of A. We denote the syntactic identity between expressions by $\equiv$. The syntactic category Id of *identifiers* is defined as in C.

In Nepi, there are four basic types: int (of *integers*), str (of *character strings*), chan (of *communication channels*), and proc (of *processes*). Let $\mathcal{V}_{\text{int}}$ $\mathcal{V}_{\text{str}}$, $(\xi \in) \mathcal{V}_{\text{chan}}$, and $(A \in) \mathcal{V}_{\text{proc}}$ be the syntactic categories of variables of types int, str, chan, and proc, respectively. Each of these is defined as a subset of Id, by specifying the starting letter of the identifiers in it: elements of $\mathcal{V}_{\text{int}}$ (resp. $\mathcal{V}_{\text{str}}$, $\mathcal{V}_{\text{chan}}$ and $\mathcal{V}_{\text{pro}}$) are identifiers starting with i (resp. w , c and p). Let $(z \in) \mathcal{V}_{\text{data}} = \mathcal{V}_{\text{int}} \cup \mathcal{V}_{\text{str}}$ and $(x \in) \mathcal{V}_{\text{val}} = \mathcal{V}_{\text{data}} \cup \mathcal{V}_{\text{chan}}$.

Value Expressions. We call int and str *built-in data types* of Nepi, and put $(t \in)$ $\text{DT} = \{\text{int}, \text{str}\}$. A set DO of *built-in operators* on these types is also provided, together with a typing function type : $\text{DO} \to (\text{DT}^* \times \text{DT})$.[1] For each $t \in \text{DT}$, let $\mathcal{L}_t$ be the set of terms of type t constructed from the signature (DT, DO).[2] We use **n** as a metavariable ranging over $\mathcal{L}_{\text{int}}$. Let $(d \in) \mathcal{L}_{\text{data}} = \bigcup\{\mathcal{L}_t | t \in \text{DT}\}$. We assume that for each $t \in \text{DT}$, a semantic domain $\mathbf{DV}_t$ is given as a subset of $\mathcal{L}_t$, and that for each operator $F \in \text{DO}$ with $\text{type}(F) = ((t_1, \ldots, t_r), \tilde{t})$, a function from $\mathbf{DV}_{t_1} \times \cdots \times \mathbf{DV}_{t_r}$ to $\mathbf{DV}_{\tilde{t}}$ is given as the predefined *interpretation* of F. We put $(\mathbf{d} \in) \mathbf{DV} = \bigcup\{\mathbf{DV}_t | t \in \text{DT}\}$. The *evaluation* $[\![d]\!] \in \mathbf{DV}$ of each *closed data expression* d is determined by the interpretations of the operators in DO.[3]

From $\mathcal{L}_{\text{str}}$, the syntactic category $(u \in) \mathcal{L}_{\text{chan}}$ of *channel expressions* is defined by $\mathcal{L}_{\text{chan}} = \mathcal{V}_{\text{chan}} \cup \{(\text{ch } d)| d \in \mathcal{L}_{\text{str}}\}$. Finally, we define the syntactic category $(v \in) \mathcal{L}_{\text{val}}$ of *value expressions* by $\mathcal{L}_{\text{val}} = \mathcal{L}_{\text{data}} \cup \mathcal{L}_{\text{chan}}$.

Process Expressions and Programs. Process expressions of Nepi are constructed as algebraic terms from the following primitive constructs plus λ-notation: (1) 'δ' for *inaction*, (2) ' $\|$ ' for *parallel composition*, (3) 'ν' for generation of a fresh channel. (4) '!' for *output*, (5) '?' for *input*, (6) '+' for *alternative choice*, (7) a set $(\mathbf{o} \in) \mathbf{OP}$ of *output ports*, (8) a set $(\mathbf{i} \in) \mathbf{IP}$ of *input ports*, and (9) 'if' for *conditionals*. Formally, the syntactic category $(P, Q \in) \mathcal{L}_{\text{proc}}$ of *process expressions* is defined simultaneously with the category $(G \in) \mathcal{L}_{\text{pref}}$ of *prefixed process expressions* by the following grammar:

$$\begin{cases} P ::= \delta \mid (\| \ P_1 \ P_2) \mid (\nu \ \xi \ P) \mid G \mid (+ \ G_1 \ \cdots \ G_n) \mid (A \ v_1 \ \cdots \ v_n) \\ \quad \mid (\text{if } \mathbf{n} \ P_1 \ P_2) \mid (\mathbf{o} \ d \ P) \mid (\mathbf{i} \ (\lambda \ z \ P)), \\ G ::= (! \ u \ v \ P) \mid (? \ u \ (\lambda \ x \ P)). \end{cases}$$

For $P \in \mathcal{L}_{\text{proc}}$, let $\text{FV}(P)$ denote the set of *free variables* contained in P. Let $\mathcal{L}_{\text{proc}}^{\emptyset} = \{P \in \mathcal{L}_{\text{proc}} | \text{FV}(P) = \emptyset\}$.

---

[1] In this paper, we use the term 'operator' as a synonym of 'operation symbol' to refer to a syntactic entity.

[2] We can introduce new data types and new operators on data by giving their definitions in C; for the syntax for doing this, see [2].

[3] An expression is said to be *closed* when it contains no free variables.

Each program of Nepi consists of zero or more declarations of processes and the *main process expression*. We define $\mathcal{D}_{\text{proc}}$ to be the set of declarations of the form $(A \ (x_1 \ \cdots \ x_n) \ P)$, which declares the process A with formal parameters $x_1, \cdots, x_n$ and the body P. From $(\Delta \in) \ \mathcal{D}_{\text{proc}}$ and $(P \in) \ \mathcal{L}_{\text{proc}}$, we define the syntactic category $(R \in) \ \mathcal{L}_{\text{prog}}$ of *Nepi programs* by $R ::= (\text{labels} \ (\Delta_1 \ \cdots \Delta_n) \ P)$, borrowing the *labels* construct of Lisp for defining mutually recursive processes.

3 Operational Semantics Based on the π-Calculus

Following [4], we define the *structural congruence* $\equiv$ over $\mathcal{L}_{\text{proc}}$ as the smallest congruence relation satisfying several laws, which are essentially the same as the six laws in [4, Sect. 2.3]. For channel expressions u_1 and u_2, we write $u_1 \cong u_2$ to mean that both u_1 and u_2 are channel variables with $u_1 \equiv u_2$ or that both u_1 and u_2 are closed terms with $[\![u_1]\!] = [\![u_2]\!]$. For expressions $P, v_1, \ldots, v_r$, and distinct variables $x_1, \ldots, x_r$, we denote by $P[\langle v_1, \ldots, v_r \rangle / \langle x_1, \ldots, x_r \rangle]$ the result of the simultaneous substitution of $v_1, \ldots, v_r$ for $x_1, \ldots, x_r$ in P. We define the set $\mathbf{E}$ of *events* by $(e \in) \ \mathbf{E} = (\mathbf{OP} \times \mathbf{DV}) \cup (\mathbf{IP} \times \mathbf{DV})$. Let $(a \in) \ \mathbf{E}_\tau = \mathbf{E} \cup \{\tau\}$, where τ is a symbol representing an *internal* (or *unobservable*) action.

The *transition relations* $\xrightarrow{a}$ $(a \in \mathbf{E}_\tau)$ are defined as the smallest binary relations on $\mathcal{L}_{\text{proc}}$ satisfying the following laws COMM–STRUCT.

COMM: If $u_1 \cong u_2$ and $\text{type}(v) = \text{type}(x)$, then
$$(\| \ (+ \ \cdots \ (! \ u_1 \ v \ P) \ \cdots) \ (+ \ \cdots \ (? \ u_2 \ (\lambda \ x \ Q)) \ \cdots)) \xrightarrow{\tau} (\| \ P \ Q[v/x]).$$
OUT: For each $\mathbf{o} \in \mathbf{OP}$, we have $(\mathbf{o} \ d \ P) \xrightarrow{(\mathbf{o},[\![d]\!])} P$.

IN: For each $\mathbf{i} \in \mathbf{IP}$, we have $(\mathbf{i} \ (\lambda \ z \ P)) \xrightarrow{(\mathbf{i},d)} P[d/z]$.
COND: If $[\![\mathbf{n}]\!] \neq 0$, then $(\text{if} \ \mathbf{n} \ P_1 \ P_2) \xrightarrow{\tau} P_1$; otherwise, $(\text{if} \ \mathbf{n} \ P_1 \ P_2) \xrightarrow{\tau} P_2$.
REC: If $(A \ (x_1 \ \cdots \ x_r) \ P)$ is in the declaration part, then
$$(A \ v_1 \ \cdots \ v_r) \xrightarrow{\tau} P[\langle v_1, \ldots, v_r \rangle / \langle x_1, \ldots, x_r \rangle].$$
PAR: $P \xrightarrow{a} P'$ implies $(\| \ P \ Q) \xrightarrow{a} (\| \ P' \ Q)$.
RES: $P \xrightarrow{a} P'$ implies $(\nu \ \xi \ P) \xrightarrow{a} (\nu \ \xi \ P')$.
STRUCT: $Q \equiv P$, $P \xrightarrow{a} P'$ and $P' \equiv Q'$ implies $Q \xrightarrow{a} Q'$.

From $\xrightarrow{a}$ $(a \in \mathbf{E}_\tau)$, we define so-called *weak* transition relations $\xRightarrow{s}$ $(s \in (\mathbf{E}_\tau)^*)$, and thereby the concept of *weak bisimulation* as in [3].

The rule STRUCT is useful in simplifying the definition of the transition relation, but imposes difficulty in distributed implementation of the π-calculus. In the next section, we introduce another calculus named the $\nu\pi$-calculus, which is shown to be equivalent to the π-calculus at an appropriate level of abstraction, and is more suited to distributed implementation.

4 Implementation Based on the $\nu\pi$-Calculus

The transition relations of the $\nu\pi$-calculus are defined as binary relations between *system configuration*, which are pairs of a process expression and an integer. We define the transition relations between system configurations as in Sect. 3, except that we replace the rules RES and STRUCT in Sect. 3 by the rules RES_ν and STRUCT_ν given below.

To give the rule RES_ν, we need to introduce distinct channel constants $\gamma_0, \gamma_1, \gamma_2, \ldots$ not appearing in $\mathcal{L}_{\mathrm{proc}}$. Let $\tilde{\mathcal{L}}_{\mathrm{proc}}$ be the set of process expressions constructed in the same way as in Sect. 2 except that the symbols γ_m may be used as channel constants ($m \in \omega$). Clearly, we have $\mathcal{L}_{\mathrm{proc}} \subseteq \tilde{\mathcal{L}}_{\mathrm{proc}}$. Let $\tilde{\mathcal{L}}_{\mathrm{proc}}^\emptyset = \{P \in \tilde{\mathcal{L}}_{\mathrm{proc}} \mid \mathrm{FV}(P) = \emptyset\}$. A *system configuration* is formally defined to be a pair $\langle m, P \rangle \in \omega \times \tilde{\mathcal{L}}_{\mathrm{proc}}^\emptyset$, where m is used as the index of the next fresh channel. The rule RES_ν is given in terms of the channel constants γ_i as follows:

RES_ν: $\langle m, (\nu\, \xi\, P) \rangle \xrightarrow{\tau} \langle m+1, P[\gamma_m/\xi] \rangle$.

To formulate the rule STRUCT_ν, we define a relation $\equiv_\nu$ to be the equivalence relation on $\tilde{\mathcal{L}}_{\mathrm{proc}}$ induced by the Abelian semigroup laws for parallel composition. In terms of $\equiv_\nu$, the rule STRUCT_ν is given as follows:

STRUCT_ν: $Q \equiv_\nu P$ and $\langle m, P \rangle \xrightarrow{a} \langle \ell, P' \rangle$ implies $\langle m, Q \rangle \xrightarrow{a} \langle \ell, P' \rangle$.

Each process expression P in the π-calculus and the system configuration $\langle m, P \rangle$ in the $\nu\pi$-calculus are bisimilar in the sense of CCS [3, Sect. 5.1]. This property is formally stated by the next theorem (see [2] for the proof).

Theorem 1. *There is a binary relation $\approx\, \subseteq \mathcal{L}_{\mathrm{proc}}^\emptyset \times (\omega \times \tilde{\mathcal{L}}_{\mathrm{proc}}^\emptyset)$ satisfying the following two clauses (i) and (ii). (i) $\forall P \in \mathcal{L}_{\mathrm{proc}}^\emptyset, \forall m \in \omega[\, P \approx \langle m, P \rangle\,]$. (ii) For every $P_1 \in \mathcal{L}_{\mathrm{proc}}^\emptyset$ and $\langle m, P_2 \rangle \in \omega \times \tilde{\mathcal{L}}_{\mathrm{proc}}^\emptyset$ such that $P_1 \approx \langle m, P_2 \rangle$, the following two properties (1) and (2) hold for every $s \in (\mathbf{E}_\tau)^*$:*

$$\forall P_1'[\, P_1 \xRightarrow{s} P_1' \;\Rightarrow\; \exists \langle \ell, P_2' \rangle [\, \langle m, P_2 \rangle \xRightarrow{s} \langle \ell, P_2' \rangle \wedge P_1' \approx \langle \ell, P_2' \rangle\,]]. \tag{1}$$

$$\forall \langle \ell, P_2' \rangle [\, \langle m, P_2 \rangle \xRightarrow{s} \langle \ell, P_2' \rangle \;\Rightarrow\; \exists P_1'[\, P_1 \xRightarrow{s} P_1' \wedge P_1' \approx \langle \ell, P_2' \rangle\,]]. \tag{2}$$

References

1. G. Berry and G. Boudol, The chemical abstract machine, *Theoretical Computer Science, Vol. 96*, 217–248, 1992.
2. E. Horita and K. Mano, *Nepi: A Network Programming Language Based on the π-Calculus*, ECL Technical Report, Vol. 11933, NTT Communication Science Laboratories, 1995.
3. R. Milner, *Communication and Concurrency*, Prentice Hall International, 1989.
4. R. Milner, *The Polyadic π-Calculus: A Tutorial*, Technical Report ECS-LFCS-91-180, LFCS, Department of Computer Science, Univ. of Edinburgh, 1991.
5. R. Milner, J. Parrow, and D. Walker, A calculus of mobile processes, I and II, *Information and Computation, Vol. 100*, pp. 1–40 and pp. 41–77, 1992.
6. B. C. Pierce and D. N. Turner, *Concurrent objects in a process calculus*, in Proceedings of International Workshop TPPP'94, Lecture Notes in Computer Science, Vol. 907, pp. 187–215, Springer, 1994.
7. G. D. Plotkin, *A Structural Approach to Operational Semantics*, Report DAIMI FN-19, Comp. Sci. Dept., Aarhus Univ., 1981.

Modelling Interoperability by CHAM: A Case Study

Paola Inverardi and Daniele Compare

Dip. di Mat. pura ed Appl., Università di L'Aquila
via Vetoio, Coppito, I-67010 L'Aquila, Italy.
(inverard@univaq.it), (compare@univaq.it)

Software architectures (SA) descriptions can be useful tool for the design, the analysis and the production of systems whose construction is based on the interoperability paradigm. In this paper we consider the SA of a system obtained by suitably assembling together existent software. The Cern Compressing Proxy (CP), has been presented in [4] and it is an interesting case study since it was obtained in two steps. The first version considered the interface mismatch between the components, which seemed to be the only problem to be solved in order to compose the existing pieces. Actually, when at work this solution exhibited a wrong dynamic behaviour since there were cases in which the whole system deadlocked. The second solution therefore removed this problem by analysing the dynamic behaviours of the components, thus suitably adapting the functionalities of the connecting new code. This example clearly shows the need of a precise description of the dynamic behaviour of the components that we claim should be retrieved from the architectural description. In the following, the descriptions of the two software architectures on which the CP was based on are given by using the Chemical Abstract Machine (CHAM) formalism [2] as introduced in [5]. A CHAM description of a software architecture consists of a syntactic description of the static components of the architecture (the *molecule*) and of a set of reaction rules which describe how the system dinamically evolves through reaction steps. in these descriptions both the origin of deadlocks in the first architecture and the ways to prevent them in the second architecture can be easily outlined and a certain amount of formal reasoning can be carried on. A CHAM is specified by defining *molecules* $m, m', \ldots$ and *solutions* $S, S', \ldots$ of molecules. Molecules are the basic elements of a CHAM, while solutions are multisets of molecules interpreted as defining the *states* of a CHAM. A CHAM specification contains *transformation rules* $T, T', \ldots$ that define a *transformation relation* $S \longrightarrow S'$ dictating the way solutions can evolve (i.e., states can change) in the CHAM. At any given point, a CHAM can apply as many rules as possible to a solution, provided that no molecule is involved in more than one rule. Thus it is possible to model parallel behaviors by performing parallel transformations. When more than one rule can apply to the same molecule or set of molecules the CHAM makes a nondeterministic choice as to which transformation to perform.

The **Compressing Proxy system** is an example of *interoperability* obtained by suitably assembling together special **http proxy servers**, composed of many filters which are connected together via a function-call-based stream interface.and **gzip**, which behaves as a traditional, standard input/output interface, Unix filter, i.e. it accepts a stream of input and produces a stream of compressed/decompressed output. The purpose of this system is to improve the performance of a Unix WWW browser connected to the Web by a slow link. This problem and its solution have been described in [4] and a formal description, in Wright [1] of the presented architecture has circulated as well [6]. The idea is to create an **httpd**-style filter, i.e. the C ompressing Proxy (**CP**), whose purpose it to compress the documents content, and inse rt this filter in an appropriate place in the **httpd** process. In order to use the **gzip** filter we have to adjust his standard input/output interface to a function-call- based stream interface like the other filters. This is achieved without modyfying **gzip** by embedding it in an ad-hoc created adaptor, the Unix Cern Adaptor (**UCA**) wh ich exhibits externally a function-call-based stream interface while internally it creates a **gzip** process and communicates with it via Unix pipes.

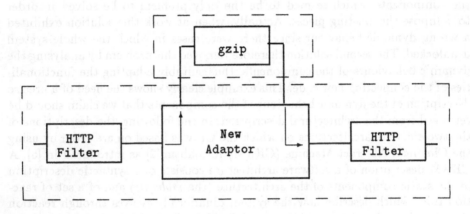

The Compressing Proxy

This system when executed will sometimes deadlock. This happens because the entire document is sent to **gzip** before any attempt to read from it is done. If **gzip** tries to output before the adaptor has finished to send data out, **gzip** will block waiting for the adaptor to read. When then the adaptor tries to send more output to **gzip**, **httpd** will block waiting for **gzip**, thus causing a deadlock. This problem can be avoided by changing the communication modalities of the adaptor towards **gzip**, i.e. by using of non-blocking read and writes.

In the first architecture the adaptor uses *blocking writes* when sending data to gzip. We must define an algebra of molecules i.e. a syntax by which molecules can be built. We start with a set of constants P representing the processing elements and an infix operator "$\diamond$" that we use to express the status of a processing element. The connecting elements for the blocking architecture are given by a the set C consisting of two operations, i and o, that act on the elements of the set N, that give the topology of the sistem, i.e. the communicating channels that connect components. The set E, introduces the costants used in the communication between gzip and the adaptor. The syntax Σ_b of molecules M is then

$$M ::= P \mid C \mid E \mid M \diamond M$$
$$P ::= CP \mid UCA \mid UF$$
$$C ::= i(N) \mid o(N)$$
$$N ::= 1 \mid 2 \mid 3 \mid 4$$
$$E ::= eof_i \mid eof_o$$

The set of syntactic elements is the initial algebra in the class of all the Σ_b algebras. The initial solution S_1 below corresponds to the initial, static configuration of a system conforming to the architecture.

$$S_1 = CP \diamond o(3) \diamond i(4), i(3) \diamond o(1) \diamond eof_o \diamond UCA, i(1) \diamond eof_i \diamond o(2) \diamond eof_o \diamond UF$$

Finally transformation rules describe the evolution of the system.

$$T_1 \equiv CP \diamond o(3) \diamond i(4) \longrightarrow o(3) \diamond i(4) \diamond CP$$
$$T_2 \equiv i(x) \diamond m_1, o(x) \diamond m_2 \longrightarrow m_1 \diamond i(x), m_2 \diamond o(x)$$
$$T_3 \equiv e \diamond m \diamond c \longrightarrow c \diamond m \diamond e$$
$$T_4 \equiv UCA \diamond i(3) \diamond m \longrightarrow i(2) \diamond eof_i \diamond o(4) \diamond UCA$$
$$T_5 \equiv eof_o \diamond m_1 \diamond o(x), eof_i \diamond m_2 \diamond i(x) \longrightarrow$$
$$m_1 \diamond o(x) \diamond eof_o, m_2 \diamond i(x) \diamond eof_i$$
$$T_6 \equiv UF \diamond m \longrightarrow m \diamond UF$$
$$T_7 \equiv UCA \diamond i(2) \diamond m \longrightarrow i(3) \diamond o(1) \diamond eof_o \diamond UCA$$
$$T_8 \equiv eof_i \diamond m \longrightarrow m \diamond eof_i$$

where $m, m_1, m_2 \in M$, $x \in N$, $c \in C$ and $e \in E$. In this architecture it is easy to show that there are derivations which exactly model the deadlock situations.

Let us turn to the second architecture. The main difference is that the adaptor can use *nonblocking writes* when sending data to gzip. Thus, any time one of those writes would have blocked, the adaptor will read any avaible data from gzip (using nonblocking reads) and then retry the write. This approach introduces a degree of parallelism by allowing the Compressing Proxy to start sending out compressed data before all the incoming data has arrived. Therefore we enrich the structure of the molecules by introducing an infix operator "||" to syntactically represent a complexly composed molecule that can be broken down into parallel subcomponents, thus allowing multiple reactions to occur simultaneously. We can simply augment Σ_b. Let us call the new syntax Σ_n and define it as follows.

$$M ::= P \mid C \mid E \mid M \diamond M \mid M \parallel M$$
$$P ::= CP \mid UCA \mid UF$$
$$C ::= i(x) \mid o(x)$$
$$N ::= 1 \mid 2 \mid 3 \mid 4$$
$$E ::= eof_i \mid eof_o$$

Comparing Σ_b and Σ_n we see that only the highest-level molecule syntax generator M are different. Let S_1' be the solution to represent the initial configuration.

$$S_1' = CP \diamond o(3) \diamond i(4), i(3) \diamond o(1) \diamond eof_o \diamond UCA \parallel$$
$$i(2) \diamond eof_i \diamond o(4) \diamond UCA, i(1) \diamond eof_i \diamond o(2) \diamond eof_o \diamond UF$$

The solution contains a molecule that represents the parallel communications UCA can perform. In this way UCA will never block during its input or output. To complete the specification, we define a new set of transformation rules.

$$T_1' \equiv CP \diamond o(3) \diamond i(4) \longrightarrow o(3) \diamond i(4) \diamond CP$$
$$T_4' \equiv m_1 \parallel m_2 \parallel \cdots \parallel m_n \longrightarrow m_1, m_2, \ldots, m_n$$
$$T_7' \equiv UCA \diamond m \longrightarrow m \diamond UCA$$
$$T_9' \equiv CP \diamond o(3) \diamond i(4), o(4) \diamond UCA \diamond m \longrightarrow$$
$$i(4) \diamond CP \diamond o(3), o(4) \diamond UCA \diamond m$$

where $m, m_1, \ldots, m_n \in M$, $x \in N$, $c \in C$ and $e \in E$.

The reaction rule T_1' is a specialization of the reaction rule T_1 from Σ_b. T_4' breaks apart a complex molecule into its (parallel) components, which can then participate in (parallel) reactions; T_7' reactivates the inert adaptor: it summarizes rules T_4 and T_7 from the previous architecture. Finally, T_9' is a reaction rule that forces CP to read compressed data from UCA when CP is in an idle state.

For brevity, we cannot show these reactions, we refer to [3] and to the full version of this paper for a complete account on the specification and analysis of the two architectures. Our specifications are kept at a rather high level of abstraction, with many details of the system behavior left unaddressed. From our point of view this is a strengh of the formalism since it provides the specifier with an explicit degree of freedom in interpreting the architectural descriptions (e.g., purposely leaving certain implementation choices up to developers). In this case our goal was to see if the CHAM descriptions of the Cern Compressing Proxy could easily outline the problems which cause the system to deadlock. From the given specifications this can be simply derived and formally proved [3].

References

1. R. Allen and D. Garlan. Formalizing Architectural Connection. In *Proc. of the 16th Int. Conf. on Software Engineering*, pag. 71–80. IEEE Comp. Soc., 1994.
2. G. Berry and G. Boudol. The Chemical Abstract Machine. *Theoretical Computer Science*, 96:217–248, 1992.
3. D. Compare. Specifica ed Analisi del Cern Compressing Proxy con la CHAM. Tesi di Laurea in Scienze dell'Informazione, Uni. L'Aquila, December 1995.
4. D. Garlan, D. Kindred, and J.M. Wing. Interoperability:Sample Problems and Solutions. Technical report, Carnegie Mellon University, Pittsburgh, Pennsylvania.
5. P. Inverardi and A.L. Wolf. Formal Specifications and Analysis of Software Architectures Using the Chemical Abstract Machine Model. *IEEE Transactions on Software Engineering*, 21(4):100–114, April 1995.
6. D. Kindred. The CERN Stream/Unix Filter Adaptor:WRIGHT Specification. Technical report.

Integrating Coordination Features in PVM

O. Krone, M. Aguilar, B. Hirsbrunner[1], V. Sunderam[2]

[1] Institut d'Informatique, Université de Fribourg
Fribourg, Switzerland
Oliver.Krone@unifr.ch
[2] Computer Science Department
Emory University, Atlanta, GA, USA
vss@mathcs.emory.edu

Abstract. In this paper we focus on coordination for parallel systems controlled by the PVM software package. We describe several extensions to PVM which allow the use of extended coordination features like generative communication or client/server programming.

1 Introduction

The coordination of distributed applications has recently become a scientific discipline in its own right and is described for example as "*managing dependencies among independent entities*" [10]. This can be achieved using a coordination language, as "*the linguistic embodiment of a coordination model*" [6], to express and describe the relationships between the active entities running in parallel.

This research has led to the development of several coordination models and corresponding coordination languages like [5, 2, 3]. Although these models deserve a lot of attention from a theoretical point of view, their implementations have shown performance problems. On the other hand, PVM [11] is an efficient system which allows the development of distributed applications using the standard message passing paradigm. Unfortunately PVM lacks some classical coordination features like generative communication or client/server programming. In this paper we are bridging this gap by enhancing PVM with a set of primitives which allow the use of classical coordination features while preserving the efficiency and programming model of PVM.

The rest of this paper is organized as follows: Section 2 introduces the extensions for PVM, and Section 3 concludes with some final remarks and an outlook on future work.

2 Advanced PVM Coordination Features

We now give an informal overview of the extensions we propose for PVM towards some "higher" programming model than pure message passing. In order to achieve this goal, we define (1) a global name space for processes, services and messages, and (2) an instance called "Post" which is responsible for high level message passing, and finally (3) abstractions to support the client/server programming model.

2.1 Global Name Space

We introduce a global *name-service* in PVM. New primitives are provided to register and unregister names in this name space. Names are used to identify either processes, messages or services.

Processes. Processes can register and unregister to and from the global name space of PVM. By registering, the user specifies a symbolic name by which the processes will be identified in the future. The process of registration is dynamic, therefore allowing a dynamic change of the configuration of the parallel machine represented in the name space. Names can be transferred to other processes so that they can communicate with formerly unknown processes. Using names has the advantage that process identification can be done independently from the underlying process management and communication platform.

Messages. One of the most well known "advanced" communication metaphors is uncoupled communication [8]. Since coupled communication is already provided by the original PVM programming model, we focus our extensions on uncoupled communication.

The extension for messages is two folded: (1) messages can be identified by a symbolic name, and (2) the semantics of messages will be extended towards uncoupled communication by allowing new message types like *persistent* messages (see Section 2.2). By giving messages a name we considerably change the standard semantics for messages in PVM. However, to avoid unnecessary blocking at sender side, we define a *stream* semantics on named messages; a message name can be reused by the sender before the receiver has performed the corresponding receive operation. Processes receive messages in the stream in FIFO order.

Services. Adopting a client/server model for PVM allows to combine two widely used coordination paradigms, namely message passing and client/server programming, in one programming tool. We do not present a classical synchronous remote procedure call interface known from, for example [4], but a combination of service invocation and service provision calls combined with classical message passing. Again, we use the global name space as a repository for the storage of symbolic service identifiers. Processes providing a service have to register their service in this name space. Processes requesting a service can use the service by addressing a service name and process name in the name space (see Section 2.3).

2.2 Advanced Message Passing: Postal Mail Delivery

Using a postal mail delivery system [1] for message passing facilitates several extensions with regard to advanced message passing. Message can now be identified – like processes or services – by a logical name. The sending of messages is not restricted to point to point communication anymore, but allows several modes: (i) *Persistent*: message will be kept by the mail delivery server and can be accessed by anybody who knows the symbolic name of the message; (ii) *Hold*: hold message a certain amount of time, after the specified time the message expires and will be removed; (iii) *Instant*: send message to destination, do not keep it (old PVM standard mode), and (iv) *Multiple-Copies*: keep multiple copies of the message; allows several, but determined processes to receive the message.

Combinations of the modes are allowed, e.g., *Multiple-Copies* and *Hold*. Processes can retrieve information by either specifying the sender and the message name, only the message name, only the sender name, or finally by a wild card. A reserved shared data space called "Blackboard" serves as a common communication space. Every process has per default access to this space which is used for the distribution of information to an unknown audience.

Beside the extensions concerning advanced message passing, a postal mail delivery system has a couple of other advantages: (i) it supports migration of processes, because it maps logical site independent process names to physical site dependent process identifiers; (ii) it hides the physical site of a process from a user, and (iii) it supports the implementation of highly portable and scalable algorithms since programs do not depend on certain physical communication structures of the target machine.

2.3 Client/Server Programming

Client/server programming will be facilitated by introducing two new primitives pvm_bind_svc and pvm_req_svc. The former primitive is used at server side to bind a service to a service name, whereas the latter primitive is used at client side to invoke the service.

In order to request a service the user calls pvm_req_svc (a nonblocking primitive) with the specification of the requested service, e.g., parameters and service identification. To finally receive the result, a receive call is used where the message name corresponds to the service name of the requested service.

3 Conclusion

In this paper we proposed extensions to the PVM programming model which allow a higher degree of expressiveness to coordinate parallel applications. We extended PVM by introducing a global name space for messages, services and processes which will be used to implement non-classical message passing semantics and client/server programming model. The proposed extensions fit into the general philosophy of the PVM programming model.

The extensions, especially the postal mail delivery service and the name space, will be used to implement a system that allows interoperability at coordination level. The idea is to define several *Coordination Spaces* which are characterized by the coordination model used inside the space [9]. Inter coordination (coordination between several coordination worlds) will be achieved by the abstract definition of *coordination performatives* like the performatives of KQML [7] for message passing. The actual interpretation and transformation of a coordination performative from one coordination space to another will be realized by the introduction of a special control instance S inside the coordination space (like the facilitators in KQML). Here the global name space and the advanced message passing capabilities of PVM can help to enable e.g. coordination between a pure LINDA like system and a pure PVM like controlled system.

A similar project is defined in [12] where a *Interoperability Architecture* is proposed which is built around a family of distributed languages. A specialized component called *Interoperability Server* is used as the interface to the different environments.

Our plans for the future include an implementation of the described extensions for a version of PVM running on the Parsytec PowerExplorer.

References

1. Marc Aguilar and Béat Hirsbrunner. Post: A New Postal Mail Delivery Model. In K.M. Decker R.M. Rehmann, editor, *Programming Environments for Massively Parallel Distributed Systems*, pages 231–237. IFIP WG 10.3, Birkhaeuser, April 1994.
2. J.M. Andreoli, P. Ciancarini, and R. Pareschi. Interaction Abstract Machines. In P. Wegner G. Agha and A. Yonezawa, editors, *Reserach Directions in Concurrent Object Oriented Programming*. MIT Press, Cambridge Mass., 1993.
3. J. P. Banâtre and Le Métayer. The Gamma Model and its discipline of Programming. *Science of Computer Programming*, 15:55–77, 1990.
4. M. Bever, K. Geihs, L. Heuser, M. Mulhauser, and A. Schill. Distributed Systems, OSF DCE and Beyond. In A. Schill, editor, *International DCE Workshop*, number 731 in LNCS, Karlsruhe, October 7–8 1993. Springer Verlag.
5. N. Carriero and D. Gelernter. Linda in Context. *Communications of the ACM*, 32(4):444–458, 1989.
6. N. Carriero and D. Gelernter. Coordination Languages and Their Significance. *Communications of the ACM*, 35(2):97–107, February 1992.
7. T. Finin and R. Fritzson. KQML - A Language and Protocol for Knowledge and Information Exchange. Technical report, University of Maryland, Baltimore, MD 21228, 1994.
8. David Gelernter. Generative Communication in Linda. *ACM Transactions on Programming Languages and Systems*, 7(1):80–112, 1985.
9. O. Krone and M. Aguilar. Bridging the Gap: A Generic Distributed Hierarchical Coordination Model for Massively Parallel Systems. In *Proceedings of the '95 SIPAR-Workshop on Parallel and Distributed Computing*, Biel, Switzerland, October 1995.
10. T. W. Malone and K. Crowston. The Interdisciplinary Study of Coordination. *ACM Computing Surveys*, 26(1):87–119, March 1994.
11. V.S. Sunderam. PVM: A framework for parallel distributed computing. *Concurrency: Practice and Experience*, 2(4):315–339, December 1990.
12. K. Zielinski, G. Czajkowski, and A. Uszok. Coordination through Interoperability in Distributed Processing. In *ECCOP Workshop on Models and Languages for Coordination of Parallelism and Distribution*, Bologna, 1994. Springer Verlag.

A Simulator Framework for Embedded Systems

Pieter A. Olivier

University of Amsterdam,
Programming Research Group,
Kruislaan 403,
1098 SJ Amsterdam, Holland

Abstract. We have developed a flexible and intuitive simulator for embedded systems stable enough to be used in a commercial setting, with an execution speed comparable to that of the simulated hardware. This extensible simulator is based on a loosely coupled set of tools that form a framework for efficient construction of new simulators.

1 Introduction

By "embedded system" we mean any computer system for which the primary development tools do not run on the system itself. Typical examples are the computer systems that are build into household appliances, cars, and airplanes.

Many embedded systems are produced in small quantities and use non-standard hardware, for which hardly any programming support is available. The costs for buying or building tools such as, for instance, a simulator are in such cases only warranted if they can be amortized over a wide range of embedded systems. This means we must achieve a significant amount of reuse, both in design and coding efforts.

This is why we deployed a software interconnection architecture based on message passing, called the *ToolBus*[BK95]. The ToolBus software application architecture was designed to control a number of heterogeneous components, possibly in a distributed environment. The ToolBus enforces formalization of the communication behaviour between the components, making the interaction between them very explicit. This leads to a set of loosely coupled tools with a well-defined input/output behaviour, greatly improving reusability. The ToolBus also provides us with the opportunity to implement each component in the most appropriate programming language.

An ideal simulator provides all the information about the state of the running program the user wants, and no more. To provide this information in a clear and concise way, a good and extensive user interface is a must. The considerable effort that must be invested into the creation of appealing and easy to use user interface components, logically focussed our attention on making these components reusable.

The framework itself consists of a user interface and a virtual machine. It has been used to build a full-fledged C development environment containing a C compiler, assembler, linker and libraries. Here, we only discuss the simulator framework itself.

2 User Interface

The user interface of the framework consists of six components, see Figure 1.

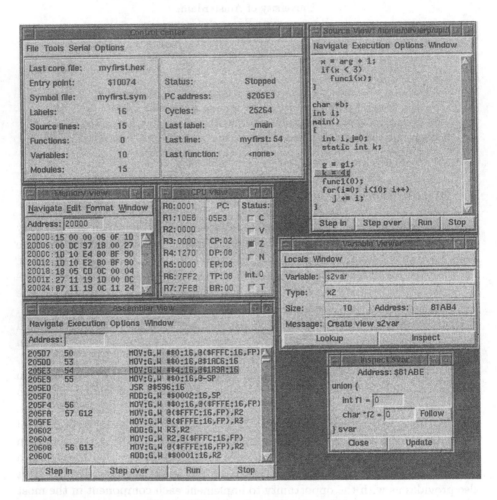

Fig. 1. The simulator user interface

When the user starts the simulator he/she is presented with the *control center*, that provides a global status view of the system and enables the user to load programs and bring up the viewer components discussed below:

- The *memory viewer* is used to inspect and change the contents of the memory of the simulated system.
- The *CPU viewer* enables the user to inspect and change the contents of the simulated CPU registers.

- The *assembler viewer* displays the disassembled memory contents. It allows the user to step through the assembler code and set and clear breakpoints.
- The *source viewer* tracks the current C source file[1] and the current point of execution within this file. Breakpoints are highlighted and can be changed.
- The *variable viewer* tracks the contents of variables and lets the user change them. This tool creates one additional window per variable that the user wants to inspect/change.

3 Virtual Machine

Central to the framework is the notion of a *virtual machine*. which takes care of the actual execution of simulated programs. To do this, the virtual machine has to keep track of the following information:

- CPU register contents;
- Memory contents;
- The status of any simulated special hardware components needed during execution, like any switches, LED's, communication hardware etc.;
- All breakpoint activities;
- Debug symbols (to map addresses to line numbers etc.).

In addition to the 'bookkeeping' tasks needed to maintain this information, the virtual machine performs the following operations:

- Simulate actual execution of machine language instructions;
- Disassemble the contents of memory on request.

The user interface components enable the user to interact with the virtual machine, and provide different views on the information maintained by the virtual machine. The ToolBus is used to control all communications between the user interface components and the virtual machine. The virtual machine simulates all parts of the system that have to run at full speed, so no ToolBus communication is needed during the high-speed execution of a program section.[2]

4 Conclusions

Performance: Because the actual program execution takes place within the virtual machine, the simulator's performance is not influenced by our distributed architecture. Although the user interface components are all separate tools, the interactive response times are good, essentially justifying the choice for the Tool-Bus concept.

---

[1] Any language can be used, as long as the virtual machine can implement a mapping between source lines and corresponding adresses in the assembler code.

[2] We use the term 'program section' in this context to indicate a portion of the program to be executed without a need for visual feedback to the user. For instance, execution of the code generated by one line of source code or by an entire routine depending on the command issued by the user.

Reusability: We implemented a simulator for a specific embedded system using this framework. This project took about six man months to complete, and resulted in the following statistics:

Simulator component size		
Component	Lines of code	Language
virtual machine (partly reusable)	17420	C++
UI components (reusable)	8252	Tcl/Tk
communication control (reusable)	1657	ToolBus script

All the user interface components are reusable when a simulator is developed for a new embedded system. This means an instant design and code reuse of over 50 percent[3], depending on the complexity of the virtual machine. Factoring out the machine independent components from the virtual machine would increase the reusability even further.

Extensibility: Because of the clear responsibilities of the different components and the open nature of the framework, the basic framework is very extensible. We have extended the simulator to simulate the special serial communication hardware that was present in the embedded system for which we developed the simulator. This only required extending the basic framework, not changing it.

A more extensive description of the discussed framework can be found in [Oli96].

References

[BK95] J.A. Bergstra and P. Klint. The discrete time toolbus. Report p9502, Programming Research Group, Department of Mathematics and Computer Science, University of Amsterdam, FWI WCW, Kruislaan 403, 1098 SJ Amsterdam, 1995.

[Oli96] P.A. Olivier. Embedded system simulation. Report p9601, Programming Research Group, University of Amsterdam, WCW, Kruislaan 403, 1098 SJ Amsterdam, 1996.

---

[3] We take into account here that the high level Tcl/Tk and ToolBus code is more compact than the C++ code of the virtual machine.

Understanding Behavior of Business Process Models[*]

Pablo A. Straub and Carlos Hurtado L.

Departamento de Ciencia de la Computación
Pontificia Universidad Católica de Chile
Vicuña Mackenna 4860 (143), Santiago 22, Chile
straub@ing.puc.cl   churtado@ing.puc.cl

1 Introduction

Business processes have intrinsic parallelism given by the relative independence of some activities. Parallelizing a process might "dramatically reduce cycle times and the resultant costs" [5], but it might lead to anomalous behavior, like deadlock or useless activities. There are three main approaches to avoid behaviorally incorrect models, a notion that is not even well defined: 1) Build a model and then verify its properties (e.g., building the space state, or finding net invariants [2]). 2) Build a model that is correct by construction (e.g., using activity annotations [1] akin to parbegin parend pairs). 3) Use only small models by abstracting models and submodels. The first approach does not explain why or where a particular model has behavioral problems. The second approach constrains the forms of parallelism: it is impossible to model a PERT chart. The third approach is just a rule of thumb that may lead to oversimplified models.

This work intends to: define a notion of correct behavior in business process models and give a framework to allow behavioral analysis.

2 A Notion of Correct Behavior

We use our Copa notation [6]; it is easy to map concepts presented here into similar languages like ICN [3], Action Workflow [4], VPL/Rasp [8], whose behavioral semantics are defined in terms of Petri nets. Fig. 1a shows a simple but anomalous process model. Connector x splits execution in two parallel activities (a and b). Activity a proceeds to c while b may choose to proceed to either c (causing a deadlock in y) or to connector y (synchronizing with c).

The semantics of Copa is given by a Petri net obtained by translating each element of the model and connecting corresponding elements (Fig. 1b). Allowable initial states have a single token in one input socket and no other tokens.

One basic property of a good model is that it does not deadlock, that is, each process of the model reaches an output socket. Another basic property of a good process model is single-response, that is, each enaction of the process produces exactly one output. Process models can suffer from prescribing too

[*] This work is funded in part by CONICYT through project FONDECYT 1940677.

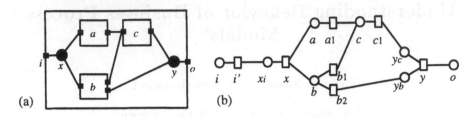

Fig. 1. Example of a Copa net with an anomalous process model.

much work, so that some activities are unnecessarily performed, because in some particular execution no output socket depends on them. For example, if there were a connection from activity b to output socket o in Fig. 1, choosing this connection would render a and c useless.

Given a process model $\mathcal{M}$ whose set of output sockets is S_o:

Property 1 (Deadlock freedom) A final state M_f is a *deadlock* if for all $s_o \in S_o$, $M_f(s_o) = 0$. $\mathcal{M}$ is *deadlock-free* if none of its final states is a deadlock.

Property 2 (Single Response) $\mathcal{M}$ is *single-response* if all final states M_f satisfy $\sum_{s_o \in S_o} M_f(s_o) = 1$. It is *multiple-response* if there is a final state M_f such that $\sum_{s_o \in S_o} M_f(s_o) > 1$.

Property 3 (Usefulness) An activity a is *useless* within a process (in the sense of Petri nets) of $\mathcal{M}$ if there is no path from a to an output socket. A process model $\mathcal{M}$ is *useful* if no activity is useless in any process.

Property 4 (Simple control) $\mathcal{M}$ has *simple control* if every final state M_f satisfies $\sum_{s_o \in S_o} M_f(s_o) = 1 = \sum_{p \in P} M_f(p)$.

Simple control implies that if a model begins with a single token in one of its input sockets, it ends with a token in one of its output sockets and there are no other tokens. Simple control implies the other properties [6].

3   A framework to understand control properties

In a sense, simple control means "at the end there is exactly one token". Place invariants capture the idea of having the right number of tokens in a system. A place invariant I is an assignment of weights to places such that for any transition t, the sum of the weights of its predecessors equals the sum of the weights of its successors, thus the weighted sum of their tokens is constant [2].

Theorem 1. *Let I be a positive invariant of a process model with an input socket s_i that has a path to an output socket s_o, then if $I(s_i) \neq I(s_o)$, the initial state that has a token in s_i leads to multiple response, an overloaded state, or deadlock.*

A necessary but not sufficient condition for simple control is the existence of a positive balanced invariant (i.e., all sockets have the same weight). The example has a positive balanced invariant but it may deadlock.

A theory of threads of control whose results are proven in [7] is an extension of the work on invariants. A thread of control captures the idea of parallel subprocesses within a process. Unlike the usual sense given in operating systems, our concept of threads is static. Within a process model, every activity should belong to one and only one thread; to tell which one, we propose a labeling that assigns a set of thread labels to each place or transition.

Definition 2 Model labeling. The labeling of a model is a function τ from nodes of the net to sets of labels, defined by: 1) The only label for an output socket is $\mathbf{1}$. 2) Each label of a transition is computed by adding a consistent set of labels[2], one from each successor. 3) The label of a place p that does not correspond to an output socket is computed by multiplying a label from a successor $t \in p^\bullet$ that leads to an output socket, by $\sigma(t, \{p\})$.

For example, part of the labeling of the model in Fig. 1b is: $\tau(o) = \{\mathbf{1}\}$, $\tau(c) = \{\mathbf{1} \otimes \sigma(y, \{y_c\}) \otimes \sigma(c_1, \{c\})\}$, and $\tau(b) = \{\mathbf{1} \otimes \sigma(y, \{y_b\}) \otimes \sigma(b_2, \{b\})$, $\mathbf{1} \otimes \sigma(y, \{y_c\}) \otimes \sigma(c_1, \{c\}) \otimes \sigma(b_1, \{b\})\}$.

Definition 3 Label equivalence. Label equivalence, denoted $\doteq$, is defined by: 1) $\oplus$ is commutative, 2) $\oplus$ and $\otimes$ are associative, 3) $\otimes$ distributes by the right over $\oplus$, 4) $\sigma(t, x) \oplus \sigma(t, y) \doteq \sigma(t, x \cup y)$ if $x \cap y = \varnothing$, and 5) $x \otimes \sigma(t, {}^\bullet t) \doteq x$.

A *thread* is a non-empty equivalence class of labels. A labeling τ such that all labels assigned to a given node x are equivalent defines a threading ψ. We usually denote a thread by a label (one of its members). Threadings are non-numeric invariants [7].

From definition 3 we see that the example has no threading because activity b belongs to two threads of control, namely $\mathbf{1} \otimes \sigma(y, \{y_b\})$ and $\mathbf{1} \otimes \sigma(y, \{y_c\})$. This fact implies the model has control anomalies.

Definition 4. A threading ψ is *balanced* if the thread of all input sockets is $\mathbf{1}$. A model is balanced if its threading is.

If a model is balanced, in all reachable states M the summation of the active threads (those that have a token) is $\mathbf{1}$; besides, only one activity is executing in a thread, that is, M marks at most one place in the same thread. The main result from this theory is that threadings capture our notion of correctness:

Theorem 5. *A model is balanced if and only if it has simple control.*

There are three possible causes for not having a balanced threading, which can be interpreted in terms of behavioral properties. First, there might be a place with no labels. If a place in the model has no label, this implies there is a proper trap in the net (i.e., a set of places that once they receive a token they always have some tokens [2]) and the model has an overloaded state, unless a deadlock upstream impedes reaching the trap. Second, there might be two

---

[2] A set of labels is *consistent* if all occurrences of a place refer to the same transition.

unequivalent labels for a place, which means that this place is an activity whose output sockets are connected to different threads: this implies either deadlock or overloaded state. Third if there a threading, but it is unbalanced, then Theorem 1 applies [7].

4 Conclusion

There are two reasons to use simple control as a notion of behavioral correctness. First, it implies there are no control anomalies, like deadlock, useless activities, and multiple response [6]. Second, a simple control model behaves like an activity; this allows consistent or-abstraction in which a process model can be used safely within a larger model. Or-behavior is the most commonly accepted from of model abstraction (as in, e.g., ICN, VPL/Rasp, Action Workflow).

Simple control is related to other behavioral properties of free-choice Petri nets. In fact we prove in [6] that a model has simple control if and only if a connected free choice net derived from the model is live and safe in the sense of [2]. This implies in turn that simple control in free choice nets (i.e., in all Copa models) can be decided in polynomial time.

Our framework formalizes threads of control in business process models and relates them to behavioral correctness, by demanding that threads of control be adequately combined. We have recognized several applications of thread theory within workflow models: diagnostic of why a model might fail, model building, advanced exception handling, unanticipated exceptions.

References

1. Giorgio De Michelis and M. Antonietta Grasso. How to put cooperative work in context: Analysis and design requierements. *Issues of Supporting Organizational Context in CSCW Systems.* L. Banon and K. Schmidt, August 31, 1993.
2. Jörg Desel and Javier Esparza. *Free-choice Petri Nets.* Tracts in Theoretical Computer Science, Cambridge University Press, 1994.
3. Clarence A. Ellis and Gary J. Nutt. Modeling and enactment of workflow systems. In *14th Int'l Conf. on Application and Theory of Petri Nets*, June 1993.
4. Raúl Medina-Mora, Terry Winograd, Rodrigo Flores, Fernando Flores. The Action Workflow approach to workflow. *Management Technology Proceedings of CSCW*, November 1992.
5. Michael Parry. *Reengineering the Business Process.* The Workflow paradigm, Future Strategies Inc., ISBN 0-9640233-x.
6. Pablo Straub and Carlos Hurtado L. The simple control property of business process models. In *XV Int'l Conf. of the Chilean Computer Science Society*, Arica, Chile, October 30th to November 3rd, 1995.
7. Pablo Straub and Carlos Hurtado L. A theory of parallel threads in process models. Tech. Report RT-PUC-DCC-95-05, Computer Science Dept., Catholic Univ. of Chile, August, 1995. In ftp://ing.puc.cl/dcc/techReports/rt95-05.ps.
8. Keith D. Swenson. Visual support for reengineering work processes. In *Proc. of the Conf. on Organizational Computing Systems*, November 1993.

Springer-Verlag
and the Environment

We at Springer-Verlag firmly believe that an international science publisher has a special obligation to the environment, and our corporate policies consistently reflect this conviction.

We also expect our business partners – paper mills, printers, packaging manufacturers, etc. – to commit themselves to using environmentally friendly materials and production processes.

The paper in this book is made from low- or no-chlorine pulp and is acid free, in conformance with international standards for paper permanency.

Lecture Notes in Computer Science

For information about Vols. 1–983

please contact your bookseller or Springer-Verlag

Vol. 1019: E. Brinksma, W.R. Cleaveland, K.G. Larsen, T. Margaria, B. Steffen (Eds.), Tools and Algorithms for the Construction and Analysis of Systems. Selected Papers, 1995. VII, 291 pages. 1995.

Vol. 1020: I.D. Watson (Ed.), Progress in Case-Based Reasoning. Proceedings, 1995. VIII, 209 pages. 1995. (Subseries LNAI).

Vol. 1021: M.P. Papazoglou (Ed.), OOER '95: Object-Oriented and Entity-Relationship Modeling. Proceedings, 1995. XVII, 451 pages. 1995.

Vol. 1022: P.H. Hartel, R. Plasmeijer (Eds.), Functional Programming Languages in Education. Proceedings, 1995. X, 309 pages. 1995.

Vol. 1023: K. Kanchanasut, J.-J. Lévy (Eds.), Algorithms, Concurrency and Knowlwdge. Proceedings, 1995. X, 410 pages. 1995.

Vol. 1024: R.T. Chin, H.H.S. Ip, A.C. Naiman, T.-C. Pong (Eds.), Image Analysis Applications and Computer Graphics. Proceedings, 1995. XVI, 533 pages. 1995.

Vol. 1025: C. Boyd (Ed.), Cryptography and Coding. Proceedings, 1995. IX, 291 pages. 1995.

Vol. 1026: P.S. Thiagarajan (Ed.), Foundations of Software Technology and Theoretical Computer Science. Proceedings, 1995. XII, 515 pages. 1995.

Vol. 1027: F.J. Brandenburg (Ed.), Graph Drawing. Proceedings, 1995. XII, 526 pages. 1996.

Vol. 1028: N.R. Adam, Y. Yesha (Eds.), Electronic Commerce. X, 155 pages. 1996.

Vol. 1029: E. Dawson, J. Golić (Eds.), Cryptography: Policy and Algorithms. Proceedings, 1995. XI, 327 pages. 1996.

Vol. 1030: F. Pichler, R. Moreno-Díaz, R. Albrecht (Eds.), Computer Aided Systems Theory - EUROCAST '95. Proceedings, 1995. XII, 539 pages. 1996.

Vol.1031: M. Toussaint (Ed.), Ada in Europe. Proceedings, 1995. XI, 455 pages. 1996.

Vol. 1032: P. Godefroid, Partial-Order Methods for the Verification of Concurrent Systems. IV, 143 pages. 1996.

Vol. 1033: C.-H. Huang, P. Sadayappan, U. Banerjee, D. Gelernter, A. Nicolau, D. Padua (Eds.), Languages and Compilers for Parallel Computing. Proceedings, 1995. XIII, 597 pages. 1996.

Vol. 1034: G. Kuper, M. Wallace (Eds.), Constraint Databases and Applications. Proceedings, 1995. VII, 185 pages. 1996.

Vol. 1035: S.Z. Li, D.P. Mital, E.K. Teoh, H. Wang (Eds.), Recent Developments in Computer Vision. Proceedings, 1995. XI, 604 pages. 1996.

Vol. 1036: G. Adorni, M. Zock (Eds.), Trends in Natural Language Generation - An Artificial Intelligence Perspective. Proceedings, 1993. IX, 382 pages. 1996. (Subseries LNAI).

Vol. 1037: M. Wooldridge, J.P. Müller, M. Tambe (Eds.), Intelligent Agents II. Proceedings, 1995. XVI, 437 pages. 1996. (Subseries LNAI).

Vol. 1038: W: Van de Velde, J.W. Perram (Eds.), Agents Breaking Away. Proceedings, 1996. XIV, 232 pages. 1996. (Subseries LNAI).

Vol. 1039: D. Gollmann (Ed.), Fast Software Encryption. Proceedings, 1996. X, 219 pages. 1996.

Vol. 1040: S. Wermter, E. Riloff, G. Scheler (Eds.), Connectionist, Statistical, and Symbolic Approaches to Learning for Natural Language Processing. IX, 468 pages. 1996. (Subseries LNAI).

Vol. 1041: J. Dongarra, K. Madsen, J. Waśniewski (Eds.), Applied Parallel Computing. Proceedings, 1995. XII, 562 pages. 1996.

Vol. 1042: G. Weiß, S. Sen (Eds.), Adaption and Learning in Multi-Agent Systems. Proceedings, 1995. X, 238 pages. 1996. (Subseries LNAI).

Vol. 1043: F. Moller, G. Birtwistle (Eds.), Logics for Concurrency. XI, 266 pages. 1996.

Vol. 1044: B. Plattner (Ed.), Broadband Communications. Proceedings, 1996. XIV, 359 pages. 1996.

Vol. 1045: B. Butscher, E. Moeller, H. Pusch (Eds.), Interactive Distributed Multimedia Systems and Services. Proceedings, 1996. XI, 333 pages. 1996.

Vol. 1046: C. Puech, R. Reischuk (Eds.), STACS 96. Proceedings, 1996. XII, 690 pages. 1996.

Vol. 1047: E. Hajnicz, Time Structures. IX, 244 pages. 1996. (Subseries LNAI).

Vol. 1048: M. Proietti (Ed.), Logic Program Syynthesis and Transformation. Proceedings, 1995. X, 267 pages. 1996.

Vol. 1049: K. Futatsugi, S. Matsuoka (Eds.), Object Technologies for Advanced Software. Proceedings, 1996. X, 309 pages. 1996.

Vol. 1050: R. Dyckhoff, H. Herre, P. Schroeder-Heister (Eds.), Extensions of Logic Programming. Proceedings, 1996. VII, 318 pages. 1996. (Subseries LNAI).

Vol. 1051: M.-C. Gaudel, J. Woodcock (Eds.), FME'96: Industrial Benefit and Advances in Formal Methods. Proceedings, 1996. XII, 704 pages. 1996.

Vol. 1052: D. Hutchison, H. Christiansen, G. Coulson, A. Danthine (Eds.), Teleservices and Multimedia Communications. Proceedings, 1995. XII, 277 pages. 1996.

Vol. 1053: P. Graf, Term Indexing. XVI, 284 pages. 1996. (Subseries LNAI).

Vol. 1054: A. Ferreira, P. Pardalos (Eds.), Solving Combinatoreial Optimization Problems in Parallel. VII, 274 pages. 1996.

Vol. 1055: T. Margaria, B. Steffen (Eds.), Tools and Algorithms for the Construction and Analysis of Systems. Proceedings, 1996. XI, 435 pages. 1996.

Vol. 1056: A. Haddadi, Communication and Cooperation in Agent Systems. XIII, 148 pages. 1996. (Subseries LNAI).

Vol. 1057: P. Apers, M. Bouzeghoub, G. Gardarin (Eds.), Advances in Database Technology — EDBT '96. Proceedings, 1996. XII, 636 pages. 1996.

Vol. 1058: H. R. Nielson (Ed.), Programming Languages and Systems — ESOP '96. Proceedings, 1996. X, 405 pages. 1996.

Vol. 1060: T. Gyimóthy (Ed.), Compiler Construction. Proceedings, 1996. X, 355 pages. 1996.

Vol. 1061: P. Ciancarini, C. Hankin (Eds.), Coordination Languages and Models. Proceedings, 1996. XI, 443 pages. 1996.